all the

Mondale

Certiles

Bert

Mode 8512 } => Mode 3a

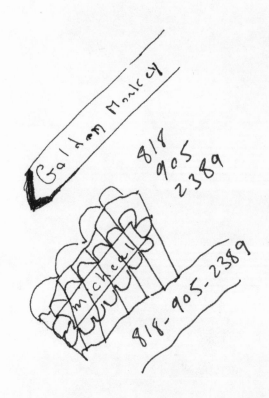

Golden Monkey

818
905
2389

michael

818-905-2389

AMERICAN HOSTAGES IN IRAN

A Council on Foreign Relations Book

COUNCIL ON FOREIGN RELATIONS BOOKS

AMERICAN HOSTAGES IN IRAN
THE CONDUCT OF A CRISIS

WARREN CHRISTOPHER

HAROLD H. SAUNDERS

GARY SICK

ROBERT CARSWELL

RICHARD J. DAVIS

JOHN E. HOFFMAN, JR.

ROBERTS B. OWEN

with commentaries by
OSCAR SCHACHTER
ABRAHAM A. RIBICOFF

under the editorial direction of Paul H. Kreisberg

YALE UNIVERSITY PRESS   NEW HAVEN AND LONDON

Published with the assistance of the
A. Whitney Griswold Publication Fund.

Designed by James J. Johnson
and set in Century Schoolbook type.
Printed in the United States of America by
Vail-Ballou Press, Binghamton, New York

Library of Congress Cataloging in Publication Data
Main entry under title:

American hostages in Iran.

   "A Council on Foreign Relations book."
   Includes index.
   1. Iran Hostage Crisis, 1979–1981—Addresses, essays,
lectures. I. Christopher, Warren. II. Kreisberg, Paul H.
III. Council on Foreign Relations.
E183.8.I55A6 1985   955′.054   84–19592
ISBN 0–300–03233–1 (cloth; alk. paper)
      0–300–03584–5 (paperback)

*The paper in this book meets the guidelines for
permanence and durability of the Committee on
Production Guidelines for Book Longevity of the Council
on Library Resources.*

10 9 8 7 6 5 4

CONTENTS

FOREWORD

Few events in recent decades have so consumed the attention of the nation and the energies of its leaders as the seizure of the United States Embassy in Tehran in 1979 and the holding of Americans hostage until 1981. For 444 days, the country was riveted. The shaping of the national agenda and the conduct of the 1980 presidential campaign were drastically altered. The world economy was triggered into a severe recession by a doubling of oil prices closely associated with the crisis. Perceptions here and abroad of American power and will to deal with crises in the world were sharply influenced. The ripples in domestic politics and international relations continue.

This book examines the crisis through the eyes of the direct participants in the making of policy. It traces the role of senior advisers to the President, the Secretary of State, the Secretary of the Treasury, and the President's National Security Adviser. It explains the agonizing human, political, military, and economic choices that had to be confronted. It describes the interaction of the policymakers with a diverse host of outside forces: the families of the hostages, private individuals pressing to involve themselves, international bankers whose interests were dramatically affected, and an aroused media and public opinion.

The genesis of this project has two separate strands that happily were joined together. In the fall of 1980, two committees of the Association of the Bar of the City of New York—the Committee on the Lawyer's Role in the Search for Peace, then under the chairmanship of John Temple Swing, Vice President of the Council on Foreign Relations, and the Committee on International Law, then under the chairmanship of Donald Rivkin, founding partner of Rivkin Sherman and Levy (now Schnader, Harrison, Segal &

Lewis)—joined forces in an examination of the role of international law in influencing foreign policy decisions. In January 1981, the two committees sponsored a discussion of the role of the Legal Adviser to the Secretary of State in the decision-making process, led by John H. Stevenson and Monroe Leigh, both former Legal Advisers. The discussion turned almost inevitably to the Iranian hostage crisis, then in its final stages, as one of those rare situations—a night scene illuminated with a flash of lightning—in which the conflict between law, politics, and force could vividly be seen. The discussion raised so many important questions that the chairmen of both committees immediately began to plan for a series of special meetings focusing on the hostage crisis to see what might be learned concerning the role of law and lawyers in the settlement of future international disputes.

At the same time, the editors of *Foreign Affairs* received two manuscripts by former U.S. government officials that touched on various aspects of the crisis. One of these, Robert Carswell's "Economic Sanctions and the Iran Experience," appeared in the Winter 1981 issue of *Foreign Affairs*. Based on his reading of the manuscripts, Paul H. Kreisberg, the Council on Foreign Relations' Director of Studies, concluded that the country would be well served by an account of the crisis written largely by the participants themselves. It is common for policymakers at the highest level—presidents and Cabinet officers—to describe their experiences and views about public office. It is far less common for those at senior working levels of government who are primarily responsible for handling the day-to-day course of negotiations, for analyzing and evaluating developments, and for preparing recommendations for policy decision by the President and his most senior advisers. Most of the government officials who had held such positions in the Carter Administration and who had worked on the release of the hostages from Iran were no longer in government and were, in principle, free to discuss their involvement.

It quickly became evident that many of the participants in the discussions at the Council and at the Association of the Bar would inevitably be the same. The Association and the Council therefore decided to join forces in a retrospective examination of the diplomatic, economic, and legal issues at stake in the fourteen-month-long crisis, the negotiations to resolve it, and possible lessons for the future both for policymakers and for lawyers directly involved with the issues of international law.

The enthusiastic agreement of the authors of this volume was obtained. The study began in the spring of 1982 with former Senator Abraham Ribicoff as chairman of the study group, which was to meet over the next nineteen months. John Temple Swing and Donald Rivkin served as study group directors and Paul H. Kreisberg as coordinating editor for the book. The joint study group was composed of members of the New York City Bar, members of the Council on Foreign Relations, and Foreign Service officers who had been held hostage in Iran.

The purpose of the group was to examine the issues and choices confronting senior American officials as the crisis began and throughout its duration and to clarify how and why specific choices were made. When the study began, the primary policymakers—President Jimmy Carter, Secretary of State Cyrus Vance, and National Security Adviser Zbigniew Brzezinski—were in the process of writing their own views of the crisis. These all became available while the group was conducting its study and served as background for the discussions. Many of the key senior sub–Cabinet-level officials involved in the crisis are among the authors of this volume. They joined with other participants in the study in assessing: the key considerations on which they and their superiors focused as they worked their way through this extraordinary national crisis; the institutional structures through which they worked; the role of economic sanctions and of the private banks; the use and nonuse of force; and a range of political, constitutional, and public information issues.

The group believed it would also be useful to have a distinguished professor of international law assess the longer-term significance of the crisis and the decisions made by the United States, Iran, and the international community as a whole for the general understandings that underlie the principles of international law.

The book consists of elaborated and refined discussion papers originally prepared for the study group. It begins with an overall review and assessment of the crisis and the issues raised during the 444 days it lasted by Warren Christopher, who as Deputy Secretary of State played a key role in the discussions within the U.S. government and in negotiations with Iran.

In chapters 1, 2, and 7, Harold Saunders, former Assistant Secretary of State for Near Eastern and South Asian Affairs, who was the senior working-level official responsible to the Secretary of State for coordinating policy recommendations on the crisis, discusses the situation in Iran from the start of the crisis and of the U.S. response from early 1979 through the collapse of hopes for the negotiated release of the hostages in early 1980.

Gary Sick, who was National Security Council staff member for the region during the crisis, then examines in chapter 3 consideration of options for the use of military force.

Robert Carswell, former Deputy Secretary of the Treasury, and Richard Davis, former Assistant Secretary of the Treasury for Operations, assess in chapters 4 and 5 the application of economic and financial pressure on Iran and the problems that arose within the government when these pressures were relaxed as part of the negotiations leading to the release of the hostages.

John Hoffman, a partner in the New York law firm of Shearman & Sterling, describes in chapter 6 the role of the private U.S. banks in negotiations with Iranian officials and their European lawyers on the complex issues involved in handling Iranian dollar deposits and bank claims.

Roberts Owen, former State Department Legal Adviser, gives his account in chapter 8 of the final negotiations in Algiers and the difficulties that arose in the concluding stages.

Oscar Schachter, Hamilton Fish Professor of International Law and Diplomacy at Columbia University, then assesses in chapter 9 the broad issues and lessons for the future relating to international law that emerged from the handling of the crisis.

Finally, Senator Ribicoff offers his observations and thoughts on the lessons of this experience for the future. His views are based on both the preceding chapters and the discussions at the ten meetings of the study group from March 1982 to April 1983.

We would like to express our deepest appreciation to Abraham Ribicoff, John Temple Swing, Donald Rivkin, and Paul H. Kreisberg and to all the members of the study group for their faithful participation in meetings and for their thoughtful and penetrating comments and questions. These were very helpful to all the authors, who regularly took part in the meetings as well, in their preparation and revision of their papers.

We would also like to thank the specially invited guests and speakers, whose views on a broad range of issues helped to clarify both the dilemmas of U.S. policy and the complexities of Iranian politics.

The rules of the Council on Foreign Relations that the comments of participants in Council meetings may not be quoted directly or attributed to the speakers in any way were strictly maintained during all the discussions. Several of the participants, however, have specifically agreed to have particular comments cited in the final chapter by Senator Ribicoff.

Even though each author has taken great care to confirm his recollections with other colleagues in preparing his chapter, it is evident that the chapters represent personal statements and that the views represented are those of the authors and not of the Council, the Association of the Bar of the City of New York, or other members of the Carter Administration.

While responsibility for the general plan of the book rests with the Council and the study group, the various chapters are the responsibility of their authors. There is inevitably overlap among the chapters, partly because each chapter is designed to be read as a separate piece and partly because each author views the episode from his own vantage point. We believe that this provides the most complete—and perhaps most accurate— record possible of a multifaceted event. It also serves to underscore the role of different departments of government in defining policy choices and in implementing policy decisions as a crisis evolves. We seek the reader's indulgence for the duplication this may occasionally entail.

Even these complementary accounts are necessarily incomplete, however. Each author had to make selections among the materials available; certain aspects of the events remain classified, and no author has continuing access to classified documents.

We believe that the authors have contributed in an important way to an understanding of this extraordinary incident in American foreign policy and to a clear view of how policies are made and implemented. But equally important, we believe that there are significant insights and judgments on the way in which the American government dealt with the crisis that may be of assistance to U.S. officials and legislators as the United States inevitably confronts in the future what will be different but no less taxing tests of national will, political judgment, and diplomatic skill.

WINSTON LORD, *President*
Council on Foreign Relations

LOUIS A. CRACO, *President*
Association of the Bar of the City of New York, 1982–84

THE AUTHORS

Robert Carswell was Deputy Secretary of the Treasury in charge of all economic issues relating to the crisis. He is a partner in the law firm of Shearman & Sterling.

Warren Christopher was Deputy Secretary of State and chief negotiator in the concluding stages of the crisis. He is a partner in the law firm of O'Melveny & Myers.

Richard J. Davis was Assistant Secretary of the Treasury responsible for the financial and economic sanctions. He is a partner in the law firm of Weil, Gotshal & Manges.

John E. Hoffman, Jr. was chief legal counsel for Citibank and the key banking figure in the negotiations between the U.S. banks and the Iranian bankers. He is a partner in the law firm of Shearman & Sterling.

Roberts B. Owen was Legal Adviser to the Secretary of State and a participant in the final negotiations in Algiers. He is a partner in the law firm of Covington & Burling.

Abraham A. Ribicoff is a former governor and senator from Connecticut and was Secretary of Health, Education and Welfare. He is a partner in the law firm of Kaye Scholer Fierman Hays & Handler.

Harold H. Saunders was Assistant Secretary of State for the Near East and South Asia and the head of the Iran Working Group during the crisis. He is currently a resident fellow at the American Enterprise Institute.

Oscar Schachter is Hamilton Fish Professor of International Law and Diplomacy at Columbia University. He is a co-editor-in-chief of the *American Journal of International Law* and a past President of the American Society of International Law. He served from 1946 to 1966 as a legal

adviser to U.N. Secretaries-General Lie, Hammarskjold, and U Thant
and as director of the U.N. Legal Division.

Gary Sick was National Security Council staff member for Iran and the
chief assistant to the National Security Adviser throughout the crisis.
He is Program Officer for U.S. Foreign Policy at the Ford Foundation.

INTRODUCTION

WARREN CHRISTOPHER

This volume is a powerful recommendation for the value, indeed the necessity, of recording and studying the history of large events. In the long sweep of history, the Iranian hostage crisis may occupy little more than a page. Yet it riveted the attention of the U.S. government for more than fourteen months and preoccupied the country as an event rarely has. It was a matter of confounding complexity, involving a myriad of financial, legal, political, and practical details and decisions.

As a result, even participants and close observers had a hard time comprehending the crisis as a whole as it unfolded. The best way to understand it is to disassemble the various pieces and look back at them one by one. Then the entire event can be seen, and, more importantly, we can begin to perceive its lessons and prepare ourselves should something similar confront us in the future. That is what this volume tries to do.

Of course the likelihood of these precise events recurring is quite remote. While hostage situations are not unprecedented in the diplomatic community, in other cases host governments quite promptly have recognized their obligations under international law to protect foreign embassies against hostile elements in their populations. Here, however, the host government condoned and then embraced what the terrorists had done, and thus made their crime its own—an almost unprecedented act and one of extraordinary repugnance.

That gave us some leverage we otherwise would not have had, for even revolutionary governments have assets and interests they want to retain. But it also worsened the plight of the Americans confined in Tehran and made their prospects for rescue exceedingly dim.

But if the exact circumstances are unlikely to recur, we can be confident that our country will be called upon again to address large and enigmatic crises in which the stakes are high, the dangers great, and the smallest decisions fateful. Reexamination of the Iranian hostage crisis can, I believe, teach lessons of more general utility.

GENERAL OBSERVATIONS

Individual chapters of this book address specific aspects of the crisis in detail. They suggest some conclusions about the crisis that were not readily apparent at the time, when the experience was being lived mostly in episodes and seen mainly in glimpses. Drawing on these chapters, my part is to make some general observations and then to propose some lessons to be taken from this national trauma. My comments are illustrative, not comprehensive. They are designed to stimulate, but by no means to satisfy, the reader's appetite for what follows.

Phases

Viewed in retrospect, the crisis can be seen to divide itself into a number of distinct phases:

THE PRE-CRISIS. For months before the hostage taking, the United States had been reassessing its relationship with Iran. The revolution there did not make Iran a less significant country to the United States. Its location on the Persian Gulf and the Arabian Sea, its status as a land bridge between the Middle East and Asia, and its energy reserves still defined it as a strategically important country and no less so because of its internal turmoil. On the contrary, now U.S. policymakers also had to concern themselves with the reality that Iran's internal divisions made it weaker and therefore more vulnerable to Soviet opportunism. All things considered, American interests argued strongly against hastily giving up on Iran. Thus, although the official American presence in that country had been drastically reduced after the Iranian revolution, nevertheless a decision also had been taken to maintain a diplomatic presence in order to continue communications and to promote a mature and correct, if considerably cooler, relationship with the revolutionary government. We were not prepared to walk away from the situation, and we should not have been. At the same time, businesses and banks with commercial contacts in Iran had begun to reassess their operations and prospects there and to adjust to the new environment.

THE IMMEDIATE AFTERMATH OF THE NOVEMBER 4, 1979, HOSTAGE TAKING. This period began with an expectation, which survived for only a matter of days, that the Iranian authorities would rescue our embassy personnel in line with their assurances and with their behavior in a similar incident the prior February. When that hope proved vain, and it appeared that the Iranian government was condoning the actions of those who took the embassy, the Carter Administration rather quickly reviewed its options and imposed economic sanctions, including the freeze of Iranian assets. In addition, our case was taken to the International Court of Justice, to the U.N. Security Council, and to other countries around the world.

THE FAILED NEGOTIATIONS. This phase lasted from late November into March 1980 and involved working out, through Paris lawyers and with the cooperation of United Nations Secretary-General Kurt Waldheim, a "scenario" under which the hostages would be released at the end of a series of reciprocal steps. In Iran this effort was backed by a Europe-oriented group—principally President Abolhassan Bani-Sadr and Foreign Minister Sadegh Ghotbzadeh. The process led to the creation and dispatch to Iran of a U.N. Commission of Inquiry that was to investigate Iranian grievances against the Shah. The phase ended when the Ayatollah Khomeini and religious elements in Iran began adding new and unacceptable conditions and when it became apparent that Bani-Sadr and Ghotbzadeh could not control the situation, even to the extent of arranging the agreed meetings with all the hostages by members of the U.N. Commission.

THE NADIR. In late March, as the Commission of Inquiry scenario collapsed, it became clear that the hostages' fate had become entangled in the internal political maneuvering of various factions in Iran. At least until the situation sorted itself out—until a new government was solidly in place— none of the competing groups could afford to take the political risk of appearing to yield to the United States by supporting the release of our people. It was under these circumstances that the ill-fated hostage rescue attempt was authorized and initiated. Later in the same period, Iranian officials with economic responsibilities, working through Iran's ambassador to Germany, began to explore with U.S. banks the possibilities for an economic settlement. It is quite possible that the Iranians involved in those talks hoped to settle economic matters separately from the hostage issue. However, under firm instructions from us, those representing the private sector on the U.S. side made clear from the beginning that any economic settlement would have to include release of the hostages as well.

REAL BARGAINING. By September 1980, the Iranian parliament, or Majlis, had been formed, a new government was in place, and the Iranians appeared ready to proceed. At this point the Iranians initiated contact with the United States through the Germans. At the outset of this phase, the Ayatollah Khomeini announced his four conditions for a settlement. Shortly thereafter, in mid-September, I had direct discussions with an Iranian emissary outside Bonn. That channel was severed after the outbreak of the Iraq-Iran war later in September. Then the negotiations opened up in earnest in November, with the Algerians serving as highly skilled intermediaries and facilitators.

THE END GAME. The closing days of the crisis were distinguished by the fact that the Iranians at last came to terms on the most disruptive issues. They plainly wanted to resolve the crisis prior to the change in administrations in the United States, and they gradually came to realize, with the help of the Algerians, that execution of the settlement, and especially of the intricate financial provisions, also would take considerable time. Therefore, while they remained deeply suspicious and often obstinate, the Iranians also made a number of far-reaching decisions rather quickly in the closing hours, permitting the release of the hostages before the day was out on January 20, 1981.

Limits on Government Power

From the outside, the executive authority of the United States may appear to be virtually limitless, especially in a crisis when the President is possessed of extraordinary powers and when he also can expect widespread political support for the steps he deems necessary to protect the national interests and honor. Even in such circumstances, however, the President is tightly bounded by legal, practical, and political considerations. Nearly all of the essays in this volume include illustrations of how these considerations confined President Carter's decisions to fairly narrow channels.

Broader foreign policy concerns played a major role. For example, as Captain Gary Sick points out, the Soviet invasion of Afghanistan on December 27, 1979, diminished the appeal of military pressure or retribution against Iran. Obviously we had no interest in forcing the Iranians to turn to the Soviets for help or in weakening Iran to the point where it could not resist leftist subversion.

Similarly, foreign policy considerations limited the scope of the freeze on Iranian assets, which was imposed ten days after the hostages were taken. Despite questions about U.S. power to do so, the freeze was extended to Iran's large dollar accounts in the foreign branches of U.S. banks, principally in Paris and London. On the other hand, while it would have been logically consistent to do so, Iranian accounts in other currencies in those same banks were not frozen. As Robert Carswell points out, this reflected a sensitivity to the fact that the extraterritorial reach of the freeze was bound to offend these friendly governments, and we wanted to limit the irritant.

The attitudes of other branches of the U.S. government also were a factor. There was concern that the scope of executive authority would be constrained and our bargaining position thus undermined if the courts or the Congress acted. As Richard Davis notes, the November 26, 1979, decision to allow U.S. claimants against Iran to initiate action in U.S. courts, despite the assets freeze, was made in part to accommodate claimants in the hope of avoiding ultimate court tests of the President's authority while the crisis continued. The strategy was not entirely successful, although it did prove possible to stay all proceedings at the court of appeals level.

To avoid adverse court rulings, we also had to take into account the legal limitations on the government's power to dispose of the assets it had frozen. This reality, present from the beginning, dictated the shape of the final settlement. Almost all Iranian assets present in the United States had been subject to attachments by businesses and individuals with claims against Iran. To convey those Iranian assets held in U.S. banks out from under the judicial attachments simply was beyond the unilateral power of the President. Even the release of funds overseas was subject to satisfactory arrangements with respect to the debts Iran owed the banks where its funds were on deposit.

As to the Congress, consideration was given to seeking new legislation to increase the President's authority to deal with the crisis, perhaps by authorizing the President actually to take title to (to "vest" rather than merely freeze) Iranian assets found here, as compensation for wrongs done the United States. The decision was made to operate within existing legal authority, in part because of concern that in the heat of the moment the Congress might attach mandates for retribution that would narrow our bargaining options. In another case, after the U.N. bargaining effort collapsed in March 1980, we considered whether Congress should be asked to declare that a state of war existed between the United States and Iran. In this case it was felt that the Congress might have objected to the extraordinary presidential powers that a declaration of war would have conferred. Sharp questioning on Capitol Hill, perhaps even a rejection of the action, obviously would have damaged our bargaining position.

Mundane practical constraints also had to be surmounted. For most of the period, Iran ruled out face-to-face negotiations, and negotiation through intermediaries—even highly skilled ones like the Algerians—created inevitable delays. To an extent, we also negotiated in the dark. It was not until very late, for example, that the government had reliable information on the sum of the Iranian bank accounts it had frozen. In mid-December 1980, as described by John Hoffman, the bank group retained Peat, Marwick, Mitchell & Company to collect financial data on a blind, coded basis, and this led to the agreed figure on consistent terms—more than a year after the assets were frozen.

In the final two weeks, geography played a complicating role, for important steps had to be taken in at least six locations—Washington, New York, London, Algiers, Tehran, and Bonn. Telecommunications were often slow or unreliable. Between the most distant points, the time change was nine hours, which meant that the action continued somewhere literally around the clock. The multicentered operation imposed great demands for experienced personnel. The escrow agreement, for example, largely was negotiated by former Treasury General Counsel Robert Mundheim, who was pressed back into service from his post as a professor of law in Pennsylvania.

As a last constraint, we were operating under a rapidly closing deadline—12:00 noon on January 20, 1981, when the new President was to be sworn in. At that moment, all of the Carter presidential appointees would lose their authority to bind the United States and even to negotiate on its behalf. Yet the Iranians did not really seem to focus on the full dimensions of the issue, with all of its technical details, until January had already begun.

Nonetheless, I am persuaded that this particular constraint was more a help than a hindrance. Laboring under a deadline produced superhuman effort from scores of people in the public and private sectors. It made some parties willing to do things that might have horrified them under a more leisurely timetable, such as the banks' payment of billions of dollars on the basis of a garbled, and at some points indecipherable, payment order from Iran. The deadline also probably made the Iranians somewhat more pliable at the end, for they knew that at a minimum, the new administration would require time to inform itself on the issues and might well take an even harder line on the settlement terms. President-elect Ronald Reagan had used some blunt language in referring to the crisis, which we did not hesitate to highlight as an added incentive for the Iranians to come to terms.

Who Can Speak for Iran?

One of the most challenging and frustrating problems of the crisis was trying to figure out who within Iran would be influential in a decision to release the hostages and what might motivate them to act favorably. As Harold Saunders describes, to a large degree these matters still are shrouded in mystery. Our information about that period in Iran remains sketchy. In many respects it is contradictory. Under the remote and erratic Ayatollah Khomeini, the government of Iran during the crisis often seemed to be a composite, with no settled identity or single voice.

This inevitably led to negotiating difficulties as Iranian positions tended to come to the fore and then, at the crucial moment, to fade. It seemed reasonable, for example, to hope that the arrangement worked out through two Paris-based lawyers in early 1980 would gradually lead toward "expulsion" of the hostages once the Iranians had been permitted to air their grievances before the international Commission of Inquiry. This scenario

was acceptable to some important elements in the government, including
Foreign Minister Ghotbzadeh. It was said to have the support of the Revolutionary Council. And it was fashioned in such a way as to appeal to the
Ayatollah. Yet in the execution it disintegrated entirely, probably because
at that stage the hostages had become an indispensable tool of the clerics in
their quest for power; therefore, they could not be let go until the power
struggle had been completed.

On another issue, the Iranian with whom I met outside Bonn in September 1980 initially suggested that shipments of military spare parts and
equipment to Iran, from stocks for which they had earlier paid, would be
important in persuading them to release the hostages. Fortunately, from
my standpoint, the issue was never raised again in the negotiations.

The same thing also happened in the financial negotiations. As John
Hoffman relates, Iran's ambassador to West Germany, Mehdi Navab, stated
in private talks with Hoffman that guarantees of outstanding bank loans by
the Iranian government and Bank Markazi would be no problem. Within a
few days, such guarantees became totally unacceptable to Iran. Fortunately, there also was a reversal in our favor in the subsequent Iranian
decision not only to bring current, but to pay off, the bulk of their outstanding bank loans that had been arranged by syndicates with U.S. banks participating. This constituted acceptance of a plan that once had been flatly
rejected.

The most reasonable conclusion to draw is that the aspirations of the
Iranians changed according to who among them was doing the aspiring.
Iranian treasury and bank officials were interested mainly in working out
the best possible financial arrangement, concentrating on the release of
Iranian assets. The radical clergy and the revolutionary "students" holding
the hostages wanted to consolidate the revolution, a process they saw as
requiring a total separation from the United States, with the result that
they placed the greatest stress on finding a forum to vilify the Shah and
castigate the country that had been so closely identified with him. The
secular officials like President Bani-Sadr wanted to get the crisis out of the
way because they saw from an early point that it was harmful to Iran, and
they probably were interested in such things as military supply and economic viability. The Ayatollah Khomeini, meanwhile, had the greatest
accumulation of power and probably the least coherent view of what procedures were feasible and what objectives were obtainable in the hostage
context.

Only in the late summer of 1980, when the parliament was seated and a
new government was in power, did the Iranians concert their attention. At
that time, it became essential for us to shift our focus from the Western-
educated Iranians to the right-wing fundamentalist group then in power. In

any case, it is clear that the difficulty and delay in solving the crisis was due in major part to the fact that the other player had no discernible fixed rules, goals, or even identity.

Role of the International Community

There were some disappointments in the way the international community responded to the hostage crisis. The Soviet Union's role was distinctly unhelpful. On January 13, 1980, the Soviets vetoed stiff economic sanctions against Iran, which otherwise would have been approved by the U.N. Security Council. The lack of Security Council action became the grounds cited by some of the other U.N. members when they failed to carry out sanctions sought by the United States. In addition, the Soviets and the pro-Soviet elements inside Iran tried continuously, through propaganda broadcasts, to inflame Iranian popular opinion against the United States and the hostages, even during the last and most delicate moments in the negotiations.

While they agreed with us formally, meanwhile, even some of our closest allies were unwilling to join us in a ban on trade with Iran when we sought agreement on that sanction in April 1980. Unquestionably this narrowed the economic pressure.

If there were disappointments, however, the United States has good reason to feel grateful to the international community as a whole and to the role of specific countries within it. From the outset, for example, the Swiss and the Germans were deeply and actively engaged in our efforts to communicate with Iranian leaders. Moreover, while they did not go all the way with us, our allies did impose sanctions that were roughly commensurate with their capabilities, given their greater dependence on imported oil. A large dose of realism is useful in evaluating another country's willingness to join in sanctions, especially in response to an episode that affects them only indirectly.

We received particular cooperation from an institution that many Americans have grown to resent and regard as hostile to our interests—the United Nations. In October 1980, when the new Iranian Prime Minister, Mohammed Ali Rajai, came to the United Nations seeking an international condemnation of Iraq for its September invasion, he received instead a steady round of reprimands from the U.N. missions of scores of countries, which made clear their lack of sympathy for a country that remained in continuous and flagrant violation of diplomatic norms and international law. This performance may be discounted as no more than a manifestation of the reality that the weak have a greater stake in the rule of law than the strong. But the fact remains that countries we often have thought to be our antagonists within the U.N. system helped mightily and perhaps decisively to let Iran know that, for its own sake, it should resolve the crisis.

Earlier the world community had taken other important steps to support our position. On December 4, 1979, all the members of the U.N. Security Council—including the Third World members—joined us in demanding the immediate release of the hostages. This was clear notice to Iran's leaders that their country would be isolated and stigmatized in the world community so long as the Americans were held captive. After hearing our case on November 29, 1979, the International Court of Justice, an institution that predates the United Nations but is now part of its structure, rendered its decision with unprecedented speed, ruling on December 15 in our favor.

By far the greatest contribution by a single country to the resolution of the crisis came from Algeria. Algeria was designated as the official intermediary by Iran in early November 1980. From that time forward, the Algerians contributed enormously to the settlement process, with no selfish reason to believe that their effort would produce any benefit for themselves.

• Algeria mobilized its most gifted public servants in the form of a four-member negotiating team led by Foreign Minister Mohammed Benyahia, whose death in 1982, on another peace mission, was a tragic loss to the cause of world order.

• They contributed heavily in the form of sheer energy. After our first meeting in Algiers, the traveling members of the Algerian team left within a matter of hours for Tehran, and from then on they moved at an exhausting pace from Tehran to Washington to Algiers and back again, finally to remain in Tehran from December 30 until they came out with the hostages on January 20, 1981.

• The Algerians served an indispensable function in interpreting two widely disparate cultures and reasoning processes to each other: convincing the Iranians, for example, that the President was powerless simply to release Iranian assets subject to legal attachments in the United States; meanwhile, interrogating us vigorously on the various elements in our position and helping us to refine our views and to repair any shortcomings. This unique role was possible because the Algerian diplomats involved had and kept the full confidence of both sides.

• And the Algerians contributed with their credibility as a country, placing themselves squarely in the middle of the settlement, as the party to whom the promises were made.

All in all, no one performed with more energy, skill, commitment, or honor than did the members of the Algerian team. It is a simple fact that the settlement could not have been achieved without them.

So the crisis demonstrated that we have much to gain from responsible international citizenship and also that ours is far from the only society that aspires to lofty ideals.

The Rescue Mission

Captain Gary Sick and others describe in some detail the planning and preparations for the April 1980 rescue mission and the decision to proceed with it. There is room for sharply contrasting viewpoints on the central question of the wisdom of the attempt and also on related issues, including the validity of military judgments on such matters as the size of the helicopter force and the overall adequacy of the rescue plan and whether excessive secrecy handicapped the making of those judgments.

But perhaps just one additional observation on the cost of the mission is in order. On the one hand, the mission was tragically expensive. It cost the lives of eight crewmen, who were killed when two aircraft collided accidentally in the Iranian desert after the President had already called off the effort. The helicopter equipment failure that required the mission to abort was a sharp blow to U.S. military prestige. Also, we know that the hostages were dispersed after the rescue attempt and that their living conditions became harsher. It is conceivable as well that the rescue effort made the Iranians still more belligerent toward the United States and therefore raised the ante for the ultimate settlement and made it harder to reach—although it is difficult to point to specific evidence of this.

On the other hand, we probably would have been forced in any event to wait out the internal rearrangement of authority in Iran—the election of a parliament, the selection of a President, the appointment of a new Prime Minister. The failed mission had no discernible impact on the timetable for those events. It cannot have had much effect, either, on the judgment of the authorities in Iran as to whether holding the hostages was harmful or helpful to their interests. And rather directly after the Iranian government was at last composed, it moved—although still with ponderous decision-making and crippling suspicion—to get the issue settled. So it may be fair to erase from the negatives of the rescue attempt at least this one factor: it probably did not substantially prolong the confinement of the hostages.

The Role of International Law

Oscar Schachter has contributed to this book a comprehensive review of the international legal issues raised by the crisis. His effort leads to a first observation that international law has much more relevance to such matters than might commonly be supposed.

At the outset, the rules of international law defined the character of the hostage taking as a lawless act. Later, they were relevant to the rescue attempt. They affected the design of the sanctions and their implementation, and they helped dictate the terms of the final agreement. The settlement itself was simplified because a reliable body of arbitration law already existed in the United Nations system and could be lifted by reference into the agreement.

International law is widely regarded as a rather nebulous sphere, in large part, I suppose, because the enforcement of international legal rights can be an uncertain proposition. Nevertheless, a vast body of legal precepts and precedents exists to guide the conduct of nations in their dealings with each other. Moreover, whether or not international rules of law are enforceable under the ordinary understanding of that term, as a practical matter they do have a prominent role in the decisions nations make.

Iran, of course, violated the law both in failing to protect American diplomats and then in failing to release them. It was in flagrant violation of the 1961 Vienna Convention on Diplomatic Relations and the 1963 Vienna Convention on Consular Relations, both of which reaffirm customary international rules on diplomatic privileges and immunities and on the host state's responsibility for protecting diplomatic missions. Ultimately, the release of the hostages came about in substantial part because Iran found itself completely isolated in the world community—not because other countries necessarily were friendly to the United States, but because they almost universally were offended at Iran's transgressions against international law. In that sense, while it took time, obedience to the Vienna conventions was imposed not legally through a judicial forum but diplomatically by the countries of the world.

For our part, it was the practice of the United States throughout the hostage crisis to test contemplated actions against international legal standards. As an example, before diplomatic relations were severed, the idea became popular in some quarters to "even the score" with Iran by confining their diplomats in the United States, as they had done to ours in Tehran. The thought did have a nice symmetry to it. It was never seriously pursued by the United States, however, not only because it likely would have been ineffectual or counterproductive in a practical sense, but also because it would have placed the United States, too, in violation of the 1961 and 1963 conventions. Those documents contain nothing to permit retaliation in kind.

There were of course much closer legal questions, for example, the rescue mission. Apart from the judgment whether the mission was wise, the question has been raised whether the rescue attempt was consistent with article 2(3) of the United Nations Charter requiring the settlement of disputes by peaceful means, article 2(4), the basic rule against threatening or using force, and article 51, which recognizes the inherent right of self-defense in cases of "armed attack." Read together, these provisions seem to require a reasonable showing of necessity before force can be employed, even in self-defense. But that leads to the further questions Mr. Schachter identifies. Is it necessary to exhaust all peaceful avenues or remedies before resorting to force? Is it necessary to show an immediate peril to life or territory before force can be used? Bringing such abstract principles down to specific cases, was the United States legally justified in undertaking the rescue mission in April 1980, even though diplomatic efforts were still continuing and even though the hostages, at that moment, may not actually have been in imminent danger?

In my judgment the answer is best found by examining what it was reasonable for the United States to believe about the risk to the hostages at the time of the rescue mission. And that must be viewed not in retrospect, with the benefit of hindsight, but at the time of the crisis, when decisions actually had to be made. Of course it may be possible to fashion a hypothetical case in which a government could satisfy itself that the hostages' lives were not in jeopardy. That might be the case, for example, if the International Red Cross were permitted constant access. It might be the case if the hostages were held by regular, well-disciplined authorities and were well insulated and protected from popular anger. Conceivably the legal picture would change if there were explicit assurances on the safety of the hostages and they were receiving adequate medical attention and other essentials.

But none of these conditions was present in the Iranian case. Neither at the time of the rescue mission nor at other times did we know with any certainty that the hostages were safe from physical harm. We rarely knew where all of them were, how they were being treated, or how they were tolerating their confinement. What we did know is that they were in the hands of unidentifiable militants who had shown little sensitivity to ordinary standards of decency. We did know that the hostages had been cruelly paraded blindfolded before the cameras and subjected to taunts from a hostile crowd. We knew that they were permitted to have only sporadic contact with the outside world and that most efforts to have them checked by neutral agencies had been rebuffed, including efforts by the U.N. Commission of Inquiry, which had gone to Iran in March with the understanding that it would be allowed to meet with each of the hostages during the course of its visit. We knew that there were long periods during which some of the hostages were never seen or heard from at all. We knew that throughout the crisis there were repeated venomous statements by the leadership of Iran, including the Ayatollah Khomeini, of a kind well calculated to foster a hatred of the United States and everything connected with it.

By any objective measure, it was certainly reasonable for the United States to operate on the assumption that the hostages were in grave, even mortal, peril at the time of the rescue mission. In the circumstances, I think

Mr. Schachter is manifestly correct in concluding that the action taken did not violate the Charter or international law.

In interpreting and applying international legal principles to events of this kind, the crucial point to remember is that international law is, and must be, rooted in practicality and common sense. That is why international law, often unenforceable otherwise, is nonetheless heeded and obeyed.

It is important to a nation that its behavior be consistent with the general rules laid down by custom or by consensus. Otherwise, over time, it simply will not be trusted. It will be unable to make agreements. It will be unable to rely on the various international institutions to help enforce its political and economic rights. And a country, unlike an individual, cannot move elsewhere and start over. It is stuck with its reputation.

Probably most Americans recognize that our comparatively great power does not immunize us from a need to rely on the rule of law internationally. Our stake in the world is so large—in trade, in security, in stability—that we are heavily dependent on a reliable legal order. On the other hand, the hostage crisis also stands as a reminder that even a society like Iran at that time, embittered against the world and drawn to iconoclasm and asceticism, cannot go on long before coming face-to-face with the reality that it too needs the protections of the international legal system.

The Iranian experience underscores the importance of refining the capacity of the international legal system both to deter hostage takings and, when they nonetheless happen, to build incentives for the humane treatment and prompt release of the captives. It would be logical, as Mr. Schachter suggests, to build further upon the foundation laid in the 1979 Convention Against the Taking of Hostages, and particularly to account for the special case when hostages are held with official connivance. The politics of any given situation—leading to the inability of the U.N. Security Council to impose sanctions even in such an obvious case as this and to the reluctance of many individual countries to go along with sanctions because of their separate interests in the offending country—also make a good case for automatic sanctions. This, however, is an area in which to tread cautiously, so that the negotiating flexibility needed in actual cases is not lost.

On the whole, however, it cannot be said that the international legal system failed us. It worked in strange and unconventional ways. It moved with frustrating slowness. But many of these same flaws and frustrations are not unheard of in our own advanced legal system. And in the end, the international structure did help bring the crisis to a close.

Costs to Iran

The taking and holding of the hostages was an enormously costly proposition for Iran. During the course of the crisis, Iran lost access to some $12 billion in assets, isolated itself from even its customary allies in the world, and invited, by its apparent weakness, a military assault from its rival, Iraq. Then, in the solution, Iran further had either to suffer the indignity of providing added security for its debts to U.S. bank creditors or else to pay them off (which it elected to do) and had to accept a claims settlement procedure that excluded major legal protections and thus promised to afford most of the other private claimants much better treatment than they could have expected in court. Meanwhile, the professed aims of the embassy occupiers went unrealized. No one was tried. The United States made no apology and confessed to no crimes. Neither the Shah nor his assets were returned to Iran.

There is a school of thought which holds that, given the mindset in Iran, the difficulty and anguish caused to the United States and its total estrangement from Iran were in themselves an achievement. In this view, the isolation created and the inability of the Americans to find or force a solution for fourteen long months gave the Iranians a psychic satisfaction that outweighed the tangible disadvantages, at least for a time and at least in the minds of the most radical elements. In view of the Iranian obsession about "the Great Satan," one cannot completely dismiss this viewpoint; still, I doubt that any nation would find such a psychic ride to be enough compensation for the massive losses Iran suffered. There is scant incentive for others to copy the Iranian action in the future.

A great deal still is to be learned, and much probably never will be learned, about the identity of the captors and their relationship with various elements in the government. However, it seems quite plausible to me that they were not initially controlled by the government but were in fact seen by it too as a dangerous element that had to be treated gingerly and then co-opted. Those struggling for power in Iran probably feared that they would lose the support of the revolutionaries holding the embassy and their followers if they moved to resolve the crisis. If that is the case, then the hostage crisis was as much Iran's quagmire as it was ours.

For other host governments, the costs to Iran teach a powerful lesson. It is to move promptly to take control of such situations and to accept whatever immediate political cost that might entail in order to avoid vast losses of almost every kind further down the road.

The Bank Negotiations

Chapters 4–6 of this book, by Richard Davis, Robert Carswell, and John Hoffman, are highly revealing in their discussion of the private bank negotiations and the financial arrangements. This is the mysterious realm that gave rise to such graphic terms as "black hole," "dentist's chair," and "Big Mullah." Much of the information here is new, because the private channel between the banks and the Iranians was pursued completely out of the public eye.

Readers of this book quickly will observe that, from the time Iran's assets were frozen, the prospects for an official settlement became closely related to a settlement in the banking sector. Any settlement dealing with the bank claims and Iranian deposits had to be agreed to by the banks, since they owned the claims and held the deposits and could not be forced, at least without extensive litigation, to give them up. The ability to resolve the crisis by Inauguration Day 1981 was greatly aided by the fact that the banks had been negotiating since the previous May, through the channel in West Germany, on the elements of a financial agreement. The banks had found authoritative Iranian representatives to talk with at a time when the government channels all were closed down.

The aspect of the financial settlement that has received the most comment is the notion that the banks were treated better than other potential claimants—Americans whose property had been expropriated by Iran, those who had contracts repudiated by the new regime, or the holders of a long list of other sorts of claims and potential claims. While the better treatment is factually correct, it was not due to favoritism on the part of the U.S. government. Where possible, the government did try to be responsive to commercial considerations for banks and others. But, as Richard Davis records, there also were cases where bank requests that made good commercial sense were nonetheless rejected on the ground of government policy. A case in point was Treasury's rejection of a bank proposal under which U.S. banks that had served as agents for syndicated loans would be replaced by non-U.S. banks, on the theory that Iran then would be more likely to make the scheduled payments. The government regarded this as a substantive accommodation to the Iranians and refused to permit it.

As Robert Carswell demonstrates, the main reason why the banks came out better was that they began better. For one thing, they held the money—the Iranian deposits—and in any dispute the party that starts out with the cash has a built-in advantage. In addition, their claims were for "liquidated," or readily discernible, amounts. In a straight loan arrangement, the amount due ordinarily is understood by both parties, and there is no real room for dispute.

In contrast, when property is expropriated, when a contract is breached, or when a personal injury is inflicted, the amount of the damage usually is a major element of the dispute. In those circumstances, no one in the government could responsibly assign a value to each of the nonbank claims pending against Iran and then add up the total. To resolve these nonbank claims, the settlement included a procedure for settling or arbitrating claims against Iran—one that promised to treat most claimants better than they could have expected in the U.S. courts, because it avoided the jurisdictional bar of sovereign immunity and such defenses as the act-of-state doctrine. In providing that avenue, the settlement probably did as much as it was possible to do to protect the interests of the nonbank claimants, whose claims were of indeterminate amounts and thus qualitatively different from the bank claims.

Paradoxically, it was not owing to the demand of either the banks or the government that the bank loans were paid off. Until January 15, 1981, both the government and the banks had assumed that they could obtain no more than an Iranian agreement to bring the loans current and to provide additional security to guarantee future payments. It was the Iranians who decided, in a dramatic shift of position only five days before the hostages were released, that they preferred to pay off the majority of the bank loans. If this was favoritism for the banks, the complaint should be lodged with the Iranians, not with the U.S. government or even with the banks themselves.

As these chapters make clear, the negotiation and implementation of the financial agreement generated both enormous complexity and compelling drama in the closing days of the crisis. In the end, implementation of the agreement involved multiple acts of faith on both sides. The Iranians entrusted enormous fund transfers to others. The banks, meanwhile, were willing to pay over $5.6 billion into an escrow account on the basis of a garbled payment instruction from Iran and an order from a lame-duck Secretary of the Treasury, despite the fact that Iran had refused to sign a technical annex to the escrow agreement. In the end, therefore, even a settlement between such disparate parties required a heavy element of trust.

Hostage Claims

One of the most difficult aspects of the settlement involved the question what to do about potential claims against Iran by the people who had been held hostage. At our encounter in Germany in mid-September, the Iranian emissary, Sadegh Tabatabai, said Iran would require a provision that neither the United States nor the hostages themselves could assert claims against Iran as a result of the embassy seizure. I objected to that demand.

Subsequently, however, we agreed to it as part of the settlement. This decision was based on several elements: advice from the Attorney General as to the remoteness of any recovery in private suits against Iran by the hostages, the preference of a great majority of the hostage families, and the judgment that the U.S. government should find a way to compensate the hostages for their ordeal. I feel that the decision on balance was a correct one, but it also generated no little agony in the process, and it leaves no little pain upon reflection.

A Working System

For some, the Iranian hostage crisis came to symbolize a failure of the United States and the incompetence of its government. The feeling of anger and frustration that such a thing could happen was not unknown in the government either. But the chapters in this study implicitly support a contrasting view of how our government functions.

This was a case, for example, in which the separate branches of the government pulled together. In the post-Vietnam era there has been growing concern about the potential foreign policy "gridlock" of the U.S. government, growing mainly out of disputes between the executive and legislative branches. The Vietnam experience inspired the Congress to fashion a comprehensive assortment of new tools for involving itself more deeply in the conduct of foreign policy (some of which have become considerably less potent with the demise of the legislative veto at the hands of the Supreme Court). In this context, it is quite extraordinary that in the Iranian hostage crisis the executive was left a relatively free hand to design and pursue its course, with a minimum of legislative strictures, second guessing, or sniping.

Of course the character of the crisis invited congressional deference. The problem was simply intractable, and promising ideas and easy solutions were no less scarce on Capitol Hill than elsewhere. With the country up against as unpredictable and quarrelsome an adversary as the Ayatollah Khomeini, and with American personnel in such obvious and immediate peril, there was an understandable reluctance on Capitol Hill to say or do things that might aggravate the situation. Moreover, the domestic political implications of the event were extraordinarily complex. Despite popular frustrations, few wanted to risk the appearance of interfering with sensitive diplomacy.

The executive, of course, also did what it could to further discourage unhelpful legislative initiatives, principally through a strategy that ought to be standard practice in such circumstances—extensive consultation with the Congress. There was a rigorous effort to keep senators and congressmen informed, both on events in Iran and on the details and rationale of our policy. Consultation with relevant committees took place almost daily during the crucial periods. This helped make the Congress a partner in our policy and also worked to dispel the sort of suspicions common in the Vietnam era that Congress was being deceived or cut out of the action. So, even in an era of intragovernmental rivalry, this was at least one case in which the two most contentious branches of the national government were able to work well together, to coordinate their efforts, and to present the world with a united front.

Similarly, as the crisis evolved the judiciary also accommodated itself to the executive's need for wide discretion in managing a complex and delicate international matter. As Richard Davis and Robert Carswell recount, a number of U.S. district court judges did reject the government's requests that cases involving attachments of Iranian assets be stayed. The appellate courts, however, supported the government's position and thus assured the negotiators wide latitude to bargain. Most importantly, in 1981 the U.S. Supreme Court explicitly affirmed the President's power during the hostage crisis to nullify attachments, order the transfer of Iranian assets, and suspend the enforceability of claims against Iran in U.S. courts.

Within the executive branch, meanwhile, there also were examples throughout the crisis not only of diligence and dedication but of resourcefulness and foresight on the part of government officials. Richard Davis, for example, notes that long before the hostages were seized the Treasury Department had made a comprehensive assessment of economic links between the United States and Iran and the President's authority to act to protect American interests. Later, when President Carter decided to impose a freeze on Iranian assets, the papers necessary to implement his decision— including a presidential executive order, appropriate regulations, and a report to Congress—already had been prepared in Treasury's Office of Foreign Assets Control.

Showing another quality, Harold Saunders's first chapter includes a description of on-the-scene reports by telephone from the embassy's political officer, Ann Swift, as the embassy was being overrun. Her cool professionalism comes through clearly. Saunders also describes how, with the usual sources of information cut off, the officers on the Iran task force working in the State Department's Operations Center used the telephone as a remarkably effective instrument for gathering intelligence.

Elsewhere, Roberts Owen describes how professionals in the Legal Adviser's office were able to reduce typically long, convoluted American legal documents into the abbreviated language of the Declarations of Algiers, making them translatable and understandable to the other parties involved without sacrificing the desired meaning or legal effect. At the same time, whenever a term changed even slightly, all the implementing orders had to be recast to reflect the change—a highly demanding technical job with no room for error.

A special example of professionalism was the interpretation of discussions and translation of documents between English and French. A major part of this enormously difficult and sensitive task fell to two professional State Department interpreters, Stephanie Van Riegersberg in the early stages and then Alec Toumayan. They were not only masterly linguists but also experts on the cultures of the region. Their translations transcended science; they were works of art.

There also was personal sacrifice. The sacrifice of the hostages them-selves was of course the clearest example of the difficulties America's public servants must be prepared to endure. The commitment, discipline, and sheer life force that brought them through the ordeal was awesome to ob-serve. Though many others did double and triple duty, the hostages were the heroes of this frustrating experience.

On the whole, it is obvious that a settlement in such unusual circum-stances, in the face of such overwhelming obstacles, simply could not have been achieved without high levels of energy, creativity, and talent. Most of the attention went to a few officials at the top of the government. Most of the credit for the success, however, belongs to the many scores of career public servants who were not visible but who made countless decisive contribu-tions to the process.

LOOKING TO THE FUTURE

While it is important to record what happened, that is only a step on the way to the still more useful purpose of this reexamination, which is to grasp whatever lessons the event has for the future. Each section of this volume makes a contribution along that line, and the interpretations and lessons drawn by the authors have been supplemented and refined in broader dis-cussions involving others who had a role in the hostage episode. In this same spirit, I propose the following, not as an exhaustive review of the lessons of the crisis but as a preliminary list of those to which I would attach importance.

Negotiating with Terrorists

One of the most controversial questions raised about U.S. policy on the Iranian crisis is whether it was right, as a matter of principle, to negotiate with the terrorists who took over the embassy. In this case, a refusal to negotiate with the terrorists would have entailed a refusal to negotiate with the government that subsequently embraced the terrorists' actions. Some still are disturbed by the remembered image of the United States constantly probing for ways to start discussions, while the hostages were being paraded blindfolded before the cameras and while the Ayatollah, rebuffing every attempt to talk, was escalating his abusive, anti-American rhetoric. It might well have been more satisfying psychologically to turn a cold shoul-der to these international outlaws, or to treat them in kind—or perhaps to pound them back to the Stone Age.

Considered more soberly, however, the most extreme of those an-swers—massive military retribution and the like—almost certainly would have cost the lives of the hostages and also would have severely damaged broader American interests. Moreover, it would be neither an accurate portrayal of our national character nor an especially appealing or useful depiction of America to have it known that when we are confronted by uncivilized groups we readily jettison our own standards.

In the circumstances we faced, seeking to negotiate, in combination with economic sanctions, was the right course. To think otherwise—to regard negotiating itself as a concession—is mistakenly to equate talking with yielding. We can and should refuse, as we did in this case, to make concessions that imply any form of victory for kidnappers. We firmly resisted the kind of outcome that would have invited similar acts in the future. Such a negotiating posture, one that shows our resolve, can produce an agreement that withholds concessions and still saves lives.

Circumstances will of course differ from case to case. Sometimes a bold and skillful military strike can be successful, as the Israelis proved at Entebbe. But there will be other, less propitious times as well. We must be prepared to adapt our strategy to suit the circumstances. A rigid "never negotiate" posture limits the government's ability to find an acceptable outcome. Any predetermined strategy, slavishly followed, could draw us to nightmarish results.

The decision to probe and negotiate was sorely tested in Iran, where our efforts to inject reason at first were met only by insolence and insults. Nevertheless, in the end it was not the force of our arms but the force of our arguments—along with our economic and diplomatic leverage and our persistence and determination in making them felt—that ultimately prevailed. It was the policy of steady, methodical probing for a negotiated result that brought the crisis to an end. And I believe we should take the crisis as a clear vindication of talking as a means to resolve international disputes.

That is a lesson we should keep in mind should similar circumstances arise again. It is also a lesson to be remembered as we apportion the national budget, so that as we build our military strength we do not neglect the diplomatic resources that are equally indispensable to our international success.

Flexibility in Negotiation

Beyond the decision to negotiate, the successful conclusion of the Iranian hostage crisis stands as testimony to the value of a flexible, creative approach in negotiations. There were numerous examples.

• In the initial phase, working through the United Nations, we moved away from the American model of a comprehensive agreement settled in advance to an evolving "scenario," with a series of mutually dependent steps. That effort ultimately failed—not, I think, because the approach was unworkable, but because political circumstances in Iran were too confused.

• Later, the United States responded flexibly to Iran's demand that all U.S. claims against Iran be canceled. Rather than reject the demand outright, we agreed to "cancel" claims that Americans then had pending against Iran on condition that the Iranians subject themselves to an international arbitral tribunal that would consider the same claims.

• In the case of the bank settlement, too, we were able to accommodate Iranian sensibilities without sacrificing substance. They wanted back all of their frozen overseas bank deposits, an outcome that would have left the bank creditors of Iran unprotected. Through an escrow arrangement, however, all of Iran's overseas deposits were momentarily given up by the banks; but the major part of the funds was immediately returned to the banks by the escrow agent to pay off the loans.

• Another example of flexibility was a dramatic departure from the American tradition of length and complexity in drafting agreements. It was clear that long and complicated documents could not easily survive translation into French and Farsi, nor were such documents likely to be comprehended in Tehran. Therefore the settlement documents were made short and simple. The claims settlement declaration was reduced to only five pages—even though it established principles for the settlement of claims running into the billions of dollars.

• Yet another example was the form of the agreements. When the Algerians came to Washington on December 27, 1980, they reported that Iran would not sign anything that the United States signed. This led to the idea of separate, parallel, mutually reinforcing promises to the Algerians by both the United States and Iran.

In these and other instances, the hostage negotiations underscored the importance of an open-minded approach. We must never be prisoners of precedent. It is essential to keep the perspective of the opponent in mind, not to make concessions but to be able to frame unalterable principles in ways that also accommodate purposes of the other side. The objective in a serious negotiation is to achieve affirmative results—in this case to win the release of the hostages in a way that would also preserve American honor, and to do so under the most favorable terms for private American claimants.

Flexibility is bound to become even more important as the international environment changes. Harold Saunders forecasts that in the decades ahead the United States will have to cope increasingly with nations whose world view is not ours, whose political and decision-making processes are unfamiliar, and whose political conditions make it impossible or unlikely that they will respond to outside pressures however compelling, or who by their very lack of power and coherent political structures can limit the capacity of the great powers to influence the course of events. Beyond learning as much as we can about the novel perspectives and cultures that are coming to play an expanded role in world affairs, one way to bridge the gulf will be through a more creative diplomacy, a constant search for new formulas for preserving and advancing our interests.

The Ease of Starting Conflicts

For all countries, the hostage crisis must be an object lesson for the proposition that conflicts and crises can be comparatively easy to begin and gruelingly difficult to end. Some accounts leave the impression that the crisis began almost by accident—that the plan of the captors had been only to hold the embassy for a short time and then withdraw. Perhaps they fully expected that the government security forces would soon arrive and drive them out.

On that front, however, no one gave the appropriate order. Various government factions may have feared a violent reaction against them if they attempted to remove the captors, and so the government decided to co-opt the action rather than oppose it. As the days wore on, the captors may have become so caught up in their own rhetoric and so enamored of their new prominence that they could not let go. We can only speculate. But it is at least conceivable that the start of the crisis grew out of impulse rather than strategic planning and that the crisis continued out of inertia. In those few hours at the beginning, however, the die was cast for a long-running ordeal that would cost Iran dearly.

The Iranian hostage episode therefore should be a reminder to those who might contemplate similar provocations that such events can tumble out of control, with bitter consequences for all concerned. What can be started easily, almost casually, often can be stopped only at enormous effort and cost.

In a wider sense, all nations should keep in mind that the same principle applies even more forcefully where shooting wars are concerned, as Iraq, Argentina, the Soviet Union, and others have discovered in tangible ways in recent years.

The Role of Military Options

The lessons of the Iranian hostage crisis with respect to military action may seem obvious, but perhaps they are deceptively so. The military options developed by the Joint Chiefs of Staff at the outset included a possible punitive strike, but this was not pursued since it did not seem likely to contribute to the release of the hostages and probably would have worsened their plight and made Iran still more obdurate. Less drastic options, such as mining Iran's harbors or otherwise imposing a blockade, also were seen as excessively risky instruments. This was especially true after the Soviet invasion of Afghanistan altered the strategic picture. The use of force also might have reversed the favorable international view of our side of the issue—the factor that led to mounting international political pressure on Iran.

On balance, the main military options available seemed potentially at least as harmful to our interests as to Iran's. So it is quite easy to "learn" from the crisis that military action is a blunt instrument, ill-suited to delicate operations, and therefore irrelevant in circumstances such as those we faced in Iran. A sledgehammer, after all, is not well suited to carve a design.

The proper lesson, however, is more complex. For there is some evidence that one precisely targeted, very explicit military threat did have some effect on the behavior of the Iranians. In the first days after the hostages were taken, their captors announced that they were to be tried as spies and executed. The White House publicly suggested that any such trials would bring a U.S. military response. Then on November 23 the President followed up with a private message to Iran which left no doubt that if the hostages were harmed or tried, there would be military retribution. Since Iranian decision-making at the time was so murky, we cannot of course be certain of a direct connection between that threat and subsequent Iranian behavior. It is a fact, however, that the talk of trials and punishments began to fade rather abruptly after President Carter's message was delivered.

So the lesson on the utility of military options might be formulated somewhat more narrowly. It probably is true that a spasm of violence in response to the hostage taking would have been counterproductive. But it also is possible to use or intimate force in measured ways, and there are circumstances in which a credible threat, aimed at a precise issue, can serve to provoke thought rather than inflame passions.

It may be most relevant to distinguish between the threat or use of force for *deterrence,* to dissuade a nation from taking undesirable action in the future, or for *coercion,* to make the object change the behavior it is engaged in now. Between the two, a threat for deterrence, which was used in the hostage case, tends to be the more promising strategy. Such factors as inertia and the general human instinct against uncertainty tend to reinforce a strategy of deterrence, because they help tip the scales against changing the status quo. So deterrence, whether geared toward preventing the Iranians from putting the hostages on trial or toward keeping the Soviets from launching a nuclear strike, has been employed with some success.

Coercion usually is more difficult. There are of course variations of a coercive military strategy. One route would be simply to issue an ultimatum, demanding surrender by a certain date "or else" there will be massive retribution. Of course it is necessary then to be prepared to carry out the threat. Bluffing is not an option, because if the bluff is called—and chances are great that it will be—backing down would entail an unacceptable loss of credibility.

Or force can be applied in increments—first a blockade, then mining harbors, then air strikes against military targets, then strikes against economic targets, and so on—with a pause after each step to afford an opportunity for compliance with the demand. But here inertia operates against the strategy, because coercion seeks to change conduct—in the Iranian case to induce the government to arrange the release of the hostages. Face also comes into play, especially if the threat is publicized. The change almost certainly will be visibly attributable to the threat, and countries are loathe to be seen yielding to force. It is possible to conceive of circumstances where coercion might work. In most cases, however, and certainly in the Iranian hostage crisis, military coercion is a strategy whose promise is uncertain and whose risks are tremendous.

The Effect of Economic Sanctions

Another lesson that should not be overlearned, in the sense of invoking it automatically, involves the effectiveness of economic sanctions. It is unquestionable that in these specific circumstances the sanctions, principally the freeze of some $12 billion in Iranian assets, placed a heavy burden on Iran and contributed to the ultimate conclusion on the part of Iranian leaders that it was in their interest to resolve the crisis. However, that impact, powerful though it was, not only was slow in coming but flowed from some unique circumstances.

In the years of the Shah's rule, U.S. business had been selling huge quantities of goods and services to Iran, and Iran maintained large deposits in U.S. banks to sustain that commerce as well as to place Iran's oil earnings. Thus the United States had access to most of Iran's available foreign exchange reserves. Access to such a vast share of another country's resources, to the point where a freeze can truly make a difference, is likely to be a rarity.

We also need to keep in mind that the imposition of such sanctions is not without cost. As Robert Carswell points out, a willingness to block dollar accounts in U.S. banks abroad can put our banks at a competitive disadvantage, since it may inspire foreign holders of dollars to deposit them in competing non-U.S. banks instead. Indeed, the scope of the assets freeze in this case has warned other countries to be more diversified than Iran was in placing their deposits. Also, foreigners may choose to shift their assets out of dollars into other currencies, which ultimately could weaken the dollar and undermine its role as a reserve currency.

Richard Davis identifies yet another cost: the fact that many of the dollars held by Iran in U.S. banks were on their way to U.S. citizens as payment for goods already supplied, debts previously incurred, or services already performed. In those cases the hardship of the freeze landed on our own people. And a freeze with extraterritorial reach inevitably creates frictions with the countries where our branch banks are located, since those countries also assert jurisdiction over institutions operating on their territory.

For these reasons, we should not take from the Iranian hostage crisis the lesson that economic sanctions are always, or even usually, an attractive tool for serving our political goals in the world or for resolving individual crises. They still should be used sparingly in special cases where the conduct to be answered is particularly egregious, where we can enlist the support of other countries, and where we can be sure economic leverage will have some effect. Iran was such a case. There will not be many others.

The Impact of the Press and Media

In the United States, news reporting not only records history but also helps compose it. In a society where the press is both free and zealous, it inevitably influences events, through the character and the extent of its coverage, even as it describes them.

If that is true as a general proposition, it was especially true of the Iranian hostage crisis. It became a preoccupation of journalists with a variety of specialties. For the entire fourteen months of the crisis, it was the dominant national news story. Throughout that time, more often than not it was the lead story on the networks' evening news broadcasts, and rarely was a program without at least some coverage. On CBS it was nightly fare, as the running count of days of the hostages' confinement became Walter Cronkite's regular signoff. On ABC, it gave birth to an entirely new news program, *America Held Hostage*, now *Nightline*. The major newspapers, wire services, and newsmagazines also reported, examined, and speculated on the crisis in abundant detail.

So whatever influence ordinary coverage would have had on the crisis was magnified because the coverage was so intense. It also was magnified by the phenomenon of television, with its capacity to display the news graphically, or bring it alive, into the American home—and also with its tendency to simplify, so that we think we are informed when in fact we are not much more than notified.

Several different kinds of press influence on the hostage crisis can be identified. First, it is quite possible that the instant celebrity and access to the media won by those who took the hostages had some impact both in convincing the captors that they were on to something and ought to persevere and in deterring the assertion of control by Iranian security officials. It was a situation reminiscent of the common demand of hostage takers that they be permitted to convey their special message directly to the world through the media. Of course this phenomenon and the proper role of journalists are subjects of continual soul-searching by the media. I do not propose here to offer any prescriptions—only the observations that it is vain to try to deflect news organizations from their job of covering events that are newsworthy and that the line between coverage and participation, especially in hostage takings, is not necessarily a clear one.

A second and still more formidable kind of influence is the impact of news coverage in shaping popular views. The Vietnam war was a particularly good example of the process—the first U.S. war that literally could be brought home to the living room each evening through satellite communications. By reporting reality much more efficiently than in the past, the media hastened the growth of domestic opposition to the war. This same process of accelerating and sharpening the development of public attitudes unquestionably played a role in the Iranian crisis. Coverage that reinforced a national sense of outrage and frustration put heavy pressure on the government to act swiftly and visibly.

Third, because our diplomacy in this case had the unusual property of being a negotiation between parties that were not speaking to each other, it was unusually susceptible to faulty press interpretation or characterization of the positions of the two sides. For example, the December 19, 1980, Iranian demand for $24 billion in financial guarantees, while the amount was excessive, contained the first indications of Iranian willingness to accept a tribunal for adjudication of claims and to accept guarantees rather than actual payments, both major concessions. But in news accounts, the favorable aspects of the Iranian statement were almost universally ignored, while the size of the demand was widely reported and of course unremittingly pummelled. Such treatment complicates the negotiating atmosphere, as negotiating partners who are not accustomed to our system ascribe press views to the government or as the media's concentration on the most inflammatory issues tends to require the negotiators to concentrate on them as well.

On the whole, I believe that the American people were basically well served by the media and the press during the crisis. There was a great deal of very good reporting—accurate accounts of events, solid background reporting, and creative efforts to explain complex financial and diplomatic issues in layman's terms. But there also were some serious lapses—a few in misreading the facts and more in failing to place events during the crisis in context.

For example, as the descriptions in this book make clear, the visit of Iranian Prime Minister Rajai to the United Nations in mid-October of 1980 was a turning point in the crisis, because he learned at first hand there that

Iran's isolation from the world community was so deep that he could find no sympathy at all for Iran as the victim of aggression from Iraq. U.S. diplomacy was geared toward precisely that objective at the United Nations, and it was successful. On the other hand, we did not place great emphasis on seeking a direct meeting between U.S. officials and Prime Minister Rajai, since we knew it was unlikely to happen and unlikely to accomplish anything if it did. Yet much of the press coverage of Rajai's visit ignored the critical message he was receiving from other countries and focused on his unwillingness to meet with representatives of the United States. The press emphasized that his refusal deflated hopes that his presence could provide an opening for high-level contacts, but no one seriously harbored such hopes.

A more serious failing was the tendency to report events outside of any historical framework. At the outset of the crisis, the American people probably knew next to nothing about Iran and its history. While a better perspective on the cultural and political traditions of Iran would not have made the hostage seizure any more acceptable or justifiable, it might have made the episode more understandable and could have encouraged a calmer and more deliberate reaction. In particular, the hatred of the Iranians for the United States could be understood only against the background of gross and prolonged abuses by the Shah and the history of U.S. involvement with him, and this perspective too often was missing.

In defense of the press, however, it is fair to say that this lack of perspective had been cultivated by many years of official intimacy with Iranian leaders and emphasis on the convergence of U.S. and Iranian interests—a kind of myopia our leaders still disport with respect to the authoritarian leaders of some other countries of strategic importance.

To put the press's performance in perspective, it must also be said that this was a story of almost impenetrable complexity, requiring expertise on such diverse matters as Iranian history and culture, the practices of international finance, and the intricacies of international law. Also, the government was not always as helpful as it could have been in providing the necessary background. As events unfolded, the most knowledgeable briefers were not always the most accessible. And with so many people involved in planning and implementing U.S. strategy, it was inevitable that some officials would interpret things differently from others, so that a reporter sometimes could find inside authority for contradictory propositions. There is always room for improvement in the way the government deals with the press, especially on the most sensitive issues.

Unquestionably, a free press can be an irritant, even as a handicap, to our diplomacy and our other operations in the world. But that views it out of context, just as the hostage crisis too often was viewed. A free press also is indispensable to democracy and among the most precious assets a free people can have. We must direct our efforts not toward limiting its role but toward dealing with it realistically and helping it perform its legitimate role with greater accuracy, enlightenment, and professionalism.

Integrating Public and Private Interests

The Iranian hostage crisis and the negotiations to resolve it raised the possibility, if not the reality, of a collision between public and private negotiating efforts. The government had as its principal aim the release of the hostages under circumstances that would protect the national honor. The banks had a distinct primary interest, which was to assure that Iran's outstanding debts to them would be repaid.

Those aims were not necessarily in conflict; as it turned out, the settlement served them all. Nevertheless, it remained possible throughout the negotiations that one set of discussions could interfere with the other. It is at least theoretically possible, for example, that if the banks had refused to discuss an economic settlement with the Iranians in May 1980, those same Iranians might have pressed their government harder to renew official contacts. Government-to-government contacts during that period would not likely have been fruitful in any event, but the speculation illustrates a generic danger.

In my view, such problems were managed or avoided because of several factors that may have broader utility in any future cases where important public and private interests are involved:

• In his discussion with Iran's counsel in Germany, John Hoffman, who conducted the bank negotiations, made clear from the outset that the negotiations would be reported to the U.S. government and that no settlement could be reached on economic matters unless U.S. government objectives were secured in the same agreement.

• The private negotiators were scrupulous in reporting the contents of their negotiations to the government, through Treasury Deputy Secretary Carswell. This made it possible for the government, if necessary, to warn the private negotiators away from dangerous areas and also to help channel them in promising directions.

• The government did not use, and resisted requests to use, the bank channel as a means of conveying information to the Iranians. Even this kind of limited, direct involvement in the diplomatic process would have invested the bank channel with more authority than it required and would have led to further confusion of an already complex process of negotiating through the Algerians.

• The bank issues were an integral part of the ultimate agreement as a consequence of the assets freeze. This gave the government good reason to recommend that the bank negotiations go ahead, even when government-to-government contacts were not possible. In other circumstances, it might be advisable to insist that government-to-government issues be settled first.

In sum, intimate linkages between private and public questions of the kind that occurred here are fraught with danger. They need to be handled with extreme delicacy and care on all sides. The success of the negotiations in this case is a confirmation that those standards were met.

A related concern arises from the phenomenon that major international events often draw volunteers of various kinds. They range all the way from cranks, publicity seekers, and opportunists (including, in this case, people who were interested in facilitating renewed armed sales to Iran, for a price) to academics and cultural experts who have important insights to offer and contributions to make. The only lesson in this is that the government cannot afford to become so offended by the pestering of the former that it neglects to take advantage of the latter. These pages contain evidence that some private individuals actually complicated the negotiations. On the other hand, the help provided by others in the private sector was of value.

A Better Way

Finally, the Iranian hostage crisis has left me thinking about processes of crisis management. Having long been impressed by General George Marshall's policy of abstention, I have no plans to evaluate or criticize the personal performance of any of my colleagues. This self-imposed rule does not prevent me from considering whether there is a better process through which to address a comparable problem in the future. My consideration is directed to that category of grave and important problems that fall just short of a full-scale military crisis, such as presented by the Cuban missile crisis, but encompassing festering issues with no discrete time limits.

For the first ten months of the hostage crisis, the President dealt with the problem almost exclusively through the National Security Council (NSC) apparatus. President Carter described this process in *Keeping Faith:*

> At least once each day my top advisers—the Vice President, Secretaries of State, Defense, and Treasury, Attorney General, National Security Adviser, members of the Joint Chiefs of Staff; my Press Secretary, Legal Counsel, Director of the Central Intelligence Agency, and others as necessary—met in the Situation Room at the White House to discuss Iran. When I did not meet with them, they prepared written minutes almost immediately after they adjourned. Any question of policy was referred to me, either during the meeting or in a series of questions within the written report. I would answer

the questions and give additional instructions, and then could feel reasonably confident that everyone would work by the same rules. In times of emergency or when there was an especially difficult decision, we met in the Oval Office or the Cabinet Room, so that I could participate in the full discussion.[1]

In this process, people participated based upon their positions, not expertise or any other criterion, and several Cabinet members were involved regularly. Since the President chose to address the problem largely through the Special Coordinating Committee (rather than the broader Policy Review Committee, which was chaired by either the Secretary of State or the Secretary of Defense), the National Security Adviser played a central role. He established the agenda for each day's meeting, assigned special studies, chaired the meetings, and prepared the minutes that went directly to the President.

For each day's meeting, the Cabinet officers and sometimes their deputies would leave whatever else they were doing and go to the White House Situation Room to meet, usually at 9:00 A.M. This group of top-level officials conscientiously went through a substantial agenda, usually consisting of an intelligence update, and then diplomatic, economic, military, and sometimes press issues. Public statements from the White House often were used to communicate with Iran as well as with our public, and they were debated extensively at these meetings. The sessions rarely consumed less than an hour, often more.

Occasionally, as President Carter noted, he would chair the meetings in order to participate directly in the discussion of an especially urgent or difficult issue. If he was not present, the National Security Adviser would summarize the meeting immediately after its conclusion and forward an action memorandum to the President, often containing split recommendations. By the end of the day, the President would act on the recommendations. And then the cycle would start over again.

This process reflected the depth of President Carter's commitment to this issue. No one who observed him during that period could have doubted the priority he gave to the twin goals of the safe return of the hostages and the preservation of our national honor.

In hindsight, the process had several unintended and probably undesirable consequences:

First, on an almost daily basis, as many as ten of the most important officials in the executive branch were diverted each day from their other duties for one to two hours or more, since preparation time had to be added.

1. Carter, *Keeping Faith*, p. 462.

The timing of the meetings, which with travel frequently consumed from 8:30 to 10:30 A.M., tended to maximize the interference with the management of other problems.

Take two hours out of the morning of the most important Cabinet secretaries to meet on an almost daily basis on any specific problem, and you will see a government so highly focused on that issue that other issues may be neglected. Such a process both tended to reinforce the Iranian militants' conviction that they had paralyzed the U.S. government and to strengthen the public impression that the administration regarded the crisis as all-important. In time of war, such a process is necessary. At other times, it is fair to ask, is there a better way?

Second, the formal NSC structure tended to cast each Cabinet secretary in his role as a spokesman for his department. On some of the subsets of issues (for example, sanctions, visa cancellations), this sometimes could result in a form of bargaining or in attempts to reach compromises. The compartmentalized approach almost inevitably led each participant to protect the area of his expertise. Some participants tended to be diffident in expressing views outside their own area, and probing questions outside one's own area sometimes were answered by a welter of bureaucratic jargon that there was no time to penetrate. And there was no devil's advocate. (Although I did not participate, anecdotal data suggests that these characteristics were even more apparent in the tightly knit group that considered and planned the rescue mission under the chairmanship of the National Security Adviser.)

Third, as a related point, the working groups within the Cabinet departments, while expert and useful, largely were circumscribed in their missions and did not cross departmental lines. For example, the State Department's Iran Working Group performed heroically over the fourteen-month period, but it had little opportunity to affect planning or execution in the phases of the crisis being managed by other departments. Because of the need for secrecy, heightened by concern for leaks, the departmental experts often had to operate without knowing the full picture. This was orderly, but was it optimal?

Fourth, reliance on the formal NSC process tended to focus the entire problem on the President and make it impossible for him to distance himself from any aspect of the matter. The President was hooked:

> Staying close to Washington quickly became standard policy. Once the custom of eliminating unnecessary travel had been adopted, to renounce it was to indicate reduced interest in the hostages or a loss of hope that they would survive.[2]

2. Ibid., p. 463.

For whatever reason, there never was a sustained effort to put the issue on the back burner. Some have argued that because of the high level of national interest it would not have been possible to delegate any aspect of the problem. Given the extent of television coverage, that point of view cannot be dismissed. What can be said, however, is that the mechanism chosen to handle the problem gave no opportunity for the President to step back from the problem. Fully aware of the daily White House meetings, the press gave the President no opportunity to deflect the pressure elsewhere.

In the fall of 1980, a different model was partially adopted, more by instinct than by deliberate choice. When we received word through the Germans on September 9 that the Iranians would at last send a representative to meet with us, President Carter asked me to meet with the Iranian, and in turn I asked the President to set up a new, special interagency task force to draft negotiating instructions. The members of this special group could be selected for their special expertise. It consisted of officials just below the top levels of the Cabinet departments; Cabinet secretaries occasionally joined our meetings, but usually did not.

After the German connection broke down, this task force remained in operation and worked out the U.S. positions, subject to approval at highest levels. This group operated with many similarities to the "ExCom" of the Cuban missile crisis. The discussions were unstructured and collegial, with the participants willing to challenge each other's positions across departmental lines and seniority levels. Members of the task force had the confidence of their principals, and they also felt free to carry back a different message from the one they brought to the meetings.

The only agenda was the task before us, and that enabled the discussions to range widely. We wrote and rewrote each other's sections of the instructions to the point where much of the technical background became common. This proved invaluable when, during the final two weeks, part of the task force was in Algiers and part in Washington. The task force assembled confidentially and remained out of public view. That served its principal purpose well. At the same time, the invisibility of the task force did preclude it from deflecting pressure from the President.

Every President must operate in a process that he finds effective for himself. It will vary from President to President, from problem to problem. Should a crisis arise comparable to the Iranian hostage matter, I think a President would be wise to consider lifting the issue out of the regular NSC process and delegating it to a senior interagency task force. He should do so as early as possible—as soon as it is apparent that the problem will persist. The membership of the task force should be drawn from the upper levels of government, with reputations that will command the respect of the bureaucracy and the press. In some instances, it may be advantageous to bring a former official back from private life to participate in the task force as Dean Acheson did at the time of the 1961 Berlin crisis or even to play a leading role as Cyrus Vance did during the 1967-68 domestic riots. Among other attributes, the head of the task force should have ready and direct access to the President.

The necessary press briefings might emanate from the head of the task force or from its own spokesman. Of course the President would be regularly involved where necessary, but he would find it easier to put some distance between himself and the day-to-day developments. No one can be sure that this would calm the public clamor, but it does seem clear that so long as the President is personally involved on a day-to-day basis the visibility will remain high—perhaps artificially high.

On the substance, such a task force could attack a vexing problem of this kind without hobbling regular government operations. Using a collegial approach, the task force could minimize bureaucratic rivalries and produce bolder alternatives for consideration by the President. Of course, no task force can diminish the President's ultimate responsibility. Indeed, a task force may often require inspiration and prodding from the President to avoid a sense of resignation about the problem. Sometimes the President will have to energize the task force by bringing in new personnel, but this should be seen as a reflection of the intractability of the problem rather than the inefficiency of the task force.

After all, if it were an easy problem, it could be handled in a routine way.

1   THE CRISIS BEGINS

HAROLD H. SAUNDERS

TAKEOVER: SUNDAY, NOVEMBER 4, 1979

The Shattering Phone Call

The hostage crisis began for the Washington crisis team, as many Middle East crises do, with a phone call in the middle of the night. Because of the large time difference between Washington and the Middle East—normally six to eight hours—the action often begins there just after Washington has gone to bed. For the State Department's Middle East Bureau in 1979, the ringing of a phone in those hours when most of the country was sleeping rarely meant good news or a simple problem. Each time the phone shattered silence and sleep, bodies and minds braced for shock. Even if the problem was manageable, it took time before minds relaxed and heartbeats returned to normal. This time the crisis was to last 444 days and nights. One staggering call followed another—one bizarre event followed another—until one night much later, hanging up the phone, I found myself asking, "Is the world unraveling?"

A few moments after 3:00 A.M. Washington time on Sunday, November 4, 1979, a call came to the State Department Operations Center from Embassy Tehran. Round the clock every day of the year, senior foreign service officers man the brightly lit "Ops Center" on the seventh floor, several dozen steps from the Secretary of State's suite of offices. From a panel of desks, by secure and open phones and by coded telegrams, they are a link between embassies around the world and action officers and senior policymakers in Washington. The phones ring constantly, and they work against the background chatter of the teletype machines and the whoosh of messages coming by pneumatic tube from the communications center several floors below.

This time it was Political Officer Ann Swift reporting that just before

10:30 A.M. Tehran time—Tehran then was seven and one-half hours later than Eastern Standard Time—a large mob of young Iranians had poured into the embassy compound, was then surrounding the chancery building, and was breaking into other buildings on the compound. Unlike the armed guerrillas who had overrun the embassy the previous February 14, shooting as they came, this mob appeared unarmed. Though technically not the senior officer in the embassy when the attack began, Swift as the senior political officer on the premises seemed to become the hub of a small leadership group that gathered quickly in the ambassador's suite on the second floor of the chancery. Chargé d'Affairs Bruce Laingen and Political Counsellor Victor Tomseth had gone with Security Officer Mike Howland to the Foreign Ministry on routine business. Swift and her colleagues had started to draft a flash telegram but decided to try to get through on the phone too.

Swift's phone call was immediately patched by the Ops Center watch officer to three Washington-area bedrooms. Having served since April 1978 as Assistant Secretary of State for Near Eastern and South Asian Affairs, I was the senior official in a bureau of 110 people in Washington and 1,000 in thirty-seven diplomatic and consular posts in twenty-four countries from Morocco to Bangladesh. Sheldon Krys, Executive Director for the bureau, was a career officer with experience concentrated in administration and management of the human side of foreign service life. His warmth in working with people, his ability to inspire trust, his capacity to get almost anything done in a complex bureaucracy along with a twinkling humor that kept life livable had already made him a central figure in dealing with any crisis of this kind. Carl Clement was Acting Director of Iranian Affairs in the absence of Director Henry Precht, who had been visiting Tehran but had left a few days before and was on his way home. Clement was an experienced and serious officer—a good steady professional with a quiet style and a pleasant manner.

For the next two hours, the three of us shared a running conversation with Swift and her colleagues on the phone in the ambassador's outer office in Tehran. She stayed on the phone while others with her moved in and out of the office reporting what they saw through the windows or learned from the Marines on the lower floors. At our end, it was impossible for us to leave our phones while the conversation continued.

Meanwhile, Secretary Vance arrived at the department where he and his senior assistant Arnold Raphel worked from his outer office. Raphel was a career officer who, as it happened, had served in two posts in Iran and spoke Farsi. The Secretary depended on his commonsense judgments, and his colleagues respected his good-humored and highly competent way of handling our business with the Secretary when time prevented our doing it ourselves. The White House Situation Room alerted the President and key members of his staff. Other watch officers in Washington alerted their principal officials.

High Stakes

Those of us dealing with the Middle East and South Asia had had more than our share of tense late night phone conversations over the previous year. During the early hours of February 14, two calls had come to the Operations Center in quick succession—one reporting the first attack on the embassy in Tehran and the other that our ambassador in Afghanistan, Adolph "Spike" Dubs, had been abducted on his way to work. By the beginning of normal working hours, the captives in the embassy had been freed, but the ambassador was, tragically, dead.

Opening a direct phone line at the beginning of such a crisis was standard procedure. An open line permits instant reporting of developments on the ground, allows Washington to authorize possibly sensitive actions promptly, and enables the crisis team at the State Department to broaden efforts to get help to the scene. For example, a few weeks later while our embassy in Islamabad, Pakistan, was occupied by attackers, Secretary Vance was able to talk directly with the President of Pakistan to urge that he speed army help to relieve the embassy. There is usually a high degree of frustration on the Washington end of such calls, because the Washington team is not always able to provide such specific and immediate help and cannot possibly have the same feel for the situation as the group in the embassy. Those under attack, however, have later said that they found some measure of calm and comfort and a useful checklist of actions to be taken from having immediate access to Washington and avoiding long silences between telegrams.

The previous year and a half had engaged us in a relentless series of high-stakes developments in the Middle East. In April 1978 the local communist party had staged a coup in Afghanistan, and by the fall of 1979 it was in deep enough trouble that Moscow had sent a top-level military team for several weeks to see how the regime could be stabilized. In September 1978 President Carter in an unprecedented stroke had invited Egyptian President Sadat and Israeli Prime Minister Begin to Camp David to discuss ways of building a comprehensive Arab-Israeli-Palestinian peace from Sadat's historic visit to Jerusalem. Six months of further negotiation followed the Camp David accords to produce the breakthrough Egyptian-Israeli peace treaty. Negotiations had been accelerating through the summer and early fall of 1979 to take the next step that had been agreed at Camp David— establishing a Palestinian self-governing authority and launching a five-year transitional period for resolving the Israeli-Palestinian conflict. In the last half of 1978, revolutionary forces had intensified with surprising speed in Iran, and by January 1979 the Shah's regime—once seen as an "island of stability" in the Middle East—had been toppled. With it crumbled the security system on which U.S. policy had relied in the vital Persian Gulf, and with the sharp decline of Iranian oil production came the second of the 1970s' great oil shocks.

Swift's call broke the early Sunday silence. What we could not know then was that the crisis would shatter that agenda, the Carter presidency, and some portion of the foundations of America's stature as an effective global power.

The Embassy Under Attack

The senior staff in the embassy had begun the day at a staff meeting with Chargé Bruce Laingen. The staff had then gone about its work while Laingen with Tomseth and Howland had driven off to the Foreign Ministry for a meeting. There had been a rising sense of apprehension in the embassy for some days over the increasing lawlessness of students in Tehran and the government's decreasing ability to control them. As Economic Counsellor Moorhead Kennedy much later recalled saying to a friend, "Look, if they are now taking over hotels and the government can do nothing about it, what will they take over next?" That Sunday morning as Laingen drove out of the compound onto the main street, there was no indication of the impending attack.

Suddenly, those at their desks were interrupted by the shout of one of the Marine guards, "There's a break-in." As Kennedy later recounted, "I went to the nearest open window because we had blast screens over most of our windows, and there was this huge sea of faces coming in—ardent, ecstatic. We learned later from one of their spokesmen that a great many had expected to be shot at and killed. Of course, that was an immediate passport to the life hereafter for them."

Swift brought those of us in Washington up to date with a quick description of what was happening. We questioned her to try to develop some feel for what the crowd wanted, whether it was armed, how effective and purposeful or how aimless it seemed to be, and how dangerous it appeared. As Kennedy later put it, "They were carrying sticks but there was not a weapon in sight. It was only afterwards that they pulled out their pistols. The whole image they were trying to convey to us was conveyed by a long streamer held up below the big plate glass windows in the ambassador's office by a bunch of women students who would not be fired on. It read: 'We do not wish to inconvenience you. All we want is a 'sit-in.'" Even though the danger of flying bullets did not seem immediate, it was quickly obvious at the Washington end that the mob intended a major demonstration, would not easily be turned away, and would probably at a minimum be able to break into some of the buildings on the compound.

We immediately focused on the efforts of Swift and her colleagues to let the Iranian authorities know what was happening and to try to get help there as quickly as possible. Ultimately, the security of every embassy depends on protection by the host government. No embassy could hold out against a hostile population for very long. For this reason, the strategy for dealing with mob attacks is to give embassy staff a safe place in the chancery to hole up until help comes, hopefully without creating an incident that would make it politically impossible for the government to come to their rescue. That is why the Marine guards at each embassy are instructed not to fire at an attacking crowd until specifically ordered by the ambassador or ranking officer. Deaths of local citizens in an attack could further infuriate the population and make it more difficult for the government to return the situation to normal.

Swift told us that Laingen, Tomseth, and Howland were still at the Foreign Ministry. Embassy Security Officer Al Golacinski had reached them on the radio in their car just as they were about to leave the Ministry at the end of their meeting. They had immediately turned around and gone back into the Ministry. Swift and her colleagues had already reached a Ministry official by phone to report urgently what had happened and to request help, but now Laingen and Tomseth took over that job. They kept a phone line open to the same office where Swift was holding down her end of the line to Washington. Laingen gave the order to begin destroying classified material.

Swift informed the Washington group and the group in the Foreign Ministry that the Marines had so far kept the mob from entering either the ground or first floors of the embassy. Most of the 70 to 80 persons working on the ground and first two floors had moved for safety to the second floor behind a steel door. Many of these were Iranian employees of the embassy and a few others who had been doing business in the chancery. When the Iranians used a truck to pull a grill off one of the windows on the ground floor and entered the building, the Marines attempted to secure the first floor. Whether used on purpose or from an accidentally dropped canister, tear gas began to spread on the first floor. After some forty-five minutes, the Marines retreated to the second floor along with the rest of the staff. They brought their weapons with them and began taking up positions at some of the windows. At one point, the Washington team, listening on the open phone, heard Swift exclaim, "For God's sake, put that down. Put away the guns. No weapons here." The Marines showed complete discipline, despite their frustration at being unable to hold off the mob.

Swift reported that Security Officer Golacinski, who had his own line to Howland at the Foreign Ministry, had courageously gone outside the embassy in an effort to talk with the attackers. It is not uncommon during attacks like this to try to make contact with the mob's leaders, to find out what they want, to get people talking about whether some reasonable response will meet their objectives, and generally to reduce passions and the chances of people being hurt. In this case, it did not work. Swift's colleagues at the windows reported at 4:11 A.M. EST, according to a rough log kept at the Washington end of the line, that the attackers had bound and blindfolded Golacinski and were also holding four Marines whom they had captured elsewhere on the compound.

Swift was also on the phone to the consular office in another building at a far corner of the compound. I instructed her to have the consul destroy visa plates so unauthorized visas for entry into the United States could not be issued if the office were taken over and the plates fell into Iranian hands. The consulate building was not immediately penetrated. As we learned later, its occupants were able to exit onto the street on a side of the compound away from the attacking mob. Five who turned one way escaped detection and eventually found refuge in the Canadian Embassy. They were later joined there by the agricultural attaché, who was working in another building near the compound during the attack. Their concealment by the Canadians and subsequent escape from Iran would become one of the many minidramas that make up the story of the hostage crisis. Those from the consular section who turned in the opposite direction were captured and joined the rest of their colleagues held hostage in the compound.

Swift reported that efforts were being made to destroy what files were still in the staff's control. Some of the files on the lower floors had simply been locked in haste as the staff withdrew upstairs. The quick break-in on the ground floor did not leave enough time for destruction. Shredding continued as long as possible on the second floor but the chaotic situation, shortness of time, and the breakdown of one of the destruction machines made it impossible to destroy substantial quantities of material. A small group remained locked separately in the embassy's top security vault on the second floor even after the rest of the embassy had surrendered, destroying communications equipment and classified papers stored there.

At 4:25 A.M. Washington time—11:55 A.M. in Tehran—Swift reported that the attackers appeared to be lighting fires on the chancery's first floor. A combination of smoke and tear gas began seeping under the steel door and reaching to the group on the second floor. They also seemed to be using some sort of torch to break through the last steel door. As it became increasingly apparent that Iranian government help might not arrive in any reasonable time, the staff in the chancery made one more effort to talk with the attackers, at least to assure the safety of the staff if it surrendered. John Limbert, an officer fluent in Farsi, volunteered to try and slipped out through the steel door. It was barricaded again behind him. At 4:46 A.M. EST, Swift reported that both Golacinski and Limbert were urging that the group on the second floor come out, that further resistance would be useless. They also reported threats to kill some of those staff members who had been taken in other parts of the embassy compound. Laingen and Tomseth by phone with Swift from the Foreign Ministry concurred in the decision to surrender.

At that point, the staff had to strike a balance between holding out longer and leaving the attackers in a mood where harm to embassy personnel would be inevitable if they had to surrender. Laingen was told in the Acting Foreign Minister's office that the mob intended only to stage a peaceful demonstration and sit-in and that the Ayatollah Khomeini would soon be on the radio telling the attackers to turn back the embassy. Swift reported at 4:44 A.M. EST, just minutes before the surrender, that the Ministry said it had contacted Khomeini's office. Faced with smoke and whiffs of tear gas drifting into their second-floor refuge, threats to harm individuals in the hands of the mob, and no immediate prospect of government help, those in Tehran felt they had no alternative to surrender. "Our whole thought," said Swift after coming home, "was to give up peacefully so we could be released peacefully." We on the phone in Washington agreed with that judgment.

Each of the parties on the phone remembered the attack earlier in the year on February 14, when the embassy staff surrendered to a heavily armed mob in an effort to prevent bloodshed. On that occasion, the embassy was taken over for a few hours but turned back to then Ambassador William Sullivan by senior officials of the revolutionary government, who came to the compound and dispersed the attackers. A key figure in the February 14 rescue was the man who was now the Foreign Minister, Ibrahim Yazdi. The expectation that any captivity would again last only a few hours conditioned the judgment that surrender was preferable to confrontation.

At 4:50 A.M.—12:20 P.M. in Tehran—Swift reported, "We have just opened the door." The Iranians on the other side looking in, she said, were not armed. They began searching staff members as they came out, telling them not to be afraid. Swift told us they were in their early 20s, quiet, controlling themselves well but that they were tying people's hands as they went out. Then Swift said simply, "We're going down." They started down the stairs into what no one at that stage could know would eventually add up to 444 days as hostages. Swift had not hung up. She had put the phone down, leaving the line open. After a long period, it went dead. The group in the security vault remained locked in, but an hour and a half later the communications center in the department reported that its teletype line had gone down too.

With the phone connection out, the three of us who had been on the phone with Swift dressed quickly and headed toward the Ops Center. At about 6:00 A.M. Washington time, Under Secretary David Newsom had taken charge of the line from the department to Laingen in the Iranian Foreign Ministry. Newsom, the top career officer in the department's hierarchy, was a veteran of many crises and had coordinated the department's activities through much of the 1978 revolution in Iran. He had also been the senior "action officer" during the Shah's admission to the United States in October.

When Laingen, Tomseth, and Howland had left the embassy for their 9:30 A.M. meeting at the Foreign Ministry, the crowds passing on their way to a demonstration at Tehran University had paid little attention to them. That demonstration was not specifically directed at the United States. Earlier that morning in a staff meeting, they had discussed the possibility of trouble as the crowds dispersed later in the day, but they had not expected trouble so early. In earlier staff meetings they had discussed the severe disruption to normal embassy operations caused by shutting the embassy down each time there was a demonstration in Tehran, and they were not inclined to close that morning.

As they turned back into the Foreign Ministry after learning of the attack on the embassy, they immediately sought out the Chief of Protocol with whom they normally dealt on security and demanded he take the necessary action. Then they moved to the Acting Foreign Minister's office. They were told that Foreign Minister Yazdi, who had just returned from Algiers with Prime Minister Bazargan, was on his way back to the ministry from the airport. When he arrived, Laingen and Tomseth moved to his office. Howland remained in the embassy car to maintain contact with the embassy over the car radio. Tomseth, inside with Laingen, manned the phone to the embassy, talked with Howland on a hand-held radio, and maintained his own line to Washington. Tomseth also was in touch with the U.S. cultural center, which was not seized until much later.

When they got into Yazdi's office, Laingen insisted that Yazdi go to the embassy compound as he had on February 14. Yazdi told Laingen that he would make every effort to free the embassy and apparently made some telephone calls. When Laingen asked him why he did not go to the embassy himself, Yazdi replied, "Then the lives of the people in the embassy were in danger but that is not true now." It was almost immediately apparent that Yazdi felt that he did not have the clout to do what he had done earlier. Not only did he recognize that his government's control was much weaker. He knew his own political position had been further hurt by photos in the

Tehran newspapers the day before showing Yazdi and Bazargan shaking hands with U.S. National Security Adviser Brzezinski in Algiers. That brief meeting was not part of any strategy plotted in Washington. But those photos dramatized to the Islamic purists in the revolution the realization of their worst fears—renewal by government leaders of a closer relationship with the United States, which they regarded as responsible for what Iran had suffered at the hands of the Shah's regime.

As State Department Director of Iranian Affairs Henry Precht wrote in retrospect, "I think the one constant theme that obsessed the movement against the Shah, both the leaders of the revolution and the followers, was a fear that the United States would repeat 1953 (when the Shah was restored to his throne with U.S. help) in destroying Iran's revolution. The secular people sometimes tried to woo us; the religious people tried to destroy all connections with us. When we brought the Shah to New York, it fueled those suspicions, which were further sparked by the Brzezinski-Yazdi-Bazargan meeting in Algiers. No government, no force in Iran, could support the United States when a question of the Shah was involved."

Precht, with considerable experience in political-military and Iranian affairs, was one of the bureau's outstanding officers. Soft-spoken with a mild southern accent, he maintained an amazing range of contacts and was capable of turning out an enormous amount of work on short deadlines. He had been quick to see in 1978 that the Shah could not overcome the forces against him and in 1979 repeatedly pointed out the consequences of inviting the Shah to the United States. In 1978, his views had irritated the White House, because he came to the conclusion early that the Shah's regime could not survive. But during the hostage crisis, Precht, as manager of the Iran Working Group and participant in critical negotiations, won the respect of key White House officials from the President down.

Yazdi remained at the Foreign Ministry until close to midnight Tehran time with Laingen camped in his office. Yazdi told Laingen that our colleagues were safe in the compound and that security forces were outside the compound. He made half-hearted efforts to get further help and at one point told Laingen that one of the religious leaders of the revolution was going to the compound—perhaps Khomeini's son. As it turned out, the Ayatollah never got there and the spiritual adviser of the captors, Hajatoleselam Khoeini, had apparently supported early planning of the takeover. Laingen and Tomseth tried unsuccessfully to reach Prime Minister Bazargan on the phone. Near midnight Yazdi escorted Laingen, Tomseth, and Howland to the room where they were to remain and left the ministry, explaining that he was going to a cabinet meeting. The group at the ministry, as one of them later said, "had no reason to believe that the structure of authority in the form of the Revolutionary Council could not come to grips with this problem." Yazdi acknowledged to Laingen that the impetus for the takeover had come from the religious element in the revolution but said the government would play a catalytic role in achieving a resolution of the crisis.

Laingen saw Yazdi Monday morning about 9:00 A.M. for the last time. Laingen continued to talk with Yazdi's deputy and was even on the phone to the Ayatollah Beheshti, one of the key figures in the revolution, urging him to go to the compound. Beheshti told Laingen that he appreciated the problem but did not know whether he could be directly involved. While he regretted the events at the embassy, he said it was a natural reaction to U.S. attitudes and actions. He reminded Laingen he had warned that the Iranian reaction to the Shah's admission to the United States would be strong, but the U.S. had refused to act accordingly. Nevertheless, he did not link release of the hostages at that stage to any U.S. action, and he acknowledged that the hostage problem must be resolved.

The hostage crisis had begun. The revolution continued. The staff of the embassy was in the hands of fanatical supporters of Khomeini—"followers of the line of the Imam"—bent on purging the revolution of secular, "pro-Western" elements. Laingen and Tomseth watched as the secular government crumbled. The Americans trapped in Tehran were now an instrument in the continuing struggle for control of the revolution.

GULF BETWEEN TWO WORLDS: WHAT STRATEGY TO PURSUE?

The Iranian Revolutionary Agenda

"You will not get your hostages back until Khomeini has put all the institutions of the Islamic revolution in place." That was the prophetic advice given to Secretary Vance and a few of his colleagues in the Secretary's office in January 1980 by a prominent Islamic statesman. Like a number of the world's true public servants, this quiet, attractive, articulate, and thoughtful visitor was trying to help American leaders understand the Iranian agenda to the benefit of both. He and others like him knew that the hostage taking tarnished the image of Islam at a time when peace in the world required sympathetic understanding among the world's great religions. He saw the wide gulf between the worlds of the Islamic Iranian revolutionaries and the well-intentioned Anglo-Saxon strategists of a Western superpower and feared the consequences for an already troubled world if the gulf could not be bridged. He had come to Washington to help the American crisis managers understand the Iranian priorities and objectives, so they could find ways to bridge the dangerous gulf between the two worlds.

In hindsight, it appears analytically correct to say that the hostages were released only when they were no longer useful as a weapon in the internal struggle to consolidate Khomeini's Islamic revolution. Career officers within the State Department had begun giving Secretary Vance equally pessimistic analyses of the situation within a week after the embassy was seized, although no one thought of the hostages' captivity dragging on as long as it did. Until late August and early September 1980, every attempt to free the hostages was thwarted by the political struggle inside Iran. That is a key part of the story.

To the public servants in Washington who man one crisis team after another, the point about having to wait out the consolidation of the revolution made sense analytically, but taken alone it missed the real-world character of the crisis. As one veteran member of the State Department crisis team wrote later,

> It would tend to impute more systematic thought, orderly procedures, and clarity of vision to the Iranian side than probably was the case—certainly in the early months of the crisis. I doubt, for example, that the students who seized the compound really had any idea where they would be the next day or what they would do with the premises if they were successful. I doubt that any of the successive members of the leadership in the first months had any clear idea or sufficient courage to carry out a plan for ending the crisis. I think the Iranians went along from day to day, motivated by a deep and abiding fear and distrust of the U.S., a personal hatred for Carter whose personal involvement focused their anger, and a lack of capability for handling complex problems. There was no unity and no leadership except that of Khomeini, and I am not sure he had a rational scheme in mind. Bitterness, righteousness, fear, suspicion, and revenge were probably the strongest motivating factors for him.

Even if Khomeini's was the principal mind at work directing the Iranian revolution, that mind could be changed by his judgment of what others on whom he depended would and would not support.

The Iranian revolution that brought Khomeini to power had momentarily united three partially incompatible elements in 1978 to achieve a single objective—toppling the Shah's regime. The moment the Shah left in January 1979 and Khomeini returned to Iran on February 1 to a welcome from millions in the streets, each group began trying to shape the revolution according to its own views.

In one group clustered secular nationalist elements who played significant roles in managing Iran's economic progress—*bazaaris* (businessmen), technocrats, Western-educated professional men and women, and nationalist politicians. Among them were political leaders who had stood against the Shah in 1952–53 to establish their wider participation in government and to reduce the role of foreign powers—the British at that time. These were people who wanted a fuller say in governmental decisions affecting the direction of the modernization process they were managing.

In quite another group were the Islamic clergy who, as large landholders, had been gravely hurt by the Shah's land reform program in the 1960s and who now also felt that the infusion of Western ways of life—dress, music, relations between the sexes, materialism—was undermining the indigenous value system defined by Islam. Their highly effective political base was the "mullah network"—their ability through cassette, radio, and the Friday sermons in the mosques to put Khomeini's views constantly before people at all levels of society.

Cutting across all groups were those who had suffered at the hands of Savak, the regime's ruthlessly effective secret police. Many of them both believed the U.S. Central Intelligence Agency was behind the repressive effectiveness of Savak and resented the rapidly growing American presence in Iran. Further complicating the situation was the fact that the groups themselves were in flux, with members shifting between groups and between subfactions engaged in continuing struggles for influence and over specific issues.

The revolution, in short, was an explosion of pent-up resentments—a deeply rooted revolution against what Iran had become and was becoming. Whereas the Islamic fundamentalists had some vision of the Iran they wanted to build, the secular participants in the revolution had no clearly painted vision. The secular people were sure, however, that the fundamentalist mullahs had little idea how to run a modern government and economy. Khomeini himself seemed to recognize that fact and appointed respected secular leaders with experience in the old National Front to run the new government. As time passed, however, the battle lines were drawn between the religious and secular revolutionaries.

In the days after the takeover of the embassy, student captors in political discussions with their captives told some of the hostages their purpose. They wanted to bring people into the streets in support of the religious elements' efforts to purge the government of secular leaders who, they feared, might be too quick to rebuild a relationship with the United States—the number one enemy of an independent Iran with a truly Islamic character. Holding the embassy hostage while demanding the Shah's return to Iran from the United States for trial seemed a way of rallying such support.

The hostage crisis, in short, was not in Iranian eyes an episode in Iran's international relations. It was one act in a nationwide struggle for control of a genuine domestic revolution. The United States was "the Great Satan"—the arch enemy of those who followed the "line of the Imam" in trying to

shape a fundamentally Islamic revolution. Islamic elements fought to gain
the upper hand over the secular revolutionaries, or "Westerners" as they
were called because of their roles in managing a Western-designed process
of modernization.

In hindsight, we can interpret events through most of the next nine
months in light of that struggle. The Iranians clearly had their own agenda
and their own world view during these 444 days.

"How Can We Deal with People Like This?"
Outrage was the American reaction. Nowhere was the gulf between the
Iranian and American worlds more angrily felt than in the American living
room, with fanatical Iranian faces daily screaming hatred from TV screens.
Immediately, Americans were torn between two feelings—the normal humane concern for the hostages and a natural desire to "show those people
they can't do this to the United States." Almost at once, the crisis team in
Washington felt the painful tension within the American agenda—the need
to bring our people home safely while protecting national interest and honor
and the principles that govern relations between nations.

The challenge facing members of the American crisis team as they
drove toward the Ops Center at daybreak through the quiet Sunday morning streets of Washington was how to bridge the gulf between the Iranian
and American worlds. How could we deal with people like this? How could
we make them see that it would best serve their revolutionary agenda to
release our people instead of holding them? Should we hit them hard in a
quick, sharp, punitive blow? Should we ignore them? Should we search out
Iranian leaders who wanted the hostages freed for their own political reasons and try to find ways of maneuvering so as to make it more feasible for
them to do what they wanted to do? Behind these questions was another
question: What approach would the American people support?

The President and his top advisers on November 4 and for months
following were faced with the challenge of how to move those other human
beings who were leaders in Iran—leaders with their own agenda and their
own world view—to do what we wanted them to do. Our textbooks picture
presidential decision-making in an international crisis as relating to major
decisions involving such forces as balances of power. In fact, the job is much
more down-to-earth. It is easy to decide in the abstract what ought to be
done; it is much harder to move human beings to do it.

In addition to figuring out how to deal with Khomeini, the President
had to build political support here at home among an angry people for what
he decided to do. The objective of President Carter and his advisers was to
cause the leaders of Iran's revolution to decide that releasing the hostages
was in their interest but to do it in a way Americans would see as honorable.

In hindsight, the issue that would burn at the center of almost every debate over United States strategy for management of the hostage crisis focuses on the stance President Carter took in trying to bridge the gulf between the Iranian and American worlds. This was *the* issue of high strategy. If in fact release of the hostages depended mainly on developing an Iranian interest in releasing them, was the President right in keeping the crisis center stage and in involving himself so directly? Was this the best way to bring the full weight of American influence to bear in persuading the Iranians to let our people go? Or was the better strategy for bridging the gap between these two agendas to establish a firm American position, develop pressures and incentives for Iran to release the hostages, depersonalize the crisis, and stand back until the Iranians were ready?

This issue works on two levels. First, it relates to the degree of the President's own deep personal tactical involvement in the crisis and the extent to which his involvement kept the issue on the front burner through the first months of the crisis and made it more difficult to deal with in Iran. Second, it relates to the substance of our strategy for dealing with the Iranians—the extent to which we should have tried actively to shape conditions for an early release of the hostages as opposed to a less active approach of simply marshalling pressure and keeping the channels of communication open. These questions arose again and again as one phase of the crisis gave way to another.

Republican opponents in the 1980 presidential campaign, as well as some less partisan critics, charged that the White House "hyped" the crisis. The critics argued that the President, by keeping the crisis center stage, gave the Iranians holding the hostages leverage they would not otherwise have had and made it more difficult to work out their release. Keeping the crisis in the spotlight also heightened popular frustration across the United States. That frustration over our inability to bring the hostages home may have limited the administration's maneuverability in negotiation, led the President to take steps like the rescue mission that he might otherwise not have approved, and caused the voters to turn against President Carter in the last hours before the election partly in reaction to developments in Iran that dramatically reminded them that election day—November 4, 1980— marked the first anniversary of the takeover of the embassy.

Members of the crisis team would later acknowledge that this argument may have some validity, but they also insist on recalling the mood in those first days after the takeover. Could the President have walked away from a crisis that had so thoroughly captured national attention? If President Carter were to have had the option of downplaying the crisis, media leaders would have had to find a way to reduce television coverage of events in Tehran. Administration officials point out that television's focus on the mobs in front of the U.S. Embassy in Tehran while the rest of Tehran lived a relatively normal life tended to elevate the crisis both in Iran and in the United States into a clash between two nations rather than leave it as the action of one group of Iranians against a small group of American officials.

Media leaders, on their side, as well as others in the foreign affairs community, respond that President Carter, by pursuing his "rose garden strategy" and refusing for months to engage personally in the presidential primary campaign until the hostages were released, made it impossible for them to allow other stories such as the democratic political contest for the presidency to take over top billing. They admit, however, that the story of the hostages was like a fire out of control. They too felt they did not have the option of giving less coverage to a story which, by their own acknowledgment, came to dominate television as no story had since World War II, with the possible exception of Vietnam.

Against that background, President Carter in his initial reactions may simply have been acting as Jimmy Carter—an outraged and concerned American who happened to be President. He was attacked as President of the United States, and he felt a deep personal responsibility for the lives of the hostages and for returning them safely to their families. Politically, for a President under challenge by Senator Kennedy for leadership of his party, it must have seemed virtually unthinkable to try to put such a problem on the back burner. Americans do not respond warmly to the leader who coldly stacks up human lives against some rational calculation of "national interest."

The basic question was which course, among various activist ones, to pursue; it was not acting versus doing nothing. As the immediate opportunities to free the hostages faded, the crisis team's longer-term responsibilities established a minimum level of activity. In any situation of this kind, the bureaucracy's role is (1) to lay out for the Secretary of State and the President the broadest possible range of workable options for dealing with the crisis and (2) to develop the capability to carry out whatever course of action the President decides to follow. Whether the President involved himself personally or not, it was still necessary to develop possible ways of turning the hostages from being an attractive lever in the internal Iranian struggle into a liability for those who advocated continuing to hold them. It was necessary to develop ways of giving the Iranians a face-saving way of releasing the hostages, should the President choose to pursue them. We felt that if an action would not make matters worse, it was at least a realistic strategy to leave no stone unturned, no lead unexplored, no reasonable approach untested.

One other thought bothers the public servant at a time like this and tends to rule out a "do little" approach. One of the most difficult issues in a crisis of this kind is to identify the moment in a heated and rapidly changing situation when policymakers should change the premises on which they are acting. For instance, in the earlier phases of the Iranian revolution the key policy call in the fall of 1978 was to determine when the regime of the Shah could no longer survive. Heads of state with influence in such a situation are reluctant to make this judgment about the fate of another leader, because the judgment itself could become a factor in worsening prospects for that other leader to resolve his political problems. In the first six months of the hostage crisis, there never seemed to be a moment when trying to show less interest in the hostages' release would not have contributed to their confinement for an even longer period. It is easier to make such a judgment in theory than it is in the real world. The natural tendency is not to make a sharp judgment but to keep all possibilities open. The issue really became a question of degree—in what measure the administration should have tried to lower the visibility of the problem in Iran and in the United States while actively but more quietly keeping open all avenues toward possible resolution.

At the other end of the spectrum of options were harsh actions such as cutting off food or bombing some important Iranian target like a major oil refinery. Cutting off food imports might have put the hostage takers in the position of undercutting the revolution's ability to assure the urban poor that the revolution could help them, but it would have hurt the innocent poor. Some individuals continue to argue that sharp military action would have caused the revolution's leaders to think twice about holding the hostages, but the prevailing view was that those holding the hostages would react by killing some of them. In hindsight, it has been asked whether we dismissed these options too quickly because we sensed President Carter wanted—and we wanted—to show the superiority of solving international crises by peaceful, humane means. Whatever the truth in this case, even raising the question underscores the point that conscientious crisis management requires rigorous analyses of all feasible options right at the start. Before the day ended on November 4, officers had been set to work laying out all realistic courses of action for "dealing with people like this."

In addition to these arguments, what the President faced daily from the media, from the Congress, and from the public at large was an angrily insistent, "Why aren't you doing something?" The crisis team, therefore, in those first days, did not feel that sitting back and waiting out the Iranians was a real-world choice. That was especially true during the first days when release still seemed an early possibility. It was natural from the moment the embassy fell to try immediately to open the widest range of possible opportunities for the Iranians to back off and to release the hostages. Particularly in those first days, we felt an urgent need to press all possibilities for immediate release.

"How Can We Even Talk to Them?"

In addition to laying out policy options, the crisis team in the Ops Center immediately began what no one could know would become an almost continuous search over the next ten months for ways to communicate between the two worlds. It was one thing to develop policy options in Washington; implementing them required ability to communicate. When the embassy was taken, the normal machinery of information gathering and communication went with it. But the challenge that began as the embassy's phones and code room went dead was not only to build a whole new network of communication but also to find a way of communicating.

The Washington crisis team had to work in two directions. Much of what the crisis managers did had to start from the fact, so well stated by our Islamic visitor in January 1980, that Iranian revolutionary groups and leaders had their own objectives and their own world views. The crisis team had to try to understand that agenda and to develop ways of communicating with those who held it. This in itself was a formidable task. One member of the team later cited as his dominant feeling from those 444 days "the utter frustration of not knowing what kind of political creature we were dealing with in Iran." At the same time, the President could not act in any way that he or an angered American people would judge inconsistent with national interest and honor. The crisis team had to help the President develop support for policy in the Congress, in the media, and among the electorate. It had to present proposals to the President that might have a chance of being workable in Iran as well as politically supportable at home.

Time and time again, we would find that the main problem was to find words and actions that would get through to Iranian revolutionary minds. Even the "negotiation" of the final agreement was not so much a conventional negotiation as a trial-and-error effort to present a necessarily complex American position so that it could be described in a politically acceptable way in Tehran. As one member of the Algerian team that worked out the eventual release of the hostages said after his roundtrips between Washington and Tehran: "These weren't negotiations. They were more like an extended seminar. In Tehran, we explained to the Iranians the American legal, banking, and political systems. In Washington, we explained the politics of revolutionary Iran."

The Iranian revolutionaries not only had a strong interest in completing the Islamic revolution, but they also marched to a code of belief and behavior that fell outside familiar international norms. The Iranians found

those norms only a reflection of what they regarded as a hostile and dec-
adent Western civilization. Each person involved has his or her own long list
of examples. For many, the outlandish nature of the differences between
world views was captured in the exclamation by one of the captors in the
embassy compound when he learned in January 1980 that six Americans
had escaped Tehran with the help of the Canadians and false documentation. He was reported by the press as saying, "But that's illegal!" How to
bridge the almost undefinable gulf between the two worlds and how to
operate in such a vastly different world was a critical problem for the Washington crisis managers.

A Uniquely Human Crisis

The domestic management of the crisis in the United States was unusually
complex, because the crisis was intensely human. Every crisis in foreign
affairs involves human beings—war, peace, trade, world finance. But this
one absorbed entire populations on both sides in a way that is unique except
in wartime.

For the crisis managers in Washington, it was a problem, to start with,
of American citizens and others close to us held hostage or trapped in
Tehran and of their families here in the United States. It was a problem of
concerned Americans watching the nightly television news and understanding that the hatred in those Iranian faces was somehow directed at
them. Individual hostages and individual captors became personalities.
Members of the hostages' families became familiar figures in their communities and even on national television. It was not just the usual clash of
national interests and national honor. The American people became
uniquely involved. The immense outpouring of relief and the national em-
brace that welcomed the hostages home more than fourteen months later
can be explained only by saying that many Americans felt their own dignity, safety, and ability to deal with the world caught up in some difficult-to-
explain way in the crisis of those seventy-two individuals initially trapped
in Tehran.

Those in Washington charged with responsibility for the crisis had to
struggle with human questions such as these: How to deal with a people
breaking the code of international principle but claiming that the code itself
was biased against the developing nations? What sanctions or pressures
might be effective in moving the leaders of such a people to decision? What is
the appropriate role and what is the potential effectiveness of military force
against a nation where power seems to reside in the streets? What effect can
economic pressures have against a nation whose economic management has
broken down and where revolutionaries seem prepared to return almost to a
subsistence level for the sake of fulfilling a political movement? What is the

effect of international isolation on a people like this? Can international persuasion move them if pressure cannot? How can the United States in such a situation protect interests ranging from its own international stature and power to a variety of private American economic interests and assets? How can one conduct a negotiation with a government that does not have a clear power base and with a group of people who are not prepared to negotiate?

For Americans outside government, there were also serious questions: What role might private Americans with contacts in Iran play in bridging the gap between the two worlds and in resolving the crisis? The same question applied to individual members of Congress. What was the appropriate role of the media, particularly television? At what point do the media themselves become actors and not just reporters? What role is appropriate for the families of the victims, both in domestic politics and relationship with the Iranians? What defines the appropriate role of private negotiating channels?

Bridging the gulf between the Iranian and American worlds came to absorb the attention of a large number of concerned Americans in and out of government. In that sense the hostage crisis posed challenges that the United States will increasingly face through the remainder of the century and beyond as the developing nations of the world increasingly influence the course of events and march to the beat of their own drummers. That does not mean hostage taking will become more common as small nations seek to increase their leverage against larger power, although we may see more of it. It does mean that the United States will have to cope increasingly with nations whose world view is not ours, whose political and decision-making processes are unfamiliar, whose political conditions make it impossible or unlikely that they will respond to outside pressures however compelling, or who by their lack of power and coherent political structures can limit the capacity of the great powers to influence the course of events. It does mean that American leaders must increasingly learn how to bridge the gulf between our world and those other worlds around us.

HOW DID WE GET HERE?

Three Issues
Public debate in the United States following the takeover of the embassy immediately zeroed in on three issues. These questions were usually put— in the media, in the Congress, and in private discussion—with the inquisitorial implication of "another failure" of the U.S. government. The executive branch had been grappling with them since the Shah left Iran in

January 1979, but to the public they seemed new: (1) Should American officials in such numbers have been in revolutionary Iran at all? (2) Had sensible measures been taken for their protection generally and particularly when the Shah came to the United States on October 23 for medical treatment? (3) Why was the Shah admitted to the United States, given warnings about the possible consequences? These are all legitimate questions, although the accusatory way they were frequently stated also contributed to the heated political atmosphere in which the President and his advisers had to deal with the crisis.

Why So Many Americans There?

During the Iranian revolution in late 1978 and early 1979, almost 45,000 Americans who had been living and working in Iran had been evacuated. With that background, the attack on Valentine's Day in 1979 had presented officials in Washington with a choice between closing the embassy altogether until the government could assure some measure of order or, alternatively, maintaining some official presence at a skeleton level. This is a familiar choice in dangerous situations. In the end, policymakers usually decide, if the country is an important one, that it is more consistent with American interests to be present than to be absent.

Given the large American and free world strategic interests in the independence of Iran, that was the decision made in February 1979. Keeping Iran out of the Soviet orbit had seemed critical to American strategists since World War II. Iran was the Soviet invasion route to Persian Gulf oil.

The period after the revolution would inevitably be a formative period for the new political regime in Tehran, and we wanted to be on the ground. The Iranian leadership, perhaps concerned by the Soviet threat, wanted us to remain despite their strong suspicions and hostility toward us. So a decision was made shortly after the February 14 attack to cut the size of the embassy to about sixty but to try to build some relationship with the new leaders. Sixty may seem larger than a "skeleton force," but the numbers rise quickly because of significant blocs of staff such as Marine guards, security officers, communicators, and consular officers and because of the need to service a large number of American businessmen with projects to straighten out or claims to pursue in the wake of a revolution.

During the months after the February takeover, the embassy moved quickly to improve physical security for those Americans who remained and began testing the extent to which it would be possible to have a businesslike relationship with the new regime. Gradually contacts expanded. We proposed sending a new ambassador, but the Iranians rejected him in reaction to what they regarded as a hostile resolution passed by the Senate on May 17. The so-called Javits resolution expressed "abhorrence of summary executions without due process." An Iranian tribunal issued a summons for the Senator, and there were demonstrations in reaction that caused concern in the embassy. Nevertheless, more than a few businessmen went back to Iran to test the water themselves and to renegotiate or to wind up their projects. Embassy and Iranian officials talked about such issues as phasing down and getting some control over the large military supply relationship left over from the Shah's regime. On June 18, Bruce Laingen—sent as Chargé d'Affaires, since the Iranians had rejected our proposed ambassador—took over the embassy. Throughout the summer Laingen and his colleagues in the embassy tentatively but gradually expanded relationships with the new leadership.

By October, the embassy had resumed consular business in order to process large numbers of Iranian students who still wanted to attend American schools, colleges, and universities and to help minority groups who wanted to leave Iran at least until conditions settled down. The Iranian government pressed us to provide these services. The consular section expanded in the newly opened office on the compound, and the embassy staff went up to about seventy.

When Foreign Minister Yazdi came to New York during the annual regular session of the United Nations General Assembly, he and Secretary of State Vance met in a small room near the General Assembly hall. The Foreign Minister later met with other American officials as part of the continuing effort to sort out the residue of the military supply relationship. In Tehran, the embassy was in touch with most of the important secular officials in the new revolutionary government as well as with some of the key religious figures.

The conversations with Foreign Minister Yazdi in New York brought home to the American participants the difficulty of communicating with Iran's new leaders. Yazdi had spent almost a decade in Texas. Those of us who sat in the small, crowded room with Secretary Vance and the Foreign Minister anticipated an Iranian polemic, but we thought that it might be possible, because of Yazdi's American experience, at least to communicate with him in private conversations. In the conversation with Secretary Vance, he returned again and again to the theme of American culpability for all that Iranians had suffered under the regime of the Shah.

Later, in a private conversation with Yazdi and some of his colleagues in the living room of the Iranian residence, Henry Precht and I tried in that less formal atmosphere to have a serious discussion of the U.S.-Iranian relationship. The Iranians were hospitable. We sat in a heavily furnished, high-ceilinged room of the large New York house, with tea and Iranian cakes and young, bearded staff members coming and going. For two hours we heard out Iranian views about the causes of the revolution and repeatedly asked, "How can we develop our relationship now?" Even in that setting, however, Yazdi and his colleagues turned every issue into a litany of complaints about the past sins of the United States. After repeated efforts to put the past behind and to focus on what kind of relationship might be possible then and in the future, I finally asked in frustration whether Yazdi thought it would be possible for his generation of revolutionary leaders ever to conduct a businesslike relationship with the United States. Yazdi did not reply, but the next day experts did meet over military supply questions. The relationship was a curious mixture of obsession with the past and some readiness to get on with the future.

Why were the numbers in the embassy not further reduced when the Shah was admitted to the United States? The embassy staff reflected two points of view. One emphasized the constant security threat and the increasing inability of the government to control such groups as the students. The other acknowledged the danger but worked from the premise that the decision had been made again and again in Washington to take the risk. "Certain bridges had been crossed," said one senior member of the staff later. "Judgments had been made that there was going to be an embassy there. It was unlikely that we would decide to take people out just because we were having another round of troubles. We had had troubles before."

Or as another member of the staff put it, referring to a similar review after an earlier round of troubles:

> We felt the government was in tenuous shape, but we had crossed that bridge back in May and June when we had problems after the Javits resolution on the revolutionary courts. The Chargé had convened several meetings to work out what our presence should be. Notwithstanding reservations some of us had about maintaining a conspicuous presence, there was a broad if not universal consensus that the stakes involved were sufficiently great that we had to take the risk of maintaining a full diplomatic establishment. When the Shah went to New York, we felt that the qualitative situation was similar. We had to take the risk.

Before President Carter decided to let the Shah into the United States, he had agreed with Secretary Vance that Laingen should tell Prime Minister Bazargan and Foreign Minister Yazdi. Laingen and Precht, who happened then to be visiting the embassy, met with them. They said the Iranian people would react negatively but acknowledged their obligation to protect the embassy. Given the real world of revolutionary Tehran, they did not give an ironclad guarantee of protection. It was more of an affirmative nod, a murmured "yes," or an impatient "of course." One member of the embassy staff said a year and a half later, "If I had known about those so-called assurances, I wouldn't have believed them. It was clear that the government was losing control." Everyone knew the situation was dangerous, but Laingen had to do what he could with Iranian officials to underscore the government's responsibility.

In a prolonged crisis like this, which had been going on for over a year, when is it time to judge that the danger has suddenly become too great to keep people in an embassy? When hostages are taken, the media, the Congress, and the public focus on the immediately preceding events. Because they pay little attention to similar dangers over a prolonged period, they show little understanding of judgments made, repeatedly reviewed, and made again over time that "we had to take the risk." Despite the murder of our ambassadors in Lebanon and Afghanistan, we have kept embassies functioning in those important countries through years of civil war. Few Americans stop to think about the dangers embassies face daily until a drama like that of November 4, 1979, focuses their attention. Then the judgments are harsh—and often without much understanding of the past.

Hardening the Embassy

After the Valentine's Day takeover the State Department worked in two ways in the spring of 1979 to improve the physical security of our embassy. First, as already mentioned, the staff of the embassy was cut to a modest level, from over 1,400 officials before the revolution to about 60. Second, steps were taken to "harden" the embassy buildings with a number of protective devices—window grills, blast shields, steel doors—that would give employees a safe haven within the building, so the government would have time to disperse an attacking mob before our people would fall into the mob's hands, as had happened on February 14. This work was completed in mid-1979. On November 4, the embassy could probably have held out a little longer if government help had been on the way.

Throughout the summer, Chargé Bruce Laingen also pressed Iranian authorities to improve the quality and discipline of the Iranian guard force around the embassy. For much of this time, an informal guard force roamed the embassy compound as well as guarded the gates. As one officer described them, "They were a totally undisciplined bunch of young men with old guns which they fired at random and dangerously." A local hero, a butcher, was in charge. They were so careless in handling their weapons that even moving about the compound was sometimes hazardous. They also occasionally tortured Iranian prisoners in their guardroom in the compound. Laingen finally succeeded in August in having uniformed Iranian police replace the informal guard force. Paradoxically, members of the embassy staff later realized that the departure of those guards, while essential, probably diminished the embassy's security, because they had more influence in the streets than the police had. They would not have made much difference against the determined attackers on November 4.

The experience of the embassy in the first two weeks after the Shah came to the United States on October 23 gave us some hope that the government understood that securing the embassy also depended on controlling crowds well outside the compound. On the evening of November 1, for instance, government authorities encouraged religious leaders to announce a change in the location of a large demonstration scheduled for the next day in order to remove it from the area around the embassy compound. This seemed to the embassy—and to those of us watching carefully from Washington—a signal that neither religious nor government leaders wanted to provoke an incident that would jeopardize the U.S.-Iranian relationship. As it turned out, there was a separate group of about 3,000 that marched past the embassy and spray-painted graffiti on the walls, but marshals kept them in order, and extra police were on duty at the compound.

There seemed to be no new reason to change the original assessment that the risk of keeping the embassy open had to be taken. Those who deal with questions of this kind in Washington are all too familiar with the difference between knowing that something may happen and believing with enough certainty that it will happen to change an earlier decision. One of the most difficult decisions policy-makers have to make is to determine when the character of a situation has changed enough to warrant a change in position.

One of the issues that remained alive for some time was the number of classified documents that ultimately fell into Iranian hands; many of them were reassembled by the Iranians from shreds with incredible patience and published. This experience raised basic questions about storage policies in dangerous posts, records retrieval systems, document destruction equipment, and management of destruction during the siege. Most of the files had been destroyed or shipped out of Iran during the revolution. Some had been shipped back as the scene calmed down, so there were unquestionably more documents in the embassy than there should have been and more than could be destroyed during the attack. The offices and files on the first two floors had to be locked and abandoned soon after the attack began. Some of the destruction equipment broke down. With the Chargé out of the embassy, no one present focused on his private safe.

Why Did We Let the Shah Come?

The sharpest question fired at President Carter and those around him was why the Shah was allowed to come to New York. In the heat of that early, angry public reaction, few stopped to ask the other question that would come to the surface in thoughtful minds much later: Was the decision to admit the

Shah the main trigger for the takeover, or would the militants in Tehran have found some other basis for acting against the United States as a means of rallying support?

The later judgment of some key embassy officers was that the Shah's entry into the United States was only a pretext. "I did not think and I still do not think," said one, "that the Shah's being let into the United States was the trigger. It was an excuse. The trigger was what was perceived among religious groups to be a reinstitution of the U.S.-Iranian ties that would turn the revolution from its course." Others would later cite the Brzezinski-Bazargan-Yazdi meeting in Algiers and the pictures in Tehran as the trigger. It seems likely that the takeover was planned as one group's effort to influence the struggle for control of the revolution and that its timing was dictated by Iranian considerations.

When the Shah left Iran on January 16, 1979, the President's first decision was to offer a haven for a leader who had over the years preserved a relationship with the United States based on legitimate common interests. In December and January we had told the Shah he would be welcome here, but he had gone to Egypt and then to Morocco. In late February, while he was in Morocco, there were inquiries about his possible travel here. By that time, it had become clear from the situation in Tehran and from the February 14 attack on the embassy that the new government in Iran could not then provide certain security for our people. It was after the February 14 takeover that professionals in the State Department first judged that Americans might be held hostage for the return of the Shah if he came to the United States at that time. The decision was made that the Shah should not come to the United States immediately, and our ambassador in Morocco, Richard Parker, was given the unhappy task of telling the Shah of this decision.

The President reached this judgment with great reluctance. As he said much later at his first press conference after the hostages were taken, the United States has always been a haven for people in distress, and it disturbed the President deeply to have to withdraw his earlier invitation. Months later in October when the unexpected news suddenly arrived in Washington that the Shah was gravely ill and indeed for some time had been suffering from a form of cancer, the President's discomfort with his earlier decision again came to the surface. The news of the Shah's illness introduced a compelling new human element into the picture and, despite the President's concern about the consequences, tipped the balance in favor of extending hospitality to him for the specific purpose of offering the medical treatment that American medical facilities were in the best position to provide.

Much has been made of the argument that the President's decision failed to give adequate weight to the alternatives of moving medical equipment to Mexico for the necessary diagnostic work. In hindsight, the point is made that, whatever the cost of such an operation, it would in the end have been far less than the cost of the hostage crisis. The argument is plausible, but in reviewing decisions of this kind it is always necessary to recapture the situation at the moment the decision was made. Time seemed important to the well-being of the Shah; there seemed little choice but to go ahead and then to take whatever preventive measures could be taken to avoid the worst consequences.

STARTING THE CRISIS MACHINERY

The Machinery

Whenever a new crisis breaks in Washington, the foreign affairs community within the government almost automatically sets in motion the bureaucratic machinery needed to manage the crisis. The various parts of that machinery have been used on many previous occasions. They are kept well lubricated and lightly mothballed to be activated on a moment's notice. Later, orders come from the top to establish a task force, but everyone knows what needs to be done and automatically starts doing it without waiting for instructions.

This machinery has two main components. One involves developing an effective operational base for dealing with the main dimensions of the crisis—channels of communication, sources of information, instruments of influence and pressure, mechanisms for working-level coordination in Washington, means for responding to the press, conducting relations with other governments, briefing and consulting the Congress, and handling the human and administrative problems that arise for the officers involved. The other involves identifying the substantive issues, preparing possible courses of action for dealing with them, reviewing the desirability and political feasibility of those options, and formulating them for the President's decision.

The operational base is centered in the State Department Operations Center. Other major departments of government have crisis rooms, including the Situation Room in the White House. By general agreement, the task force or working group formed in the State Department Operations Center normally becomes the coordinating center for the working levels of the government.

The Ops Center is a complex of interior rooms designed to provide working facilities on a continuing basis for the twenty-four-hour watch of the State Department and, during crises, to provide office space for as many as three special task forces working simultaneously. The concept behind establishment of the task force areas was that, in a crisis, it is important to have people from various parts of the State Department and other parts of the government together in one place for the sake of rapid communication and consultation. It is also essential to have equipment at their fingertips to permit them to communicate rapidly with almost any part of the world.

The main task force rooms are medium-sized conference rooms with long tables in the middle and banks of telephone lines at several positions around the table. Just off the conference rooms are several small offices where the heads of the task force and key colleagues can work and space for the invaluable secretaries who often sign up to work eight-hour shifts at night in addition to their regular jobs. Many officers volunteer to help man the three shifts on top of doing their assigned work, since the normal country desk is far too small to man a round-the-clock operation for a long period. The complex also includes sleeping rooms. In a long crisis it can become home away from home.

Little did those who assembled in that area early Sunday morning know that the Iran Working Group, as it came to be called, would eventually challenge all records for the task force longest in continuous operation. It would not close down until after the return of the hostages in late January 1981, almost fifteen months later.

As it settled in, the Working Group expanded into a large adjacent briefing room for a unique purpose. As time went on, it became important to stay in close touch with the families of the hostages. Volunteers from the hostages' families living in Washington or from among the wives of the Working Group or other department officers manned the telephones to stay in touch with each of the families. Eventually, cards were kept on contacts with each family, so that those in the family working group would know of special problems and when last contact had been made. The medical division within the department also assigned counselors to each family, so they would have someone to turn to for help if necessary and so the counselor would be better prepared to ease the hostages' transition to normal living after their release.

In March 1980, the family members decided to organize, and FLAG (the Family Liaison Action Group) was formed, but that is a later part of the story. The fact that a group to communicate with the families was set up immediately in a room adjacent to the operating task force was another first in the department's growing attention to the human side of diplomatic life. Louisa Kennedy, wife of Economic Counsellor Moorhead Kennedy, was the first to come in.

The decision to set up the "family branch" of the Working Group was spontaneously made by the officers responsible for dealing with the people problems in the crisis. Sheldon Krys, who had begun his day on the phone with Ann Swift, and Ben Read, the warm and politically sensitive Under Secretary for Management, both knew that they needed no approval from Secretary Vance, who had long since made known his determination to make the State Department compassionate in dealing with individual needs and representative of the rich variety of backgrounds in the American people. Others later expressed some reservations about having even a few family members in the task force areas because of the potential shock of bad news suddenly breaking there and because of the occasional difficulty of dealing with highly classified information with outsiders nearby. But that Sunday morning it seemed obvious that "we'd better get somebody in here to talk with the families." We never seriously regretted that decision.

The other component in the State Department crisis machinery is the group that draws together to formulate policy decisions for the President. When the machinery is working well, there is considerable overlap between a working group and this less formal policy group, but it is normal for a separate center of activity to develop around the office of the senior policy official who will take charge of the crisis. In the State Department, the Secretary, the Deputy Secretary, or the Under Secretary for Political Affairs normally becomes the center, with the responsible Assistant Secretary and Deputy Assistant Secretary as the principal linchpin between that group and the working group.

In the hostage crisis, Secretary Vance personally assumed the leadership position within the State Department. As Assistant Secretary and also the head of the Iran Working Group, I worked directly with him. Peter Constable, my principal deputy, was a senior foreign service officer whom Deputy Secretary Warren Christopher had come quickly to respect during a visit to Pakistan when Peter was deputy to the ambassador. In our division of labor among the deputies in the bureau, he had special supervisory responsibility for Iranian affairs and for the administrative affairs handled by Sheldon Krys, as well as for acting as Assistant Secretary during my many absences and preoccupations. His judgment was soundly based on wide experience, he conducted personal and official relationships with warmth and humor, and his work was highly respected at the top of the department and in the White House.

In a crisis of this magnitude, Deputy Secretary Warren Christopher was naturally by the Secretary's side and functioned as his alter ego. It was Christopher, a slender, good-humored, highly effective, problem-solving lawyer-diplomat, who a winter later would rightly come to national prominence when he led the negotiating team that finally succeeded in freeing the hostages. Under Secretary for Political Affairs David Newsom continued in his normal role of assuring that all elements of the department with responsibility for some part of the problem were appropriately involved. Under

Secretary for Management Ben Read was also heavily involved because of his responsibility for personnel, funding, and the administrative underpinnings of a number of unique activities. Tony Lake, trusted by Vance since the transition period in late 1976 for his advice on a variety of global issues, marshalled knowledgeable members of his Policy Planning staff and others to put the crisis in a larger perspective.

At the level of the career officers, the working group under the Assistant Secretary coordinates the drafting of policy studies for which the State Department has primary responsibility. Those studies, with their policy options, are reviewed by the Secretary or one of the other senior officials in the department before being sent to the White House. Where the State Department does not have primary responsibility, it works with the staff of the government department or agency that does.

Moving beyond the State Department, the National Security Council (NSC) at the White House provides the forum for bringing all parts of the government together to coordinate the formulation of the President's policy choices and the effective execution of his decisions.

To begin with, our system of government is built around two groups of public servants. One is a cadre of career officers and staff whose profession is to master the business of managing the many sometimes complex aspects of the foreign relations of the United States. They include the Foreign Service, the military services, the career services of the Central Intelligence Agency, and other departments and agencies that may have specific responsibilities in some aspect of foreign affairs. Most of these people staff the government from one administration to the next. They are the continuity and the source of expert knowledge in government. The other group—the administration—consists of the President and Vice President, their Cabinet officers and White House advisers, and a number of other appointed officials picked from outside government or from the career services to play a special role in setting and managing policy directions. An assistant secretary in the State Department frequently has a foot in each camp, since he is often a career officer, but he is nominated by the President and appointed with the advice and consent of the Senate.

These groups of course interact within each department. But it is the NSC system, when it is working properly, that provides a meeting ground for what I often called "a continuing conversation between the President and the government professionals." The President and his advisers inject their sense of the general direction they believe the nation should take. That sense of direction is presumably rooted in what they regard as their political mandate. The professionals add their sense of the opportunities and constraints imposed by the real world and their knowledge of how to get things done.

The two groups often start from different premises. That fact is twice true when one also considers the wide range of responsibilities in the different departments of government, ranging from agriculture and the price of bread in American supermarkets to political, economic, and military responsibilities and the conduct of our relations abroad. It is easy to understand how presidents quickly come to feel that "the bureaucracy" is bent on telling them why it is impossible to do what they want to do or even to frustrate them by not wholeheartedly carrying out presidential orders. It is also easy to understand how the professionals would find some political leaders with no experience in foreign affairs quite out of touch with the real world in setting their goals and ways of achieving them. The NSC system was established after World War II with the formally stated purpose of assuring that our foreign policy goals were consistent with our resources for achieving them and assuring coordination among departments. In the clanking of the day-to-day machinery of government, a place was needed for the perspectives of different politicians and sets of experts to meet.

In the Carter Administration, four groups constituted the policy review, coordination, and decision-making machinery within the NSC system.

The normal crisis management group of the NSC in the Carter Administration was the Special Coordinating Committee (SCC). It was chaired by the President's National Security Adviser, Zbigniew Brzezinski. The normal membership of this group included the Secretaries of State and Defense or their deputies, the Chairman of the Joint Chiefs of Staff, and the Director of the CIA. The Budget Director and other senior White House staffers often attended as well as the senior NSC staff member and the Assistant Secretary of State, who headed the Working Group. During the hostage crisis, the Secretary of the Treasury, the Attorney General, and sometimes the Secretaries of Energy, Commerce, or Agriculture attended when the crisis spun off problems in their areas of responsibility. This group's job was to develop a picture of all aspects and consequences of a crisis such as this and to have studies prepared quickly on them.

A second group working under the National Security Council was the Policy Review Committee (PRC). This group included essentially the same officials, but it was chaired by the Secretary of State or Secretary of Defense as appropriate. Its responsibilities were less those of crisis management than of policy formulation and planning. In that group, issues of longer-term strategy would normally be discussed. Since the membership of this group was essentially the same as that of the SCC, in practice most of the meetings took place as SCC meetings with Dr. Brzezinski in the chair. It is a measure of the degree to which the hostage crisis absorbed the top levels of the government that one or the other of these groups met almost daily, including many Saturdays and some Sundays, for the first four months of the crisis and several times a week after that. Dr. Brzezinski met consistently and confidentially with a few members of this group as an informal subgroup to develop and consider military options.

The SCC and the PRC met in the basement conference room of the White House Situation Room. It was an interior room with adjacent offices where the twenty-four-hour watch office of the White House provided a round-the-clock picture of the global situation. The furnishings in the conference room were simple but seemed designed to provide an atmosphere of calm. For the most part, the discussions that took place around the table were serious and businesslike. Even where there were sharp differences, the atmosphere was normally one of honest people of high integrity sorting out their differences in the interests of the nation. During the hostage crisis, there was an even greater than normal sense of seriousness and common purpose, perhaps imposed by a special sense of responsibility for the lives of the hostages. The purpose of the meetings was to cover an agenda of issues that required immediate attention and to work out quickly how the issues would be presented to the President. Gary Sick, a naval captain responsible on the NSC staff for Iran and one of the government's leading experts on that area, reduced the judgments reached in each meeting to a memo from Dr. Brzezinski to President Carter, and the President's views were reported at the next meeting.

A third group was the National Security Council itself in which the President met with the key Cabinet members involved in the crisis. The NSC was an advisory, not a decision-making body. The President met with the NSC, normally in the Cabinet Room, to discuss options and considerations affecting decision, but the President alone decided. These formal meetings were usually held when some decision of major significance needed to be addressed. Despite the formality of the setting—the formally furnished room with its french doors leading out into the White House rose garden— the discussion was relatively informal among men who had worked personally with the President in dealing with many of the nation's international problems. President Carter came to these meetings well briefed and in detailed command of the issues to be discussed. He normally began the meetings with his own statement of what he wanted to accomplish and his own view of the issues to be discussed. Throughout the discussion, he did not hesitate to express his own judgment, and his advisers seemed comfortable in stating different points of view. At the end of the meeting, the President often made a general statement about his conclusion, but frequently his decisions were left to be put in precise written directives later. An atmosphere of civility pervaded the discussion, and even those who might be overruled by a presidential decision normally left the room without any sense of loss of stature.

But it was in a fourth group more than any other that the President brought together those responsible for helping him build political support in the nation for his policies and those running the departments charged with the responsibility for managing the conduct of policy. This group functioned as a less formal variant of the NSC and usually took the form of a Friday foreign policy breakfast at which the President, some members of the NSC, and key members of the White House staff met for discussion of current issues. In some cases, one could argue that this gathering functioned as the real NSC at a particular moment. It was in these informal gatherings that the President sifted out his own views of the national interest and what national policy should be. In addition to the regular Friday breakfasts, the President met frequently with one or several advisers in his office, at his residence, at Camp David, in the Situation Room, or simply on the telephone.

The Agenda

As the crisis team began its work on that Sunday morning of November 4, members made mental notes of actions and issues that belonged on a checklist for managing the crisis. Inevitably, the President or some other senior figure would be called on to make a statement about the crisis. Military planners in the Pentagon would need to canvass the the options available for military action. A check would be necessary to assure that security for the Shah at his hospital in New York was adequate. Planners in the State Department group experienced in dealing with terrorist acts would begin contingency thinking about how the United States should respond if the Iranian captors started killing individual hostages. Finally, the search began almost immediately to compile a list of emissaries, American and foreign, who might have particular influence with the revolutionary authorities in Iran.

When the SCC met on Monday, November 5, the members added their own thoughts to the agenda. In addition to putting the crisis into the larger context of global U.S. interests, particularly relations with the U.S.S.R., the members of the group focused on problems peculiarly related to this crisis. These included issues such as the effects on international oil supply, how to deal with the thousands of Iranian students in the United States, how to handle demonstrations by Iranians here, a review of major exports to Iran including military supplies and means of stopping them, the status of Iranian diplomats and diplomatic missions here, the effect on the international financial situation, monitoring of unusual Iranian transfers of bank assets, and military options including a rescue attempt. The SCC dealt mainly with the continuing basic elements of the crisis that required interdepartmental coordination. Diplomatic efforts were often discussed directly with the President or at the Friday breakfast.

As the agenda for dealing with the hostage crisis jelled, other important issues were gradually crowded off the agendas of each of the principals involved. Even in my own case the impact was clear. Before the hostage crisis, I had traveled with the President's special representatives in pursuing the post-Camp David negotiations on autonomy for the Palestinians in the Israeli-occupied West Bank and Gaza. I never took another trip with that team. Twice I planned to attend meetings of our ambassadors in South Asia; twice I canceled, because Secretary Vance did not want me to travel on any but hostage-related business. The same fate befell my plans to visit the Persian Gulf. In Washington, many days I did little but hostage-related business, leaving our bureau's other issues to deputies. If this was true at my level, the effects of the displacement were certainly much greater at higher levels.

The Approach

In a crisis, the quick initial decisions made without a lot of deliberation begin to set in place the main elements of an approach for dealing with the problem. Some of those actions meet obvious operational needs and are almost automatic. Others are slightly less so and begin to set the direction of a strategy.

Even before the embassy surrendered and direct communication was cut off, for instance, steps were taken from the Operations Center to open telephone communication with as many other sources of information at other points in Tehran as we could reach. It was critical to get the broadest possible picture of what was going on in Tehran, to know how Americans not in the compound were faring and whether this was an isolated attack against the U.S. Embassy or part of a larger series of demonstrations. The telephone line opened to Laingen at the Foreign Ministry was critical to our efforts to persuade the Iranian government to help. But lines were also open to other American offices in Tehran until their capture as well as to other embassies and individuals around the city. Through that network, for example, we were able to track the six officers who escaped the compound and were able to hide in Tehran until January, when the Canadians helped them escape.

With those initial steps taken in the heat of the need to stay in touch with what was happening, members of the Working Group began to develop ways of using the telephone that, over the months of the hostages' captivity, produced remarkable results. The normal way of doing business is to ask an embassy to gather the information we needed in Washington. With the embassy out of action, we had to develop new approaches. The telephone network the Working Group developed—made possible by the existence of direct dialing equipment in Iran—came to include direct or indirect contact with people across the full spectrum of Iranian society from cabinet officers to members of parliament, the captors in the embassy compound, prison and hospital officials, doctors, businessmen, journalists, academics, foreign diplomats, military figures—all from telephones in the Operations Center. As time passed, the Working Group estimated that it had as many as a dozen and a half significant channels of communication for gathering information from authoritative sources active at any given time throughout the 444 days during which the hostages were held.

Early in the crisis, for instance, a small group of Persian-language officers and psychiatrists experienced in hostage situations teamed up to call the embassy compound to see whether they could find ways of approaching the captors and get messages to and from the hostages. For a time until the Iranians closed this channel, they got to know some of the captors as individual personalities. When the Iranians suddenly announced the following July that one hostage was ill and would be released, it was possible within minutes to locate him and to confirm that he would be leaving.

Key officers in the Iran Working Group maintained an active set of cards on current telephone contacts. In moments when no other work was more pressing, they went through the cards and called each number periodically to get the latest news or insight. Later, for example, it became possible through two or three different channels to get immediate reports on important meetings with Khomeini or within the Revolutionary Council, to determine the health of individual hostages who had not been heard from for a time, to get a picture of the health of Khomeini, to get a sense of the line-up in the Revolutionary Council on issues important to us. When thought was briefly given by planners to the option of cutting Iran off from international telecommunications access to satellites as a possible sanction, it was almost instantly discarded as more damaging to our own communications access to Iran than to the Iranians themselves.

In addition to opening as many channels of communication as possible, we began almost immediately to seek the help of individuals, organizations, and governments around the world that might have influence with the revolutionary leadership in Iran. We turned early to Islamic countries like Pakistan and Saudi Arabia with mutually respectful relations with Iran's revolutionary leadership, to revolutionary governments like Algeria's, to movements like the Palestine Liberation Organization that were close to Khomeini, and to international organizations like the Organization of the Islamic Conference, the United Nations, and the Vatican. Channels of influence changed in usefulness, depending on the political fortunes of the Iranians at the other end of the channel, but the search for those who might have influence never ceased. At the end of December 1979, for example, the Working Group sent the Secretary a list of twenty-two such channels active at that time.

As time went on, these channels fell into two categories. Most of our contacts, particularly world figures with some connection or influence in Tehran, were simply encouraged to make general arguments with key Iranians for release of the hostages and to help change the climate among Iranian decision-makers to one more favorable for release. From time to time a few became channels for specific exchanges between the United States government and Iranian authorities about positions and steps designed to free the hostages. Playing this role required a degree of precision, commitment, and perseverance that we could not expect from many who were willing to be helpful in a general way.

As usually happens in a crisis, "round robin" messages—so called because the same instruction went to multiple addresses—were sent to embassies in a number of key capitals around the world instructing ambassadors to inform their host governments of what had happened and what the American position was. In this case, governments were asked to use their influence in Tehran to persuade the government of Iran to free the hostages and to turn the embassy back to American officials. This initial round of messages also served as a quick probe to determine who might be willing to help and who might have special influence. Developing a dialogue with those governments that showed readiness to help became part of the ongoing charge of the Working Group.

One of the purposes of those early messages was to develop international pressure on Iran by marshalling a series of approaches to the Iranian authorities by governments with influence in Iran. These pressures ranged from encouraging Islamic statesmen to try to change Iranian authorities' attitudes toward release of the hostages to votes in the United Nations and economic sanctions. As time passed, it was possible to increase Iran's isolation from the international community. But in these early hours of the crisis the objective could only be to open the dialogue by trying to engage as many others as we could in our behalf.

Other factors uppermost in the minds of policymakers were the need to gain access to the hostages to try to assure their safety and the need for care not to take any action that could trigger attacks on individual hostages. Those making decisions in Washington assumed that in that early volatile period the lives of the hostages were in hourly danger. Television pictures of the mobs outside the embassy underscored the danger.

Two important extensions of the crisis management machinery involved presenting the administration's position to the public and its representatives in the Congress. An unusual amount of time was spent in the Iran Working Group dealing with the inquiries of the press and in the SCC developing a posture to take with the press. The Iran Working Group had available at all times, especially in those daily predawn hours when the morning television news programs were being put together, a press spokesman to take calls checking on overnight developments. The President's press secretary, Jody Powell, and Secretary Vance's spokesman at the State Department, Hodding Carter, required special guidance for shaping a view of developments on a number of occasions to deal with stories that seemed to be distorting the picture. In addition to dealing with the press, Secretary Vance and Deputy Secretary Christopher briefed leading members of the Senate and of the House of Representatives frequently and regularly—almost daily at some points during the crisis. It was the candid sharing of problems and thoughts about dealing with them that, for the most part, assured strong support from the Congress in sensitive moments.

The leadership and members of Congress raised many questions about the role of the Congress in this crisis. In one sense, it seemed initially the kind of foreign policy problem that uniquely required executive branch management and minimal congressional action. However, in a crisis that provoked such widespread popular concern, the members could not appear inactive. The detailed briefings by the Secretary and Deputy Secretary of State were valuable simply in enabling the members to show their constituents that they were on top of the problem, even if the Congress was unable to take action on its own. At later stages of the crisis, the Congress found itself presented with opportunities to play an institutional role, because the question was raised whether or not, as the representative body, it could take positions apart from the executive branch that would be seen in Iran as reflecting the views of the people of the United States and not of the President. In the end, these options were not chosen, but the Congress from time to time had to deal with them.

By the end of the day on Monday, November 5, the operational machinery was in full swing, the President had met with his advisers, and the SCC had canvassed the wider implications of the crisis and launched the necessary studies for coping with each. The crisis machinery was already working in high second gear to help the President and his advisers set a course for dealing with what no one at that time could know would be one of the most unusual crises in the nation's history.

In many ways, it was a crisis of the future. As more actors influence events on the world stage in this century's closing years, the old instruments of power and influence will not work as they used to. With societies showing increasing political awareness, those who conduct our nation's foreign relations will have to pay increasing attention to the internal dynamics of how others' decisions are made. They will need to pay far more attention to psychological and cultural ways of influencing whole bodies politic than to the classic instruments of economic, diplomatic and military power used to move states in the past. If we learned nothing else from this unique experience, we should have learned one lesson. Our effectiveness as a global power will increasingly depend on our effectiveness in bridging the gulf between our world and the world where most of the globe's people will live.

What actually brought about the release of the hostages in the end? What did we learn about dealing with situations like this? First, the massive effort we made to construct an international environment unsympathetic to Iran as long as it held hostages undoubtedly had an effect in a variety of ways, including the concrete pressures of economic sanctions and $12 billion in frozen assets. Second, it was important that we kept a number of channels through which we conveyed to Tehran constantly that the terms of a reasonable settlement were available along with mechanisms for implementing them. Third, we could perhaps have done better if we could have reached the Islamic centers of power earlier, but we tried and failed. All of those actions—perhaps like basketball's "full court press"—helped keep the stage set for a breakthrough because they denied the Iranians the option of setting the hostage issue aside. While our continued attention to the hostage issue may have marginally helped those in Iran who wanted to keep the spotlight on the hostages for their own political purposes, we felt that it was important to deny the Iranians the option of ignoring their obligations to release the Americans being held. In the end, the timing of key steps was governed by the shifting strengths of the key protagonists in the Tehran power struggle.

2 DIPLOMACY AND PRESSURE, NOVEMBER 1979—MAY 1980

HAROLD H. SAUNDERS

SETTING A COURSE: NOVEMBER AND DECEMBER 1979

A Two-Track Strategy: Pressure and Providing a Way Out
Time rarely hangs as heavily as it does on an open telephone line in the middle of a crisis when nothing is happening. You wait hours for good news, but you suspect deep inside that nothing good is happening. Speakers from the crisis scene keep themselves busy, partly to try every door and partly because they cannot do nothing. Listeners grasp every detail in the hope that any action may be significant. Sometimes they have to wait out endless silence at the other end. Sometimes they have to chatter on endlessly for fear a telephone operator will cut in, hear nothing, and break the connection. That is how the members of the Iran Working Group spent those interminable night hours between sunset on November 4 and dawn on November 5.

By Monday morning in Washington—well into the day on November 5 in Tehran—it became apparent that the first efforts by Foreign Minister Yazdi to persuade other Iranian authorities to free the hostages would not succeed. When Laingen, Tomseth, and Howland at the Foreign Ministry saw Yazdi for the last time early Monday morning Tehran time, they began to conclude that he was not going to be able to produce results. A statement by Khomeini and the presence of his son, Ahmad, at the embassy compound made clear that the Ayatollah was endorsing, not opposing, the takeover. On Tuesday, news reached Washington that the Bazargan government had resigned. Khomeini gave power to the Revolutionary Council, which had been a shadowy body with unknown membership. President Carter himself repeated several times that day the grim frustration that would increasingly grip everyone trying to free the hostages—the frustration of not being able to deal with anyone in Tehran who could speak and act with authority.

Almost as soon as policy discussions began on Monday, the members of the crisis team in both the White House and the State Department focused on a two-track strategy. On one track would be all those efforts designed to maximize communication with Iran about conditions and arrangements for release of hostages and even to open the door to negotiation. With Secretary Vance's approval, the Iran Working Group had already instructed our ambassadors to make approaches in several dozen capitals around the world to generate a broad international outcry and to open the doors for communication. On the other track would be efforts to increase the cost to Iran of holding the hostages. Many decisions would hinge on the timing of specific steps on one track as they related to actions on the other. For instance, economic sanctions were imposed before and after but not during negotiation. The President took military action when the prospects for negotiation seemed to have dried up.

The elements of this strategy began to take shape in a series of SCC and NSC meetings on Monday and Tuesday, November 5 and 6. The first meeting of the SCC on the hostage crisis took place Monday morning with Dr. Brzezinski in the chair. At the beginning of a new crisis, each participant is eager to trade perceptions of what is happening and to begin getting the pieces of the new puzzle in order. In this case—a nonmilitary situation—they looked to Secretary Vance or Under Secretary David Newsom and to CIA Director Stansfield Turner for the latest reports from Tehran. After a review of the situation in Iran, there was general agreement that we had to show restraint in any public comments in order to avoid exacerbating the situation, and there was discussion of the possibility of sending an emissary to try to talk with key religious figures in Tehran. Responsibility was also assigned for a series of contingency plans for the group to review at a later meeting. Most of these involved various kinds of military action that the President might at some point wish to take.

Tuesday, November 6, saw a series of meetings that gradually produced the outlines of a strategy. The first began at 8:00 A.M. in the Oval Office with the President and his key advisers. Upholstered chairs and a sofa are normally grouped around the fireplace opposite the President's big desk. Advisers pull up chairs from the wall to complete the circle. The men in that group have learned to discuss even the most complex problems in a few words. Time is valuable. They know each other and can talk in shorthand to save time without sacrificing meaning. The group quickly agreed on the importance of urging American companies still operating in Iran to pull their employees out and then turned to the question whether the administration should issue some statement of the U.S. position. The President rejected the idea of a statement that went beyond repeating that we expected the Iranian authorities to make good on their assurances that our people would be safely released. There was some tentative discussion of possible punitive military actions that might be taken if Iran harmed any of the hostages.

At 8:30 A.M. all of the participants but the President went to the SCC meeting downstairs in the Situation Room, where the group discussed again some of the issues that had come up in the Oval Office and then turned to a review of the possible effects of the crisis on energy supplies. In addition to the usual membership of the SCC, present that morning were Vice President Walter Mondale, Attorney General Ben Civiletti, and Secretary of Energy Charles Duncan. Contingency planning was undertaken to review ways of coping with a reduction in Iranian oil production. The group further refined its job assignments for military contingency planning, and the Attorney General was asked to look into questions arising from the large number of Iranians then in the United States.

The third meeting of November 6 took place again with President Carter, this time in the Cabinet Room at 4:00 P.M. after news of the Bazargan government's resignation reached Washington. By the time this meeting ended, the President and his advisers had identified the key elements of the two-track strategy, including as the ultimate sanction drawing up plans for punitive military strikes. President Carter interrupted that last meeting of the day to meet with two emissaries he had decided to try to send to Tehran, and with that effort began the first direct efforts to open the door to negotiation.

The First Tries at Negotiation

As soon as it became clear that Laingen had no one in authority in Tehran to talk to, attention in Washington shifted to ways of reaching those who held real power. For a time, Laingen could make contacts in Tehran by phone, but Foreign Ministry officials made clear that he, Tomseth, and Howland would be detained in the ministry "for their own protection." As early as Sunday, members of the Working Group had begun listing prominent figures who might get a hearing in Tehran.

On Tuesday morning, President Carter decided to send two special emissaries to Tehran quickly in the hope that they might see Khomeini. Right from the start, we assumed that Khomeini's voice would be decisive. Yazdi's ineffectiveness and Bazargan's initial unwillingness to move and subsequent resignation underscored the point. Since the Iranian revolutionaries regarded the government in Washington as the enemy because of its support for the regime of the Shah, we had to find someone whom the Iranians would see as representing the American people and not the administration, yet someone who would forcefully argue the case for releasing the hostages. The President chose former Attorney General Ramsey Clark and former Foreign Service officer William Miller. As a supporter of civil liberties causes, Clark was seen in Iran as someone who would understand the grievances of the Iranian people against the regime of the Shah and the United States' relationship with him. He had visited Tehran and had met with the Khomeini group. Miller had served in Iran in the early 1960s and had been sensitive to the concerns of the political opposition in Iran. Although as he later said in a personal communication to me, "The Khomeini group were made up of men I did not know well and in most cases had never met," he had followed Iranian politics with care long after he left Iran in 1964, had close Iranian friends, and had visited Iran a number of times since his departure. He was in 1979 staff director of the Senate Intelligence Committee. The previous summer word had come from Iran that he would be an acceptable U.S. ambassador in Tehran. For a variety of personal and professional reasons, he had declined.

Late in the afternoon of Tuesday, November 6, President Carter left his meeting in the Cabinet Room to sit down by the fire in the Oval Office with Clark and Miller. He had not met Clark before but had seen Miller in a number of meetings in connection with Miller's Senate duties. Gary Sick from the NSC staff joined them. The conversation was brief. The President was clearly disturbed by the turmoil in Iran and inability to communicate with anyone who could speak for Iran or affect the dangerous situation. Carter gave them a brief four-paragraph letter on the traditional pale green White House stationery addressed, "Dear Ayatollah Khomeini." Anticipating that Clark and Miller would be able to reach Tehran, Carter wrote that "Based on the willingness of the Revolutionary Council to receive them," he was asking Clark and Miller "to discuss with you and your designees the situation in Tehran and the full range of current issues between the U.S. and Iran."

The President's letter reflected the first written effort to formulate an American position on the two key issues that seemed to require resolution before the United States and Iran could resume efforts to build a normal relationship—release of the hostages and some sensitivity on the American side to Iran's grievances:

> In the name of the American people, I ask that you release unharmed all Americans presently detained in Iran and those held with them and allow them to leave your country safely and without delay. I ask you to recognize the compelling humanitarian reasons, firmly based in international law, for doing so.
>
> I have asked both men to meet with you and to hear from you your perspective on events in Iran and the problems which have arisen between our two countries. The people of the United States

desire to have relations with Iran based upon equality, mutual respect, and friendship.

The letter was signed in the President's large precise handwriting, "Jimmy Carter."

The President wished them success as they left the Oval Office for Andrews Air Force Base, where a plane from the President's fleet of special aircraft was waiting for them. Their trip became the first of many efforts during the crisis to find the right channel to those who could make decisions in Tehran and have them carried out.

Both Laingen in Tehran and the Iran Working Group sought by phone the agreement of Ayatollah Beheshti, one of Khomeini's key colleagues, to receive Clark and Miller. They left Washington Tuesday night before Iranian agreement was assured and flew as far as Istanbul. The President had wanted to keep the mission a secret, because he believed it would be easier for the Iranians to receive Clark and Miller if it did not look as if they were bowing to American pressure. But it is hard to keep travel movements secret in Washington, and when Clark and Miller arrived at Andrews they were confronted with a battery of reporters and TV cameras. The story, including pictures of the departing plane, broke on the NBC Tuesday evening news, despite Jody Powell's efforts to dissuade NBC from carrying the story. The publicity, in part, caused the Iranians second thoughts, and on Wednesday word came that Khomeini had ordered that no one in Tehran should talk with them.

In some critical situations during the hostage crisis, individual journalists acted with great restraint and integrity. This was one instance, however, where those of us in government could not understand how a network or newspaper could run a "scoop," knowing it would jeopardize a sensitive mission, as it did the Clark-Miller mission.

While waiting in Istanbul Clark and Miller stayed under heavy security in the Consul General's house, symbolically located just above the bridge across the Bosporus between Europe and Asia. Figuratively, it was a bridge they could not cross. All of Turkey was under martial law at the time. There were bombings and killings every night they were there. From there, they contacted Tehran. As Miller would write three years later,

> Since there was no government in Tehran, and it was not at all certain what powers the Revolutionary Council had, we set about calling the key members of the Council—Beheshti, Ghotbzadeh, Yazdi, and the Prime Minister's office—as well as contacts in the bazaar with access to Khomeini's group and the Revolutionary Council. We also spoke with the captors in the American Embassy. The Turkish government gave us first priority on all telephone lines

going from Turkey to Iran. We soon came to know the voices of a number of international telephone operators in both Turkey and Iran as they placed call after call from 8:00 A.M. in the morning until 2:00 or 3:00 A.M. the following morning over a ten-day period. . . . We also made calls to Iranian officials at the U.N. and at the Iranian Embassy in Washington where Ramsey Clark was well known—but to little effect.

The lines of communication gradually closed down. Miller observed,

They politely listened, said they would try to help and raised in turn the list of familiar demands concerning the Shah, admission of U.S. guilt, return of the Shah's assets to Iran, and so on. . . . We said we were sent by President Carter to discuss all of these matters. The response was that they would consult with the Ayatollah and would have an answer in a day or two. The next stage was very frustrating because the Revolutionary Council, we were informed, had been ordered by Ayatollah Khomeini to have no contact with us. . . . A curious tactic developed at this point. We would call Beheshti or Ghotbzadeh or Bani-Sadr's office. A secretary or assistant would answer, say that their principals would not speak to us, but relay our messages and their answers in turn. We could hear voices in the background which in some cases were clearly those of Ghotbzadeh, Beheshti, or Bani-Sadr. This indirect dialogue by telephone, undoubtedly overheard by all the interested intelligence services of the world, was but one of the bizarre chapters in Iranian diplomatic annals.

Clark was also on the phone to a number of Palestinian contacts both in the United States and in Lebanon. They were hard to track down in Beirut, because they constantly moved around for security. Sometimes they did not come to rest for the night until 2–3:00 A.M. During one of his midnight calls to Beirut, Clark suggested as a first step in resolving the crisis the release of the women and marine guards among the hostages who did not have the same political involvement as some of the regular Foreign Service officers.

As time passed, Miller later concluded, "It became increasingly clear that there would be no movement in Tehran until the new government had given itself legitimacy through adoption of a new constitution, later parliamentary elections, and eventually the formation of a government." Despite the fact that their telephone contacts in Tehran gave them unique insight into the developing power struggle among the revolutionaries in Tehran, they eventually advised Washington that there seemed to be no useful purpose in staying on in Istanbul. The mission was called back to Washington on November 15. Carter's letter was never delivered.

Perhaps because of Clark's contacts and perhaps on their own insight, one of the groups that began almost immediately to address the hostage problem was the Palestine Liberation Organization (PLO). The PLO had provided security for Khomeini's group in Paris, and Yasir Arafat had been one of the first foreign figures to pay a much-publicized formal visit to Tehran after Khomeini's return in February. Through several indirect channels abroad and in the United States, word reached the State Department that Chairman Arafat was looking closely at the situation. He sent an emissary to Tehran and also worked through the PLO representative already in Tehran. Information from several sources confirmed that the Palestinians were active in Tehran and were meeting with Khomeini on the subject. Key Palestinians told their American contacts, including individuals outside the executive branch like Congressman Paul Findley from Abraham Lincoln's old district in Illinois, that the PLO sought no quid pro quo from the United States in return for their efforts, although for reasons obvious in the larger Middle East context they hoped for some kind of private acknowledgment of what they were doing. They told the Iranians and stated publicly that they were not mediating between the United States and Iran. In Washington, Secretary Vance authorized me to tell those transmitting these PLO views that constructive help from any quarter would be appreciated in Washington. The PLO continued to act on its own and not as a direct mediator.

Toward the end of the first week, we began to receive what the inner circle of the crisis team regarded as the first significant response to our many probes. Top members of the team, as well as Clark, had put into several channels the idea that it would be important to see an Iranian demonstration that the revolutionary authorities could deliver on a decision to release the hostages, because the chaos in Tehran raised suspicion about whether the militants holding the hostages would indeed respond to orders to release them. As David Newsom said, "We badly need some kind of indication that the Ayatollah *could* achieve release of the hostages." About November 9, word began to come through our most authoritative channel from the top PLO leadership that Khomeini was seriously considering ordering the release of women and black hostages "not considered spies." The United States was notified through the PLO on November 14 that the Iranian authorities were prepared to make the release but that they expected a U.S. statement on departure of the Shah from the United States. That idea was later dropped, and word came on Friday, November 16, that a decision was expected momentarily on this partial release. We expressed through a private channel our appreciation for continuing efforts on behalf of the hostages.

Thus it was that, among the many channels through which support was initially sought for release of the hostages, the PLO in the first phase pursued the issue in Tehran more actively than any other and with apparent results. In January 1981, just after the hostages had been released, some members of the House of Representatives Foreign Affairs Committee in open hearings about the agreement with Iran expressed outrage that the United States had included the PLO among those organizations from which it sought help. Some of that outrage was obviously for the record, since the hearings were being broadcast, but some of it went to the serious substantive question of whether we should have dealt with the PLO on this issue.

Those dealing with the crisis knew that the United States had stated openly on a number of past occasions that, while it would not negotiate with the PLO in the Arab-Israeli context until the PLO accepted the objective of peace with Israel, it would deal with the PLO on matters of security. That was essential, and we made no effort to hide it. The PLO provided security in much of the area around the American Embassy in Beirut. It had guaranteed security when Americans were evacuated in 1976 after the Lebanese civil war broke out. In this first week of the hostage crisis, the judgment was made that the fate of the hostages in Tehran was equally a matter of security of Americans, and the channel to the PLO was opened along with a number of others.

With Secretary Vance's approval, I sent an oral message to the highest level of the Israeli government explaining the PLO role. Word came back from Jerusalem that, while their position on the PLO was well known, they would not complicate our efforts to release the hostages. The Israelis themselves have dealt with the PLO on occasion about exchange of prisoners. It was obvious to all those involved that constructive PLO help on the hostage crisis might be relevant at some later stage in the Arab-Israeli context, but both U.S. and Palestinian officials were scrupulous in never involving in this exchange any subject but the hostages.

PLO officials remained active for more than two months. Early in 1980, they apparently judged that the situation in Tehran was so chaotic that not even they would have much luck producing decisions until the political struggle worked itself out.

The release of the thirteen hostages on November 18 and 19 was not negotiated. It was an Iranian gesture unilaterally taken. Whether they made their decision at PLO urging or because they recognized the need to improve their position we were never sure. Whoever took the initiative, the move was probably seen in Tehran as a step to portray the regime as humanitarian and intent only on exposing the U.S. government and its "nest of spies."

From the first hours of the crisis, as in President Carter's letter to Khomeini, we began to develop a position in response to Iranian demands that was communicated to and through all active channels. In response, we began to get a more precise picture of exactly what the Iranians wanted in return for release.

The United States' position throughout the first week of the crisis was simply to demand the release of the hostages and, as long as they remained in captivity, some access to them to determine their condition. As the President wrote Khomeini, his instructions to Clark and Miller had been to gain release of the hostages and then to discuss ways of establishing some base for relations between the two countries. They were to tell the Iranians that the Shah was in serious condition and could not immediately leave the United States. They were authorized to offer to arrange for a confidential exchange between Iranian authorities and doctors treating the Shah in order to confirm his condition. Clark and Miller could tell the Iranians that they were free to pursue claims against the Shah's assets in U.S. courts; that the United States supported the independence and territorial integrity of Iran and opposed any external involvement in Iran's internal affairs; that progress could continue in sorting out the U.S.-Iranian military supply relationship. The hope was that their mere presence in Tehran and readiness to listen to Iranian grievances might provide a way out for the Iranians.

We also had to take a position on the Shah's departure from the United States. Even during the first week of the crisis, people on both sides began to discuss whether and how his departure might affect the situation. The Shah had let it be known as early as November 7 that he was prepared to leave New York as soon as he was well enough. Later, as mentioned above, when word first came that Khomeini was considering releasing female and black hostages, the message to the crisis team indicated that the Iranians expected in return a statement by the United States explaining exactly when the Shah would be leaving the United States. We responded that there was no way to provide a date because the Shah's health was unpredictable—he still had tubes in him—and his treatment required additional time. That idea was dropped, but it was obvious that the Shah's departure, whenever it took place, might be a significant moment for breaking the impasse or, conversely, might cause a negative reaction in Tehran. On November 9, President Anwar Sadat's offer to welcome the Shah in Egypt was repeated to the Shah.

When the effort to make contact through Clark and Miller failed, attention shifted to a second channel. That approach focused on the United Nations, where Secretary-General Waldheim met with Iranian representatives in the first of a series of efforts to work out arrangements for release of the hostages. The President decided that in discussions with the Secretary-General and in the United Nations the United States should take the position that Iran should release the hostages first; only then would the United States be prepared to discuss, in the United Nations or elsewhere, Iran's grievances and other issues necessary to resolve the crisis.

The thought behind this position was that Iran was not entitled to use the U.N. platform to air its grievances while it was violating the very principles on which the United Nations was founded. Some members of the crisis team were uncomfortable with this position. Some pointed out that the United States had always supported the right of U.N. members to discuss the causes of conflict in the Security Council, whether the United States agreed with their positions or not, so this reversed a long-held principle. Others felt that it might help resolve the crisis if Iran could be drawn into the U.N. process early to learn how its action was isolating it.

The Iranian authorities' demands, stated on November 12 by the new Foreign Minister, Abolhassan Bani-Sadr, developed around three points: return of the Shah's assets, an end to interference in Iran's affairs, and an apology for past U.S. "crimes" against Iran. Bani-Sadr had assumed the functions of Foreign Minister after Yazdi stepped aside with Bazargan's resignation. His later formulations dropped his November 12 repetition of the demand that the Shah be returned to Iran for a "fair trial," which had been the rallying cry of those Iranians in control of the embassy compound. On November 16, Washington was studying a press report of an interview with him in which he stated as Iran's only demand U.S. acceptance of the principle of an international commission charged with investigating the behavior of the Shah during his reign. As policymakers discussed how to respond, a difference of approach surfaced among them.

One school of thought started from the premise that the authorities in Tehran, however disorganized, had to be held responsible for their acts. Because they themselves constituted the government of Iran, they had to be made to see, through a variety of pressures, that interests important to them would be damaged if they continued to hold the hostages. With that premise in mind, the discussion focused on more or less traditional thoughts about what those interests were and how they might be threatened as a means of increasing the pressure on Iran. Those who held this view took the firm position that there would be no discussion of Iran's concerns until the hostages were released. People who leaned toward this position tended initially to be close to the American political scene and to have limited experience dealing with other political systems.

Other members of the team, mainly those whose jobs were to deal with other peoples and cultures, felt that a solution would have to provide Iranian leaders with some development they could use politically to claim "victory" and to justify releasing the hostages. They started from three thoughts:

1. Whatever the correctness of holding the revolutionary authorities accountable before international law and opinion, the political fact was that the revolution in Iran was still in process, and even Khomeini could not be assumed to have a political base strong enough to force his will in all cases. The hostages were a weapon in their power struggle.

2. The priorities of the revolutionary leaders started with consolidating the revolution, not with meeting Iran's international responsibilities and not even with keeping the Iranian economy much above necessary subsistence. In any case, revolutionary Iran did not define Iran's responsibilities in terms of Western law and morality, which themselves were targets of the revolution.

3. Whatever steps might be necessary to increase pressure on Iran as pressure is classically conceived, it would also be necessary to think of actions that would play into the internal political dynamics of Iran in ways that might generate internal arguments for the release of the hostages.

As early as November 9, the Iran Working Group was developing a "basket of proposals" which, if presented to the Iranians by an intermediary, might offer a face-saving way of releasing the hostages. Whatever the decision, career officers on the crisis team and Secretaries Vance and Christopher in the SCC urged a thorough discussion before any decisions were made on the relationship between actions to pressure Iran and efforts to establish some kind of negotiation or mediation.

When I speak of tension between two points of view, I am not setting the stage for the classic media description of hostile advisers and bureaucratic forces locked in mortal combat over opposed strategies. The point is an intensely human one. Each of us had to argue within himself the proper balance at a given moment between two unavoidable ingredients of policy— pressure and providing a way out. Minds changed as conditions changed. Differences were with only a few exceptions handled honestly and respectfully. The normal approach for high policymakers in a situation of this kind is to consider the classic instruments of economic, political, and military pressure. The problem in Tehran was that no normal government existed that could respond to pressure by making decisions and making them stick. While external pressure over time might have some influence, it seemed to some of us that we would also have to find ways of building a constituency in Tehran for release of the hostages. We had to find steps that could make it advantageous in the Tehran power struggle to release the hostages. In the early stages of the crisis, the White House tended to see any such steps as appearing to the American people to be appeasement or surrender.

These differences were always discussed reasonably and within the appropriate policymaking circle. Whereas there had been acrimony and many press leaks in the policy debate during the Iranian revolution a year earlier, that experience was not repeated during the hostage crisis. The different approaches that were discussed reflected a normal difference, often found in Washington, between those who are particularly sensitive to the political dynamics of a foreign situation and those who have to build political support for foreign policy in the United States. It is a familiar argument between those who say that the United States should simply get tough and let the other side respond and those who recognize that foreign leaders also have political constituencies even though their political systems may be different.

At the beginning of the second week of the crisis, I had asked a number of my colleagues in the Working Group for individual reflections on Iran's internal political developments and their relationship to the hostage crisis. The responses painted a picture of the Iranian revolution as having moved into a new phase with the resignation of the Bazargan government. This phase was marked by the removal from authority of those secular individuals who had been in Iran during the revolution. A few like Ghotbzadeh, Bani-Sadr, and Yazdi, who had been with Khomeini in Paris, remained a part of the inner group. No threat to Khomeini's tenure seemed likely in the near future. Some voices stated with varying degrees of certainty that the prospect of a stalemate after the end of the first week loomed larger and larger as long as it seemed impossible for emissaries to develop a serious dialogue with the religious leadership in Tehran. Some of the more pessimistic voices categorically stated that neither diplomatic action nor pressure would produce a release of the hostages and that their captivity could continue for months. On the other side of the ledger by November 15 were the impending release of some of the female and black hostages and the prospect for serious discussion through Secretary-General Waldheim at the United Nations. While it looked like an uphill struggle, with frustration at each step of the way, we felt there were openings we could use to build momentum for release.

This was a familiar situation for those of us who spent our professional lives dealing with intractable problems. My bureau had its share—the Arab-Israeli-Palestinian conflict, the India-Pakistan tension, the Lebanese civil war, and personalities like Khomeini and Qadhafi, to name just the more notable ones. In each of these, we face pressures from two directions. We face the observers—in the press, in the academic world, sometimes intelligence analysts—who explain how intractable the problem is and how unlikely it is to be solved soon. There seems to be a certain smug, macabre satisfaction in painting a "realistic" picture, which is usually a gloomy one. On the other side are those line officers who understand perhaps better than anyone how tough the problem is but who in the national interest are trying to find openings for making the situation a little better or at least minimizing the danger. I used to tell my colleagues, "Our job is to take a 10 percent chance of success, try to turn it into a 20 percent chance, and hope for a break." So it was in the hostage crisis.

As the United States refined its position for possible exchanges at the United Nations, those who felt that the United States should demand release of the hostages before responding to the Iranians' concerns in any way prevailed. On November 17, Secretary-General Waldheim gave to Iranian representatives the United States' position, which by then was stated in terms of these four points:

1. The release of all American personnel held in Tehran
2. The establishment of an international commission to inquire into violations of human rights in Iran under the previous regime
3. The availability of United States courts to the Iranian government to hear its claim for return of the assets it believed had been illegally taken from Iran
4. Affirmation by the governments of Iran and the United States of their intention to abide strictly by the Declaration of Principles of International Law Concerning Friendly Relations and Cooperation Among States in accordance with the Charter of the United Nations and to abide by the provisions of the Vienna Convention on Diplomatic Relations

Despite U.S. opposition to discussion in the Security Council at that stage, Secretary-General Waldheim, Ramsey Clark, and other private intermediaries in New York held intensive conversations with Iranian representatives. Some of these took place as informal consultations of the Security Council, and documents were developed. As a result, arrangements were made for Bani-Sadr to come to New York. We hoped that he would meet with Secretary Vance. Ostensibly his purpose in coming to New York was to join in the deliberations surrounding possible meetings of the Security Council. First, Bani-Sadr postponed his visit, and then word came on November 28 that he had been removed as Foreign Minister and had been replaced by Sadegh Ghotbzadeh. That same day, Ramsey Clark reported that the Iranian representatives in New York with whom he had been working were leaving for Tehran and that no one would be coming to the United Nations from Tehran.

Throughout this period, there was a proliferation of private groups and individuals who felt that their going to Tehran in an unofficial capacity could provide an American sounding board for Iranian expression of grievances against the United States. Some of the groups that talked about going but did not included prominent public figures like Andrew Young and Jesse

Jackson. Other groups that did go were built around scholars who knew Iran well and were sensitive to the feelings of the revolutionaries. Ramsey Clark himself began considering going to Tehran in a personal capacity and eventually went the following June. At each holiday season—Christmas and Easter—groups of clergymen offered to go and conduct religious services. The administration urged the secular groups not to go to Tehran unless they had a commitment in advance to bring the hostages out with them. In another vein, the thirteen hostages who left Tehran in November issued a statement saying what the captors in the compound had told them about Iranian grievances, without commenting on it. In that way, they hoped to use their departure to try to improve the atmosphere in Tehran. On Thanksgiving Day, Congressman George Hansen was in Tehran, raising the question whether congressional hearings into the situation in Iran might provide a vehicle for allowing Iran to express its grievances. Some consideration was given to this approach in the House Banking Committee, but most members disapproved and wanted to dissociate themselves from the Hansen initiative.

These private efforts raised questions both for the private individuals and for us in the government. On the one hand, we welcomed any opportunity to open new channels to Tehran. But some of those who went risked cutting across policy actions by the government that were unknown to them, especially when they refused to talk with the administration before departing. In their own college and religious communities, the activities of some of these people were questioned. Were they naively assuming responsibilities beyond their capacity and beyond their authority? Some even violated American regulations in going to Tehran. The Working Group was often frustrated by the attitude among some of these groups that they would tarnish their credentials by talking to the State Department before they went. From the Working Group's viewpoint, the groups could have been much more effective in bringing back word about individual hostages for the families hungry for reports of contact if they had been briefed beforehand on those about whom we were particularly concerned. Some saw hostages and came back unable to recall whom they had seen. The hostages themselves, in some cases, were bitter that the efforts of some individuals to appear sympathetic to Iranian militants and critical of the United States actually made their position as American officials even more difficult. While many of these groups acted as they did out of their own frustrated convictions that the government was not doing everything it could, the answer seemed to be that there was a place for private emissaries but that any approach to hostage takers in a situation like this should be coordinated so as to assure maximum effectiveness from all channels that worked.

The thirteen female and black hostages arrived at Andrews Air Force

Base on a bright, sunny Thanksgiving morning to the gratefully warm welcome of family and colleagues. Their captivity of two weeks seemed distressingly long then. That afternoon around Thanksgiving tables across Washington, we gave thanks for their safe return and asked a blessing on those still in Tehran and their families who could not share in the happiness of reunion.

The return of "the thirteen" to Washington gave us the best early picture of the deplorable conditions under which the hostages were being held and of the condition of individual hostages. We also began to get a sense of the dimensions of the collection of classified material now in Iranian hands. Although the returned hostages were careful in their statement to the press, we decided that it would be a good idea to allow some stories about the conditions of their captivity to get into the press in order to fuel negative international reactions about what the Iranians were doing. For long periods many of the hostages had been blindfolded with hands tied and were not permitted to speak. The enforced immobility and silence were particularly difficult to bear. Stories were told of mock executions. We were able to get some sense of how the captors in the compound were organized.

When Bani-Sadr was dismissed and the negotiations at the United Nations suspended, the crisis team in Washington recognized that the momentum they had hoped was building through the release of the thirteen hostages and the New York exchanges would be lost. Analysts in the Working Group pointed out that Khomeini was using both the hostages and the height of religious fervor, which culminated in Iran November 29 and 30, to build support for the nationwide referendum on the new constitution for the Islamic Republic, which was scheduled for December 2–3. After three weeks of intense efforts to build momentum, we had to suffer the frustration of watching it trickle away.

This moment also showed how we repeatedly looked for opportunities even in the most discouraging situations. Some of our analysts suggested that the completion of the constitution could be a moment when the Iranians might look for an opportunity to proclaim victory and to expel the hostages. In the months ahead, we would look again and again at those events in the Islamic calendar that might be occasions for pardoning prisoners and releasing captives. Other more pessimistic analysts suggested that instability in the Iranian ruling group would not be so quickly overcome by the referendum and that the insecurity of members of the Revolutionary Council would continue to undermine a consensus for release of the hostages. Finally, there were those who pointed out that Khomeini might simply be seeking revenge and the humiliation of the United States over a period of time.

In this forced lull in efforts to begin a negotiation, members of the crisis team reviewed the three main channels then currently active—Secretary-

General Waldheim, the PLO, and Ramsey Clark in his capacity as a private citizen. By now the list of Iranian "demands," apart from those of the militants holding the compound, added up to these: First, U.S. recognition of injustices in Iran under the Shah. Various Iranians differed about whether they would be satisfied simply with an inquiry into those injustices or whether they also required the United States to accept the principle of the Shah's guilt. Second, U.S. acknowledgment of some responsibility for the Shah's actions and commitment to noninterference in Iranian affairs in the future. Third, timing release of the hostages to coincide with some U.S. act recognizing the Shah's guilt. Fourth, an opportunity to recover some portion of the Shah's assets. By this time, demands for extradition of the Shah had dropped from the Iranian list.

Throughout these first weeks, humanitarian concern for the safety of the hostages was in the minds of policymakers at all levels. The wild mobs that continued to demonstrate in front of the embassy and reports of the harsh conditions under which the hostages were held underscored the conviction that any sudden move by the United States could well provoke execution of some of the hostages.

The President had to balance his concern for those human beings in Tehran and their families against the national humiliation and the evidence that the United States was impotent to protect its people or to force an outlaw group to abide by international law and practice. One of the most difficult challenges a President faces in conducting foreign policy is to set a course between conflicting sets of pressures and to stick to it. Many of the toughest problems can be dealt with only by wearing them down. As in the hostage crisis, the test for a lot of us became whether we could outlast the Iranians. For the President that was harder than it was for the rest of us, because his efforts to show restraint and to keep a steady course were buffeted by high political winds blowing across the country. Often the challenge to the President in public debate was whether he was going to be soft and put the safety of the hostages above national honor or whether he was going to show our strength and pursue honor regardless of the consequences for the hostages. The deep frustration of knowing that you are doing the sensible thing while being publicly berated is one of the personal problems public officials have to live with.

In addition to coping with these difficult issues, we pursued our concern about the hostages' safety in three ways.

First, we pressed through a number of diplomatic and international channels for visits to the hostages themselves to account for them, to provide medical care, and to determine the conditions of their captivity. One hostage, we knew, was an older man with a heart condition. Others wrote to families about various symptoms, mostly brought on by the strain. The

Iranians permitted a visit to the hostages on November 10 by the Swedish and Syrian ambassadors in Tehran and the French and Algerian chargés, but over time such visits were few and far between. Christmas and Easter visits by clergy were allowed, but there was to be no formal visit by diplomats until the Algerian mediating team visited the hostages in December 1980. Families eagerly awaited the reports of those visitors.

Second, there was a continuous effort from the first day of the takeover to account accurately for the whereabouts of each person known to have been in the embassy compound or in the American official community in Tehran on the day of the takeover. The Iran Working Group had begun maintaining a master list of each individual and everything that had been heard about him or her. As the 444 days accumulated, it became a matter of considerable concern when individuals had not been heard from for some time. Since some of them were held in solitary confinement, those cases were too frequent for comfort.

Third, President Carter met as early as November 9 with members of the hostages' families, who had been invited to the State Department. Hundreds of hours would be spent helping families deal with their family, personal, emotional, financial, and other needs as an integral part of managing the crisis.

When word was received that the thirteen hostages would be released, once again actions taken in these early days of the crisis set a pattern for U.S. handling of the crisis until the last of the hostages was free. The decision was made that the freed hostages would be taken to the U.S. Air Force hospital in Wiesbaden, Germany, for prompt medical care and for a brief period of unwinding before coming home. Organizing the reception in Wiesbaden was no simple job. Every element in the bureaucracy wanted somehow to be involved. At the outset, firm guidelines were set down that protected the hostages from becoming guinea pigs in larger efforts to advance medical research or intelligence analysis. A U.S. team put together by Sheldon Krys and led by Under Secretary of State David Newsom, which included medical specialists and top-level administrators, went to Wiesbaden November 18 to work with hospital personnel to establish procedures for helping the freed hostages return quickly to normal lives. The team included psychiatrists who had studied the problems of prisoners of war as well as others who had helped and counseled the families of the hostages in the United States. Their purpose was to ease the transition as hostages and families were reunited.

During this period, a special relationship developed with the government of Switzerland. Among the staff papers prepared in the early days of the crisis was the usual legal memorandum on appointing another government to look after U.S. interests if diplomatic relations were broken. It is a customary step when diplomatic relations are broken for each government to appoint a "protecting power" to do its business in the other's capital. Although relations between the United States and Iran were not broken till later, the Washington team developed close working and personal relationships with the Swiss that became central in later dealings with Tehran. The Swiss ambassador in Tehran and his colleagues in Berne and Washington were gradually drawn into the crisis.

When it was announced that the thirteen hostages would be released, the Swiss immediately offered an aircraft to fly them to Europe. They offered communication with Tehran through a channel beginning with Ambassador Raymond Probst and his deputy, Franz Muheim, in Washington, going through Edouard Brunner, the senior ministry official responsible for the Middle East in Berne, and Foreign Minister Pierre Aubert, and ending with Ambassador Erik Lang in Tehran. Increasingly, Lang became the bearer of sensitive U.S. messages to key Iranians, a principal analyst of the political dynamics in Tehran, and an independent source of judgment on other negotiating channels. Probst would bring Lang's thoughtful analytical messages into David Newsom's office or mine and read them to us. When we had replies, we would often drive them to the Ambassador's office late in the day, keeping him and his communicators at work well into the evening. Eventually, the following April, when the United States broke relations with Iran, Switzerland formally became the protecting power, but help far above and beyond the call of that duty had by then come to characterize the relationship.

Meanwhile, concern for the safety of the hostages remained deep. At the time of the release of the thirteen, the Iranians threatened to try the remaining hostages as spies. In the atmosphere of religious frenzy in Tehran, summary trials and executions seemed real possibilities. By November 18, widespread talk of trials caused us through our many communication channels to press friends to weigh in against trials and to convey to Iranian authorities that harm to any of the hostages would bring grave consequences for Iran. The United States sought a statement by the U.N. Security Council against trials and tried to marshal approaches from Islamic states that trials would be contrary to Islamic law and tradition.

After discussing these threats at some length with his advisers at Camp David, the President approved on November 23 sending a private message to Bani-Sadr making our position clear. Secretary Vance brought it back to the department and told me to have it delivered through the most reliable secret channel available. The message made four points:

1. As the President had previously stated, the U.S. preference remained a peaceful solution that the United States would pursue through channels available to it.

2. Any public trial or governmental trial of U.S. personnel in Iran would result in the interruption of Iranian commerce.

3. Any harm to any hostage would result in direct retaliatory action.

4. This message was being conveyed privately by a highly secure channel. The United States did not want any misunderstanding about the seriousness of the message.

Because Bani-Sadr was removed from office shortly after that message was delivered to him, it was not clear who in Tehran knew of it. However, the President met with hostage families on December 7 and stated that Iran had been warned that the United States would interrupt its commerce if the hostages were tried. The President spoke confidentially to a closed meeting, but one of the family members recorded his remarks and passed them to *The New York Times*, which reported them.[1] In any case, talk of trials in Tehran stopped for awhile, and some of the President's advisers attributed the halt to the President's tough message. I was not so sure.

Throughout December, intermediaries seeking the "bridging mechanism" between the U.S. position and Iranian demands frequently discussed the possibility of some kind of tribunal in Tehran that would dramatize the wrongdoing of the Shah and the U.S. support for him but end in "expulsion" of the hostages. The crisis team in Washington considered at length whether and how legal counsel might be provided the hostages if a trial took place. The Association of the Bar of the City of New York offered to do extensive preparatory studies on Islamic legal procedures and preliminary defense work for individual hostages. The United States continued to take a strong stand against any such tribunal because of both the principle of protecting diplomatic immunity and deep concern that any such situation could get out of control and lead to killing some of the hostages on the spot.

The tension in Washington over the safety of Americans was not confined to Tehran during this period. The atmosphere in some other parts of the Middle East was charged with anti-Americanism partly in resonance with the events in Tehran.

On November 20, an armed group of conservative Muslims took over the Grand Mosque in Mecca, Saudi Arabia, the holiest shrine for all of Islam. This shocking act had nothing to do with the hostages in Tehran. As it turned out, the group opposed the pace and path of modernization in Saudi Arabia. But Khomeini charged the United States with responsibility. Radio reports of the attack in Mecca and Khomeini's charge, when they reached Pakistan, seem to have triggered a mob of Muslims to attack and burn the U.S. Embassy in Islamabad on November 21. Before the Pakistani army arrived to free the compound, most of the staff was holed up in a secure area

1. *The New York Times,* December 8, 1979, p. 1.

on the top floor with the building burning under them. The floor became so hot that the carpet was turning brown. When they finally climbed up to the roof, they found that attackers whom they had previously heard there had miraculously disappeared. By the time the compound was cleared, two Americans and two Pakistani employees were dead. On December 2, the embassy in Libya was attacked and burned. Fortunately, everyone was able to escape through a carefully planned escape route not obvious to the attackers. An attack on the embassy in Kuwait was thwarted by alert local authorities.

Shortly after these attacks, one evening around 11:00 P.M., Secretary Vance called me apologetically and asked if I could come to his home. As we sat in his study, he shared with me his agony over the safety of other Americans in Islamic countries. "I'm deeply concerned," he said in effect, "over what would happen to our people if the White House decided to take military action against Iran. I can't responsibly just leave them there." I knew he was asking himself how he would explain to himself, to Congress, to the press, or to families why he had left so many Americans exposed to danger if the flames of a violent reaction swept the Islamic world. I could not disagree. My conscience raised the same questions. We could not be confident that the attacks we had just lived through would not become common experience.

When I left Vance's home after midnight, I called the Working Group to start people on studies for him on the implications of the use or threat of force for U.S. personnel throughout the Near East and South Asia. These studies considered the possible reaction throughout these areas to several kinds of U.S. military action—a quick and successful strike to free the hostages, an unsuccessful effort causing loss of life, retaliation for execution of hostages, extended military operations against Iran, and the simple perception that the United States was considering the use of force. I also asked for separate papers laying out recommendations for reducing the numbers of Americans at particularly exposed posts—what posts were particularly vulnerable; what Americans could be brought out without crippling our presence; what the host government's reactions would be; whether the evacuation should be ordered or left to ambassadors' discretion; where the evacuees would go. After he had discussed these memos with his senior colleagues the next day, Secretary Vance decided to draw down the number of Americans throughout the area, without reducing essential activities. Instructions were sent on December 2, and over the next several weeks more than 900 American officials and family members left the area with no certainty about when they could return and with serious disruption to their personal lives.

With that act, we created human problems little noted by the American people but on a scale even greater than those generated by the hostage crisis. Mothers and children as well as employees returned to the United States in the middle of the school year to dig in with families or in temporary furnished apartments. We could give them no idea how long they would have to stay. Many of them—and their ambassadors—were angry and seriously questioned our judgment. From their perspective, they saw no signs of unrest around them and felt no danger. We in Washington, on the other hand, had read too many telegrams from ambassadors on how stable their situations were ("it can't happen here") only to end up on the telephone with a beseiged embassy a few days later. We did what we had to do, knowing full well that our caution could prove unnecessary. But none of those families would ever fully understand what Secretary Vance felt at that moment was the real possibility of a sudden U.S. military move.

As Dr. Brzezinski himself recounts, this was a period when he was pressing for review of military options, which had been discussed at the November 23 NSC meeting at Camp David, and arguing that we had to give fuller attention to our strategic interests.[2] He urged enhancing the U.S. security presence in the Persian Gulf and even recommended steps for unseating Khomeini. Secretary Brown wrote the President on December 1 that he did not see how to avoid military action for more than another few weeks.

By the end of November, we were still looking for a way to bridge the gulf between Iranian and American requirements and to make it possible for the Iranians to act. The wide range of decisions and actions taken during the first month of the crisis to define and come to grips with the problem provided the base for the more measured strategy that became necessary as the crisis dragged on. During the last week of November, the Working Group drafted a scenario in which the Secretary-General of the United Nations would determine the willingness of the Shah to leave the United States, Iran would allow medical examinations of the hostages, the Secretary-General would offer to approach television networks with the idea of their taping a one-hour presentation by the militants holding the hostages, the Secretary-General and some leaders from the Third World would go to Tehran to hear Iranian complaints, a friendly government would assume control of the American Embassy compound, the hostages would be "expelled," and the U.N. Security Council would resume its sessions to hear Iran's complaints. In that context, the United States would pledge noninterference in Iranian affairs, discussion of the future of Iranian-U.S. relations, thawing the freeze on assets after release of the hostages, and no retaliation against Iran. Many of these thoughts originated not only in the Working

2. Zbigniew Brzezinski, *Power and Principle: Memoirs of the National Security Adviser, 1977–1981* (New York: Farrar, Straus, and Giroux, 1983), pp. 483–84.

Group but also with private American academic specialists. Some of them were in touch with Iran daily by phone or actually went to Tehran to talk with contacts there at high levels and to report informally to the crisis team.

There was a feeling by the end of November that the United States needed to give more attention to how it would be possible to work within the Iranian political situation, but American anger at the Iranians still made it very tricky to take any step that would look as if we were "dealing with kidnappers." As one friendly ambassador in Tehran described the problem, "The U.S. and Iran are addressing each other on different planes. Iranian rhetoric is revolutionary and religious, whereas U.S. rhetoric is primarily legal." We needed to bridge the gulf while protecting our honor.

Systematizing the Pressure

The strategy in place by the end of the second week of the crisis combined pressure with the efforts to open the door to negotiation.

Many of the steps taken were steps that it would be normal to take at the beginning of any such crisis. We had encouraged other governments to make their views known to Iran, and we had their support in significant numbers. We had consulted at the United Nations, where the President of the Security Council had issued an appeal for release of the hostages on November 9 and repeated it on November 27. The President of the General Assembly had issued a consensus statement.

We had approached the Soviet Union as well as a host of other governments. We knew that in 1978 and 1979 the Soviet Union had worked intensively to penetrate the new Iranian government and to strengthen the Tudeh (Communist) Party, which was now operating openly. Pleased with our expulsion from Iran, it was doing its best to improve its own position for the long run. Nevertheless, it had normally taken a position against such acts as hijacking and hostage taking, and it was important to put the Soviet Union on record, too, even though that was the extent of the help we expected from it. So while its subversive activities in Iran—and eventually its invasion of Afghanistan—were constantly on our minds in the larger strategic context, the Soviet Union did not figure prominently outside the United Nations in our management of the crisis.

President Carter had also taken unilateral steps to demonstrate to Iran that its actions would have concrete costs. In order to nip in the bud any thought that Iran could use its oil as leverage in settling the crisis, the President on November 12 had ordered that U.S. purchasers could no longer buy oil from Iran. Secretary Duncan's studies for the SCC had shown that a cutoff of Iranian imports was manageable. When Iranian authorities said they would withdraw Iranian bank deposits from the United States, the President ordered on November 14 that all Iranian assets be frozen, including deposits in U.S. banks and their foreign branches and subsidiaries. (This complex action is discussed in detail in chapter 4.) Military shipments to Iran and most trade, with the exception of food, were stopped. The administration had had to introduce greater discipline into the handling of Iranian students in the United States by requiring them to register to determine whether their papers were current, because they were the object of some resentment in American communities. Some of us were uncomfortable with this decision, which we felt caught many innocent and even antirevolutionary Iranians who were honestly pursuing their studies in the United States.

On November 29, we had petitioned the International Court of Justice at The Hague for a prompt legal decision that Iran's action in taking and holding the hostages violated international law. The idea of taking such a move had crystallized in the second week of the crisis and had been agreed on in SCC discussions. State Department Legal Adviser Roberts Owen and his colleague Steven Schwebel had flown to The Hague and on November 29 filed the necessary court papers. They requested "provisional measures"— an early order to release the hostages.

As November gave way to December, it was a time of stock taking. In hindsight, when we look back at November 1979, even those of us who were involved find it hard to believe how much we actually did in those three short weeks. For all that, a solution still seemed far from reach.

As Gary Sick later wrote:

The American campaign of persuasion and pressure which was mounted in the days and weeks following the hostage seizure was probably the most extensive and sustained effort of its kind ever to be conducted in peacetime. No nation in the world had more resources at its command than the United States, and all of those resources were mobilized to bring the maximum political, economic, diplomatic, legal, financial and even religious pressure on the revolutionary regime in Tehran. The result was a virtual onslaught of messages, pleas, statements, personal emissaries, condemnations, and resolutions of all natures from governments, institutions and individuals around the world, descending in torrents on Iranian officials and representatives wherever they might be.

From a technical point of view this campaign was an extraordinary achievement. Seldom if ever has world public opinion been so universally aroused and spoken with such a single voice in opposition to the action of one nation against another. No Iranian of any political persuasion could appear in any group or any forum virtually any place in the world without being questioned and

criticized about the seizure of the American hostages in Tehran. Iran
became an instant pariah in the world community, and its conduct of
relations outside its own borders was severely impaired. There are
probably few nations in the world which would have been willing to
sustain the battering of national pride and national interest to which
Iran was subjected in the long months of the crisis. In one sense, this
campaign was a convincing demonstration of the powers of moral
and political suasion which can be mustered by the world
community. Unfortunately, it was also a demonstration of the
inherent limitations of international public opinion to deal with a
renegade nation in a state of revolutionary euphoria.

Despite this pressure campaign, policymakers had to face the fact that
the internal political struggle in Tehran had already removed two of the
officials with whom they would normally deal in seeking release of the
hostages. The Shia religious observance of a month of self-flagellation
reached its height at the end of November, not only making it politically
impossible for anyone in authority to consider release of the hostages then
but also sharply increasing concern for their safety. That concern was
heightened by the grim descriptions of the hostages' treatment and increasing talk of trials. Finally, the referendum on the Islamic constitution was
scheduled for December 2–3, and decision-making in Tehran seemed in
suspense. Against that background of mounting frustration and concern for
the hostages, when the negotiating track at the United Nations came to an
end on November 28 with the dismissal of Bani-Sadr, it was natural for the
crisis team in Washington to take stock and to consider ways of broadening
its strategy and systematizing its pressures.

As the first week in December began, the SCC met to review the pressures already mounted on Iran and to discuss what else we might do. Growing national impatience increased pressure on the President to "do something." The SCC also considered new ways to open a negotiating track. The
key issue at this stage was how to tighten the noose without making it
impossible to persuade the Iranians to negotiate. Decisions made in
November were reaffirmed or developed to increase pressures on Iran and to
give the U.S. actions the strongest possible base in international law and
approval. These actions in the economic, military, and international legal
fields are described and analyzed in separate later chapters. The purpose
here is to discuss the strategy they reflected and to put them in the larger
political and diplomatic context.

During the policy review in the first week of December, several options
were discussed. Secretary Vance outlined one approach, which would maintain the current level of economic pressures but avoid significant new steps

while attempts were made to develop diplomatic avenues that had been opened. He proposed pursuing the debate in the U.N. Security Council, which had begun late on Saturday evening, December 1, despite new Foreign Minister Sadegh Ghotbzadeh's announcement the day before that Iran would not attend. He also believed that pressing our case at the International Court of Justice would hold the initiative in the eyes of the American people while we discussed through existing channels a possible scenario that could lead to the release of the hostages. Reports of conversations in Tehran between intermediaries and Ghotbzadeh suggested that it would be very difficult to reach agreement on all elements of a package settlement, because Khomeini's mind did not work that way. The approach suggested in these conversations was that the United States should take some action to show that it understood Iran's grievances, and then those in Tehran prepared to argue for release of the hostages could present that gesture as a new element to Khomeini.

This was our first significant exposure to Ghotbzadeh's thinking. We had been told that Khomeini treated Ghotbzadeh like his own son. Frequently in the following weeks Ghotbzadeh was to prove in a variety of circumstances that he had access to the Ayatollah and insight into his thinking, never complete as it turned out but authentic enough to make us pay attention to him. We knew we had to find access to the group around Khomeini, and Ghotbzadeh seemed to have the double advantage of that entrée and of holding the position of Foreign Minister. The American people got to know him too, because he willingly spoke with the television correspondents. Many Americans found him repulsive. What they did not know at that time was that—for reasons that have never been entirely clear— Ghotbzadeh seemed to have decided that it would serve his personal political purposes to get rid of the hostage problem. Perhaps he figured astutely that the hostages were a club in the hands of the religious purists who wanted to purge secular revolutionaries like him. In any case, he was a contact we had to pay attention to at a time when routes to Khomeini were rare.

During December, other intermediaries with other channels to the Khomeini group explained Khomeini's mental processes in much the same way Ghotbzadeh did. It almost seemed that they were having as much trouble learning how to lead him to decisions as we were. The art, we were told, lay in presenting a picture of a situation to Khomeini in a way that would lead him to a desired conclusion about it. If he responded as hoped, a decision was made, but one was never sure how firm the decision was. In any case, those of us who spent a lot of our time with these intermediaries began to think of the problem in terms of devising steps we could honorably take that would enable those around Khomeini who wanted to free the hostages to present those steps positively to Khomeini.

As more and more channels opened, Secretary Vance was increasingly able around the SCC table to argue for holding off new harsh measures until the new channels had been further explored. At this stage in the crisis team's early December deliberations, however, it proved to be asking too much for the decision-makers to risk any conciliatory step before release of the hostages, so trying the scenario Vance suggested was set aside to be revived later. The SCC turned to measures for tightening the noose.

Other possible options discussed by the SCC were breaking diplomatic relations with Iran, asking allies to withdraw their missions from Iran, encouraging foreign banks to block Iranian assets abroad, other economic sanctions such as a total U.S. trade embargo including food, and a naval blockade. We had not broken diplomatic relations when the hostages were taken, because we thought the Iranian Embassy in Washington might provide a useful channel of communication. As it turned out, embassy officials reported inaccurately and were not useful. As is discussed in detail in chapter 4 on economic sanctions, decisions were made to pursue the consolidation of the freeze on Iranian assets and discussion of other economic sanctions, but military action and a break in diplomatic relations were deferred. The one military step taken at that time was sending AWACS (Airborne Warning and Control System) to Egypt with the connotation that it might be a forerunner of a rescue attempt.

The United States continued to restrict formal U.N. Security Council action to calling for release of the hostages. The debate, which had begun on December 1, ended with the passage of Resolution 457 on December 4. The resolution simply called for release of the hostages, the peaceful settlement of differences between Iran and the United States, and the Secretary-General to lend his good offices. Iran's refusal to attend removed for that moment the issue of an Iranian effort to use the Security Council as a forum for airing its grievances before the hostages were released.

The discussions leading to these decisions were not easy. Secretary Vance, always the patient negotiator, faced rapidly mounting pressure in the White House for tougher steps. In each discussion, he argued persistently that diplomatic doors were still open and that harsh U.S. action would not only close those doors but increase the danger of a violent reaction against the hostages. When possible military steps were discussed, no one could argue persuasively that they would free the hostages. Through those discussions a balance for our strategy was established. Frustrations with lack of movement were vented, but the arguments for restraint, steadily mounting pressure, and persistent attempts to open the door to a political solution prevailed. Those of us who believed in the grind-them-down approach to problem solving rather than the clobber-them approach felt we were gaining ground. To this day, many of us feel this was the only realistic approach, but we always have to ask ourselves whether a quick and early threat of massive military action would have changed even Khomeini's mind. I continue to believe it would only have provoked the hostages' execution.

Out of those deliberations in the SCC and with the President, decisions were taken in this period to move on two fronts to build a legal and international political base for systematizing the pressures on Iran.

First, the United States pressed its case before the International Court of Justice. Acting with unprecedented speed, on December 15, the Court directed that the hostages should be released immediately and that Iran should return to the United States its diplomatic properties in Iran. The Court's unanimous decision was welcomed in Washington because the fifteen judges, including a Soviet judge, represented all the world's major regions. Iran ignored the order. The State Department then turned to preparing its briefs for the Court's study and judgments, which would be passed down the following May.

Second, meeting on December 6, the SCC assessed Security Council Resolution 457, which had been passed two days earlier, as reflecting four achievements: the further isolation of Iran, establishment of a strong mandate for the Secretary-General's good offices, proof that the nonaligned states would not support Iran's action, and provision of an argument to those Iranians in favor of releasing the hostages to restore broad international support for the Iranian revolution. Together with the ruling of the International Court, the resolution's call for release of the hostages provided a base for stronger nonmilitary actions against Iran.

It is reasonable to ask what impact, if any, these steps had in Iran. The answer is, probably very little in the winter of 1979–80. Iran's sense of international isolation was a factor when Iran decided to negotiate the following September. In this second month of the crisis, however, the Iranians saw the United States as manipulating Western-controlled international organizations to its own advantage, and they ignored the judgments of those organizations as irrelevant. Some members of the crisis team understood this but recognized that the steps were important nevertheless, because they provided a necessary legal base for trying to enlist the cooperation of allies in imposing sanctions. They also provided some measure of satisfaction in the United States that we were "doing something."

Against the background of the World Court and Security Council actions, the United States launched an intensive effort in December to put in place a broad system of international economic sanctions. At a meeting of the National Security Council on December 4, the President had given his blessing to the strategy hammered out in the SCC. Secretary Vance, in visits to European capitals during the second full week in December, sought to build support there for this effort and began a dialogue that was to continue over almost five months and to sharpen tension between the United States and its allies. The frustration of watching allies find ways not to join in imposing sanctions intensified in later weeks, but at this exploratory stage Vance was able to report European cooperation in trying to gain Security Council approval of formal sanctions. The dialogue with our European allies was further complicated by a new set of strategic issues after the Soviet invasion of Afghanistan on December 27, but that is a later part of the story.

While these efforts to build the base for systematizing international pressures were under way, two other steps were taken to clear the stage of other issues and to increase bilateral pressure.

First, we had learned from the Shah's entourage on November 28 that his doctors had decided that he was medically ready to leave New York and could leave the United States on December 2. We had to consider concretely whether the Shah's movement, coinciding with the constitutional referendum in Iran and the end of the religious month of Moharrem, could be handled so as to let individuals in Tehran use it as part of their own scenario for freeing the hostages. At that moment, the administration still believed that Mexico was ready to have the Shah return to his house there. Then the bottom dropped out of this scenario. The Mexican government suddenly reversed its decision and without any warning told us that the Shah's visa was no longer valid. For days, all our energies were absorbed not in trying to work out a scenario with the Iranians but in finding a new home for the Shah. We put out informal feelers to a number of countries through a variety of channels. Among them, I flew secretly to Vienna to talk with Chancellor Bruno Kreisky, who had also been one of the parties maintaining close contact with the PLO. President Sadat's invitation was still outstanding, but we feared the Shah's going to Egypt could increase Sadat's political difficulties at a time when he was already isolated by his peace with Israel. Hamilton Jordan, the President's Chief of Staff, also talked with Panamanian representatives with whom he had worked during ratification of the Panama Canal Treaty.[3] While these efforts were under way, the Shah left New York on December 2 to continue his recuperation at Lackland Air Force Base in Texas. In the end, the government of Panama agreed to receive him, and he flew there on December 15. But whatever opportunity

---

3. See Hamilton Jordan, *Crisis: The Last Year of the Carter Presidency* (New York: Putnam Publishing Group, 1982), pp. 72–98, for a full account of these discussions.

there might have been to try to build a scenario around his departure had been lost.

Second, on December 12, the President issued orders cutting Iranian diplomatic and consular staffs in the United States to a total of thirty-five persons. Expulsion was considered but rejected in order to keep open whatever communications channel embassy personnel might offer and, more important, to maintain consular services and a channel for financial support for thousands of Iranians living here. It was argued that cutting the flow of support would have increased the burden on already angry American communities. The cutting of the staffs was the least that could be done.

While these actions were being taken, the authorities in Iran seemed no closer to responding to U.S. actions. Successful completion of the referendum on the constitution in the first week in December did not seem to free their minds to get back to the hostage problem. Instead, they began to turn their attention to the election of a President, which was eventually scheduled for the end of January.

The shocking plight of the hostages again exploded in American living rooms at the height of quiet family Christmas observances. A small group of clergymen visited the hostages, and some pictures of their Christmas meetings were released. The strain showed in their faces. Even worse, the clergymen counted only forty-three hostages. Christmas afternoon, I was besieged in the Ops Center at the State Department by journalists angrily asking why we did not know how many hostages there were. The reply was that we knew exactly how many there were and that the confusion was in Tehran. The Christmas evening newscasts were dominated by the "missing hostages." Confidence further eroded when Ghotbzadeh said he did not know how many hostages there were. At one point in our midnight phone talks with the captors in the compound, our count had been confirmed, but it was upsetting to learn both that Ghotbzadeh did not know what was going on in the compound and that seven of the hostages had been kept away from the clergy. Only when they came home did we find out that some were in solitary confinement and some simply did not want to see the clergy, because they feared their captors were somehow manipulating the clergy's visit for propaganda.

With no responsiveness in Tehran and fresh concern for the hostages, the administration felt that it had no alternative but to take the next steps in notching up international pressure. Ambassador Donald McHenry at the United Nations had written to the President of the Security Council on December 22, citing the action of the International Court and Resolution 457 and asking that the Council consider means of causing Iran to fulfill its international obligations. The Council was convened for that purpose during the holiday week, and Secretary Vance personally went to New York the weekend of December 29–30 to represent the United States.

By this time the Council members were considering a two-stage action in which the Council would, in a first resolution, agree on the scope of economic sanctions and instruct Secretary-General Waldheim to go to Tehran. Then, if he could not report any progress after his return, the Council would pass a second resolution putting the sanctions into effect. Meeting Saturday morning with Waldheim, Secretary Vance said it was essential that the first resolution spell out the sanctions in detail. He argued also that the deadline implied in the second resolution was vital in containing American domestic reaction. Secretary-General Waldheim reported from his talks with Iranian representatives that they were not ready for a mediating effort. The Revolutionary Council wanted it, Waldheim had been told, but Khomeini rejected mediation. Waldheim was still trying to work out a possible visit to Tehran. Vance replied quickly and sternly that the Security Council needed to be told authoritatively that Khomeini was rejecting mediation. Persuading the allies to stand by us was becoming grim business—even more so in the wake of the Soviet invasion of Afghanistan. They were not ready to risk significant financial assets. The vote was by no means a foregone conclusion. Sunday was a day of intense activity. The President himself telephoned the heads of government in Nigeria and Jamaica and was in touch by message with other state leaders.

On Monday, December 31, the Council passed Resolution 461, which began the process of formalizing economic sanctions. The resolution reaffirmed Resolution 457 and decided that the Council would meet again on January 7, 1980, to review the situation and to adopt "effective measures" under articles 39 and 41 (sanctions) of the United Nations Charter if Iran did not comply. The resolution did not spell out those measures; the days while Waldheim was in Tehran were to be used in drafting them. By the time the vote was taken shortly before noon Waldheim was already flying to Tehran. Vance left the Security Council chamber mildly buoyed by the successful outcome. In his refreshingly simple way, he celebrated by stopping off on the way to LaGuardia Airport to take a couple of us to lunch at his favorite short order restaurant.

The vote on Resolution 461 was 11–0 with four abstentions (U.S.S.R., Czechoslovakia, Kuwait, Bangladesh). The discussions surrounding the Council deliberations revealed an important combination of elements that characterized the international consensus as it had developed in the light of the Iranian actions and intensive American efforts to develop a wide range of pressures on Iran. Allies were supportive but, with no end of the crisis in sight, were increasingly restive with the idea of committing themselves to a long-term interruption of economic relations with Iran. Many nonaligned nations stated with conviction their concern that the smaller nations of the world had more at stake than the great powers in protecting the principles of the U.N. Charter and international law. They saw U.N. action as the alternative to the superpowers taking matters into their own hands. The two-stage approach was important, allowing for U.N. mediation. Islamic nations privately voiced the view that Iran's actions were tarnishing the image of Islam but found it difficult to act against Iran in any concerted way. The Soviets continued their opposition to hostage taking, but after we took a tough stand against their invasion of Afghanistan Moscow became increasingly reluctant to side with the United States. The Soviets also became interested in strengthening their own political position in Iran. We never expected much help from Moscow on the hostage issue, but we made clear its obligation to support international law and practice.

Resolution 461 represented the culmination of December's efforts to lay the foundation for economic sanctions in the absence of concrete prospects for negotiation. Before the Security Council could hold its follow-up meeting, the diplomatic track was opened again, and the progress of economic sanctions became intimately interrelated with the ups and downs of the negotiating course.

SCENARIO FOR RELEASE: JANUARY–EARLY APRIL

A Shift in Approach: Early January
The intensely frustrating lack of movement in Iran in the month after the December 2–3 referendum on the Islamic constitution—frustration heightened by the emotions of Christmas—led President Carter to begin thinking about whether some shift in approach might help pry open the door to negotiations. Almost simultaneously, in the closing days of December and in January, a series of developments came together to crystallize a revised approach to trying to break the stalemate.

At the end of that dreary after-holiday week—on Thursday afternoon and Friday morning, January 3–4—Secretary Vance, Under Secretary Newsom, and I and other colleagues spent several hours with a senior Islamic statesman who had come secretly to Washington. He was a person broadly committed to building bridges between the Islamic world and the West and had spent time in revolutionary Iran. He wanted the Iranian revolution to succeed and knew Iran was losing international support.

"The way out is some kind of deal worked out by a third party," our visitor told us. "In Khomeini's eyes, the United States is a kind of 'global Shah'—a personification of evil. Khomeini is the 'government.' Legal and diplomatic arguments won't persuade him. Sanctions won't persuade him. He sees Iran conquering by defeat—martyrdom. You need an intermediary—someone who can talk both with you and with Khomeini. The trouble with your trying to reach Khomeini directly is that he is aloof and outside the whole system of things."

"How should we proceed now?" Vance asked. "Would the Ayatollah ever meet with a representative of President Carter? Or is resolution possible only through a third party? We've tried to establish a dialogue, but everyone we talk to turns out to be an interlocutor not able to speak for his government. It makes us think the only possible dialogue is with Khomeini."

"The matter at this stage should be taken up by a third party—one who recognizes both Iranian grievances and the mistake of holding the hostages," came the reply. "An intermediary won't be helped by threatening noises. They will limit his room for maneuver. If a third party does his work well, maybe it can pave the way for a direct confrontation between Khomeini and a representative of President Carter." Among possible mediators he mentioned the Syrians, the Algerians, and the PLO or maybe a group including some of them with other Muslims like a Nigerian or a Pakistani. Among those few inside Iran who understood the West but who could also talk with Khomeini and whose opinion he felt carried some weight with the Ayatollah, Bani-Sadr and Ayatollah Beheshti were at the top of his list.

"What are Iran's *real* grievances against the U.S.?" Vance inquired.

"For one thing, the Iranians believe there are organs of the U.S. government that carry on activities to change the course of political affairs in Iran," our guest explained. "The Iranians believe the documents found in the embassy prove that the U.S. is working with minorities and other groups to replace the regime. Telling the Iranians they can sue for the Shah's assets in U.S. courts isn't enough. You should approach the Shah himself to help defuse the situation. He should abdicate for himself and his son—dismantle the peacock throne. He could buy his own security by declaring his assets and returning them to Iran."

"What realistic forum could be established for allowing Iran to air its grievances?" Vance asked.

"If the U.S. agrees to a mediator," our visitor replied, "his first task would be to discuss a forum with the Iranians. It could take the form of an international tribunal. Or maybe the U.S. could meet initial Iranian needs simply by acknowledging them in a public statement. The U.S. could start by saying for its own purposes that the U.S. will not hand back the Shah, that taking hostages is illegal, and that those responsible will be punished if the hostages are harmed but go on to say the U.S. accepts that Iran has grievances, is prepared to talk about them, and will turn over a new leaf on the basis of findings about them."

"Could such a statement be part of an agreed plan?" David Newsom asked.

"Yes. There is a consensus in Tehran for such an approach. The question is how to make it happen."

"How can we crystallize a decision?" I asked.

"You need to create a current by talking with a multiplicity of people. Most of those people would simply try to change the climate in Tehran. One would try to build support for a specific proposal."

We in the Working Group had had a number of such conversations in November and December. I had traveled secretly to New York twice in December, for instance, to meet with a serious senior Iranian who had been brought to Warren Christopher's attention by a high-minded American lawyer who gave hours to keeping this relationship alive for the next year. The Iranian proposed a scenario revolving around searching out the Shah's assets and proposed a meeting with a member of the Khomeini family. Vance ordered us to pursue all reasonable leads. By the beginning of January the message emerging from these channels was coming through loud and clear—the United States had to be prepared to engage in a political process without assured success and would do best working through intermediaries who could win some trust in Tehran.

The policy debate throughout December over how to move the Iranians had hung on a key question of tactics—how to time the release of the hostages in relation to some opportunity for the Iranians to air their grievances against the United States. Which would come first?

The four points in the U.S. position paper that Secretary-General Waldheim had given the Iranians on November 17 and the position taken by the United States with other governments held that the hostages' release would have to take place before any discussion of Iran's grievances. According to this view, Iran would have to put itself into compliance with international law before it was entitled to recourse to any of the normal machinery for airing its grievances. As I mentioned earlier, the United States had opposed allowing Iran to air its grievances in the U.N. Security Council in early December without assurance that the hostages would be freed.

Increasingly, through December, however, the point had been made in policy discussions among members of the Working Group that the United States would have to be prepared to engage in a political process and not simply stand fast, exerting pressure and waiting for Iran to give. The more we heard about the chaotic situation the "authorities" in Tehran had to cope with, the clearer it became that conventional diplomacy and pressure tactics by themselves had little chance. We could not be sure any tactics would, but we kept looking for openings. As mentioned, we drafted an illustrative scenario as early as November 27. There were few strong arguments that the steps to systematize pressure taken in November and December were wrong. To the contrary, most members of the crisis team agreed it was essential to stake out a strong U.S. position, to build international pressure on Iran, and to develop channels of possible influence on Iranian leaders. At the same time, strong feelings were building that a more flexible political track was now needed—that our decision-makers had to focus on the political base of the leaders they were trying to influence.

Before a December 19 National Security Council meeting, the Iran Working Group had written an options paper spelling out two ways of developing a political track. The first would be to go on letting the Iranians flounder in trying to develop their own mechanism for airing their grievances and expelling the hostages when they were ready to respond to our pressures. The second would be to give them specific suggestions on how to organize airing their grievances and releasing the hostages. The argument for the first approach was that nothing would work until the Iranians themselves had strong enough reasons for releasing the hostages to put together their own course of action. The argument for the second approach was to divert Iranian thinking from some kind of tribunal—their then predominant thought—to an approach the administration would find safer and politically more manageable and to try to speed up their dragging decision-making.

The Working Group concluded that if the President decided to develop the second approach, we would have to find a way to build into the same scenario an assurance of the hostages' immediate release and some steps to establish the forum for airing Iran's grievances. The art in developing a scenario like that was to devise a series of steps on both sides that could reinforce each other and gradually establish a momentum toward release.

The dilemma the crisis team was grappling with was captured in a later exchange between a senior member of the team and an American professor in regular touch by phone with high officials in Tehran.

"The administration does not seem to comprehend that there is not going to be agreement in advance on all the elements of a specific package," the professor explained. "Because the U.S. government wants immediate release of the hostages, it is not sensitive to the need for atmosphere-building in Iran. Khomeini may acquiesce in a general approach, but his advisers will not know his specific answer until they ask him for a decision. It is essential to them when they approach him for a decision to be able to cite new developments that create an atmosphere for releasing the hostages."

"We understand," the American official responded. "But our problem is in giving everything away up front with no assurance that the hostages will actually be released when Khomeini makes that decision."

Early in the afternoon of December 28, the pastors who had visited the hostages on Christmas day met with Secretary Vance and several of us in the Secretary's large conference room. The atmosphere was one of intense human concern. This was our first direct report on the hostages since before Thanksgiving. The report underscored the difficulties we faced. They found the "students" in complete control of the compound. They were very reminiscent of American students in the 1960s—a clear sense of purpose and difficult to reach with any message. Their religious leaders could not negotiate; they saw releasing the hostages as an act of weakness. The pastors identified the hostages they saw on the basis of our careful briefings, including pictures, and reported most in reasonable physical condition, with a handful "visibly stressful."

Right after New Year's, Secretary Vance one morning asked me urgently to plot in columns on a long sheet of paper the main points in several conversations with significant international figures who had been in and out of Tehran. All of them were describing the need for a fluid scenario designed slowly to change the political atmosphere in Tehran. Late one afternoon—the bleak Friday afternoon of January 4 after the talks with our Islamic visitor—Secretary Vance presented that tabulation privately to President Carter.

We found the President alone in the Oval Office. Remember that this was the week following the Soviet invasion of Afghanistan—"the most serious international development that has occurred since I have been President," as Carter had written in his diary the night before.[4] He faced difficult decisions on curbing or interrupting normal trade with the Soviet Union, on putting ratification of SALT II on the shelf, on withdrawing from the Moscow Olympics, and on the conduct of his political campaign in the primaries then about to start. He had just told his staff and that evening was going to announce that he had decided to embargo grain exports to the Soviet Union, with all the consequences that would have for the Iowa caucuses. Warren Christopher had left for Europe the previous Sunday—my deputy, Peter Constable, was with him, stretching our bureau thin—to coordinate reactions with the allies.

Despite those other issues on his mind, the President listened carefully to Vance's report on our recent conversations. He had already agreed in the closing days of December that we could tell Secretary-General Waldheim that we would be willing to discuss a scenario before the hostages' release.

---

4. Jimmy Carter, *Keeping Faith: Memoirs of a President* (New York: Bantam Books, 1982), p. 473.

That decision had been made without a lot of argument. When the President approved the two-step approach to the Security Council resolution on economic sanctions—allowing time between two resolutions for Waldheim to explore a negotiated solution—he introduced enough flexibility into the U.S. position for Waldheim to discuss any reasonable proposal that might come up. Now we were beginning to talk about how such a scenario might work. He promised to think about the advice that was reaching us in a steadily mounting drumbeat.

The questions of whom to communicate with and what communicating mechanism to use remained unresolved. Members of the crisis team recognized that authority in Tehran rested with Khomeini and the clerical figures around him, but they also had to face the facts that Khomeini had charged the Revolutionary Council to act as a government and that we had no access to Khomeini. As our Islamic visitor told us, it was doubtful that we could communicate with Khomeini even if an American emissary met him. By early January, the team had mentally divided its more than two dozen channels to Iran into three categories. One consisted of sources of information and analysis. The other two already reflected the advice of our Islamic visitor on January 3–4. One group of individuals who had access to Khomeini and other religious figures in Tehran could be useful in trying to create a climate among the religious leaders for release of the hostages. The other, if we could put together the right mechanism and combination of people, might be able to talk with responsible members of the Revolutionary Council, including key religious members, to begin formulating steps leading to the release of the hostages. Finding the right mechanism was the next step.

The Mechanism: A U.N. Commission

The mechanism began to come into sharp focus during Secretary-General Waldheim's chaotic visit to Tehran.

"I am quite uneasy about the outcome of my mission," Secretary-General Waldheim had told Secretary Vance on Saturday, December 29. The visit had been discussed with the Iranians by a senior official of an Islamic country. Waldheim told Vance it was clear that Khomeini was reluctant to work with the United Nations, because it was "dominated by the big powers." The intermediary had disagreed, stressing the role of the smaller nations there. The Iranians were willing to receive the Secretary-General out of respect, but they made clear their concern about his mission being judged a failure. "They are unable to give anything and do not want the Secretary-General to return with nothing," the intermediary said. It was clear that some Iranians opposed his coming, but Waldheim felt that he had to try. The specters in his mind, I assumed, were harsher economic or military action against Iran, execution of the hostages, U.S. retaliation, and the possibility of a Soviet counter move. At 3:05 P.M. Sunday afternoon, Waldheim had called Vance to say he was about to announce that he had been formally invited to Tehran and would leave Monday.

Late on the morning of December 31, shortly before the Security Council vote on Resolution 461 and Secretary-General Waldheim's departure for Tehran, I stopped briefly in the Secretary-General's 38th-floor office to give a new five-point statement of the United States' position, which the President and Secretary Vance had approved for this purpose, to Rafeeuddin Ahmed, Secretary-General Waldheim's Chef de Cabinet and principal assistant on this issue:

1. All U.S. personnel held hostage must be released from Iran prior to the institution of any international tribunal.

2. The United States was prepared to work out in advance a firm understanding on arrangements for the airing of Iranian grievances before an appropriate forum after the hostages had been released.

3. The United States would not object to any Iranian suits in U.S. courts to recover assets allegedly taken illegally from Iran by the former Shah.

4. The United States would affirm jointly with Iran its intention to abide by the Declaration on Principles of International Law Concerning Friendly Relations and Cooperation Among States in Accordance with the Charter of the United Nations and by the provisions of the Vienna Convention on Diplomatic Relations. The United States stated that it accepted the present government of Iran as the legitimate authority in Iran and reaffirmed the view that the people of Iran had the right to determine their own form of government.

5. The United States was willing, once the hostages were safely released, to seek, in accordance with the U.N. Charter, a resolution of all issues between the United States and Iran.

At this stage, there was no departure from the position that the hostages had to be released before Iran gained satisfaction, but one new idea was introduced when the administration stated readiness to *work out in advance* how Iran would air its grievances. The President's decision during the first week of the crisis to send Ramsey Clark and Bill Miller to Tehran reflected recognition in the administration that it would be necessary to find an American approach that could be presented in Tehran by those leaders who wanted to release the hostages in such a way as to make release a step that could be seen to work to Iran's advantage. Pierre Salinger in *America Held Hostage* suggests that in his discussions in Tehran Waldheim undercut the United States' position.[5] As Secretary Vance and others stated pub-

5. Pierre Salinger, *America Held Hostage: The Secret Negotiations* (Garden City, Doubleday, 1981), pp. 110–16.

licly before the TV cameras of Salinger's interviewers after the hostages were free, the Secretary-General, in exploring mechanisms for allowing Iran's grievances to be heard in connection with the hostages' release, was acting in accordance with the American position he was given before departure.

During a chaotic visit to Tehran, the Secretary-General was directly exposed to the frightening Iranian mobs and to the Iranian decision-making process in the Revolutionary Council. On the eve of his arrival, opponents of his visit published pictures of him with the Shah and his sister. Hostile mobs threatened him wherever he went. On a visit to the Cemetery of the Martyrs he described an angry mob appearing over a nearby hill, a dash for his helicopter, and a takeoff just as the mob arrived. He was also taken to a meeting of people the Iranians told him had been maimed by Savak.

Despite the chaos swirling around him, Waldheim did confirm, during his conversations with Foreign Minister Ghotbzadeh, that Ghotbzadeh was prepared to explore creation of an international commission as a mechanism for airing Iran's grievances, for reducing tension in Tehran, and for creating an environment in which release of the hostages might become possible. They even discussed possible members on the commission—individuals who enjoyed international respect and credibility and would also be credible in Iran. Ghotbzadeh by then was a candidate in the presidential elections. Whatever his rationale may have been, for some months from that moment on Ghotbzadeh's interest in the hostages' release for Iranian revolutionary reasons became a central point in U.S. efforts to win their release. That interest, plus his well-known closeness to Khomeini, seemed at that time to offer the best hope of establishing conditions for release. Although we knew that religious figures like Beheshti were important, they had stopped talking with us in November, saying the Foreign Minister would deal with us, and Khomeini had charged the Revolutionary Council with the responsibility of government. Later, as the religious factions gained strength and pushed Ghotbzadeh aside, it was easy to say we should have been using other channels, but at that moment in January, given our need for go-betweens who could operate in the Tehran environment, Ghotbzadeh seemed a logical avenue.

After his return from Tehran, Secretary-General Waldheim reported to President Carter and Secretary Vance at the White House late on Sunday, January 6. He urged the President to hold off on the follow-up vote in the Security Council on economic sanctions to allow time to develop a diplomatic track. He reported his talks with Ghotbzadeh about a possible commission of inquiry to include perhaps three representatives of developing countries and one or two independent international figures. During his discussion of the commission with the Revolutionary Council, he reported that the Iranians proposed that the hostages be released after the commission had completed its work. For us, that posed the question of whether some series of steps could meet both our needs and theirs. The President told the Secretary-General that he did not believe the Secretary-General's finding warranted delaying economic sanctions further, but he would consider his report. Waldheim also relayed his view that militants holding the American hostages were quite independent of Khomeini's control.

The Secretary-General also reported to the Security Council. As the Council was preparing its resolution on economic sanctions, he received word on January 11 that Iran was requesting consideration of a commission of inquiry to help improve the atmosphere for a settlement. The United States agreed to allow time until January 13 for the Secretary-General to probe the Iranian request but insisted that the Council take up the sanctions resolution when it became clear that the Iranian proposal was not linked to release of the hostages. There were ten votes for the resolution, but the Soviets vetoed it. The United States indicated it would go ahead with sanctions and urged its allies to do so as well. At this point the allies, in addition to saying that sanctions would be legally difficult for them without a U.N. resolution, urged that the United States defer sanctions until after Iran's presidential elections, scheduled for January 25.

Progress had been made during the Secretary-General's trip in focusing Iranian attention on a mechanism for airing their grievances, but the question of how to link that mechanism to the hostages' release remained. He himself was not the appropriate mediator, but he had opened a door and offered United Nations auspices for a commission. A commission of the composition discussed could bring to Tehran a group of individuals who would listen sympathetically but argue Iran's interest in releasing the hostages. This is what we had been trying to achieve since the first week of the crisis. The problem we had to solve now was how to avoid making all of our concessions up front—how to assure ourselves that if we embarked on such a process the hostages would definitely be released as part of it. In our view, we needed to agree with the Iranians in advance on a scenario that would include both something for the Iranians and release. We had been told that Khomeini's mind did not work this way—that we could only try to create an atmosphere for release and hope Khomeini's colleagues could successfully present the case to him. Uncertain as this course was, it seemed better to try to influence Iranian decision-making this way while tightening the economic screws than to rely solely on economic or military pressures.

As it turned out on January 12, wheels were already turning in Tehran that would open the door to discussing a scenario to be built around the U.N. commission Secretary-General Waldheim had discussed. The idea of working through intermediaries flew in the face of the normal U.S. practice of insisting on face-to-face negotiations. While we had worked hard in other contexts such as the Arab-Israeli conflict to bring such negotiations about, it seemed to me from our experience in dealing with revolutionary Iran that direct conversation might well prove unproductive. Working through third parties can be time-consuming and has many disadvantages, but trying to negotiate when two parties are talking past each other is next to impossible. A U.N. commission seemed a mechanism that might offer both a cover for an Iranian decision to release the hostages and an intermediary to make communication possible.

The New Strategic Setting: The Carter Doctrine

On December 27, the Soviet Union began to move substantial military forces into Afghanistan—an act with consequences reaching far beyond the hostage crisis for U.S.-Soviet relations, for our relations with our European and Japanese allies, for Soviet and U.S. relations with the nations of the Middle East and the Islamic world, as well as for our efforts to enlist cooperation in pressing Iran to release the hostages.

The collapse of the Shah's regime at the beginning of 1979 had abruptly brought down the security system in the Persian Gulf—the vital reservoir for much of the non-Communist world's oil. When the British had reduced their protective presence in the Gulf at the beginning of the 1970s, the Nixon Administration had tried to establish cooperation between Iran and Saudi Arabia as the "twin pillars" of a new Persian Gulf security system. Iran's military buildup became the muscle of that system. So the revolution in Iran had already set the military planning machinery turning in Washington to look at ways for the United States to project its forces into this critical area quickly if they were needed. The key to conducting military operations in the area was the availability of support facilities there, and the administration began exploring possible arrangements with Oman, Somalia, Kenya, and Egypt and continued its discussions with the Saudis about enhancing their security. The Soviet invasion of Afghanistan, coming so soon after the collapse of the Gulf security system, gave urgency to those explorations, and agreements were negotiated during the first half of 1980.

In his State of the Union address before a somber Congress on January 23, 1980, President Carter underscored the historic and global significance of the Soviet attack against the background of other serious developments in the Middle East, including the hostage crisis:

> These last few months have not been an easy time for any of us. As we meet tonight, it has never been more clear that the state of our Union depends on the state of the world. And tonight, as throughout our own generation, freedom and peace in the world depend on the state of our Union.

The 1980s have been born in turmoil, strife, and change. . . .

At this time in Iran, 50 Americans are still held captive, innocent victims of terrorism and anarchy. Also at this moment, massive Soviet troops are attempting to subjugate the fiercely independent and deeply religious people of Afghanistan. . . .

Three basic developments have helped to shape our challenges: the steady growth and increased projection of Soviet military power beyond its own borders; the overwhelming dependence of the Western democracies on oil supplies from the Middle East; and the press of social and religious and economic and political change in the many nations of the developing world, exemplified by the revolution in Iran. . . .

. . . now the Soviet Union has taken a radical and an aggressive new step. . . . The implications of the Soviet invasion of Afghanistan could pose the most serious threat to the peace since the Second World War.[6]

After discussing the implications of the Soviet move for U.S.-Soviet relations and world peace, the President returned to the Persian Gulf. In measured words, he set down a fundamental statement of U.S. policy that came to be called the Carter Doctrine: "Let our position be absolutely clear: an attempt by any outside force to gain control of the Persian Gulf region will be regarded as an assault on the vital interests of the United States of America, and such an assault will be repelled by any means necessary, including military force."

This is not the place to discuss in detail how the Carter Doctrine was drafted or implemented.[7] The points to stress here are that the hostages in their agonizing confinement were now sitting in the center of a raging strategic whirlwind that had nothing to do with them or with the Iranian revolution but that could not be separated from their plight. Much later, Secretary Vance would wonder whether sharper warnings to the Soviet Union before the invasion might have headed it off—warnings that were not given because of our absorbing immersion in the hostage crisis. To the tensions already brewing with our allies over economic sanctions against Iran were added the even more painful tensions over the far-reaching sanctions against the Soviet Union. On the hostage problem itself, we had sought Soviet support in the interest of international order, and while they

6. *Weekly Compilation of Presidential Documents*, Monday, January 28, 1980, vol. 16, no. 4, pp. 194–96.

7. See Christopher Van Hollen, "Don't Engulf the Gulf," *Foreign Affairs*, vol. 59, no. 5 (Summer 1981), pp. 1064–78, and David Newsom, "America Engulfed," *Foreign Policy*, no. 43 (Summer 1981), pp. 17–32.

had not been actively helpful, they had not been obstructive either. Their veto of the resolution on economic sanctions at the United Nations was an early casualty of the new situation.

The Carter Doctrine was not directed at the hostage question, but the Iranians were not immune to its implications. Some of them saw increased discussion in the United States of the Rapid Deployment Force and the feasibility of U.S. deployments to the Gulf area as a prelude to American military action against them. In other quarters in Tehran the Soviet invasion shocked Iranian leaders, who immediately recognized the implications for Iran. What were long-term Soviet intentions? Would Iran be next?

In order to give those Iranians who were concerned about Soviet action a possible additional handle on the hostage problem, the President approved a revision of the U.S. position paper. The purpose of the revision was both to develop the idea of the commission of inquiry from Secretary-General Waldheim's talks and other recommendations on a political process and to add readiness to discuss the Soviet threat with concerned Iranians. The new statement now contained six points:

1. The safe and immediate release from Iran of all Americans held hostage was essential to a resolution of other issues.

2. The United States understood and sympathized with the grievances felt by many Iranian citizens concerning the practices of the former regime. The United States was prepared to work out in advance firm understandings on a forum in which those grievances might subsequently be aired, so that the hostages could be released with confidence that the grievances would be heard in an appropriate forum after the release had taken place. The United States would not concur in any hearing that involved the hostages. The United States was prepared to cooperate in seeking through the auspices of the United Nations to establish such a forum or commission to hear Iran's grievances and to produce a report on them. The U.S. government would cooperate with such a group in accordance with its laws, international law, and the U.N. Charter.

3. The U.S. government would facilitate any legal action brought by the government of Iran in courts of the United States to account for assets within the custody or control of the former Shah that might be judged to belong to the national treasury of Iran by advising the courts and other interested parties that the government recognized the right of the government of Iran to bring such claims before the courts and to request the courts' assistance in obtaining information about such assets from financial institutions and other parties.

4. Once the hostages were safely released, the United States was prepared to lift the freeze of Iranian assets and to facilitate normal commercial relations between the two countries, on the understanding that Iran would

meet its financial obligations to U.S. nationals and that the arrangements to be worked out would protect the legitimate interests of U.S. banks and other claimants. The United States was prepared to appoint members of a working group to reach agreement on those arrangements.

5. The United States was prepared to appoint a representative to discuss with Iranian representatives the current threat posed by the Soviet invasion of Afghanistan and to recommend to their governments steps that the United States and Iran might take in order to enhance the security of Iran, including the resumption of the supply of military spare parts by the United States to Iran.

6. The Carter Administration was prepared to make a statement at an appropriate moment that it understood the grievances felt by the people of Iran and that it respected the integrity of Iran and the right of the people of Iran to choose their own form of government. The U.S. government recognized the Government of the Islamic Republic of Iran as the legal government of Iran. The United States reaffirmed that the people of Iran had the right to determine their own form of government.

Secretary Vance gave Secretary-General Waldheim this elaboration of the basic U.S. position on January 13 to pass to the Iranians.

Working Out a Scenario

"The way out is some kind of deal worked out by a third party," Secretary Vance's Islamic visitor had told him on January 4. The President and the Secretary now had the option of trying to achieve that deal by working with Secretary-General Waldheim to put a U.N. Commission of Inquiry on the ground in Tehran. The President did not feel the American people would tolerate sending a high-visibility commission to give the Iranians a hearing without any prior understanding that the hostages would be released as part of their visit. He still needed some way to work out an understanding up front that a commission could go only if authorities in Tehran could use its visit to produce a decision to let the hostages go.

As it happened, it was at precisely this moment that a more direct channel to Iranian authorities opened from an unexpected direction. It was not without significance that Sadegh Ghotbzadeh, the key figure at the Iranian end of this new channel, was keenly concerned about the implications of the Soviet invasion of Afghanistan as well as of the increasing strength of the Tudeh (Communist) Party in Iran.

A call came to Hamilton Jordan, President Carter's Chief of Staff, on Friday, January 11, in Laurel Lodge, where meals are served to staff guests at Camp David, from an aide to Panamanian leader Omar Torijos, whom Jordan had come to know during the debate on ratification of the Panama Canal Treaty. Torijos wanted Jordan to fly to Panama the next day. Jordan was reluctant to go, but he and Christopher agreed that he could not turn

Torijos down. As a convenience, Jordan arranged to meet the Panamanian emissaries half-way by flying to Homestead Air Force Base in Florida on Saturday, January 12.[8]

After his meeting Jordan called from the plane through the Situation Room and asked if I could meet him in the White House that night toward midnight as soon as he got back. We sat down immediately to go over his lengthy notes. The Panamanians had told him a story of two Paris-based lawyers close to the revolutionary authorities in Tehran who had visited Panama just after Christmas on Ghotbzadeh's behalf to explore the legal possibilities of filing suit for the extradition of the Shah. One of the Panamanians had followed up the lawyers' visit by going to Tehran himself. To his surprise, he had found the Parisian lawyers to be solidly connected in Tehran. The Panamanians felt the lawyers would be well worth talking to and urged that the White House send someone to meet with them. A few days later, the Panamanians came through Washington to underscore their point.

The connection was not implausible. First, the Shah in Panama remained a potential element in any Iranian scheme, even though we did not want to pursue that approach. Second, one of the contacts the Iran Working Group had already established in Paris was with a lawyer known to have worked with the Khomeini group before Khomeini returned to Tehran. So with the approval of the President and Secretary Vance a meeting was arranged for Saturday, January 19, in London at the home of United States Deputy Chief of Mission Ed Streator. Ham Jordan and I, with tickets purchased under assumed names for security reasons, flew to London on Friday. Saturday morning in the Streators' study we met the two lawyers— Christian Bourguet and Hector Villalon—accompanied by two of the Panamanians, former Ambassador in Washington Gabriel Lewis and businessman Rori Gonzales. That meeting was the first of more than 100 hours of detailed discussion and meticulous drafting with the lawyers in London, Washington, Berne, and Paris.

The London morning was gray, but the setting was convivial. Jordan and the Panamanians had become friends during the Panama treaty fight, and their banter quickly broke the ice. One of the lawyers was with them. The other, it was explained with an air of immediacy, would arrive momentarily from Heathrow airport, where he had just landed from Tehran. As we settled down to talk, with the help of an embassy officer pressed into service as an interpreter, three questions were uppermost in our minds: Did the lawyers really have the contacts in Tehran that they claimed to have? Could they deliver? Why were they doing this?

"We are meeting at Iranian initiative. The Revolutionary Council has

8. See Jordan, *Crisis,* pp. 102–08.

approved this contact. The Revolutionary Council does not conduct business without the approval of Khomeini." The lawyers' presentation began with these words, which hung over all subsequent transactions with them. Then Villalon launched into what turned out to be the first of many sweeping sketches of political conspiracy and intrigue in revolutionary Tehran. His picture on this occasion was painted for the purpose of providing an overview of the competing figures and factions in the governing group. It began with the explanation that the takeover of the embassy was carried out by the religious right for the purpose of removing Western-oriented officials, whom he called the "European group."

This squared with interpretations we had received from diplomats remaining in Tehran. But Villalon and Bourguet provided in an hour and a half personality and political sketches of each of the figures in the leading group that were consistent with our own intelligence but showed a far more comprehensive and direct familiarity with the current scene than any other individuals we had talked to. They characterized another of the power struggles in Iran as a struggle against Soviet domination via indigenous communists. I wondered skeptically at the time whether this was a sophomoric effort to attract what they assumed would be naively anticommunist American listeners. As time would prove, however, while it may have contained a quotient of the views of Villalon, a Peronist exile, it also reflected a view of the world as seen by Sadegh Ghotbzadeh.

Villalon and Bourguet explained that they had gone to Panama in December at Ghotbzadeh's request to determine whether, by seeking the extradition of the Shah, they could generate symbolic action that would give Ghotbzadeh a political context in which to arrange the release of the hostages. According to their scenario, the Shah would not actually be extradited, but the U.N. Commission, which Ghotbzadeh had discussed with Waldheim, meeting to hear Iranian grievances against the backdrop of a move for extradition might be able to argue successfully in Tehran for the hostages' release.

It was at this point that we began to sense through Villalon and Bourguet that Ghotbzadeh, too, was trying to devise a series of events that could come together in such a way as to precipitate a decision in Tehran to expel the hostages. Villalon's descriptions of the battle among revolutionary groups for control of television and Ghotbzadeh's daily manipulation of radio and television to shape perceptions gave us a picture of a man with a keen sense of tactics engaged in hourly struggle. They also gave us more concrete understanding of Ghotbzadeh's reasons for believing that getting rid of the hostages would wrench from the radical religious groups one of the weapons they were using against the secular revolutionaries. They had already felled Bazargan and Yazdi with it, and Ghotbzadeh saw himself as the next target. He was then a candidate in the presidential elections. The two lawyers, at least, seemed to be already engaged in trying to build a scenario for the release of the hostages.

The question was whether they were really speaking with Ghotbzadeh's authority and whether, if so, he was speaking with Khomeini's. While he was known to be close to Khomeini, this second question could never be satisfactorily answered. But toward the end of the afternoon, as we broke for a social hour in the living room with Ed Streator joining us, Bourguet asked to use the phone, and within minutes he was reporting to Ghotbzadeh in Tehran in a cryptic French shorthand on the day's discussions.

During the social hour, we began to get a fuller sense of the lawyers' own personal motivation for involvement in an effort to free the hostages. Bourguet, it turned out, was a partner of the lawyer whom the Iran Working Group had already contacted in December when we learned of his earlier relationship with the Khomeini group. A slim, soft-spoken, bearded man, Bourguet gave an impression of serious commitment in a Roman Catholic context to human rights causes. Villalon described himself as an Argentinian exile from the Perón period who had fallen in with the Iranian community in Paris "out of sympathy for fellow exiles." Both lawyers were doing what sounded like a highly profitable legal business for Iran—one in dealings with the European nuclear power community and the other in oil and securities—when they were paid.

One evening a month later over dinner in a Berne hotel, one of them only half jokingly commented on the tremendous expenses they were running up with their trips to Panama, the United States, and back and forth between Europe and Tehran without any reimbursement yet from the inefficient Iranian bureaucracy. By that time they were a lot more deeply into the hostage release effort and had given it many midnight hours.

"Why are you doing this, anyway?" I asked them, seizing the opening to try to get a more exact picture of what they expected to get out of it.

There was no question that, to begin with, they were doing what lawyers normally do for clients—trying to help them achieve their objectives. Through Villalon's Latin American contacts, they had been able to work their way through the Panama connections to the White House itself. Satisfying Ghotbzadeh seemed one reasonable way of assuring continuation of what sounded like big-stakes legal and financial accounts. But three compelling human factors also came through strongly in that conversation. First, they had become gripped with the more high-minded aspirations of the Iranian revolution and saw the hostage taking as a serious obstacle to the revolution's achieving wide international acceptance. Second, the more deeply they got into the exercise and the more possible it seemed to achieve results, the more difficult it became for them to let go. Third, besides enhancing reputations, success would have provided that combination of internal gratifications that success gives any human being—some noble and some ego-centered.

In any case, the long day's discussion ended with an understanding that the President would be interested in listening to proposals for a scenario that included assurance of the hostages' release, although we made clear that we had no authority to commit the President. They agreed to explore the idea more concretely in Tehran. We arranged to be back in touch promptly, and the two lawyers left with the Panamanians. We still could not be sure, but we were at least convinced that the channel was well worth pursuing.

The next morning I took advantage of being in London to meet with senior Egyptian journalist Mohammed Heykal before we flew back to Washington. We knew Heykal had been in Tehran earlier in the winter working on a book about Khomeini. As a prominent columnist read all over the Middle East, he was one of those figures in the Islamic world who might be able to help in changing the climate in Tehran, especially among those around Khomeini. Given his acceptability there and our previous acquaintance in the Egyptian context, I thought it unwise not to talk with him and had been authorized by Secretary Vance to see him. I went to his luxurious suite, driving with a friend through the early Sunday quiet of the London streets.

In that initial discussion, we exchanged pleasantries over coffee about a variety of common interests surrounding Arab-Israeli diplomacy. In January 1974, we had flown the same plane from Aswan to Cairo after the first Egyptian-Israeli disengagement agreement emerged from the first of the Kissinger shuttles. I had read his weekly columns for some years. I explained that there were two jobs to be done in Tehran. One was the general work of trying to persuade Khomeini and other Iranian leaders that they should release the hostages for Islamic and revolutionary reasons. The other task was actually to negotiate details of the release. A number of individuals could work on the first track, while the negotiating track required one authoritative channel.

Knowing Heykal's reputation as a man with his own interests, I probed to see whether his own views of the hostage crisis would make him a natural advocate in Tehran for release of the hostages. I explained our position in detail as it had already been passed to the Iranians in our position papers. I asked whether he would be going again to Tehran, and he indicated that he might. In any case, he was frequently on the phone to Tehran. I tried to put him in a position to say he thought the United States was prepared to work out a way to air Iranian grievances in the context of the hostages' release. We never had any thought that Heykal would become a negotiator, because he was not the kind of person we could be sure would reflect our position accurately and precisely in a prolonged detailed exchange. That Sunday morning, too, Ham Jordan and I were ready to recommend to the President that we explore seriously concentrating our efforts through the Paris-based lawyers, so I had no desire to muddy the waters by activating another channel. But we hoped Heykal would add his voice to those arguing for the hostages' release with an accurate understanding of the U.S. position.

Jordan and I returned to Washington that afternoon. We gave a detailed report of our meeting to President Carter and Secretary Vance and recommended that we continue these discussions. The President and the Secretary shared our caution, but they agreed that what we had learned in London justified another meeting without any commitment on our part. That next meeting with Bourguet and Villalon—this time without the Panamanians—was arranged for the following Friday and Saturday, January 25–26.

These meetings took place in Ham Jordan's spacious corner office on the main floor of the White House's west wing, just down the hall from the President's Oval Office. We brought our visitors in through the west basement door without exposure to the press, although they would hardly have been recognized, and had meals brought up from the White House Mess downstairs so as to avoid curiosity among the staff. In these meetings, we were now joined by Henry Precht and Stephanie Van Reigersberg, the superb French and Spanish interpreter at the State Department who had earlier worked with Jordan during the Panama Canal Treaty ratification. Before this exhausting exercise ended, Stephanie had not only proved her stamina by interpreting through sixteen-hour days almost nonstop but had become a trusted and valued member of the team to the point where our intermediaries would often call her with reports, because they could avoid a government number by calling her family home and speaking in Spanish.

We sat down to these meetings with cautious hope that maybe we had at last found a workable channel. Bourguet and Villalon had been to Tehran and Panama since the London meeting. They were impressed by being in the White House, and Ham showed them the President's office during a break when the President was out. To further establish their own credentials, they had brought from Ghotbzadeh a cassette tape recording of Secretary-General Waldheim's meeting with the Revolutionary Council at the beginning of January in Tehran.

Bourguet and Villalon began by describing Ghotbzadeh's report of the Revolutionary Council meeting at which they gave their report from our London meeting. They said that the Revolutionary Council had designated Ghotbzadeh as the single negotiator until a new government could be formed after the presidential election and inauguration. Ghotbzadeh was in a position to report directly to Khomeini. In response to Jordan's question about Khomeini's involvement, they implied that Khomeini understood the drift of the situation. According to Ghotbzadeh's description of Khomeini's "oriental method of work," Ghotbzadeh transmitted information to Khomeini and proceeded if nothing came back. Bourguet indicated that the principal presidential candidates in Iran were briefed on this exchange. When asked directly whether the idea of a scenario that we had discussed in London was Ghotbzadeh's alone or whether it was more widely accepted, the lawyers said Ghotbzadeh was very cautious, and they imagined it was not his idea alone.

We recognized that these answers were well short of the certainty we would have liked, but we knew we were playing in a game with unknown rules, and the issue was whether to try to play or to wait for a day, which might not come, when the rules might be clearer. In any case, we seemed now to have the opportunity to engage in the kind of political exercise the Iranian specialists in and out of government had been urging on us for some time. We knew the split between the secular and clerical figures further increased uncertainty, but trying to work out some scenario of events leading to the hostages' release could at least give us the vehicle for exchanges with important figures in Tehran that had been lacking since November.

At the end of a long afternoon of "preliminary" discussion on January 25, Ham turned on the evening television news to hear reports that Bani-Sadr was claiming victory in the Iranian presidential election. The lawyers stated that, if his victory were confirmed, he would allow Ghotbzadeh to continue working for the release of the hostages. Completion of the election would also help us crystallize a new time frame for our planning. We recognized that Iran would not have a full-fledged government until the new parliament could be elected and formed to give that government a vote of confidence. As of the end of January, those parliamentary elections were still scheduled to begin February 15, although the Working Group felt that they might be delayed until later in the month. In any case, the period between the presidential election and the formation of parliament seemed to be a defined period during which steps might be taken to pave the way for release.

The election of Bani-Sadr as President also seemed to offer the possibility of supplying one of the key missing ingredients in the situation we had been dealing with to date. We had been repeatedly frustrated by the absence in Tehran of both a firm commitment to resolve the crisis and negotiating partners who could negotiate with authority. Now it seemed worth testing further whether Bani-Sadr with a strong popular mandate along with Ghotbzadeh with his own interest in releasing the hostages might become receptive and even effective partners in working out a release. At that moment, we could not foresee the rivalry that would emerge between those two men or the fact that Khomeini himself would later begin to shift his support behind the Islamic faction that eventually established superiority in the parliamentary elections. At that moment, they were, under Khomeini, the "authorities" in Tehran, and a review of eight other possible mediating channels that might then have been used revealed no more promising approach.

We had spent the afternoon hearing a lengthy review of the intrigue in Tehran, which Villalon described with great drama and relish. Finally, Ham and I tried to bring the talk down to practical steps. "Where do we go from here? How do we put together a scenario?" we asked. Through the evening and the next morning we talked in excruciating detail about each step of a scenario. We turned each move over and over in our minds to decide how it could be designed to play to the advantage of those in Tehran who would be trying to build support for releasing the hostages, while remaining politically manageable in the United States. We talked about how each step could be described in ways and revolutionary language to have maximum appeal in Tehran. To move us forward, I began writing our decisions in the format of a series of matching steps to be taken in agreed sequence in New York at the United Nations, in Tehran, and in Washington. After several hours, I had an English text running over a number of legal-sized yellow pages. By lunch time Saturday, I thought we were just about finished. Then we started translating it into French, and I discovered we had only just begun. We agonized again over every turn of phrase, changing the English and producing a French text. As a veteran of the Kissinger shuttles, Camp David, and the Egyptian-Israeli peace treaty negotiations, I had learned infinite patience with endless hours of straining over details, but by early Saturday evening even I thought we had done enough for a first cut. Finally, we wrapped it up, agreeing to take the English version to the President and Secretary Vance.

Before we sought the President's decision, the Secretary again reviewed the two possible approaches we had been discussing more or less continuously over the previous month. The first was the approach we had been concentrating on through mid-January in which all parts of a package would be agreed in detail in advance, and the hostages would be released at the same time the first steps were taken to meet Iranian concerns. The alternative approach was based on the repeated reports that the way Khomeini's mind worked made it impossible that all details in a scenario could be assured in advance. Those reports argued that a sequence of steps would have to be taken to change the climate in Iran a little at a time before Khomeini would be asked to release the hostages. When asked, he might disapprove, so there would be a major risk in starting down such a path.

The issue Secretary Vance now had to put to the President was whether the President felt he could manage politically a situation in which steps would be taken that would appear to respond to Iranian grievances before the hostages would be released and before these steps could publicly be explained as designed to lead to the hostages' release. In fact, if the President were to approve the scenario we had drafted, he would have to risk taking the first steps without any assurance that the later steps would turn out as we envisioned. The scenario that emerged from the talks with Bourguet and Villalon was a series of paired reciprocal steps, each pair including a move by Iran and a move by the United States, with the built-in opportunity to abort the process if either side elected. The first steps would be defined precisely; later steps could be outlined at the beginning but might have to be refined or changed as the situation evolved. But there would be agreement at the outset that the purpose was to proceed within the framework of the scenario to the soonest possible peaceful resolution of the crisis.

The steps envisioned at that point included these:

• The United States would drop its opposition to Waldheim's sending a commission of inquiry to Iran, provided the Iranians would request it as a means of airing Iran's grievances *and* of helping achieve an early end of the crisis and would request that the commissioners meet each of the hostages. The United States would oppose any interrogation of the hostages.

• After the Iranians had made their request in those terms, Waldheim would announce the commission. The Iranians would announce their cooperation in seeking an end of the crisis and in arranging for the commission to meet each of the hostages.

• The commission would hear Iranian grievances in Tehran and visit the hostages. The commission would report to the Revolutionary Council that the conditions in which the hostages were held were inhumane and that no report to the Secretary-General would be credible until the conditions were changed. The Iranian authorities would transfer the hostages to a hospital under the joint custody of the Revolutionary Council and the commission.

• The commission would report to the Secretary-General, and the hostages would be pardoned and expelled.

The key element in this approach was agreement in advance with the Revolutionary Council, presumably with Khomeini's concurrence, to accept the principle of establishing a scenario and proceeding within that framework by stages, each involving reciprocal actions to be agreed in advance. The precision with which each step would be taken as formulated was designed to provide evidence of good faith and to enhance confidence that later steps would be carried out. Private agreement on the approach would mean that Iranian authorities had agreed secretly to work toward releasing the hostages before any steps were taken to institutionalize the airing of their grievances, yet they would have a visible forum for airing their grievances before their commitment to release the hostages became a political issue in Iran.

Secretary Vance recommended that the President approve asking the Paris lawyers to discuss this approach in Tehran. The President concluded that this seemed the best opening to date and that it could be managed politically provided the commission conducted itself properly as a serious commission of inquiry committed to withholding any public report on its findings until it was assured of the hostages' release.

With the President's approval in hand, Secretary Vance and I flew secretly to New York on January 28 to brief Secretary-General Waldheim over lunch at his residence on our efforts to develop a scenario. The Secretary-General indicated his willingness to cooperate but expressed his concern whether President-elect Bani-Sadr was fully involved. Bani-Sadr had been present when Waldheim had his discussion with the Revolutionary Council in Tehran, but that had been almost a month earlier. We could only repeat what the lawyers had told us and agreed that Waldheim should take his own soundings. It was clear to us that Waldheim was well along in his thinking about possible members of the commission from his discussions with Ghotbzadeh in Tehran, but it would be necessary for him to settle the details with Ghotbzadeh and assure Bani-Sadr's support. Meanwhile, Bourguet and Villalon had left Washington and were on their way to Tehran with a draft of the proposed scenario for discussion with Ghotbzadeh.

At this time, we established a second line of indirect communication with Ghotbzadeh through an American professor in order to give us a way of checking independently on Ghotbzadeh's current thinking and on the lawyers' account of it. This produced a series of almost daily phone conversations which, most of the time, seemed to support the lawyers' general picture of the situation. We realized of course that we were depending on Ghotbzadeh's analysis in both channels, so we also put the lawyers in touch with the Swiss ambassador in Tehran to open through that channel yet another perspective on their activities. Then we settled down to await the results of the lawyers' efforts to gain agreement of the Revolutionary Council to the scenario.

During this period another drama momentarily affected the situation. On January 29, the six Americans who had escaped capture in November and who had been hidden by the Canadian Embassy left through Tehran airport with fabricated identities and documents provided by the Canadian government. Anticipating a sharp Iranian reaction to the escape of the "Canadian six," the Canadians closed their embassy and withdrew all their personnel. The Iranians were outraged at this "illegal" behavior. We could only watch in amused awe at their sudden concern for legality and in somber recognition once again at the deep gulf that separated us. In retaliation, the Foreign Ministry further limited our phone contact with Bruce Laingen and his two colleagues being held at the ministry. Although we had occasionally experienced difficulty getting through, we had maintained fairly steady phone contact with them since November. Despite the momentary reaction, Ghotbzadeh's discussions with the lawyers seemed to remain on track.

It was also during this period, while the American team waited for word from Tehran, that President Carter met on February 7 with a group of American scholars on Islam. Since the beginning of the hostage crisis, considerable effort had been put into understanding the tenets of Shia Islam and of the fundamentalist Islamic revival. The President wanted at a minimum to be sure that, in dealing with the Iranian revolutionaries, we did not do or say things that would make us seem at odds with the whole Islamic world. Even more, he wanted to understand how we might be seen in Iran to understand the best in revolutionary aspirations there. The President also wanted to take whatever advantage could be taken of the Soviet invasion of Afghanistan, a nonaligned Islamic nation. Naturally we were looking, among other things, for those principles that were inconsistent with holding hostages.

Scholars present that day in the Roosevelt Room of the White House described a conceptual framework for American foreign policy reaching well beyond security issues posed by the U.S.-Soviet conflict. They saw the United States ideally as a partner in a global interdependence with other nations and not just as a security partner with some nations against Soviet aggression. They also described the risk of the United States identifying too much with governments and inadequately with peoples—an obvious reference to what they saw as the overpersonalization of the President's relationships with leaders like the former Shah of Iran and Egyptian President Sadat. In any case, all agreed that the American public needed every opportunity for a better understanding of Islam and the diversity of Islamic nations. Like a lot of White House meetings, this one showed a few key people the President's concern. Meanwhile, the Iran Working Group was in almost daily contact with members of the American scholarly and Islamic communities.

Finally word came from Bourguet and Villalon in Tehran that they were ready to review the scenario as developed in talks with Ghotbzadeh and on the basis of what they reported had been approved by the Revolutionary Council. The Swiss offered to arrange a secret meeting for us, and close to midnight on Saturday, February 9, our foursome—Jordan, Precht, Van Reigersberg, and I—sat down with the Paris lawyers in a suite they had reserved for our meetings at the Hotel Bellevue in Berne. As was becoming the pattern, the session began with a detailed account by the lawyers of maneuvering within the Revolutionary Council. We began at breakfast and worked through Sunday past midnight into Monday in the same meticulous way that had characterized our meetings at the White House two weeks earlier. As the hours wore on, Stephanie's voice wore thin, and the attention to detail produced a real endurance test as I repeatedly tried to distill from the talk a simple written understanding of what had been agreed. Sometimes I wondered whether we were negotiating with ourselves or with the absent Ghotbzadeh. In the post-midnight hours, when we had nearly finished our work, the conversation lightened, and the voluble Villalon's voice began to rise in hilarity. Finally, the hotel manager called and asked us to go to bed.

By the time we went to bed, we had a document with three headings: (1) a day-by-day schedule of actions for the next five days, (2) a description of the commission's procedure in Tehran, and (3) steps for the later stages of the scenario.

The concept for the first stage of the scenario was stated in these words: "It is agreed in the approval of this scenario that the Secretary-General of the United Nations should establish a Commission of Inquiry to hear Iran's grievances and to allow an early solution of the crisis between Iran and the U.S. and that Iran desires to have the Commission speak to each of the hostages." The scenario would be set in motion as soon as we could fly to New York, talk with Secretary Vance, and gain Secretary-General Waldheim's agreement. On Monday night, if possible, Secretary-General Waldheim would send a message to Ghotbzadeh confirming his readiness to send to Iran within a week the commission of five to seven members that he had discussed in Tehran early in January "to hear Iran's grievances and to allow an early solution of the crisis between Iran and the U.S." On Tuesday, Ghotbzadeh would respond by agreeing that the commission should come to Tehran within a week and stating "Iran's desire to have the commission speak to each of the hostages." That same Tuesday night, the United States, by direct private communication to the Secretary-General, would remove its objections to the establishment of this commission. In that communication, the United States would state the importance of the commission's looking into the grievances of both sides and working for early release of the hostages. We would say publicly that, while we had opposed the formation of a commission under past conditions, we would support any steps by the United Nations "that might lead to the release of the hostages while protecting essential international principles."

Next, Secretary-General Waldheim would send a second message to Ghotbzadeh that would (a) state briefly the purpose of the commission as a fact-finding mission (not a tribunal) to help end the crisis and (b) recommend a membership of five to seven persons, including suggested names.

Between the dispatch of that message and Friday, either Bani-Sadr himself would confirm by phone to the Secretary-General or the Imam (Khomeini) would issue a statement that he had authorized the Revolutionary Council to resolve the crisis. The Secretary-General would not proceed with the commission until he had received confirmation from Iran. Once he had received confirmation, he would announce "Friday at 1600 hours" the establishment of the commission and its purposes, including Iran's desire to have the commission speak to each of the hostages. After Waldheim's announcement, the President of Iran would publicly present the establishment of the Commission of Inquiry as a success of Iranian diplomacy, would interpret the visit to the hostages as one of the elements in the investigation into Iranian grievances, and would state the desire of the Imam to see the Commission conclude its work rapidly. The Iranian President would instruct government administrations to place their documents at the disposal of the Commission. After the Iranian statement, the United States would state that the Commission was going on a fact-finding mission to Tehran to hear the grievances of both sides, to meet with each of the hostages, and to report to the Secretary-General. The United States would object publicly to having the Commission subject the hostages to interrogation in connection with its inquiry during any of its meetings with them.

Once the Commission had begun work in Tehran, it would hold its meetings in private and receive evidence and documents to be submitted to it by Iranian authorities. It would visit the embassy as soon as possible to meet with the hostages. As soon as it had concluded its work and drafted its report, it: (a) would tell the Revolutionary Council that the credibility of its report would be seriously limited unless the hostages were released immediately or at least moved from the compound to a hospital; (b) would inform the Revolutionary Council that it was ready to return to New York to submit its report to the Secretary-General.

The final stages of the scenario envisioned transfer of the hostages to the protection of the government of Iran either in a hospital or in the embassy compound after the students had left the premises; return of the Commission to New York; submission to the Secretary-General of the Commission's report and its publication as a U.N. document; and release of the hostages and their departure from Iran. The idea discussed at this time was that statements by President Bani-Sadr and President Carter, which had been previously drafted and given to the Secretary-General, would be released after the hostages' departure. By prior understanding, these statements would aim at creating an atmosphere that would begin to close the books on the crisis and provide a basis for looking toward a new relationship. The Iranian statement, as conceived, would acknowledge that holding the hostages had been wrong, express regret, promise to respect international law, and affirm a desire to establish normal relations based on mutual respect and equality and international law. The U.S. statement would, as we already had, note Iran's right to pursue the Shah's assets in U.S. courts; express understanding and regret for the grievances of the Iranian people, including the widespread perception of U.S. intervention in Iran's internal affairs; affirm the right of the Iranian people to make decisions governing their political future and the policy of the United States to respect that right; and affirm a desire for normal relations based on mutual respect, equality, and the principles of international law. Finally, a joint commission could be established to resolve all unresolved bilateral problems.

After hours of tedious talk in three languages and laborious drafting in two, it looked as if we had an understanding on a course of action. We knew the outcome was far from assured. On balance, however, this approach would at least allow us to put a small group of highly capable and experienced international figures acceptable to the Iranians on the ground in Tehran to work directly with leaders in the revolution to see whether they could make themselves catalysts for the hostages' release. Since we could not produce an Iranian decision from the distance of Washington with the conventional instruments of influence and the Iranians did not seem able to decide by themselves, this effort seemed worth the risks and much better than sitting on our hands and waiting for something to happen. Despite our sober recognition that we were walking into uncertainty multiplied by all the bizarre characteristics of the Tehran scene, we had to try as long as there seemed some chance of success and we could see no irretrievable costs of failure.

Launching the U.N. Commission
Early Monday, February 11, Jordan and I left Berne for Paris and then took off for New York. We left Henry Precht and Stephanie Van Reisenberg in Paris to maintain communication with the lawyers, directly while they were there and through their offices or homes when they went to Tehran.

In New York, Jordan and I first met with Secretary Vance. Then all three of us and Ambassador McHenry met with Secretary-General Waldheim and his assistant, Rafi Ahmed, to present the latest version of the scenario. It was recognized that details of the later stages would have to be worked out as time passed and were only suggestive as drafted. The purpose was to treat that day, February 11, as the starting point of the scenario with the first of the agreed messages. The Secretary-General agreed to proceed and sent the first message.

While he was waiting for the formal Iranian response, Waldheim intensified his telephone exchanges with Ghotbzadeh about the membership of the Commission. After many exchanges and midnight calls halfway around the world, the Secretary-General gathered a Commission that included the following five men: co-chairman Andres Aguilar, Venezuelan Ambassador to the United States and Permanent Representative to the United Nations and former Justice Minister; co-chairman Mohammed Bedjaoui, Permanent Representative of Algeria to the United Nations and former Minister of Justice; Adib Daoudi, Foreign Affairs Adviser to President Hafez al Assad of Syria; Harry W. Jayewardene of Sri Lanka, member of the main U.N. body dealing with the protection of minorities; and Lewis Edmond Petitti, a former president of the French bar known for his work on international human rights. The co-chairmen met with the Secretary-General and with Secretary Vance in New York on February 18 and were briefed on the scenario. This was a delicate moment for us, because these men had accepted the appointment with only the most general knowledge of their terms of reference and certainly without knowledge that the outlines of their script had already been written for them without ironclad assurance that it would be followed in Tehran. The co-chairmen responded well individually. They seemed in fact to take the scenario in stride and almost to be pleased that we had done some homework before asking them to step in. Before their mission in Tehran ended, the interpretation of their freedom to maneuver within the scenario was to become a cause for contention between the two co-chairmen. Their apparent decision not to tell other members of their group about the scenario until Bani-Sadr hinted at its existence in Tehran also added to cross-currents among them. The Commission finally began assembling in Geneva on February 20.

Before the Commission ever left Geneva—indeed in the first instance even before the Commission was announced—the Iranians had departed on two significant occasions from the scenario. These departures underscored our doubts about just what Khomeini's understanding and approval of this approach was. There was no question from the second day on that this was going to be a rocky road requiring a lot of forebearance on our part.

The first occasion was the very first Iranian response to the Secretary-General's message offering to send the Commission to Tehran. That response used wording to describe the purpose of the Commission that was not in the scenario and was not acceptable either to the United States or to the United Nations. We got on the phone immediately with our colleagues in Paris. They roused the lawyers, who tracked down Ghotbzadeh, then traveling in Europe. After a number of exchanges Ghotbzadeh succeeded in having his office in Tehran send a second message consistent with the terms of the scenario. At that point, we could still blame the hitch on Ghotbzadeh's absence from Tehran and take comfort that the second message did go back to the scenario.

The next departure was more serious. At 1:30 A.M. on Wednesday, February 20, I received a call at home from Rafi Ahmed. A message had arrived at the United Nations from the Iranians giving a go-ahead for the Commission to come to Tehran but stating its terms of reference in language far from that agreed upon and quite unacceptable to the United States. The message in its convoluted wording said: "Now that the wish of the Imam and the people of Iran regarding a study and investigation into the past interferences of the U.S. into the internal affairs of Iran through the regime of the deposed Shah and with a view to establishing a tribunal to determine their treason, crimes and corruption has been accepted, the Commission whose establishment and functions have been agreed upon by the Revolutionary Council of the Islamic Republic of Iran and the Imam can come to Iran."

I called Acting Secretary Warren Christopher, and together we had the Operation's Center patch through a call to Secretary Vance, who had to step out of a meeting with Foreign Minister Genscher in Bonn to talk with us. The Secretary felt that the Iranians should be required to stick scrupulously to the script before the Commission proceeded to Tehran. Christopher and I then called the President. It was probably 3:00 A.M. by then. He said he would be in his office at 5:00 A.M. and suggested we join him.

We met in the deserted State Department garage and drove in Christopher's car to the White House. As we climbed the stairs to the main floor and walked toward the President's office, we found the halls darkened, with the exception of a small light and one guard outside the Oval Office. When we entered, we found the President wearing a heavy cardigan in a dimly lit room with the fire blazing. I had been in that office on many occasions at moments of deep crisis and exhilarating success, but never had I been struck by so vivid a picture of the loneliness of the man in that office, surrounded by darkness in the empty west wing with the flickering firelight. How human and forsaken he seemed in that moment.

We went over the situation in detail, explaining Secretary Vance's views. Ham Jordan had been called. Jody Powell came in later and possibly Zbig Brzezinski. In the course of the discussion over whether to proceed, reasonable points were made on both sides of the argument. Some argued against proceeding until the Iranians demonstrated their capacity to stick precisely to what was agreed. Others felt that, if we were going to engage the Iranians, we would have to take the situation in stride when they acted in their own way rather than with Anglo-Saxon legal precision.

On balance, the President decided that it would be better to have an active process in motion with responsible men of international stature on the scene in Tehran consciously playing a role on behalf of the hostages' release. Their presence itself was designed to give the proponents of release an important development around which to build steps leading to "expulsion" of the hostages. By 9:00 A.M., after the President had talked with Secretary-General Waldheim, he agreed that the Commission should go ahead after the Secretary-General had told both the Commission and the Iranians that he was proceeding on the basis of the original terms of reference.

The Commission members left Geneva for Tehran about noon on Saturday, February 23. They were accompanied by Diego Cordovez, Assistant Secretary-General of the United Nations. (Their departure had been delayed for two days pending word from Ghotbzadeh that Tehran was ready for them.) While they were in the air, the most significant departure from the scenario exploded like a bombshell in Tehran. Press reports suddenly hit our desks in Washington midway through that Saturday quoting Khomeini as saying that the elected representatives of the people would decide the hostage question. Key Iranians did their best to put a positive face on this development, but it appeared to have taken them by surprise too, and it was unclear to everyone how this would affect the Commission's work and playing out the scenario. It was one more jarring reminder that the scenario might serve as a framework but, as one Iranian said, the scenario "cannot be carried out like something abstract and it will be necessary that each step is deliberately prepared as a basis for the following step." As the steps unfolded, the Iranians urged particular care in Washington about all public statements that could affect the atmosphere in Tehran. That advice was received with further grim and tired shorthand reflections on the Iranian revolutionary mind. At least we were launched!

As the Commission settled into its first meetings in Iran, the atmosphere was positive. In fact, as it was reported to Washington, the meetings went so well that a problem surfaced within the Commission when Bani-Sadr referred to carrying out the "secret plan." Other members of the Commission were momentarily upset to learn that they had not been told about the scenario, but the co-chairmen overcame the problem. The group was told that it would see the hostages the following Wednesday morning, each commissioner visiting ten of the hostages. Ghotbzadeh began talking about moving the hostages "to a hospital" as a means of taking them into government custody. According to Laingen, Ghotbzadeh also began making preparations for housing them in the Foreign Ministry. Laingen and his colleagues even began figuring out how they could schedule use of the limited bathroom facilities by fifty more "guests." The Commission began meeting with other Iranians, who spilled out their accounts of human rights violations during the rule of the Shah. Secretary-General Waldheim stressed to the co-chairmen that they must see all of the hostages and not leave Tehran until the hostages had been transferred to government control.

Although the Commission's meetings with President Bani-Sadr went well in the first few days, indications of difficulties began to surface over the Commission's visit to the hostages. By Wednesday, February 27, it became obvious that Bani-Sadr was having real difficulty arranging the visit to the embassy compound. Reports from Tehran indicated that the militants holding the compound had said the Commission could see only some of the hostages, because not all were in the compound. The Commission insisted on seeing all of them. The date for the visit to the compound kept slipping, while the Revolutionary Council tried to gain control of the embassy. As day after day passed, the Commission was reassured daily that they would indeed see all of the hostages after one or two more details were worked out. For its part, the Commission held to the position that there would be no report until all of the hostages had been transferred to custody of the government.

By Wednesday, March 5, the Commission recognized that the Revolutionary Council was not succeeding in its efforts to gain the agreement of the militants in the compound to the Commission's visit to the hostages. The militants insisted on limiting the Commission's visit to six of the hostages and appeared to be setting up a situation in which those hostages would be interrogated about their activities. The Commission began to discuss leaving Tehran with its mission not completed.

In the late afternoon, Secretary-General Waldheim's assistant, Rafi Ahmed, and a half-dozen of our crisis team gathered in Ham Jordan's office. We began to discuss the announcement that would be made if the Commission had to leave. Telephone lines were opened between Waldheim at the United Nations and the Commission's co-chairmen in their hotel suite in Tehran, between Waldheim and his assistant, Diego Cordovez, who was with the co-chairmen, between Waldheim and Ahmed in Jordan's office, and between Jordan's office and the Paris lawyers in an adjacent room in the same hotel where the Commission was headquartered in Tehran. Because of differences between the co-chairmen, Waldheim's instructions often had to be passed to Cordovez to be negotiated carefully with the co-chairmen and other members of the Commission to assure some measure of consensus. Both parties in Tehran—the co-chairmen and the lawyers—reported on their separate lines that the situation was serious. Ghotbzadeh came to the hotel to ask the Commission on behalf of the Revolutionary Council to stay another twenty-four hours. Secretary-General Waldheim advised the co-chairmen to wait until 2:00 P.M. the following day.

Thursday, March 6, began with a surprise Tehran radio report of an announcement by the militants holding the embassy that they would turn over custody of the hostages to the Revolutionary Council. Ghotbzadeh, after a Revolutionary Council meeting, said the Council had accepted the militants' decision and that a committee would be formed to work out details of the transfer. With considerable frustration and exasperation, we can say that we have never understood why Bani-Sadr and Ghotbzadeh did not move without hesitation to take charge of the hostages. Many of us believed at the time that a lightning move at that critical moment could have resulted in the hostages' transfer and brought the scenario nearer to completion. We seemed so close, but the move did not come. Key members of the Revolutionary Council supported the agreed course of action, but others around Khomeini were apparently working against success. Again, the struggle between clerics and secular authorities turned out to be critical.

On Monday, March 10, after four days of exchanges between the militants and the Revolutionary Council, Khomeini made a statement that the documents in the embassy should be turned over to the Commission, that a meeting with those hostages implicated by the documents would be permitted, and, if the Commission declared its viewpoint in Tehran about the crimes of the United States and of the Shah, that a visit with all of the hostages would be permitted. The Commission responded that it could not operate under conditions contrary to its mandate. Later that day, Ghotbzadeh proposed that the Commission stay and meet with the Revolutionary Council and that a joint declaration on the crimes and intervention of the United States be issued. Bani-Sadr indicated to Ambassador Bedjaoui, the Algerian co-chairman, that he would be flexible about this statement. Some members of the Commission favored trying this approach, while others were doubtful, because they were not sure what Khomeini wanted. Secretary Vance agreed to the Commission's staying for meetings but with the understanding that the Commission issue no such statement. Once again, the co-chairmen recommended leaving Tehran that night. The Secretary-General asked them to wait until morning, which they did, leaving Tehran on March 11.

Regrouping for a Second Try

When it was known that the Commission might be returning to New York without completing its mission, the Iran Working Group was asked through the SCC to prepare papers on a number of options for next steps. These included a return to the Security Council, going ahead with hearings at the International Court of Justice, breaking relations with Iran or further restricting the role of Iranian diplomats, going ahead with economic sanctions, and an assessment of the potential impact of various kinds of blockades.

Jordan and I arranged to meet with Bourguet and Villalon in Berne on March 12. The meeting began late that evening before Jordan's arrival the next morning. Our purpose was to assess whether the scenario could be revised and revived. In the end we worked out a revised scenario, called

"Berne II," contingent on developments in Tehran, all on the hypothesis that Bani-Sadr would receive a mandate in the parliamentary elections.

In the meantime, a message had reached Washington that Bani-Sadr had promised the President to transfer the hostages within fourteen days. It is possible that Bani-Sadr expected the parliamentary elections on March 14 to produce a result that would strengthen his hand. As our group in Berne continued meeting on Thursday, March 13, Secretary Vance and his assistant, Arnold Raphel, met with the Commission in New York. The Secretary expressed the belief that it would be necessary to allow a period of time for the Iranians to complete the first round of their parliamentary elections and to make their own decision to transfer the hostages. When they had completed the transfer, the United States would support the Commission's return to Tehran to complete its work if that would still be useful, provided Iran gave assurance that the visit to the hostages would take place on a specified date. The Commission shared his view that no report should be prepared until next steps, if any, were arranged.

In the days following our Berne meeting, Secretary-General Waldheim made contact with Bani-Sadr to pave the way for the return of the Commission if that would help in the release of the hostages. During that period Bani-Sadr was preoccupied with the parliamentary election. He expressed a desire to continue to work but was indecisive about the Commission's return.

At this same moment, Panama's end of March deadline for completing the case for extradition of the Shah was approaching. Shortly after the Commission's departure from Tehran, officials in Washington learned that the Shah was scheduled for surgery in Panama to remove his spleen. With a move on extradition likely, the Shah became concerned about pursuing urgent medical treatment in Panama. The administration hoped that he could be persuaded to stay. He feared that the squabbling among Panamanian and American doctors would make it impossible for him to receive reliable treatment there, and he accepted President Sadat's outstanding invitation to move to Egypt and to have his operation there. There was serious concern in Washington about the effect on Egypt, but in the end the President concluded that the impact of his return to the United States would be worse.

When it became known that the Shah would leave Panama on March 23, Bourguet and Villalon, in close touch with Ghotbzadeh in Tehran, saw an opportunity for a dramatic event that could provide a trigger for the hostages' release. They urged that the Shah's flight be turned back to Panama from the U.S. base in the Azores where it would refuel. They felt a situation could be constructed in which the Shah would appear momentarily to have been subjected to judicial process and they could capitalize on the moment of "victory" in Tehran. From the lawyer's first mention of the extradition ploy in London in January, we had told them we could not concur in any such action. Now when they raised it again against the background of our frustrating efforts in Tehran we had to listen to them, but by this time it seemed to me they were grasping at straws. In the end, the Revolutionary Council could not provide concrete assurance of the hostages' transfer, even if the Shah's plane were turned around. The Shah proceeded to Egypt, where he eventually died on July 27 with little notice in Iran.

After the Commission's departure from Tehran, efforts continued in Tehran to pick up the elements of the now broken scenario. A fabricated letter from President Carter to Ayatollah Khomeini, presumably written by Villalon and containing language designed to look like an American admission of guilt, was published in the Iranian press. It was a cleverly assembled collage of earlier private messages sent by Jordan to Bani-Sadr and Ghotbzadeh. Those two earlier messages had been handwritten by Jordan to convey our seriousness of purpose. President Carter had agreed to his doing this, and Jordan showed them to me before completing them. Both stated U.S. views, but neither implied that it was a message directly from the President. The White House accurately denied that any such message from Carter to Khomeini had been authorized. Then Bani-Sadr released two actual messages from Washington urging the Revolutionary Council to take custody of the hostages.

Bourguet, on his way back from Panama, met the President on March 25. Jordan's purpose in arranging the meeting was to enable Bourguet to carry back to Tehran a firsthand report that U.S. patience was wearing thin. March 25, as it happened, was the day in which the President lost heavily to Senator Kennedy in the New York and Connecticut primaries, partly as a result of an earlier vote in the U.N. Security Council that had angered Israel. The President had no difficulty making his irritation clear to Bourguet.

Word suddenly came from the Paris lawyers on March 30 that Bani-Sadr would announce at noon the next day that the Revolutionary Council, with the Imam's agreement, had approved the transfer of the hostages on April 1. They wanted the administration to acknowledge somehow that the decision on eventual release would be taken by the new parliament. Another source also reported a talk in which Ghotbzadeh said on March 31 that the transfer should take place the following day. The lawyers reported that members of the Revolutionary Council and the militants holding the embassy had met. Bani-Sadr remained concerned about the actual step of taking the hostages into governmental control.

During the first morning hours of April 1—the day of the presidential primary election in Wisconsin—the Iran Working Group learned that a message was coming from the Swiss ambassador in Tehran through the Swiss channel. About dawn, Swiss Ambassador Probst in Washington telephoned me at the White House, where the President's advisers were gathered with him awaiting news on the reported transfer. The word was that Bani-Sadr had announced that the hostages would be transferred to governmental control if the United States would recognize the role of the Iranian parliament in the hostage crisis and refrain from propaganda, provocation, or claims against Iran. On early morning television President Carter welcomed Bani-Sadr's statement and said we would again delay imposition of sanctions until this development could be assessed.

Charges were subsequently made that the President's announcement was timed to influence voting in Wisconsin. The President and his senior White House staff obviously had the Wisconsin primary very much on their minds that morning, but those charges do not take into account that they had been intensively involved almost hour by hour for several weeks in the effort to push the Iranians over the line in taking custody of the hostages. In that context, a quick response to Bani-Sadr that could be made public in Tehran that day seemed essential. The response could have been given in the President's name by Press Secretary Jody Powell, but it was thought that a statement by the President himself could have a greater impact in Tehran. The relationship of the statement to voting in Wisconsin was mentioned, but no one even considered that the President might be charged with trying to use the hostages for political purposes.

Nothing happened in Tehran on April 1, but reports began to come from Tehran that the transfer would take place April 5. After an 8-3 vote in the Revolutionary Council, the issue was taken to Khomeini on April 6. Confirmed reports told us that Khomeini had asked whether the recommendation of the Revolutionary Council was unanimous. When he was told that there were three negative votes—Ayatollah Beheshti and two other clerics—Khomeini refused to approve the Council's recommendation.

Once again the religious elements within the leadership had thwarted the efforts of the secular leaders to end the crisis. By the time the National Security Council met in Washington on Monday morning, April 7, momentum for a negotiated solution seemed to have run out. Later in the month, on April 19, Ghotbzadeh, who was visiting Paris at the time, provided his own assessment of the situation to the Paris lawyers. His morale was low. He felt that it was unrealistic to think of achieving anything before the new Iranian parliament was elected and formed. The second round of elections was put off to May 9. That meant a probable delay in forming the new assembly, so that late June seemed to be the earliest that progress on the hostages' release could be achieved. The lawyers thought Ghotbzadeh seemed defeated. One of them described the situation that day in terms of a power struggle involving the left, the moderates in the "European" group, and the religious elements. Until there could be some kind of governing coalition, he did not see much prospect of a solution.

As this negotiating track petered out, it became more and more obvious that the so-called moderates could not get their way and were losing out to the religious elements, who since November had viewed the hostage crisis as one of their instruments for gaining control of the revolution and of the machinery of the revolutionary government. The administration was criticized for having attempted to work through the secular elements in the government rather than trying to reach directly to the religious figures. The fact was that extensive efforts had been made in November and December to find channels to the religious leaders but without success. Even groups like the PLO, which had direct access to Khomeini and those around him, seemed to have reached the conclusion in December and January that their access would not produce results until the power struggle had sorted itself out. Since none of the few channels to the religious leaders seemed likely to produce results, the administration fell back on the one approach available to it—working with secular figures on the scene who did have access to the religious leadership, in the hope that they could present the case for releasing the hostages in such a way as to persuade the religious leaders that it would serve their purposes. They did not succeed, presumably because the religious figures could not allow the secular leaders to have a success.

Against those odds, should the administration have tried the negotiating track through the unusual channel of the Paris-based lawyers? As often happens in a situation of this kind, we had to choose among available alternatives and chose one that offered direct access to one of the centers of power at the time. Much of the time there seemed to be at least some significant chance of success. Some would argue that Ghotbzadeh and Bani-Sadr came very close to gaining control over the hostages at two moments. Those of us who had shared the risks of negotiation with President Carter at Camp David and on his bold trip to the Middle East to conclude the Egyptian-Israeli peace treaty the previous March were convinced that it was preferable to negotiate if at all possible. We did so, having made the judgment that trying to negotiate and failing would leave matters no worse than they would otherwise have been, and we could not be sure we would not succeed.

The Families Organize

"No matter how compassionate others may be in supporting the families; no matter how concerned others may be about the hostages, they cannot know what we are going through and they cannot maintain the interest in the hostages to the same degree as we who are so directly involved," wrote Penne Laingen in early April for the first issue of the *FLAG Bulletin*. FLAG, the Family Liaison Action Group, was the new organization of the "families of the American captives in Tehran."

From the families had emerged such ideas as the ringing of church bells at regular times and then the widespread practice of displaying yellow ribbons as signals of hope for the hostages' return. Many of those ribbons stayed in place for more than a year until, tattered and torn, they were finally taken down after the hostages were welcomed home. In an expression of the concern of all American families at the first Christmas celebration after the hostages were taken, President Carter decided to leave the national Christmas tree dark as a reminder of those who could not be with their families during that normally happy season.

In the first meetings of the families with government officials, there was frequently a sharp display of hostility toward the government for their plight and for the failure to produce a prompt solution. In a large meeting in the State Department auditorium in January, officials made a determined effort to try to overcome the hostile "we-they" atmosphere of the first meeting and to establish an atmosphere of common concern for friends, colleagues, and loved ones in Tehran and a spirit of shared effort to gain their release. With the help of a number of family members who, because of their residence in Washington, were closer to the day-to-day operations of the State Department, some progress was made on that front. While a few families continued to show distrust, most gradually placed at least guarded trust in those responsible for efforts to release the hostages.

Even those who worked closely with us came to feel that they should have some organization of their own for dealing with this situation. As the first issue of the *FLAG Bulletin* explained the organization's birth, "FLAG was originally conceived by Penne Laingen, who, after talking with former POW wives, realized there was a need for the families of hostages to band together." The Defense Department had had great difficulty working with the Vietnam POW family organization and was initially very reluctant to see FLAG organized. As Defense officers began to attend their meetings, they became supporters. Why the acronym, FLAG? As Louisa Kennedy, who became spokesperson for the organization, had said earlier: "The fifty stars represented the fifty hostages held at the American Embassy compound; the three colors in the flag represented the three hostages held at the Foreign Ministry; and the thirteen stripes represented the thirteen released hostages."

Feelings among the families were varied and complex. For some, FLAG was a channel for their anger, through which they could be critical of the State Department with the protective organizational covering they felt would reduce the danger to husbands' careers. For others, it was an institutionalization of the human support mechanisms they found so important.

For still others, it was a potential source of help and advice in dealing with the practical problems of day-to-day life. Finally, some thought establishing cohesiveness among the families might prevent individual actions that most of the families saw as harmful. The *Bulletin* formally described FLAG's several purposes this way:

> As a group under the name FLAG, we will have more influence on public opinion. . . . FLAG can be decisive in communicating to Iran that the American public will no longer tolerate their actions.
> There is strength and comfort in sharing our feelings with each other. FLAG members in the Washington area, who are close to the seat of government, will by necessity form the nucleus of the group, pressing for answers to questions that can be disseminated to families who live in other parts of the country. . . .
> FLAG was also established to have greater input from the families into decisions which directly affect the hostages and the families. Questions relating to administrative, legal, medical, repatriational, etc. decisions have already been submitted to the Undersecretary of State for Administration, Mr. Ben Read, for his answers and signature. When these are received, they will be disseminated. . . .

The organization began to take shape in Saturday meetings at the State Department on March 15 and 22. The spotlight began to fall for the role of president on Katherine Keough, whose husband was one of the two nonofficial hostages. He had been head of the international school in Tehran and had moved to a similar job in Pakistan. He had been in Tehran simply trying to collect and assure the safety of the records of the Tehran school. Both Katherine Keough and Louisa Kennedy took the view that there was more advantage in working in ways complementary to government efforts than in doing battle with the government, and they also became valued partners in the larger effort to manage the public aspects of the crisis to the benefit of all.

As we worked through these months in close touch with most of the families, we became increasingly aware of how deep the frustration and resulting anger ran among family members. These emotions ebbed and flowed with the news from Tehran. The ups and downs of the emotional roller coaster were a major problem for many families, especially when fragments of news hit them without at the same time providing context for assessing the stories. FLAG was formed in a period of optimism, while there still seemed some hope from negotiations, and was in its organizational stages in the emotional low point after the military rescue mission. Hopes rose again when Richard Queen was released in July. The families who fared best—and we later learned this was true of the hostages themselves—were those who took a long view and tried not to get swept up in the daily torrent of reports.

Some of the frustration came from the fact that husbands and family members had gone to Tehran in the first place. Since it was difficult to be angry at a hostage, some of that anger was directed at "the system" and at the State Department. In other cases some of the anger vented at the department was born of the frustration of years of coping as Foreign Service wives with the difficulties of regularly uprooting home and family to live in often inhospitable parts of the world. There was a feeling among some wives, who rightly felt they had invested a great deal of themselves in the conduct of our nation's foreign relations, that all of their effort had been for nothing if the Iranians' actions were any measure of success. In yet other instances, it came from frustration at feeling they were not fully informed. It was difficult at best to keep everyone informed up to the minute. Yet the moment any family felt that information was being withheld was the moment it began seeking other channels to make feelings heard—calls to congressmen, talking to the press, seeking their own organizational outlet.

Some of the reason for the mainly cooperative rather than potentially hostile relationship between the family organization and the department resulted from the families' access to government officials. They talked often with Secretary Vance and with the President. In April, several of the wives traveled to Europe and met with heads of government and heads of state there. They had day-to-day access to members of the Iran Working Group. Sheldon Krys, through his hours of attention and his way of dealing with the families, gradually won their confidence in the department. The importance of this cooperative relationship can be underscored only when one imagines what it would have been like had the families been in open and vocal opposition to the government.

FLAG was officially incorporated on June 9. During its early weeks, it was offered office space in the State Department Task Force area. The advantage of being there was that a number of families took comfort from the fact that FLAG officials could easily be in touch with us on an almost hourly basis as necessary. The families felt at that time that their mere presence was a daily reminder of their concern. This was particularly important to families who lived far from Washington and wanted to feel that their concerns were represented in the department. Some of the families felt, however, that they would be better off in offices of their own, and finally they moved to a Washington office building. FLAG continued to pursue a variety of practical concerns. Among them was support for passage through Congress of the Hostage Relief Act of 1980, which provided educational and medical benefits for the hostages and their families. FLAG representatives

appeared at congressional hearings on the bill held by Congressman Fas-
cell's Subcommittee for International Operations within the House Foreign
Affairs Committee. Passed in the spring of 1980, that act became law in
October.

Much of the department's work with the families throughout the crisis
was geared to the hostages' return. The medical division of the department
had become involved within the first days of the crisis and had already
assisted in the return of the first thirteen hostages and the "Canadian six."
As time went on, it became apparent that we were really dealing with two
different groups of families—one consisting of parents and the other of
spouses and children. The distinction would make a difference, not during
the captivity but after the hostages' return. In the intimate relationship of
marriage, the hostages would return to spouses who had been forced to cope
on their own and who in some cases had become figures on the national
stage. Their relationship in the future would have to take account of that. In
the case of parents, the adjustment would be simpler. Their sons and
daughters had earlier established their separate lives, and parents had
come to terms with their independence.

As the summer wore on, the department and FLAG held regional meetings with family clusters. At one of these in California in August, the families met the new Secretary of State. Later in the year, they made important
suggestions about arrangements for the hostages' homecoming.

INCREASING PRESSURE AGAIN: APRIL AND EARLY MAY

After the collapse of the diplomatic track pursued since January, a feeling
pervaded the administration that the patience of the American people was
running out and that firm and decisive steps had to be taken. I did not feel
that pressure, but I was not out on the primary hustings. At the same time,
the efforts since January had provided intensive experience in dealing with
the revolutionary leadership in Tehran and made clear, if it was not already
clear, that the administration could not succeed by dealing only with the
secular authorities. The intensifying power struggle in Tehran made it
increasingly fruitless to put the secular leaders in a position to deal with the
religious faction. For the moment, however, attention in the SCC turned
back to the question of how the costs to Iran of continuing to hold the
hostages could be further increased.

On April 7, the President announced a number of new decisions:

• Diplomatic relations with Iran were broken, and all Iranian diplomatic and consular personnel and military trainees were compelled to
leave. (The United States then formally asked the Swiss to protect U.S.

interests in Iran, while Algeria was designated to act for Iran in Washington.)

•The United States formally put into effect the economic sanctions in the vetoed Security Council resolution of January 13. Subsequently, the administration urged European and Japanese allies to impose sanctions as well, and their sanctions went into effect shortly after agreement was reached on May 17. The sanctions added to Iran's difficulty in purchasing supplies. Iran's imposition of higher oil prices in any case reduced Western European and Japanese purchases.

•A formal inventory of Iran's frozen assets and of Americans' claims against Iran was ordered.

•Visas held by Iranians were invalidated, and new visas were to be issued only for strong humanitarian reasons.

While broadening the sanctions would have a potential effect in the long run, the other measures seemed to us in the State Department as designed more to satisfy Americans that we were getting tougher than to influence decisions in Tehran.

Like so many other somber moments in those 444 days, this too was broken by unintended comic relief. It was decided that Warren Christopher would call in the Iranian Chargé to give him the formal note breaking relations and ordering the Iranian diplomats to leave. My deputy, Peter Constable, was preparing the note, which had to be retyped, when the Iranian arrived. So Henry Precht met the Chargé, Ali Agah, and a colleague, Mohammed Lavasani, at the entrance to the State Department and took them to his own office until Constable was ready. Lavasani had attended the Vance-Yazdi meeting the previous fall and was assumed to be the revolutionary leadership's watchdog. While waiting, they were talking about the hostages.

"The hostages are really quite happy in Iran," Lavasani said, "Some of them even want to stay."

"Oh bullshit!" Precht exploded in exasperation.

"I'm not going to be talked to like that!" the Chargé retorted angrily, heading for the elevator.

Precht, knowing the purpose of the visit, did not want the Iranian to leave without the note formally expelling him. He followed the Iranian into the elevator, pushed the stop button, and tried to reach Constable on the elevator phone to have him rush the note to the elevator. The Chargé fumed about being "held hostage." He got the elevator started down before Constable arrived and left the building to return to his embassy, where he told reporters that he had been insulted.

Next, Constable and Precht put one of the officers from the Working Group in a car and sent him to the Iranian Embassy to deliver the note.

When they told Deputy Secretary Christopher what had happened, he tried to recall the officer for fear he would end up a hostage in the Iranian Embassy. Fortunately, he had accomplished his mission and was safely on his way back to the department before word of Christopher's concern reached him.

When the newspapers described the episode the next day, Precht began receiving strongly worded fan mail from all over the country. The American Legion commended him. But his most prized note was penned on top of one copy of the story:

> One of the elements of good diplomatic language is to be concise, accurate and clear. You have shown yourself to be the master of all three. (Jimmy Carter)

Ten days later, on April 17, the White House announced economic measures to increase the pressure on Iran: financial transfers to Iran were prohibited without Treasury Department license; imports from Iran were banned; American travel to Iran was banned except for journalists and others with individual authorization from the Secretaries of State and Treasury; military equipment previously purchased by Iran but still in the United States was made available for purchase by other users. Again, these steps seemed more a tidying of the books than significant new applications of pressure.

On April 11, the President had approved military action designed to rescue the hostages. The President had obviously instructed Vance that no one else in the State Department should be involved in planning the rescue mission. The reason was presumably a concern for secrecy, although we in the department had consistently opposed military action. We felt that punitive military action would probably trigger execution of some of the hostages and would not produce a decision by the divided Iranian leadership to release the hostages. We also continued to be deeply concerned about hostile reactions against Americans elsewhere in the Middle East. Finally, we thought a rescue effort would only leave a lot of Iranians, a number of the hostages, and some of the rescuers dead.

It was clear to a few of us from Vance's repeated questions about the exact whereabouts of the hostages and the layout of the embassy compound that some sort of rescue mission was being actively discussed. I knew from months of working closely with Vance and his deep concern expressed on a number of earlier occasions that he opposed any military effort. I had also taken each opportunity to explain in those conversations why we in the Working Group recommended strongly against military action. I also knew from our close cooperation before, during, and after Camp David that he was open and straightforward in confiding in me the President's instructions, decisions, and objectives. So when he said nothing to me about military action despite his obvious questions I knew that the President had instructed him to say nothing. Experience had taught me that the decent way to work with a colleague under such instructions was to find ways to make my views known but not to put him on the spot by asking questions. I knew he would speak strongly against military action, so there was nothing more to be said.

Our one operating dilemma was that, in ignorance of the earlier stages of planning the rescue mission, we had decided that some of the families evacuated from other posts in the Middle East because of concern over reactions to U.S. military action could return. Fortunately, the decision had not resulted in the movement of any significant numbers.

It is time now to interrupt this account of the diplomatic and political framework to go back and discuss in detail the economic and military options and actions considered and taken since November and accelerated in April.

3 MILITARY OPTIONS AND CONSTRAINTS

GARY SICK

One of the most hotly debated issues of the hostage crisis was whether the Carter Administration properly used the military capabilities at its command. That debate has been muddied by the tight security screen drawn around the subject during the course of the crisis and, to some extent, in subsequent accounts. It is evident from the public record that President Carter and his chief policy advisers rejected direct military action against Iran during the crisis, with the key exception of the attempted rescue mission. It is less obvious that the potential resort to violence was present throughout the crisis as a palpable reality in the minds of American decision-makers, in the calculations of America's allies, and in the interplay with Iranian revolutionary politics.

The military dimension is important as a backdrop to the dynamics of those fourteen and one-half months. The following account attempts to trace that subterranean policy theme, identifying key decision points and the implications in each instance for the overall conduct of U.S. policy.

In the Beginning

Almost from the first moment of the seizure of the hostages in Tehran, a military response was actively considered. On November 6, the second day of the crisis, the Joint Chiefs of Staff presented to the Special Coordinating Committee (SCC) of the National Security Council (NSC) the general outlines of three potential courses of military action. These were: first, a possible rescue mission to extract the imprisoned Americans from the beseiged embassy in downtown Tehran; second, a possible retaliatory strike that would cripple Iran's economy; and third, considerations of how the United States might be required to respond if Iran should disintegrate.

In the meetings of November 6, most attention was paid to the first two.

The possibility of a rescue mission was examined in considerable detail. However, even the most cursory analysis of the embassy complex, its location in the center of a large city whose population was inflamed, and the great distances between Tehran and facilities that might be available for U.S. military use suggested that such an operation would be enormously complicated and would involve unacceptably high risks.

The Chairman of the Joint Chiefs recommended against any immediate attempt at a rescue mission, since reliable intelligence was unavailable and a complex plan would require time to develop. His judgment was supported by the Secretary of Defense, who had discussed the prospects with a high Israeli military official intimately associated with the Entebbe operation.

After a careful review, President Carter ordered the Department of Defense to proceed with preparations and planning for a rescue mission, while postponing any such attempt for the time being. He recognized that even a high-risk rescue attempt might become necessary if it appeared that the hostages were going to be killed by the Iranians.

Also at the meeting on November 6, President Carter was presented with a preliminary analysis of possible targets for a retaliatory strike. It was obvious that a purely punitive strike would not set the hostages free. On the contrary, it might well result in some or all of them being killed by their captors. Thus a punitive strike was viewed as retribution in the event the hostages were harmed. The President ordered that planning for such a strike be perfected and held in reserve, stressing that the objective would be economic targets, with the minimum possible loss of life among Iranian civilians.

Two other alternatives were examined in the context of a possible military strike. The seizure of a discrete piece of Iranian territory, for example an island, was considered. However, it was estimated that taking and holding a significant piece of Iranian territory would risk incurring sizable casualties—Iranian, American, or both. It could set off a continuing naval and air battle in the Persian Gulf that would be enormously costly to the broader interests of the United States, its Western allies, and the oil-producing states of the Gulf. Moreover, it was not considered likely to produce the freedom of the hostages. Rather, it might incite Iran to unite in a nationalistic visceral response and turn to the Soviet Union for protection. As a consequence, this option was never pressed much beyond the conceptual stage.

The possibility of dropping naval mines in Iranian harbors or otherwise imposing a military blockade was given serious consideration from the very beginning. For a variety of reasons, the mining option came to be regarded as the most likely policy choice if a decision should be taken to use limited military force against Iran. Mines could be planted on very short notice by naval forces already in place in the region. They would impose very high economic costs on Iran with little or no loss of life on either side. And the process was reversible, either by setting the mines to deactivate after a specific period of time or, if necessary, by physically removing them. As U.S. policy moved progressively toward an embargo on all trade with Iran, the ability to mine one or more Iranian harbors was increasingly regarded as a potentially classic example of the extension of diplomatic strategy by military means.

There were, however, negative consequences associated with a mining operation. Mining is an act of war, and its use against Iran would have legal, moral, military, and political consequences that could not be predicted with certainty. For example, Iran might choose to react by sinking U.S. tankers in the Persian Gulf, thus setting off a much wider and more destructive conflict. Certainly the oil-producing states of the region would have regarded such an operation with alarm, as would many of America's oil-dependent allies. At a minimum, insurance rates would probably rise sharply, affecting the movement of tankers into the Gulf and adding a further increment to the price of oil, which had soared to devastating levels in 1979. The Soviet Union could have offered minesweepers and point air defense assistance, which Iran might have found difficult to refuse, thus increasing the possibility of direct Soviet penetration. Although it would have greatly increased the pressures on the regime in Tehran, there was no basis for assuming that such an operation would result in the prompt release of the hostages.

Nevertheless, as a limited display of military power in the context of a strategy of pressure, the mining option involved relatively fewer risks than other forms of military action. It afforded a degree of policy control that permitted it to be integrated into a political and diplomatic strategy, and it was consequently retained under active consideration at each of the escalatory points during the crisis.

As a result of the NSC meeting of November 6, a number of guidelines were developed that served as the basis for U.S. policy throughout the crisis. Five of these guidelines were related to the question of the use of force:

•The United States would attempt to increase the cost to Iran of its illegal actions, until the costs outweighed whatever benefits it might hope to achieve.

•Peaceful means would be explored and exhausted before resort to violence.

•The United States would retaliate militarily if the hostages were put on trial or physically harmed.

• The U.S. government would make no threats it was unable or unwilling to carry out.

• No military action would be taken that was not reversible. Specifically, President Carter was determined to avoid a situation where a limited military action would trap the United States in an open-ended escalatory cycle leading to land combat in Iran.

These guidelines were never codified and were never intended as declaratory policy. Rather, they were articulated by President Carter as objectives and policy boundaries for his advisers in developing U.S. strategy. They established the framework for consideration of military options throughout the entire course of the 444-day drama.

The Warning Note

On November 18 and 19, Iran released thirteen of the hostages—five women and seven blacks—after intervention by the PLO. At the time of the release, there was a new burst of belligerent rhetoric from the student militants and from the Ayatollah, threatening that the remaining Americans would be tried as spies and executed if the United States failed to return the exiled Shah to Iran. Washington had very limited information about the condition of the hostages within the embassy, and these threats were taken with deadly seriousness.

On November 20, the White House released a statement suggesting the possibility of U.S. military action should Iran put the hostages on trial. The statement said that a peaceful solution "is preferable to the other remedies available," but it pointedly drew attention to the self-help provisions available under the U.N. Charter.[1]

The statement was underlined by the dispatch of the aircraft carrier USS *Kitty Hawk* and its supporting battle group from the Pacific to the Arabian Sea. The carrier USS *Midway* and its battle group were already present in the area. With the arrival of *Kitty Hawk*, the United States had at its disposal the largest naval force to be assembled in the Indian Ocean since at least World War II and the most impressive array of firepower ever deployed to those waters. Two carrier battle groups remained in or near the Arabian Sea throughout the remainder of the crisis.

On the following day, November 21, a band of fanatics overran the Grand Mosque in Mecca. A mob in Islamabad, Pakistan, reacting to the

---

1. *The Iran Hostage Crisis: A Chronology of Daily Developments,* Report Prepared for the Committee on Foreign Affairs, U.S. House of Representatives, by Clyde R. Mark, Foreign Affairs and National Defense Division, Congressional Research Service, Library of Congress (Washington: GPO, March 1981), pp. 40–41. (Hereafter cited as *Chronology*)

news and to inflammatory rumors of U.S. involvement, attacked the U.S. Embassy, killing two Americans and two Pakistanis. This event coincided with the beginning of the Shi'i Muslim month of Moharram, which is always the occasion for mass flagellation, deep mourning, and high religious fervor. In addition, this particular date commemorated the beginning of the Fourteenth Century of Islam, giving it added symbolic importance.

The Soviet Union chose this date to announce, in a statement by Foreign Minister Andrei Gromyko, its "positive attitude toward the revolution" in Iran and to warn that no outside state should intervene in the internal affairs of Iran.[2] An East German diplomat let it be known that the socialist states would meet Iran's food needs should Iran become the target of an economic blockade.

On Friday, November 23, President Carter met with his senior foreign policy advisers at Camp David to review the situation. He let it be known to the press that the consequences would be "extremely grave" for Iran if even one of the remaining American hostages was harmed.[3] At the same time, and without publicity, a very blunt private message was sent to the leaders of Iran explicitly warning them of the U.S. intention to respond militarily if the hostages were harmed or subjected to trials. Once more the full array of military options was reviewed, and contingency planning was accelerated toward operational readiness if required.

Because only indirect channels of communication were available to the United States to send a private message to Iran's leaders, and because the power structure in Iran itself was so chaotic, it was impossible to confirm that the formal U.S. message was ever conveyed to Khomeini personally. However, there is no doubt that the message was received at a very high level in Iran and that its thrust was understood.

No Iranian official ever referred to the message, but perhaps significantly neither was its seriousness questioned—publicly or privately. Subsequent speeches by Khomeini continued to denounce the United States in the most vitriolic terms; however, he ceased his threats to execute the hostages. Instead, he focused on the Iranian nation's willingness to suffer martyrdom in the event of an American attack, warning that a U.S. military attack would result in the deaths of the hostages.

This was an important shift, and it marked a turning point in Iranian rhetoric. In the cacophony of voices emanating from Tehran, it was difficult to know with any degree of certainty whether a genuine change of policy had occurred, particularly since the Ayatollah and others chose to envelop any profession of moderation in the most inflammatory language. Nevertheless,

2. Ibid., p. 43.
3. Ibid.

the casual threats to the lives of the hostages that had been common in mid-November ceased to be a staple element of political bombast. Later, when one of the hostages developed a severe medical problem that could have resulted in death, he was hastily evacuated, possibly to avoid the danger of U.S. retaliation.

On balance, there is reason to believe that the U.S. threat of retaliation was received in Tehran, that it was considered credible, and that it was heeded by those in authority. If so, it was one of the few such instances in the history of the crisis. This episode suggests that Iran's leadership was not immune to threats of the use of force. It also raises the question whether military threats or a military ultimatum during those first months might not have convinced Iran to release the hostages and terminate the crisis.

The answer to that question illustrates the fundamental asymmetry of U.S. and Iranian objectives and underscores the limits of military instrumentalities in such an emotionally charged political environment. The Ayatollah regarded "Westernization" as the primary cause of the evils of the Shah's reign. The United States was viewed as a sinister influence that had diverted Iran from the path of Islamic purity. Thus, the eradication of ties with the West, particularly with the United States, together with the establishment of a truly Islamic state were the core values of Khomeini's revolutionary doctrine. The taking of the hostages served both purposes. By creating a total confrontation with the United States, it progressively severed the many links that remained from the days of the Shah. At the same time, it mobilized Iranian opinion behind extremist revolutionary objectives just at the moment when moderate elements in Iran were seriously beginning to question the principle of a theocratic state. In the defense of those central principles, Khomeini and his followers were prepared to sustain enormous sacrifices.

In his speech of November 23, Khomeini stated that the Iranian nation would gladly suffer martyrdom if the United States should attack. "This is not a struggle between the United States and Iran," he said, "it is a struggle between Islam and blasphemy."[4] Khomeini's willingness to risk the very destruction of Iran in the pursuit of revolutionary principles was repeatedly demonstrated as the crisis unfolded. Any lingering doubt on this point was definitively removed by the absolute intransigence that Iran displayed when faced with a full-scale military invasion by Iraq in September 1980. Despite massive losses, Khomeini steadfastly refused all offers of compromise and mediation, and Iranian forces eventually rallied to push Iraqi forces back to the frontier.

American objectives, however, were much more modest. There were

4. Ibid.

limits to the sacrifices the United States could reasonably accept in the effort to free the hostages. The President constantly had to weigh the welfare of the hostages and the defense of American honor against the risk of a widening war in the Persian Gulf and the attendant danger of drawing the Soviet Union into Iran. The United States had it in its power to force Iran into a suicidal conflict, but it was clear that Iran's "suicide" would undermine fundamental U.S. interests in the Persian Gulf and elsewhere. It was an uneven contest.

For Khomeini's purposes, it was enough to hold the hostages; it was not necessary to execute them or even to put them on trial. Consequently, he was susceptible to pressure on those secondary issues. In effect, the military option provided the United States with at least a limited veto over certain potential excesses of Iranian behavior. But it is doubtful that the application of military threats, however skillfully employed, could have persuaded Iran's revolutionary leadership to abandon core values and to release the hostages before essential internal political objectives had been achieved.

The Soviets Change the Environment

When President Carter stated publicly in late November that the release of the hostages would not "wipe the slate clean,"[5] he was expressing not only his personal view but also the view of many of his closest advisers and probably most of the American public at the time that America had suffered a grievance that could not be rectified merely by a return to the status quo ante. This deep anger was a constant and inescapable element of policymaking at the time, and it was fueled by the endless hours of television coverage from Iran, featuring interviews with disdainful Iranian spokesmen, punctuated with lengthy shots of the seemingly permanent mobs swirling outside the occupied U.S. Embassy.

As the weeks dragged on with no sign of progress, pressure mounted in public opinion and within the administration itself to take some action. In practice, this took the form of two parallel tracks, as Harold Saunders described in chapter 2. One approach focused on the United Nations Security Council, the World Court, and U.S. efforts to develop an international consensus for the imposition of sanctions against Iran.

A second approach involved the use of pressure on Iran, of which one component was a heightened level of military planning within a small circle of senior officials in Washington who met regularly in the office of Zbigniew Brzezinski, taking extraordinary precautions that their deliberations remained entirely secret. It was during this period that the rescue mission began to take shape as a practical possibility. A team was assembled, re-

5. Ibid., p. 45.

hearsals began, intelligence support began to take shape, and special equipment was developed specifically for the mission. Matériel for a military operation began to be positioned in various locations, and the operational lineaments of weeks of military planning began to come together.

The Soviet invasion of Afghanistan on December 27, 1979, abruptly altered both tracks—the diplomatic and the pressures (including military)—of U.S. Iranian policy. On the diplomatic side, Soviet truculence in the U.N. Security Council resulted in the vetoing of sanctions against Iran, and the United States was unable to muster the support of its allies to impose far-reaching sanctions in the absence of a U.N. resolution. On the military and strategic side, attention was directed away from the hostage crisis. The Iranian leadership responded sharply to the Soviet invasion, and the United States and Iran suddenly found themselves quite independently pursuing parallel efforts to mobilize opposition to Soviet aggression.

The Afghan invasion transformed the strategic environment in the region and provided a compelling set of reasons for seeking a negotiated settlement with Iran instead of pressing the situation toward possible conflict. As we saw in chapter 2, it was at this critical moment that a new set of possible intermediaries appeared on the scene, credibly offering the possibility of initiating a dialogue with the revolutionary forces close to Khomeini. Consequently, the military plans were shelved, and a new round of secret negotiations was begun that lasted until April 1980.

Military Pressure, Sanctions, and the Rescue Option
By March 10, the complex negotiating scenario developed through the efforts of the French and Argentinian intermediaries had collapsed. Nevertheless, President Bani-Sadr and his Foreign Minister, Sadegh Ghotbzadeh, continued to improvise desperately in an attempt to salvage the negotiations. No one in the U.S. government wanted to see the negotiating effort collapse, especially since the two Iranian principals had staked their political lives on the issue. So the process was nursed along for nearly a full month, until April 7, when President Carter announced the imposition of an economic embargo and other sanctions.

During this same period, official attention once again began to shift toward the possibility of military action. Operational planning had proceeded throughout the intervening months, and the rescue mission in particular was taking shape as more than a desperation measure. As the negotiating process faltered and then collapsed entirely, Zbigniew Brzezinski took the initiative to place the military options back in the center of the policymaking process. On March 22 at Camp David, President Carter and all his key aides received "a full briefing . . . about the latest plans for a rescue mission," and the President "authorized the flight of a small airplane to the site (of the proposed staging area in Iran) for a close visual observation."[6]

The shift back toward the military option was an acknowledgment of the fact that, once the secret negotiations had definitively collapsed, Washington's policy choices were quite limited:

• The U.S. government could choose to do nothing at all, in the belief that Iran would eventually release the hostages when Khomeini concluded there was no further benefit to be gained by holding them.

• A patient new effort could be launched to locate alternative channels of communication to Khomeini and the ruling circles in Tehran, with the objective of launching a new round of negotiations.

• The United States could impose additional unilateral sanctions on Iran, recognizing that these would be essentially symbolic, since all trade and other state-to-state activity had already ceased.

• An international effort could be launched to persuade other nations to impose sanctions on Iran in the absence of a U.N. resolution.

• The United States could unilaterally extend the scope of economic sanctions by a blockade of Iranian ports or by selectively mining Iranian harbors.

• An independent effort could be launched to extract the hostages forcibly by a rescue mission.

• A punitive military action could be carried out against selected Iranian targets, for example, refineries, rail facilities, power stations, docks.

The first two choices, which would have required the Carter Administration to exercise quiet patience while seeking new channels of communication to Tehran, were supported only by Secretary of State Vance. Then and later, Vance argued that, once an elected Majlis was in place, Iran would find that the hostages were becoming an intolerable burden and would begin to seek ways of resolving the crisis. As he expressed it later: "Our only realistic course was to keep up the pressure on Iran while we waited for Khomeini to determine that the revolution had accomplished its purpose, and that the hostages were of no further value. As painful as it would be, our national interests and the need to protect the lives of our fellow Americans dictated that we continue to exercise restraint."[7]

That view did not prevail. Five months had been spent working through the United Nations, with the international community, with intermediaries, and with a negotiating scenario consciously designed to give

6. Jimmy Carter, *Keeping Faith: Memoirs of a President* (New York: Bantam Books, 1982), p. 501.
7. Cyrus R. Vance, *Hard Choices: Critical Years in America's Foreign Policy* (New York: Simon and Schuster, 1983), p. 408.

Iran a dignified way out of the impasse without sacrificing fundamental U.S. honor and interests. In each instance, these had been rejected contemptuously by Iran's revolutionary leadership. President Carter made it very clear to his advisers that he was unwilling to sit passively for another three or four months in the vague hope that the revolutionary chaos in Iran would eventually resolve itself.

This deep sense of anger and frustration was shared by most of the President's advisers and by much of the American public. I recall vividly my own experience in April after the last shreds of the negotiating effort were swept away in a new statement by Khomeini. As usual, I arrived early at the White House to review the latest message traffic and then have breakfast in the staff mess. At eight in the morning, I wrote a memorandum that began: "The hawks are flying. I had two unsolicited suggestions (from White House staff members) for a blockade of Iran before breakfast this morning."

Similarly, the search for new negotiating channels was viewed as the functional equivalent of doing nothing. Obviously Washington would remain alert for any signals coming from Tehran, but having enlisted the President and Foreign Minister of Iran in an unsuccessful effort to solve the problem, it was difficult to believe that a new negotiating track was likely to appear in the near future.

The strategy adopted during the first two weeks of April 1980 was a combination of all except the first and the last of the policy choices listed above. Doing nothing was rejected, as was a punitive military strike. The former was considered too little; the latter too much. A punitive strike, it was believed, would put the hostages' lives in danger and would risk pushing the new Iranian regime into the arms of the USSR.

As we saw in chapter 2, President Carter announced on April 7 the breaking of diplomatic relations with Iran, a total economic embargo, an inventory of frozen Iranian assets in the United States, cancellation of all outstanding entry visas for Iranians, and expulsion of remaining Iranian diplomatic officials. The President added that, if the hostages were not promptly released, "other action" would follow.

At the same time, a major international effort was undertaken, largely through the Department of State, to persuade other nations—particularly America's allies in Europe and Japan—to join the United States in an economic embargo. The Europeans were extremely reluctant to sever their own economic relations with Tehran. As a means of bolstering European resolve, Washington let it be known through a veritable torrent of leaks, public hints, and private statements that the alternative would be a unilateral interruption of Iranian commerce through some military action, specifically the mining of Iranian ports. The Europeans and Japanese could read for themselves the grim mood in Washington, and by mid-April they had begun to move toward the adoption of a package of sanctions that were useful, although much less stringent than the United States had sought.

This flurry of diplomatic activity in turn provided an effective diversion from the preparations to launch a rescue raid. The decision to proceed with the operation was taken by President Carter on April 11, and it was scheduled to occur on the Iranian weekend evening of Thursday, April 24.

The Rescue Mission

There was never any illusion on the part of anyone close to the planning of the rescue mission that it was anything but a high-risk venture. It was understood to be a highly complex and daring raid that would not only strain the limits of technology but would also press the endurance of men and machines to the outer margins. As Secretary of Defense Harold Brown commented in his press conference after the mission failed, there was no other country in the world that could even have attempted such an operation.

Ironically, the very improbability of attempting to extract more than fifty prisoners from a well-guarded site in the center of a major, hostile city halfway around the globe and more than 500 miles from the nearest available military facility was a factor in the plan's favor. One of the students in the embassy, when informed on Friday of the rescue attempt the previous evening, was reported to have replied: "Impossible!" In fact, the student captors had long before concluded that a rescue attempt was not feasible, and they had relaxed their security to such a degree that a raid was no longer the unattainable goal it had appeared in the earliest days when the student guards were suspicious of every shadow.

Millions of words have been written about the abortive raid. This brief account cannot possibly deal with all the issues that have been raised. Instead, it provides a description of the general concept of the operation, a skeleton account of the actual events, and some summary observations.

The rescue was designed to be conducted in a series of related steps, each of which would be reversible without escalation and with minimum casualties should something go wrong. The need to be able to terminate and withdraw at any point, together with the need for absolute secrecy, added to the complexity and difficulty of both planning and execution. The first stage of the plan involved the positioning of men, matériel, and support equipment at key locations in the Middle East and Indian Ocean. This movement had to be accomplished under the cover of other routinely scheduled activities to avoid signaling that an operation was being prepared. As a matter of security, the bulk of this matériel was held back until political authorization was granted to proceed with the operation. The practical effect of

Iran and the Desert Rendezvous

this decision was to extend the time lapse between the decision and the actual launching of the raid.

The insertion of the force into Iran was a grueling and technically difficult operation. Under cover of darkness, eight RH-53D helicopters and six C-130 aircraft were to depart from different locations, fly into Iran, and rendezvous at an airstrip some 500 miles inland. This airstrip, near the small town of Tabas, had been secretly prepared in advance and was known as "Desert I" in the plan. At Desert I, the helicopters were to be refueled and loaded with the men and equipment transported by the fixed-wing aircraft. Following the refueling and loading, the C-130s would leave Iran. The helicopters, still under cover of darkness, would proceed to a remote site in the mountains above Tehran, where they would be camouflaged and remain in hiding throughout the following day. This delay was required to insure that the assault on the embassy itself could be carried out under the cover of darkness. Because of the distances involved, it was impossible to insert the necessary forces, release the hostages, and depart in a single night.

For the nonspecialist, it is difficult to appreciate the demands this critical first phase of the operation placed on men, equipment, and technology. Simply flying 600 miles nonstop over sea and land in a helicopter is a remarkable feat. To do so at night, without lights, in complete radio silence, and at very low altitude is quite simply an heroic achievement. Many of those associated with planning the rescue mission believed—quite rightly as it turned out—that this was the most difficult segment of the entire operation.

Assuming the successful insertion of the team and its survival undetected during the following day, the actual rescue operation would be conducted under cover of darkness on the following night. The entry of the team into Tehran would be in local vehicles to attract minimum attention, with the helicopters making the briefest possible appearance to pick up the team and the hostages. The helicopters would then fly to an abandoned airfield near Tehran (called "Desert II" in the plan), where they would rendezvous with transport aircraft. The helicopters would be abandoned, and the personnel would be flown out of the country under heavy U.S. air cover.

A great deal of attention has been focused on the actual assault on the embassy, where many believe there would have been an unacceptable loss of life among the hostages. The truth will never be known, but there is good reason to believe that these fears were exaggerated. The success of the entry into the embassy depended almost entirely on surprise. If the students guarding the embassy were alerted to the operation in advance, the risks to the lives of the hostages would have been very great, probably unacceptably so. If, however, the first twenty-four hours passed without detection of the team *as part of a rescue attempt,* the odds would have shifted substantially in favor of a successful extraction of the hostages with minimum loss of life.

It must be remembered that the student guards were in fact students, not trained military personnel. After nearly six months of guard duty, activities had settled into a comfortable and generally relaxed routine. How would these individuals react in the wee hours of a weekend night when confronted suddenly and without warning by seasoned combat troops?

No one could say with certainty that the students would not react by immediately beginning to shoot the prisoners they had been guarding for months, but human nature and past experience suggest otherwise. There was a curious parallel only a week after the rescue attempt, when a group of terrorists invaded the Iranian Embassy in downtown London and held its

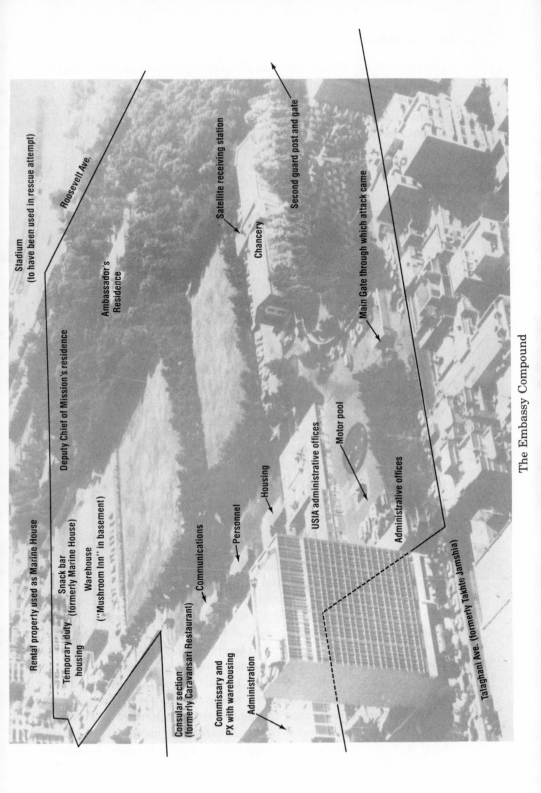

Stadium
(to have been used in rescue attempt)

Roosevelt Ave.

Rental property used as Marine House

Temporary duty housing

Snack bar (formerly Marine House)

Warehouse ("Mushroom Inn" in basement)

Deputy Chief of Mission's residence

Ambassador's Residence

Satellite receiving station

Chancery

Second guard post and gate

Main Gate through which attack came

Communications

Consular section (formerly Caravansari Restaurant)

Personnel

Housing

USIA administrative offices

Motor pool

Administrative offices

Commissary and PX with warehousing

Administration

Talaghani Ave. (formerly Takhte Jamshia)

The Embassy Compound

occupants hostage. On the sixth day of the seige, in broad daylight, with the terrorists on guard and alert, and with crowds and TV cameras filling the streets below, a small group of British commandos suddenly attacked and overcame the five terrorists with no loss of life to the hostages. Would a U.S. commando team have achieved the same success, striking without warning in the middle of the night in Tehran? We can only speculate.

The actual rescue mission failed long before it arrived at the embassy walls. Eight helicopters took off from the carrier USS *Nimitz* in the evening of April 24. Some two hours into the flight, while over Iranian territory, helicopter number 6 of the formation began receiving warning signals in the cockpit of a possible impending rotor blade failure. The pilot landed and, in accordance with normal operating procedures, abandoned his craft. The crew was picked up by one of the other helicopters and the flight continued.

The warning signal on the RH-53D helicopter is intended to provide advance warning of a crack in the rotor blade. However, it can be triggered by a number of nonthreatening circumstances. In the flight history of this aircraft, a total of forty-three warning light episodes had occurred. Subsequent investigation revealed that in none of those cases—or in any other case in the 38,000 hours of total flight experience with the RH-53D—had a rotor crack actually been present. Even if a crack is present, it does not prevent the craft from flying for a considerable period of time. Peacetime safety regulations prescribe that an RH-53D not fly more than five hours after appearance of a warning light. At the time this helicopter was abandoned, the craft was approximately three hours from Desert I.

Shortly after this event, the helicopter flight unexpectedly encountered a cloud of suspended dust, making visual observation extremely difficult. Since the helicopters were observing strict communications silence and were unable to maintain contact with each other visually, they became separated. The flight broke out of the dust cloud, only to encounter another shortly thereafter that was more dense than the first. Because of the dense, swirling dust, the helicopters were forced to rely almost entirely on the inertial navigation equipment and instruments specially designed for this operation. Approximately four hours into the flight, helicopter number 5 began to experience malfunction of essential flight instruments. The pilot reversed course, flew back for more than two hours through the dust cloud, and returned safely to the carrier. The crew of helicopter number 5 was unaware that, at the moment when this decision was taken, they were only twenty-five minutes from the end of the dust cloud and that the weather conditions at Desert I itself, less than one hour away, were clear.

At approximately the same moment when helicopter 5 reversed course, number 2 was beginning to experience hydraulic problems. Number 2 continued on to the rendezvous site and arrived safely. However, inspection after arrival revealed that a hydraulic leak had occurred, leading to contamination of the hydraulic system and the failure of a pump. Repair of this malfunction required not only replacement of the pump but a thorough flushing of the entire hydraulic system, a process that could not be accomplished at the desert site. The helicopter would have to be abandoned.

At this stage, the mission commander at Desert I was faced with a critical situation. Because of the dust storms, the helicopters had arrived as much as eighty-five minutes late. Dawn was fast approaching, and he had only five workable helicopters. It had been determined in advance that a minimum of six helicopters was required in order to proceed with the second stage and to assure the availability of sufficient lift to conduct the actual mission the following night. As a consequence, the mission commander at the site determined that the operation should be aborted. This decision was relayed to the White House, where President Carter approved, and the force prepared to withdraw. During the refueling operation preparatory to withdrawal, one helicopter collided with the C-130 refueling aircraft, which immediately burst into flames. Eight crew members died, and five others were wounded. The remaining helicopters were abandoned, and the force withdrew on board the C-130s.

At 1:00 A.M. on the morning of April 25, the White House issued an announcement that a rescue mission had been attempted, and President Carter later went on national television to take personal responsibility for the failure. The purpose of the announcement and its timing were intended to insure that Iran would not mistake the events at Desert I for an invasion attempt and retaliate against the hostages. From all accounts, Iran became aware of the raid only when officially informed of it by President Carter.

This account is in no sense a complete reconstruction of the events of that tragic night. The formal critique of the mission identified twenty-three issues of concern or controversy about the planning and execution of the raid.[8] Most of the issues raised in the critique and in the press, however, were largely subsidiary to what I consider to be the central issues of weather and helicopter availability.

If one wished to identify a single factor that was ultimately the cause of the failure, it would have to be the clouds of suspended dust, which had not been foreseen and which interfered disastrously with the timing and execution of the raid almost from the start. The flight path of the helicopters was, by necessity, across virtually uninhabited desert, where regular weather observations were sporadic or nonexistent. Satellite observations were used extensively but were incapable of identifying low-level dust clouds. Histor-

8. The "Rescue Mission Report" was distributed to the press and others in Washington, D.C., in a photocopied version in August 1980.

ical information about the phenomenon was available and was even incorporated into the weather annex to the operational plan; however, its importance was not adequately appreciated, and crews were not briefed. Ironically, two international meteorological stations that would normally have been providing a continuous stream of data about the region had broken down and were no longer operational, as Iranian technical services had collapsed after the fall of the Shah. If the seriousness of the dust problem had been understood in advance, there were relatively simple remedies available even on short notice to overcome the problem.

A great deal of attention has been paid to the question of providing a larger number of helicopters. Indeed it would have been possible from an operational perspective to employ up to twelve helicopters without unduly straining existing support capacity. The decision to proceed with only eight was based on exercise experience with the RH-53D over desert terrain and was consistent with the lean military profile adopted for the operation as a whole in order to preserve security and minimize the risks of detection.

Was it a fatal error? Accounts of the raid seldom point out that, of the eight helicopters sent on the mission, only one suffered an irreparable mechanical failure. Two others encountered significant problems, but their withdrawal from the operation was due to *pilot discretion* rather than mechanical necessity. Again, one may ask what would have happened if the two pilots had chosen to press on, rather than abandon ship in one case and reverse course in the other. There is no way to know.

Historically, American military forces have not demonstrated a capacity to plan and conduct successful raids. The reasons for this less-than-impressive record are not immediately apparent, and it would be presumptuous to generalize from the particular circumstances at Desert I. Nevertheless, there are some broad observations about the rescue mission that may be worth pondering in connection with any future small unit action of this nature.

The first, and perhaps the most important fact to emerge from a close review of the operation is that human judgment was decisively influenced, even overridden, by technology. The men who conducted the operation had all volunteered, and all were aware that they risked their lives. Yet in two critical cases, when machines failed to operate as expected the mission was abandoned. In one case, a warning light in the cockpit led a helicopter crew to leave the craft in the desert. In the other, a failure of instruments led the commander of the second helicopter to turn back when he was only one hour away from the objective. In both cases, the machines were technically capable of going on, though with reduced reliability. The decision to abandon the mission was a purely *human* response to technological uncertainty.

That is also a thoroughly American response. One of the first lessons learned by anyone who drives an automobile or operates complex equipment is that the erratic functioning of a machine or a flashing warning light is not to be ignored. As members of the premier technological culture, we have been trained from infancy to heed and even to subordinate ourselves to machines. They assert their precedence in the commonplace acts of our daily lives, as when an insistently ringing telephone is permitted to intrude on the most solemn conversation.

If either pilot had chosen to ignore the malfunction and to proceed with the mission, the nature of the decision at Desert I would have been changed. That is not to say that the rescue would have succeeded—only that the odds would have been altered slightly in favor of success. But in an operation skirting so close to the outer margins of human and technological endurance, even tiny changes in the odds are not to be discounted.

The second issue concerns the relationship between a civilian commander-in-chief and his professional military advisers. To what degree should a President have confidence in the professional judgment of his military advisers and to what extent should he question it? John F. Kennedy was widely criticized, especially within military circles, for insisting on civilian control over military operations in the Cuban missile crisis down to the most minute detail. Lyndon Johnson was similarly criticized for asserting presidential control down to the unit level during operations in Vietnam. Jimmy Carter consciously attempted to avoid these extremes. He spent many hours with the military planners and members of the rescue team, educating himself about the plans in advance. Once the decision was taken to undertake the operation, he left the details in the hands of his military specialists. Yet the postmortem of the operation by Admiral Holloway and his military colleagues is extremely critical of the planning, coordination, and training for the operation on a purely military professional level.

How does a civilian President assure himself that the advice he is receiving from his military advisers is based on the best possible military judgment and experience? No military leader wants to be put in the position of telling his President that his forces are incapable of carrying out a mission that is important to the national interest, and every President should be aware that the "can do" spirit so characteristic of the military is a mixed blessing. It may get the most difficult and dangerous tasks done, but it may also involve an almost unconscious tendency to understate the risks, once a commitment is accepted. Presumably it was his disastrous experience at the Bay of Pigs that led President Kennedy to insist on civilian control of every detail during the Cuban missile crisis.

In the case of the hostage rescue mission, there would have been great merit to an independent review of the plan by a small group of professionals in advance of the operation. An independent check by several respected experts not personally committed to the plan could have revealed weaknesses that unfortunately became evident only during the mission itself.

A military raid is by definition a high-risk venture that operates on the margins of the possible, relying on skill, daring, and a goodly measure of luck. When a raid succeeds, it is regarded as a stroke of genius. Hence the appeal. When it fails, it invites ridicule and the second-guessing of armchair strategists. All of those involved in the rescue operation were conscious of the risks of failure, and the dignity with which they accepted their bitter disappointment did them no disservice.

The larger policy issue of whether a rescue mission should have been undertaken at all, in view of the inherent risks, is a question that admits no easy answer. The negative consequences were tangible and of great moment. Eight brave men lost their lives. The hostages themselves were dispersed to remote sites, in some cases with considerable discomfort and danger. America's allies, who had been led to believe that their imposition of more stringent sanctions would forestall any unilateral U.S. military action, believed with some justification that their trust had been abused. America's military reputation was dealt a devastating blow. And the President of the United States was politically wounded, perhaps fatally.

Some severe critics of the operation have maintained that it may have been fortunate that the operation failed at the beginning. Even a successful operation, it is argued, would have entailed unacceptably high costs to the United States for three essential reasons: (1) There was a very high risk of an armed confrontation within Tehran itself, which could have resulted in very high loss of life among the rescue team, the hostages themselves, or the Iranian population; (2) The Islamic world might have reacted by sparking a conflagration with the West generally and the United States in particular; and (3) Even if all the hostages had been removed successfully, Iran might have retaliated by imprisoning a new set of American hostages, specifically the many American journalists who were present in the country. These are essentially the arguments that Secretary Vance advanced in opposition to the mission before it was launched and that subsequently led him to resign when his counsel was rejected by President Carter. For obvious reasons, there was substantial support for this position among journalists, particularly those in Tehran, who were furious to realize not only that they had been taken by surprise by the rescue attempt but that they might have been its victims.

Those who supported the rescue attempt did not share this assessment. They believed that, if the rescue team could be delivered without warning to the embassy, it would succeed in carrying out its task with a minimum of bloodshed. They did not believe that Iran had much support even within the

Islamic world for its actions and felt that most Islamic states would be secretly pleased to see the crisis terminated. If the operation could be conducted with little loss of *civilian* lives in Tehran, there seemed to be a reasonable prospect that most Islamic states would stop short of making it a major international incident.

There was indeed a significant risk that other hostages would be taken, possibly including journalists. In the weeks prior to the mission, the administration made it illegal to conduct even the most routine financial transactions with anyone in Iran. Paying a hotel bill in Tehran became a criminal offense under U.S. law. Repeated warnings were issued that individuals traveling to Iran did so at their own risk and that the U.S. government could offer no protection or support. However, journalists, because of first amendment protection of freedom of the press, were exempted from the travel ban (although they were supposed to report their travel to the Treasury Department), and they were accustomed to traveling in areas where there was significant risk. It is uncertain whether the Iranian students would have launched a massive search for other Americans to replace the hostages at the embassy, and it is not clear that the government would have acquiesced in such an effort had it been attempted. The only thing one can say with certainty is that the very nature of the crisis would have been changed if the original hostages had been spirited out of Iran in April 1980.

The views of both the critics of the rescue mission and those who supported it have tended to harden in subsequent years. It is an argument that is not likely to be settled authoritatively, since the operation failed before these hypotheses could be tested. However, even the failure was not without its silver lining. It must be reiterated that the actual policy choice made by President Carter was not between a rescue mission and no action at all. On the contrary, given the relatively weak response of our allies to the U.S. call for sanctions, even after some fairly severe armtwisting, a decision to impose a partial or total economic blockade by military force would have been virtually impossible to resist in the face of Tehran's persistent flouting of its responsibilities under international law. The rescue attempt, though unsuccessful, lanced the boil, removing the pressures that had been building with deadly inevitability toward a wider military confrontation.

Though unintentional, the failure of the rescue attempt created a quieter policy environment that permitted Washington to de-emphasize the crisis and allowed time for the peculiar rhythms of Iranian internal politics to play themselves out. By the end of August, an Islamic government consistent with Khomeini's theocratic vision had been installed. Very shortly thereafter, the Iranian leadership concluded that the continued retention of the hostages was a net liability, and they took the initiative to seek a solution. The fact that those four critical months passed without resort to violence must be attributed to the tragic experience of the rescue attempt.

Military Equipment as a Negotiating Element

From the failure of the rescue mission on April 25 until the release of the hostages on January 20, 1981, there was no further policy consideration of the use of military force, although contingency preparations for a possible rescue effort continued in the event it was required. In the last few months before the presidential elections, there were spurious reports that the Carter Administration was planning a spectacular military operation against Iran. This so-called "October Surprise" allegedly would be intended to win votes for the President. The story was a total fabrication. It was promptly denied by the White House, and a number of responsible newspapers refused to print it. Nevertheless, the story received widespread attention and soon developed a life of its own.

The story was fueled and embellished by developments in Iran, particularly after Khomeini outlined the possible terms of a settlement in the course of a long, rambling speech on September 12. The Iraqi invasion of Iran's Khuzestan Province on September 22 sparked new speculation about a possible deal in which the Carter Administration would exchange military equipment, badly needed by Iran, for the hostages.

Some of these stories no doubt reflected genuine fears of some on the Reagan campaign staff that the Carter forces planned to pull off a foreign policy coup just before the election. As the date of the election approached, the stories and inventions assumed an almost hysterical note. Those individuals within the White House who were called upon to respond to each new story began to speak of the "daily denial," for it was an unusual day that passed without a columnist—usually one who supported the Reagan candidacy—providing a convincing new story of plane loads of military equipment moving from the United States to Iran. All of this may have been effective politics, for it discredited in advance any sudden breakthrough in the hostage situation as mere political manipulation. As journalism, it was simply shabby. None of the reports had the slightest basis in fact.

The contacts and discussions with the Iranians during this period are examined elsewhere in this volume, but it is necessary to touch on them briefly here in order to complete this survey of the military dimension of the hostage crisis. On September 10, less than three weeks after the installation of an "Islamic" government under Prime Minister Rajai, two relatives and a third close associate of Khomeini met with West German Ambassador Gerhard Ritzel in Tehran to outline the terms for a possible settlement of the crisis. The terms were remarkably mild—at least in comparison with past rhetoric. They included no demand for a U.S. apology for past crimes against Iran and no insistence on a trial of the hostages. Two days later, Khomeini repeated the terms essentially verbatim in what was obviously an inserted passage in an otherwise unremarkable speech. President Carter nominated Deputy Secretary of State Warren Christopher to meet with an Iranian representative in Germany, and a position paper was prepared for those talks, which occurred on September 16 and 18.

Throughout the late summer and fall of 1980, the Carter Administration had been approached by private individuals claiming to speak for the Iranian authorities and seeking military spare parts and equipment. Washington was also aware that Iran was actively seeking military items in Europe and elsewhere. Although there were hints that a deal might be worked out involving the release of the hostages in return for the release of military equipment, the evidence strongly suggested that these were private entrepreneurs who saw the possibility of some lucrative business for themselves. The U.S. response was the same in each case. Before any discussions, it would be necessary for the intermediary to establish clear bona fides as an authorized representative of Khomeini, and no arms or spare parts would be released to Iran until after the hostages were safely released. Neither condition was ever fulfilled, and nothing ever came of these shadowy contacts.

There was no reason to doubt that certain circles in Iran were genuinely interested in locating supplies for the American equipment in the Iranian inventory. Prior to the hostage taking, formal talks had been held with Iranian defense officials in New York about the vast pipeline of contracted and undelivered equipment that was frozen at the time of the fall of the Shah. In the month prior to the seizure of the embassy, as part of the effort to normalize relations with the new regime in Tehran, the United States had agreed to release a small quantity of spares. However, the embassy attack occurred before any deliveries could be made, and any consideration of arms transfer was dropped.

By the time Warren Christopher met with the Iranian representative in mid-September 1980, the military conflict with Iraq was escalating rapidly. As a consequence, the negotiating team anticipated that some assurances about supply of military equipment would be required as part of a settlement. In fact, the issue was raised briefly in the initial talks in Germany, and Christopher did not rule out the possibility that some military equipment might be transferred to Iran in the context of a settlement.

The specific equipment at issue, in the eyes of the negotiating team in Washington, was the matériel that Iran had contracted for under the Shah and that had subsequently been paid for but withheld, as a matter of policy, after the collapse of the Shah's regime. Technically, this equipment belonged to Iran. By September 1980 it consisted of several hundred million dollars' worth of assorted military items stored in military depots and ware-houses throughout the United States. A survey of this matériel was pro-vided to the team by the Department of Defense, and some contingency planning was undertaken in the event some or all of it might be sent to Iran. However, none of the matériel was ever moved or even consolidated within the United States.

The larger issue of a military supply relationship with Iran, beyond this inventory of frozen equipment, was understood to be a policy question that could be addressed only in the context of a wider political relationship after resolution of the hostage issue. In mid-September, there were press indica-tions that Iran might wish to reestablish such a relationship eventually; but that issue was never broached, either in the negotiations themselves or in the development of the U.S. negotiating position.

Iranian interest in retrieving its frozen arms and spare parts was con-firmed on October 10, when the Iranian representative requested, via the German Embassy, a detailed inventory of military equipment ordered un-der the Shah but not yet delivered by the United States. It was obvious that the Iranian government, in the chaos following the Shah's collapse, was unable to determine either the nature or the value of the frozen military pipeline. The negotiating team responded to the query with a very general message that identified some dollar totals but revealed neither the composi-tion of the military inventory nor the total dollar value. The objective was to whet their interest without relieving their ignorance.

Press reports from this period suggested that a debate was under way in Iran about this very sensitive political issue; however, signs began to ap-pear that the Iranians found the question too hot to handle. When Prime Minister Rajai returned to Tehran from his visit to the United Nations on October 22, he was closely questioned on this issue. He flatly dismissed any connection between military supply and the release of the hostages. At the same time, the U.S. government was receiving unmistakable evidence that Iran was taking desperate measures to circumvent the boycott through middlemen in Europe. In each case, these semiclandestine efforts were halted by U.S. contact with the countries and the companies involved. The negotiating team continued to believe that military equipment might be an essential part of any final settlement, and the option was preserved. On October 28, during the campaign debates, President Carter mentioned that the United States would release military equipment that Iran owned if the hostages were released.

When the Iranian Majlis presented its formal terms for the release of the hostages on November 2, the document contained no reference to mili-tary equipment. However, the demand that the United States release all frozen assets and place them at the disposal of Iran could be interpreted as including the military as well as the financial assets held by the United States. The question was finally answered on November 5 when the Speaker of the Majlis, Ali Akbar Hashemi Rafsanjani, stated flatly that "we have decided not to import weapons from the United States."[9]

The negotiating team continued to hold in reserve a list of nonlethal military items owned by Iran, in the event the issue should arise. However, Rafsanjani's policy declaration proved to be final. In the three months of intensive negotiations that followed the November elections, the Iranians never alluded to the military equipment being held by the United States. One can imagine that there was a heated policy debate within Iranian inner circles on this issue. There was no doubt that the Iranian military was badly in need of spares in their desperate effort to halt the Iraqi advance. However, in this instance as in the case of the hostage crisis itself, revolutionary political aims triumphed over mundane pragmatism. Reopening a military relationship with "the Great Satan" ultimately proved too high a price to pay, regardless of immediate material needs. In the end, revolutionary purity was maintained, and the United States was spared an agonizing and controversial policy decision.

Declaration of War

In the long list of "might have beens" that emerged during and after the hostage crisis, the alternative that gained perhaps the widest attention and support among responsible observers was a formal declaration of war against Iran. A strong case can be made that such a declaration would have expressed in proper form the national outrage experienced by the people of the United States, that it would have strengthened the President's hand in dealing with the crisis, and that it would have increased the level of uncertainty in Iran to the benefit of the United States. There were three points of decision during the crisis when such a declaration might have been feasible or desirable. Without undertaking an elaborate assessment of its relative advantages or disadvantages, it may be helpful to review the reasons why such a declaration was never approved.

The first logical opportunity for declaring war on Iran would have been during the first few weeks of the crisis. There is little reason to doubt that such a declaration would have been extremely popular with the American people and the Congress. It was not, however, considered as a primary option by the President and the National Security Council. Throughout at least the first month the crisis was expected to be relatively short-lived, and the President and his closest advisers did not wish to take a step that might have irrevocably severed U.S. relations with one of the most important

9. *Chronology,* p. 373.

nations in the Persian Gulf or pushed Iran toward the Soviet Union. On the contrary, as noted earlier, the decision was made to exhaust peaceful remedies before resorting to the self-help provisions available to an aggrieved state under the United Nations Charter.

There is no doubt that a declaration of war would have removed many of the frustrating obstacles that President Carter encountered in his attempts to prohibit demonstrations, to control fractious Iranian students in the United States, and to take drastic economic measures, such as freezing Iranian assets. Nevertheless, the President found the means to take the steps he felt were required during those first weeks, and the image of the United States as a nation of laws, responding with restraint to an outrageous breach of international law, was extremely helpful in mobilizing world opinion and isolating Iran. On several important occasions that effect was of more than symbolic value—in enlisting the support of Third World diplomats to serve on the U.N. Commission that went to Iran; in seeking private and credible channels of communications with Iranian revolutionary authorities; in shaking the confidence of a committed revolutionary such as Mohammed Rajai when he visited the U.N. session and discovered that the entire world was opposed to Iran's actions; and, most importantly, in retaining the invaluable assistance of Algeria in conducting the arduous and delicate final negotiations. None of these would have been possible if the United States had not projected an image of balance and restraint in its initial response to provocation.

Once the initial decision had been taken to seek peaceful redress through the United Nations and the World Court, the question of a declaration of war did not again arise until early January 1980, when the Security Council resolution on sanctions was vetoed by the Soviet Union. As indicated previously, American decision-making at that time was overwhelmingly influenced by the Soviet invasion of Afghanistan. A U.S. declaration of war against Iran at that juncture would have disrupted the Islamic consensus building against the Soviet Union and would have provided the U.S.S.R. with a golden opportunity to pose as the protector of regional states against the "aggressive" designs of the United States.

The third decision point came in late March and early April 1980, when the secret negotiations collapsed and the United States moved to impose new sanctions on Iran. During this period, the option of declaring war was seriously discussed in the White House, although it was not, to the best of my knowledge, presented as a recommendation to President Carter. The reluctance to move toward a declaration of war at that stage was conditioned largely by the anticipated reactions of the Congress. The crisis was by that time five months old, and there had been ample time for reflection and second thoughts. Although there was a mood of militancy rising in the country, there was also a deep sense of concern within the Congress and elsewhere about the dangers of involving the United States in a shooting war in the Middle East. There were also vivid memories of the Tonkin Gulf Resolution. In the congressional hearings that certainly would have preceded any vote on a declaration of war, the elected representatives could scarcely have overlooked the point that they were waiving their rights under the War Powers Act to review presidential actions. In effect, a declaration of war would have given the President a blank check to take actions of the most far-reaching character, not only in Iran but even in the domestic economy.

It was feared in the White House that a declaration of war would be met with a burst of initial enthusiasm, followed by severe second doubts and internal debate, which would not only fail to strengthen the President's hand but conceivably could even splinter the spirit of national unity that had prevailed throughout the ordeal. In short, since the declaration of war was neither essential to the pursuit of U.S. policy nor likely to change dramatically the circumstances of the hostages, it was concluded that the better part of valor would be to avoid the exercise entirely. In retrospect, that judgment appears valid.

Were the Choices Right?

This account has attempted to clarify the role of military options during the hostage crisis and to explain some of the reasons why these options were either accepted or rejected by the Carter Administration. The key point to be made is that the military options were an integral, if generally imperceptible, element in the decision-making process throughout the crisis. At each critical turning point, the knowledge that coercive instruments were available influenced policy decisions, occasionally in subtle and unexpected ways.

Some will conclude that a more vigorous application of force would have better served essential American interests. Others may believe that even the limited use of force employed was ill-advised. The strategy of the Carter Administration led to the safe release of all the hostages and the conclusion of a framework agreement to resolve the vast array of economic and legal conflicts created by the emergence of a revolutionary regime in Tehran. However, it required 444 days for the strategy to succeed—a length of time many would regard as unacceptably humiliating to a great power.

Could a different strategy—relying on a greater, lesser, or more imaginative use of force—have resulted in an earlier resolution of the crisis and less corrosion to American self-esteem? The answer to that fundamental question cannot be a simple one. It must be rooted in a firm understanding of the strategic and psychological context in which decisions were taken, as well as the political and moral dilemmas encountered in dealing with a society in the throes of revolutionary upheaval.

American performance during the hostage crisis revealed no shortage of public lapses, errors in timing and judgment, and failures of execution, the most tragic of which was the aborted rescue mission. With regard to negotiating strategy, it can be argued that a greater degree of public reticence on the part of the President and his chief advisers might have heightened uncertainties in Tehran and created doubts about possible U.S. use of force.

By openly proclaiming the hostages' physical safety as the central concern of U.S. policy and by focusing almost exclusively on diplomatic rather than military instrumentalities during the first critical months, the United States may have unnecessarily relinquished a useful psychological weapon. Khomeini and others were able to conclude rather early in the crisis that, as long as the hostages remained physically safe, the United States would limit its response primarily to the realm of economic sanctions and international public opinion. Iran was of course prepared to suffer extraordinary economic and diplomatic losses in the pursuit of revolutionary political objectives.

There is no convincing evidence that Khomeini and the radical students would have yielded to direct military threats. Nevertheless, a case can be made that one of the elements of a U.S. negotiating strategy should have been to generate as many doubts as possible in Tehran about U.S. intentions. At a minimum, that would have required "playing it closer to the chest." In terms of negotiating *style,* the United States might have benefited from the deliberate projection of an image of greater unpredictability— what one colleague described as "bloody-mindedness"— to lend an air of gravity to the economic and diplomatic offensive.

In the latter stages of the crisis, an element of uncertainty was injected into the situation by the Reagan presidential campaign and subsequently by the anticipated change of power in the White House. Although Reagan, while a candidate, had endorsed Khomeini's terms of September 12 as an acceptable basis for a settlement of the dispute, the Iranians were aware of his heavy emphasis during the campaign on military action. The uncertainty of what Reagan might do if elected was probably a significant factor in Iran's almost frantic rush to complete formal action by the Majlis prior to November 4.

After the elections, the negotiating team deliberately exploited Iran's uncertainty about the Reagan Administration by drawing attention to the fact that a new team of negotiators would take over, possibly with a new set of criteria for a settlement. It must be recalled that this sequence of events occurred *after* Iran had independently decided that the continued holding of the hostages was a national liability. As a consequence, the negotiating balance gradually shifted more and more toward the United States, with Iran becoming increasingly willing to make concessions in order to bring the situation to an end. In that context, Iranian apprehension about the appearance of a new administration in Washington was valuable in establishing a credible deadline and enforcing it. Iran's uncertainties about President Reagan were not responsible for Iran's decision to terminate the crisis; however, those uncertainties did help to strengthen the American negotiating position. It is possible that the deliberate projection of an element of unpredictable menace could have had a beneficial effect at earlier stages of the crisis.

That being said, it is not easy even in retrospect to construct realistic negotiating scenarios in which the messianic leadership in Tehran would have been persuaded to abandon what they regarded as sacred revolutionary principles in response to American use, or threat of use, of military force. President Carter never lost sight of the fundamental truth that, painful as it was to have American diplomats held prisoner in Tehran, there were other possible outcomes that were even worse. Bluster, threats, and tough talk, though emotionally and politically satisfying, carried a potentially heavy price tag. For a President in office, it would almost surely have become necessary at some point either to make good on the threats or else to admit that there was nothing behind the rhetoric. Either outcome would have entailed severe costs to U.S. interests.

President Carter was unable to devise a strategy to secure the prompt release of the hostages, but he avoided other outcomes—a shooting war in the Persian Gulf, great loss of Iranian or American lives, the introduction of a Soviet presence into Iran—any one of which could have affected the course of Middle East history and politics for many generations. When the political stalemate became intolerable, he approved a rescue mission. He gave the military planners everything they asked for; he resisted meddling in the operational details; and when the mission failed he accepted full responsibility. The mission was a failure, but it was a failure of military execution, not of political judgment or command.

To lead is to choose. The President of the United States largely chose to forego the use of the violent means at his command. Iran remained intact, but the hostages spent an agonizing 444 days in captivity. Partly as a consequence, the President was defeated at the polls, but the United States thereby preserved certain policy options whose importance may not become fully apparent for a generation or more.

Iran did not escape unscathed. As a precedent, it is safe to say that there are few nations in the world that would willingly undergo the political and economic punishment Iran sustained as a result of the hostage crisis just to prove a political point. If much greater physical damage had been inflicted on Iran, would the circumstances today and in the future be substantially improved?

The Iranian hostage crisis touched directly on American national values and raised questions of profound, even philosophical, importance. How does a nation or its leadership reconcile the contradictions between the protection of innocent human lives and the preservation of national honor? To what extent should a great nation be prepared to accept short-term humiliation in the interest of long-term strategic objectives that are themselves uncertain? At what point does such humiliation itself begin to acquire strategic consequences? It is questions such as these—honor versus life—that endow great events with qualities of heroic or tragic proportions, and it is the lessons to be derived from such stark choices that draw the historian, the policymaker, and the student back again and again.

These are not questions that will be answered so close to the event. As participants and observers, we are entitled to our opinions, but final judgments are the province of history.

4 THE ECONOMIC AND FINANCIAL PRESSURES: FREEZE AND SANCTIONS

ROBERT CARSWELL AND
RICHARD J. DAVIS

The fall of the Shah led to more than an upheaval in the political and strategic alliance between the United States and Iran; it strained and ultimately broke an entire range of economic relationships that had developed between them. U.S. companies serviced and supplied the oil fields of Iran and purchased large quantities of oil. U.S. banking institutions held most of Iran's dollar deposits and were major lenders (both individually and as members of syndicates) to Iran. U.S. suppliers of military equipment and services had very substantial contracts in process. U.S. companies were involved in numerous construction and manufacturing projects in Iran and operated major subsidiaries there. And U.S. firms were major sources of varying types of goods imported into Iran.

It is not surprising that each of these relationships ultimately was placed under severe strain by the revolution. Writing now, however, there is a tendency to forget that in its early days the final path of the revolution did not appear so certain. The Bazargan government was in place, and just as the U.S. government adopted a "wait and see" attitude on political and military matters, so it and the U.S. private sector did in the economic area. Thus for example, in February 1979, after consultation with both State and Treasury Department officials, the Federal Reserve Board of New York decided to honor payment instructions from the new officials of the Iranian central bank. Once this decision was taken, U.S. commercial banks, holders of substantial Iranian deposits, followed suit.

At the Treasury Department, consistent with procedures followed in other international crises, the departure of the Shah from Iran was the stimulus for extensive activity. Existing knowledge about the United States-Iranian economic links, including deposit and loan exposure information, was assembled and reviewed. The legal authority of the executive branch to act to protect American economic interests was analyzed.[1] And Treasury participated in a special working group chaired by Under Secretary of State David Newsom designed to monitor and maintain a range of options for dealing with the developing situation in Iran.

The nine months leading up to the seizure of the hostages on November 4, 1979, were difficult ones for those who had been doing business with Iran. Some contracts and agreements were blatantly breached by Iran; some were made impossible to perform; and others were left in limbo. Payments of debts were often late, and the long-range security of those obligations was, at best, uncertain. The taking of the hostages, however, became the death knell for all these relationships. Oil imports from Iran were banned; U.S.-run projects ground to a halt; subsidiaries in Iran were lost; Iranian assets were frozen;[2] and nearly all trade was stopped. A virtual economic miniwar raged between Iran and the United States.

Chapters 4–6 describe how the U.S. government conducted this miniwar. This chapter describes how it began and how it was fought, emphasizing the imposition, enforcement, and administration of the freeze, the pursuit (only marginally successful) of international sanctions, and the second wave of United States sanctions imposed in the aftermath of the failure of the first phase of political negotiations in early April 1980. Chapter 5 then examines how this economic miniwar was brought to an end—how and why the freeze was resolved as it was; the relationship between the government and the so-called bankers' negotiations, which John Hoffman elaborates in detail in chapter 6; and the economic aspects of the final negotiations from September 1980 through their frantic and improbable completion in the early morning hours of Inauguration Day, January 20, 1981.

Chapters 4 and 5 are not a moment-by-moment chronology of the fourteen months of the crisis. Rather, they are a discussion of the significant economic issues that emerged during this period, explaining how and why they were resolved as they were. The authors participated extensively in these events as Treasury Department officials, and that is the perspective

1. In a report published in July 1981 the House Banking Committee described this legal review as representing some form of serious consideration of the possibility of imposing a freeze in February. See House Committee on Banking, Finance and Urban Affairs, *Iran: The Financial Aspects of the Hostage Settlement Agreement,* 97th Cong., 1st sess., July 1981, Committee Print 97-5, pp. 5–6. The work undertaken during this period, however, constituted only routine staff work and such an action was not seriously considered at that time at the policy level.

2. When assets are "frozen" an order is issued instructing the holders of all affected assets to hold them as they then are. Any form of disposition—whether to the purported owner or a third party—is prohibited unless permission is received from the government. Permission customarily is granted in the form of licenses. A general license, in the form of a regulation, grants permission to all holders of property falling within its terms. A specific license is issued on a case-by-case basis.

from which the events are described. While there was often agreement over the resolution of these issues, in some instances there were real differences of view within the government. Chapter 6 on the bankers' negotiations discusses some of the same issues and events but from the viewpoint of a lawyer for one of the principal banks.

The Decision to Freeze

During the first days of the hostages' captivity, top-level executive branch attention was devoted primarily to diplomatic efforts aimed at both acquiring reliable information about events in Iran and securing immediate release of the hostages. The application of military force, discussed by Gary Sick in chapter 3, was considered and determined to be impractical. And the application of economic force, while recognized as an obvious policy option, was deferred until the nature of the events in Iran became clearer.

In Treasury's Office of Foreign Assets Control (OFAC), however, detailed planning to implement a full range of economic sanctions began immediately. This fourteen-person office, headed at that time by Stanley Sommerfield, had been involved in waging economic warfare since before World War II.[3] Sommerfield, an OFAC veteran of over thirty years, understood that the seizure of the hostages presented the type of situation where a President might ultimately look to economic weapons, finding they satisfied a need for action when military force was considered either impractical or unwise. Thus OFAC, with the approval only of Assistant Secretary Richard J. Davis, prepared necessary papers to implement a freeze—a presidential executive order, regulations, and a report to Congress. Since this work was commenced with no policy guidance, the first draft papers contemplated the broadest possible economic measures, including a freeze of all official and private assets, as well as a trade embargo. Once this was done, modifications could be made to reflect decisions on the kind of sanctions program that would be most effective in the instant situation.

Interest in a potential freeze escalated when press reports on Friday, November 9, suggested that the head of Bank Markazi, the central bank of Iran, had either quit or had been discharged over his resistance to a plan to remove all Iranian assets immediately from United States banks. Receipt of this information was accompanied by expanding indications that the seizure of the hostages was not to be a momentary crisis.

During the weekend of November 10, review of the draft sanctions

---

3. Among the programs administered by OFAC were the blocking of German assets in World War II and freezes and trade embargoes directed at the Peoples' Republic of China, North Korea, Cuba, Vietnam, Rhodesia, and Cambodia. The other principal members of the OFAC office during this period were Dennis O'Connell, Chief Counsel, and Susan Swinehart, Chief of Licensing.

continued. While policy decisions as to their scope remained to be made, at this point other Treasury officials, including Secretary G. William Miller, were briefed on the preparations under way. Secretary Miller also requested that the Federal Reserve Bank of New York contact the principal banks holding Iranian deposits to determine the status of the deposits.

On Monday, November 12, a group assembled at Treasury, including Secretary Miller, Deputy Secretary Robert Carswell, General Counsel Robert H. Mundheim, Assistant Secretary Davis, and OFAC Director Sommerfield and his Chief Counsel Dennis O'Connell, to review the scope of, as well as the mechanics of implementing, a potential freeze. The key issues, discussed in more detail below, were whether any asset freeze would apply to U.S.-controlled institutions abroad and whether private as well as government-owned assets should be frozen.

The next morning the President promulgated the first of his economic measures designed to react to the Iranian action—the prohibition of oil imports from Iran. Although it was widely recognized that the then existing nature of the oil market (there remained many other willing buyers for Iranian oil) meant the action was largely cosmetic, this step was intended as a clear public declaration that the United States would not be influenced in this crisis by Iran's traditional role as a major supplier of oil.[4] While no further economic measures were announced at this time, the option of imposing a freeze had been presented to the President, but he had made no decision on whether to proceed. So that he would be able to act on short notice if events so dictated, later that day draft presidential executive orders were sent to the White House Counsel's office and to the Justice Department for review. As far as the authors know, prior to the decision to freeze Iran's assets, no person outside the U.S. government was told that such a freeze was under consideration or had been decided.

Early in the morning of November 14 a news report was received that Acting Foreign and Finance Minister Bani-Sadr had announced that Iran was removing all its dollar deposits from U.S. banks. Upon being notified by the Treasury watch offices, Treasury Secretary Miller conferred by telephone with Secretary of State Vance and the President, and the decision was made to implement the freeze immediately. Calls went out, and by 7 A.M. the responsible Treasury officials (including those attending the Monday meeting, Under Secretary for Monetary Affairs Anthony M. Solomon and Treasury Public Affairs Assistant Secretary Joseph Laitin) were already at work. Key congressional leaders were consulted by telephone, at 8:10 A.M. the President signed the required executive order, and by 10 A.M. the first reg-

---

4. Another factor was a desire to take this action in the context of demonstrating American strength rather than wait for Iran to implement its own embargo, a not unlikely possibility.

ulations implementing the freeze were filed at the Federal Register. During the balance of the day, Secretary Miller, Under Secretary Solomon, and others called relevant foreign financial officials in order to explain the action taken by the President. A number of U.S. banks were called by Deputy Secretary Carswell, while officials of the New York Federal Reserve Bank briefed members of the banking community.[5]

While the Bani-Sadr announcement provided the final impetus for ordering the freeze, it was not its primary cause. The decision was based on a political judgment that the United States could not be continually passive in the face of repeated hostile acts by another country (taking hostages, attacking our financial institutions) without responding with some form of action. It is clear that if there had been no hostages, there would have been no freeze at this time. While protection of U.S. claims was one of the articulated bases for the action, implementation of the freeze had not been urged on the government by private U.S. interests. In fact, insofar as the major U.S. international banks were concerned, many of them had deposits sufficient to cover their direct loan exposure to Iran. The freeze was also not predicated on a belief that financial calamity would flow from the withdrawal of these deposits. In fact, most of the bank deposits were time deposits that could have been withdrawn only over many months and thus could not be used effectively in an attack on the dollar or on U.S. financial institutions.[6]

The Scope of the Freeze

When promulgated, the freeze order reflected two principal policy decisions: it applied only to assets owned or controlled by the government of Iran, and its reach extended to those assets in the custody or control of U.S. persons overseas.

The first of these decisions was a departure from the practice generally applied in earlier freezes (for example, Cuba, China, Vietnam), which also included assets belonging to the nationals of the country involved. The decision to limit this program was based on three basic factors, none of which involved any desire to reduce the impact of the freeze on Iran. First, the overwhelming percentage of Iranian assets frozen (then grossly underestimated at around $6 billion) belonged to Iranian government-owned entities such as the National Iranian Oil Company (NIOC), Bank Markazi, and other Iranian government instrumentalities. Adding private entities

---

5. Throughout the freeze the Federal Reserve Bank of New York played a major role in dealing with the banking community and in advising Treasury on technical issues involved in its administration. The principal actors for the New York Fed were James Oltman, General Counsel, and Ernest Patrikis, Deputy General Counsel.

6. Though this was not a major concern, protection of the dollar was occasionally articulated by Treasury spokesmen as an added reason for the freeze.

and individuals to the order would thus have resulted in no meaningful additional pressure on Iran.

Second, a freeze applicable to private Iranian nationals would have affected a very large number of Iranians living in the United States, many of them refugees and friendly to the United States. While licensing programs could be developed to allow some use of frozen assets by Iranians living outside Iran, past experience strongly indicated that trying to do so would create a bureaucratic nightmare and be impossible to police effectively.

Last, but not articulated at the time, was a desire to avoid having to deal with the Shah and any assets he might have in the United States. While there was never any belief that the Shah maintained any substantial assets in the United States,[7] this approach temporarily put off the day when the United States would have to focus on his possible assets within its jurisdiction. Also, any application of the freeze to the Shah could have been interpreted as U.S. acquiescence in the Iranian demand for the return of the Shah's assets or an indication that it was legally capable of doing so. From a policy perspective, either of these interpretations was obviously undesirable.

The second major policy decision was to extend the scope of the freeze to Iranian assets outside the United States. That decision had its principal impact on U.S. banks that had booked very large amounts of Iranian deposits in their overseas branches. Past experience with this issue provided little guidance in dealing with the question. While prior U.S. freeze orders had purported to reach assets in the possession of United States persons and corporations abroad, as a practical matter they did not catch much—countries like Cuba and China simply did not keep meaningful deposits in the overseas branches of U.S. banks. But in this case it was thought that over $3 billion was involved, and that proved to be a gross underestimate.

At the same time, there were downside risks to applying the freeze overseas. Our allies, particularly Great Britain, where most of Iran's overseas deposits were concentrated and where there is a long tradition of free financial markets, were likely to resent or oppose any U.S. effort to control deposits held by U.S. branch banks operating in their territory. Applying the freeze extraterritorially could cause an undesirable deflection of allied complaints from Iran's actions to those of the United States. Treasury was also concerned that overseas application of the freeze could adversely affect both the position of the U.S. dollar and future prospects of U.S. banks. Foreigners might conclude that investments in U.S. dollar assets or in U.S.

---

7. It was later determined that neither the Internal Revenue Service nor other governmental agencies had significant information on the location of the Shah's assets.

banks were too vulnerable to U.S. government action and switch their assets and deposits to areas believed to be more secure.

But the amounts involved were simply too large to leave untouched. If the freeze was to have any impact, the Iranian overseas deposits had to be tied up. In the end, on Treasury's recommendation, the President and his advisers concluded that they could not allow United States-controlled banks and corporations abroad to continue doing business as usual with Iran. It was also expected that the presence of the hostages in Iran likely would cause our allies to mute any criticism of U.S. action.[8]

The Structure of Decision-Making

For the fourteen months following November 14, 1979, the Treasury Department had the responsibility of implementing the freeze and the additional economic sanctions imposed in April 1980. This required decisions on an extraordinary variety of commercial and financial transactions involving many billions of dollars. OFAC had the primary operating responsibility.

Key operational and planning decisions were made or forwarded to higher authority by a relatively small working group chaired by Deputy Secretary Carswell. Meeting daily for over six months and three times a week thereafter, this group included Assistant Secretary Davis, General Counsel Mundheim, Russell Munk and Leonard Santos of his staff, Jerry Newman from the Office of the Assistant Secretary for International Affairs, the Deputy Secretary's Executive Assistant (first Paul L. Lee and later William Anawaty), and Foster Collins, the head of Treasury's Intelligence Office. Figuring out how to react to the available intelligence was another major purpose of these meetings. Secretary Miller and Under Secretary for Monetary Affairs Solomon, as the situation warranted, also attended.

Significant decisions obviously also had to be discussed with others within the executive branch. Initially this was done at the nearly daily meetings of the Special Coordinating Committee (SCC) of the National

---

8. Concern over allied reaction and the position of the dollar was a factor, however, in not fully applying a previously used OFAC theory—the cover account theory. Under this theory any (even non-U.S.) bank holding an Iranian dollar account overseas would be deemed to be holding a corresponding amount in the United States. This corresponding amount in the bank's U.S. accounts would then be blocked. It was concluded that if the United States attempted to apply the freeze to U.S. cover accounts of Iranian dollar deposits held by non-U.S. banks operating outside the United States, our allies would voice major (and not fanciful) complaints and that the risk to the dollar would be maximized. Moreover, enforcing such a freeze without access to the foreign bank's books would be difficult. The decision not to apply the cover account theory to U.S. dollar deposits at non-U.S. banks was made at Treasury.

Security Council, which forwarded recommendations to the President. Later an attempt was made to resolve the more technical issues through a special subgroup of the SCC organized to deal with the economic aspects of both the Iranian and the Afghanistan situations. When this system began to create bureaucratic delays in necessary decisions, a small working group at the Assistant Secretary level of representatives from State, Treasury, and the NSC was created to expedite necessary actions. Decisions of this group were deemed final unless additional questions were raised within two days by participants in the group.

Presenting the Freeze to the World

One of the most difficult early problems was how to explain and justify the freeze to the world and thus to minimize any sense that the U.S. dollar and U.S. financial institutions were unreliable or insecure. Throughout the freeze the U.S. government argued that the hostage seizure and other aggressive acts by Iran represented a unique set of circumstances unlikely to be repeated.[9] But there was a nagging concern about the possible impact of tying the freeze to protection of U.S. claims as opposed to attributing it principally to the political struggle with Iran. Some argued that relying on the former rationale might create fewer problems with Saudi Arabia and other major investors who themselves had sensitive political relationships with the United States. During his previously scheduled November trip to the Middle East, Treasury Secretary Miller thus stressed this nonpolitical factor. Ultimately it became clear, however, that the political nature of the freeze could not be ignored, and it was generally included in later explanations.[10] For example, in a December 27, 1979, letter to the International Monetary Fund (IMF), emphasis in defending the freeze was placed on the Iranian taking of the hostages and the subsequent U.N. and International Court of Justice actions.

A second issue was how the United States would publicly describe the relationship of the freeze to release of the hostages. While in the immediate aftermath of the freeze Treasury assumed that the assets would be unblocked as soon as the hostages were released, the public position was al-

9. The initial report to Congress referred both to the hostages and the need to protect U.S. claimants in the face of the Iranian actions. *International Emergency Economic Powers Act Authority Taken with Respect to Iran—Message from the President of the United States to the Congress,* November 14, 1979 (H. Doc. No. 96–226).

10. Some may question the need to "justify" our actions to the Saudis and others. For at least a decade Treasury has consistently taken the position that the presence of OPEC and other investments in the United States and in U.S. institutions does not pose a problem to U.S. security. Nonetheless, any action that could lead others to believe that it is dangerous to invest in the United States and/or in U.S. institutions could have adverse long-range consequences for U.S. interests and could not be ignored.

ways less precise, and as time passed some effort was made to separate the two issues. The December IMF letter contains an often used formulation of this position—*once* the hostages were released, the United States would move to resolve *all* other differences with Iran, presumably including the freeze.[11] Ultimately, however, as discussed below, release of the assets became inextricably linked with release of the hostages.

Dealing with Iranian Entities and Individuals in the United States
The day the freeze was announced, Thomas Shack, an attorney representing Iran, came to Treasury to discuss the freeze's impact on bank accounts operated by Iran or its entities within the United States. First were those accounts used by the Iranian Embassy, its consulates, and its United Nations Mission.[12] Here the United States immediately declared that, unlike Iran, it would respect diplomatic immunity and therefore authorize payments from such accounts. Licenses were then issued authorizing payments for diplomatic purposes and, in exceptional circumstances, for student emergencies.[13]

Periodic problems nevertheless did arise with these accounts when various banks refused to make payments from them, either because they wanted to hold the money as security for their own claims (even though offsets against Iranian property in the United States were not allowed) or for fear that these accounts were covered by various attachments (despite the fact that Treasury licenses said the contrary). At the request of the State Department, Treasury representatives, with uneven success, at varying times urged banks to continue operating these accounts. No effort was made, however, to have U.S. courts require banks to make these payments from these accounts, because of a general desire (discussed in more detail below) to avoid premature litigation over the President's authority, as well as an unwillingness to appear to be supporting the Iranians against U.S. commercial interests.

Licenses were also issued to allow various Iranian entities (the oil company [NIOC], the gas company, Iran Air, and various banks[14]) to keep

11. In late December consideration was given to what could be done to help claimants if the hostages were released and the freeze was simply ended. One possibility considered was legislation removing Iran's sovereign immunity and other roadblocks to private litigation. But the Treasury working group tentatively concluded that, in the absence of negotiations with Iran, no attractive alternatives were available for protecting U.S. claimants once the freeze was lifted.

12. The United States did not break diplomatic relations with Iran until April 7, 1980.

13. Treasury did require submission to it of monthly statements for these accounts. While individual transfers were not investigated, they were reviewed for unusual patterns.

14. Treasury also used its authority under the freeze to prevent the N.Y. Banking Department from seizing the Iranian bank branches operating in that state, believing that such action was unnecessarily provocative.

operating in the United States. These licenses generally permitted new money to be brought into the United States for designated purposes but allowed previously frozen funds to be used only in very limited circumstances. The underlying rationale for these licenses was a desire to avoid the elimination of all sources of contact with Iran. This policy continued until April 17, 1980, when, following the failure of the first negotiating phase, all Iranian entities except the Iranian banks were ordered closed and their licenses revoked.

An added motivation for licensing the Iranian banks was their role in transmitting tuition and support payments to the over 50,000 Iranian students in the United States. Shortly after the freeze the continuation of such payments was authorized.[15] There were some radical, and potentially violent, supporters of the Khomeini regime among the Iranian student group, but the specter of tens of thousands of Iranian students forced onto welfare or out of school was unacceptable. Not only would it risk diverting foreign sympathy from the hostages to the students, but there was concern at the State Department that ill treatment of Iranians in the United States could adversely affect how the hostages were treated in Iran.[16]

While issuing these student payment licenses Treasury did seek to retain certain controls. First, the licenses were for specific amounts, so that the need for repeated applications would enable a periodic review of the policy. And second, as a condition of the license, copies of every payment order had to be submitted to Treasury. These in turn were transmitted to the Justice Department for use by the FBI and the Immigration and Naturalization Service.

Dealing with Interrupted Commercial Transactions

The freeze interrupted a wide array of ongoing transactions and relationships, virtually all in some stage of decay. This required the government, in administering the freeze, to make a variety of judgments affecting the rights of various parties. Treasury policy was, to the extent possible, to protect legitimate U.S. commercial interests but to avoid actions that might adversely affect the hostages or reduce the future flexibility that might be needed to resolve the crisis.[17]

---

15. While individual student assets had not been blocked, most of the students had little money and were supported by Iranian government or parental payments transmitted through Iranian banks that were subject to the freeze.

16. In fact, during the weeks it took to negotiate the necessary licenses and convince some U.S. banks of the appropriateness of participation in the payment structure, various sympathetic media stories about the plight of individual Iranian students did appear.

17. As discussed more completely in the analysis of the final negotiations in chapter 7, another interest throughout was not to take any action that so removed existing rights or benefits from U.S. persons that it could be perceived as paying ransom to Iran.

One of the first issues to arise involved so-called setoffs. Various U.S. banks, with over $2 billion in loans outstanding to various Iranian entities, wanted to use the traditional banker's remedy, called a "setoff," to pay off the loans from the Iranian deposits they held, both in the United States and overseas. The freeze as first promulgated prevented such setoffs.

Various banks immediately telephoned Treasury requesting reversal of that policy, and on November 15, 1979, the prohibitions on setoffs against assets held outside the United States at the time of the freeze were removed. Shortly thereafter Treasury also ruled that the freeze did not bar moving claims against Iran to overseas offices where assets might be available to set off. In taking these actions the government was not, however, ruling on the validity of any setoff; that remained for resolution between Iran and the banks, either through agreement or litigation.

There was some concern within Treasury that permitting the banks to take setoffs overseas would provide them with an unfair advantage over other potential claimants against Iran. The setoff decision, however, was simply a recognition that, given the legal and political difficulties involved, it would be at best extremely difficult to use overseas assets in a general claims program. It seemed uncertain that the United States could keep these overseas assets frozen indefinitely and very unlikely that it could force their transfer to the United States.[18] On the other hand, by removing the obstacle to setoffs in this limited fashion and using these otherwise unavailable Iranian funds, substantial bank claims against Iran would be resolved. This would materially reduce the volume of claims potentially to be satisfied out of the U.S.-based assets pursuant to either a later claims program or any available judicial remedies.

Authorizing overseas setoffs had another benefit. Shortly after the freeze, the Iranians sued the U.S. banks in London and Paris seeking to compel return of the frozen deposits. As discussed below, a primary goal of the U.S. government was to delay these actions and deprive Iran of the use of the assets while it held the hostages. Allowing the setoffs enhanced both the banks' motivations and their ability to litigate and defend the overseas application of the freeze, something which otherwise was not necessarily in their purely commercial interests.

The initial decision on setoffs seemed relatively simple, but it led to a largely unforeseen set of issues that the attorneys soon called the "black

---

18. The legal issues involved in requiring a British-chartered branch of a U.S. bank to transfer its assets from London to the United States, where they would be used to satisfy U.S. claims, are far more troublesome than the already difficult issues associated with a freeze of those assets. Given the practical problems of accomplishing this in the face of the inevitably intense opposition of other governments, such assets simply could not be considered available for use in a U.S. claims program.

hole" problem. Most syndicate loan agreements contain so-called sharing clauses. Those clauses require any member of a syndicate that receives an unequal payment on the syndicate loan to share the payment proportionally with other members of the syndicate. Thus, when a U.S. bank set off its portion of a syndicate loan against a deposit, arguably it had to share the amount set off with the rest of the syndicate. If it did so, that meant most of the setoff went down the "black hole" to the other syndicate members, and the bank theoretically had to keep setting off until the whole loan was paid off, even though some members of the syndicate—for instance, foreign banks—might not want to be paid off. Despite requests for rulings from various banks, the Treasury stayed above the tangle and declined to rule on the legitimacy of "black hole" setoffs in the hope that the situation would somehow get resolved, as it did on January 16, 1981. Similarly, in order to maintain future flexibility, Treasury throughout the freeze also deferred responding to other questions concerning specific setoffs. (See chapter 6 for further discussion of the black hole problem.)

Another intellectual bog that the freeze created—one that unlike the setoffs has not yet been drained—involved so-called standby letters of credit. When a U.S. contractor entered into an agreement with the Iranian government, it was typically asked to provide a bank guarantee that would secure its receipt of advance payments and its performance. These guarantees, usually issued in the form of standby letters of credit, frequently provided that, if the contractor did not complete the job or deliver the goods as agreed, Iran could demand payment of a specified sum from the bank that issued the standby letter of credit.

A review of these agreements indicated that the Shah's representatives had been tough bargainers; on their face the Iranians had the ability to call upon the banks to make payments under these letters of credit for any reason whatsoever. It was estimated in November 1979 that there were over $1 billion in these instruments outstanding.

In the aftermath of the hostage seizure and the freeze, various U.S. companies—in meetings, telephone calls, and letters—sought protection from Treasury against potential Iranian calls of these obligations. While these companies had bargained away various rights in order to secure contracts in Iran, they argued in meetings with Davis, Mundheim, and Carswell that the revolutionary changes there and the risk of politically motivated actions as part of an Iranian effort to strike out at U.S. interests justified protective action by the U.S. government. The actions proposed varied, with some suggesting nullification of these obligations. Nearly all urged that at a minimum some procedure be developed that, in the event of Iranian calls, would not require them to provide funds to issuing banks, which would then simply create additional frozen bank accounts for Iran.

The commercial banks, however, had a different view. They had actually issued these obligations, and anything that prevented them from honoring calls pursuant to their literal terms would, they felt, cast doubt upon their standing in the international financial community. While they could accept—as the freeze generally required them to do—holding all payments in a frozen account in the name of Iran, they strongly objected to any further restrictions. Concern was also expressed by banks and others that, given the wide use of such instruments in varying parts of the world as a precondition to the awarding of contracts, action by the U.S. government undermining the security they provided could adversely affect U.S. companies seeking overseas business.

The U.S. government's desire to avoid irreversible actions at this stage made nullification of these obligations an unacceptable alternative. But it also seemed somehow inequitable to leave the companies vulnerable to a politically motivated attack from Iran, the effect of which would be to drain over $1 billion from various U.S. corporations. So, as is often the case in government, an awkward compromise was fashioned. Treasury ruled that in the event of a call by Iran on a standby letter of credit issued by a U.S. bank, the company involved could apply for permission to open a frozen account on its own, rather than the bank's, books, thus avoiding the need to deposit money in a bank account. Although this did not finally resolve the issue, it avoided immediate harm to U.S. companies.[19]

It was possible to produce a compromise on the letter of credit issue that fully preserved future flexibility. The next sticky issue that arose in the action-packed early days of the freeze, however, led to an early and occasionally regretted Treasury position. That issue involved the ground rules for U.S. claimants who wanted to sue Iran in U.S. courts and satisfy any judgments they secured out of the frozen assets. The freeze prohibited any action that would affect the title to the frozen Iranian property. Traditionally OFAC had interpreted similar prohibitions as barring nearly all forms of litigation, since such legal actions ultimately could have an effect on title to frozen property. Nevertheless, in the implementing regulations, Treasury had allowed the preliminary phases of litigation to proceed, including the filing of prejudgment attachments, while prohibiting such attachments from actually becoming effective. The entry of judgments affecting the frozen property was also barred. The true scope of the executive branch's ability literally to close the courthouse door remained uncertain.

On November 26, 1979, Treasury filed a regulation authorizing litiga-

19. Intricate rules were also developed during this period to deal with a variety of pending situations under commercial letters of credit associated with Iranian exports to the United States. These rules were the product of extensive consultation with bank lawyers and others concerning the array of such transactions interrupted by the freeze.

tion to the same extent allowed under previous asset freezes. The decision had three fundamental bases (which were ventilated in interagency debate):

1. In the midst of this crisis there was a strong desire to avoid legal challenges to any aspect of the President's authority, both for the sake of appearance and to avoid premature judicial judgments that might (contrary to executive branch arguments) place restrictions on powers that might be required ultimately to resolve the crisis. A total bar to litigation might encourage such a challenge and provoke a judgment on presidential authority in a less than ideal factual context.

2. Such an approach was consistent with past practice.

3. The U.S. government, particularly in the first months, could not assure claimants that, if the hostages were released, their interests would be protected by maintenance of the freeze or some other action. This made it fundamentally unfair simultaneously to prohibit potential claimants from putting in place available judicial protections that could become effective if the freeze order was rescinded.[20]

An underlying assumption of the litigation decision was that any litigation would remain in a very preliminary phase for the period required. It soon became clear, however, that neither the hostage crisis nor the freeze was to be quickly resolved. With the Justice Department playing the coordinating role, a Justice-Treasury-State-White House Counsel group was therefore created to develop a strategy for dealing with the ever-increasing volume of domestic litigation.[21]

The overriding policy goal was to avoid actions in particular litigations from affecting the U.S. government's ability to secure the hostages' release as quickly as possible. This meant avoiding judicial decisions on major issues. Any decision would be viewed by Iran, unable to distinguish judicial from executive or legislative action, as reflecting deliberate U.S. policy choices. For example, a judicial decision on whether the prejudgment attachments were valid, no matter what the result, would create unneeded risks. A judgment that they were valid—a step that a judge would be taking without any coordination with overall diplomatic strategy—would be perceived by Iran as an additional U.S. sanction. The contrary judgment, however, would provide the Iranians a benefit for which they had not been forced to bargain. It would also reduce the effectiveness of an important argument that the United States wanted to (and did) make—that the pending attach-

20. Treasury also believed and stated that this limited authorization would not later prevent it from ultimately exercising control over these assets if necessary.

21. The total number of cases ultimately exceeded 200, and although the largest number were pending in the Southern District of New York cases were pending in courts throughout the country.

ment litigation made it imperative for the Iranians not to condition release of the hostages on resolution of the status of the blocked assets in the United States. To avoid this problem the executive branch asked the courts to defer acting upon these cases while the hostages were being held.[22]

Not surprisingly, given the U.S. constitutional system, the judiciary did not uniformly accept the executive branch's sense of a need for caution. An attempt to consolidate all the cases from around the country in one court was rejected. And then, over time, various U.S. district court judges rejected pleas by the Justice Department that the cases before them be stayed.

The most publicized situation developed in the Southern District of New York, the site of the greatest number of cases as well as a substantial percentage of the Iranian assets in the United States. The judge, considering whether to confirm the attachments, acquiesced in some delays but ultimately rejected strenuous pleas from the Secretaries of State and Treasury, which were contained in documents filed with the Court, to continue to stay his hand. Instead, in September 1980 he ruled against Iran, finding that by imposing the freeze the President had somehow removed Iran's sovereign immunity. This ruling came at the critical moment when the first secret official United States-Iranian contacts were under way and was a most unwelcome complication in an already unbearably complicated negotiating situation. Not only was his finding about the intent of the freeze wholly inaccurate, but saying that the President had by executive decision removed Iran's immunity suggested that it could similarly be restored. The official U.S. position, however, tried to stress the contrary—the difficulty of the President effecting a transfer to Iran of the domestic assets without lengthy judicial proceedings.

While those of us in Washington were undoubtedly looking at the issue from a quite different perspective from that of a federal district judge, we felt that this action was an uninformed and imprudent attempt by a federal judge to override the judgment of the Secretary of State and President as to how to deal with a complex political confrontation with a foreign power—a classic exercise of the foreign relations power granted to the President under the Constitution.[23] Fortunately, the Court of Appeals reacted differ-

22. The government did not intervene in these cases. It wanted to minimize discovery burdens and did not want to be required to take positions on all potential issues in the litigations. For example, the United States wanted to avoid having to take a stance on the sovereign immunity of the Iranian government and other entities being sued, since the traditional executive branch position—important to preserve in other contexts—would have tended to support Iran, something the executive branch was simply not prepared to do. Instead of intervening, the government therefore simply filed suggestions of interest urging the stay of all litigation.

23. It is of course difficult to determine whether the district court ruling ultimately did have impact on the final settlement. At a minimum, it likely added to the Iranians' already great distrust of the United States position on the domestic assets.

ently and ultimately stayed the proceedings. Similarly, in those other instances where U.S. district court judges chose to act, the appellate courts supported the government's position urging a stay.

At various times during the freeze, in response to concerns that U.S. district court judges would ignore requests for continued stays, consideration was also given to issuing a new executive order seeking to bar all further litigation involving Iran. This might have assisted in avoiding the risks associated with litigation but would have generated other problems. First, it could have provoked a premature challenge to the President's authority.[24] Also, without some clear positive Iranian action, which was not forthcoming, it would undercut the United States' bargaining position by providing them with an unreciprocated benefit. While the issue was frequently considered within the executive branch, in the end such an order was not issued and, as discussed below, despite problems along the way the litigation was not a major complication to completion of the hostage release agreements.

One inevitable by-product of a freeze is that it catches funds intended for U.S. companies. Traditionally during freezes these payments are not allowed, since the operating policy has been that all frozen assets should be held available for possible claims settlement purposes, and preferences should not be given to individual creditors. Also, if too many exceptions are made to a freeze, the political purpose underlying it can be undercut. This was particularly true in the context of the Iranian situation, where it was recognized that allowing the release of even selected frozen assets would demonstrate an undesirable lack of resolve in the face of the Iranians' continued holding of the hostages.[25]

While we refused generally to allow payments from frozen funds, an effort was made to try to reduce the potential impact on U.S. companies. First, a regulation was issued on November 20, 1979, authorizing new money (that is, money not previously caught in the freeze) to come into the United States to pay obligations to U.S. persons. Such new monies were later also made immune from attachment. In addition, as a policy matter Treasury generally agreed to issue any necessary specific licenses that would facilitate payments to U.S. persons from unblocked funds.[26]

Limited payments from frozen funds were also allowed in exceptional circumstances. Initially certain payment transactions were allowed to be

24. Litigating the President's authority in the context of an overall settlement with Iran would be substantially more advantageous than doing so in other contexts.

25. In the latter part of 1980 lists of potential licenses that could be issued to release selected Iranian assets as a positive signal to Iran were developed. None of these licenses was, however, ever issued.

26. An exception to this was in the syndicate loan area, which is discussed below.

completed where the amounts were relatively small (that is, a check in the collection process for $50,000 or less). Later on, payments to U.S. persons pursuant to letters of credit were authorized on a case-by-case basis where the amounts were $500,000 or less *and* where special hardship could be shown. This provision, intended to benefit small exporters, proved to be only marginally helpful, since attachments—not only the freeze—constrained most banks from making these payments.

The freeze undoubtedly complicated payment problems and caused real hardship to some smaller businesses. While Treasury, through its licensing policy and other means,[27] sought to minimize these impacts, they are one of the inevitable costs of imposing a freeze, a fact not generally focused upon when deciding whether to take such an action.

Monitoring the Freeze

Another early requirement in implementing the freeze was development of the capability to monitor the affected assets.[28] It was immediately recognized that the dimensions and significance of this freeze required Treasury to take a more active role than normal in determining the amount and nature of the frozen assets.

One of the first areas to receive attention involved the monies owed by U.S. oil companies to Iran. On the day the freeze was announced, the Energy Department provided a preliminary estimate of slightly over $1 billion in such debts (the amount ultimately turned out to be substantially more). Treasury immediately sent a telex to all the oil companies making certain they understood that the freeze applied to all debts they might have to Iran and inviting them to a meeting at Treasury several days later. There the substance of the telex was reiterated, and information was obtained concerning the status of all oil shipments from Iran and all monies owed to that country. For the duration of the freeze period, reports to OFAC were required updating the information.[29]

A second area receiving special attention was the frozen assets held by banks, which accounted for the majority of all types of assets affected by the freeze. To monitor these assets all banks were required to submit weekly

27. Treasury, with little success, urged the Small Business Administration to be more active in assisting small companies being severely harmed by the confrontation with Iran.

28. Criminal and civil penalties apply to any violation of a freeze order. Treasury also received some assistance in monitoring compliance with the freeze, consistent with applicable rules, from the intelligence community.

29. Oil payments were made through letters of credit. Like others, oil companies, where they otherwise were legally entitled to do so (for example, because of defects in the letter of credit documents), blocked accounts payable on their books instead of making payments under the letters of credit into frozen bank accounts. Nonetheless, substantial portions of these debts were paid into frozen bank accounts.

reports to the Federal Reserve Bank of New York. These reports covered the amount of assets held in the United States, the amounts held in overseas branches, and the amount of offsets taken. While generally helpful, these reports proved only partially satisfactory, since, particularly in the first months, some banks reported on the basis of undisclosed legal theories that produced some underreporting. The reliability of the available statistics was improved somewhat by the later formal census of all assets, but, as discussed below, totally precise figures were not developed until shortly before the final settlement.

While Treasury gradually developed more precise information about the frozen assets, very little of this was released to the public. On November 14 an estimate of the frozen assets amounting to $6 billion was announced, and several days later this was modified to "in excess of $8 billion." Even though it was soon clear to those in the government that the dollar value of the frozen assets was substantially greater, no further numbers were disclosed until the final settlement.[30] Iran was uncertain about the amount frozen, and we had no desire either to assist them or to present as a precise number a figure that we knew to be imprecise.

Another issue that affected the amount of frozen bank assets was what rate of interest the banks should pay on the frozen deposits. A large percentage of these deposits were either demand deposits (on which no interest is customarily paid) or expired time deposits. Given the large amount of assets affected, by the time of the final settlement nearly a billion dollars was involved.

Few issues were more hotly debated during the freeze than the interest question. The banks had the use of Iran's money during the period of the freeze, and nondeposit bank claimants against Iran were not reticent in suggesting that interest should accrue, presumably for the claimants' benefit, on the money the banks held. Treasury was prepared to require the payment of interest as it had done in 1979 with respect to other frozen assets (for example, Cuba and Vietnam). But a decision concerning interest, depending on how it was characterized, could send a variety of signals to Iran—that the freeze would be of long-term duration, that the United States was building up the assets for vesting and to use them to satisfy claims, or that the United States wanted to assure fair treatment of the Iranians.

It was clear that interest would ultimately have to be credited to the frozen assets. Any other result would have provided the deposit-holding banks with an indefensible windfall. The problem was timing, since for a

---

30. The only breach of this came in the fall of 1980, when a former Treasury official discussed his understanding of the assets involved. While the information given was not accurate, because his estimate was significantly higher than $8 billion, it was widely reported in Iran and was not helpful to the U.S. negotiating position. *The New York Times,* November 3, 1980, p. A19, col. 1; *Kayhan International* (Tehran), November 5, 1980, p. 1, col. 2.

substantial period the sending of any of the above signals was not desired. In December 1979, however, a regulation was issued authorizing the Iranians to transfer their assets to interest-bearing status.[31]

Finally, in July 1980, Treasury issued a regulation in proposed form that, if adopted, would have required interest to be paid as of December 1, 1979. Treasury characterized this step as a possible precursor to application of the assets to satisfy U.S. claims. The regulation was issued in proposed form because of a need for additional information concerning the appropriate rate of interest and other details.

Opposition to any interest requirement from those banks holding deposits was vigorous. While it remained clear that, despite this opposition, interest would be required, it was determined that fixing the precise level should await the inevitable negotiations with Iran. The level fixed thus could be a bargaining chip available to the United States. The ultimate resolution of this issue is discussed below.

Finally, monitoring also involved ruling on the wide range of interrupted transactions, which produced, to say the least, a variety of complicated factual situations. Goods were caught by the freeze at various stages of shipment to Iran. For example, goods being shipped by one company were located in a European warehouse at the time of the freeze. While customarily the U.S. company had arranged for further shipment to Iran, arguably the buyers had the legal right to come to the warehouse and simply claim the goods. Throughout the freeze, we told the U.S. company to take no action and, as was generally the case, they complied even though they had a different legal view. And while Iran complained about not getting the goods, it never realized that it probably could have just picked them up.

The Freeze Overseas

The freeze also had effects outside the United States. Once the U.S. government decided to apply the freeze extraterritorially, it was important to avoid losing control over the overseas assets, particularly while the hostages were being held. To minimize the difficulty of obtaining at least acquiescence from foreign governments, on November 21, 1979, Treasury exempted from the freeze nondollar deposits held outside the United States. By restricting the freeze to dollar assets, the United States avoided the far more difficult task of, for example, convincing Great Britain not to object to a U.S. effort to restrict movement in British pounds at U.K. branches of U.S. banks.[32]

31. Banks might choose of course not to follow instructions. What to do in this situation was not decided but was left for future consideration. Banks following this course arguably made themselves vulnerable to future claims by Iran.

32. The substantive impact of this distinction was not significant, because most banks continued to hold their nondollar deposits pending resolution of lawsuits commenced by Iran in London and Paris.

The Iranians made numerous efforts to recover their blocked overseas assets. In some countries they commenced litigation; elsewhere they sought the intervention of local banking authorities. As it learned of each of these situations, the U.S. government sought the cooperation of the relevant governments in avoiding actions that would affect the general U.S. position vis-à-vis Iran. Whether as a consequence of these requests, or, just as likely, because of ordinary bureaucratic or judicial delays, all these attempts were unsuccessful. During the fourteen months of the freeze Iran did not succeed in obtaining one dollar of its blocked overseas assets.

One issue addressed soon after November 14 was whether the United States would seek to intervene in the litigation against the banks commenced in London and Paris. The United States decided not to do so; it was even more dangerous to assume in another country the risks of being a party to a lawsuit than it was in the United States. Ultimately, the banks, which aggressively defended the cases, were able to create a series of imaginative delays in all these cases, and adverse decisions were avoided.[33]

The Spreading of the Economic Miniwar

The freeze became but the first shot in what ultimately became an economic war that raged between the United States and Iran for over fourteen months. While often far less visible than the dramatic political struggle being openly waged, it did not lack for intensity, particularly in the early months.

One battleground in this war was the syndicated loans that United States and other banks had made to Iran and its various entities. At the time of the seizure of the hostages, while payments were often late and future prospects were uncertain, these loans (which involved over $3 billion) remained in place.[34]

The freeze, however, had several immediate impacts. First, it complicated the payment mechanism, particularly for those loans where U.S. banks acted as agents for the syndicate members. Some monies intended for

33. The only other litigation outside the United States involved the effort by some U.S. banks and companies to secure attachments (or their equivalent) in Germany and Great Britain. The most notable of these attempts involved efforts to obtain the Iranian interest in Krupp and the debts owed by the British Water Board to Iran. These efforts generated complaints from the countries involved, which did not like the continued extension of the U.S.-Iranian economic battles across their borders. Generally, however, because prejudgment attachments are a less effective remedy outside the United States, the amount of this litigation was not very great.

34. Some have asked why Iran, a country with substantial foreign reserves in the form of liquid deposits and gold, had engaged in extensive borrowing activities abroad. Two possible answers have been suggested. One is that Iran desired a sizable liquid reserve for contingencies. The second is that some Iranian entities that did not have access to oil revenues utilized external borrowings to fulfill their cash needs and capital requirements.

syndicate loan payments were themselves caught by the freeze. And while Treasury authorized new monies to be used for these payments, the Iranians refused to entrust additional funds to U.S. institutions. Second, as discussed below, the Iranians adopted a policy of not using dollars for their various payments, even though the loan agreements required payment in dollars. Finally, the Iranians created real doubts as to whether they intended to continue honoring their obligations. Shortly after the freeze, Bani-Sadr told the press that Iran was in fact repudiating the debts incurred during the Shah's reign. While Iran almost immediately sought to repudiate the repudiation statement, it never fully succeeded in overcoming the impact of Bani-Sadr's statement. And even in later statements, Iran qualified its commitment to repay its debts by excepting "Shah debt," an unclear term that it did not define.

In the beginning the banks split on whether defaults could or would be called on any of these loans. If defaults had been declared, the financial pressure on Iran would have been immeasurably increased. As a consequence of such defaults, over $3 billion in syndicate (and unknown amounts of nonsyndicate) loans would have become immediately due. Virtually every major bank in the world would then have had an arguable right to seize any Iranian deposits it held to set off against its claims; as a result, the freeze would have in reality extended to nearly all Iranian bank deposits wherever held.

While this scenario of escalating default was discussed within the executive branch, the attitude of other governments, non-U.S. banks, and a number of U.S. banks was to limit disruption.[35] Default was declared on a $500 million loan to the government of Iran where a majority of the participants were U.S. banks, but this failed to ignite a chain reaction.[36] There was simply a reluctance by the necessary parties to apply this kind of pressure to Iran. They were concerned both about the further isolation of Iran from the West and, more broadly, about the precedent of using international syndicated loans for political purposes.[37]

Both U.S. and foreign banks were unhappy about Iran's attempt to boycott the dollar and its reluctance to make payments through U.S. banks acting as agents for other banks in syndicated loans. In early December a foreign and a U.S. bank, at a meeting with Mundheim and Davis, presented

35. No formal decision was ever made by the U.S. government to seek the implementation of this scenario; the expressed attitudes of these necessary "players" made it an unrealistic option.

36. Although informed of the decision to declare a default on the loan, this action was not undertaken at Treasury's request.

37. As discussed below, other governments also were desirous of maintaining as good commercial relations with revolutionary Iran as possible, which for some involved maintaining a source for oil.

to Treasury a proposal whereby U.S. agents would be replaced by non-U.S. banks. The rationale for this was simple: it would make continued Iranian payments of funds to agents for all syndicate members (U.S. and non-U.S.) more likely. Treasury rejected the suggestion and asserted it would refuse to issue any necessary licenses. It similarly refused to authorize a U.S. agent to modify a syndicate loan agreement by accepting payment overseas in nondollars.

While these proposals certainly made commercial sense, the United States at this point was unwilling to take any action that would suggest to Iran that it was willing to make any substantive accommodations while the hostages were being held. Acquiescence in Iranian economic demands designed as hostile acts aimed at the United States could not help but undercut the U.S. position in dealing with the hostage crisis.[38] Instead, Treasury repeated its position that appropriate licenses were available to authorize Iran to use new funds to make payments to U.S. agents in accordance with the syndicate loan agreements.

Ultimately Iran chose to bypass all agents; to pay directly to non-U.S. banks; and to take what they were owed out of the frozen assets, which, as Iran knew, was effectively nonpayment. While the impact of this was less on those banks with Iranian deposits available to set off, it produced real hardship for non-deposit banks. This disparity, however, was not a consequence of government policy; it derived in some circumstances from commercial decisions concerning lending and deposit policies made by individual banks, with those banks that had made substantial loans without compensating deposits being in the worst position.

Iranian reaction to the freeze involved a series of financial measures that went beyond syndicate loans. In addition to boycotting the dollar as a form of payment, Iran sought to convert its dollar reserves to nondollars.[39] Both steps were apparently designed as a form of attack (which had no discernable impact) on the stability of the dollar. In addition, Iran sought to secure premium prices for its oil and in general to use its role as oil supplier to prevent U.S. allies from more actively supporting the U.S. position.

Both in response to the Iranian actions and to apply additional pressure on Iran, the United States in November and early December sought more active support from other Western nations and Japan. This was among the

38. While those affected by the economic warfare—bankers and businessmen—generally understood that all U.S. actions had at their core the struggle with Iran over the hostages, there were times when specific requests seemed to ignore this reality and focus only on the commercial needs of the parties.

39. This could be done only over time, since most Iranian reserves were held in time deposits. During this period, in order to shield its assets, Iran also began to invest certain of its funds through the Algerian Central Bank.

purposes of a series of trips by high-ranking representatives of State (Under Secretary Richard Cooper and Assistant Secretary George Vest) and Treasury (Carswell and Solomon) to meet with the leaders of various European governments and Japan.

Although this effort produced agreement on certain measures, the program developed must at best be described as modest. While offering strong public support and diplomatic assistance, U.S. allies remained at least as concerned about not adversely affecting long-term relations with Iran and the Muslim world. No agreements on a multinational freeze, on a cessation of oil purchases from Iran, or on the declaration of defaults on various loans were possible. Eventually, in December 1979, the following limited multinational measures were agreed upon:

1. No military equipment to Iran. This sanction was generally adhered to by Western nations, although Iran continued to obtain some military supplies from black market, North Korean, and other sources.
2. No premiums for Iranian oil. Although this was agreed to, for a number of months the United States had to intercede with Japan and to some extent Great Britain to ensure that this policy was truly adhered to by nationals of those countries that continued buying oil from Iran.
3. No new deposit facilities and no substantial increase in existing nondollar accounts. These were designed to reduce the ability of Iran to transfer its reserves from dollar to nondollar form. While some questions about compliance existed at the outset, in general it appears that these restrictions were followed. Determining the extent of compliance during this period was complicated, however, by the fact that the aggregate level of Iran's reserves was falling much of this period.
4. No new extensions of credit. This appeared to be generally adhered to throughout the period, in part because no one really wanted to lend new money to Iran.

The political impact of these actions was reduced, however, by the unwillingness of our allies to announce that they had been taken. While many of these items became part of the proposed U.N. sanctions (discussed in detail below), other countries were at this time simply unwilling, for the reasons discussed above, to have it known that they had undertaken any actions outside the U.N. context.

Development of Additional Sanctions
The next phase of the Iran-U.S. economic war was played out during the course of deliberations at the United Nations in December 1979 and Janu-

ary 1980. After the Security Council had called upon Iran in November 1979 to release the hostages and had set the stage for the implementation of U.N.-mandated economic sanctions, discussions were undertaken with other governments as to what the content of these measures would be.[40]

The U.S. approach in these negotiations was simple. It desired, first, to secure the strongest possible measures that would apply pressure to Iran. At the same time, however, in order to maximize the economic and political impact on Iran, it desired the broadest possible international support for any actions, and that inevitably led to compromise. Foremost among these accommodations was the omission of a ban on imports from Iran. Other countries were simply unwilling to deny themselves Iranian oil over the hostage issue. While these compromises, extracted by our allies as much as by Third World countries, produced an imperfect result, the agreed-upon sanctions, if broadly implemented, would have been a meaningful expression of international repugnance with Iranian actions.

The sanctions developed included the following:

1. A ban on exports to Iran, except food, medicine, and medical supplies.
2. The informal financial sanctions discussed above. Once again, however, attempts failed to secure a meaningful commitment to declare defaults whenever possible.
3. A ban on new service contracts. Because various countries were unwilling to abandon substantial ongoing property in Iran, these were ultimately deleted from the proposed sanctions.

The Soviet veto in the Security Council on January 13, 1980, however, prevented the adoption of these sanctions and stymied this effort to secure broad international participation in the campaign to apply pressure on Iran.

As discussed in chapter 2, after the Soviet veto the United States deferred unilateral implementation of the vetoed sanctions while the "secret" negotiations continued.[41] Finally, on April 7, after they failed, the President promulgated a new executive order implementing these new prohibi-

40. These negotiations were conducted primarily by Secretary of State Vance and Under Secretary of State for Economic Affairs Cooper.

41. While efforts were made to preserve imposition of an export embargo as an additional step the United States could take, during this period nearly all exports had already been effectively halted. The freeze complicated the payments system and itself prohibited transferring of property in which Iran, under the terms of export contracts, had "an interest." 31 C.F.R. §535.201 (1980). And a longshoremen's boycott effectively curtailed trade in authorized items, such as grain. Throughout the freeze, special care was taken to police potential exports for military hardware and for use in Iranian energy production, since these were the areas of greatest Iranian dependence on the United States.

tions. At the same time a census of all Iranian assets and of all claims against Iran was announced. This census was essential to improving the government's knowledge and providing the kind of detail essential to any future negotiations. This action was also presented as a signal to Iran of U.S. capability to apply the Iranian assets to satisfy U.S. claims if future events should make that necessary.[42]

The most significant policy issue associated with this new round of sanctions was whether these prohibitions should apply to foreign subsidiaries of U.S. companies. Traditionally a source of friction between the United States and its allies, the extraterritorial reach of the freeze had already created some problems with U.S. allies. Exacerbating these tensions at this time would, it was felt, undermine the more important ongoing effort to convince other governments to apply the sanctions to all persons within their borders. Thus while members of the White House staff urged stronger action, the President decided to follow the recommendations of the State and Treasury Departments, which were to forego a possibly broader impact and not to apply the new sanctions to subsidiaries incorporated outside the United States. When making this decision, the President instructed Treasury, however, to attempt to seek some of the benefits of wider application by actively discouraging such exports.

U.S. companies were accordingly required to inform Treasury ten days before any overseas subsidiary exported any item covered by the new sanctions. On receiving these notices Treasury, with very few exceptions,[43] aggressively urged the U.S. parents to prevent these exports. This approach prevented such exports in nearly all situations, as companies generally decided to forego the exports rather than risk adverse publicity.

Within days of the imposition of the April 7, 1980, sanctions the President determined to apply added measures as soon as options could be developed. These new sanctions were announced on April 17 and, while they represented growing impatience with Iran, they had little real impact. The new actions included:

1. A ban on imports from Iran. Since oil shipments already had been banned, only very small quantities of rugs and pistachio nuts were affected.
2. No remittances to people living in Iran, except for family members.

42. The President also announced on April 7 the breaking of diplomatic relations with Iran, expelled Iranian diplomats, and imposed new restrictions on visas for Iranians seeking to enter the United States. Executive Order 12205, Prohibiting Certain Transactions with Iran, dated April 7, 1980.

43. The only exceptions were some isolated situations where a special problem existed in connection with limited nonsensitive exports from some countries and other subsidiaries were foregoing far more substantial exports.

The impact was minor, and ultimately licenses were required to allow severance and other payments to current and former employees of U.S. companies in Iran.

3. Revocation of operating licenses for all nonbank Iranian entities in the United States. The banks were excluded largely because of their ongoing role in transmitting support payments to Iranian students in the United States.

The last, and most controversial sanction was a ban on travel to Iran.[44] Motivated by a concern over potential danger to U.S. citizens in Iran (the rescue mission was undertaken less than two weeks later, although none of us at Treasury were aware of this potential consideration), this prohibition was implemented despite serious misgivings about the inevitability of creating troublesome legal and compliance issues.[45] The first of these problems arose right away—the mother of one of the hostages left for Iran immediately after April 17—and was resolved by issuing a license. A second problem arose when Ramsey Clark led a delegation to attend a conference in Iran. The conference was sponsored by the Iranian government to examine U.S. conduct in Iran as a precipitating cause of the hostage seizure. A license was refused. Following the trip, a limited investigation was conducted, but concern over the distraction a prosecution would generate resulted in no action being taken.

Following the unilateral imposition by the United States of the U.N. sanctions vetoed by the U.S.S.R., substantial efforts were undertaken to convince the European Community and Japan to follow suit. Initially, these efforts bore sparse results. The allies, while continuing to voice their public support for the U.S. position, remained wary of imposing concrete sanctions against Iran, particularly without the protective shield of a U.N. vote.[46] They continued to be concerned about the impact of such measures on their relations with other Muslim governments and about the potential further isolation of Iran from Western influence. These concerns and the resulting reluctance to act were increased by the failed rescue mission in late April.

Finally, in June, the European Community and Japan agreed to adopt

44. Technically, this was accomplished by State Department action and by prohibiting payments in connection with any such travel or with living in Iran.

45. In an attempt to avoid one potential legal challenge, journalists were exempted from this ban. A requirement that those taking advantage of this exemption report it to Treasury was ignored by the press. This requirement was intended simply to enable the government to identify U.S. citizens in Iran in the event of additional problems that could threaten their security. The press chose, however, to ignore the requirement, and the government did not make an issue of it.

46. Some claimed that the absence of a U.N. resolution made imposition of sanctions legally more difficult. This objection never seemed very weighty to us.

an embargo on exports to Iran. While this represented a public action demonstrating unity with the United States against Iran, its impact was substantially weakened by its tardiness.

The agreed-upon sanctions affected only those export contracts entered into after November 4, 1979, the day the hostages were seized. Earlier agreed-upon nonmilitary exports could continue. Great Britain, in implementing this broader agreement, further reduced the effectiveness of its sanctions by applying them only to contracts entered into after the date of the European Community agreement in June. It also excluded any new contracts that reflected continuation of a previous supply relationship so long as the level of exports remained at the earlier levels. The British program thus was wholly symbolic and involved no commercial sacrifice.

The Issue of Legislation

In the spring of 1980, the administration considered seeking legislation to grant the President standby authority to resolve hostage, commercial, and U.S. government claims against Iran. Those opposing legislation, which included Treasury, believed that adequate authority existed and that pursuing legislation risked congressional action setting requirements for any settlement, thus reducing the President's flexibility in future negotiations with Iran. Not only could the emotions of the situation cause the inclusion of unrealistic demands in any legislation, but domestic economic groups with their vast and varied interests were surely prepared to seek provisions protecting their own "just" claims. The prospect of a debate over these competing economic issues while the hostages remained in captivity was unappetizing. These risks, it was argued, outweighed any possible value that would derive from adding this as another signal to Iran of U.S. determination.[47]

Nonetheless, frustrated by months of unproductive action, the President initially decided to seek legislation. Along with the new sanctions and the claims-assets census, the President therefore announced on April 7 that legislation was being prepared. No timing for submission of the legislation was announced and its substance remained unclear, with the President suggesting only that it would be designed to facilitate the payment of claims of hostages and others, including those of the U.S. government.[48]

---

47. While not a major factor in the discussion, the possibility that any legislative proposal would become submerged in the legislative process and not pass, which would send an enormously negative signal to Iran, was another risk.

48. Among the U.S. claims referred to was the added cost of maintaining our fleet in the Indian Ocean as a result of the hostage seizure. The potential enormity of this claim concerned some claimants, who feared it would absorb all available Iranian assets. This claim has not been pursued.

Following the April 7, 1980, announcement the debate moved to one principal issue: Should any legislation include standby authority for the President to vest title to the frozen Iranian assets in the United States? Members of the White House staff who advocated this position properly pointed out that such authority was not available under existing law and could be useful at some point. By taking ownership of the assets, the United States could apply them to U.S. claims or, alternatively, return them to Iran as part of a negotiated settlement. Others, including Treasury, argued that using, and even seeking, such authority would renew and extend concern already created abroad by the far less severe act of freezing the assets that the United States was not a secure place for foreign investment.

The President decided that, given the enormous breadth of his existing powers, it would be unwise to seek this additional authority. In a regrettable failure of staff work, however, on the same day that this presidential decision was received at Treasury, the President in his statement announcing the April 17 sanctions (which statement had not been cleared at Treasury) left the impression that any legislation would include such a vesting provision.

In the end, no legislation was submitted. As the drafting process stretched out, it became clear that the risks outweighed the uncertain benefits. In fact, except for the congressional consultations required by the International Emergency Economic Powers Act and one brief hearing, there was no formal congressional participation in the freeze or the final negotiations. While various members were of course briefed periodically about the hostage crisis, all but a few members of Congress appropriately recognized the wisdom of restraint.

The period from May through September followed a depressing routine. Numerous rulings on specific regulations were sought and provided. The considerable task of processing the claims-assets census continued. Meetings and telephone conversations with claimants of all types continued as Treasury, State, and the White House listened to everyone who had a view as to what should be done or had information about what was transpiring.[49] And while the various sanctions continued in place, with uncertain impact and increasing complication, the hostages remained in Iran.

---

49. In fact, to make certain it had adequate information about the range of claims against Iran and any ongoing commercial contacts with that country, Treasury and State throughout the freeze initiated a number of meetings with potential claimants of all types.

5 CRAFTING THE FINANCIAL SETTLEMENT

ROBERT CARSWELL AND RICHARD J. DAVIS

To recapitulate, at the end of the summer of 1980, after the failure of the rescue mission and once the Iranians had sorted out their own internal political struggle, President Carter named Deputy Secretary of State Warren Christopher to coordinate the negotiations with Iran. For months before that step in September, while there was still hope that at some point Iran might unilaterally release the hostages, the more realistic and generally held view was that release would come in the context of a negotiation in which at least some of Iran's grievances against the United States would be addressed. These grievances had accumulated over the previous decades but escalated in the aftermath of the hostage seizure and the retaliatory measures taken by the United States. The dilemma for Christopher and those who worked with him[1] was how to reach agreement on a complex and changing array of issues with an adversary that had publicly declared it would not talk directly to the United States, "the Great Satan." One obvious answer was to find some acceptable intermediary, but until that could be accomplished all that could be done was to prepare for an elusive advent of negotiations.

High on the list of questions certain to arise and likely to bog down any negotiation was how to handle the claims that the U.S. government and

---

1. Christopher decided to form a small, high-level negotiating team. Members of the original team were: from the White House staff, Lloyd N. Cutler, Counsel to the President; from the National Security Council staff, Capt. Gary Sick USN; from the Department of State, Harold Saunders, Assistant Secretary for Near Eastern and South Asian Affairs, Roberts Owen, Legal Adviser, and Arnold Raphel, Special Assistant to the Secretary; from the Treasury Department, Robert Carswell, Deputy Secretary; and from the Justice Department, John M. Harmon, Assistant Attorney General, Office of Legal Counsel, or his deputy, Larry Simms. Also an important contributor to the work of the group was Douglas Dworkin, then Special Assistant to Christopher.

U.S. individuals and companies had against Iran and that Iran had against the United States. As discussed in the preceding chapter, when Iran's assets were blocked on November 14, 1979, U.S. public statements linked the freeze not only to the taking of the hostages but also to the protection of the interests of U.S. nationals with claims against Iran. As the months went on, Iran's leaders repeatedly asserted that release of the hostages was linked to return of the blocked assets and the settlement of mutual claims. Historically there was plenty of precedent and reason for concern about how to resolve the claims issue. Almost from the hour of its birth the United States has dealt with a parade of international claims involving British privateers, Barbary pirates, Latin American revolutionaries, and a host of others. Sometimes the United States has obtained full value for its claims; sometimes it has obtained nothing; most often, after a decade or more of negotiations, compromise has been the outcome. In reaching agreement with Iran, the administration faced the added complexity of needing to achieve a result that would not be characterized as the payment of ransom.

Various approaches and forms of judicial and arbitration procedures have evolved over the years to handle and settle international claims. None, however, was clearly applicable to all aspects of the U.S.-Iran confrontation. Here the claims involved more than just a wide variety of commercial and financial matters. There were also U.S. government claims asserted against Iran by the Export-Import Bank of the United States for nonpayment of loans, claims by the Defense Department covering military equipment purchased or contracted for by the Iranians, claims by the State Department for embassy property confiscated, and lastly—and clearly the most sensitive— claims on behalf of the hostages for their unlawful detention.

Governor Ali Reza Nobari of Bank Markazi, the central bank of Iran, and other Iranians had publicly and privately asserted as early as June 1980 that Iran was prepared to arbitrate all claims. But they offered no specifics. It was apparent that something had to be worked out, and starting in the summer of 1980 lawyers at the Legal Adviser's Office at the State Department began to design an arbitration procedure. In conferences with Treasury and Justice lawyers, who also had experience in the area, various general approaches were considered. The hope was that the details of an arbitration procedure could be put off until after the hostages had been released. That hope proved illusory; nevertheless, the dogged drafting at State and the frustrating internal discussions that continued through the fall did sharpen issues and in the end provided groundwork for a quick resolution of an extraordinarily complex set of problems.

At Treasury, preparations meant focusing on the unique financial issues that were likely to confront the negotiators, as well as on the more traditional claims settlement issues. The group that would form the special negotiating team had a good idea by the end of August of the magnitude of both the Iranian assets that had been blocked and of the claims of U.S. persons against Iran; the team had also recognized the necessity of preserving as much flexibility as possible to respond to unknown demands to come; and it had formulated preliminary ideas about unblocking the assets and resolving the claims. An understanding of the course of the final negotiations requires elaboration of the positions from which the process started.

In April, Treasury had been cleared by the White House and the State Department to conduct a census of the blocked assets and the claims of U.S. persons against Iran. It is at best imprudent to negotiate about issues without understanding, or at least having some knowledge of, the underlying facts. Hence it was agreed that detailed information on the assets and the claims was a prerequisite to substantive negotiations. The results of the census, plus reports submitted to the Federal Reserve Bank of New York by banks holding Iranian deposits, would, it was hoped, provide that information. By the end of July Treasury had pretty well completed compiling the returns from the census, and the N.Y. Fed had verified the deposits reported by the banks. But the results were of limited assistance. Some of those responding to the census submitted incomplete information. Many resolved all doubts in the manner most favorable to their own interests, with the consequence that claims against Iran were overstated and blocked assets were understated, for instance by not including any interest on deposits held. That left Treasury with a general idea of the amounts of claims and assets but also with a shifting factual base from which to conduct the negotiations.

The uncertainties in the numbers forced two early conclusions: first, to avoid giving numbers to the Iranians or making any data public for as long as possible, and second, to continue efforts to the date of final settlement, if necessary, to obtain accurate data. On the first point, it was a foregone conclusion that if any numbers that were given to the Iranians subsequently proved inaccurate, this would thereby convert their suspicions to paranoia. Withholding the numbers also had the potential advantage of giving the United States negotiating leverage, because crucial Iranian financial records had apparently disappeared or been destroyed during the course of the revolution. It also avoided providing a focus for pending or threatened litigation in the United States or for ill-considered congressional action.

The administration was in fact able to keep the constantly shifting numbers confidential until the press conference held shortly after the settlement, even though, as mentioned in the preceding chapter, there were two newspaper stories during the fall that printed inaccurate figures, one of which identified a former Treasury officer as its source.

During the fall, Treasury tried several approaches to improve the factual data base. In September, Treasury asked a special committee of the Association of Reserve City Banks, a prestigious association composed mainly of large banks, to try to get agreement on the fair rate of interest that should be paid to Iran on the blocked deposits and for suggestions on how to improve the accuracy of the census reports. They reported back that they had been unable to make significant progress because of lack of agreement among the banks, particularly on the interest issue. Representatives of the Office of Foreign Assets Control and of the Federal Reserve Bank of New York who continued, on Treasury's behalf, to discuss the reports with the banks also encountered difficulties with changes in previously reported numbers, presumably in part because of reassessments by individual banks of their legal positions.

On the claims side, Treasury interviewed representative classes of claimants to try to understand the basis of each type of claim and assess their value. The census reports filed by U.S. persons identified claims aggregating more than the available blocked assets in the United States; Treasury's rough assessment, however, was that these claims were probably worth substantially less than asserted.

The numbers on the claims of U.S. banks against Iran were reasonably solid, even though they changed from time to time, for example when new loans were discovered or interest due was recalculated. The bank claims were mainly for loans then in default, consisting of about $1.2 billion in syndicate loans (or about one-third of the $3.6 billion of the international syndicate loans to Iran) and about $1.0 billion in direct loans to Iranian entities, some of which might be disclaimed by Iran as personal debts of the Shah.

The balance of the claims involved all manner of factual issues: breach of contract questions, jurisdictional disputes, claims of harassment and torture, and wide disagreement as to the value of assets seized or allegedly seized. As discussed in chapter 4, a particularly nettlesome issue involved how to deal with almost a billion dollars in performance bonds (and similar letters of credit), which U.S. contractors had taken out in favor of Iran and which were being called by Iran claiming that projects or sales contracts had not been completed.

Even a cursory study of the roster left no room for doubt: Treasury could not evaluate the nonbank claims with certainty. Many claims had real substance, but they were so complex and varied that only a court of claims, arbitration commission, or the like, after holding hearings and studying the facts, could establish fair values. This could not be done by the U.S. government in any kind of time frame consistent with an early release of the hostages. Hence the U.S. position from the beginning was that the nonbank claims would have to be settled after the hostage release. It was also a U.S. objective to obtain reliable assurance of payment, regardless of the procedure by which the fair value of claims would eventually be determined.

Treasury knew in September 1980 that considerably more than $8 billion had been blocked and that it was basically in four pots: (1) at the N.Y. Fed, (2) at the overseas branches of U.S. banks, (3) at the domestic branches of U.S. banks, and (4) in the hands of a relatively large number of companies (principally oil companies) and individuals, both here and abroad, most of whom also had claims against Iran. Differences from the Treasury September figures continually developed, but they were not significant enough to affect planning. For the sake of simplicity in the discussion that follows, the final numbers will be used. The blocked assets on the date of settlement are shown in the accompanying table.

		U.S. dollars (millions)
At Federal Reserve Bank of New York		
Deposits and securities	$1,418	
Gold (at $576/oz.)	940	2,358
At overseas offices of U.S. banks		
Deposits and securities		5,579
At domestic branches of U.S. banks (exclusive of accrued interest)		
Deposits		2,050
Other assets held in the U.S. or overseas by U.S. individuals		1,000–2,100
TOTAL		$10,987–$12,087

(The figures shown for the N.Y. Fed and the overseas offices of U.S. banks include interest.)

In November 1979 the President had linked the blocking to both release of the hostages and protection of U.S. interests. In the negotiations he faced the dilemma of how to use return of the assets to obtain release of the hostages but at the same time avoid nullifying any rights U.S. claimants might have to obtain payment of their claims from the blocked assets. The composition and legal status of the blocked assets helped to resolve that conundrum.

Commencing shortly after the blocking, U.S. corporations and individuals with claims against Iran went to court and got orders attaching all the assets of Iran they could find in the United States to secure payment of their claims. The attachment orders demanded that the assets remain tied up until the claims awards were paid. Justice lawyers had concluded that, while it would be possible in the context of an overall settlement to have the attachments nullified, that would require going to courts all over the country and, taking into account likely appeals, it would be a lengthy and fractious process. However, the attachments effectively covered only the two pots of assets in the U.S. private sector: the deposits in the domestic branches of U.S. banks and most of the miscellaneous assets. Those assets were simply not available for quick release in exchange for the hostages. But the status of the other two pots of assets left more room for negotiation.

The assets at the N.Y. Fed and the deposits at the overseas (principally London) branches of U.S. banks had a different legal status. By the end of August lawyers in Justice, Treasury, and the N.Y. Fed had tentatively concluded that the N.Y. Fed could legally comply with an order of the President to return the blocked assets that it held to Iran. The attachments served on the N.Y. Fed were without legal substance and could safely be ignored.

The blocked Iranian deposits and securities at the overseas branches of U.S. banks were similarly free of attachments, because the attachment process of U.S. courts does not reach assets located outside the United States. No comparable process was available in the United Kingdom, where Iran held most of its overseas deposits. Thus these two pots of assets were theoretically available for a quick settlement.

In practice the deposits held by the banks abroad were not so clearly available. The $4.8 billion (plus accrued interest) of overseas Iranian deposits was at ten large U.S. banks—half at the London branch of the Bank of America. Those same banks had made considerably more than $1 billion in loans to Iran, all of which were by then in default. They were not anxious to return the deposits unless some provision was made for payment of these loans, not just to themselves but also to other banks (both U.S. and foreign) that were members of the same syndicates. Their concern for other members of syndicates was not charitable; rather, they were fearful that because of provisions in the syndicate agreements they would be required to share anything they received with the others.

Most of the U.S. bank branches in London had, in any event, already paid off the loans on their books from the blocked deposits they held by using the banker's traditional legal remedy, the setoff described in chapter 4. While it is uncertain that the use of setoffs in this situation was legally authorized under English law, the fact was that setoffs had been taken. The President might have the authority to reverse the setoffs and to unblock these overseas deposits and order them paid over to Iran, but he could not deprive the banks of their day in court to contest any presidential order, and that would more likely be three months than a day. On the other hand, the banks might not want to assume responsibility for keeping the hostages locked up in Iran if the settlement was even a marginally acceptable one.

To sum up the situation in September when the negotiating team was formed, it was fairly certain the President could deliver about $2.3 billion of assets at the N.Y. Fed as part of a quick settlement. It had concluded the President could direct the immediate return of some significant part of the $5 billion held by ten U.S. banks in their overseas branches, but only if the banks did not contest his order in court. Acquiescence by the banks would probably be dependent on a reasonable settlement of their defaulted loans to Iran. It also seemed clear that the other blocked assets could be released only after a court battle, probably a lengthy one, and then only in the context of an overall settlement. To do simple justice and to avoid the precedent of paying ransom, it was also clear that any overall claims settlement with Iran on its face would have to be favorable to the United States. It was in that uneasy context that the negotiations got under way, both on an official level in Bonn and on an unofficial level with the bankers through their German contacts.

The Bank Channel

In chapter 6, John Hoffman describes in detail his and the U.S. banks' parallel negotiations with Iranian officials and their attorneys. In this chapter, the details of the bank negotiations are referred to only as they became substantively critical to the overall negotiations.

When Hoffman first reported to Deputy Secretary Carswell by telephone on May 3, 1980 that there had been an Iranian approach, he was asked to come to Washington to discuss the matter with Carswell and Roberts Owen, Legal Adviser to the State Department. After subsequent discussion with Christopher and others, Carswell was authorized to inform Hoffman that the U.S. government had no objection to his proceeding with negotiations with the Iranians, but only on the condition that he inform the Iranians that there would be no settlement with the banks until the hostages were released and with the clear understanding that he was not authorized to represent the U.S. government. He was also requested and agreed to keep the U.S. government informed of the status of his negotiations.

In the ensuing months Hoffman periodically came to Washington and reported to Carswell, Owen, and Davis. Since Hoffman was a former law partner of Carswell and was also known to others at Treasury and State, the meetings were informal, but memoranda were kept of each meeting and guardedly disseminated. Hoffman was requested, for security reasons, not to report by telephone, although by the late fall the acceleration of events forced abandonment of that limitation.

It was also decided from the start that Hoffman would not be briefed as to the progress—or lack of progress—of the official negotiations, and until the end, so far as the authors know, he had no access to official information.

During the fourteen months, a number of other banks or potential claimants or their attorneys reported contacts with Iranians to Treasury. Indeed a number talked periodically by telephone or in meetings in Europe or the United States with Iranian customers or Iranian government officials. Those who asked for guidance from the U.S. government were all given the same conditions as Hoffman. While other bank contacts and discussions with Iran continued through the period, so far as the authors know only the Hoffman channel was pursued by Iran.

The Tabatabai Contact

On Monday afternoon, September 15, 1980, the State and Treasury members of the Christopher team left by special Air Force plane for Bonn, Germany. The next day a State Department spokesman noted that Christopher had gone to Europe for routine consultations. Other members of the team were not identified, and they had returned to Washington before their absences attracted attention. The German government, through its ambassador in Tehran, had arranged for a meeting with Sadegh Tabatabai, an inlaw of Ayatollah Khomeini, who was represented as having authority from him. (See also chapter 8.)

Christopher met twice with Tabatabai and West German Foreign Minister Hans-Dietrich Genscher during the team's three-day stay and outlined general terms for release of the hostages. Tabatabai was reserved but not hostile and indicated he would transmit the proposal and be back in touch. He also made a few comments and outlined Khomeini's four conditions for release of the hostages.

Christopher's terms were simple and designed to meet, or at least to deal with, the substance of Iran's generalized demands as they had appeared in the press on September 12. When Iran released the hostages, the United States would: (1) unblock and return Iran's assets on deposit at the Federal Reserve Bank of New York (about $2 billion); (2) unblock (but take no action to return) the assets of Iran on deposit at the foreign branches of U.S. banks ($5.5 billion) and (3) prohibit removal of the Shah's assets from the United States pending the outcome of any litigation. The balance of Iran's assets would be unblocked in the context of an overall claims settlement program that would be worked out later. To emphasize that the United States was ready to proceed, he exhibited draft executive orders that would carry out the actions described. With the approval of the President, the team had drafted the orders in planning sessions held in September.

Tabatabai never again made direct contact with the United States. Subsequently contacted by the German ambassador in Tehran, he raised the issue of spare parts and Iranian-owned equipment in the United States but fixed no date for a second meeting. The Iran-Iraq war had started, and the establishment on September 16 by the Majlis of a parliamentary special committee to investigate the hostage issue (the Nabavi Committee) led to a conclusion that the Iranian government would henceforth play the central role. In Washington it was assumed that the terms outlined to Tabatabai had reached those in authority in Tehran, but one could only speculate on the effect, if any, the Tabatabai meeting would have on later events.

By then the presidential campaign was in full cry. President Carter's handling of the hostage issue was clearly a principal issue. There was talk in the press of an October surprise. It was obvious to all that a hostage settlement would be of enormous, perhaps decisive, help to the President. The Iranians might have reasoned that this was a time of maximum leverage for them. Instead, they chose to issue inflammatory statements in Tehran and to try to rally international support to their cause in the war against Iraq. Their Prime Minister, Ali Rajai, addressed the United Nations in New York and, as we have seen, received a frigid reception from the delegates. Nevertheless, he rebuffed approaches designed to get negotiations started.

Members of the negotiating team spent the month of October in Washington negotiating with each other, talking guardedly with claimants and advisers and developing a comprehensive framework for settlement consistent with the terms proposed to Tabatabai. But there was no one with authority from Iran to talk to.

The Algerian Intermediation

Just before the U.S. presidential election, the Majlis ratified the text of terms for release of the hostages that had been recommended by its special committee in charge of investigating the hostage issue (the Nabavi Committee). Iran then asked the government of Algeria to deliver the text of the resolution to the U.S. authorities and to act as the intermediary in future hostage negotiations. (See also chapter 8.) Ronald Reagan was elected President on November 4.

On November 11, the State and Treasury members of the Christopher team arrived in Algiers. After two days of detailed discussions with Algerian Foreign Minister Benyahia and his team of experienced diplomats (including the head of Algeria's central bank), Christopher delivered a written proposal, revised to take into account suggestions by the Algerian team, for presentation to the Iranians. The Algerians left that night for Tehran with the proposal.

The First U.S. Proposal

The U.S. proposal of November 13 consisted of a memorandum, together with draft declarations and executive orders to implement the terms outlined in the memorandum. The President had actually signed the orders, so that Christopher could show them to Benyahia as evidence of the seriousness of our preparations and intentions. The orders addressed the demands in the Majlis' resolution, but on the financial side limited U.S. government action to the return of $2.3 billion at the New York Federal Reserve Bank, the simple unblocking of Iran's assets both domestically and abroad, and a commitment to enter into a comprehensive claims settlement procedure after the hostages had been released "in accordance with recognized procedures for international arbitration."

Translated into the realities of the situation, that meant Iran could expect to get back the $2.3 billion at the N.Y. Fed but not much else. The banks and various other claimants against Iran had already tied up most of Iran's assets in the United States with attachments and other legal process, so that a simple order rescinding the U.S. blocking orders would not free them. Rather, Iran would have to go to court in the United States to get the attachments lifted, or it would have to settle with the claimants before it could recover excess assets that had been blocked. To recover its blocked overseas deposits after they had been unblocked, Iran would have to work out an agreement with the U.S. banks. That type of settlement would leave our nationals in the best possible bargaining position. There was no way to predict Iran's response.

Twelve days later, on November 25, the Algerian team came to Washington with Iran's response, but prior to their return we had some notion that they would not be bearing unqualified acceptance. John Hoffman's clandestine bank negotiations had proceeded through the fall, and by the middle of November he had worked out a fairly detailed proposal identified as Plan C (Plans A and B having been previously discarded or rejected). The proposal was that when the hostages were released and the blocking orders terminated, the U.S. banks would use Iran's deposits in their overseas branches to pay off its loans and then return the excess deposits (estimated at $2–3 billion) to Iran. (See also chapter 6.)

On November 14, the day the Algerians had arrived in Tehran with our formal proposal, the Iranian representatives informed Hoffman in Germany that Plan C was unacceptable. Hoffman returned, and his report to us in Washington signaled that on a technical level there was no bank agreement in sight. On the other hand, in spite of strenuous efforts in courts in England, France, and Germany, Iran had made virtually no progress in obtaining the release of its blocked assets. In Washington it was assumed that the Iranians understood that the prospect of success in the courts was not high so long as they continued to hold the hostages and that a recognition of that fact might cause some movement toward settlement.

In meetings that ran over into Thanksgiving morning the Algerian team went over Iran's comments on our November 13 proposal. Many of the comments were substantive. The Algerians also suggested that it would be helpful, as a matter of grace and cosmetics, if our proposal could be framed in a manner that would highlight acceptance of as many as possible of the Majlis' conditions. On the financial side, the Algerians reported—as Hoffman had earlier—that Iran did not want to pay off the bank loans and that mere assurances on return of its assets were inadequate.

The December 3 U.S. Proposal

In a series of drafting sessions the negotiating team repackaged the November 13 proposal, so that in a memorandum of understanding the United States agreed to virtually all of the Majlis' points but in accompanying comments added necessary qualifications. That weekend the State and Treasury members of the team left for Algiers, and on Monday, December 1, discussions started on the repackaged próposal with Benyahia and the Algerian team. That took two days and produced two significant changes.

The Algerians felt that about all the United States could hope for was that Iran would bring all its bank loans current—that is, pay the amounts necessary to put the loans in good standing—but it would not give additional security to guarantee future payments on the loans.[2] Christopher pointed out that the U.S. banks might not release excess deposits in their overseas branches without some assurances that the outstanding loans would be paid off as they matured. Eventually an uneasy compromise was formulated whereby Iran would bring the loans current and, in that context, would "consult concerning the normalization of banking relationships." The Algerians were repeatedly informed that the U.S. government could not force the banks to return the excess deposits without a protracted court battle. Hence, whatever the document said, Iran would have to make its own settlement with the banks before the relationships could be normalized and the excess deposits returned.

The Algerians also felt that the United States must broaden its proposal on claims settlement. The negotiating team was very reluctant to do that, because the prospect of working out detailed procedures seemed too complicated to accomplish. But Christopher did agree that the process should cover all claims, not merely those in litigation, and in a so-called nonpaper general principles were spelled out on which the formal claims procedure would be based.

2. Seghir Mostefai, a member of the Algerian team and head of Algeria's central bank, had earlier explained to members of the U.S. team that, under the terms of Algeria's settlement with France, loans from French banks to Algerian entities had been brought current—not paid off—and no special guarantees had been given by Algeria with respect to future payments. The authors do not know whether any similar statement was made to the Iranian negotiators and therefore whether this precedent had any influence on the Iranians.

On December 4 the Algerian team returned to Tehran, and rumors surfaced that Iran wanted to get the hostages home by Christmas. To meet that hypothetical deadline, an extraordinary amount of technical underbrush would have to be cleared away. Treasury still did not have accurate figures on bank loans and deposits; yet a bank settlement would require that those numbers be available. If the Iranians refused to trust the United States to make payments directly, an escrow agent (probably the central bank of another country) would have to be found and arrangements worked out with the agent. If billions of dollars of transfers were to be made simultaneously with release of the hostages, the Federal Reserve Bank of New York would have to play a significant role, and the complex details of that would have to be worked out. Special problems of various banks and claimants would have to be accommodated. Treasury started to get ready.

On December 5 Carswell and Davis went to New York and met with senior officers of Chase Manhattan Bank, Morgan Guaranty Trust Company, and Citibank. Later in the week they met either in Washington or New York with senior officers from the rest of the ten banks that had large deposits from Iran on the books of their overseas branches or had significant loans outstanding. The message to all was the same: Iran is still insisting on a deal where the loans are not paid off but only brought current, and it is unclear what security, if any, they will give with respect to future payments. We are not sure whether there is any real chance for a deal, but if there is, it will come on short notice. Each bank will then have to produce accurate numbers on the Iranian deposits and loans it holds, and it will have to have a senior officer ready to come to Washington and participate in decisions that will bind the bank.

All the banks agreed to those requests, and within a week they had hired the accounting firm of Peat, Marwick, Mitchell & Co. to collect and organize the numbers from all the banks. Each bank designated a senior officer as its point of contact and also a senior lawyer to act for it.

Carswell and Davis also spent two hours on December 5 with Anthony Solomon, President of the Federal Reserve Bank of New York, and brought him up to date on the precise status of the negotiations. The N.Y. Fed acts—at least in a technical sense—as the central bank of the United States for foreign transactions. It has banking relationships and a communications network with the central banks of other nations. We discussed the role it would play in the financial transfers that loomed ahead, as well as the legal issues involved in paying out the $2.3 billion of gold, securities, and deposits that the N.Y. Fed held for Iran and the problems of maintaining security. Solomon had been involved in Treasury's year-long effort to get the numbers organized, and as a former Under Secretary of the Treasury for Monetary Affairs was familiar with the landscape. He assigned his best people to the effort and stayed in close touch until the final dawn.[3]

Our next efforts were directed at finding skilled people to help. A lame duck, the status bestowed on President Carter by the electorate on November 4, faces diminished loyalties in his administration, and by the time he leaves office most of his aides have already departed for greener pastures. At Treasury, the problem was compounded because the circle of those working on Iran had deliberately been kept very small to minimize the chances of deliberate or inadvertent leaks. Those in that small circle had to assume the duties of those who departed during the fall. By December it was clear Treasury would have to find help. First, orders went out that the bright but inexperienced lawyers in other areas of the Treasury were to be made available as required. Next contacted was Robert H. Mundheim, who had resigned as General Counsel at Treasury in September to resume his teaching career at the University of Pennsylvania Law School. Almost enthusiastically, he agreed to give up his Christmas and mid-term vacations if he should be needed.

Meanwhile, Hoffman kept us informed at Treasury on his continuing negotiations with Iran's lawyers on the bank issues. He had expanded his group to include attorneys from several of the other large banks and together they had developed a Plan D, the alphabetical successor to the rejected Plan C. The new plan was based on Iran's bringing all its loans current and providing some kind of security for future payment of outstanding loans. The banks would then release Iran's excess foreign deposits. They reported signs of progress, but it was difficult to tell what was going on or even if they and the Algerian team were talking with a coordinated government group in Tehran.

As the days before Christmas passed by, it seemed increasingly doubtful that the hostages would be home for the holidays. Nevertheless, Christopher called a meeting of the team for Sunday morning, December 21, to go over what was left to be done and to brief Secretary of State Muskie, who was to appear on the *Meet the Press* television program that morning. As we arrived, the wire service stories began to come in with the chilling news that the Iranians had made parts of our proposal public in violation of their commitment to the Algerians, had rejected it, and were demanding

3. At the Federal Reserve Bank of New York, the principal officers who worked on the settlement were James H. Oltman, General Counsel, and Ernest T. Patrikis, Deputy General Counsel, but dozens of others under First Vice President Thomas M. Timlen worked on collection of data and transfers of funds and securities. In the last days the N.Y. Fed was kept open around the clock, so that the necessary final transfers of funds could be put through if the time finally came.

that the United States put $24 billion in escrow. Muskie promptly characterized the Iranian demands as "unreasonable and beyond the powers of the American Presidency." This time, rather than making comments through the Algerians, the Iranian reply to our proposal took the form of a detailed written response released to the public. The response was confusing and placed heavy emphasis on return of the Shah's assets, an issue about which we could do almost nothing. It was hard to be optimistic, and with little enthusiasm the members of the negotiating team bought last-minute presents and looked forward to a less than joyous Christmas. But there was in fact a little gleam of hope.

In their reply the Iranians had reduced their demands on the amount of assets they wanted returned to a little less than $10 billion. That was still high, but there were ways of narrowing the gap and still protecting those with claims against Iran. The President wanted to have one last try.

The Final U.S. Proposal

In a lengthy communication to the Algerians, sent just before Christmas, Christopher transmitted suggestions that addressed what appeared to be some of the principal Iranian concerns and simply ignored others, such as their demand for a $10 billion escrow to ensure return of the Shah's assets. In particular, the suggestions indicated agreement to the concept of an escrow of funds that would be paid over to Iran when the hostages were released. There would also be an arrangement whereby $2 billion of Iran's deposits held at the domestic branches of U.S. banks would not be paid over but would initially be placed in escrow as security to pay the claims of U.S. nationals. The suggestions also included a statement that a claims settlement agreement was being drafted, and a copy of Hoffman's Plan D was transmitted as a proposal to settle the commercial bank loan-deposit side of the negotiation. Christopher suggested that the Algerian team come to Washington if they thought the suggested revisions provided a basis on which to proceed. The team then dispersed for a brief and somber holiday. The Algerian team arrived in Washington on December 27.

The two teams met at the Department of State periodically over the next three days. Between sessions the U.S. team drafted new papers. First, the Algerians went through in detail their understanding of the Iranian response, and the U.S. side commented on areas where something could be done and where it could not. The Algerians reported that Iran would not sign anything that the United States signed. Eventually parallel declarations were suggested to the Algerians, who would announce receipt of adherences to the declarations from both the United States and Iran signifying their effectiveness. That form proved acceptable to both sides, and by December 30, when the Algerian team departed, it took with it drafts of the two declarations that eventually became the basic final agreements. The first declaration covered the principal political and financial issues. It was basically a reformulation of positions previously arrived at and provided that Iran's deposits in the overseas branches of United States banks would be unblocked when Iran's loans had been brought current and after Iran had provided affirmations and assurances sufficient to restore the loans to good standing. That dovetailed with Plan D but in effect made release of the deposits dependent on Iran and the banks reaching an understanding on the necessary assurances. It also provided for escrow accounts and for various U.S. government actions to obtain the release of Iran's other blocked assets.

The second declaration, which covered claims, was mostly new and set out the broad framework of an international claims arbitration process. To secure payment of arbitral awards, Iran would establish an escrow deposit of $1 billion (down from our original proposal of $2 billion, which the Algerians reported had not been accepted). The deposit would be replenished by Iran when it fell below $500 million.[4] We knew that any draft of arbitration procedures would likely raise some thorny issues that, from our standpoint, would be better addressed after the hostages were out, but the Algerian team was clear that Iran insisted they be faced before the release.

We also supplied the Algerian team with a background paper giving for the first time some general estimates of Iran's assets blocked in overseas branches of U.S. banks and of Iran's outstanding loans to U.S. banks. Finally, but perhaps more important than any of the details, the response made it clear that unless there was an acceptance by January 16, 1981, the whole proposal was withdrawn, and Iran could deal with President-elect Reagan, who had ten days earlier characterized the Iranian response as a demand for "ransom" and their leaders as "barbarians."[5]

Preparation for Settlement

The Algerian team went over our reformulated proposals in detail and departed for Algiers. After reporting to Algerian Foreign Minister Benyahia, they flew directly to Tehran and did not return until twenty days later on the plane carrying the hostages out of Iran.

During this period the Justice Department (with assistance from State and Treasury) was engaged in conducting a holding action in various foreign courts, where Iran was suing to get its assets back, as well as in various U.S. courts, where U.S. claimants were still attempting to reach Iran's frozen assets. As discussed in chapter 4, any court ruling had the potential of changing the basis of the negotiation either by encouraging Iran that it

4. This escrow proposal was based on the pre-Christmas Iranian response.
5. *The New York Times,* January 17, 1981, p. 10, col. 1.

might ultimately prevail in court or by tying up Iran's assets so thoroughly as to preclude a settlement in the few weeks left. Although there had been a few close calls, including the puzzling lower court decision in New York described in chapter 4, the status quo was maintained. A similar holding action was successfully conducted with an endless stream of claimants, members of Congress, and advisers, who were understandably nervous about the course of the negotiations.

On a more positive note, the team decided to move ahead with the selection of an escrow agent and the negotiation of forms of escrow agreements with appropriate indemnifications, tested communications, and all the paraphernalia that facilitates large banking transactions. Since there were no experienced personnel left in Treasury who could be spared, Carswell called Mundheim, who agreed to come to Washington on January 6 to be briefed and then to take on responsibility for negotiating an escrow agreement. He left for London on January 7 with Ernest Patrikis, Deputy General Counsel of the Federal Reserve Bank of New York, to talk with the Bank of England. They ended up going from there to West Germany, then back to London, thence to Algiers, and did not return until the day following the hostages' release.

Selection of the escrow agent proved awkward, presumably because the Iranians were suspicious. We told the Algerians that either the central bank of the United Kingdom (the Bank of England) or of West Germany (the Bundesbank) was acceptable to us, but the Algerians were unable to get a decision out of the Iranians. Mundheim had to negotiate with officials of both central banks until on January 12 the Algerians suggested that the Bank of England be designated.

Negotiation of the agreements was also difficult, principally because there was no precedent to follow: no central bank had ever been called upon to act as an agent in a similar situation. There might be some unquantifiable risk involved, and the amounts involved were enormous. It ultimately took the combined efforts of U.S. Ambassador Kingman Brewster in London and Prime Minister Margaret Thatcher, as well as all the negotiating teams, to settle the escrow details. The extraordinary physical awkwardness of conducting negotiations in several different cities simultaneously also caused problems and delay. That awkwardness materially but unavoidably increased on January 7, when the President sent Christopher and the State Department members of the U.S. negotiating team to Algiers to work directly with Benyahia.

Christopher to Algeria

Christopher's departure came after the Algerians notified us on January 6 that Iran had reduced its demands for assets to be released immediately to

$9.5 billion but would not agree to the January 16 deadline. It was clear the United States would not be able to produce more than the $2.3 billion at the Federal Reserve Bank of New York and the $4.8 billion of deposits plus interest in the overseas branches of the U.S. banks. Even if a little more money could be found in the U.S. banks, there was no chance of reaching $9.5 billion. It was, however, clear that, even if specific mention of the January 16 deadline were dropped, because of the technical problems we faced it was in fact about the last realistic day for negotiation. The President therefore decided to drop the explicit deadline but otherwise to stand pat. He sent Christopher and his associates from State to deliver and explain the U.S. position to Benyahia in Algeria. They did not return until after the hostages had been released.

The result of this redeployment of personnel was that in the last two weeks of down-to-the-wire, twenty-four-hour-a-day negotiations, six locations were involved. The President, his counsel Lloyd Cutler, and others on his staff, and those involved in the financial side of the negotiations stayed principally in Washington. The banks eventually had personnel in Washington, New York, London, and Algiers. Christopher and his group were in Algiers with Benyahia, where the final papers were being written. The Algerian negotiating team was in Tehran with the Iranians. Attorneys representing Iran were in London, New York, and Frankfurt, Germany.

Obstacles also emerged in communications, which were frequently slow or unreliable. The telephone links between Germany and Tehran seemed to be better that those between London or Algiers and Tehran. Iran's German counsel frequently had better luck reaching Tehran than anyone else. The bank group in London frequently had better luck getting through to Algiers, because U.S. telephone calls to Algiers had to go through London, and locally originated calls seemed to have priority. Time zone differences also compounded the problems. Washington and New York were five hours behind London, six behind Algiers, and nine behind Tehran. As a practical matter, that meant twenty-four-hour-a-day negotiations at the end.

Language difficulties also persisted throughout the last days. We kept our documents in English, and that was the preference of the bankers, the Bank of England, and some of the subordinate Iranians. The Algerians did not feel comfortable working in English, so everything had to be translated into French for them. The political level in Iran insisted on working in Farsi.

After Christopher and Mundheim departed, attention at Treasury focused on trying to push along the bank negotiations. With time running out, unless the U.S. banks went along there was no way to complete the negotiation. If the U.S. government tried to force the banks to give up the Iranian deposits in their overseas branches, there was little doubt they could precipitate a court challenge that would extend well beyond January

20. If they simply dragged their institutional feet, they could probably delay matters beyond January 20. On the other hand, most of the banks genuinely wanted to resolve the matter and get the hostages out. None wanted to face the public consequences of having frustrated release of the hostages or to miss the chance of payment on doubtful loans.

On January 8, there was a meeting at Treasury with key lawyers from the twelve deposit banks (those holding virtually all the overseas deposits of Iran) to review the open issues and how to solve them. The banks were still trying to resolve the numbers, to agree on the rate of interest Iran should receive on its deposits while they were frozen, and to hammer out the final details of Plan D. There were continuing disagreements among the banks, but the U.S. government could help with some of their problems by drafting changes in the executive orders lifting the freeze and reformulating directives covering the return of Iran's assets. That consumed most of the next day.

On Saturday, January 10, Carswell and Davis went to New York to continue the discussions with the bank lawyers. One important point was resolved, namely, that the banks were willing to turn their Iranian overseas deposits over to the escrow agent and then have the agent make the agreed-on payments on Iran's defaulted loans. That meant Iran would get all the money back—crucial for them as a matter of pride—but the banks would get their loans, or some part of them, paid off immediately from the returned deposits. Iran's U.K. and German lawyers had arrived in New York the day before, but Carswell and Davis decided not to meet with them at least until they had completed their first round of talks with the banks. It was important that a consensual negotiation not be turned into one grounded on government mandate. Saturday ended with some progress but with many points still open.

On Sunday, January 11, the bank lawyers were informed that Iran would probably not accept the security aspects of Plan D. The banks were asking for too much; the plan was too complicated. Herbert Wagendorf (one of Iran's German attorneys) returned to Germany apparently to try to clarify instructions. Roger Brown, Iran's U.K. counsel, remained in New York to meet with each bank separately on the interest rate it would be willing to pay retroactively on Iran's frozen deposits, as the banks could not agree on a joint proposal. Treasury continued to monitor the situation and to answer questions from Christopher about technical issues raised by the Iranians through the Algerians.

On Monday, January 12, Carswell returned to New York and met with representatives from the twelve banks. Carswell outlined the proposal that the United States had tabled through the Algerians, including the portion that in effect required that agreement with the banks be reached before the

United States would order the banks to return Iran's assets in the foreign branches. He stated that Christopher had been informed that morning (Algiers time) that Iran was insisting on a substantially better offer from the banks, or it would transfer the bank negotiations to the government negotiators and the Algerians. Carswell urged that a final offer be agreed on and made, or the last chance to negotiate a deal before a new and probably less informed U.S. technical team took over would be gone. Comments from various banks ranged from supportive to guardedly hostile. Carswell stated that the government would give the banks all the protection it could through executive orders but that it had no power to guarantee or indemnify the banks for any loan losses they might suffer. He stated that most of the other outstanding issues, such as the nonreturn of the Shah's assets, seemed to have been resolved.

Carswell then talked in New York with Leonard Boudin, one of Iran's U.S. lawyers, and outlined at his request the facts on Iran's assets that had been previously transmitted to Iran through the Algerians. Carswell also made it clear that without a consensual bank settlement there would be no deal before January 20.

Carswell next talked with Roger Brown, Iran's U.K. attorney. Brown was guarded and complained about his inability to get accurate numbers. Carswell repeated the generalized numbers previously supplied but declined to be more precise, because the U.S. government could not stand behind the accuracy of the numbers on any assets except those held by the Federal Reserve Bank of New York. He concluded by urging that very little time was left, and it would be in no one's interest to follow the pattern of Cuba, where the assets were blocked in 1962 and Boudin was still litigating about them on Cuba's behalf.

Davis replaced Carswell in New York the next day and continued to work on drafting and mechanical issues with the banks. Brown returned to London, and after Prime Minister Thatcher personally intervened the Bank of England resolved most of its technical problems with the draft of the escrow agreement.

On Wednesday, January 14, in New York the banks concluded, with Treasury's encouragement, that if this transaction was to be done, it would be necessary to have an operating group in London. A party of bankers and lawyers took an overnight plane to England and the next morning set up an operations office at Coward, Chance and Company, London solicitors for some of the banks. Two days later, two of them, Thorne Corse, representing Bank of America, and Frank Logan, representing Chase Manhattan Bank, went on to Algiers with Mundheim, Patrikis, and representatives of the Bank of England. The preparations were moving ahead on many fronts, but there was still no basic deal.

On the morning of Thursday, January 15, the negotiations remained stalled. Iran had not formally rejected a modified but still complex Plan D, but it was apparently not acceptable.

The day before, in Tehran, the Majlis had acted to approve commercial arbitration of claims, but a tricky and long disputed issue remained open: the jurisdiction of the arbitral tribunal over contracts providing specifically for an Iranian judicial forum. Washington members of the negotiating team worked on the problem in Lloyd Cutler's office. After awhile, he came up with a brilliantly Delphic formulation that ultimately was accepted and has been the subject of an inevitable interpretative dispute in the Hague Tribunal.[6]

The Turning Point

Just before lunch on January 15, Christopher called and said Washington would shortly get a message containing a modified proposal submitted by the Algerians. The message came in about 2:00 P.M. At 2:10 P.M. Cutler and Carswell called John Hoffman and told him to get on the 3:00 P.M. shuttle to Washington. He did not return to New York until after the hostages had been released five days later.

The message stated that Iran had decided (1) to pay off all its bank loans, $3.4 billion of which it agreed posed no problem and $1.4 billion more that would be deposited in an escrow account and be paid out after verification of figures; (2) to return the hostages upon receipt of $8.1 billion ($2.5 billion from the Federal Reserve Bank of New York; $4.8 billion in overseas deposits; $800 million interest on the overseas deposits); and (3) to accept in principle the U.S. proposal that $2.2 billion in deposits in the United States be returned later, with a $1 billion replenishable escrow account providing security for a claims program. That was very close to the Plan C that Iran had rejected in November.[7] It was an offer that, even though it raised some

6. Several phrases were inserted in paragraph 1, article II, of the Declaration Concerning the Settlement of Claims to provide a basis for arguments by U.S. claimants that would permit them to escape the consequences of having entered into contracts that provided for some type of exclusive jurisdiction for Iranian courts. See also chapter 8.

7. Neither the bankers nor the U.S. government negotiators were clear at any point during the negotiations whether it was in Iran's interest as part of the final settlement to pay off its bank loans or simply to bring them current. Iran had ample frozen reserves with which to pay off all its bank loans, and it was quite unlikely that it could earn a higher rate of interest on the reserves than it was paying on the loans. Interest charged on the bank loans was typically a floating (or changing) rate keyed to the cost of funds in the London interbank market plus from 0.75% to 1.5%. On the other hand, reserves could typically be expected to earn only London interbank rates or a little less. Thus it "cost" Iran 0.75% to 1.5% to continue to borrow under the loan agreements when it had funds to pay off the loans. Nevertheless it might have been prudent for Iran not to pay off the loans if it expected to run short of reserves in the near future and thus need to borrow. The floating rates charged on Iran's bank loans

problems, unambiguously signaled Iran's desire to reach agreement. But everyone would have to act very rapidly if the documents were to be re-drafted and the deal closed in the four days remaining.

With the approval of the President, Secretary of State Muskie sent telegrams to the twelve deposit banks inviting each to send an officer who could commit the institution to a meeting on Iran at 11:00 A.M. the next morning (January 16) at the Department of State in Washington. When Hoffman arrived at 5:00 P.M., everyone turned to preparations for the meeting.

There seemed to be three substantive difficulties with the offer. First, Iran had offered to pay off $3.6 billion in loans and to secure payment of the rest with $1.4 billion. The loans totaled about $5 billion, but the open ques-tion was which would be paid immediately and which designated for future payment or arbitration. Second, would the banks be willing to pay $800 million in back interest? Third, would the total of the frozen assets to be returned to Iran reach $8.1 billion?

The loan situation was complex. In the years preceding the Iranian revolution, U.S. banks had made hundreds of loans to the government of Iran, to Iranian governmental corporations, and to entities guaranteed by the government or by governmental corporations. The loans were of two types: those made by individual banks and those made by syndicates of banks. As described in chapter 4, the members of the syndicates were some-times exclusively U.S. banks, but more typically they included both U.S. and foreign banks. It was clearly not going to be possible, in the time avail-able, to examine and make judgments about hundreds of individual loans even if someone could figure out criteria on which judgments would be made and who would be the judge.

Fortunately, fate in the form of an arithmetic coincidence intervened. The banks' best estimates were that the syndicated loans aggregated about $3.6 billion, or a little more than Iran had offered to pay off. It was easy to conclude that those should be the loans paid off. That decision had other reasons to recommend it. By and large the syndicated loans were potentially the least controversial, as they were made largely to finance various public projects. Their payment would also take care of the smaller U.S. banks, few of which had made individual loans, and the foreign banks, which had restricted their lending activities to syndicated loans and were very vocal in

---

were no bargain by 1980 market standards, but it would have been difficult for Iran to borrow at any rate while it continued to hold the hostages. This state of affairs made it particularly puzzling when Ali Reza Nobari, governor of Iran's central bank, declared that Iran had ample excess reserves but called the bank loans "cheap" and recommended that they not be paid off. In retrospect, it seems likely that factional politics in Iran had more to do with Iran's indeci-sion on this issue than economic considerations.

demanding they not be forgotten in any settlement reached. But that decision would leave a number of the larger banks waiting for payment on their individual loans. They might balk.

The second question, whether the banks would pay $800 million in interest, was puzzling. No one knew where the number had come from. The best guess was that the Iranians had produced the number by taking the highest interest rate that any U.S. bank had offered to pay during the negotiations with Roger Brown in New York and then applying that rate to the estimated deposits. A quick calculation showed that $800 million of interest meant an annual rate of about 14.2 percent. That was higher than some banks wanted to pay but not outrageous.

The third issue—whether $8.1 billion could be produced—would depend entirely on the final deposit numbers from the banks.

After going over the offer and discussing the issues with John Hoffman, Cutler and Carswell asked him to brief his group and have them talk to each of their banks before the next morning. He was also instructed to tell each bank it would be expected to produce, and then stand behind, its deposit and loan figures at the meeting. Everyone at Treasury then spent the rest of the evening preparing for the meeting, redrafting documents, and answering questions from various bankers and lawyers who called during the night.

Meanwhile, in Algiers, Christopher was concerned that the documentation on the escrow agreement was not going fast enough and was not being properly coordinated. That was partly because the Algerian central bank, which was to be a signatory, had not sent a representative to London. The Algerians then proposed that the escrow negotiations be shifted from London to Algiers. On the morning of January 16, Christopher's plane flew up from Algiers to London, picked up Mundheim, Patrikis, the two bank lawyers, Deputy Governor C. W. "Kit" McMahon of the Bank of England, David Somerset, Chief Cashier of the Bank of England, and Peter Peddie of Freshfields, the Bank's counsel, and returned to Algiers. They worked there until the hostages were out.

In Washington, January 16 started with breakfast at the White House, at which the President was briefed and a tentative decision was taken to send a signal of good faith to Iran by transferring Iran's gold to London, where it would be available for delivery in any settlement reached. The Federal Reserve Bank of New York had about 1.6 million ounces of Iranian-owned gold, valued then at about $940 million, in its New York vaults. Since one monetary gold brick is like any other monetary gold brick, Treasury had decided that, rather than ship the gold to London, it would swap the Iranian gold in New York for gold that the Bank of England had in London. After the swap, the Bank of England would own 1.6 million ounces of gold in the

United States,[8] and the N.Y. Fed would hold Iran's 1.6 million ounces of gold in London. It could then be turned over to the escrow agent in London as part of the settlement.

In concept the swap was simple enough, but a key Bank of England messenger was delayed in a Trafalgar Square traffic jam; a very long time was required to count and retag gold bricks and pass the inevitable receipts and certificates. It took till 3:00 P.M. to get the transfer completed, almost too late to make the evening news in the United States and the morning news in Tehran. The President, who checked periodically all day, was understandably concerned that if Treasury and the N.Y. Fed could not get that relatively uncomplicated gold swap mechanical business done efficiently, what would happen when they had to transfer the deposits and loans without a dress rehearsal. He was right to be concerned.

The 11:00 A.M. meeting at the State Department on January 16 was high theater. All twelve of the banks and their lawyers were there, some scrubbed and well-barbered, others bleary-eyed and unshaven from having flown all night. At least a dozen government officials were there as well, including the Secretaries of State and the Treasury and the Counsel to the President (who did not come himself only because his presence might have been regarded as coercive). The location was the Secretary of State's large conference room, with chandeliers and dark leather chairs.

The Secretary of State opened the meeting by stressing the national interest and gravity of the situation. Treasury Secretary Miller then outlined the Iranian offer and the issues. After a half hour or so of general discussion, Secretary Muskie suggested the banks caucus without government officials present and that the meeting then take up the question of which loans would be paid first. After fifteen minutes of caucus, side conversations, and telephone calls to home offices, it was agreed that the syndicated loans would be paid first, and the meeting turned, after another caucus, to the interest issue. There the agreement was to pay 14.2 percent, which would produce the needed $800 million, but the government side agreed to try to change the documents, so that any bank could pay any part of the interest under protest and then go to arbitration later with the Iranians for the amount disputed. (In the end $130 million in interest payments were disputed.)

It took about an hour more to get agreed figures on bank loans and deposits. This process involved some of the leading bankers in the country

8. To minimize the possibility of attachments directed at Iranian property, the Bank of England preferred to hold gold that had no history of being owned by Iran, so in the end a three-way swap was conducted, with the Bank of England ending up with 1.6 million ounces in Fort Knox, Kentucky, rather than the ex-Iranian gold in New York.

sitting around the large conference table at State, running calculators and preparing schedules, a job many of them had not done in twenty years or more. By 3:00 P.M. they had agreed to stand behind the payment of $4,733,417,403.68 of principal and $800,017,007.42 of interest. They had also produced final loan figures aggregating around $4.8 billion.[9]

In less than four hours, agreement in principle had been reached, but Christopher would have to go back to the Iranians and ask for several modifications. He would ask that Iran pay off all its syndicated loans, which would cost $3.67 billion rather than $3.4 billion; the banks would pay $800 million in interest, but they wanted the right to dispute $130 million in binding arbitration; and the grand total was $200 million short of the $8.1 billion Iran had demanded.

It took until early the next morning to draft the cables to Christopher and the suggested amendments to the agreements.

The Final Hours

From then on there was very little sleep for anyone. State had set up a twenty-four-hour operations center at the start of the Iranian crisis, but it was not until Saturday, January 17, that the Treasury staff went on a twenty-four-hour rotation. Some Treasury officers simply stayed and napped occasionally on their office couches. Food was irregular, but morale was high.

The volume of drafting and redrafting required during this last period dangerously stretched waning resources. Not only did the basic documents have to be continually reviewed and modified to pick up changes, but the dozens of implementing executive orders and regulations of Foreign Assets Control also had to stay on the same cycle. The Justice Department had to produce a lengthy Attorney General's opinion and be prepared to go to court at any point to defend the proposed or actual settlement. Releases and background material had to be prepared for the press and interested members of the public, all in accordance with an endless array of procedural requirements and Freedom of Information Act considerations. At the same time an extraordinary number of calls from the press and various people who wanted to help also had to be dealt with.

At Treasury, most of Saturday was spent straightening out errors that had crept into the documentation because of communications and language difficulties. Vacant offices were turned over to the banker-lawyer team and arrangements made for extra secretarial and telephone service for them.

---

9. This total included certain loans the Export-Import Bank of the United States had made to Iran. Some banks had suggested they be collected only after the bank loans had been satisfied, but that suggestion was rejected.

The draft executive orders and Attorney General opinion were gone over line by line in meetings that lasted all day. The bankers' room at Treasury was hooked up by open line to their operations rooms in New York at Shearman & Sterling (John Hoffman's firm), at the Federal Reserve Bank of New York, and in London. The N.Y. Fed and the Bank of England both arranged to stay open after business hours to pass necessary transfers. By the end of the day, although the escrow agreement had not been completed, and there was some unhappiness among the bankers, the overall signs looked good. Just before midnight Christopher reported that the basic terms of the Declarations were agreed upon except for the amount of assets Iran would receive.

The negotiating team knew that the Department of Defense was holding a significant amount of frozen Iranian funds on deposit at Treasury. These were funds Iran had advanced DOD for the purchase of military equipment that would not now be delivered. Although they had been attached, they, like the Iranian assets in the New York Fed, could be transferred pursuant to a settlement with Iran. Lloyd Cutler decided the time had come to be in a position to transfer those funds if necessary. By 1:00 A.M., January 18, DOD had agreed, and by 9:30 A.M. the New York Fed had received the funds. In the end, $40 million was transferred.

Sunday morning started auspiciously with word that Iran had agreed on $7.955 billion as the amount it would receive—an amount it appeared certain would be produced. Various documents and orders were put in final form. The President and Secretary Muskie signed an order delegating authority to Christopher to sign the adherences to the Declarations in Algiers. The bankers, Treasury, and N.Y. Fed officials worked on the mechanics for completing the transfers of funds. The text of the Escrow Agreement seemed finally to be agreed. Just after midnight, in Algiers, Christopher initialed the Declarations and an Undertaking (which included precise figures and which, at Iran's request, would not be immediately released to the public).

Early in the morning on Monday, January 19, the Algerians reported that Iran had initialed the Declarations, the Undertaking, and the Escrow Agreement. At 4:45 A.M. the President appeared on TV and announced the agreement and the expected return of the hostages. The glow of success did not last long.

About an hour later it developed that, although Iran had initialed the Declarations, the Undertaking, and the Escrow Agreement, it had refused to sign a document called Implementing Technical Clarifications and Directions (ITCD), which amplified the more general provisions in the Escrow Agreement. Included as Attachment B to the ITCD was the form of payment order that Iran would send to the banks to direct them to pay over the deposits. This was an important document to the banks.

As a general rule, a bank will not pay out a depositor's money without a written order from the depositor. In this instance, the banks were being asked to pay out over $5.5 billion, some of which they would get back through an escrow arrangement to which they were not parties. They understandably felt they needed something, and to satisfy that need they drafted Attachment B, a draft payment order, and sent it to Iran's lawyers in London and to the escrow agreement team in Algiers.

When the draft payment order reached Tehran, Ali Reza Nobari, the head of Iran's central bank, objected to sending it. He pointed out that the order contained a clause releasing the banks from any further liability to Iran if they made the payments as directed. He took the position that, if Iran later found that banks had deposits they had not turned over, Iran had a right to those deposits and that the inclusion of the release clause amounted to perfidy or worse.

As soon as the problem was understood in Washington, Treasury called the banks, and they readily agreed to drop the offensive release. Substitute language was drafted, telephoned to Christopher, to Iran's lawyers, Brown in London, and Wagendorf in Germany. That was all done by 10:00 A.M. on Monday, January 19, but the atmosphere had apparently been poisoned. Christopher reported that Benyahia was depressed and that the Iranians were charging there had been bad faith. It did not help to point out that the Iranians had received the draft order on Saturday and never said anything about it until Monday. The ITCD had not been signed, and it seemed unlikely that it ever would be. The situation was grim, and no word came through all day. Treasury did, however, continue discussions and reached agreement with the banks that they would pay over even if the ITCD was not signed, so long as they received an adequate payment order.

About dinner time on Monday, Mundheim called from Algiers to report that further discussions had produced an Iranian insistence on a short-form payment order that probably would not be acceptable to the banks. He said they would try to draft something.

At 8:30 P.M., Roger Brown, Iran's lawyer in London, called to say he had drafted a long-form payment order that was acceptable to bank counsel in London and that he was reasonably sure Tehran would accept. Mundheim called at 8:52 P.M. suggesting amendments to the ITCD and a short-form order that he would send back through the Algerians. There really was not much choice. We simply did not have time to renegotiate the ITCD, so we told Mundheim to suspend his approach but to try to get the ITCD signed without any Annex B. We would rely on Brown to produce a payment order.

After an hour's silence—a very long hour for everyone—Brown called to report Tehran's acceptance of his procedure and of the text. The order would soon be transmitted by telex from Tehran and on its receipt in London, New York, and Washington, the transaction could go forward.

As it was set forth in the documents, consummation of the financial settlement involved a number of precise steps, none of which had been fully rehearsed. When the twelve deposit banks received the proper payment order, each would pay over the Iranian deposits it held in its overseas branches to the Federal Reserve Bank of New York. That step involved payments by twelve banks aggregating $5.5 billion from overseas branches, principally in London, Paris, and Germany. When the N.Y. Fed had received the payments, it would transfer the payments to, and hold them in, an account that it had opened with the Bank of England, which was to act as escrow agent, in London. When the N.Y. Fed had deposits in its London holding account plus gold and securities totaling at least $7.955 billion and when all the necessary instructions and agreements had been signed, it would transfer that amount of deposits and assets to the Bank of England as escrow agent.

The Bank of England would then notify the Central Bank of Algeria that it was holding the amount required under the Undertaking and that it was ready to act as provided in the Escrow Agreement. The Algerian central bank would then notify the governments of both Iran and the United States that all preliminary steps had been completed. Iran would then release the hostages, and when the Algerian government notified the governments of the United States and Iran that the hostages had left Iran, then the Algerian central bank would instruct the Bank of England to return those Iranian assets that were left after paying off the syndicated bank loans and setting up the $1.4 billion escrow account to secure payment of the nonsyndicated bank loans.

But before that process could move ahead, the payment order had to be received. For more than four hours the telex was silent. Every half hour or so one of the bank lawyers in London would call Tehran and receive an evasive or discourteous reply. At 2:35 A.M. on Tuesday, the telex chattered, and by 3:00 A.M. the coded test words had been confirmed. By 3:16 A.M. a payment order in the correct form had been received, but it contained many errors and omissions (see p. 276). At 3:20 A.M. Mundheim called to report that Iran would not sign the ITCD. After twenty minutes the banks were still deliberating about what to do. Treasury Secretary Miller, with more spirit than authority, directed them to pay. By 4:10 A.M. all the bank transfers had been received by the Federal Reserve Bank of New York, and by 5:20 A.M. deposits, gold, and securities with an agreed value of $7.977 billion were ready in the London holding account of the N.Y. Fed to be transferred to the Bank of England as escrow agent.

But the Escrow Agreement still had not been signed by all the parties, so the Bank of England still had not been appointed as escrow agent. The open issue was whether the existing documentation, without the by then infamous ITCD, was complete enough to give needed protection to all participants. Lawyers for the banks, the Treasury, and the N.Y. Fed had been looking at the issue of protection all night. In Washington and New York they had concluded the protection for the United States and for the N.Y. Fed was adequate. There were difficulties in communicating this conclusion to the U.S. team in Algiers, but with the President urging everyone on in periodic telephone calls, Solomon finally was able to achieve a consensus and ordered the N.Y. Fed representative to proceed. At 6:18 A.M., the Escrow Agreement and a supplement called Technical Arrangements, but not the ITCD, were executed by all parties. The last open points had been resolved.

Our log of the final mechanical steps reads as follows:

6:18 A.M.   Escrow Agreement and Technical Arrangements signed by Christopher and Patrikis.

6:43 A.M.   Account with Bank of England opened.

6:45 A.M.   Fed holding account funds, gold, and securities transferred to Bank of England escrow.

7:27 A.M.   Written confirmation of transfer to escrow completed.

7:45 A.M.   Algiers typist started typing escrow agent's certificate.

8:00 A.M.   Certificate conditionally delivered to Algerian central bank.

8:06 A.M.   Algerian central bank notified Algerian government of the deposits.

before
12:00   Algerian central bank notified Iranian government of the deposits.

12:00   Ronald Reagan sworn in as President.

12:05 P.M.   Algerian central bank notified U.S. government of the deposits.

12:33–
42 P.M.   Aircraft departed Tehran with hostages aboard.

1:35 P.M.   Government of Algeria certified to U.S. and Iran that hostages have departed from Iran.

2:00 P.M.   On instructions of Algerian central bank, Bank of England (1) disbursed $3.67 billion to the Federal Reserve Bank of New York, which then disbursed the funds to the agent banks for the loan syndicates, (2) disbursed $2.88 billion to Iran, and (3) held balance ($1.42 billion) in escrow pending settlement of outstanding loan and interest claims of U.S. banks.

When the Algerian central bank had certified its receipt of the funds called for in the Undertaking, there was nothing more we could do. The hostages' release depended on others doing what they had agreed to do. So the rumpled, dog-tired bankers and lawyers and government officials gradually left for home and sleep and were replaced by well-tailored, vivacious guests invited by the new President to view his inaugural parade from the capacious windows of the Treasury.

Evaluating the Financial Settlement

The settlement obtained the release of the hostages. It would be difficult to overestimate the importance of that. Their detention had distorted foreign policy objectives of the nation and diverted the attention and energy of the President and his advisers for more than a year. A new President might well have been able to obtain their release, but that release might not have come quickly. The status of the blocked assets would have continued to grow more complicated and more difficult to unravel. The courts might have sustained attachments in pending cases, or in frustration the Congress might have taken action. While the hostages remained in Iran the diversion of presidential and governmental attention would have continued.

More speculative but perhaps more important was the continuing risk that the hostages might be harmed. The situation in Iran was unstable. Only three months after the settlement, Iran's Prime Minister and many key members of its Majlis were assassinated by a bomb. Ayatollah Khomeini denounced the assassination as the work of the United States. Would he or could he have prevented acts of revenge against the hostages? Where might that have led?

But even assuming the desirability or even the near necessity of achieving a settlement by January 20, it is still fair to consider whether the settlement was a good one from the standpoint of protecting U.S. interests. Three types of exceptions have been taken to the financial terms of the settlement. The first was that the President had exceeded his legal authority in making the settlement. On July 2, 1981, the Supreme Court unanimously held that the actions taken by the President were within his authority.

The second exception taken was that the banks had received more favorable treatment than individuals with claims against Iran. That is certainly true, but in the authors' view the course of the negotiations demonstrates that it was inevitable. The banks were holding $5.5 billion of Iran's assets in their overseas branches, and there was no way to obtain the release of the hostages without simultaneously dealing with the return of those assets. In the end it was Iran that decided on January 15 to pay off its bank loans, so that it could recover part of the $5.6 billion of overseas deposits, and it was that decision—more favorable to the banks than they or the U.S. government had demanded—that produced the apparent inequality of treatment. It was not, nor should it have been, U.S. policy to force any class of U.S. creditors to settle for anything less than the most favorable possible terms. As a class, the banks came out well, but those who hold cash usually do. The smaller banks in particular came out well. Since the Iranian loans made by virtually all of them were of the syndicated variety, they were paid off in full immediately.

The third exception taken was that the United States should have obtained more favorable terms for other U.S. claimants against Iran. In our view the chronicle of the negotiations makes it extremely doubtful that better terms were available, but some claimants assert that at least the United States should not have agreed to cancel the claimants' attachments and return the $2.2 billion of Iran's assets blocked in the domestic branches of U.S. banks.[10] The assumption apparently is that U.S. claimants would have fared better in U.S. courts than in international arbitration and would have been able to satisfy judgments from the $2.2 billion in blocked deposits. Both assumptions are open to question. Many claimants had signed agreements providing that the law and the courts of Iran would decide any disputes under the agreements. Iran also had other defenses that U.S. courts might well have accepted.

Equally important, it is by no means clear that the courts would have enforced the claimants' attachments. Most of the funds attached were accounts in the name of either Bank Markazi or the National Iranian Oil Company, but most of the claims were against other Iranian entities. Iran would undoubtedly have argued that the attached deposits were immune from attachments by reason of sovereign immunity. They would also have asserted that Bank Markazi and NIOC were not legally responsible for the actions of other governmental entities and hence that their funds were not attachable. There is considerable legal support for at least the latter position. The claimants would have had to argue that Iran was not entitled to sovereign immunity and that all Iranian entities are the same or, as the argument was summarized by the lawyers involved, that Iran was one Big Mullah.

Obviously, the situation varies from claimant to claimant, but overall the claimants appear to be faring as well as if not better than they would have in the U.S. courts. One should also remember that under the Declarations many nonbank claimants who, like banks, held Iranian assets are permitted provisionally to retain those assets (which aggregate over $1 billion) until their bona fide claims against Iran have been resolved.

---

10. Under the Declarations of Algiers, the blocked domestic deposits of Iran were to be returned by July 20, 1981, except for $1 billion that was deposited in the escrow fund to secure payment of arbitral awards. The six-month delay in returning those deposits was to provide time for U.S. courts to rule on challenges to the President's executive order directing such return. It should also be noted that an additional $1 billion or more in assets (mostly on the books of oil companies) remained in the United States in situations where Iran's title to such assets was subject to contest.

Our personal judgment then was and remains that the financial settlement overall, and in historical perspective, was favorable to U.S. claimants against Iran.

The Effectiveness of the Economic Sanctions

Economic sanctions are a deceptively attractive means by which a nation or group of nations can exert pressure on another. They are nonlethal; they are simple to impose; and they often appear to be without cost. They have been considered and used in a wide variety of international situations through the centuries. But with the exception of measures taken as a corollary to military action, the sanctions imposed against Iran were the most comprehensive imposed by the United States in this century. The obvious first question is: did they work?

Modern history does not contain many illustrations of situations where sanctions have demonstrably worked to effect a change in a nation's position or conduct. That may in part be because the relevant facts are elusive. Evaluation of the effectiveness of sanctions necessarily involves judgments about the states of mind of political leaders. That is a difficult undertaking, because no political leader is likely to admit publicly he was forced to make an important decision because of pressure from abroad. Such an admission from the political leadership in Iran would not seem likely. It is however clear from both public and private statements of Iran's leaders during tbe period that they bitterly resented the sanctions. It is also clear that by the end of 1980, in part because of the drain on resources caused by the war with Iraq, Iran was beginning to feel adverse effects from the sanctions. Its foreign exchange reserves were dangerously low, and it was having difficulties obtaining spare parts. But it was also feeling the pressure of its political isolation, and the detention of the hostages was no longer the domestic political asset it had been. Historians may be able at some point to answer the question whether in fact these pressures did cause a change in mind of Iran's political leaders. Our view, based more on surmise than evidence, is that the sanctions did have a considerable, albeit delayed, impact, but perhaps not a decisive one.

Chapter 4 discussed in detail the two types of sanctions against Iran: trade and financial. The trade sanctions were directed at interdicting the flow of physical goods to and from Iran, particularly goods vital to important sectors of Iran's economy and government. Trade between the United States and Iran was effectively shut down by U.S. sanctions, but except where military equipment was involved some of our allies did not impose effective trade sanctions. Nonallied nations conducted trade as usual. The result was that, although Iran apparently had to pay more for many types of goods and some types of goods (particularly replacement parts) remained in short supply, it was only toward the end of 1980 that there were indications of significant problems. Available reporting, however, was not comprehensive. Accordingly, it is hard to conclude more than that the trade sanctions contributed to a feeling of isolation in Iran, to increased costs, and to some disadvantage on the battlefield as the Iran-Iraq war dragged on.

Evaluating the effectiveness of the financial sanctions involves less guesswork. The financial sanctions (none of which were imposed by our allies) effectively immobilized $12 billion of Iran's assets, including most of its available foreign exchange reserves. In the beginning, proceeds from the sale of oil provided ample new foreign exchange resources. But as time went on, oil sales steadily fell. The trade sanctions began to have some effect, mechanical breakdowns occurred in the oil fields, and the Iran-Iraq war forced closure of some facilities and scared off prospective purchasers. By late fall it appeared doubtful that foreign exchange proceeds from oil sales were covering Iran's foreign currency needs, particularly the need to pay cash for military supplies. Their reserves were declining, and the quickest and most obvious source of relief was to recover some or all of the blocked $12 billion. Western logic—a thought process somewhat removed from Islamic philosophy—leads to a conclusion that the financial sanctions must have had some impact. What they did not do, however, was force an unwilling Iran to return the hostages until it was politically ready to do so.

Lessons on the Use of Economic Sanctions

Whether they worked or not, the economic sanctions against Iran were the highwater mark in U.S. use of this weapon since World War II. On that basis alone they deserve attention for any lessons they might teach for the future.

Our first conclusion flows from the unique level of U.S. economic relations with Iran. For some years the United States had been Iran's largest supplier of manufactured goods, both military and civilian. Iran held the bulk of its foreign exchange reserves in U.S. dollars on deposit in U.S. banks. There were substantially more Iranian assets under U.S. control than U.S. assets under the control of Iran. The imposition of sanctions in that context was certain—at least over time—to have an impact. It is also the kind of leverage unlikely to be replicated, if only because countries saw what happened to Iran and will now be less likely to put the bulk of their liquid assets within U.S. reach.

Since World War II the United States has imposed various types of trade sanctions with varying degrees of impact against the U.S.S.R. and Eastern Europe, the People's Republic of China, North Korea, Cuba, Vietnam, Rhodesia, and Cambodia. It also imposed financial sanctions against some of the same nations, but with little impact, because their financial assets were meager or largely beyond U.S. reach. U.S. financial sanctions against Iran not only were unprecedentedly successful, but they also represented a significant expansion of U.S. power, namely, unprecedented extraterritorial reach.

The United States was able, for nearly fourteen months, to block $5.6 billion of Iran's deposits in overseas branches of U.S. banks, mostly in Europe. That extraterritorial reach provided the real leverage. In other post-World War II financial sanctions programs, the United States blocked virtually no financial assets outside the United States. The Treasury Office of Foreign Assets Control occasionally asserted that the United States had the power to block dollar accounts wherever they might be located, but there were virtually no Chinese, Cuban, or Vietnamese deposits in overseas branches of U.S. banks, so the issue never really arose. The United States' assertion of extraterritorial power was challenged by Iran in the courts of the United Kingdom, France, West Germany, and Turkey, but no decisions were reached before the settlement.

To state the lesson more generally, the Iranian episode demonstrated to the world that the United States has the potential capacity to block dollar accounts wherever they may be located. That capacity remains to some extent unproven, because in future episodes foreign courts or governments might attempt to nullify U.S. actions, and their legal foundation has never been judicially validated either in the United States or abroad.

The blocking of overseas assets was justified on two grounds. The first was that every country has a right to legislate and exercise power over its nationals wherever they may be. This was a conventional U.S. assertion, and it has led in the past to bitter confrontations between the United States and other countries, a recent illustration being the attempt by the United States to prevent overseas subsidiaries of U.S. companies from honoring contracts to supply compressors and other equipment to the U.S.S.R. for use in the proposed Soviet gas pipeline to Western Europe. That rationale has not had an unbroken record of success.

The second ground is based on the unique nature of Eurodollar deposit accounts. Those are accounts denominated in dollars maintained by offices of banks located outside the United States and principally in Europe (hence the name "Eurodollar"). For reasons rooted in history and practice, virtually all banking transactions in Eurodollars clear through New York. Thus a payment by Iran from a dollar account in London to an exporter in Germany is made through the bank payments clearance system in New York. The payment is electronically routed through New York: Iran's London bank tells its New York correspondent bank to pay the New York correspondent bank of the German exporter.

Since Eurodollar accounts operate through New York, the United States asserted that it could effectively block those accounts without resort to extraterritorial power simply by blocking the use of the U.S. clearing or "cover" accounts, that is, the dollar accounts all foreign banks maintain with their U.S. correspondent banks in New York to cover or facilitate payments. Theoretically this market structure would permit the United States to block dollar accounts not only at the overseas branches of U.S. banks but also those at foreign banks. As a practical matter, however, a U.S. blocking order could not be effectively extended beyond U.S.-controlled overseas branches, and no attempt was made so to extend the Iranian blocking order. The U.S. Treasury has no power to visit the offices of Barclay's Bank in London to find out whether Iran (or some other sanctionee) has dollar accounts there. It could and does examine U.S. branches in London, but to examine a U.K. bank in London it would need the cooperation of the Bank of England. That might not be forthcoming.

These practical limitations mean that blocking of dollar accounts abroad will ultimately put U.S. banks at a competitive disadvantage. If a foreigner can deposit London dollars in Barclay's for the same rate as Chase Manhattan Bank pays, he may well bank with Barclay's rather than take the risk that his London account with Chase Manhattan Bank could be blocked by the U.S. government. That means Chase Manhattan Bank will lose a deposit and, more important, a customer relationship. It can buy the dollars from Barclay's, but it cannot get the rest of the customer's banking business, because it does not know who he is. In the longer term that loss of business can be important.

A further consequence of indiscriminate future U.S. blocking of dollar accounts would likely be to cause some foreigners to shift assets out of dollars and ultimately to weaken the dollar as a reserve currency and as the mainstay of the international monetary system. That would not be in the interest of either the United States or its allies, and a recognition of this potential cost will, one hopes, lead to very selective use of this type of sanction.

Finally, the Iranian episode illustrates once again the familiar lesson that the more universally nations support sanctions the more effective they are likely to be. There is no real doubt that if our allies had imposed sanctions comparable to those the United States deployed, Iran's economy could have been shut down quite quickly. Whether or not that would have been productive in resolving the crisis amicably can be debated. But it is clear that economic sanctions that are not effective are costly to the country imposing the sanction and likely to have only limited political impact on the target country.

6 THE BANKERS' CHANNEL

JOHN E. HOFFMAN, JR.

The Role of the U.S. Banks

Confidential contacts and negotiations between U.S. bank lawyers and Iranian representatives began shortly after the failure of the rescue mission in April 1980 and culminated in the structuring and execution of a multibillion-dollar financial transaction in January 1981 that was essential in freeing the hostages. The lawyers for the U.S. banks in these efforts were a small coterie, mostly well known to each other and accustomed to working together under pressure toward resolution of complicated domestic or international financial tangles involving their major banking clients. These activities involve a highly technical and inbred legal practice, where the familiarity of the lawyers and their clients with one another and past experience with similar problems are important factors in their ability to "work out" of such situations. As the title of the scene changes from Iran to Chrysler to the Falkland Islands to Mexico or Brazil, many of the same faces are seen around the table and are known to the government officials who are apt to be involved. The New York law firm of Shearman & Sterling, of which I am a partner, represents Citibank in such matters. My responsibilities for Citibank's Iranian litigation led to encounters with the Iranian representatives and the ensuing financial negotiations that were an important element in the hostages' release. This chapter relates those events from my perspective as one of the bank lawyers.

The unusual role of U.S. commercial banks in the resolution of the Iranian hostage crisis emerged as a consequence of the substantial pre-existing financial relationships between the banks and Iran and of the U.S. government's imposition of economic sanctions, including the protracted Iranian asset freeze, affecting those relationships.

It was apparent from the outset that any negotiated solution would require some resolution of the financial imbroglio, which could not be accomplished without the direct involvement of the banks that held most of the billions of dollars in frozen assets. Early signals from the Iranian side in the spring of 1980 regarding conditions for release of the hostages included financial terms, and of the celebrated four conditions announced publicly by Ayatollah Khomeini on September 12 three were financial or economic demands. It would have been foolish, if not impossible, to try to deal with the financial tangle without the participation of those most directly involved, those whose knowledge and expertise could be of significant assistance to the government negotiators. The structure and implementation of the financial settlement would not have been possible without the active participation, support, and cooperation of the banks.

It was also evident from the start that the very existence of worldwide litigation over Iran's external assets would involve regular contact between representatives of U.S. and Iranian interests at a nongovernmental level. The opposing lawyers would have to be together in courts in the United States, England, France, and Germany, where litigation over Iranian assets had been commenced, and there evolved through bank lawyers a regular line of communication with the lawyers representing Iran and thence to the principal factions in Iran.

Intriguing legal issues arising from the asset freeze remain unresolved. Nevertheless, the Iranian experience serves to focus new attention on many important aspects of international financial relationships. How those relationships were used to help free the hostages is the main topic of this chapter. The story also provides a case study in productive cooperation between the government and the private sector at a time when such cooperation was badly needed. The success of that cooperation provides a vital lesson to be taken from the hostage crisis.

The Financial Relationships

The Shah's aggressive development program, funded by vastly increased oil revenue, engaged Iran in a variety of large-scale financial relationships with U.S., European, and Japanese banks. Just before the revolution in 1979, oil revenues were running at a rate of $50 million per day, and in 1978, the last full year before the revolution, aggregated $22.6 billion. This enormous U.S. dollar income was largely recycled through the international banking system to finance imports and capital development projects, with multibillion-dollar balances being held by Iran in accounts with U.S. banks' overseas branches, principally in London. In addition, substantial Iranian investments had been made in West German industries during the Shah's regime. At the time of the freeze on November 14, 1979, Iran held a 25 percent equity investment in Krupp and in Deutsche Babcock. These investments were to figure in the financial link that led to the bank line of negotiations in 1980. Also, Bank Markazi, the central bank of Iran, had approximately $1.2 billion-worth of securities, as well as 1.6 million ounces of gold, on deposit with the Federal Reserve Bank of New York.

Augmenting direct revenues from exports, the government of Iran, as well as public and private sector Iranian enterprises, were substantial borrowers from U.S. and other foreign banks. More than 200 banks, either alone or acting in syndicates of international banks, loaned money to Iran during the boom years of the 1970s. The syndicated loans especially, most of which were led by Chase or Iran Overseas Investment Bank in London, were sizable. While details regarding the amounts borrowed were not easily ascertained, Iranian external debt was roughly $5 billion, of which about $2 billion was owed to U.S. banks (including the Export-Import Bank of the United States).

U.S. banks had a variety of other financial relationships with Iran. Some—particularly standby letters of credit in the nature of performance guarantees and documentary letters of credit issued in favor of the National Iranian Oil Company financing U.S. oil imports—involved very large amounts and had produced postrevolution litigation even before the seizure of the U.S. Embassy.[1] Some U.S. banks had offices or other investments in Iran. For purposes of the hostage negotiations, however, Iran's deposits and the banks' loans to Iran were the critical relationships.

Prefreeze Activity of U.S. Banks

The events of November 4, 1979, sharply concentrated the attention that U.S. banks had already been giving their Iranian relationships for many months. Although syndicated debt payments were more or less current, the turbulent conditions in Iran throughout 1979 did little to inspire confidence among the bankers, and the seizure of the U.S. Embassy and the hostages caused urgent reviews of loan exposure and coverage.

Loan agreements were analyzed for provisions allowing for declarations of default based on events other than nonpayment, such as "adverse changes" in debtors' circumstances, changes in ownership due to possible nationalization, and war or other military action. Assuming that loans could be declared in default and "accelerated," so that the total outstanding balances would be due and payable immediately, from what sources could satisfaction be obtained? U.S. lawyers were comfortable with local U.S. laws providing for setoffs or court orders of attachment of debtors' assets.

---

1. U.S. commercial relations with Iran suffered disruptions throughout 1979, and some of these events precipitated litigation in U.S. courts, seeking to block bank payments to Iran under various letters of credit.

However, the major Iranian deposits were booked in London and Paris branch accounts. The banks and their lawyers immediately began a crash study of the relevant laws of those countries.

Few of the syndicated loan agreements had default provisions that accommodated the circumstances prevailing during the days immediately following November 4. However, one potentiality (in addition to the obvious possibilities of repudiation or nonpayment) seemed to offer a theoretical legal trigger. An Iranian asset freeze plainly was an option for the U.S. government. All major banks had previous experience with situations in which the Treasury Department had acted to block the assets of, or had imposed economic sanctions on, a number of foreign countries. Some bank lawyers developed a theory that such a freeze would be analogous to the appointment of a receiver for a debtor, which, under New York law (§151 of the debtor-creditor law), authorizes a bank to set off immediately all accounts of the debtor against all outstanding loans, both matured and unmatured. Papers were drafted to implement this action, should a freeze occur.

Speculation that some U.S. banks may have urged or at least had some advance knowledge of a freeze led the House Banking Committee to consider that question in connection with its 1981 report on the financial aspects of the hostage crisis.[2] The report found no evidence to support such speculation. Because of their experience with Cuba and similar countries, the banks needed no advance notice and in fact had initiated a logical course of contingency planning well before any government decision. I personally had no advance knowledge of the freeze, had not lobbied for it, and know of no one else who did.

The Blocking Order: Early Days

U.S. banks holding the largest Iranian deposits received word of the freeze early on the morning of November 14 by telephone calls from Deputy Secretary of the Treasury Robert Carswell.[3] The banks' European offices had already heard of announcements made earlier in the day by President Bani-Sadr in Tehran that, in response to the November 12 decision of the United States to prohibit further oil imports from Iran, Iran had decided to remove its deposits from U.S. banks, later estimated to be more than $12 billion, and to transfer them to banks in countries that had not joined in the U.S. sanctions. Iran justified this action by claiming that U.S. banking interests were responsible for the admission of the former Shah to the United States.

2. House Committee on Banking, Finance and Urban Affairs, *Iran: The Financial Aspects of the Hostage Settlement Agreement*, 97th Cong., 1st sess., July 1981.

3. Carswell and I had been partners at Shearman & Sterling before he was appointed to the Treasury. With that fact in mind we took special care and precautions during the course of the Iranian events to maintain our contacts at arms' length, although our previous experience did provide a basis for trust and confidence.

The banks had been closely monitoring their Iranian accounts for any significant movements of funds[4] and were able to implement the blocking order immediately. Overseas bank branches were told by telephone to block Iranian accounts, pending clarification of which accounts were actually affected. At the request of the Treasury Department, the banks instructed their foreign offices to report the effect of the freeze on the money and foreign exchange markets.

Soon after the freeze, U.S. banks with substantial overseas deposits took action, licensed by Treasury, to set off all syndicated and nonsyndicated loans against their overseas Iranian deposits. There were a number of manifest problems with these setoffs, however.

Few of the Iranian overseas deposits were in the name of an Iranian debtor or guarantor. It would clearly be difficult to set off the account of one entity against the debt of a separate, unrelated entity. This problem was met through invocation of the "Big Mullah" theory, under which it was argued that, as a result of the Iranian revolution and its subsequent nationalization programs, all elements of the Iranian economy had become one. The theory was further strengthened by one of the principles of the new Islamic constitution, which gave control of all "major and mother industries," including banking, to the governmental sector. Thus it was argued that a bank was justified in applying the deposit accounts of Bank Markazi, the government-owned central bank, against the debts of NIOC, the government-owned National Iranian Oil Company. The validity and legal effect of the Big Mullah theory was a critical issue in much of the Iranian litigation that ensued.[5]

4. Indeed, some banks had received telephone calls over the previous weekend from the Federal Reserve Bank of New York inquiring whether there had been recent unusual activity.

5. It was by no means a novel issue. Cuban claims litigation has been a hardy perennial on the court dockets in the United States, England, and elsewhere for more than twenty years, and in June 1983 the U.S. Supreme Court handed down a decision in one of the Cuban cases where the "identity issue" was crucial. In *First National City Bank v. Banco Para el Comercio Exterior de Cuba,* 103 S. Ct. 2591 (1983), the Supreme Court confronted whether, under the circumstances before it, a Cuban government agency was identical to the Cuban government for the purposes of a counterclaim. In that case, a Cuban government agency known as Bancec in 1961 sued Citibank (then called First National City Bank) in New York under a letter of credit. Citibank sought to counterclaim for the value of its Cuban branches that had been expropriated by the Cuban government, contending that Bancec and the Cuban government were identical for the purposes of the counterclaim.

On June 17, 1983, the Supreme Court sustained Citibank's counterclaim, holding that, on the facts before it, the Cuban government was the true beneficiary of the letter of credit, and Citibank was entitled to an offset. The Court noted that, within days of the commencement of the action, the Cuban government had transferred the assets of Bancec (including the letter of credit claim against Citibank) to a Cuban ministry or other governmental entities that could be held responsible on Citibank's expropriation counterclaim.

The Big Mullah issue was never decided in the Iranian cases, and the propriety of banks' Eurodollar setoffs on that ground remains uncertain. As part of the Algiers Accords in January 1981, Iran assumed responsibility for government-sector debts and authorized Bank

Another problem concerned the maturity of the loans. Even with the imposition of the freeze, there were few clearcut events of default. In fact, only one syndicated loan was ever formally declared in default by a vote of the requisite majority of banks. The banks did take ironic comfort in a statement attributed to Bani-Sadr on November 23 that overseas debts contracted under the Shah would not be honored. The banks claimed that this statement amounted to repudiation.

Yet another problem related to some of the Iranian deposits, such as Dutch guilder accounts in Paris or Swiss franc accounts in London, which were not in the currency of the debts (largely denominated in dollars). Setoff of these accounts would present problems under applicable local laws.

These issues and more were apparent to the banks. It was equally apparent, however, that speed in effecting setoffs was vital. The formidable legal arguments could be dealt with later, and with greater comfort, if the deposits had not disappeared in the meantime.

It was the objective of both the banks and the U.S. government that the accounts remain intact. Since there was considerable uncertainty regarding the effectiveness of the purported extraterritorial reach of the freeze, application of the bank setoffs provided additional assurance that the accounts would remain blocked, while brigades of lawyers battled over the issue in the months or years to come.

The setoffs by themselves would not have consumed all the Iranian overseas deposits but for the effect of sharing provisions of the loan agreements that created the "black hole" problem, briefly discussed in chapter 4. As explained there, syndicated loan agreements commonly provide for sharing recoveries or payments pro rata among syndicate members. Thus a bank that recovered its debt by a setoff could be obligated to share that recovery among other less fortunate syndicate members that held no Iranian deposits. An example illustrates the ensuing problem:

Say a bank has a 10 percent participation in a $100 million loan but is lucky enough to have $100 million on deposit from the debtor. On default, the bank sets off its $10 million claim against the $100 million deposit and would be paid but for a sharing provision that would require it to share 90 percent of any payment or recovery with the other members of the syndicate. Thus it must give up $9 million of the $10 million setoff to the syndicate. Now having retained only $1 million of its $10 million claim, it sets off again for $9 million against the remaining $90 million deposit. But again it must give up 90 percent, or $8.1 million. It then sets off that amount. The

---

Markazi to negotiate with U.S. bank creditors on behalf of all Iranian debtor entities. Those negotiations have led to debt settlements that reach the extreme fringes of the Big Mullah theory. That result was due in part to the leverage effected at the outset of the crisis by the Big Mullah setoffs.

process continues until the bulk of the $100 million deposit disappears into the black hole of the sharing mechanism.

The U.S. banks with foreign deposits faced actual and sometimes strident demands by syndicate members for sharing of any setoffs. Accordingly, many banks with foreign deposits claimed setoffs not only to cover their own participations but also their black hole exposure to the syndicates.

Through the application of the freeze order and the setoffs, all Iran's dollar deposits in overseas branches of U.S. banks were effectively immobilized.

Litigation Begins and Escalates

As anticipated, Iran promptly demanded payment of its overseas accounts, focusing at first, not surprisingly, on the larger London accounts. On November 28, Bank Markazi telexed payment orders for small U.S. dollar transfers out of its London accounts with various U.S. banks. These orders were not honored, and Markazi thereupon demanded transfer of its full balances in these accounts within two days. The freeze prevented U.S. banks from complying with Markazi's demand, and as a result, on November 30, 1979, Bank Markazi brought suit against five U.S. banks in the English courts. Several weeks later, Bank Markazi added to its claims against the banks the contention that it had intended to use the blocked funds to buy gold on November 30, 1979, and therefore intended to hold the banks responsible for any losses suffered as a result of not being able to do so. Bank Markazi initiated similar litigation in the French courts in December.

In turn, the U.S. banks, on the basis that their overseas setoffs might not be entirely upheld, sued Iran for the unpaid loans and attached Iranian assets in the United States and Europe, principally in Germany, where Iran had substantial capital investments in German companies. Nonbank creditors also sued Iran. These included, among others, various U.S. contractors and other companies involved in the ambitious modernization programs undertaken during the Shah's regime and persons who had had their property destroyed or confiscated during the revolution and subsequent nationalization programs. Very quickly all discoverable Iranian assets in the United States were blocked, not only by the presidential freezing order, but also by layer upon layer of judicial attachment orders. Since domestic setoffs had not been permitted by the Treasury, banks obtained attachments, permitted by amendments to the freeze regulations. The banks also booked setoffs "subject to Executive Order 12170" to preserve their legal position that the banks had a claim against their own domestic Iranian deposits superior to that of other attaching creditors.[6]

6. The express reference to Executive Order 12170, 44 Fed. Reg. 65, 729 (Nov. 15, 1979),

While there were obvious legal difficulties with these domestic attachments, not the least of which involved sovereign immunity, the risk of liability for wrongful attachments seemed minimal, because all the attached property was already blocked by the presidential freezing order.

Banks Consider How to Avoid the Cuba Syndrome

As 1979 came to a close, battalions of lawyers began to dig in for trench-warfare litigation that gave ample promise of dragging on for years, or even decades, as in the case of the postrevolution Cuban lawsuits, which after twenty years are still being litigated in U.S. courts. As they considered the vast amounts at stake and the uncertainties of litigation prospects, banks and lawyers began thinking about ways out of the legal-financial thicket.

Starting the day of the freeze, regular contact had been maintained with the banks by the U.S. government, which was closely monitoring the domestic and overseas assets litigation. In the course of these contacts, a series of meetings took place in early 1980 between banks and the Treasury Department to review the situation.

Hans Angermueller, then Senior Executive Vice President of Citibank, and I attended one such meeting with Treasury Deputy Secretary Carswell, Treasury General Counsel Robert Mundheim, and State Department Legal Adviser Roberts Owen on February 20, 1980. We discussed the possibilities of debt settlement structures using frozen overseas deposits to liquidate bank loan claims. Our general ideas at the time were later labeled "Plan A" and (a slight variation) "Plan B." Under Plan A, the United States would lift the asset freeze overseas upon release of the hostages, and Iran's dollar debt to U.S. banks would be paid off from previously frozen foreign deposits. The banks would then release their claims to setoffs or attachments on domestic deposits, freeing them for satisfaction of nonbank claims. While no agreement on these procedures was reached, the mechanics of such a plan appeared feasible and could include elements that had been used in previous analogous situations. Bank letters of credit had been pivotal, in a similar situation, in working out the Cuban prisoner exchange after the Bay of Pigs fiasco in the early 1960s. But any such arrangements required the agreement of the third necessary player—Iran—which was missing from the table.

We believed that because of the extraordinarily large sums of Iranian external assets that had been blocked, there was a substantial incentive for Iran to agree to such arrangements. Iran had been trying to recover from the

---

was intended to reserve the legal question of the effect of the executive order, while at the same time satisfying the requirements of legal precedents governing the manner in which the priority of a setoff is established over other competing claims, private or governmental.

debilitating aspects of the revolution and of drawn-out strikes in the oil fields. While the war with Iraq had not yet begun, nevertheless, Iran, with a 35 percent unemployment rate and a virtually stagnant economy, could hardly afford to lose such large sums of money. The enticement of a solution involving the return of these much-needed assets could be a meaningful bargaining chip in any hostage negotiations.

From the first, we had frequent contacts with lawyers representing Iran in the United States, London, Paris, and Germany. My own responsibility for supervising Citibank's litigation in all of these countries afforded many opportunities to look for signals indicating Iranian interest in settlement. In March, I was invited to speak at Harvard Law School about the Iranian asset litigation, and I suggested that Tom Shack, Iran's lead U.S. lawyer, be included, in order to give a balanced presentation. This event provided me with an opportunity to discover that there actually was sentiment favoring settlement on the Iranian side. Later in March, I attended a hearing on our Iranian case in Paris, hoping that some contact might develop there. In the meantime, we continued to reflect on possible settlement structures and found similar considerations under way at other major banks.

Shortly after the failure of the hostage rescue mission in April 1980, Citibank and I discussed going back to the U.S. government with some more concrete settlement proposals. On May 1, Angermueller and I reviewed these possibilities with Robert Douglass, General Counsel of the Chase Manhattan Bank, and Chase's lead outside attorney, Frank Logan of Milbank, Tweed, Hadley & McCloy, who had called to discuss the situation.

Meanwhile, the litigation struggles continued, and in Germany a hearing was scheduled early in May on Iran's motion to vacate Citibank's court attachment of Iran's Krupp shares.

The German Connection Opens

On May 2, Citibank's counsel in Germany, Peter Mailander, informed me that his partner, Klaus Gerstenmaier, who was handling the litigation, had been asked on April 29 by Peter Heinemann, German counsel for the government of Iran, whether Citibank would be willing to discuss an "economic solution."

Peter Heinemann, who practiced law in Essen, had worked at Shearman & Sterling in 1961 as a foreign trainee in New York, where he had known Angermueller (who is fluent in German). Heinemann was active in Social Democratic Party politics and was soon to be elected a member of the North Rhine-Westphalia parliament. In his forties, he was the son of Gustav Heinemann, who helped form the Christian Democratic Party and later served as President of the Federal Republic of Germany from 1969 to 1974.

Peter's political heritage was relevant, as I later heard that he had been selected by the Iranian Embassy in Bonn to handle the postfreeze legal problems in part because it was sensed that he would have appropriate political skills and might be understanding of the current Iranian revolutionary regime because of his father's opposition, while President of the Federal Republic, to the Shah's human rights policies.

Heinemann's colleague, Herbert Wagendorf, was in his fifties and was reported to be an expert business lawyer with experience in the Middle East.

These German lawyers, who reported to the Iranian Embassy in Bonn, said that they had recently met several times with the Iranian Minister of Finance and Economics, Reza Salimi, who was Iran's delegate on the Krupp board of directors, and with Governor Ali Reza Nobari of Bank Markazi. They asserted that Nobari and Salimi had instructed them to open confidential negotiations toward a pragmatic economic solution of the worldwide litigation and removal of the attachments on Iran's German investments. Iran was willing to consider confirmation of the validity and enforceability of Citibank's debt claims against Iran and its controlled entities. According to Heinemann, Iran was willing to consider any feasible solution put forth in the context of settlement negotiations. Specifically, he mentioned the possibility that Iran would accept the setoffs by Citibank in London and elsewhere as legally binding, thereby validating the Big Mullah theory and adopting the Plan A concept of paying off debt to U.S. banks with frozen sovereign deposits. Alternatively, Bank Markazi might purchase Citibank's debt claims against Iran, again by using the frozen foreign deposits.

Two important conditions had to be met before Iran would agree to enter into negotiations with Citibank. First, the negotiations and all topics discussed within the context of the negotiations were to be kept strictly secret. If any leak resulted in publicity, the tenuous link would be broken, and Iran would deny any involvement. Further, Iran would not put up any fresh funds. Given these conditions, Iran would favor total setoff of all debt claims by U.S. banks against deposits with U.S. banks. A deal struck with Citibank would break the ice and set a more general process in motion. (Similar feelers were put out to Bank of America and Morgan Guaranty at about the same time.) Contact with Iran would be maintained through Heinemann and Wagendorf, whose mandate to negotiate was backed by President Bani-Sadr. Heinemann asked for our response by the following week, when Nobari would be in Geneva.

I immediately informed Angermueller and Citibank's chairman, Walter Wriston, of the contact with the German lawyers. Wriston was intrigued by the possibility of settlement negotiations. He insisted, however, that any negotiations had to be conducted with an eye toward an overall settlement; Citibank would not work for a deal for itself alone. Furthermore, the U.S. government would have to be informed of and approve every move we made.

In this context, Wriston admonished us to be mindful of the Logan Act, which makes it a crime for a private individual to negotiate with a foreign government on issues directly affecting U.S. government policy. He instructed me to contact Carswell immediately.

I reached Carswell on Saturday morning, May 3. He requested that Angermueller and I come to Washington as soon as possible in order to give him a more complete report. In the meantime, we began to elaborate and refine the Plan A concept we had discussed with the government in February. On May 6, Angermueller and I met with Carswell and Owen in Washington. Carswell, with Owen's agreement, cautioned us to take no steps without the express approval of the U.S. government. He instructed us to keep the lines of communication to the Iranians open but to make no substantive response to their proposal until given the green light by the U.S. government. He further instructed us to find out more about the German lawyers and attempt to determine why the initial signal came to Citibank.

I believed that Citibank was a logical point of contact for the Iranians, as it was involved in litigation with Iran on all fronts and had attachments and court proceedings pending in Germany. I did not learn until after the first meeting with the Iranians' lawyers that they had contacted Bank of America and Morgan Guaranty as well. Those banks also were involved in the Iranian asset litigation in Europe.

Heinemann suggested to Gerstenmaier that we should negotiate for simple fixed terms that could be presented ready-made to appropriate "officials" in Tehran for signature. While this made some sense, it also raised the question that was to plague us to the end: who were we really negotiating with, if anyone? That question was never satisfactorily answered, but the doubt it occasioned dictated the form the negotiations had to take. We simply had to keep putting plans forward until someone in authority on the other side decided to act. It was up to us to design a feasible system and hope that some day someone in Iran would push the starting button.

On May 12, Heinemann told us he had a clear mandate to get as much resolved as possible, provided there was no input of new funds. Six billion dollars—apparently the amount Iran thought had been frozen—was all we had to work with. The Iranians were concerned about prospects for new U.S. legislation, presumably regarding authority for vesting Iranian assets in the U.S. government.

The next day Carswell informed me that my meeting with Iran's counsel had been cleared. I was reminded that the early release of the hostages was of the utmost importance.[7] There could be no economic settlement that did not specify their release as the first principle. Carswell cautioned me

7. Release of the hostages was the trigger event under the Plan A and B concepts we had discussed with the government in February and all other plans we considered for an economic settlement.

against calling in on transatlantic phone and asked me to report to him in person upon my return to the United States. I received clearance from Angermueller, and the first meeting was arranged for May 15 in Kronberg, a small town—with a large and quiet castle turned hotel—near Frankfurt.[8]

The number of people at Shearman & Sterling and Citibank who were informed about the pending discussions was kept severely restricted. My secretary, Helen Lee, who handled logistics and typed the plans, one associate, Margaret Wiener, who had been with me when Mailander called on May 2 and whom I kept briefed in case of emergency, and my senior partner, Robert Clare, were the only ones at my firm who knew of the negotiations for the next several months. At Citibank, only Wriston and Angermueller were informed. While it was personally awkward at times, particularly since most of those working on our Iranian team at Shearman & Sterling, at Citibank, and at our attorneys' offices in London and Paris did not know of the negotiations, I did have the advantage of a plausible cover story for the trips, since I was in fact supervising Citibank's Iranian litigation in all the countries involved. Thus I was able simply to inform my colleagues that I was going to Europe on the Iranian matter, without arousing suspicions.

On May 15, Mailander, Gerstenmaier, and I met Iran's lawyers in Kronberg. I emphasized:

• There would be no separate Citibank deal. Any negotiations must protect other parties similarly situated, whether as claimants against Iran or holders of frozen Iranian assets.

• The U.S. government would be kept completely informed. There could be no deal without its approval, and there would be no financial settlement without the release of the hostages. This was the practical and political reality.

In addition to these conditions, I said it would be necessary to obtain early approval of any tentative deal from the other essential players, specifically (in addition to the U.S. government) the other banks holding the foreign deposits that would be used to fund a settlement.

With those basic parameters, the discussion began. I stressed that a global settlement was feasible and certainly desirable, despite the possibility that it could leave substantial issues unsettled in the United States.

8. Germany frequently had a role in the hostage drama, deriving from a history of commercial and other relationships between it and Iran. As noted above, Iran under the Shah had made substantial investments in Germany. The Iranian chargé d'affaires, later ambassador, in Bonn monitored Iran's commercial relationships there and in Western Europe and thus assumed a major role in dealing with the U.S. economic sanctions. Even Ayatollah Beheshti, a leader of the Islamic Republican Party, had once run a mosque in Hamburg.

The next chapter touches upon the important involvement of the German diplomatic corps in the development of the final negotiations.

The alternative could be years, perhaps decades, of litigation with the attendant expense, uncertainty, and risk of economic destabilization, as worldwide litigation and attachments interfered with any attempt Iran might make to rejoin the international financial and economic community. In this context, I repeatedly referred to the continued pendency of the Cuban litigation.

I reiterated that any settlement would require the involvement of both the U.S. government and the banks, since neither simply lifting the freeze nor removing the setoffs alone would free the deposits. Indeed, basic settlement concepts had in fact been discussed earlier in the year, both with the U.S. government and also among a number of sophisticated bank lawyers who had worked together in the past and who had great confidence in each other. I concluded by reminding Iran's representatives that it was in everyone's best interests to relieve the disruptions to the payment system.

I then proposed a four-step scenario: (1) agreement on a plan stated as a sequence of steps capable of effecting an economic settlement; (2) presentation of the plan, as a "heads of agreement" with possible variations, directly to the principals with authority; (3) having received, from these principals, a confirmation of authority to proceed, presentation of the plan to the other banks holding foreign deposits; and (4) establishment of the mechanism and documents providing for simultaneous release of the hostages, tender of payment, release of the freeze, and release of lawsuits and attachments.

It would be possible, I said, to work these procedures out in a small group, without a "Congress of Vienna." If Iran signaled that it was willing to work toward the same goals, we would set to work any time in any suitable place. A small group could best do this work and could better preserve security. Wagendorf replied that such an arrangement would be better for their side as well, and they need only consult Tehran—whatever that meant. However, they also planned to inform Tom Shack and Leonard Boudin (the Iranian government and Bank Markazi lawyers in the United States), and Bank Markazi counsel in London and Paris.

At the start of the afternoon session, the lawyers for Iran brought up the hostage issue, observing that, if the hostages were released, the freeze would be lifted and settlement would be easy. They believed current progress in our talks could be useful in resolving the hostage crisis. Heinemann said he would go to Tehran to discuss our meeting with Bani-Sadr, commenting that "he and the others are very interested to see such small steps because they make it easier to do something for the release of the hostages." Thus, they said, they wanted a general structure to present to their client.

I replied that we had a number of plans but that it was premature to discuss details. The plans, however, all involved using frozen foreign deposits to pay liquidated claims[9] and establishing some structure satisfying unliquidated claims out of the net overseas balances and frozen assets in the United States. Bearing in mind each government's political problems and their mutual distrust, we still believed that procedures were available to accomplish these goals.

Heinemann said that on his return from Tehran, where he would seek a green light for further talks, we could set the time of our next meeting, which we agreed would be in Germany. Heinemann was sure the answer would be positive. Future meetings could be held in other secure locations or even in New York.

While the negotiations were always conducted in English, our counsel would repeat the essentials in German to be sure there was adequate understanding.

As the meeting finally broke up, Iran's counsel urged us to convey both to our client and to the U.S. government their conviction of Iranian intentions to effect the swiftest possible release of the hostages. It was necessary for us and for our government to understand that the taking of hostages was an act of self-defense in a revolutionary process. Iran wanted only to protect itself against a recurrence of the sort of counterrevolution that had occurred with the help of the C.I.A. in 1953. The Germans assured us that the hostages were well cared for and were in every way healthy. The United States, they continued, was hardly in a position to accuse Iran of violations of international laws, having supported as it did the illegal excesses of the deposed Shah.

They further noted that Bani-Sadr was interested in seeing how the new Iranian parliament would respond to the hostage issue before taking any definitive action. In conclusion, they mentioned that they had informed certain officials within the German government of our discussions and had sought their backing in the efforts to work toward the release of the hostages.

I promised to report all of this to the U.S. government immediately upon my return home the next day. When I returned to New York on May 16, I briefed Carswell in summary by telephone and met with him, Mundheim, and Owen on May 19 to report in detail on our meeting. At Carswell's request, I wrote out a report of the German meeting with a copy of Plan A and Plan B. It was decided that if we received a green light from Iran, I would go back and start discussion of a deal involving simultaneous release of the hostages and release of the freeze on foreign deposits. We noted

---

9. Liquidated claims are those of a determined or readily ascertainable amount, such as claims for an unpaid loan or for payment for goods delivered at an agreed price.

that a great deal of work needed to be done to develop good figures for the loan claims (see chapter 5).

Plan C

On May 20, I was informed that Heinemann had received a green light to proceed with our discussions. His authorization was said to have come from Bani-Sadr through the Iranian Embassy in Bonn. Iran's lawyers proposed that we meet in Kronberg on June 5 and 6. In preparation for this meeting, I prepared the early drafts of "Plan C," and reviewed them in Washington on May 29 with Carswell, Mundheim, and Owen.

As I presented it on June 5 in Kronberg, Plan C had a preamble stating:

> This proposal consists of a series of procedures, whereby
> *Iran would—*
> (1) Release the hostages;
> (2) Pay or establish a mechanism for payments by a neutral
> party of
>
> (i) liquidated debts to certain specified lenders electing to accept
> such payment,
> (ii) liquidated obligations to, or settlements with, certain other
> specified U.S. persons, such payments to come from blocked Iranian
> accounts in London; and
> (3) Receive amounts remaining in London and other overseas
> branches after payments pursuant to (2) above;
> —and—
> *The United States would*
> (1) License release of all overseas blocked accounts; and
> (2) Commit to a good faith negotiation to establish a claims
> program that would settle other U.S. claims and release the balance
> of blocked accounts.

A three-phase sequence of procedures was then set out:

> *Sequence of Procedures*
> *Phase I* established a mechanism whereby when the hostages
> were released, the U.S. freeze as to Iranian property outside the
> United States would be withdrawn and certain debts would be paid
> with a portion of Bank Markazi balances with London branches of
> certain U.S. banks.
> *Phase II* followed immediately upon Phase I, and provided a
> mechanism for payment within a very short period (e.g. 2 weeks) of

additional claims with further portions of the London balances. Since the freeze as to Iranian property outside the United States was withdrawn as an element of Phase I, all such property as well as the London balances remaining at the end of Phase II would become available to Iran.

Phase III also followed immediately upon Phase I, and involved the negotiation and establishment of a claims settlement program, funded with Iranian blocked property in the United States.

Under Plan C, the debt claims of the U.S. banks holding foreign deposits would be satisfied out of those deposits, and the net balance owing to Iran would be transmitted to a "Neutral Bank" in a third country. The Neutral Bank would then issue a letter of credit in favor of Iran, funded by the excess balances and payable upon presentation of (1) a certificate of the International Red Cross evidencing safe return of the hostages; (2) a U.S. Treasury license lifting the freeze outside the United States; and (3) commitments from the U.S. and Iranian governments to enter into immediate negotiations toward setting up a claims settlement process funded out of blocked assets in the United States.

The Neutral Bank would also make a tender offer on behalf of Bank Markazi for the purchase of other liquidated claims against Iran. This procedure was intended to deal with the black hole problem. The essential characteristic for a claim to be included in this phase was that it be "liquidated," that is, for a readily ascertainable amount. While this meant primarily bank claims, it was not exclusive, and it was planned to cover nonbank claims as well.

At the June 5 meeting, Iran's counsel said that, in any event, most if not all of the hostages would be released before the U.S. elections, noting that Iran did not want to see a change in the U.S. government. At this and every subsequent meeting I pressed them to identify precisely for whom they were speaking. It became clear that most of their communications were through Mehdi Navab, Chargé d'Affaires and later Ambassador at the Iranian Embassy in Bonn. This varied on occasions when the German lawyers met with other Iranian officials in Europe or on trips to Tehran. There had been a meeting in London the preceding week among various Iranian representatives regarding our discussions. Attending were Wagendorf, François Cheron from Paris,[10] Roger Brown (of the Stephenson, Harwood law firm, Bank Markazi's solicitors in London), Leonard Boudin from New York, Morteza Abdullahi (of Bank Markazi) and Saeed Abtahi (of Bank Melli). All were reported to be in favor of the settlement talks and most of them to want a big

10. Cheron's partner was Christian Bourguet, who had figured prominently in the abortive negotiation attempt in March. See chapter 2.

meeting. The German counsel preferred to continue negotiating with the present group, plus Tom Shack from Washington. I agreed to the limited discussions but again stressed that Tehran must further clarify the German lawyers' authority.

We then began our examination of Plan C. Wagendorf noted that both Nobari and Bani-Sadr, while understanding that the release of the hostages was a requisite condition of any settlement, felt that their actual release was beyond the purview of Bank Markazi. After all, it was not the bank that held the hostages. To be politically acceptable to Bank Markazi, any settlement document would have to reflect that understanding.

We all agreed that we badly needed better information on the numbers and that we should try to develop these facts jointly from any available sources of information. From this meeting in June, until Plan C was eventually rejected by Iran in November, a general modus operandi was followed:

I would meet with Carswell and Owen in Washington before each trip and brief them personally on my return.

Between the meetings, we worked on refining Plan C and drafting all the necessary operational documents. We started preparing the financial schedules necessary to effectuate the plan. This was, to the end, a prosaic but most difficult job, in which we received no meaningful assistance from the Iranian side at any stage.

I enlisted the behind the scenes help of a leading bank finance lawyer, Frank Logan of Milbank, Tweed, Hadley & McCloy, who I knew had great discretion as well as skill as a legal craftsman. More visibly, my partner, J. J. Stevenson, a bank finance expert, joined Margy Wiener of my office, who had been involved in the project from the beginning. The Iranian side added Roger Brown. While I consulted frequently with Logan and Shack, they did not directly participate in the group discussions until late in the fall.

Meetings on Plan C were held throughout the summer and fall, variously in London, Paris, New York, Bermuda, Bonn, Düsseldorf, and even at my home in Chappaqua, New York.

On September 16, while in New York, Roger Brown reported that he had suddenly been summoned to Germany. This event, it turned out, coincided with Deputy Secretary of State Warren Christopher's first meeting with Sadegh Tabatabai in Germany. I was not informed of those meetings at the time by anyone and in fact did not learn of them until an account was published in a press interview with Christopher after the hostages' release. The arrangement with Carswell was such that I was never told what other lines of negotiation were open, and it was not until the government negotiations through the Algerians had commenced and were reported upon publicly that I was much aware of activities beyond those in which I was personally involved. However, through my constant communication with Washington on the progress of the bank discussions, it was possible for Carswell to keep that process on a course consistent with other U.S. government plans and activities.

Brown proceeded from Frankfurt to Tehran, where he and his colleagues were immobilized when the Iraqi war started and the whole settlement process was temporarily suspended. When Brown re-emerged, we continued working on Plan C in the hope that it could proceed and that the war might in fact provide an additional incentive to settle.

By late October, while the Iranian parliament was engaged in procedural wrangles over how to debate the hostage issue, Wagendorf was preparing to go to Tehran with what was to be the last draft of Plan C. By that time, Plan C had evolved into a three-inch-thick book of plans, schedules, and implementing documents, although many of the critical financial statistics remained to be filled in.

On November 2, Iran announced that the Majlis had voted to release the hostages if the four conditions proposed in September by Khomeini, and later by the special Iranian parliamentary commission, were met. Iran appointed Algeria to act as an intermediary with the Great Satan, with whom they would not deal directly.

On November 3 Wagendorf informed our counsel in Germany by telephone from Tehran that they had met with an Iranian government interministerial committee. This committee, consisting of sixteen members from the Ministries of Economics and Finance, Justice, Foreign Affairs, Energy, and elsewhere did "not favor" Plan C because it was too complicated. Specifically, the involvement of third-party central banks as intermediaries was considered unnecessary.

Meanwhile, Governor Nobari of Bank Markazi gave a telephone interview to the *Washington Post,* announcing that Iran was prepared to pay its debts to American banks and corporations and to put money into escrow accounts for that purpose. It was not clear what authority Nobari had to interpret the hostage release conditions, and his statement seemed to conflict with the third Iranian condition requiring cancellation of claims against Iran. Cryptic telephone communications with the German lawyers in Tehran during the next several days provided scant enlightenment. There were apparently strenuous disputes among the principal factions of moderates and radicals.

There was a persistent misunderstanding in Tehran regarding the ability of the President to nullify private U.S. claims and U.S. court orders of attachment. I had been informed by one of Iran's lawyers in March that the Iranian authorities did not understand the constitutional separation of powers in the United States. As the year rolled on, I concluded that the

Iranians were being informed, by at least some of their advisers, that the U.S. court attachments could be readily expunged through executive action. The Iranian misunderstanding of limits on U.S. executive power led them to misjudge the speed with which assets could be freed, even assuming a U.S. government commitment to take such a course.

While disputes among factions in Iran apparently continued, a more positive note was struck by the expressed willingness of the Western attorneys representing the interests of the principal factions to work together. U.K. counsel for Iran Roger Brown informed me that he and Bank Markazi's U.S. counsel, Leonard Boudin, were in accord on the issues we were discussing. Through their reports to Nobari, we had a regular line of contact with the central bank people parallel to the line of communication through the German counsel to the Iranian Foreign Ministry via its embassy in Bonn.

On November 7, Brown called me from London saying that he had discussed the settlement prospects with his client, who recognized that the Iranian hostage release conditions announced on November 2 were "too vague" and believed that aspect was delaying the U.S. government response. A response had been expected in Tehran in twenty-four hours, and Brown's client now realized that some clarification was needed. Brown said his client suggested that I "informally" find out what problems the U.S. government had with the conditions and pass that information to him orally. The information would be reported through Nobari to Bani-Sadr and might thus enable Iran to provide clarification. Brown said he was willing to come to New York for my response. He further reported that no steps would be taken in Tehran until a response had been received from the U.S. government and that Iran's delay in taking a position on Plan C was due to a lack of response from the U.S. government on the Majlis' conditions. In addition, I was informed that there was concern in Tehran over the legal consequences of the change in the U.S. government as a result of the November 4 election and over the powers President Carter had at present to act by executive order.

I reported the message from Brown to Carswell, who told me that the U.S. government was working on this matter through the Algerians and that he was skeptical about opening up another line of communications regarding the Majlis' conditions.

Heinemann returned to Germany on November 10, traveling as far as Vienna with the Algerian ambassador to Iran, who was on his way to Algiers to meet Warren Christopher. Heinemann said that while 80 percent of the problems were solved, the authority of the German lawyers to continue negotiations with us would be unclear until Iran received the U.S. government response to the Majlis' conditions. Despite this uncertainty, which Roger Brown also reported after speaking to Wagendorf in Tehran, it appeared that we might be able to make some progress in assembling the financial data, which was still woefully incomplete. Brown reported that Ali Manavi-Rad, head of the international department of Bank Markazi in Tehran, had expressed his willingness to provide some of the loan data we had been requesting unsuccessfully since August.

While we awaited further word from the Iranian side regarding Plan C, we prepared two alternate versions (predictably called "Plan C-1" and "Plan C-2"), attempting to read between the lines of the vague messages relayed from Tehran through the European lawyers. These plans sought to reduce some of the complexities inherent in Plan C that seemed to be troubling the Iranian authorities.

On November 12, I received a lengthy report from Citibank's German counsel, Gerstenmaier, regarding Heinemann's trip to Tehran. The overall impression I received was of continued disputes among the factions, each blaming the others for poor handling of the hostage situation. There appeared to be some consensus, however, that the taking of the hostages had been a bad political mistake, one that should be righted as soon as possible. The Council of Ministers would have the final say as to whether the Iranian conditions had been met by the U.S. government and the U.S. banks, but the Council would act only if backed by the Islamic Republican Party (I.R.P.), headed by Ayatollah Beheshti. There was a temporary stay of formal negotiations through the bank channel pending analysis and evaluation of the U.S. government response to the four conditions.

The I.R.P. apparently took a hard line, negating the effects of much that had already been resolved, however tentatively, as a result of the financial negotiations thus far. With regard to the financial issues, it held the view that debt claims should be reinstated as of November 14, 1979, and all litigation terminated at the banks' cost. All Iranian assets and credit balances should be paid to, or put at the disposal of, Iran, except those that were presently due on loans without default interest. Iran would guarantee performance under the loan agreements but would provide no security for such guarantee. The party believed that, if any banks required such security, it should come from the U.S. government. Regarding nonbank claims, their position was that obligations would be met when court attachments were lifted. Litigation could continue in the courts, whose judgment Iran was willing to accept. The hostages would be released only after an understanding was reached on the procedure of meeting the Iranian conditions on the assets. There would be no release prior to a deal on bank claims and attachments.

Iran's German lawyers recommended to the Iranian authorities the continuation of our negotiations, as we were said to be best informed on the subjects at hand and objective in the negotiations. The Bani-Sadr/Bank

Markazi faction reportedly wanted to renew the negotiations as soon as possible. Heinemann proposed resuming our discussions in Germany on November 14.

I advised Carswell of Gerstenmaier's report. Carswell said that the U.S. government had delivered its response to the Algerians, but he would not inform me of the contents, despite the fact that the people I would meet in Germany later that week might themselves be informed.

There were manifest difficulties and frustrations in trying to work out financial arrangements without knowing the context into which they would have to fit. I made sure that Carswell was fully briefed on all our plans and discussions and expected to be nudged if the bank talks moved out of phase with the Algerian negotiations. Thus, while operating essentially in the dark, I had confidence that I would be guided if my financial talks diverged too far from the path being followed through the Algerian intermediation. Naturally the course became much clearer late in December when the two sets of negotiations were essentially merged.

I went to London on November 13 to consult with Brown and proceeded with him to Düsseldorf to meet Heinemann and Wagendorf, who was just returning from Tehran, on Friday and Saturday, November 14 and 15. In light of the Algerian negotiations, the questions of negotiating authority and reporting lines had become even more puzzling, yet essential to define. Wagendorf said he was not authorized to negotiate "officially"—whatever that meant. Indeed, one day he had been told to halt the negotiations altogether, only to be told the next day to continue, but "unofficially." There appeared to be great anxiety over the possibility of a leak regarding our talks, and the whole process had to be deniable. The three lines of communication were to Bank Markazi, through Nobari and Manavi-Rad; to the Ministry of Economics and Finance, through Deputy Minister for Foreign Investment Akhavi; and most importantly to the Foreign Ministry, which had always approved Wagendorf's contact with me. This principal channel went through Mehdi Navab, the Iranian Ambassador in Bonn, and now was confirmed by the Acting Foreign Minister, Khoda Panahi, one of six ministers nominated by Prime Minister Rajai. I continued to press the authority question and said that I could not negotiate for my client, Citibank, without confirmation of their authority, and I would not even talk to any of the other banks without it.

Wagendorf replied that he had also met in Tehran with a "litigation committee," which formerly had been headed by Abdullahi as Nobari's delegate, but which was now headed or advised by a Pakistani lawyer from Lahore named Reza Kazim. Kazim was said to have been recommended to the Iranians by an unindentified Algerian who had been active in working on postrevolution financial settlements for Algeria. Wagendorf concluded his comments on authority by recommending that we continue to develop plans as before, pending more formal authorization for direct negotiations. For his part, Roger Brown said he had been authorized by Bank Markazi to approach all the U.S. banks, and he noted that, while there had been other bank contacts by Iranian lawyers, principally Boudin, no other line was active at present.

Wagendorf suggested that we design a plan that seemed to fall within the second and third Iranian hostage conditions, noting that noninterference and disposition of the Shah's assets were not within our scope. He then declared bluntly that Plan C could not be a basis for agreement with Iran, as they wanted to reconstitute financial relations, not pay off loans.

The rejection of Plan C required a fundamental change in our negotiations. Up to this time, we had been working on a deal that would pay off all bank liquidated claims in full, with interest. No bank could reasonably be expected to object to this. Thus we felt justified in conducting the negotiations without consulting the other banks, and the considerations of security and efficiency favoring a small working group prevailed. With the demise of Plan C, however, I made it clear to Iran's lawyers that we could no longer go it alone.

Plan D

Apart from the need to bring the other banks more directly into the process, radical changes were required in the plan, and we started discussing new possibilities immediately. The Germans felt a plan might be worked out using the Iranian overseas deposits to pay matured, liquidated claims as of November 14, 1979, as well as amounts that had fallen due since that time. A guarantee of the remaining debt by Iran and Bank Markazi might be feasible and could be approved by the Majlis. Wagendorf suggested that the U.S. government might guarantee the Iranian guarantee. I said that was out of the question.

Regarding the other issues, I reminded him that, although I was keeping the U.S. government fully informed, I had no authority to speak for anyone other than Citibank. I was furthermore unsure whether even my own client would accept anything other than Plan C, but I was willing to explore a new structure that might include the following elements:

1. Authorization of London deposit setoffs of all U.S. banks' matured claims
2. Use of London deposits to pay all other banks' matured claims
3. Guarantees by Iran and Bank Markazi of remaining unpaid Iranian public sector debt
4. Agreement by Iran to maintain advance debt service deposits, for example, one year's debt service in advance

5. Agreement that if debt service deposits were not maintained, banks could accelerate maturity of remaining debt
6. Waiver of sovereign immunity by Iran and consent to jurisdiction of non-Iranian courts
7. Maintenance of the current debt service deposits at a creditor bank and backup funds in a secure bank, for instance at the Bank for International Settlements

While deeply discouraged over the rejection of Plan C, which had been developed with great effort over many months, we started to work on "Plan D," which would provide for bringing loans current and would contain some measures to provide security for future payments. I returned to the United States on November 15 and briefed Carswell, Owen, and Counsel to the President Lloyd Cutler on the new Plan D. We all recognized that other banks, whose Iranian deposits would fund the settlement, now had to be brought directly into the process.

The Bank Group

During the last days of November, efforts were made at Treasury's initiative to develop a U.S. bank position regarding interest on domestic frozen accounts and to collect better financial data through the Federal Reserve Bank of New York. These efforts were not particularly productive, although the need for a compilation of accurate information on claims and deposits was clear. The problem was lack of workable criteria for compiling the data, coupled with some resistance from the bank side by those who believed the U.S. government was preparing to "give away" to the Iranians the banks' security.

Angermueller and I started talks with other banks about Plan D, informing them of our activities over the last months. As noted previously, until this time only Frank Logan, who happened to represent Chase, had been involved in the process. In our briefing of the other banks, no one expressed disapproval or resentment of the fact that Citibank had in effect been negotiating without their consent.

Meanwhile, Carswell and Richard Davis, Assistant Secretary of the Treasury, had started meeting with the banks during the week of December 5 in order to brief them regarding progress of the Algerian negotiations and warn them of the prospect that high-level decisions might be required on very short notice.

Prompted by these contacts, the "Iran Bank Group" coalesced. The composition of the group was determined by the principle that frozen overseas Iranian deposits in U.S. banks would constitute the bulk of any financial settlement leading to release of the hostages. Thus the twelve banks that held virtually all those deposits eventually came into the discussions. The actual participants were a group of lawyers[11] and bankers[12] many of whom were well known to each other and had frequently worked together in other similar, though less dramatic, situations. The amalgamation of such a group, frequently operating with no charter other than certain common interests, is a normal occurrence in banking. Someone usually takes the lead in getting the group together and handling logistics, but the procedures are more apt to reflect a kaffeeklatsch than a case study in *Robert's Rules of Order*.

While the Bank Group discussed Plan D options, Iran's lawyers met in London to consider their approach. We were told that, if the U.S. banks could accept payment of matured debts and agree to a Bank Markazi guarantee of unmatured debt, with some undefined provisions for maintaining external deposits, a deal could be done. Roger Brown had now begun working with Iran Overseas Investment Bank in London, the agent on a number of the syndicated Iranian loans, to compile some of the required financial data and was preparing to come to New York to continue our negotiations. That meeting, proposed for early December, was abruptly dropped with no explanation other than "lack of authority" from Brown's client, Bank Markazi. There were hints that one of Bank Markazi's U.S. lawyers, who was not participating directly in our talks, was advising against our negotiations and suggesting a different approach, which involved a general rescheduling of Iranian debt, with some Iranian deposits to be maintained in Algeria. In the course of our contacts with the U.S. banks, we learned that Leonard Boudin had recently approached at least one of the banks with such a proposal, which was manifestly in disharmony with our line to Bank Markazi through Roger Brown.

It was a troubling fact that throughout the financial negotiations the

11. The principal participants in the bank lawyers group were: James Rassweiler, for Bankers Trust; Thorne Corse, for Bank of America; Frank Logan, Margaret Liddle (Grieve), and Norman Nelson, all of Milbank, Tweed, Hadley & McCloy, for Chase, with Robert Douglass, its General Counsel; Richard Simmons, of Cravath Swaine & Moore, for Chemical Bank; J. J. Stevenson, Margaret Wiener, Mark Zimmett, and myself, of Shearman & Sterling, for Citibank, with Hans Angermueller and Patrick Mulhern, its General Counsel; Frank Shine, for Continental Illinois; Hamilton Potter, of Sullivan & Cromwell, for European American Bank; Robert von Mehren, of Debevoise, Plimpton, for First National Bank of Chicago, with its General Counsel, David Earle; Robert Webster and John Pritchard, of Winthrop, Stimson, Putnam & Roberts, for Irving Trust Co., with its General Counsel, Elliott Vestner; Thomas Cashel and Henry Landau, of Simpson, Thacher & Bartlett, for Manufacturers Hanover Trust; John Dickey, of Sullivan & Cromwell, for Marine Midland Bank; and Bruce Nichols, Bart McGuire, and Donaldson Pillsbury, of Davis, Polk & Wardwell, for Morgan Guaranty, with its General Counsel, Boris Berkovich.

12. The Bank Group was heavily populated by lawyers, consisting of both inside and outside counsel for the banks, but the lawyers of course reported to their client bankers, who often participated directly in the lawyers' meetings.

Iranian side received conflicting advice from their own foreign counsel, further confusing what was already an elusive and uncertain negotiating process. Not only were there different sets of lawyers involved on the Iranian side, who often approached our negotiations with disparate attitudes, but there were different sets of clients, principally characterized by the Bank Markazi-Nobari-Bani-Sadr line and the line through our German connections to the Foreign Ministry, Rajai, Nabavi, and Ayatollah Beheshti. It often happened, however, that when progress on one line was temporarily stalled, the other would open. On this occasion, the German line leading to the Iranian government opened, and a meeting was set in Europe for December 11 to follow consultations in Bonn among German counsel, Navab, and the Iranian Deputy Minister of Finance, Dr. Nobakht.

In preparation for this session, we discussed the Plan D concept among the Bank Group, focusing on a December 1 draft. The plan called for payment of matured liquidated debt claims from frozen London deposits and release of the balance of frozen overseas deposits upon guarantees by Iran of the remaining unpaid debts, together with some sinking fund provisions, such as maintenance of an account at the Bank for International Settlements of no less than twenty-four-months' debt service requirements.

On December 8, I met with Carswell, Davis, and Owen to discuss the upcoming meeting with the Iranian representatives in London. Carswell was skeptical about the feasibility of Plan D, because of its complexities, and worried that the time remaining would not allow anything other than a rough and ready deal that would leave the difficult details to more leisurely negotiation after release of the hostages. I saw Tom Shack later that day and urged him to attend the London meeting, as the Iranians clearly needed U.S. legal counsel in those discussions.

On December 11 and 12, I met with German, U.K., and U.S. counsel for Iran at the Dorchester Hotel in London. The Germans had just met in Bonn with Nobakht, who had recently discussed with Prime Minister Rajai our upcoming meeting, and I understood his instructions were to press toward a quick solution. It appeared, however, that while the Iranian government favored our settlement, Nobari was equivocal at best. I informed the group that we had now been in contact with other U.S. banks, as necessitated by the demise of Plan C. I then laid out Plan D line by line during a private dinner in my hotel suite. I stressed the time urgency and was informed that some of the key Iranian participants were intent on getting the deal done before Christmas.

The general response to Plan D was favorable, the main point of contention being the sinking fund provisions. No one seemed troubled by the guarantees. We concluded that Brown would brief Bank Markazi; Wagendorf and Heinemann would inform Rajai, through Ambassador Navab; and

I would brief the Bank Group in New York on December 15. If we all received a green light on the new plan, we would reconvene immediately in Europe.

Over the weekend, the Germans reported on our London meeting and Plan D to Nabavi and Nobakht. We were told that the reaction was favorable but that financial provisions would have to be part of the overall settlement being negotiated through the Algerians.

The U.S. Bank Group met on December 15 and 16. While we had yet to reach an agreement on the precise terms of Plan D, Frank Logan and Tom Cashel had already begun drafting the operative documents. Equally important, and critical to the process of the final negotiations in January, the banks retained independent accountants—Peat, Marwick, Mitchell & Co.—to collect financial data on a blind, coded basis to preserve confidentiality and to develop a data processing program to handle calculations necessary to implement a settlement.[13] Hiring Peat, Marwick had, we understood, a beneficial impact in Tehran. They apparently had done work for Bank Markazi and were regarded as providing an element of objectivity and professional neutrality in the "number crunching" process.

Procedurally, our plans involved a settlement based only on mutual acceptance of a set of operative documents—essentially payment instructions to the U.S. foreign deposit banks—accompanied by a set of schedules listing the relevant figures. We believed this would be the simplest way to handle the transaction, which would in fact involve moving around billions of dollars and under normal circumstances would be the subject of elaborate and thoroughly negotiated documentation. Wagendorf agreed with this approach, but the attitude at Bank Markazi remained uncertain, although Brown discussed the plan with Nobari and informed the other Bank Markazi lawyers, Cheron in Paris and Boudin in New York.

During the Bank Group consideration of various forms of security for those unpaid debts that would become unsecured by release of the foreign deposits, it became evident that a central bank guarantee was greatly favored by the bankers. No country could satisfactorily participate in the international financial community if its central bank reneged on its obligations. A Bank Markazi guarantee of unmatured Iranian debts was therefore set as an essential objective for our negotiations. Without it, there could be no assurance that the U.S. banks would reverse their overseas setoffs and in effect return to Iran security they now held.

Roger Brown did not attend the next meeting in Bonn on December 19, although he sent his colleague, Nigel McEwen. We considered Brown's ab-

13. The Bank Group appointed a financial subcommittee, the "figure team," to coordinate this work. This vital operation was headed by Tom Cashel and included Peggy Liddle (Grieve) and Margy Wiener.

sence to be another signal that Bank Markazi did not support the settlement. However, I reported that Plan D now had the support of the entire
Bank Group. There followed a lengthy and inconclusive discussion over the
need for any guarantees at all. I pointed out that the banks, when they
extended credit to Iran, in fact held security in the form of substantial
Iranian deposits, into which Iran's oil revenues flowed. Those revenues no
longer existed, yet the banks were being asked to release the deposits without liquidation of the debts. A request for some substitute form of security, I
argued, was only fair and reasonable.

Friday night, December 19, I met with the Iranian Ambassador to
Germany, Mehdi Navab, for two hours. This was the first occasion on which
an Iranian government official participated directly in the bank negotiations. Night had fallen when I arrived at the Iranian Embassy entrance,
which reminded me of a drive-in bank teller's window. I worried whether I
would have to slip my U.S. passport into the mechanical tray, but we were
expected and passed through immediately. As the electric door clicked shut
behind us, we paused for a moment before a large version of the familiar
glowering portrait of Ayatollah Khomeini. At that moment more than any
other time I felt awed by the encounter that now brought me into direct
negotiations with the government holding my countrymen hostage. The
meeting, conducted variously in German and English, was cordial, even
though Navab (who spoke only in German) at one point delivered a lengthy
statement to the effect that the U.S. banks were responsible for the oppres-
sion of the Iranian people. Much of the discussion was a repetition of points I
had already been over with German counsel, but it enabled me to present
our position directly to the other side. I had in fact hoped to meet Navab on
this trip, and the meeting had been cleared in advance with Carswell.

Navab was familiar with our negotiations and had accompanied Prime
Minister Rajai to New York in October for the United Nations session,
where an abortive effort was made for the two of us to meet. He impressed
me as intelligent and personable and introduced some human touches early
in the meeting by talking about his daughter's sixth birthday the next day.
With all this, however, his revolutionary attitudes and distrust of the
United States permeated the discussion. At the same time, he could not
understand why the U.S. side should distrust Iran. Here, as in all other talks
during the bank negotiations, there were only passing references to the
hostages. The prompt release of the hostages clearly was understood to be a
prime goal, but I limited my own efforts to arrangements for the necessary
financial settlement, rather than entering into more political and emotional matters.

No conclusions were reached at the meeting, although I became convinced of the need to make an effective case with Navab, who was reporting

directly to the authorities apparently making the decisions in Tehran, principally Rajai and Nabavi. As we left the embassy, Navab gave me a Christmas card, with related quotations from the Old and New Testaments and
the Koran.

As I waited at the Düsseldorf airport on December 20 for a flight back to
New York, Wagendorf and I worked over language for guarantees from
Bank Markazi as well as the Iranian government. The latter document we
called a "Confirmation," whereby "The Islamic Republic of Iran adopts and
commits itself to the punctual payment when due of all debt obligations,
including any Bank Markazi guaranty thereof, listed on the attached schedule." The Confirmation provided for English law to control, submission to
the English courts, and a waiver of sovereign immunity. This was a rather
exotic document, clearly drafted with political and psychological considerations in mind. In contrast, the Bank Markazi guarantee was to be a normal
form of commercial guarantee. I returned home believing there was a realistic prospect that these guarantees were practicable. The main problems on
the Iranian side seemed to be with the sinking fund, or security deposit,
issue.

On Sunday, December 21, Iran announced its "$24 billion demand,"
and while the whole picture darkened once again I had reason to suspect
that the demand for an additional $14 billion escrow would not remain on
the table for long. On Monday, December 22, I briefed Carswell, Owen, and
Davis in Washington regarding the meetings in Bonn, and the Bank Group
met in New York through the remaining days before Christmas trying to
reach a common position on acceptable terms for a Plan D settlement.

Merger of the Negotiations

The Bank Group was trying to coordinate directly with the U.S. government
team engaged in the Algerian negotiations, and in the first explicit recognition of the interaction of the negotiations Carswell passed Plan D to the
Algerians as illustrative of a proposal to handle the bank issues.

The prospects for a Plan D settlement oscillated wildly over the Christmas holiday and ensuing weekend. It appeared that the reaction in the
United States to Iran's $24 billion demand was being well noted in Tehran,
and a flurry of meetings to deal with the financial settlement were scheduled, unscheduled, and rescheduled, sometimes within hours. I had planned
to return to Bonn on December 29 to start detailed discussion of the security
provisions. Those discussions were canceled the morning of the twenty-
ninth and immediately reset after Wagendorf was convinced of the need to
tailor a financial package that would fit into the now publicized Algerian
settlement framework.

After an overnight flight from New York on the twenty-ninth, I was driven by Wagendorf from the Düsseldorf airport to Bonn, where we immediately commenced a nonstop session that lasted well into the night of the thirtieth. Ambassador Navab again participated. Roger Brown also attended this meeting but was generally noncommittal, apparently reflecting Nobari's continued position astride the fence.

Wearying hours were spent rearguing the issue of security. Navab, however, appeared satisfied with the need to structure an acceptable financial package, and I was sure that, if he were convinced, he would recommend it to Nabavi. A most significant point that Navab stressed was his view that the bank settlement could be accomplished simply by means of appropriate payment orders from Bank Markazi to the U.S. banks. That concept became critical in the final settlement negotiations.

As authorized by the Bank Group, I presented the latest version of Plan D, noting that the only significant changes related to the sinking fund. All agreed that there was no controversy about the other provisions, which included the government and Bank Markazi guarantees. It is worth taking note of those provisions, seemingly accepted at that time, since the same provisions were apparently the reason for rejection of Plan D on January 11.

II. *Iranian Confirmation and Guaranty of Iranian External Debt.*
Bank Markazi will deliver to the Foreign Deposit Banks, its joint and several guaranty, together with the confirmation of the Islamic Republic of Iran, of the punctual payment at maturity, with interest thereon, of all outstanding debts of Iran in which a U.S. bank is a participant. The Iranian Guaranty and Confirmation will include suitable provisions with respect to irrevocable waiver of sovereign immunity and consent to the jurisdiction of the Courts of England and the courts of each country in which an External Guarantee is issued. Plan D 12/23/80(B).

Navab had to be convinced of the economic basis, as well as the legal basis, of the financial package. He probed the issue intelligently and in the end seemed to support the concepts. Since we were negotiating over the amount of deposit coverage, this meeting also entailed the first focused discussion of overall loan claim figures. Our estimate was that $1.2 billion to $1.3 billion was required to bring the bank loans current. No one was surprised. Navab noted that they had been planning for $1 billion, but he believed that $1.2 billion was not out of line. I said that would leave $2.722 billion unpaid on the syndicate loans, for which security had to be provided. I gave them a maturity schedule, showing the aggregate amounts falling due each year through 1988. This was the first time these figures had been discussed, but while there was some surprise there appeared to be no shock.

The hangup over a sinking fund, or security deposit, seemed to be more political and psychological than substantive. The Iranian side appeared willing to establish deposit coverage but did not want to agree to do it. This led to consideration of a transaction simply on the basis of irrevocable payment instructions, which when implemented would trigger other events. I agreed that we would try to design such a procedure, while continuing to negotiate on an acceptable amount for the security deposit.

Navab said he would go to Tehran immediately with Plan D and asked for a German and English summary that he could take with him. The officials he planned to meet with were not interested in detailed lawyers' papers.

The next morning, December 31, we met at the Iranian Embassy and gave Navab the summary, which included a provision reading, "5. Bank Markazi will give a standard commercial guarantee of such [unmatured] debts." After reviewing the summary Navab said "Kein Problem" (no problem) and added that he would go to Tehran the next night, January 1, and take it up with Nabavi and the interministerial council Friday and Saturday. He hoped to have a response that Wagendorf could relay to me in time for a Bank Group meeting in New York on Monday, January 5. We also agreed that Brown's colleague, Nigel McEwen, would come to New York, starting on January 5, to work full time with the Bank Group "figure team" developing payment schedules with Peat, Marwick. The rest of the bank negotiating team (Brown, Wagendorf, and Heinemann) would come to New York on January 8 prepared to work until the deal was finished. Navab was also prepared to come over, if necessary. I returned to Chappaqua via Frankfurt the night of December 31 in time to note the expiration of 1980, feeling somewhat expired myself.

Telephone discussions with various bank counsel through the New Year's weekend revealed that at least one major bank had serious misgivings about the adequacy of the banks' protection under Plan D, although most indicated encouragement and some flexibility in the negotiations over the critical security provisions.

On Monday, January 5, German counsel told me that Navab had called from Tehran Sunday evening as scheduled but that no decision had been reached regarding a bank settlement. Wagendorf seemed puzzled by the absence of any direct reference to the bank negotiations in the U.S. government's response through the Algerians and also urgently requested English versions of various arbitration procedures.

By January 6, the Iranian demands had been reduced from the highly inflammatory $24 billion to a more manageable $9.5 billion, and the members of the Bank Group had agreed to put their claim figures into the data bank and to tell me their range of negotiating authority for the security provisions. Although I was sure that some of the banks' limits would be unacceptable to the Iranians, we were ready to go to work if and when the Iranian team arrived in New York.

On Thursday, January 8, Frank Logan and I went to Washington to review the plans with Carswell and others at Treasury, though we still had received no word from Bank Markazi. As our meeting began, I received a call from Brown in London saying that he had received detailed orders to proceed at once to New York to negotiate the bank settlement and to join us in calculating the amounts required to bring the loans current. His instructions did not come from Nobari but rather from an unnamed official on a Bank Markazi committee. Brown said that Plan D was being looked on favorably in Tehran and had been approved by the hostage committee, headed by Nabavi. A more ominous note was Brown's view that the guarantees we had been discussing would need approval by the Majlis.

Brown arrived and started work with us immediately on the night of the eighth. He was followed by Wagendorf and Heinemann on the ninth. Leonard Boudin, representing Bank Markazi in the United States, and his partner, Eric Lieberman, also came to some of our meetings.

Logan, Cashel, and I started a crash program on the ninth and tenth to complete the necessary paperwork. Carswell and Davis came up from Washington to follow our progress more closely, meanwhile staying in touch with the Christopher team in Algiers and with Bob Mundheim and Ernest Patrikis, Deputy General Counsel of the New York Fed, who were scouting European capitals in search of a suitable and agreeable escrow depository. As President Carter's January 16 private deadline for a hostage deal drew painfully close, an immense amount of work remained to be done to prepare for handling a mammoth financial transaction, the structure of which had not yet even been determined or accepted by any participants.

The banks agreed that their deposits would be released initially to an escrow account, but while the current plans envisioned such accounts no one yet knew in what bank or even in what country the escrow would be held. Throughout the preceding months, our preliminary investigations provided some understanding of relevant laws in, for example, the United Kingdom, Germany, and Switzerland, so that as Mundheim sought out a central bank that would agree to handle the documents we were able to advise Carswell in New York regarding aspects of local law. Thus, on the weekend of January 9–11, with our German attorney, Gerstenmaier, and Bill Tudor-John, Chase's London solicitor, present, we were able to give Carswell direct information on attachment laws that led the U.S. government to choose London, where court attachment orders are not available.[14]

---

14. We were worried that some claimant against Iran might secure a court order tying up Iranian assets overseas that would be used to fund the settlement. The possibility of such an

Saturday and Saturday night, January 10, were spent with the Iranian representatives in our Citicorp Center offices refining Plan D documents and conforming them to the present state of the Algerian negotiations.

Yet even at this late date, some of the basic financial elements remained completely undetermined—for example, interest on the frozen foreign deposits. Interest rates had fluctuated wildly during the freeze, ranging from 9 percent to over 20 percent on some standard maturities in the Eurodollar market. No universally accepted principles were at hand to determine how interest was to accrue on a "seven-day call" deposit account that happened to have been frozen for fourteen months. The Majlis' conditions and U.S. responses had left the matter open; negotiations with Iran had to provide the solution. No governmental fiat could assure immediate acceptance. Further complicating the issue, we felt that the interest rates had to be worked out in bilateral, rather than collective Bank Group discussions with the Bank Markazi representatives. Everyone recognized that there could be U.S. legal problems for a group of competitors jointly negotiating a price structure. Thus we set up an arrangement called the "dentist chair," whereby a group from each U.S. bank met privately with Roger Brown and his colleagues to settle on the principal balances and to negotiate the interest rate each bank would pay on its frozen overseas deposits. No one in the Bank Group knew until later—specifically at the celebrated State Department meeting on January 16—what individual amounts of interest had been agreed upon by the various banks or what they aggregated.

On Sunday afternoon, January 11, after unexplained delays through the day, the Iranian delegation, which included Abdullahi of Bank Markazi, returned to Shearman & Sterling. The Iranians' lawyers—Brown, Wagendorf, Heinemann, and Lieberman—were all present, but this time the Iranian official did the talking. Apparently speaking only for Bank Markazi, Abdullahi declared that Plan D was "totally unacceptable" and asked for the banks' "last and best offer."

This numbing announcement followed weeks of talks in which the acceptability of a Plan D settlement had been the acknowledged basis of our discussions. I replied that I had no reason to believe we could produce another plan at this late hour, let alone one more favorable to Iran. Wagendorf and Heinemann returned that night to Germany, leaving behind an atmosphere of dismay and gloom. Nevertheless, the behavior of the Iranian delegation, whom I had gotten to know well during the last six months, gave me reason to believe that Abdullahi's announcement was no more than a nego-

---

attachment interfering even temporarily with the intricate payment mechanisms we were considering haunted the financial negotiations until the end.

tiating tactic or further evidence of a split between Bank Markazi and the
I.R.P. faction, probably both.

Brown and his team stayed in New York, and we agreed to continue
working together on the figures and schedules in the hope that they could
still be used. Meanwhile, we also started working on revisions to Plan D that
might be acceptable, even though we had received no real specification of
the problems. We did hear, however, that the governor of the Algerian
central bank, who was in contact with the Iranians in Tehran, was entirely
unsympathetic to the idea of security for the U.S. banks. However, the
guarantees and some deposit provisions had always been identified as essential elements of the plan, and we continued to hope that the dramatic
last-minute rejection of a plan that had virtually been completed the night
before was more political than substantive. We had been informed that
Nobari's position was that Bank Markazi would not go along without a
written order from Prime Minister Rajai. The Majlis, we were told, would
consider the Bank Markazi guarantee the next day, the thirteenth, and
there seemed to be some basis to believe that a political decision favoring the
plan would lead to Nobari's acceptance.

The Bank Group met for eight hours the next day, formulated a "Plan D
(1/12/81 B)" that was given to the Iranians, and waited. Contacts with the
various Iranian representatives during this time indicated that, as usual,
conflicting legal advice regarding the bank settlement was being given to
Tehran. When no formal response came by the fourteenth, we sent an
urgent reminder that, in order to set up the machinery for processing the
multibillion-dollar money transfers involved, we would have to start work
at once. Those messages were passed through all three channels: through
Brown and Boudin to Bank Markazi, through Wagendorf and the Iranian
Embassy in Bonn to the Iranian Foreign Ministry in Tehran, and through
Christopher in Algiers also for transmittal to Tehran. Part of the Bank
team, led by Frank Logan and Thorne Corse (both of whom would soon end
up in Algiers) and Tom Cashel, headed for London the night of January 14,
and most of the banks arranged to have representatives at hand both in
London (where we expected the financial deal to be closed) and New York.

While I was informed that Nobari still had not made up his mind on our
latest proposal, nevertheless, early on the morning of the fifteenth I received a call from one of the lawyers in Germany reporting that the situation in Tehran was viewed as "positive" and "optimistic." The Iranian authorities, under the direction of Prime Minister Rajai, were said to be
preparing a satisfactory reaction to our proposals, even though there did
appear to be continuing disputes between the Rajai group and Bank
Markazi.

At 10:00 A.M., Thursday, January 15, the New York Bank Group met at Shearman & Sterling. Five hours to the east, A.M.D. ("Tony") Willis of Coward, Chance, solicitors for Citibank as well as some of the other U.S. banks, had set up shop for the London contingent of the Bank Group; liaison was established with the U.S. Embassy and the Bank of England. All systems were being put in place to process Plan D, if accepted. Night and weekend telephone lists for chief executives of the banks and other key players were circulated.

The Turning Point

At 2:10 P.M. Carswell and Cutler called from the White House and said that a new Iranian proposal had just been received through the Algerians. They quickly outlined the message, telling me to get the 3 P.M. shuttle to Washington.

Apparently Iran had offered to pay off the bank loans up to $3.6 billion and put into escrow what they held to be the disputed balance of loan claims, said to total $5.1 billion. While the proposal sounded promising, some mention was made of arbitration, which is usually taboo to bankers.[15] I threw a few papers and a pocket calculator in a brief case and ran out the back door of our office, telling my secretary to excuse me from a visitor who was waiting in the reception area and to cover my disappearance until we knew better what was happening.

I called Peggy Liddle (Grieve) of the Bank Group figure team from the airport and got from her a summary of the latest Peat, Marwick data. I told her we now urgently needed the figures for principal and interest to pay off all bank loans in which a U.S. bank was a participant, both syndicated and nonsyndicated, rather than merely to bring them current.

After a record slow taxi ride from National Airport, I arrived at the Treasury, and following a briefing from Carswell and others we set about arranging a meeting of bank principals for the next day. The State Department was selected as the site rather than the White House, a location thought to signal excessive arm-twisting that might backfire. I was to contact the twelve deposit banks, brief them on the new Iranian proposal, and assist the government team in responding to the proposal, which seemed to offer a real prospect for solution to the crisis.

In the proposal, Iran appeared to recognize that it was impossible to reach an agreement between Bank Markazi and the U.S. banks within the

---

15. Bankers believe loans should be paid. Loan payments may be renegotiated, rolled over, or stretched out, but the obligation to pay a loan should be recognized, not arbitrated. Therefore arbitration clauses do not appear in loan agreements, and the suggestion of arbitration, I believed, would alarm the Bank Group.

next forty-eight hours. Iran acknowledged owing $3.6 billion but said the banks were claiming $5.1 billion. They proposed to pay off both installments due and balances outstanding on all loans, paying the $3.6 billion from an interim escrow account immediately upon release of the hostages and transferring the balance, equivalent to 100 percent of the remaining U.S. bank loan claims, into another escrow account pending resolution of the amounts owed by negotiation or arbitration. They also revealed a difference regarding how much interest was owed on the $4.8 billion principal of frozen foreign deposits, which was to be transferred from the banks as an element of the hostage deal. The Iranian proposal demanded $800 million interest, which we estimated was about $150 million more than the aggregate offered by the banks in their dentist chair sessions.

Despite these two major problems, the proposal to pay off the loans was welcome and reflected more than anything a return to Plan C, which had obviously been the most attractive plan, as well as the most feasible one to execute. We did not know—and still can only speculate—why the Iranians reverted to a full pay-off proposal. One simple reason may be that it represented the quickest and surest way to get the deal done in the limited time remaining.

The loan calculations seemed feasible, as we had, or at least were soon to receive in the Peat, Marwick computer, the required data on syndicated loans and had only to change the computer program to call for figures to pay off, rather than pay current. On the other hand, the Bank Group had no collective data on deposits, and in the end much of that computation was done by hand calculators in the Secretary of State's conference room the next day. All we could tell on the night of the fifteenth was that the banks would apparently have to cough up another $150 million or so to make the deal fly.

It was impossible to tell from the Iranian proposal how they had done their loan calculations. The figures we had did not work out to loan claims aggregating $5.1 billion. The $3.6 billion of acknowledged debt, however, was close to our current figures for total syndicated debt, including interest to date, and the balance appeared to cover the aggregate nonsyndicated debt, although our data for those claims were less reliable. It seemed logical and desirable to conclude that syndicated debt was to be paid off first, particularly since that would resolve the U.S. banks' "black hole" exposure to foreign syndicate banks. I discussed such a breakdown with Roger Brown on the phone in London, and he agreed that it made sense.

The reactions from the Bank Group to my Thursday night calls ranged from interested to enthusiastic, and there was no trouble in rounding up a top-level delegation to drop everything for the crucial meeting the next morning.

The bankers and their lawyers assembled at 11:00 A.M. in an appropriately impressive crisis atmosphere at the State Department. After opening exhortations from the Secretary of State, Secretary of the Treasury, and other senior U.S. government officials, the Bank Group was left to caucus regarding a response. Agreement was quickly reached that the syndicated loans should be paid first. There were some problems in this area, as some syndicated loans came to light that had not previously been identified to the group, but the problems that surfaced were manageable and more or less familiar to participants in international lending syndicate activities. In the ensuing days the Bank Group figure team, with Peat, Marwick's support, was able to work with the Federal Reserve Bank of New York to handle the syndicated loan payments with remarkable facility.

The deposit interest issue displayed another dimension. Each bank had handled its own interest negotiation separately. The Iranians demanded $800 million from the banks. We knew we were short, but we did not know by how much or for whose account. We had no choice but to pool our information, and when each bank in turn recited its principal deposit figure and the interest that it had agreed to pay, the sums totaled $4,733,417,403.68 and $669,658,102.06, respectively. There was no substantial debate whether the banks would produce the $130 million shortfall. The issue, rather, was how to divide the ante and how best to preserve the banks' right to contest the additional amount. There were suggestions that the excess be split evenly twelve ways or that it be prorated by amount of deposit. In the end, a formula was adopted that applied to each bank's principal an additional "disputed" interest figure representing the difference between the rate the bank had agreed to and a flat rate derived from applying the $800 million to the aggregate principal deposits. Thus for some banks no additional interest was called for; for others there were additions ranging from the hundreds of thousands to over $91 million for Bank of America.

The precise figures were worked out with pocket calculators wielded by bank chairmen and unmathematical Wall Street lawyers aided finally by a small twelve-digit electric desk calculator that no one was quite sure how to operate. Nevertheless, the job got done, a schedule was prepared and given to the government, and the bankers departed through a gauntlet of reporters and TV cameramen in the State Department lobby. A few from the Bank Group remained to recheck the figures and assist the government team in translating the banks' response into a cable for Christopher in Algiers. It was also necessary to prepare for the sessions to come, in which documentation for this multibillion-dollar transaction would have to be invented, structured, drafted, negotiated, and implemented in three languages on four continents, all in less than ninety hours.

I tuned in with Roger Brown in London from time to time during this session and once again heard distant thunder in the form of comments that Nobari seemed to be disclaiming the figures in the January 15 Iranian proposal. Even now, Bank Markazi appeared to be withholding support or at least remaining aloof. These ominous signals were accurate warnings of a storm that would break during the last hours of the crisis.

The Bank Group now divided further. Many returned to New York, where an operations center was set up at Shearman & Sterling's office in Citicorp Center. Others proceeded to London, where the advance party had already set up shop at Coward, Chance's office in the City. Frank Logan and Thorne Corse were hauled off from London to Algiers to participate directly in preparing the escrow arrangements with representatives of the Bank of England, Patrikis from the New York Fed, Mundheim and others from Christopher's team, and, of course, the Algerians. Support staffs were assembled, computer operators put on standby alert.

The Final Hours

Those who remained in Washington reassembled at Treasury Saturday morning, January 17, in Secretary Miller's conference room to work on necessary payment mechanisms and documents to move the billions back and forth as provided in the underlying agreements. Open telephone lines connected the bank teams in Washington, New York, London, and Algiers. Separately, from Washington, I maintained liaison with our German lawyers, who kept in touch with Wagendorf and Navab—a communications link that allowed information to be relayed directly to Tehran.

The bank lawyers team at Treasury worked through Saturday, interrupted only by a brief "photo opportunity" Treasury afforded a clamoring press corps.

Dick Simmons and Bruce Nichols took a leading role in the drafting effort, helped by many others present, including Angermueller, Douglass, Richard Puz (Executive Vice President, Bank of America), Bob Webster, and Peggy Liddle. A somewhat lengthy and intricate payment order was drafted and sent over the Treasury wires to Logan, Corse, and Mundheim in Algiers and to the Bank Group team in London through the Treasury liaison officer at the U.S. Embassy, Jim Ammerman.

As the day wore on the notion grew that this increasingly complicated legal document would be difficult, if not impossible, for the Iranians to understand and accept in the few hours remaining. I suggested to Angermueller that we ought to give up trying to design a perfect wheel and settle for something that might at least roll. We talked it over with Bob Douglass, who agreed, and then took it up with the drafting group. They decided to continue working on the more detailed draft, while Angermueller would try to create a "one pager," consisting of a simple composite payment order: first from Bank Markazi to the twelve deposit banks, with an attached, and incorporated by reference, payment order from Markazi to the New York Fed. The essential directions for moving the funds into the escrow accounts would be included in this composite payment order, thereby providing assurance to the banks, which would pay out over $5 billion, that a portion would in fact be held in escrow as agreed. Simmons and Nichols approved and made further revisions through the afternoon and into the evening. The draft payment order was transmitted to London that night (the seventeenth) after it had been discussed on the telephone with the team in London and with Frank Logan in Algiers. A copy was relayed to Algiers from London on Sunday, January 18. Most of the Bank Group returned to New York Saturday night, leaving a few of us at Treasury to act as liaison with the U.S. government and Fed teams operating out of the otherwise nearly deserted Treasury offices.

The Treasury Secretary's wing now began to look like a battle zone. People napped occasionally on couches or at desks. A half-eaten bucket of fried chicken collected waste paper by a couch in the Deputy Secretary's office; an unshaven, unwashed Wall Street lawyer grumbled about the lack of hot coffee at 4:00 A.M.; and an incessant question plagued all—was there enough time?

Meanwhile a "litigation subcommittee" in New York was discussing with the litigators in London the subject of documentation terminating the overseas litigation. Bank Markazi was suing the U.S. banks in London and Paris for over $3 billion; those cases ought to be dropped when the accounts were paid. There was some discussion of relating the payment order to the termination of litigation. Drafts of the latest (January 17) version of the payment order prepared in Washington were handed to Christopher Gibbons of Stephenson Harwood, Bank Markazi's counsel in London, at 8 A.M. Sunday morning, January 18, by Tom Cashel and relayed by Stephenson Harwood to Bank Markazi in Tehran. Later in the day the text was modified based on changes dictated from Algiers by Frank Logan to make it more consistent with the documents being drafted there.

The New York and Washington groups later received, from Algiers through London, a draft of the Escrow Agreement prepared by Mundheim, Patrikis, and the bank lawyers in Algiers, with the related and more detailed Implementing Technical Clarifications and Directions (ITCD). That document carried, as Attachment A, the form of payment order from the Central Bank of Algeria to the Bank of England disbursing the funds after the hostage release and, as Attachment B, the telex payment orders from Bank Markazi to the twelve deposit banks and the New York Fed. The ITCD, with Attachment B, constituted the notorious "eleven-page appendix" that was widely publicized as a sudden snag in the negotiations on

Monday, January 19. It is clear, however, that Stephenson Harwood and almost certainly Bank Markazi in Tehran had the final draft of the proposed payment order for at least twenty-four and probably thirty-six hours before any complaint was made regarding its substance. Having heard no adverse comments from Bank Markazi or its lawyers by the afternoon of Sunday, January 18, the Bank Group operating in London, New York, Washington, and Algiers believed that the required pieces were in place, and we were ready to proceed with the transfer of funds upon signing of the basic documents by the governments and receipt of the apparently acceptable payment order.

On Sunday afternoon Secretary Miller asked me to alert the Bank Group to be prepared to move the money Sunday night or Monday morning. The bank computers were turned on to warm up; the operations people were briefed, and code words for the fund transfers were cleared; the New York Federal Reserve Bank was held open starting at 4:00 P.M. Sunday afternoon, and everybody waited expectantly. We heard vague reports of trouble in Algiers regarding the still incomplete Escrow Agreement, and at 1:30 A.M. Monday the New York group was allowed to stand down temporarily, subject to recall on a half-hour's notice. Some left for rest or refreshment; others napped on couches and floors throughout Shearman & Sterling's Citicorp Center office.

We recalled the New York group at 4:30 A.M. Monday when word was received in Washington that the Algiers Declarations had been initialed, and the basic intergovernmental agreements were apparently in place. Ominously, however, the Escrow Agreement was still being negotiated. When we heard nothing further by about 8:00 A.M. regarding the payment order, I called Roger Brown in London. He said he thought the Iranians now had some problems with certain figures in the payment order and believed that our deposit figures were short by $500 million. Great confusion ensued. Repeated calls to Brown and his colleagues brought no enlightenment. They were "awaiting instructions." We made many attempts to uncover the real nature of the Iranians' problems, including asking the Germans to take it up directly with Tehran. To emphasize the urgency of resolving the problem, I asked Secretary Miller to speak directly with Wagendorf. At one point we were told that the papers could not be located at Bank Markazi in Tehran and that Nobari had vanished. Finally, on Monday afternoon, the objections were made more specific; we were informed that the Iranians were objecting to certain language of the payment order, claiming that the banks were asking for a general release.

I discussed this report with Brown, emphasizing that the banks wanted no such thing. If there were U.S. bank deposits that had not been provided for, they would of course be paid. Language to make that clear should be no problem, and we started drafting at once. Then, with no advance notice, three of the banks received tested telexes[16] constituting what came to be known as the "short-form payment order." They simply directed the banks to pay all overseas Iranian assets to the Fed to be transferred to the Bank of England. The telexes read:

> PURSUANT TO THE DECLARATION OF THE GOVERNMENT OF THE DEMOCRATIC AND POPULAR REPUBLIC OF ALGERIA CONCERNING THE SETTLEMENT OF CLAIMS BY THE GOVERNMENT OF THE USA AND THE GOVERNMENT OF ISLAMIC (REPUBLIC) OF IRAN WE HEREBY INSTRUCT YOU TO TRANSFER IMMEDIATELY AND UNCONDITIONALLY ALL ASSETS (MEANING FUNDS OR SECURITIES) BELONGING TO BANK MARKAZI IRAN AND IRANIAN ENTITIES HELD WITH YOUR BANK AND OTHER BRANCHES AND SUBSIDIARIES OF YOUR BANK OUTSIDE THE U.S. TERRITORY TO FEDERAL RESERVE BANK OF NEW YORK, NEW YORK FOR CREDIT TO THE ACCOUNT OF BANK OF ENGLAND LONDON FOR THE ESCROW ACCOUNT IN THENAME [SIC] OF THE BANQUE CENTRALE D'ALGERIE AND TELEX CONFIRM IT TO US.

We understood this approach had been urged on Bank Markazi by its U.S. lawyer, Leonard Boudin. While this payment order would establish an escrow account for the benefit of Iran, there was nothing in the order to provide for payments into escrow accounts to be established for the U.S. bank claims as required by the Declarations and Undertakings. The banks were being directed to turn over everything they held overseas, with no provisions for paying the loans as had been agreed by Iran. Such an approach was unacceptable. We continued discussing the substance of the payment order with Brown on the telephone from Washington; Tony Willis, of Coward, Chance, also met personally with him in London. We hoped there was still a chance of resolving the language difficulty on the long-form payment order in a manner satisfactory to both sides. About 10:30 on Monday night, Carswell and Cutler came to the Treasury from the White House and told Bruce Nichols and me that we might have to forget the long-form payment order. Cutler asked how many banks had received the short-form order. I said three, but that I had been told by Brown that we could ignore the short order since we now believed we could get agreement on the long-form payment order, with some acceptable modifications.

---

16. A tested telex contains a special code authenticating the message. Such authentication is a normal and indeed necessary element to confirm the propriety of telex payment instructions. The test code serves a function similar to the signature on a check.

Stephenson Harwood had sent a redraft of the long-form payment order to Willis at Coward, Chance at 11:19 P.M. London time (6:19 P.M. EST). It was simultaneously sent by Stephenson Harwood to Bank Markazi for their comments, despite our London team's request that we see it and comment first. The text of that proposed payment order was also sent to us in New York and Washington and was the basis on which Bruce Nichols and I considered and agreed with Brown's changes to the long-form order.

The banks decided to ignore the short-form orders for the time being, and the question then became whether Bank Markazi in Tehran would in fact send the long-form payment order we had agreed upon with Brown. Cutler and others remained skeptical.

From that point on, shortly before midnight on Monday, until 2:35A.M. EST on the twentieth, when the telex machine in Coward, Chance first lit up, we anxiously waited to see if the long-form payment order would come in. During those deadly hours, we had ample time to regret the fact that we had been unable to arrange the financial closing the way we hoped, with all interested parties around a table in London working together. Such practical but optimistic expectations did not take into account the political realities. The Algerians wanted to work in Algiers, and the Iranians wanted to act only in Tehran. Thus the payment order, which now seemed acceptable, had to be typed and sent by Brown from London to Tehran, there to be retyped and sent from Bank Markazi back to London. In that awkward process, other pitfalls were soon to open.

On our side, all machinery for processing the payments was in place, and Stephenson Harwood was so notified at 5:05 A.M. London time (12:05 A.M. in Washington).

Shortly thereafter, our London group was informed of a news broadcast from Tehran reporting a press conference by Nobari in which he gave the U.S. banks thirty minutes in which to transfer the deposits. Nobari threatened the hostages with dire consequences if the funds were not transferred during that period. A similar statement, although attributed to Nabavi, was picked up in Washington:

> We have asked the Algerian Delegation to meet with us in 30 minutes so that we can tell them our latest views and give a deadline to the American banks to put the deposits in the account of the Bank of England. If the assets of Iranians are not put into the Iranian accounts, harsher decisions will definitely be made.[17]

Still no payment order came in, and calls to Brown provided no relief. Miller

17. Iranian External Broadcasting Service, in Farsi, January 20, 1981, 0433 GMT (U.S. Foreign Broadcasting Information Service).

kept asking for current news for the White House, but we had nothing positive to report. Carswell paced about, glumly repeating "We're dead in the water"; Davis stood by hopefully clutching the presidential executive orders and "Directive Licenses" he would hand to me for the Bank Group as soon as the telex started coming in. Willis, in London, had the telex operators periodically send messages to Tehran to check the lines but received no worthwhile replies. While the negotiating and operating teams huddled in nervous anticipation, hidden from sight, in Washington, New York, London, and Algiers, the hostages in Tehran were facing new "harsher decisions," and a new administration committed to a harder line was preparing to take the reins in Washington. Less than twelve hours remained.

Finally, at 7:25 A.M. in London (2:25 A.M. in Washington) the telex lights blinked on and a message started to arrive. Willis was on an open phone line connecting him with me in Washington and our team in Algiers; he was standing in the telex room at Coward, Chance reading the telexes as received and repeating to me over the open telephone line what was happening; I repeated it to the group in our communications center at Treasury which, at that time, consisted of Secretary Miller, Carswell, Davis, and virtually everybody else floating around. There had been in fact a false alarm shortly before in the form of a wrong number, and the atmosphere was properly supercharged as the first words of the agreed text addressed to the twelve banks began to clatter out on the London telex: "BANKERS TRUST COMPANY, BANK OF AMERICA . . ."

Our cheers relieved some of the tension, but the elation dampened as I heard that the first few lines of the telex now contained the wrong test code. The connection was immediately broken off by Bank Markazi. The Coward, Chance operators soon reestablished the connection, and after a number of other interruptions and errors the entire payment instruction finally came through. Still, some numbers were missing, and other portions were totally garbled. Thus, what should have been an instruction to one bank to pay $60,000,000 read:

> FIRST   0,000,000.00
> .-589,-) ?-,
> 9% :25: -39

In this strange form, the telex was completed at 3:10A.M. EST. (See appendix C for full text.) At the end of the message, Bank Markazi asked "WELL RECEIVED PLS?" Willis replied that some corrections would be necessary and that our operators would run a corrected tape of the payment order to Markazi, so they could run it back to London. That was standard bank telex procedure, and Markazi said they understood.

A few minutes later Markazi telexed, asking for a formal reply to their telex. Willis replied, "MOM PLS," that is, "moment, please." This was immediately followed by a message from Markazi, this time with no typographical problems, reading:

> OUR TELEX WITH TEST NO 210998 WAS TRANSMITTED TO
> YOU CONTAINS OUR OFFICIAL INSTRUCTION FOR WHICH
> WE HAVE AUTHORIZATION FROM THE GOVERNMENT OF
> ISLAMIC REPUBLIC OF IRAN AND NONEXECUTION OF OUR
> INSTRUCTION WOULD ENTAIL SERIOUS CONSEQUENCES
> FOR THE RELEASE OF 52 AMERICAN NATIONALS BEING
> DETAINED IN IRAN AND THE RESPONSIBILITY FOR THIS
> RESTS ENTIRELY WITH YOU.

The bank operator replied that we were discussing the text of their telex and would be back to them shortly. Markazi replied, "MOM PLS," and then said, "PLS WE ARE WAITING FOR YOUR REPLY AS SOON AS POSSIBLE." London said, "UNDERSTOOD. WE WILL REPLY AS SOON AS POSSIBLE." Markazi said, "THANKS" and went off the line.

I told Carswell of the threat and said our inclination was to ignore it; if the banks decided to act on the payment instructions, they would simply inform Bank Markazi that the payments had been made.

The garbled payment order caused consternation in the Bank Group, and debate raged in New York whether the banks could pay $5 billion on inadequate payment instructions, even though we were rather sure that the errors were in transmission and not in substance. Bob Douglass from the group in New York got on the phone with Miller, saying he thought that the banks would pay on these scrambled instructions if Miller ordered them to do so. I had in fact taken delivery from Davis of the presidential executive order requiring payment of the overseas deposits and a "Directive License" for the exact amount of each bank's payment. At 3:40 A.M. Miller said he was ordering the banks to pay. I suggested to Douglass that we needed an icebreaker, not an agreement. Douglass, for Chase, followed by Morgan Guaranty, announced over the speaker-phone that they were paying. The others promptly joined, and by 4:10 A.M. EST the U.S. banks had transferred $5,533,434,413.10 from their accounts in London and Paris to the Fed in New York. At 6:18 A.M. the Escrow Agreement was signed in Algiers; at 6:43 A.M. the escrow account was opened in London; and finally at 6:45 A.M. $7,977,143,433.97 was transferred from the Fed holding account to the escrow account; "Dollar Account No. 1" had been established at the Bank of England.

I immediately informed Peter Mailander in Stuttgart over an open line to Germany; Mailander relayed the message to Navab through an open line to the Iranian Embassy in Bonn, and he in turn informed Navabi in Tehran that the agreed $8 billion had been transferred into escrow and was out of the hands of the United States.

The scene now shifted to efforts, primarily in Algiers, to translate the fact of payment into certificates and other steps required by the Algerian Declarations and Undertakings. I became a weary observer, puzzled by the ensuing troubles in Algiers with consummating the preconditions for the hostages' release. When it appeared that all the certificates had finally been completed, Miller, Carswell, and I dropped down to the Secretary's dining room for breakfast. Members of the new administration were beginning to arrive at Treasury to watch the inauguration parade from the well-placed windows. They were a well-scrubbed and groomed contrast to our grungy lot, who had now been holed up for most of the last ninety hours.

Before we had finished our scrambled eggs, Roger Brown called from London wondering what was happening, since the planes had not yet left Tehran. It seemed that the certificates attesting to receipt of the required funds in escrow had been completed but not delivered, as required, to the governments of Iran, Algeria, and the United States. Those deliveries would trigger Iran's obligation to release the hostages.

We returned to Carswell's office, where we watched the inauguration preparations, parade, and ceremony from the windows and on television. Hours ticked by with no explanation, while visitors came to bid farewell or inspect their new quarters. Noon came, the United States had a new President, but the hostages remained inexplicably grounded in Tehran. Certain of the executive orders, which President Carter had signed, by their terms became effective only after the hostages had "safely departed from Iran." Were these executive orders valid? Would President Reagan ratify them? Would the new administration repudiate the whole deal? These questions haunted us, and exhausted Justice Department lawyers struggled to find answers or at least legal precedents as we waited for further word.

Finally, between 12:33 and 12:38 P.M. we heard that the planes had taken off from Tehran. I left Treasury for the first time since Saturday and took the Eastern shuttle back to New York. By the time I reached my office about 3:00 P.M. Peggy Liddle called to say that the $3.667 billion had been received by the New York Fed back from the Bank of England as planned and that the first of the distributions paying off the syndicated bank loans had already been made.

The deal had worked.

Reflections

The final development of the Algiers accords settling the hostage crisis took place in a framework bearing no resemblance to the American traditions favoring face-to-face negotiations. However, the financial aspects of the settlement had been struck as a result of such negotiations during the previous six months through the bankers' channel, and the U.S. and Iranian representatives conducting the financial negotiations had grown to know, understand, and respect each other. Those relationships, and the advance work in thinking through the financial problems together, were in the end essential elements in closing the deal.

From the start it had been clear that some form of commercial and financial settlement would be a prerequisite to the release of the hostages. Direct participation of the private sector in that process, within guidelines set by the government to ensure consistency with U.S. policy, supplied a useful channel of communication out of the glare of publicity and provided the U.S. government ready access to knowledgeable and experienced professionals who had necessary skills not widely available within the government. In that process, confrontation between governmental and private interests was either avoided or limited through cooperative analysis of the problems and a joint search for creative solutions.

The U.S. government and Iran were openly hostile and engaged in a serious conflict. On the home front a different kind of conflict loomed constantly during the hostage crisis and always jeopardized a prompt solution. The U.S. government's prime objective was the safe return of the hostages in a manner consistent with our national honor. Private parties, while sharing the government's interest in the hostages' return, also sought the valid objective of having their Iranian claims satisfied. These objectives were potentially in conflict. Bankers and other potential claimants reasoned that return of Iran's frozen assets in exchange for the hostages might not appear to be the payment of ransom and therefore would be politically acceptable to the U.S. government. Thus the release of Iranian property from the asset freeze and from other legal restraints had to be appealing to government planners. But release of the freeze also meant release of funds out of which claims might be satisfied.

Banks and other parties with claims against Iran anxiously watched developments threatening what they saw as security for their claims. A strain of suspicion existed in the private sector that, as pressure increased on the U.S. government to "do something" for the hostages, "something" would be done to the claimants' security. The self-protective interests and instincts of the private claimants thus represented a potential threat to government planners. Even in a crisis situation, courts will be attentive to complaints involving the taking of private property for public use, and the U.S. government cannot simply ignore court injunctions. Delays inherent in litigating constitutional issues naturally would imperil a speedy solution to the crisis. As the stalemate wore on, private claimants and government officials followed each other's moves with keen interest and wariness.

Throughout the Iranian experience, the U.S. government maintained regular liaison with all affected areas of the private sector. However, the active participation of those involved in the bank channel provided special benefits both to the government and private parties and relief from potential tension and conflicts between them. Some essential characteristics of that process illustrate those benefits:

•The financial and economic data and active cooperation from the banks needed to work out any settlement affecting those areas were more readily to be obtained through voluntary efforts than extracted by bureaucratic demands from the government.

•Contacts of the government within the private sector reduced the need for overt threats of government action that were as likely to inspire resistance as cooperation. Such contacts fostered mediation between competing interests and facilitated solutions without excessive confrontation.

•Private communication lines augmented government channels.

•The bank negotiations were conducted over an eight-month period with no leaks and no publicity. As Warren Christopher points out in his introduction, that kind of privacy is more easily maintained in the private sector.

A replay of the Iranian financial negotiations may not be a likely event. A parallel experience, involving vast privately held assets that may be useful to the government in solving an international incident, is only a remote possibility. But there are sure to be international conflicts that involve both governmental and private U.S. interests, and cautious, discreet, and guarded involvement of the private sector can provide the government with valuable resources.

U.S. transnational enterprises must be responsible and responsive to the governments in all areas where they operate. Businessmen and lawyers working daily in the international arena are not trained, professional diplomats, but they frequently have developed diplomatic as well as technical skills to succeed in their private endeavors. Those skills, coupled with their existing and potential network of contacts, can provide a useful complement to regular governmental channels.

7 BEGINNING OF THE END

HAROLD H. SAUNDERS

THE CHANGING POLITICAL SCENE: MAY–AUGUST

Policy Stock-taking

To return to the account of the crisis as seen from the State Department—the failure of the rescue mission, the resignation of Secretary Vance, and the appointment of his successor made a full policy reassessment essential in early May 1980 as Edmund Muskie took hold as Secretary of State.

Vance's resignation came as a blow to the State Department for many reasons. Basic were his decency as a human being to work with and the depth and soundness of his judgment on how people and nations should deal with each other. Equally important was the conviction of his colleagues in the department that he stood firmly for the resolution of conflict through determined negotiation and other peaceful efforts rather than by impetuous use of force.

In the middle of the night when we had taken the many steps necessary to pick up the pieces after the rescue mission was aborted, Vance told a small group of us gathered in his office that he had submitted his resignation to the President. Shocked, some of us probed with questions designed with the helpless purpose of somehow reversing that act. It is appropriate to let his own book record his reasoning and the relationship of his resignation to the state of the Carter Administration and others in it at that moment.[1] But it is important here to capture how his departure fitted in the context of efforts to release the hostages.

That night, he explained his opposition to the rescue attempt on

---

1. Cyrus Vance, *Hard Choices: Critical Years in America's Foreign Policy* (New York: Simon and Schuster, 1983), pp. 407–13.

grounds that he did not believe it would succeed; it would cost a number of lives; even if it did succeed, it would leave other Americans in Tehran vulnerable to seizure as a new group of hostages; and it was wrong to use military force to achieve what might be achieved by peaceful means. I do not recall his mentioning concern about possible reaction against Americans elsewhere, perhaps because he saw a rescue mission as distinct from punitive action.

His precise explanation was clear enough that night, but the full weight of his position was more dramatically expressed nine months later in Wiesbaden, Germany. As part of our effort in January 1981 to help the newly freed hostages pull together the threads of what had happened in the rest of the world during their captivity, Vance sat down with them for a whole evening in a classroom at the U.S. Air Force Hospital in Wiesbaden to review in detail all the efforts that had been made to free them. After almost an hour of describing one effort after another, when he explained his resignation simply and straightforwardly, he was applauded. The weight of his commitment to a peaceful solution and his concern for them as human beings struck deeply resonant chords in the majority of that group. To individuals held hostage in hourly face-to-face dealings with captors who represented a chaotic and sharply divided political "system," the abstract use of force on the international chessboard seemed far less relevant and realistic than patient and dogged diplomatic efforts to persuade key individuals and to put them in a position to persuade those around them to release the hostages. As I listened, I was struck by the memory of how Vance's tireless perseverance had outlasted even the most exhausting negotiations to help produce the Camp David accords and the Egyptian-Israeli peace treaty. Without *both* Jimmy Carter *and* Cyrus Vance on the American side, neither agreement would have been achieved.

Secretary Vance's resignation and preparation for his successor created a moment when it was natural for each of us to review privately the touchstones for the policy we had been following. It was not a gossipy interest in the Vance-Brzezinski or White House-State Department differences that prompted thought. Except for the rescue mission, most of those differences during the hostage crisis were well contained within the expected range of civil disagreement among concerned men. There were sharper differences in other areas, but that is not our interest here.

The issue for many of us was at its roots how nations—and the human beings who lead them—can most effectively deal with each other. The two men reflected different approaches. It was not mainly that Zbig Brzezinski was more concerned with national interest and honor, while Cy Vance emphasized humane values. Although there was that difference of emphasis, both men recognized that policy had to encompass both concerns.

As seen during the hostage crisis, it was a difference between impatience with a crisis that dragged on and the determined perseverance of a marathon runner who set his sights and tried to maintain a balanced and steady course. It was a difference between a desire to administer periodic shocks to keep a crisis from solidifying and a strategy of putting all the pieces of policy in place and then trying to wear the other side down by gradual escalation of pressure coupled with opportunities for negotiation. It was a belief in the classic use of force to change adversaries' minds versus questioning what point force would make in a society where leaders made decisions on any but a classic basis. It was a belief that arraying a disadvantageous balance of forces would be decisive versus conviction that identifying substantive common advantages was essential in breaking an impasse. It was a tendency to assess shorter-term developments and to propose frequent mid-course adjustments versus setting a long-term strategy and patiently grinding out one step after another on that course. It was a difference between force and firmness. It was also the gut difference between a man whose professional experience had taught him to deal incisively with the abstractions of international relations and one whose life had been spent in working with other human beings toward partially shared objectives.

It was probably because many of these differences reflected strong convictions about how human beings should treat one another that the two approaches often reflected deeper feelings among the American people. Perhaps it is natural that the White House is more sensitive to popular impatience—maybe even to the point of magnifying it—whereas the State Department also needs to take account of the popular mood and political constraints in other countries—even to the point of underemphasizing American moods. Finally, Cy Vance seemed to his colleagues to believe that a leader's ultimate resources in dealing with another leader are the steadfastness and steadiness of his position, the absolute trustworthiness of his word, and the soundness and firmness of his commitment to his own goals.

We quickly found out that Secretary Muskie was equally committed to a negotiated resolution of the problem. Months later, after the hostages' return and after many of us had left the government, Muskie spoke eloquently at a small dinner for the crisis team about the demonstration that diplomatic solutions can often achieve what military solutions cannot.

Muskie settled quickly into his seventh-floor office at the State Department and plunged immediately into the policy review that we had already launched. He used his new colleagues well to put himself in command of the issues, and his firm leadership—always with an open mind and readiness to listen—calmed concerns about a serious interruption in our efforts.

With economic sanctions in place and tension in the United States strangely diffused by the aborted rescue mission and perhaps by the wind-up of the primary elections, a full reassessment of the administration's approach was both necessary and possible. The Iran Working Group began its presentation to the new Secretary with the proposition that the administration was dealing in Iran with "an outlook that differed fundamentally from our own and a chaotic internal situation." The Working Group explained the two-part strategy that had been followed, combining pressures and efforts to provide a political opportunity for the Iranians to release the hostages. Its analysis underscored that a policy of pressure could not by itself produce a solution, because the religious leadership in Iran did not seem to respond to Western-style pressures. "We are not in a classic bargaining position," one paper concluded with modest understatement.

Analyzing the political situation in Iran, the Working Group pointed out that the new Iranian parliament would probably be divided and lack effective leadership. In any case, the period between the May 9 elections and the convening of the parliament would be a period of intense political struggle. It remained an open question whether a determined group in Iran might use that period of flux to push through a solution to the crisis, although no one viewed that as by any means likely. It seemed a time for broadening the U.S. approach in order to work with the three main elements in the leadership: President Bani-Sadr, who would be responsible for putting the government program before the new parliament; Foreign Minister Ghotbzadeh, who continued to be committed to release of the hostages; and the clerics, who had been so difficult to reach yet who had blocked previous diplomatic efforts.

Among other possible approaches, the Working Group proposed stepping back from the hostage issue and trying to broaden our approach to discuss wider issues, such as longer-term Iranian-European and U.S.-Iranian relationships. The full range of options was laid out in meetings of the Policy Review Committee in the White House—the forum urged by Muskie to put him rather than Brzezinski in the chair. Detailed papers describing the options and potential channels were discussed. The strategy that emerged from this in-house policy review by May 8 affirmed three main points:

• The economic sanctions would be strictly enforced, and the Iranians would be given time to judge their effect.

• A broader foundation would be developed for renewed diplomatic activity, this time with redoubled effort to open channels to the religious leaders in Tehran. Henry Precht and I, with Stephanie Van Reigersberg, were sent to Paris, Bonn, Vienna, London, and Berne with two missions. First, we took with us a list of seventeen key figures in Tehran and asked each government to examine its own channels to each of those leaders. Second, we also took the text of a general message the United States hoped might be conveyed to those Iranian leaders through all serious channels. As it happened, Secretary Muskie in a separate European trip was able to meet the German ambassador to Iran, who was in Europe on consultation, and to add his own voice to this new effort.

• A period of quiet in public diplomacy would be observed as the Iranians digested the results of the parliamentary elections and set about forming their parliament and a new government. The families of the hostages, who met with some of my colleagues, with Secretary Muskie, and with me in various smaller groups in a series of regional meetings at the end of April and in early May, concurred in trying to move the hostage issue from the center of public attention.

Just as we were in the process of laying plans for a new effort to develop a negotiating track, word came that encouraged us to believe that Bani-Sadr's interest in finding a route to negotiation remained alive. On Saturday, May 3, Deputy Secretary of the Treasury Robert Carswell received a call from John Hoffman, a New York lawyer at Shearman and Sterling, then retained by Citibank for litigation connected with Iran's frozen deposits. Hoffman reported that he had been approached by German lawyers representing Iran to determine whether Citibank would be interested in secret negotiations looking toward a practical economic settlement. At the Tehran end of this inquiry were reportedly President Bani-Sadr and Governor Nobari of Bank Markazi. What followed in this critical channel has already been recounted in chapter 6. Suffice it to say here that the news of this feeler provided one more argument for persevering in new efforts to reopen a negotiating track. John Hoffman's account also revealed how the political struggle in Tehran in May and June was apparent in the "bankers' channel," as we called it, just as it was in diplomatic channels.

As we set the stage for this new longer-term diplomatic approach, we recognized that one of the consequences of the rescue attempt was to complicate enormously our efforts to find Iranians willing to negotiate and to keep track of the hostages' whereabouts and well-being. The immediate reaction of Iranian authorities was to treat the aborted rescue attempt as an assault to overthrow the Iranian government and to dramatize the failed attempt as an example of the United States' depravity and impotence. Anti-American demonstrations again broke out in Iran, and barbarity characterized the treatment of the bodies of the eight military men killed at Desert One. Archbishop Hillarion Capucci, who had a relationship with a number of the leaders in Tehran, and the Swiss ambassador in the end played critical roles in negotiating the return of these bodies.

Precht and I met with Capucci in a private lounge at the Zurich airport arranged for us by the Swiss government as part of our European swing to assess channels available to us in this new diplomatic chapter. He was a dynamic bearded man with an open and friendly approach, whom I had known by name because he had at one point been jailed by the Israelis, allegedly for facilitating arms shipments to Palestinians. I learned in just one more strange coincidence that Christian Bourguet had defended him. With roots in the Arab-Israeli area, he recommended that we use our influence to facilitate his attempts to to encourage an Arab diplomatic effort to help Iran release the hostages. But he cautioned that he had promised to avoid political activity when the Israelis had freed him. We did not press this approach as a priority matter, because chances of pulling it together seemed remote.

In Iran, the captors' next step was to disperse the hostages to various sites around Tehran, as well as to other Iranian cities. It was not until late in the year that the location of most of the hostages was again known. Prior to the rescue attempt, the crisis team had had a reasonably good overall accounting as a result of several visits with the hostages and TV films of the Easter religious services. The dispersal of the hostages greatly increased the risk to their safety—both the risk of accident as they were moved around the country and the risk of harm as they were exposed to other and perhaps less disciplined Iranians.

Political Crisis in Iran

What pervaded reports from Tehran through almost all channels during May and June was the intensification of the internal political crisis. One contact reported that Khomeini was very ill, power was fragmented, there was total lack of coordination among the principal power centers, and Bani-Sadr was losing power rapidly. One of the best analysts still in Tehran described leadership "in a greater state of paralysis than ever before," a "cumbersome and inefficient administration decimated by purges," and a "President being undermined by fundamentalists."

Another analyst reported that, as a result of the internal power struggle, the hostage issue had become "a secondary matter" in Tehran. He added, however, that the issue remained "a useful, if not necessary focus of fixation for many power circles. . . . Often the leadership has not been displeased that this issue became a focus for the underlying dissatisfaction which otherwise would be directed against the government." Many counseled against any new initiatives while the government was so disorganized that no one could react. Most analysts with whom Precht and I talked the third week in May in Europe agreed that the release of the hostages would not come until the power struggle was resolved.

Despite the power struggle, or maybe because of it, substantive contacts between Iranian authorities and foreign figures increased in June. Some of them came about in the context of a new round of talk about trying the hostages after the rescue mission. The administration had again pressed a number of friends to take a stand against such trials. At the same time, several proposals were circulating in Tehran for some sort of international conference as a possible vehicle for releasing the hostages. Bani-Sadr was considering a meeting of nonaligned, Islamic, European, and various private groups to examine evidence of "U.S. aggression." Ghotbzadeh, on the other hand, was talking about a seven-nation conference that would invite the United States and Iran to Switzerland to discuss the full range of problems between them with several Middle Eastern and Mediterranean nations (Saudi Arabia, Algeria, Kuwait, Syria, Greece, and Spain). He told one of his nongovernmental American contacts that the Arab radicals had a better chance than anyone else at that time to get Khomeini's attention. This was presumably the track Archbishop Capucci was pursuing.

The idea of a conference of the nonaligned prevailed and was called for June 2–5 in Tehran, and the administration had to cope with the question of how to deal with Americans who attended that conference despite the ban on travel to Iran. The Working Group recommended that the administration allow a responsible group to see what it could do on the ground in Tehran, but the predominant view among members of the SCC was that it was necessary to try to stop anyone from going to Tehran at that time. Several went anyway. The conference produced two substantive documents (which we never saw), but Bani-Sadr could not muster the support necessary to use them for any constructive purpose.

It was at this time also that Adib Daoudi, the Syrian member of the earlier U.N. Commission, returned to Tehran as an individual after consultation with Secretary-General Waldheim. Waldheim had also talked with Ghotbzadeh about Daoudi's visit when they both attended the funeral of Marshall Tito in Belgrade. Waldheim announced Daoudi's trip on May 17. Daoudi's talks led to the conclusion that there seemed to be no opportunity for the U.N. Commission to return to Tehran at that time. It appeared as if Ghotbzadeh might have agreed to Daoudi's visit in the hope of heading off European economic sanctions and lost interest when the Europeans went ahead anyway.

In addition to the international conference to publicize evidence of "U.S. complicity" in the Shah's regime and alleged actions to topple the revolutionary regime, European Socialist leaders—Bruno Kreisky of Austria, Olof Palme of Sweden, and Félipe Gonzalez of Spain—went to Tehran in a separate effort. Precht and I had talked with Chancellor Kreisky during our trip a few days before his departure and had shared fully our need to open channels to the religious leadership in Tehran.

The atmosphere in Iran gradually calmed. By the third week in June, reports from Tehran began to indicate that key Iranians sensed a change in

Khomeini's attitude. They felt he now wanted the hostage issue resolved. From his vantage point in the Foreign Ministry, Laingen also sensed "a gradual movement toward the day when the Majlis will come to grips with the hostage issue."

The new parliament had been inaugurated on May 28, but it immediately fell into a long period of examining the credentials of its members. Part of that process was devoted to consolidating the positions of the Islamic representatives. At the beginning of July, a friendly diplomat in Tehran judged that another four weeks would pass before the parliament could be fully formed and that September would be the earliest time when the hostage issue might be dealt with constructively. It seemed from other reports that the political process then in motion was something like a process of coalition formation in a Western parliamentary system, though much more chaotic.

A Western visitor to Tehran reported in mid-July: "The Majlis already shows all the signs of being a shambles. It will not be an efficient legislative instrument because its members lack experience, because of the lack of discipline in the various parties and groups, and because many of its members will use it as a debating chamber rather than as an instrument of government. There is no clear link between Deputies and Ministers." In the light of these political preoccupations, he concluded: "To the west, the hostage issue comes first; to the Iranians it has slipped down the list."

On July 20 a key step was taken in the formation of the parliament when Ali Akbar Hashemi Rafsanjani was elected permanent Speaker or President of the Majlis. Analysts in Tehran concluded from this step that Khomeini had begun the final confrontation and purge of non-Islamic elements. He appeared to have sided with the Islamic Republican Party led by Ayatollah Beheshti against Bani-Sadr. Despite these discouraging reports, the crisis team sent cables to forty-six capitals urging friendly governments again to weigh in for release of the hostages and again sent its position paper to key figures in Tehran through friendly ambassadors. The modest success of these approaches was indicated perhaps when a plaintive report reached the crisis team on September 1 that Bani-Sadr and Ghotbzadeh were displeased with these efforts to reach Islamic leaders such as Rajai, Rafsanjani, and Beheshti.

On July 11, hostage Richard Queen had been permitted to leave Iran after Iranian medical authorities determined that he was seriously ill. He had contracted multiple sclerosis. Welcome as his release was in the United States, it seemed to have little significance for the larger effort to release all of the hostages. Queen was able to provide new information about the condition and whereabouts of some of the hostages. U.S.-Iranian relations again momentarily heated up the atmosphere late in July, when an Iranian opponent of Khomeini was murdered in Bethesda, Maryland, and a number of Iranians were arrested as a result of demonstrations in Washington.

Through all of the mixed signals from Tehran there gradually emerged a sense that a moment of new opportunity might be presenting itself. By the end of August, the prolonged struggle for control of the revolutionary movement seemed to have achieved a new center of gravity, with the Islamic Republican Party more firmly in control and the power of key secular leaders diminished. On August 11, Mohammed Ali Rajai was approved by the Majlis to be Prime Minister, and the new government too was on its way to being formed.

SETTING THE STAGE FOR NEGOTIATION: SEPTEMBER–OCTOBER

Iranians Begin to Respond

As a result of our approaches in European capitals in May, statements of the U.S. position began to find their way into the bands of clerical leaders in Tehran. In July, as the Majlis began to take shape, and then in August when a Prime Minister was named, a series of personal messages went from Washington to the new leaders in Tehran.

In the U.S. House of Representatives, 187 members signed a letter to Speaker Rafsanjani urging that the new parliament give priority to the hostage problem. Rafsanjani's oral reply did not close the door on further exchanges. He described the letter privately as "a first step that could permit clarification of the hostage problem." To build on that reaction, a second letter was sent August 15, signed by Congressmen Benjamin Gilman and Lee Hamilton in the interest of a prompt response during a congressional recess. The families of the hostages sent a message to Rafsanjani on August 13 offering to meet with him. All these letters were informally coordinated with the State Department. Secretary Muskie himself wrote to Prime Minister Rajai. Each of the letters was presented by the Iranian recipient to the parliament, so it appeared that they were willing to have a picture of increasing communication develop.

Against that background, we received on September 9 the first expression of interest in negotiation initiated entirely by the Iranians. The German ambassador to Iran, whom Secretary Muskie had met during his European trip, relayed a message from a well-known Iranian with ties to the Khomeini camp, the new Prime Minister, and President Bani-Sadr. The message said in effect that Khomeini was very ill, and they wanted to resolve the hostage crisis promptly. A few days later, Deputy Secretary Warren Christopher, whom the President had put in charge of negotiations, met secretly outside Bonn with the Iranian emissary. The details of that meeting and the negotiations that followed are discussed by Roberts Owen in chapter 8, but some broader points can be made here.

Moving Toward Negotiation

The preparations for that secret meeting in Bonn set a pattern of work in Washington that was to characterize the Washington management of the negotiations until the hostages' release. Three points are relevant:

First, as we had learned in our earlier efforts to develop a scenario, it would remain critical in these final negotiations to state the U.S. position in ways that would be politically and legally sound in our own country.

The challenge to the Christopher negotiating team from the outset was to find ways to present these positions so as to give Iranian leaders working for release of the hostages the opportunity to tell Iranians that they would get what justice entitled them to. As the "negotiations" wore on, it became more and more obvious that the critical element in the negotiation would be how the United States' position could be presented in Tehran. It was not the hard exchange between differing negotiating positions that is normally characteristic of negotiation. What made the exchanges possible was the judgment of key Iranians that keeping the hostages had more disadvantages than advantages for the revolution now that revolutionary leadership had been consolidated. What was critical to them was their ability to keep Khomeini and the parliament behind them as they negotiated. As the negotiations proceeded, the crisis team in Washington had reports through several confirming channels that the major power centers in Tehran continued to be actively involved. It was essential to produce something they could use politically while protecting our own interests.

This point may seem self-evident to politicians, but it was not always so to some of the American lawyers involved. Their concern understandably was whether a particular formulation would stand up in an American court of law. For the diplomats in Christopher's group, the issue was whether a formulation could be presented to win political support in Tehran. It was Warren Christopher, lawyer and diplomat, who had to marry these concerns. It was the highly competent Algerian mediating team, selected in November as the channel for the final negotiations, who sharpened our understanding of what would be useful in Iran. In the end, it was the device of developing two documents that bridged the gulf. One document appeared to say "yes" to the Iranian demands; the other laid out the fine print explaining how we would respond in ways that would meet our own requirements.

Second, the outbreak of the war between Iran and Iraq on September 22 affected the efforts to move toward agreement in several cross-cutting ways. Most immediately, the closing of the Tehran airport delayed the return to

Tehran of the emissary with whom Christopher had met in Bonn, and conduct of the war diverted and absorbed the attention of Iran's leaders. It is remarkable that they did not set the hostage issue aside altogether. In the slightly longer term, Iran's leaders became acutely aware in concrete ways of the consequences of Iran's diplomatic isolation, their inability to resupply Iran's military forces, the impact of further reductions in oil sales on dwindling financial reserves, and the economic sanctions which had begun to make themselves felt.

Previous chapters have mentioned that the consequences of Iran's international isolation were brought home to Prime Minister Rajai when he flew to New York to present Iran's case against Iraq at the United Nations October 16–19 and learned firsthand the lack of sympathy for Iran as a result of its holding the hostages. We could say that, in part, our long campaign to build international opinion had paid off. In addition, during long talks in New York, the Algerian ambassadors in Washington and at the United Nations apparently discussed with him the consequences of what Iran had done for its role as a revolutionary nation on the world stage. Ambassador Redha Malek in Washington, who was responsible for representing Iran's interests in the U.S., was a man of stature in Algeria's own independence movement. Ambassador Bedjaoui at the United Nations had been co-chairman of the U.N. Commission of Inquiry in Tehran the previous March. Rajai presumably heard more of the same during a stop in Algiers on the way home, which Khomeini had authorized as an expression of sympathy for the victims of a serious earthquake there. These contacts led Rajai subsequently to ask the Algerians to serve as the channel for exchanges on the conditions for releasing the hostages.

Rajai's stay in New York also brought him into human contact with the hostages in an extraordinary way. Katherine Keough, President of the organization of hostage families (FLAG), went to New York and asked to meet with Rajai. As mentioned earlier, the families had sent a message to Tehran when the new Iranian government was formed. After long hesitation, Rajai agreed to meet, and the moment came after a long and harrowing session at the U.N. Security Council. Mrs. Keough went to the Iranian residence in New York.

After a wait, she was told that the Prime Minister had returned, and she was ushered upstairs. At the end of her climb, she found herself sitting beside the Prime Minister on the edge of his bed while he took off his shoes. There they sat side by side while she told him of the agonies of the hostages' families. She spoke of her husband as a former school teacher, and Rajai as a school teacher himself responded warmly. Despite the gulf between them, Mrs. Keough felt that there was a moment of profound human communication. No one will know what effect that encounter had on this man with no experience on the international stage and under seige for his government's behavior. Perhaps that human moment in the loneliness of a day's battering had its own impact.

Third, despite heavy preoccupation with the war, Iran's parliament went ahead with its deliberations on the four conditions for release of the hostages put forward by Khomeini on September 12. Illustrating that the internal struggle was far from finally resolved, the Majlis held a number of closed sessions on the issue, and opponents repeatedly showed their capability to block a decision. One evening we were told that a decision would surely be made in the Majlis session the following morning. I went home for dinner and returned to sleep in the Operations Center to be on hand when the news came. Sometime during the night, I was awakened to be told that the Majlis had been recessed "for lack of a quorum." The irony of that chaotic body recessing for so Western a cause as lack of a quorum was overwhelming. "Oh, God," I said. "They've thought of still another reason for not deciding." Finally, skillful management by Rafsanjani of a series of decisions produced a resolution on November 2—two days before the presidential election in the United States—further developing Khomeini's four conditions.

Following the passage of the Majlis resolution, the Iranians formed a committee in the Prime Minister's office headed by Minister of State for Executive Affairs Behzad Nabavi to coordinate the Iranian end of the negotiations that were about to begin. The Prime Minister formally named Algeria as the sole authorized channel for negotiation, and Redha Malek, the Algerian Ambassador in Washington, on November 3 formally delivered the text of the Majlis resolution to the State Department. The Nabavi Committee would be the Algerians' point of contact in Tehran. The stage was set for the final negotiations.

THE HOSTAGES AND THE NEGOTIATIONS

Even then, more than two and a half months of grueling negotiation still lay ahead to bridge the gulf between our separate legal, financial, and political worlds. During that period, we began to receive reports that the hostages were being returned to Tehran. Throughout the summer we had received fragmentary reports from sources all over Iran about groups of hostages here and there—seen on an airplane, visited by a doctor, seen in the garden of one of the closed U.S. consulates. Some of the hostages got letters out to their families and used family references to hint at their whereabouts. After their release, one group told of being driven crazily along a deserted road when their van turned end over end. The Iranian driver was killed, but none of the hostages was hurt. It came as a relief when we began to hear that they were being returned to Tehran.

During their mid-December visit to Tehran, the Algerian team actually visited with a number of the hostages in their new hotel-like quarters. When the Algerians came to Washington at Christmas time, Ambassador and Mrs. Malek graciously invited the families of the hostages to their home for a late afternoon reception and an opportunity to talk individually about the hostages with whom the Algerian team had spoken. The Algerians had been meticulous in identifying the hostages they met and in noting something about each conversation for the families. The warmth of the Maleks' hospitality and the human concern shown by all the Algerian team made a deep impression on the families. Seeing the quality of the Algerian delegation also increased the families' confidence in the seriousness of the intense negotiations then almost through their second month.

One development in Tehran was disturbing. We suddenly received word at Christmas time that Bruce Laingen and his two colleagues at the Foreign Ministry had been moved from the ministry. As it later turned out, they had been moved to solitary confinement in a prison. If we had not felt that we had a chance to gain the release of all the hostages in the immediate future, we would have spent a lot more time tracing them.

Late in the afternoon of January 20, Algiers time, members of the Christopher team moved in and out of the ambassador's suite in Embassy Algiers. The agreement at long last had been completed. We were listening distractedly to President Reagan's inaugural address over the Voice of America with one ear while following periodic intelligence reports on the hostages' movements in Tehran. As far as we could tell, they were aboard the Air Algérie plane at the end of the runway at Mehrabad Airport in Tehran but were holding. We had been told that no night flying out of Mehrabad was allowed, so we were fully prepared for word to come that it was too late in the day for the plane to take off and that departure had been delayed. Then miraculously the report came that they had taken off. Still there was uncertainty. Would some crazy Iranian pilot try to thwart their flight to freedom? Finally, about an hour later the unbelievable report came in through intelligence channels—the flight had left Iranian air space.

Only then did we dare to talk about opening a bottle of champagne. Later we learned from the hostages aboard the aircraft that cheers had rocked the plane when the pilot announced their crossing into Turkish air space, and the Algerian crew had also broken out champagne.

In Washington, key members of the Iran Working Group had been up much of the night, as had the group with the President in the White House.[2]

2. For the White House, see Jimmy Carter, *Keeping Faith: Memoirs of a President* (New York: Bantam Books, 1982), pp. 3–14; and Hamilton Jordan, *Crisis: The Last Year of the Carter Presidency* (New York: Putnam Publishing Group, 1982), pp. 15–17 and 395–406.

Foreign Service Officer Ralph Lindstrom had by then succeeded Precht as director of the group, with Andy Sens and Larry Semakis as his principal deputies. Katherine Keough and Louisa Kennedy were there waiting too that morning. As the morning wore on, the group was gripped with tense anticipation, braced for the shock of yet another disappointment. No one could tell why the hostages were not moving. Many were convinced that something new had gone wrong. One officer dialed all the numbers for Mehrabad Airport that had worked on previous occasions. The phones rang—but no answer. Only later would they be sure from the freed hostages that the Iranians were just slow, perhaps even wisely cautious, in getting their dangerous act together.

Precisely at noon Lindstrom noticed a workman by the main elevator in the hall outside the Ops Center methodically removing the names of department officers from the big wall directory there. The board was blank. The Carter Administration was history. And the hostages were still in Tehran.

It was not until some thirty-five minutes later that word finally came through our own channels that the planes had taken off, but there still was no assurance that all fifty-two hostages were aboard. Then Lindstrom began receiving unbelievable crank calls—the planes would be shot down in flight. Iranian F-4 Phantom fighters were by then known to be escorting the Algerian planes to the Iranian border. But would they be attacked then? A flurry of checks revealed no evidence. Still they worried: Were all the hostages aboard?

About an hour after the "wheels up" from Mehrabad, word came from the aircraft trackers that the planes had left Iranian airspace. Then the critical call came from the Swiss Embassy. It was deputy Franz Muheim with a message relayed by phone through the Swiss Foreign Ministry in Berne. Lindstrom took the call. The Swiss ambassador in Tehran had boarded the Algerian plane before takeoff and had in hand the signatures of all fifty-two hostages! Having been burned by false hopes so many times before, only then could members of the Working Group begin to let themselves believe that the moment they had waited so fervently for had come. Lindstrom walked down the hall with that last round-robin message everyone had dreamed so often of sending, telling our colleagues around the world that the hostages were free.

Several hours later, as the exhausted group watched TV coverage of the hostages landing in Algiers, some of the television crews came into the Ops Center to film the scene there, bringing sandwiches and, at last, champagne. The Iran Working Group itself would stay in business through the hostages' return and formally shut down on January 29.

Shortly after 6:45 P.M. in Algiers, Arnie Raphel drafted the following unclassified telegram for Christopher to send to Washington:

1. Formal notification of departure of hostages given to Deputy Secretary Christopher in Algiers January 20, 1981 at 1845 local.
2. In atypical State Department fashion, your most dutiful, respectful and deferential negotiating team ends its mission with an unequivocal—Hooray!!!

Shortly after, the department sent us a copy of a more formal message from the Algerians. Algerian Chargé Debagha had telephoned the following message from Foreign Minister Benyahia at 2:10 P.M. (EST) January 20, 1981:

"In the name of the Government of Algeria, I just addressed the following letter to the Governor of the Central Bank of Algeria: I have the honor to inform you that the Ambassador of Algeria in Iran has just informed me that the 52 American nationals have left safe and sound the Islamic Republic of Iran. This letter constitutes the certification provided for in paragraph 3 of the Declaration of Algiers of January 19, 1981. Signed Mohammed Ben Yahyia, Minister of Foreign Affairs."

The State Department telegram was signed by David Newsom, who was by then Secretary of State Ad Interim—a reminder to several of us in Algiers that we were private citizens in the Reagan Administration.

The champagne celebration was more reverent than exuberant. We were too tired and had been through too much not to know how close the arrangements for release had come to falling apart at the last moment. While jubilation was the response at home, we walked quietly across to the embassy snack bar. The first words that passed among some of us as we sat there were: "Think how we'd be feeling if we hadn't made it." After 444 days, that was a thought that could easily make the bottom drop out of one's stomach.

Our minds were already turning, too, to the question: "What will they be like? Will they have been destroyed as human beings?" For the next few hours, our thoughts turned to that somber question. A few hours later, standing in the rain at the foot of the long stairs down from the cabin of the Air Algérie plane, I looked for the answer in each face and in each handshake. Only then could I be sure that we had welcomed fifty-two sound colleagues back to freedom.

In the airport lounge, after carefully accounting for each of the hostages—the Algerians had given each a card with a number—Foreign Minister Benyahia and Deputy Secretary Christopher exchanged welcoming remarks and, in his final official act in Algiers, Christopher signed and handed to the Foreign Minister the following note:

I have the honor and pleasure to acknowledge the return of the fifty-two United States nationals who have been detained in Iran. The Government of the United States hereby confirms the safe arrival of all fifty-two and assumes responsibility for returning them to their homes.

Mr. Minister, I want to express to your President, to you and your colleagues, and to the Algerian people the deep gratitude and respect of the people of the United States for bringing us to this moment of profound relief that these fifty-two men and women and their families have emerged from the chasm of fear. You and your government have demonstrated an inspiring commitment to humane values, and have provided the world with a singular example of the art of diplomacy.

Indeed the entire experience had "provided the world with a singular example of the art of diplomacy."

8 THE FINAL NEGOTIATION AND RELEASE IN ALGIERS

ROBERTS B. OWEN

On the morning of January 19, 1981, two extraordinarily tired government officials sat down, side by side, across the table from a huge mass of reporters in the Algerian Foreign Ministry in Algiers. The two were Mohammed Benyahia, Foreign Minister of Algeria, and Warren Christopher, Deputy Secretary of State of the United States. Neither one had had a real night's sleep in the preceding two weeks, and understandably they kept their morning's business short. As a tremendous battery of television and press cameras rolled and flashed, Benyahia invited Christopher to indicate, by initialing three brief documents, the United States' adherence to certain arrangements under which Iran would bring about the immediate release of the fifty-two American hostages.

Although the three documents initialed by Christopher were remarkably brief—they totaled only about eleven short typewritten pages—it had taken approximately four months of tremendously concentrated effort to bring them into existence. This chapter describes that four-month process from the perspective of one member of the Christopher negotiating team.

The Underlying Question: To Negotiate or Not

As earlier chapters have shown, the process began on September 9, 1980, when a German Embassy official came to the State Department in Washington and reported to Secretary of State Muskie and Deputy Secretary Christopher that, according to a message received in Bonn from the German ambassador in Tehran, a high-ranking Iranian official wanted to meet secretly with a high-ranking American official in West Germany to discuss a settlement of the hostage crisis. Muskie and Christopher proceeded immediately to the White House to inform the President of what they thought might be the critical break in the crisis.

At that White House meeting two decisions were quickly made. First, it was decided that the United States should engage in discussions with the as yet unidentified Iranian official *provided* we first obtained some assurance that, when he arrived at the proposed meeting in West Germany, he would have authority to negotiate on behalf of his government. Second, assuming that such assurance would be obtained, the President decided that Christopher should serve as the U.S. representative, to be assisted by a small group of senior U.S. officials.

Although these decisions were taken quickly, they obviously rested upon an unspoken premise adopted well before, namely, that it was in the national interest of the United States to negotiate with the government of Iran for the release of the hostages, rather than to refuse to negotiate at all. Although Carter, Muskie, and Christopher regarded that premise as sound, it was later questioned by various commentators, and for that reason it seems worthwhile to pause briefly at the threshhold of this chapter to ask: Can it be persuasively argued that in September 1980 the proper responsive position for the United States would have been to say in effect that it would not enter into discussions of any kind with the government of Iran until the latter had set the hostages free?

After the hostages' release, the new Reagan Administration provided its official answer to that question: On February 18, 1981, the State Department issued a formal statement on behalf of Secretary of State Alexander Haig asserting flatly that "The present Administration would not have negotiated with Iran for the release of the hostages."[1] The underlying rationale, presumably, is that "you should never negotiate with terrorists," because, if you do, you will be conceding something, which will serve as a signal that acts of terrorism can produce a profit to the perpetrators. If crime is rewarded by concessions, so the theory runs, it will lead to further crimes.

Although I cannot speak for President Carter and his immediate advisers, I suspect that they would respond by making at least two basic points, one in the abstract and the other in concrete practical terms. As an abstract principle, I think all would agree that, if a government negotiates with—*and* makes significant concessions to—the perpetrators of acts of international terrorism, that course of conduct may well do more harm than good over the long run. On the other hand, negotiation or (to use a more neutral term) discussion need not involve concessions, and it can certainly be argued that discussion that defuses an international crisis without concessions is worthy of international applause.

On a more concrete plane, those of us who were on the scene in September 1980 are presumably entitled to ask whether, when Secretary Haig

1. *Department of State Bulletin*, vol. 81, no. 2048 (March 1981), p. 17.

stated flatly that he would not have negotiated with Iran, he was taking into account both Iran's prior conduct and our own. If the problem we confronted in September 1980 could have been solved by a simple unilateral act by Iran (the release of our hostages), then a simple stonewall approach might have been the appropriate course. But as has been pointed out in preceding chapters, well before September 1980 the United States had taken a series of rather drastic countermeasures against Iran and thus, for better or for worse, had created an enormously complicated situation. The full complexity of the problem can be understood only after recalling the commercial consequences of the Khomeini revolution itself.

One of the fundamental precepts of the Shah's regime, of course, was that Iran should gear up rapidly to take its place in the modern industrial world. As part of that ambitious program the Imperial Government of Iran had entered into a massive complex of commercial contracts with American companies, which were to supply billions of dollars worth of goods and services to Iran on a continuing basis. Starting early in 1979, however, the revolutionary regime began to seize American properties and cancel contracts with American suppliers, thus bringing into existence a huge mass of claims on the part of hundreds of different American companies.

Many of these American claimants did not stand idle in the face of this attack. Recognizing the presence within the United States of some billions of dollars of assets belonging to the government of Iran, American claimants began to bring lawsuits against Iran in U.S. courts and to obtain judicial orders (so-called prejudgment attachments) under which Iran was precluded from removing the assets from the United States until the underlying controversy had been resolved. Prior to the seizure of the American Embassy on November 4, 1979, judicial attachment of Iranian properties in this country had been moving slowly, but the sharp rupture in American-Iranian relations resulting from the embassy seizure brought a landslide of new lawsuits and attachments. And then, on November 14, President Carter added his executive freeze order, the cumulative result being a complete and complex lock—judicial and executive—on more than $12 billion-worth of Iranian assets both in this country and abroad.

I doubt that the proponents of the Haig argument have taken these events into account. Their presence in the equation in September 1980 points to the conclusion that it would have been virtually a political impossibility for officials of the Iranian government to release the hostages without first obtaining some commitment from the United States for a corresponding release of Iranian assets within U.S. control.

In one sense the situation was like a mutual taking of hostages. It was as though, in April 1980, when President Carter decided to sever diplomatic relations with Iran and expel all Iranian diplomats from the United States, he had decided instead to seize those diplomats and hold them in custody pending release of our fifty-two nationals.[2] In such circumstances, I would suppose, even those who share the Haig philosophy would probably have been willing to work out reciprocal commitments for release of both groups of prisoners, even though some negotiation and a "concession" would have been involved, simply because the only alternative, a more or less permanent stalemate, would have been unacceptable.

One counterargument might be that in September 1980, even if some release of Iranian assets was in the interests of the United States, it should have been proffered unilaterally, without negotiation. In fact, however, as further explained below, it would have been literally impossible for the U.S. government at that time to make a simple and unadorned commitment to release all encumbered Iranian assets upon release of the hostages. For various legal reasons the encumbered assets could be released only over time and only if Iran were willing to accept a number of stringent conditions, none of which could be made understandable to Iran without a good deal of explanation at the negotiating table. In short, by September 1980 the prior actions of the judicial and executive branches of the U.S. government had made it impossible for the United States to issue any unilateral statement of position that would satisfy the political necessities of the decision-makers in Tehran. We believed we were faced with a choice between entering into discussions with Iran or settling down for an indefinite wait.[3]

Moreover, although I think that the assets-release problem was by itself sufficient to compel negotiation, there were additional factors pointing in the same direction. In mid-November 1979, only a few days after the seizure of the embassy, my colleagues and I in the State Department's Legal Adviser's Office recommended to Secretary Vance that the United States bring a proceeding against Iran in the International Court of Justice[4] at The

2. In April 1980 some Americans felt strongly that the U.S. government should have taken the Iranian diplomats prisoner. Indeed, I well remember a midnight telephone call from a distinguished and irate member of the Washington bar, demanding to know why I, as the Legal Adviser, was not recommending such a course. My answer was that, in the view of the State Department, Iran's flagrant violations of international law could not be regarded as justifying equivalent violations by the U.S. government.

3. Some commentators have suggested that the United States made a fundamental error in allowing Iran to link the return of the encumbered Iranian assets to the release of the hostages; the thesis seems to be that it was within the power of the United States to prevent any such linkage from taking place and that, if the suggested separation had occurred, the negotiations leading to the release of the hostages would have been vastly simpler and less time-consuming than they were. I believe, however, that all who have looked at the facts agree that the two sets of issues became irretrievably linked many months earlier when the attachments took hold and the freeze order was put in place. Delinkage had become impossible.

4. Senator Daniel Patrick Moynihan is mistaken in claiming—in *Loyalties* (New York: Harcourt, Brace, Jovanovich, 1984), pp. 86–90—that it was outside prodding starting in mid-November that got the State Department to consider going to the Court.

Hague, and the Secretary quickly approved. The Court, moving with spectacular speed (especially given the fact that, when the case was filed on November 29, 1979, the fifteen members of the Court were scattered throughout the world), declared in early December that Iran's seizure and detention of the hostages constituted the clearest possible violation of international law. In May 1980 the Court's preliminary ruling was followed by a final judgment declaring, among other things, that Iran was liable to the United States and to the hostages individually for damages in an amount to be determined through subsequent judicial proceedings. Although I regard the Court's pronouncements as having served a useful purpose in terms of mobilizing world opinion and persuading our allies to join with us in the imposition of at least some modest economic sanctions against Iran, it must also be recognized that both the judgment and the economic sanctions added to the complexity of unraveling the dispute between the two governments. Those two factors clearly contributed to Iran's later decision, as indicated below, to set certain difficult conditions for the hostages' release.

Finally, there was the matter of the ultimate collectibility of the commercial claims of American nationals against Iran. There was considerable doubt that our courts would be able to bring about actual collection, so that without some outside assistance the claimants faced the prospect of losses of billions of dollars. Although the release of the hostages was far and away the top priority of the U.S. government, we also wanted to avoid, if we possibly could, leaving our claimants without a remedy, and a remedy could be arranged only if Iran could be persuaded, through negotiation, to join in a responsible arrangement for adjudicating the claims. Indeed, for the U.S. government to have abandoned the claimants in the context of the hostage crisis might well have been regarded as a payment of ransom for the hostages' release, and the payment of ransom of any sort had long since been ruled out by President Carter as totally unacceptable.

The Drawing-up of the Agenda
As to what was to be discussed at the proposed meeting in West Germany, the Christopher team got its first inkling of Iran's agenda when Christopher sent a message through the German government cautioning that, before we committed ourselves to a meeting, we needed some assurance that the Iranian representative would have authority to speak for his government. In response the German Embassy soon telephoned to say that the Iranian delegate had volunteered a prediction which, if it came true, would clearly establish that he could speak for the Ayatollah Khomeini himself. The prediction was that within days Khomeini would publicly articulate four conditions for release of the hostages: that the United States would have to (1) pledge that it would not intervene in the internal affairs of Iran, (2)

return all of the frozen Iranian assets to Iran, (3) cancel all U.S. claims against Iran, and (4) return the wealth of the Shah of Iran.

Within three days the prediction was fulfilled. On September 12 Khomeini made a lengthy speech that rambled on about various Iranian domestic issues, but near the end—seemingly without any logical connection to what went before or after—he suddenly articulated precisely the four conditions that had been predicted. By this time Christopher had assembled his small negotiating team,[5] and I well remember the slightly baffled smiles around the table when we realized that the Germans' message seemed clearly to reflect a decision by the highest authority of Iran, the Ayatollah himself, to move forward toward a solution to the crisis.

The next step was to arrange as quickly as possible for a secret meeting in Germany with the Iranian delegate (now identified as Sadegh Tabatabai, brother of the wife of Khomeini's son, whom we quickly labeled "the Traveler") and to develop a response to each of the four Khomeini demands. These responses, which became integral parts of the U.S. position for the next several months, were in substance as follows:

1. As to the demand for a pledge of nonintervention, Christopher was prepared to say, "no problem." The United States would not apologize for anything; we would not acknowledge any prior improper behavior; but we saw no objection to a public statement that it would be contrary to U.S. policy to intervene politically or militarily in the internal affairs of Iran.

2. As to the demand for the return of the frozen assets, Iran was obviously assuming that all that President Carter had to do in order to return the assets was revoke the freeze order of November 14, 1979, but this overlooked the additional encumbrance of the judicial attachment orders, which probably could not be set aside until a number of legal issues had been resolved by the Supreme Court of the United States—a process that would take many months. On the other hand, since we did not wish to take the position that the United States was powerless to return any of the frozen $12 billion (all of which Iran perceived as lawfully belonging to Iran), we reviewed the various groupings of assets making up the $12 billion total and identified two categories that seemed to be relatively releasable. One consisted of the offshore assets—approximately $4.8 billion (plus accrued interest)—which, since they were on deposit in branches of U.S. banks in Europe, were not encumbered by any U.S. attachments. We recognized, however, that Iran had failed to pay interest and principal on many loans made to Iran by the same banks that held the deposits. Those banks would therefore be unlikely to return the deposits without some agreement with Iran on payment or refinancing of the loans. At best, we estimated, some $3

5. See chapter 5, note 1, for the members of this team.

billion of the deposits could be made available for release immediately upon release of the hostages.

The other promising category of frozen assets consisted of approximately $2.5 billion in gold bullion and securities which the Iranian government had on deposit with the Federal Reserve Bank of New York and which, although arguably subject to certain attachment orders, were at least in federal hands. Accordingly, Christopher went to Germany prepared to say that we were in a position to release several billion dollars (perhaps as much as $5.5 billion) immediately upon the release of the hostages but that the remainder of the frozen assets could not be released until something had been done about Iran's borrowings and the judicial attachments previously obtained by U.S. claimants—thus bringing us face to face with the third of Khomeini's demands: that the United States cancel all U.S. claims against Iran.

3. We never for a moment considered the possibility of acceding to the third demand, simply because cancellation of valuable commercial claims by the U.S. government would surely have been regarded as a payment of ransom, conferring a multimillion-dollar financial benefit on Iran at the expense of U.S. nationals. On the other hand, ironically, Iran's dissatisfaction with the litigation pending against it in our courts was matched, in a sense, by a corresponding concern about the same litigation on the part of the Christopher negotiating team. The lawyers among us were very much aware that in the pending federal suits Iran was going to claim sovereign immunity under our Federal Sovereign Immunities Act, which meant that, even without any cancellation of claims, our claimants were in a very vulnerable position. At the same time, however, we thought that it would be difficult to persuade our federal judges to lift their judicial attachments from Iran's assets unless we could give some assurance of alternative protection for claimants' rights.

From this complex of considerations we developed, after much brainstorming, the following response. "Your primary objective," we were prepared to say to Iran, "is to obtain the release of your assets from the freeze order and the judicial attachments, but the U.S. government will face serious legal obstacles in achieving that objective unless we can show our federal courts that some sort of a reasonably fair remedy is going to be provided for the claimants involved. Accordingly, in response to your third demand the U.S. government will bring about the cancellation of all commercial claims against Iran *provided* Iran agrees (1) to allow the claimants to submit essentially the same claims to an international arbitral tribunal and (2) to pay any awards made by the tribunal."

We had not paused to make a complete historical study of prior U.S. experience with international arbitral tribunals, but we knew that the

United States had joined in somewhat similar programs for adjudicating American claims on a number of prior occasions. In the late 1860s, for example, Mexico and the United States had established a three-man tribunal to adjudicate the claims of nationals of one country against the other, and the program had worked out very satisfactorily. Although a later Mexican-American claims settlement program in the 1920s met with much less success, a post-World War I German-American claims settlement tribunal (German-American Mixed Claims Commission) adjudicated almost 20,000 claims of U.S. nationals against Germany in the 1920s with relative satisfaction on both sides. With these experiences in mind, our hope was that, if Iran would accept the basic principle of international arbitration of commercial claims, it should then be possible to design a workable arbitration mechanism. (Since the Iranian government was being advised by American counsel, we did not feel any obligation to point out to Iran that, because of the legal obstacles faced by American claimants in our own federal courts, an agreement by Iran to allow such claims to be submitted to an international arbitral tribunal might place our claimants generally in a better position than they would have been in if the hostage crisis had never arisen.)

4. The last of Khomeini's four conditions—the return of the Shah's wealth—was particularly troublesome, both for practical reasons (we doubted that any substantial portion of his estate remained within U.S. control) and because we felt very strongly as a matter of principle that we could not agree to any program to confiscate his family's U.S. assets, if any, and transfer them to Iran. Nevertheless, our assessment was that the issue was one of great political importance to the Iranian side and that it behooved us to permit Iran to point to at least some token accomplishment with respect to the Shah's assets. Accordingly, we developed the position that (a) since the only entity within the U.S. government that would have the legal power to transfer the allegedly stolen property to Iran would be the U.S. courts, Iran's only means for recovering any such property would be to bring suit in our courts and ask them to order the transfer, and (b) the executive branch of the U.S. government could offer no more than some facilitation of Iran's litigating efforts. As Christopher approached the meeting in Germany, he was prepared to say that, if Iran were to undertake such litigation, the U.S. government would take legal steps to prevent the Shah's property from being removed from the country pending the outcome of the litigation, to assist Iran in its efforts to collect information about such property, and to advise the U.S. courts that the members of the family of the Shah did not enjoy any special immunity from suit in our courts. Such an offer, we believed, would not provide Iran with any significant litigating advantage that it would not otherwise have enjoyed.

These positions were hammered out during marathon meetings of the

Christopher negotiating team immediately after September 9; they were then approved by Secretary Muskie and President Carter; and on September 13 a five-man delegation—Christopher, Carswell, Saunders, Owen, and Raphel—boarded a special plane at Andrews Air Force Base and took off for Germany.

The Initial Discussions

The following morning we landed at a West German Air Force Base, were swept into four black government Mercedes limousines, and rocketed off at tremendous speeds to a "guest house" maintained by the German government outside Bonn. In fact, "guest house" was too modest a description: Our temporary residence turned out to be the Schloss Gymnich, a magnificent old palace set in one of the most beautiful private parks any of us had ever seen. The German security around the grounds could not have been more inconspicuous or more effective.

There then ensued a twenty-four hour wait while the Traveler completed his trip to Bonn; we killed the time walking the grounds of the Schloss and admiring the stately portraits of the aristocratically long-nosed Gymnich family. Conveniently, after we had caught up on our sleep, the German government informed us that the Traveler, contemplating only preliminary and generalized discussions, had arrived in Germany alone and had requested that the talks be attended by the German Foreign Minister, Hans-Dietrich Genscher—a suggestion that we welcomed. On the evening of September 15 Christopher, accompanied by Arnold Raphel, Secretary Muskie's Special Assistant and an expert on the Middle East, met secretly with Genscher and Tabatabai at a small German government residence just outside Bonn.

At the outset Christopher pointed out that political speech-making would be a waste of time, and when the Traveler in effect acquiesced Christopher proceeded with an explanation of the U.S. responses to Khomeini's four points. Some of it was received without counterargument; in other instances questions were raised; and in the end three particular points of tension emerged. First, although the Traveler made no objection to the U.S. proposal with respect to the handling of U.S. commercial claims against Iran, he took the position that Khomeini's third demand (for the cancellation of all U.S. claims) required a waiver by the United States of any claims that either the United States or the hostages themselves might want to assert against Iran as a result of the embassy seizure (for example, claims for monetary damages for the hostages' ordeal). Needless to say, Christopher objected, and the matter was left unresolved.

Second, the Traveler demanded to know whether the United States, following the hostages' release, would be prepared to supply Iran with the

spare parts it needed for its vast arsenal of American military equipment—
a demand that Christopher parried and the Iranians later abandoned after
the Algerians were asked to be intermediaries. And finally, the Traveler
expressed dissatisfaction with the U.S. position on the Shah's wealth. Although Christopher carefully explained the nature of the obstacles standing
in the way of the Iranian demand, it apparently was difficult for the Traveler to accept the notion that the executive branch of the U.S. government
lacked the power to seize and transfer private property.

At the end of the meeting, unsure how well the Traveler had understood
the various aspects of the U.S. position, Christopher suggested a second
meeting two days later, leaving an interval for each to check in with his own
government. The suggestion was accepted, and at the second meeting (at
breakfast) Christopher reviewed the U.S. position once again. The Traveler,
making clear that he had talked to his superiors in Tehran and that in
general the U.S. approach was "not unwelcome," focused hard on the problem of the Shah's assets, explaining that it was a tremendously emotional
and politically sensitive issue for the Iranian government. At that point,
however, Genscher made a significant contribution. He told the Traveler
directly that the kind of litigation facilitation being offered by the United
States was more than the West German government would have been in a
position to offer in similar circumstances and that it was all that Iran had
any right to expect. Genscher's comments helped to ease the tension, and it
was then tentatively agreed that, after Christopher and the Traveler had
returned home for further instructions from their governments, they would
resume their talks in late September. At that point it seemed possible that
the hostages might be promptly released on the basis of nothing more concrete than a bilateral acceptance of the general principles presented by
Christopher in Bonn.

That possibility was promptly obliterated by the Iraq-Iran war, which
broke out on September 22. The Traveler could no longer travel, and this
hopeful channel dried up. Although it was a serious blow, we took what
comfort we could from the realization that, with a war on its hands, Iran
would be feeling the pinch of the sanctions more than ever and would thus be
forcefully reminded, on a daily basis, of the harm that the detention of the
hostages was doing to Iranian national interests. As previous chapters have
made clear, the same point was reemphasized in mid-October when Prime
Minister Rajai traveled to U.N. headquarters in New York to seek, unsuccessfully, international support for the Iranian cause against Iraq.

The Algerian Role
On November 2, 1980, after a discouraging six weeks of negotiating inac-
tivity, the Iranian Majlis, in whose hands the Ayatollah had placed respon-

sibility for deciding the fate of the hostages, came forward with a lengthy resolution spelling out, in new and very complicated language, its own version of the four conditions previously laid down by the Ayatollah. For the preceding six months, following President Carter's severance of diplomatic relations with Iran in April, Algeria had been serving as Iran's diplomatic agent (or "protecting power") in the United States, and on November 3 the very able Algerian Ambassador in Washington, Redha Malek, delivered to the State Department a diplomatic note setting forth the terms of the new Majlis resolution and designating the government of Algeria as the official intermediary through which all further negotiations were to be conducted.

This news was both bad and good. The Majlis' resolution was discouraging on its face, because it seemed to ignore several of the fundamental problems that Christopher had so painstakingly explained in Bonn and that stood in the way of U.S. compliance with the Ayatollah's four conditions. For example, the resolution continued to call for return of the frozen assets before release of the hostages, thus completely ignoring the obstacles created by the U.S. judicial attachments; it called upon the United States to waive the hostages' right to prosecute damage suits against Iran, despite Christopher's protests against that demand;[6] and it completely failed to take into account the legal reality that Iran's only hope of recovering properties belonging to the Shah was through litigation in the U.S. courts.

The heartening aspects, however, were that, despite its preoccupation with other matters (including particularly the war with Iraq), the erratic Iranian government seemed to be continuing on a relatively steady course toward active negotiations and had selected as an intermediary a government whose diplomatic corps enjoyed a very high reputation. Within a matter of hours after Ambassador Malek's delivery of the note, the Christopher team was busy formulating a new U.S. response—an amplification of the position taken in Bonn—and Christopher had made arrangements for the U.S. team to fly to Algiers to explain it.

A brief description of the first negotiating session in Algiers will give some flavor of the negotiations as a whole. Upon landing at the Algiers Airport, we were shepherded into a string of black Foreign Ministry Peugeots and proceeded at high speed, with motorcycle escort, to the residence of U.S. Ambassador Ulric Haynes, Jr., where we were told that we

---

6. Ultimately the Departments of Justice and State concluded that, if the hostages were to try to sue Iran to recover damages, there was no court that could require Iran to pay, which meant that a waiver of such claims would not give up anything of real financial value. Since the hostages' families preferred to accede to the Iranian demand for a waiver rather than allow the issue to delay the release of the hostages, President Carter ultimately decided to waive the claims and establish a special commission to deal with the problem of compensating the hostages for their ordeal.

were expected within the hour to meet with the Algerian negotiating delegation. We were also told that that delegation would consist of four extraordinarily able men. Suggesting the importance of the matter in Algerian eyes, their delegation was to be headed by their young Foreign Minister, Mohammed Benyahia, who was to be supported by three other "stars": Ambassador Malek, perhaps Algeria's most experienced diplomat (who had participated, as had Foreign Minister Benyahia, in the negotiations by which Algeria won its independence from France); Algeria's Ambassador to Iran, Abdelkrim Gheraieb, who had been in prison almost a decade during the revolution and subsequently served as Algeria's contact with Algerians in Europe; and Seghir Mostefai, the Governor of Algeria's central bank for seventeen years and clearly one of the Algerian government's leading financial figures. We were vastly encouraged to hear that the Algerian government was prepared to go to work so quickly and with such a commitment of top-flight personnel.

Proceeding to a lovely Moorish villa used by the Foreign Ministry, we were introduced to the Algerian team, and Benyahia promptly suggested that he and Christopher withdraw for a short preliminary conference. After a brief pause, during which the rest of us chatted informally with Ambassador Gheraieb about current conditions in Tehran, the Foreign Minister invited both teams to follow him to a conference room. At a long table with a green baize cover, on which were placed two miniature flags, one of Algeria and one of the United States, the Algerians took their seats on one side, and we on the other. Seated in the center of the Algerian side of the table, the Foreign Minister delivered a courteous opening statement of welcome, while official photographers held a brief photographic session, and Christopher then was invited to present the U.S. response to the Majlis' resolution of November 2.

Christopher opened his presentation by distributing a notebook to each of the Algerians. Each book contained, in French and English, a statement of the Majlis' position and a statement of the U.S. response. Speaking through the State Department interpreter, Stephanie Van Reigersberg, Christopher painstakingly explained our understanding of the Majlis' position, the legal obstacles which the Iranian proposals confronted in terms of U.S. law, and the reasoning underlying the U.S. response on each issue. Interspersed throughout the discussion were questions from the Algerian side, which had to be translated from French into English. Christopher would then either answer the question or call upon another member of the U.S. team to do so, with a subsequent translation from English into French. It was a laborious process (the sessions frequently went on for hours at a time), but the pace provided ample time for careful analysis on both sides of the table.

One of the most productive elements in this procedure, which was repeated many times during the next two months, was the Algerian "cross-examination." Our Algerian interlocutors were highly intelligent and essentially impartial individuals who were studying our positions with care and questioning us, in a most courteous but thorough way, to find out exactly why the U.S. position was constructed as it was. They were making sure that they fully understood the problems, partly in order to make a clear presentation to the Iranians. One of the beneficial side effects was to bring home to the U.S. team the points at which our own position had not been adequately thought through or was less than clearly phrased or vulnerable to a powerful response by Iran. The process amounted to a kind of dress rehearsal, giving us an opportunity to identify ways in which we could improve our position and its articulation before the Algerians carried it to Tehran for the real presentation.

Our first session in Algiers occupied two working days, at which point both sides agreed that the U.S. position was sufficiently clear and ready for presentation. When Christopher politely inquired how soon the Algerian team could go to Tehran and commence its talks with our counterparts—the "Nabavi Committee"[7]—Minister Benyahia replied, with typical Algerian readiness, that his three colleagues would leave for Tehran at once. After a magnificent feast of whole roast lamb with our Algerian counterparts, we returned to Washington. Several anxious days later, we received word from the Algerian Embassy that Malek and his two colleagues were ready to fly from Tehran to Washington to report. This procedure—alternating the U.S.-Algerian discussions between Algiers and Washington, with a Tehran visit in between—continued for the next several weeks, and at each U.S.-Algerian session, at least through mid-December, we found that the Algerians had managed to narrow the issues and draw the two antagonists closer to an understanding.

The $24 Billion Demand

On December 17, 1980—after several weeks of apparently steady progress and almost exactly a month before the expiration of President Carter's term—Iran came forward with a dramatic new pronouncement. In a statement delivered to the Algerian delegation in Tehran and then publicly announced by Tehran radio on Sunday, December 21, Iran finally accepted the U.S. proposals for the international arbitration of claims (and also agreed to provide a revolving fund to secure the payment of arbitral awards) and then stated flatly that the hostages would be released only after the United States had placed in the hands of the Algerian central bank approx-

7. See p. 292.

imately $14 billion in frozen assets *and* an additional $10 billion cash guarantee to insure that the Shah's wealth would be returned to Iran.

The reactions of the U.S. team were mixed. On the one hand, those experienced in direct dealings with Iranians (particularly Raphel, who had served in Iran for several years) were able to find some rays of hope in the new Iranian position. Raphel emphasized that for many weeks Iran had been demanding a return of the Shah's wealth in cash as a precondition to the release of the hostages, and he argued that the Iranian willingness to accept a "guarantee" of payment *later* might well represent a significant and promising change in position. If the bargaining process continued, he said, we might be able to persuade the Iranians to release the hostages in return for future commitments rather than for cash. When others pointed to the outrageous dollar figure being suggested—$24 billion—Raphel's response in substance was, "Yes, that is an outrageous opening position proffered by people who are used to haggling in the bazaars, and the probabilities are that it will change significantly if we press on."

Others were considerably less optimistic. By this time, we had to assume, the Iranian negotiators were fully aware that the total of the frozen assets could not be released until after many months of litigation and that an outright return of the Shah's assets was out of the question. This meant that, if Raphel was wrong and Iran stuck to its newly stated position, the hostages were not going to be released for many months to come and certainly not before the expiration of President Carter's term on January 20.

A previously scheduled event required Secretary Muskie to react immediately to the new development. Appearing on *Meet the Press* only a few hours after the announcement was made from Tehran, Muskie quietly but firmly asserted that the new Iranian demands were "unreasonable" and that Iran was demanding that President Carter take steps that were beyond his constitutional authority. Our hope, of course, was that in the face of this response the Iranian position would soften, but on that particular Sunday our morale was uncomfortably low.

Indeed, on the same Sunday the President and his advisers met to consider whether the time had come to give up the negotiation process entirely and leave the hostage problem to the next administration. With all of the apparently wasted effort thus far expended, the temptation to quit was certainly there. Standing in the way of that temptation, however, was a keen awareness of the continuing ordeal of the hostages and their families and of the probability that if a release was not achieved within the thirty days remaining to the Carter Administration, the consequences might be severe. Obviously, if the Reagan Administration inherited the problem, it would need time to study it and work out its own plan of action, which would necessarily leave the hostages in captivity for a long additional period.

There was also a deep concern that, if we broke off negotiations, powerful elements in Iran would demand immediate criminal prosecution of some if not all of the hostages.

For several of us the possibility of such criminal trials had been a haunting specter ever since the early days of the crisis. Indeed, in the early days a great many lawyer-hours had been expended analyzing the options open to the U.S. government if such trials were commenced. For example, if Tehran were to announce that certain hostages would go on trial on a specified date, should the United States retain Islamic counsel from another Moslem country and seek to inject them into the trials to defend the hostages' rights? What principles of law would apply in a prosecution before a revolutionary court in Iran? And if we were to provide counsel, would the U.S. government be prepared to supply the lawyers with a full array of information as to what could and could not be said on behalf of individual hostages? While government lawyers pondered these questions, members of the private bar in Washington and New York contributed many hours preparing an extensive private file of defensive materials to be made available to counsel if the need should arise. The fact that no criminal trials were ever held was almost surely the result of a private message that President Carter had sent to Iran early in the crisis making clear that the reaction of the U.S. government would be severe. Nevertheless, throughout the crisis the Iranian revolutionary courts were conducting summary trials and ordering summary executions of hundreds of Iranian citizens, and we were never sure from one day to the next whether such revolutionary zeal would be turned loose on our people.

Faced with these hard realities on December 21, 1980, President Carter decided that, no matter how remote the prospects of success, we had to mount one last crash campaign to resolve the matter within the thirty days remaining.

Preparations for the Final Drive

Christopher immediately began to look for new ways to convey to Iran the urgency of the situation and to focus the attention of the parties on the remaining open issues. Thus far the operative documents had taken the form of unilateral position statements by each side, but at this stage Christopher called for a new, unified document stating concretely and clearly the mutual obligations of the two governments. Since we knew that Iran would not sign an "agreement" with "the Great Satan," we invented the device of a "declaration," which would be issued by the government of Algeria and to which each of the two antagonists would then "adhere." In fact, for mechanical drafting reasons, two separate declarations were prepared. The first set forth what each side would do before, during, and after the release of the hostages (the so-called basic declaration), and the second set out the understandings on the arbitral mechanism for the settlement of claims (the so-called claims settlement declaration). Christopher accurately anticipated that new documents of this kind would crystallize the open issues and thus expedite the negotiating process.

One of the challenges for the draftsman, incidentally, was to deal with the complex problems involved in simple terms so as to allow the documents to survive translation into French and Farsi and be clearly understood by (among others) laymen who had not been trained in the Anglo-American legal system. We recognized that, if either of the two declarations became long and complicated, it would be slightly comprehended and highly mistrusted in Tehran. For example, although the initial draft of the claims settlement declaration as prepared in the Office of the Legal Adviser of the State Department was some twenty-five pages long (very short and simple by ordinary standards), it was ultimately revised down to about three-and-a-half typewritten pages—surely one of the most concise legal documents of its kind ever written.[8]

The entire drafting process was fraught, to put it mildly, with technical problems. Just as one example, we were then aware that during the Shah's regime many U.S. companies, in contracting with the Iranian government, had agreed to contractual clauses (so-called Iranian-courts clauses) to the effect that, if any dispute subsequently arose under the contract, the parties would have to litigate the matter in the courts of Iran. Few, if any, of these companies had foreseen an Islamic revolution and the establishment of a radically different judicial system in Iran, and the U.S. negotiating team did not want these companies to be required to litigate their claims against the Iranian government in Iran's new revolutionary courts. We had been forewarned by the Algerians that Iran might insist on literal enforcement of all Iranian-courts clauses, but we deliberately drafted the claims settlement declaration in such a way as to allow a U.S. claimant an opportunity to try to persuade the proposed international arbitral tribunal that an Iranian-courts clause should not be treated as binding (that is, that the tribunal itself should hear his case), because the Iranian revolution had effectively destroyed the remedial mechanism to which the parties had agreed. In this and other respects the drafting of the new declarations inevitably raised the possibility of new technical disputes, but we nonetheless regarded preparation of the declarations as an essential step in accelerating the negotiations.

Christopher's next step was an urgent request for a new round of meet-

8. The principal credit for this feat of draftsmanship belongs to former Deputy Legal Adviser Mark Feldman and the State Department's then Counselor on International Law, Gerald Rosberg.

ings with the Algerians, and their three-man traveling delegation came to Washington on Christmas Day to start educating themselves as rapidly as possible on the new declarations. During a series of marathon meetings in the next several days, the Algerians cross-examined us and our documents at length—a process that led to some redrafting and improvement. Specifically, the Algerians suggested a number of ways in which the U.S. drafts could be made more attractive to the Iranian side without any sacrifice on our part.

For example, in response to the first Iranian demand we were proposing a statement that, "The United States pledges that it is the policy of the United States not to intervene, directly or indirectly, politically or militarily, in Iran's internal affairs." The Algerian delegation helpfully suggested that we augment the pledge by adding, after the phrase "it is," the words "and from now on will be." Again, although the United States was inclined to favor London as the site of the proposed international tribunal, the Algerians urged us to suggest The Hague on the theory that it would be somewhat more palatable to the Iranians. And when we suggested the possibility of enlarging the membership of the proposed tribunal from three to nine (to allow for three chambers of three members each and hence increased productivity), the Algerians strongly urged us to do so. Although in hindsight none of the resulting modifications seems to have been of critical significance, the process did produce some clear improvements in the U.S. position before its presentation by the Algerians during their meetings in Tehran.

During these late December meetings, apart from technical drafting problems, we placed particular emphasis on two points. The first was that time was running out. If a final settlement could not be agreed to by January 16, we said, the whole project would have to be abandoned, simply because there would not be sufficient time thereafter to complete the contemplated transactions before President Carter left office. Second, we reemphasized the legal limits on the ability of the United States to release frozen Iranian assets without awaiting the outcome of protracted litigation. We said again that (1) we could arrange for the release of the $2.5 billion in the Federal Reserve Bank of New York on very short notice, prior to the release of the hostages, (2) if Iran quickly arranged to bring current its loans from U.S. banks holding Iranian deposits overseas and ensure their eventual payment in full, an additional $4.8 billion offshore (plus accrued interest) could be quickly released, but (3) as eager as Iran might be to recover the approximately $2.2 billion on deposit in banks in the United States, that amount could *not* be released for many months. In terms of immediately releasing Iranian funds to Iran, what we had to offer was in the neighborhood of $8 billion.

The Algerian team conveyed these urgent messages to Tehran in the first days of January, and Iran's response was prompt. On January 7 Iran flatly refused to release the hostages until it had received (or until the United States had placed in escrow with an agreed banking institution) a total of $9.5 billion—some $1.5 billion too high. Although no explanation was given of the figure, it seemed clear that Iran had simply added up the $2.5 billion in the Federal Reserve, the $4.8 billion on deposit in U.S. banks abroad (apparently ignoring the accumulated interest), and the $2.2 billion in bank deposits in the U.S. Obviously this represented a significant retreat from the $14 billion demand in December, as well as an apparent abandonment of the simultaneous $10 billion guarantee demand, but with only days remaining to complete the cumbersome negotiating process the Iranian insistence on the immediate release of the $2.2 billion in bank deposits in the U.S.—a legal impossibility—imposed a potentially insurmountable obstacle. On the afternoon of January 7 President Carter directed Christopher to fly immediately to Algiers to enlist the personal assistance of Foreign Minister Benyahia in dislodging Iran from its unrealistic position.

On a personal note, I well remember how I received word of what turned out to be our last trip. At about 6:30 that evening Raphel called me at my office in the State Department and said cryptically, "Wheels up, Andrews, nine o'clock." I assumed the destination was Algiers and replied, "O. K., I'll see you tomorrow." "No," he said, "Tonight. Pack for 36 hours"—and hung up. I went home, packed one suit and two shirts, drove rapidly to Andrews Air Force Base, and climbed aboard a large Air Force plane a few minutes before 9:00 P.M., joining Christopher, Saunders, Raphel, interpreter Alec Toumayan, and one of Christopher's personal assistants, Dorothy French. It never occurred to me that it would be a full two weeks before the same group (except for Saunders, who went to Germany with the hostages) would arrive back at Andrews from Algiers, all of us exhausted and two of us (Christopher and myself) unemployed.

Fourteen Days in Algiers

The process in which we were engaged during those final two weeks in Algiers was essentially that of amending and supplementing the two declarations (which the Algerian team had presented to the Nabavi team in Tehran) through an extraordinarily cumbersome communications process. Since we had drafted the declarations, virtually every new proposal came from the Iranian side, and each was conveyed by the Nabavi Committee to the Algerian team in Tehran, cabled by the latter to their Foreign Minister in Algiers, hand delivered by the Foreign Ministry to the U.S. team in Algiers, translated by Alec Toumayan, and cabled to Washington. Typically, the U.S. team in Algiers would then develop a proposed response, cable it to Washington for modification and approval, receive Washington's cabled or telephonic reaction at our embassy in Algiers, translate the agreed response into French, and then discuss it with Foreign Minister Benyahia, who might then authorize that it be cabled by his ministry to the Algerian Embassy in Tehran.

The substantive work broke down essentially into three categories: (1) arriving at an agreement as to what the Iranian proposal actually meant (frequently it was garbled or otherwise obscure); (2) reaching agreement among ourselves and with Washington as to what the U.S. response should be; and (3) seeking to demonstrate to Foreign Minister Benyahia and his colleagues the reasonableness of the U.S. position. Benyahia's keen intellect would quickly reveal any weaknesses or counterarguments, and his instincts as to what would and would not be acceptable in Tehran were magnificent. Although he seemed to operate for two weeks virtually without sleep, he pursued the ultimate objective with incredible vigor, knocking heads together as necessary to get the job done.

The demands made by the Iranians during those final two weeks created a staggering set of difficulties as the clock ticked on toward January 20. Each new demand created a potentially insurmountable obstacle; each gave rise to a tremendous amount of work; and each was ultimately resolved. In almost every case, however, just when we concluded that we had worked through a particular problem successfully, having developed a solution that was tacitly accepted in Tehran, Iran would came back with a new and unforeseen problem, which in turn had to be solved on a crash basis and through the same cumbersome mechanism.

My impressionistic recollection after the fact is that, because of the time differences between Tehran, Algiers, and Washington, each new crisis invariably arose at 4:00 in the morning. (This was not literally true of course, but that is the way it felt.) Typically I would be in bed in my room on the third floor of the Ambassador's residence—frequently having assumed a horizontal position only an hour or two before—and would hear a loud knock on the door, which would then open to reveal Ambassador Haynes in robe and pajamas. His usual message: "The Foreign Ministry has just called. There is a new cable in from Tehran. Chris will be leaving in fifteen minutes." Get up. Shave. Dress. Join Christopher, Toumayan, Haynes, et al., in the Ambassador's car. Rocket through the dark deserted streets to the Foreign Ministry. Be ushered silently through heavily carpeted corridors to the Foreign Minister's luxurious conference room on the seventh floor. Listen with sinking feelings to a new, complicating Iranian objection or proposal. Drive wearily back to the Embassy to cable Washington and start work on a new response. Endless conversations with Washington and London as to what could and could not be done with various legal and financial problems. Return to the Foreign Ministry to explain. And so on, day after day after day. What kept the effort afloat, from the Algiers end at least, was the absolutely indomitable determination of Christopher and Benyahia to do everything humanly possible to achieve success.

Without attempting anything like a complete account of each crisis as it arose, I shall describe a few of the major episodes of those final days.

1. Upon our arrival in Algiers Christopher's immediate task was to convince the Algerians on the issue of the $2.2 billion in bank accounts in the United States. Proceeding directly from the airport into a private conference with Foreign Minister Benyahia, Christopher asked the Foreign Minister to consider the dilemma in which a particular U.S. bank would be placed if, in compliance with the Iranian demand, President Carter were to order all U.S. banks holding Iranian deposits in the United States to transfer those funds immediately to Iran (or to an agreed escrow agent, which would in turn transfer the funds to Iran immediately upon the release of the hostages). Christopher reminded Benyahia that the $2.2 billion involved had already been encumbered by attachment orders, which forbade any transfer without judicial approval, and he pointed out that any responsible bank, confronted with such conflicting orders, would have to go to court and ask for judicial direction as to which order to obey—a litigating process that could not possibly be completed within the time remaining available to the Carter Administration. In short, said Christopher, if we in the Carter Administration are going to achieve the release of the hostages "on our watch," Iran is going to have to content itself with a U.S. commitment to bring about the release of the $2.2 billion *after* the time reasonably required to complete anticipated litigation. The Foreign Minister quickly saw the point, and within a matter of days the Iranian demand for immediately available funds was modified downward from $9.5 to $8.1 billion (by dropping $2.2 billion and adding an estimated $800 million in interest accumulated on the offshore deposits).[9]

2. By this time the two sides were agreed on the escrow principle: that is, to guard against any breach of faith, the funds to be released to Iran in the immediate future would initially be placed in the hands of a neutral banking institution as escrow agent. If the hostages were released, the agent would transfer the funds to Iran, but if the Iranian side failed to release the

9. Within a few days, however, another controversy arose with respect to the $2.2 billion. Although Iran accepted the notion that those funds could not be released until a litigating process had been completed, it began to insist on a U.S. commitment to release the funds by May 1981. As a result of another private session with Benyahia, Christopher was able to extract an extension from May to July, thus allowing a six-month litigation period, justified on the ground, which Benyahia quickly understood, that no decision by the Supreme Court of the United States could be expected in less than six months.

hostages within a given period the funds would be returned to U.S. custody. It was also agreed that our hard-working intermediary, the government of Algeria, would determine when the hostages had actually left Iran, and an Algerian certification that the departure had taken place would trigger an instruction by the Algerian central bank to the escrow agent to release the escrowed funds to Iran.

Fortunately, despite some expectations to the contrary, the selection of the escrow agent never became a real problem. For a variety of legal and financial reasons the United States proposed the Bank of England or the Bundesbank, and after some delay Iran agreed on the Bank of England. This meant, however, that executives and attorneys representing the Bank of England had to be intimately involved in formulating the escrow arrangements, and in early January Robert Mundheim, former General Counsel of the Treasury, went to London to start working out such arrangements with the Bank.

One result was a logistical problem that arose shortly after our arrival in Algiers. The Algerian central bank, which was to be giving instructions to the escrow agent, needed to have a voice in formulating the escrow arrangements, but the operative meetings were going forward in London. When Christopher offered to fly appropriate officials of the Algerian central bank to London to expedite the process, they responded with a preference that the London participants come to Algiers. Fortunately, the Bank of England took the suggestion in good grace, and within a matter of hours Christopher had his Air Force plane make a roundtrip to London, returning with Christopher McMahon (Deputy Governor of the Bank of England), David Somerset (Chief Cashier), Peter Peddie, a British solicitor, Robert Mundheim, William Lake (Deputy Legal Adviser of the U.S. Department of State), Ernest Patrikis (Deputy General Counsel of the Federal Reserve Bank of New York), and two attorneys representing U.S. banks (Frank Logan representing Chase Manhattan Bank and Thorne Corse representing the Bank of America). For the next several days the ground floor offices of the U.S. Embassy in Algiers were the scene of a flurry of paperwork and urgent telephone calls as the escrow arrangements were completed.

3. The group on the ground floor was instrumental in keeping the Christopher team upstairs informed about the crucial banking negotiations going on simultaneously in New York. As previously noted, we had repeatedly emphasized to Iran that, if it wanted to achieve the immediate release of some $5.6 billion of Iranian funds in the European branches of U.S. banks, to which Iran was heavily indebted and in arrears on its debt-servicing, Iran was going to have to get current on its debts (that is, come forward with overdue payments of principle and interest), a step that could be accomplished only through direct negotiations between the appropriate U.S. and

Iranian banking officials. Under pressure Iran had indeed entered into such negotiations in New York, but in mid-January, with time running out, Christopher was informed that the Iranian representatives had cut off the negotiations and demanded that the banks produce a better offer, which did not seem likely. As of January 14 it looked very much as though it would be impossible to achieve the release of the $5.6 billion in Iranian funds in Europe and that the entire settlement project was about to founder on that rock.

Reflecting the roller-coaster course of the negotiations, the situation was completely reversed the next day. An Iranian memorandum of January 15 suddenly declared, to our enormous relief, that Iran was prepared to pay off $3.4 billion of its bank loans immediately and guarantee payment of the rest, thus eliminating from the New York negotiations many of the most divisive issues. Although this change was going to require a nightmarish amount of revision and reformulation, there was elation in our ranks because of what it told us about Iran's desire to achieve a settlement before time ran out. Indeed, Iran went so far as to agree that of the $8.1 billion it was to receive upon the hostages' release, approximately $4.8 billion would be used, insofar as necessary, to pay off all of Iran's obligations to U.S. banks and their syndicate partners.

4. At one point, just when we thought we were about to nail down the essential terms of the basic declaration, the Iranians suddenly appeared to focus, perhaps for the first time, on the fact that the agreed terms were giving them considerably less (to put it mildly) than they had originally demanded. To our dismay, they suddenly demanded that the basic declaration be amended to include a statement of certain "general principles" which, if broadly interpreted and given effect, would have radically changed the entire transaction. For example, Iran demanded that the United States agree generally to "restore the financial position of Iran, insofar as possible, to that which existed prior to November 14, 1979," the latter being the date of the assets freeze order. Obviously, that proposition, if given the maximum effect, would effectively have neutralized all of the concessions we had wrung from Iran in preceding weeks.

After giving the matter some thought, however, the assessment of the group in Algiers was that the demand for a set of "general principles" was not really intended to revoke the earlier concessions. Our strong impression was that the Iranian negotiating team was feeling a last-minute need for the insertion of some political rhetoric to create the public impression in Iran that Iran was going to achieve its originally stated goals, despite the fact that it would be achieving far less under the specific provisions of the agreement. In an effort to accommodate that need, we quickly drafted the "General Principles" section that appears on the first page of the basic declaration, but we stated the principles in such a way as to make clear that they were to be applied only "within the framework and pursuant to the provisions of the two" declarations. We thus provided the Iranians with some of the rhetoric they apparently thought they needed while at the same time making clear that no substantive change in the contemplated transaction was intended.

5. Interspersed among these relatively dramatic developments were a host of less important but still serious difficulties that had to be resolved quickly. Just as one example, the Nabavi Committee in Tehran suddenly decided that it could not proceed with the proposed arbitration program without authorization from the Majlis, which promptly came forward with a resolution approving the claims settlement approach generally but then stating, to our dismay, that the proposed arbitral tribunal should not be permitted to hear any dispute arising under a contract containing an Iranian-courts clause. The Nabavi Committee then drafted language designed to implement the Majlis' position and forwarded it to Algiers with a demand that it be included in the claims settlement declaration.

This led to a series of intense telephone conversations among the U.S. government lawyers in Washington and Algiers. As previously noted, we were determined that in any case involving an Iranian-courts clause the arbitral tribunal, instead of giving automatic effect to the clause, should decide whether it should be treated as binding in light of the changes Iran had made in its judicial system. After much discussion Christopher advised Benyahia that the issue could be resolved only by including in Iran's proposed language some modifying words designed to preserve the tribunal's authority to decide whether specific Iranian-courts clauses should be considered binding or not. Benyahia asked Christopher directly whether he would "insist" on the inclusion of the word "binding"—he anticipated an Iranian objection—and Christopher said flatly that he would. Fortunately, the Iranians accepted the revisions proposed by the United States, and this potentially destructive issue was laid to rest. By January 15 we seemed to have resolved most such technical problems.

6. At this point, however, we were running right down to the wire. President Carter's self-imposed negotiating deadline of January 16 was only hours away, and our authority to act for the United States would come to an end ninety-six hours after that. And yet at this critical juncture Iran came up with still a new obstacle.

Thus far in the negotiations, we had carefully referred to the frozen Iranian assets by categories (the Federal Reserve funds, the offshore assets, and so forth) and as much as possible had referred only to general dollar amounts. At the last moment, however, Iran suddenly came up with a demand for a new and separate document—a side agreement that was not to be made public but that would set forth the exact dollar amounts to be placed in escrow as a precondition to the release of the hostages. We responded by inventing and drafting a new instrument, which became known as the "Undertakings"—a process that caused us to focus with great precision on the exact amounts of the funds to be transferred.

The target, as previously noted, was to transfer $8.1 billion, but because most of the Iranian funds held by the Federal Reserve Bank were in the form of gold bullion we had become increasingly concerned that over time the price of gold had declined by some $150 million below the October 1980 value that both sides had been using in their discussions. Other troublesome variables also affected the figures (for example, fluctuations in the value of the securities held by the Federal Reserve), and by January 17 it had become quite doubtful whether, if we were to be held to the precise figure of $8.1 billion, we would really be able to meet it in the time remaining. A series of worried telephone conversations on this subject took place through the night of January 17 between President Carter and his advisers in Washington, New York, and Algiers.

Once again Foreign Minister Benyahia was able to help. On the morning of January 18 Christopher and Mundheim explained the value fluctuations problem, went through a long set of computations on the final number that could really be achieved within the time frame, and emerged with the ultimate target of $7.955 billion. Within a matter of hours Benyahia and his colleagues in Tehran persuaded the Nabavi Committee to accept that figure. On January 18 it was written into the Undertakings and became the trigger for the hostages' release, the understanding being that, as soon as the Bank of England had certified to the Algerian central bank that it had in hand cash, gold, and securities in the aggregate amount of $7.955 billion, "Iran shall immediately bring about the safe departure of the 52 U.S. nationals detained in Iran."[10]

7. In the final hours, with the chances of success increasing, Benyahia raised with Christopher the subject of "transportation"—the mechanics of physically moving the fifty-two hostages out of Iran. Implicitly assuming that Algeria would supply the necessary planes, Benyahia proposed to send two Air Algérie 727s that together would have enough capacity to carry not only the fifty-two hostages but also a substantial number of Algerian security personnel who might be needed to provide assistance and protection at the Tehran Airport. When Benyahia pointed out that the 727s did not have "long enough legs" to make the return trip without refueling and asked for Christopher's assistance in arranging for an intermediate stop on the return trip from Iran (an Air Algérie 747 with longer legs had been ruled

10. See Documentary Appendix D.

out because it was a chartered plane with an American crew), consultations with the Pentagon led to the conclusion that Athens would be the logical refueling point.

Benyahia also privately informed Christopher of the elaborate security precautions being taken by the Algerian government. It proposed, for example, that the 727s not take on fuel in Tehran because of a fear that the fuel might be contaminated. It also proposed that during their stay in Tehran the two crews file flight plans indicating proposed stops on the return trip in Damascus and Ankara respectively—and that when the planes had left Iranian air space the flight plans of both planes be changed to take them into Athens. The existence of these plans reemphasized to the U.S. team how close we were to success, and our hopes soared.

8. The night of January 18 was the longest of my life. By that time, so far as we could tell, we had worked our way through to a solution to all of Iran's problems and had reached agreement in substance, but Benyahia, while agreeing that we seemed to be at the brink of success, cautioned us against taking further steps until we had received some confirmation from Iran that there was a complete agreement. We were told that the Nabavi group was going to be meeting during the night (it would be early morning in Tehran), and in such circumstances sleep was impossible. Moreover, there was still work to be done at the Foreign Ministry. Christopher and Saunders remained in conference with Benyahia, and Alec Toumayan and I spent most of the night working with one of Benyahia's colleagues on a painstaking (and painful) line-by-line review of the Algerians' French version of the operative documents to be sure that it corresponded precisely with our English version. It was not until almost 7:00 A.M. on January 19 that we were all back at the embassy.

Within a matter of minutes—at 7:05 A.M.—Benyahia summoned Christopher back to the Foreign Ministry and then told him that Iran had agreed. After months of work, we finally had a deal. I doubt that any of us has ever felt such relief and exhilaration as when we heard that news. Foreign Minister Benyahia promptly organized a brief public ceremony at which Christopher initialed the two Declarations and the Undertakings on behalf of the United States, and at that point the banking wheels began to turn, moving frozen Iranian funds into the escrow account in the Bank of England.

9. A few hours later, as we waited for the escrow account to grow to the "trigger" point, we received unbelievable news: Benyahia sent word that a technical supplement to the basic escrow documents, which had been delayed in transmission to Tehran, had just been read and *rejected* by the Iranians. Within a matter of hours, moreover, another "glitch" occurred when an interbank telex message from Tehran to London came through in

garbled fashion and created a doubt as to whether the private arrangements for the transfer of the offshore deposits into escrow were going to go forward (see p. 276). The result was a flurry of agonized telephone conversations among all concerned, with President Carter using the full weight of his office to straighten out the misunderstandings, and by mid-morning (Algiers time) on January 20 it became apparent that these last technical obstacles had been cleared away. The amounts in the escrow account were growing; President Carter's term of office would expire at five o'clock that afternoon, Algiers time; and at that point there was nothing further for the U.S. negotiators to do except wait and see whether the escrow account would hit the top—$7.955 billion—in time.

January 20, 1981

There are two scenes that will always bring back, for me, the drama of the final hours of the crisis.

At 11:00 A.M. on January 20, 1981, Algiers time (the sun was just coming up in Washington), Christopher, Toumayan, and I were seated in a small room on the top floor of the Algerian Foreign Ministry with the two senior officials of the Bank of England, McMahon and Somerset. It was their responsibility to notify the Algerian central bank when the escrow account in London had grown to exceed the trigger amount, and Somerset was seated at a small desk with a telephone in one hand, connected to London, and a pencil in the other. A colleague in London was listing to Somerset certain categories of funds in hand, together with their dollar amounts, and Somerset was reading the entries aloud and manually adding them up. Starting from zero and trying to reach $7.955 billion, the process seemed absolutely glacial.

For those of us listening to the Algiers end of the conversation, it was excruciating. "That brings us up to $6.956, is that right? . . . Yes, but that group of securities is only worth $51 million, so that brings us down again. . . . Ah, now, we're getting there: $7.232—but we still have a way to go."[11] And so on. I do not believe that I have ever perceived time moving so slowly.

And yet the moment eventually came. Somerset looked up at us, smiled gently, and quietly announced that the Bank of England was now in possession of $7.956 billion, just enough to trigger the Iranian obligation to place our fifty-two citizens on the Algerian airplanes in Tehran. I looked out over the crowded white rooftops of Algiers and wondered if the moment was real.

I did not become sure of the answer until some hours laters, when I

11. Although the figures actually spoken were probably somewhat different, the indicated range and mood are accurate.

found myself standing at the Algiers Airport in the rain, in the dark, watching the lights of two 727s circle for a landing. Irrationally there was still a question in my mind as to whether those planes really carried the hostages or whether they might land and disgorge nothing but Algerian security police. And then it happened. The planes landed, together with a smaller plane carrying the tired but jubilant Algerian delegation—Malek, Gheraieb, and Mostafai. The door of the lead 727 opened under the glare of the lights; there was a painfully long delay as we waited for some American, any American, to emerge; and then at long last, at the top of the ramp, we could plainly see the two women, Ann Swift and Katherine Koob, walking out of the plane door with bouquets and yellow ribbons in hand, arm-in-arm with Bruce Laingen between them. Millions of Americans watched that scene on television with enormous relief, and I can only hope that they fully appreciated that it would never have occurred if foreign governments had not rendered extraordinary service throughout the crisis—service to the hostages, to the U.S. Foreign Service, to the nation itself, and to the international community at large.

Recap

Now that it is all over, we should be able to make at least some tentative judgments on these basic issues: Did we advance or injure the interests of the United States by engaging in negotiation, and how well did we do in the process itself?

To my mind, these questions are quite separate and distinct from the much broader and more popular issue—whether the Carter Administration did a good job in handling the crisis as a whole. It has been argued by some, of course, that stronger U.S. actions at the outset, immediately after the embassy seizure, would or might have brought a much more rapid ending to the crisis. Conversely, a different school of thought holds that after the early stages the United States should have virtually ignored Iran's conduct, putting the entire hostage problem on a far back burner and simply waiting until Iran released our people. These are much harder questions, in my view, than the separate issue whether, given the situation we faced in September 1980, we were right in embarking upon the negotiating process. As indicated at the beginning of this chapter, it is apparently former Secretary Haig's judgment that the United States should simply have stonewalled the situation until Iran finally abandoned its four demands of September 12, 1980, and released the hostages, whereas I personally adhere to the judgment of the Carter Administration that that would have led to an indefinite stalemate and would not have been in our interests. No one will ever know which view is right.

At any rate, given our decision to negotiate, how well did we do? I am hardly impartial about the matter, but I think that we substantially achieved all of our negotiating objectives, over and above the basic threshold of achieving the hostages' release. In response to the four Iranian demands, we gave away nothing of value that was ours; we simply returned a relatively small part of what was theirs and had the balance held back to pay off much of what Iran owed to our claimants. Moreover, before the negotiations began, our commercial claimants were in serious trouble in terms of the collectibility of their claims, and the negotiations created for them a remedial mechanism which, although it may never produce perfect results, is widely considered now to have placed our claimants in a substantially better position than they were in before the hostage crisis arose. Arguably, therefore, if substantial concessions were made by anyone during the negotiating process, virtually all were made by Iran.

Finally, through our negotiating conduct did we convey the message to the world that international terrorism pays, thus creating an incentive for future acts of terrorism? My own answer is that, although some may perceive a pay-off to Iran as a result of its hostage taking, that pay-off did not result from the negotiating process. Undoubtedly there were Iranian politicians, and indeed many members of the Iranian general public, who derived significant domestic political gains and great satisfaction from the prolonged captivity of the hostages and the resulting humiliation of "the Great Satan," and in that sense the pay-off was real. It seems relatively clear to me, however, that we could have avoided or eliminated that "humiliation" only by waging war or its equivalent, and there would seem to be very few Americans who were or are prepared to go that far in such circumstances. That being so, I assume that we will continue to face the risk of similar "humiliations" in the future, but I am inclined to doubt that the negotiations conducted in the fall of 1980 did anything to increase that risk. It is simply inherent in our position in the world as it exists today.

9 INTERNATIONAL LAW IN THE HOSTAGE CRISIS: IMPLICATIONS FOR FUTURE CASES

OSCAR SCHACHTER

In a sense, international law was at the very heart of the crisis. The seizure of the embassy and detention of the hostages were clearly flagrant violations of accepted rules of international law and treaties. The unanimous decision of the Security Council and the International Court of Justice left no room for doubt. Ironically, on the Iranian side international law was also perceived as relevant though in a different light. Iranian leaders charged the United States with violations of principles laid down in the U.N. Charter and general international law. In their bill of particulars, the role of the United States in the 1953 overthrow of the Mossadegh regime was a salient feature. Added to that were allegations of espionage and intervention by diplomats in abuse of their status. They also asserted that U.S. protection for the Shah from Iranian justice and the denial of access to the Iranian assets illegally taken by the Shah and his family violated international law principles. Underlying the legal contentions in these charges was a broader indictment of the existing system of international law as a legal system that favored the powerful against the weak.

While both sides cited violations of international law by the other as the cause of the crisis, they shared a skepticism about the ability of the international legal system to redress the wrongs suffered. The Iranians expected no help from a system they considered subservient to the powerful states and to "the Great Satan." In the United States recourse to the United Nations and the International Court were regarded as useful steps in a political process, but they were not seen as likely to bring about Iranian compliance. The other U.S. countermeasures were in the nature of self-help and were not viewed as remedies of law. One might conclude from this that law had only a marginal role in the resolution of the crisis.

Yet it would be shortsighted to assume that this is all we can learn from the hostage crisis about the role of international law. A deeper look at the issues and the action taken may reveal a more complex picture. For one thing, the attitudes and conduct of the U.S. government (and indeed most governments) reflect in some measure their conceptions of legitimacy and propriety. How far these conceptions conform to and are shaped by legal norms is a matter for inquiry. Ideas of what is permissible and impermissible may be inferred from state conduct and are often made explicit in the justifications advanced for such conduct. States may and do act on the basis of power and interest, but generally they require a basis of legitimacy to justify their action to their own citizens and, even more, to other states whose cooperation or acquiescence will be needed. While claims of legitimacy will sometimes be dismissed as self-serving, the significant question is whether they influence conduct by the actors, both by those to whom the justifications are addressed and those who put them forward. If we bear this in mind, the Iranian hostage crisis furnishes an unusual opportunity to examine contemporary perceptions of international legality. It may be likened to a flash of lightning that reveals the familiar features of the landscape in a new guise. It gives us an opportunity to take fresh bearings as to where we are in the endeavor to build a stable and just international order.

From that perspective it is not enough to ascertain what legal rules were regarded as in force and whether they were correctly applied. Of greater interest is what may realistically be proposed in the way of rules and procedures to meet future situations that are analogous to the hostage crisis. That crisis is not likely to be replayed in the future, but cases with cognate elements will almost surely arise. Beyond that, it should be enlightening to consider other, perhaps more profound, issues of international order that have been suggested by the crisis. The issues presented by the actual and proposed use of military force are obvious candidates for examination as are the inadequacies of the collective machinery of the United Nations. It may be possible to reach out from the hostage crisis, not only to a list of what-to-dos, but to a searching consideration of the role of law and of the risks and costs of the effort to achieve international order.

These ambitious goals will not be achieved in this essay, but it is hoped that the observations that follow will stimulate further thought in that direction. They will be presented under three broad headings, each treating several issues:

1. The right to use armed force in response to the seizure
2. The protection of diplomats and other nationals
3. The use of economic and other nonmilitary measures

A final comment addresses the issue of the validity under international law of the settlement agreements between the United States and Iran.

THE RIGHT TO USE ARMED FORCE IN RESPONSE TO THE SEIZURE

I begin with this issue, not only because the use of force was the most controversial question faced in the United States, but also because it leads us most deeply into the complexity of establishing a rule of law in present international society. Whether the United States should use military means in response to the seizure was sharply debated both in official circles and in the press. However, it cannot be said that the question of legality was in the forefront of that debate. The prevailing assumption, it is fair to say, was that force could be used legally if it became necessary and was likely to be effective. Whether this assumption was well-founded should be our first question. Our starting point must be the relevant provisions of the U.N. Charter, namely, articles 2(3), 2(4) and 51.[1]

Article 2(4), the basic rule against the threat or use of force reads as follows:

> All Members shall refrain in their international relations from the threat or use of force against the territorial integrity or political independence of any State, or in any other manner inconsistent with the Purposes of the United Nations.

Article 2(3) requires recourse to pacific settlement of disputes. It reads:

> All Members shall settle their international disputes by peaceful means in such a manner that international peace and security, and justice, are not endangered.

Article 51 authorizes self-defense in the following terms:

> Nothing in the present Charter shall impair the inherent right of individual or collective self-defense if an armed attack occurs against a member of the United Nations, until the Security Council has taken the measures necessary to maintain international peace and security. Measures taken by Members in the exercise of this right of self-defence shall be immediately reported to the Security Council and shall not in any way affect the authority and responsibility of the Security Council under the present Charter to take at any time such action as it deems necessary in order to maintain or restore international peace and security.

---

1. For a general analysis of these provisions of the U.N. Charter and their application in particular cases, see Oscar Schachter, "The Right of States to Use Armed Force," *Michigan Law Review*, May/June 1984.

Since self-defense is clearly authorized in response to an "armed attack," article 51 seems on first blush to provide an adequate legal basis for the employment of military force after the seizure. Several questions need to be considered in determining the application of this provision to the facts of the case.

The Requirement of an "Armed Attack"

First, there is the question of whether the seizure should be regarded as an armed attack on the United States. An affirmative answer has been suggested on the ground that an embassy and its premises constitute, in legal effect, territory of the United States. However, that view would be inconsistent with the legal position long maintained by the United States and others that an embassy does not become the territory of the sending state, although it is entitled to inviolability and protection under general international law and the Convention on Diplomatic Privileges and Immunities, to which the great majority of states (including Iran) adhere.

But even if an embassy is not legally U.S. territory, an attack on it could reasonably be considered an attack against the United States, particularly in the circumstances of a political action such as that in Tehran. It would not be unlike an attack on a naval vessel or military base abroad. Clearly, the United States could use force to repel the attack. A more complicated question is whether and how much force could be used after the armed assailants had taken over the embassy. The complications arise because self-defense is conditioned on its "necessity"and "proportionality," and these standards give rise to various questions.

Before considering the application of these standards to the hostage situation it may be useful to examine the assumption that an armed attack is a condition of a self-defense response. Not that there was any doubt about the armed attack in Tehran. But there were prior threats, and we might ask whether self-defense warrants military action to meet threats of takeover. This hypothetical question may be realistic in future cases. It leads us to two other questions.

First, is there an "inherent right" of self-defense outside the terms of article 51; second, if so, what conditions are required to allow self-defense? On the first question, there has been a long-standing difference among legal scholars as to whether article 51 was intended or may be read to preclude self-defense in anticipation of attack (as a preemptive use of force). Governments by and large have held that article 51 allows self-defense only when an actual attack has occurred. (It may be recalled that in the 1962 Cuban missile crisis the United States deliberately refrained from relying on self-defense as the legal basis for its quarantine backed by force; instead, it relied on an Organization of American States "authorization.")

If one is prepared to accept the contrary view (namely, that an actual attack is not necessary), then the second question is relevant: when is self-defense justified in anticipation of attack? Customary law based on state practice is murky. The most quoted generalization on anticipatory defense (often cited as customary law) is taken from a diplomatic note by Daniel Webster in 1842 when he was Secretary of State. The note responded to a British claim of a legal right (in 1837) to attack a vessel (the *Caroline*) on the American side of the Niagara River, because the vessel contained insurgents intending to assist an insurrection in Canada. Secretary Webster denied the "necessity" for self-defense in this case, asserting in oratorical style that self-defense must be confined to cases in which "the necessity of that self-defense is instant, overwhelming, and leaving no choice of means and no moment for deliberation."[2] On this restrictive principle, anticipatory defense would be permissible only if an attack were imminent, "leaving no moment for deliberation."

The requirement of "necessity" for self-defense is not controversial as a general proposition. However, its application in concrete cases requires judgments on facts and intentions that often involve diverse perceptions. A case for self-defense is not persuasive either on the political or legal level unless a reasonable basis of necessity is perceived. Those to whom a justification is addressed (that is, other governments or the public) will consider whether it is well-founded; they will not regard the use of force as a purely discretionary act.

When Does the Use of Force Become "Necessary"?

When we apply the test of necessity to the hostage crisis, an important dimension is the temporal: at what time did use of force become necessary? Also pertinent is whether the force to be used is for rescue or reprisal.

Some in the United States maintained that the use of force was justified at the very outset of the hostage crisis as necessary either to obtain the release of the hostages or to serve other ends such as the prestige and security of the United States. Insofar as the government considered the matter in legal terms (as well as on a political level), it presumably took the position that force was not needed as long as there appeared to be a reasonable chance to obtain the release of the hostages by negotiation or third-party efforts. That these means proved to be futile during the first year, though successful in the second, underlines the element of conjecture. It is arguable (indeed, it has been argued) that the failure of pacific means was evidence of the need to have used force in the early stages. Had the harbors

2. *The Caroline Case,* J. B. Moore, *A Digest of International Law,* vol. 2 (Washington: GPO, 1906), p. 412.

been mined or an oil installation bombed (so the argument runs), the Iranian government would have been induced to negotiate the release. This conjectural line of reasoning—whatever its persuasiveness—sharpens the legal issue. It poses the question whether nonforceful means of redress must always be sought before the use of force in self-defense can be regarded as necessary. A corollary question, phrased in lawyers' terminology, is whether pacific means of settlement must be "exhausted" before force may be legitimately employed.

The issue turns on the meaning to be given to the prohibition of force in article 2(4). That provision, it will be recalled, does not say that *any* use of force is forbidden; it qualifies the prohibition by referring to the threat or use of force "against the territorial integrity or political independence" of the target state or "in any manner inconsistent with the purposes of the United Nations." The vague language may seem to allow for an argument that a state may use force for a "good" cause, provided such force is not against a state's "territorial integrity or political independence." But can one plausibly maintain that a rescue action in the circumstances would not contravene the territorial integrity or political independence of the detaining state? Does the fact that that state is clearly violating international law affect the answer? If these questions are answered in the affirmative, the prohibition against force in article 2(4) would be significantly narrowed. It would then permit forcible self-help measures in numerous cases where a stronger state considered a weaker state to be violating international law and where the military action sought satisfaction of the legal claim. However this construction of article 2(4) is difficult to sustain in the light of the interpretation given to the article by its drafters and subsequently by the member states of the United Nations. The provision was viewed from the very outset as a general bar to the unilateral use of force (except for self-defense) even if the aim of such force was to redress a legal wrong. The entry of armed forces into the territory of a state without its permission for the purpose of frustrating that state's legal processes would generally be considered as a violation of that state's authority over its territory and its right to decide its own affairs. To argue that "territorial integrity" and "political independence" are not impaired, because the aim of the action is limited and its duration short, is not likely to convince most governments. It would open up vulnerable states to invasions to free prisoners considered by other states to be held in contravention of international rules. In my judgment this would not be an acceptable interpretation of the Charter article.

Endangerment to Life

But let us consider the case where lives of foreign diplomats and other foreign nationals are endangered. They may be threatened by mob violence or by official action that is clearly in violation of the host state's obligations under international law. Does an imminent threat in these circumstances open up an exception to the prohibition of article 2(4)? Respected authorities on international law have maintained that it should. For example, as far back as 1952, Sir Humphrey Waldock (who later served as a judge and President of the International Court of Justice) wrote that force may be used to intervene in another state to protect its nationals from injury if there is (1) an imminent threat of such injury, (2) a failure or inability on the part of the territorial sovereign to protect them, and (3) measures of protection are strictly confined to the object of protecting them from injury.[3] Waldock later observed that:

> cases of this form of armed intervention have not been infrequent in the past and, where not attended by suspicion of being a pretext for political pressure, have generally been regarded as justified by the sheer necessity of instant action to save the lives of innocent nationals, whom the local government is unable or unwilling to protect.[4]

Examples of such cases of armed action to protect nationals in peril include the U.S. action in the Dominican Republic in 1965, the Belgian action in the Congo (Stanleyville) in 1961, and the Israeli rescue action in Entebbe, Uganda, in 1976. The last example is perhaps the clearest precedent, since there was no suggestion that Israel took the action as a pretext or intended to remain in the country (both the U.S. and Belgian cases raised such questions). When the Security Council considered the Entebbe case, Ambassador William Scranton, speaking for the United States, declared:

> Israel's action in rescuing the hostages necessarily involved a temporary breach of the territorial integrity of Uganda. Normally such a breach would be impermissible under the Charter of the United Nations. However, there is a well-established right to use limited force for the protection of one's own nationals from an imminent threat of injury or death in a situation where the state in whose territory they are located either is unwilling or unable to protect them. The right, flowing from the right of self-defense, is limited to such use of force as is necessary and appropriate to protect threatened nationals from injury. . . .
>   The requirements of this right to protect nationals were clearly met in the Entebbe case. Israel had good reason to believe that at the

3. H. Waldock, 81 *Hague Academy Recueil des Cours* (Leyden: Sijthoff) 467 (1952).
4. H. Waldock, 106 *Hague Academy Recueil des Cours* (Leyden: Sijthoff) 240 (1962).

time it acted Israeli nationals were in imminent danger of execution
by the hijackers. Moreover, the actions necessary to release the
Israeli nationals or to prevent substantial loss of Israeli lives had not
been taken by the Government of Uganda, nor was there a
reasonable expectation such actions would be taken. In fact, there is
substantial evidence that the Government of Uganda cooperated
with and aided the hijackers.

. . . The Israeli military action was limited to the sole objective
of extricating the passengers and crew and terminated when that
objective was accomplished. The force employed was limited to what
was necessary for that rescue of the passengers and crew.[5]

We may reasonably conclude that, as a matter of law, an armed rescue
action to save lives of nationals (whether or not diplomats) is not prohibited
by article 2(4) when the territorial government is unable or unwilling to
protect them and the need for instant action is manifest.

Let us put forth a hypothetical case in which hostages are taken and a
demand is made for concessions by the state of which they are nationals
(whether or not diplomats). Let us assume the hostages are not subjected to
threats and they are not ill-treated. There is no indication that their lives
are in danger. Should force be allowed on the ground that hostage taking is
in itself an "act which endangers innocent human lives," as stated in the
preamble of the 1979 Convention on the Taking of Hostages? The answer to
this, I would suggest, must depend on whether the hostages are in fact in
imminent danger. The illegality of their detention and the failure of international organs to obtain their release should not be enough to legitimize
the use of force to effect their release. To allow the use of force in the absence
of imminent peril would imply a "necessity" to use force to redress a legal
wrong. It would be significantly different from the necessity of self-defense
to repel an attack or to save lives.

May one take a different position and hold that any taking of hostages is
so grave a criminal act that a rescue action is instantly justified in law? On
that view, the question of whether a rescue should be attempted would be
solely a matter for prudential and political consideration. One can readily
see why that position would have appeal. It appears realistic and practical.
By removing legal restraint it allows the question of rescue to be considered
on its merits. The aggrieved state remains free to negotiate or not, as it
chooses. Whether or not it uses force is in its own discretion.

It is not entirely clear from the record of the hostage crisis whether the
U.S. government tended toward this position or whether it considered that

5. *Digest of U.S. Practice in International Law,* at 150–51 (1976), McDowell, ed. (Dept. of
State Publication 8908, September 1977).

it was legally required to seek a solution through pacific means. Probably both views were represented in the higher echelons, and in the circumstances no choice was required until the later period when the military rescue was agreed upon. However, the legal issue may be significant in future situations and for other countries.

With that in mind, it is pertinent to affirm that the use of force in a rescue attempt, like any self-defense action, must meet the test of necessity and that such necessity cannot be assumed as long as negotiations or third-party proceedings offers credible hope of solution and there is no manifest need for instant rescue action. The basic reason for this position lies in the importance to international order of prohibiting unilateral recourse to force when peaceful means are available and there is no compelling emergency need to act to save lives. The alternative view, that any hostage taking in violation of international law gives the victim state (that is, the state of nationality) the immediate right to use force, would further weaken the already attenuated restraints of articles 2(3) and 2(4) of the Charter.

Was the Rescue Mission Legal?

This brings us to the specific question whether the April rescue effort was legal under the conditions stated. Clearly, the circumstances in April were materially different from those in November and December. The protracted efforts of intermediaries and of the United Nations had produced no significant change in the Iranian position. Iran ignored the Security Council resolution; it failed to cooperate with the U.N. fact-finding commission; and it refused to comply with the order of the International Court of December 15 calling for the release of the hostages.[6] There was no doubt about the frustrations felt in the United States over the lack of any opening toward release of the hostages. Was it not reasonable to conclude at that time that all peaceful avenues had been exhausted? Some doubt on this point may arise from the fact that the case brought by the United States was before the International Court on the merits and that in March the United States had asked the Court for an early judgment. The hearings in the Court were held

---

6. The U.S. Action against Iran in the International Court of Justice had two stages. In the first stage, the Court, acting on application of the United States, indicated "provisional measures" to preserve the rights of the parties, pending final judgment. These provisional measures (sometimes referred to as interim measures) directed Iran to release all the hostages, to extend protection, privileges, and immunities to all the diplomatic and consular personnel, and to restore the embassy to U.S. possession and exclusive control. The United States and Iran were both ordered not to take any action that might aggravate the tension between the two states (Order of 15 December 1979, International Court of Justice). In the second stage the Court considered the U.S. claims on the merits. In its final judgment made on May 24, 1980, the Court ordered Iran to release the hostages, return the embassy and consulate to the control of the United States, and also to pay reparations. (Case citation in note 9.)

on March 18, 19 and 20. The Court was in the course of preparing its judgment in the case when the rescue mission took place on April 24. It might have been reasonable to conclude, in view of the judicial proceedings, that the United States had not exhausted its peaceful means. Moreover, as later events showed, bilateral negotiations (with the aid of the Algerians) proved possible and in the end successful.

However, the question also depends on the danger to the hostages. If they were in imminent danger of serious injury, and the United States had good reason to believe that this was the case, the pursuit of remedies through the court or through negotiations would not avert that danger. A rescue mission employing the necessary degree of force and confined to the rescue would then be legally justified. "Exhaustion of remedies" is not required when almost certain to be futile.

Can we say that the hostages were actually in imminent peril in April 1980? That question is probably not answerable even today. The pertinent point is whether, at the time, the U.S. government had reason to fear that in the emotional atmosphere of Iranian revolutionary ferment the hostages would be executed, with or without a trial. As a general rule, it seems reasonable to recognize that the state whose nationals are imprisoned as hostages should have wide latitude to make the decision whether they are in extreme danger. In effect, this would place the burden on the state responsible for the illegal act of hostage taking to demonstrate that the hostages are not in grave danger. It might do this by assurances made publicly and to international organs and by placing the hostages under the authority and control of disciplined military or police units. This was not the case in Iran. Verbal attacks and threats against the hostages were made by prominent figures, and custody was exercised by emotional "militants." Fears as to the safety of the hostages were an inevitable reaction. The fact that negotiations later proved successful does not show that these fears lacked plausibility.

My conclusion therefore is that, whether or not the hostages were actually in extreme danger, the conditions were such as to lead the U.S. government to believe they were. Faced with this fact and the not unrealistic conclusion at the time that peaceful means offered no promise of release, the United States had reasonable grounds to consider military action necessary to effect a rescue. On these premises, the action taken did not violate the Charter or international law. Whether or not the rescue action was wise in a political and military sense is, of course, a different matter.

The Use of Force as a Reprisal

Up to now, I have been concerned with the permissibility of force to effect a rescue. However, questions have been raised going beyond that issue into the hypothetical but not unrealistic question of the use of force as a reprisal. One grim scenario envisaged the execution of some or all of the hostages. Would the United States then have been entitled to have had recourse to force? Would such executions be a legal *casus belli*? One can assume that there would be strong public sentiment in the United States for punitive military action.

It seems clear that present-day international law and, in particular, the U.N. Charter do not permit the use of force as a measure of reprisal by an injured state against a state that has violated a basic legal obligation. The Declaration of Principles of International Law adopted unanimously by the U.N. General Assembly in 1970 declares categorically: "States have a duty to refrain from acts of reprisal involving the use of force."[7] That principle was regarded by the member states, including the United States, to reflect established practice as evidenced by Security Council resolutions adopted in earlier cases. The U.S. government supported the principle, and like others it has considered reprisals as unlawful, in contrast to acts of lawful self-defense.[8]

The difference between self-defense and reprisals lies essentially in the aim of the action. Self-defense is protective; its purpose is to protect the security of the state and its essential rights of territorial integrity and political independence. Reprisals are punitive; they seek to compel a delinquent state to pay reparations or make a settlement or obey the law in the future. However, the dividing line, while clear in principle, may become obscure as cases move from a particular incident to a series of acts of violence. In the latter situation, the response of the wronged state in taking military retaliatory measures is plausibly protective in that the measures seek to deter the law violator from future attacks. The most prominent cases of such overlap of defensive and retaliatory action are found in the Israeli-Arab hostilities. In the face of continuing attacks, the parties (Israel in particular) have retaliated with the express aim of punishing the adversaries or those lending support to them. Such retaliatory reprisals are justified as deterrent action intended to prevent further attacks and therefore as defensive.

Would this line of reasoning support a reprisal in the hypothetical case of executions of the hostages? It might be argued that a retaliatory action of a suitably punitive character would deter future hostage taking in Iran or elsewhere. An argument on similar lines was advanced in the Boxer Rebellion incidents prior to World War I. Probably many in the United States (and elsewhere) would consider a single act of retaliation (for example,

7. U.N. General Assembly Resolution 2625 (1970).
8. See, for example, the statement of the Secretary of State in 68 *American Journal of International Law* 736 (1974).

bombing oil installations or a military base) as a way of teaching a lesson to the wrongdoer, so that the illegal act would not be repeated. They would therefore perceive the retaliation as lawful self-defense. However, if the defensive character of the retaliatory act is to be justified as a deterrent (rather than for rescue), there should be reason to believe that future seizures or attacks by the delinquent state have some degree of probability. A purely punitive reprisal could not be justified as legitimate defense, nor would there be any other legal ground for use of force. The face that redress (for example, reparations) is not available through peaceful means would not constitute a sufficient basis for armed action.

Although this conclusion will seem unsatisfactory to some, it is relevant that in the several situations in recent years of unlawful seizures and attacks, none of the aggrieved governments actually sought to use force for punitive purposes. Rescue efforts were made but, whether successful or not, they were not followed by punitive action. Gunboat diplomacy in that respect has not been revived. It therefore does not seem excessively unrealistic to affirm that states are limited to defensive action and that punitive reprisals are prohibited.

How Much Force May Be Used?

There remains the question of the extent and nature of military means that may be used to effect a release of the prisoners. Would aerial bombing or military occupation be justified in order to force release of hostages?

The legal criterion most pertinent is proportionality, a standard that may be defined generally as requiring that the acts done in self-defense must not exceed in manner or objective the necessity provoking them. Obviously, this abstract formulation may leave a wide area of differences with respect to particular cases. Yet the uncertainty of application in particular situations does not impair the essential validity of the standard of proportionality as a general rule of restraint. Uncertain as it may seem, it is a standard of conduct that is widely respected. This may be seen in the many cases in which attacks have been repulsed (as in frontier incidents or in naval and aircraft clashes) and the "defending" state has refrained from large-scale hostilities. In such cases, it seems safe to say, defensive action has been more or less proportional to the necessity provoking it. Admittedly, political or military factors (rather than legal) are usually seen as the main reason for such restraint. However, the existence of those reasons does not negate the fact that defensive action has met the test of proportionality. The linkage of practical reasons with an international law norm cannot be said to weaken the norm.

Moreover, there is ample evidence that international opinion is sensitive to disproportionate use of force in self-defense. Retaliatory force tends to be condemned when the damage inflicted by it is grossly excessive in comparison to the damage of the provocation. Many of the U.N. Security Council decisions condemning retaliation as reprisals rather than as legitimate defense have stressed the considerable casualties caused by the retaliation compared to those caused by the attack provoking it. Another factor in judging proportionality has been the geographic element. In general, a defensive action physically distant from the original attack is suspect. Thus a frontier attack would not justify an aerial bombing of the capital city. The question may be more debatable when the force responding to an attack has as its objective the removal of the source of that attack. A notable example occurred in 1964, when the Vietnam attacks on U.S. naval vessels in the Gulf of Tonkin were answered by U.S. air strikes against bases and installations deep in North Vietnam.

These general observations suggest that military measures taken to free hostages would have to avoid action that would be considered excessive in manner or purpose. There would probably be broad agreement that bombing of population centers would be a disproportionate defensive action to a seizure of hostages. Nor could one justify as proportionate self-defense a military campaign to bring back a former friendly ruler. The fact that the new government was the "source" of the wrongful actions would not mean that its ouster was justified as the objective of self-defense action. No doubt there will be borderline cases that present problems. But it remains a salutary and not unrealistic rule to prohibit force in self-defense that is excessive in aim or means to what is necessary for protection.

Must Peaceful Remedies Be Exhausted Before the Use of Force?

We still need to address the larger question whether the legal restraints laid down by the U.N. Charter and contemporary international law should be observed by a wronged state when all other means of redress have failed. It has been argued by some jurists (and probably widely believed by the public) that, in the absence of effective collective machinery, a state that has been substantially wronged by a clear violation of international law should be free to use force if necessary to vindicate its legal right. It this is not permitted, it is said, a law-breaking state protected from sanctions, for political motives (in some cases by a veto exercised by one or two states), can commit grave wrongs with impunity. The rules against force in the Charter are premised on an effective system of collective security and eventual enforcement by international organs. The contention is that, where these conditions no longer hold, it is no longer appropriate to seek to maintain the rules against force if to do so would deprive the injured state of an effective remedy.

There is no doubt that this argument has a wide appeal both to the public at large and to government leaders. Support for it is strengthened when the collective organs, particularly the U.N. Security Council and General Assembly, fail to take action they are empowered to take for reasons that have nothing to do with the merits of the case. A widespread perception of political bias, double standards, and weakness of will as dominant motives in the U.N. organs has increased a tendency to consider self-help, including the use of force, as permissible when other means of redress are not available. The legal rules expressed in the Charter and in the customary law of self-defense are then considered as irrelevant or, more precisely, as conditional rules that are not operative when a state gravely wronged by an illegal act of another state has no effective remedy. Underlying and supporting this legal argument is the idea—widely held—that the vital interests of a state cannot be subordinated to a rule of international law in the present system.

These arguments have considerable cogency, and they cannot be easily dismissed by an appeal to the ideal of a rule of law in international society. They do require, however, an assessment in the light of the interests of the world community at large, and the United States in particular, in maintaining a minimal commitment to abstain from the use of force except in legitimate self-defense. The adherence of the United States to that Charter commitment has been considered a basic element of U.S. foreign policy since 1945. It has been supported in political terms as an expression of the long-term U.S. interest in a secure and peaceful world order. Virtually all states have proclaimed their adherence to the Charter rules and have declared them as peremptory norms (*jus cogens*) that must prevail over international agreements or other understandings. To accept the contention that these rules may be disregarded or superseded when a state finds it necessary to vindicate a legal right would result in so extensive an exception as to deprive the basic rules of any value. Any state seeking to recover "lost" territory could claim that right; any grave wrong resulting from an alleged violation of an international rule would provide a ground for unilateral force. Is it in the interest of the United States to adopt a position that would allow states to assert these rights to use force?

The analysis of the legal position in the hostage crisis does not show that the United States was legally impotent to use force when necessary to seek to save the hostages from imminent peril. An exception of this kind, based on an emergency situation and limited in its aim and execution, would not open a far-reaching breach in the rules on force. However, to broaden the exception, to include punitive reprisals or such disproportionate use of force as to constitute full-scale warfare, would go a long way toward eliminating the basic prohibition contained in article 2 of the Charter. A consideration of the hostage case and analogous cases does not provide any good reason to support such far-reaching exceptions. On the contrary, my reflections on the questions raised lead to an affirmation of the desirability of maintaining the restraints of article 2(4) and of self-defense in the common interest of all states.

The Use of Force Pendente Lite: *The International Court and the Rescue Attempt*

As mentioned earlier, the rescue attempt took place when the International Court was in the course of preparing its judgment in the case brought by the United States against Iran. The Court took note of this in its judgment of May 24, 1980, and declared:

> The Court therefore feels bound to observe that an operation undertaken in those circumstances, from whatever motive, is of a kind calculated to undermine respect for the judicial process in international relations; and to recall that in paragraph 47, 1B, of its Order of December 15, 1979 the Court had indicated that no action was to be taken by either party which might aggravate the tension between the two countries.[9]

It will be noted that this passage mentions two grounds of censure for the rescue mission. One was that the operation was "of a kind calculated to undermine respect for the judicial process." This was linked by the Court to the fact that in March the United States had asked the Court to expedite its decision after having earlier requested the Court to defer oral argument. The second objection of the Court implied that the attempt to rescue the hostages was incompatible with the injunction against "aggravating the tension" included in its order for interim measures of December 15, 1979.

The censure of the Court did not lead to any sanctions against the United States. The Court expressly noted it was not passing on the legality of the rescue attempt and that it did not consider that the rescue attempt affected the right of the United States to judicial relief (para. 94). Two dissenting judges (one from the U.S.S.R., the other from Syria) implied that the rescue operation was not justifiable as self-defense, because there was no evidence that an armed attack had occurred against the United States. The Syrian judge (Tarazi) concluded that Iran should not be held responsible unless the Court also found that the United States "by reason of its conduct both before and after the institution of proceedings has equally incurred responsibility."[10] The Soviet judge (Morozov) declared in his dis-

9. *Case Concerning United States Diplomatic and Consular Staff in Tehran,* Judgement of 24 May 1980, *I.C.J. Reports 1980* (The Hague: International Court of Justice), p. 43, para. 93.
10. Ibid., at 65.

sent that various U.S. actions (such as the rescue operation, the freeze of assets, and the trade boycott) resulted in forfeiture by the United States of its legal right to reparations. The observations of the Court itself on the propriety of the rescue attempt (quite apart from the two dissents referred to) raise the following questions:

1. Whether recourse to the Court imposes restraints on a party's conduct that would otherwise be legal
2. Whether, in particular, recourse to judicial proceedings suspends the right to the use of force in self-defense *pendente lite* (during the proceedings)
3. Whether an interim measures order of the Court may preclude the lawful exercise of the right of self-defense
4. Whether an interim measures order includes an implied condition of reciprocity
5. Whether the Court may vindicate its authority by imposing sanction, by withholding relief (a "clean hands" principle), or by censure

As these questions have import for future cases, they merit consideration here.

The general proposition that the Court may impose restraints on the conduct of a party when such conduct is incompatible with the proper functioning of the judicial process cannot be denied. It has its counterpart in contempt of court and similar powers universally accepted in domestic legal systems. International tribunals have similarly taken action against parties for conduct that impedes the proper functioning of the tribunal by obstructing or frustrating the judicial process. This applies not only to procedure before a court but also to conduct that prejudges the merits of the case or impedes execution of a decision of the tribunal. Consequently, measures of self-help normally allowed in international law to obtain reparation for a wrong may become impermissible once judicial proceedings are under way. As one commentator stated:

> Whether measures of self-help will impede the ability to comply with an adverse judgment depends on the particular circumstances; even if they do not have this effect, they too are impermissible, for they are designed to bring about the termination of the conflict without regard to the impartial determinations the parties agreed to seek when they assented to the tribunal's jurisdiction.[11]

As applied to the rescue attempt it is apparent that the Court consid-

---

11. Stein, "Contempt, Crisis and the Court," 76 *American Journal of International Law* 499, at 512 (1982).

ered the attempt incompatible with the commitment of the parties "to seek an outcome according to law rather than power."[12] Note that the Court made a point of linking this to the U.S. request to the Court first for delay and then for expedition of the case. When the United States decided to go ahead with the argument in court, it can be held to have represented to the Court that the proceedings would run their course and that Iran would have the opportunity to act upon the final judgment. Even if the United States had no confidence that Iran would comply, its acting on the premise of the futility of the litigation can quite plausibly be interpreted as undermining respect for the Court. It can be no surprise that the Court so considered it.

The right of a party to a case to take countermeasures against a wrongful act *pendente lite* may be recognized in certain exceptional circumstances. For example, as indicated in an arbitration between France and the United States, countermeasures would be permissible if the tribunal is not in a position to provide interim measures of protection.[13] When the tribunal is able to protect a party from irreparable harm by ordering interim measures, the party's right to countermeasures disappears.

The hostages case presented a variant of this issue. Since Iran flouted the Court's order of interim measures, it can be said that the Court's protection was no longer available and the situation for the United States was akin to that prior to the proceedings. Therefore its right to take countermeasures may be said to have revived (as was argued by the United States in the Court hearings). But note the distinction between the Court's attitude toward the rescue mission and toward nonforcible measures. The Court referred to the rescue mission as calculated to undermine respect for the judicial process but not to the freeze or trade embargo as likely to have that effect. (In contrast, the two dissenting judges considered the economic countermeasures as also disrespectful of the Court's authority.)

It is also significant that the Court drew the distinction between the question of the legality of the rescue mission and the question of its compatibility with respect for the judicial process. By not passing on the legality of the action, the Court avoided taking issue with the U.S. position that the rescue was justifiable self-defense. If they had seen it as a reprisal to vindicate a legal right, other judges might have felt compelled to take the same position as the dissenting judges and to declare the rescue action unlawful. The main point in the Court's condemnation of the rescue mission was that, even though the use of force may have been legitimate self-defense, it conflicted with the obligation of the litigating state to conduct itself so as not to impair the judicial resolution of the controversy. The Court, by its silence,

12. Ibid.
13. *Case Concerning Air Services Agreement,* 54 *International Law Reports* 304.

implied that the economic countermeasures were different in this respect from the use of force. Force, as the Court indicated, is calculated "to aggravate the tension between the two countries" and "to render the existing dispute more difficult of solution." Hence a party using force violates its duty to the Court.

The Court regrettably did not refer to the possibility that in some crises the judicial process would not protect a state from attack or imminent threats to the lives of its nationals. This was the case in the "cod war" between the United Kingdom and Iceland; in its 1974 decision in the Fisheries Jurisdiction Case the Court did not question the British use of naval force to protect its vessels.[14] In the hostage case, the Court might well have observed in its obiter dicta relating to the rescue mission that the United States had reason to believe that its hostages were in serious jeopardy and that its rescue mission was conceived as an emergency action to save lives. It might at least have left open the inference that in such circumstances an exception to the obligation to refrain from force was necessary. Perhaps some of the judges thought that, having waited so long, the United States might have deferred the rescue attempt another month until the Court gave its judgment and Iran failed to comply. Viewing the issue in retrospect, we may reflect on the dilemma faced by a government that invokes judicial authority to protect its rights in a crisis involving use of force. Respect for the judicial process surely requires it to avoid impeding or prejudicing that process. Yet one must allow for the fragility of international judicial authority and its inability to provide adequate protection against a defiant government. If such allowance is not made so as to permit the protective use of force in emergency cases, governments may be even less willing than they are to have recourse to the Court.

Two other issues remain to be considered under the heading of the use of force *pendente lite*. One relates to the question of reciprocity in respect of the Court's order of December 1979 indicating provisional measures, including the injunction to the parties to refrain from aggravating the tensions between them. The most important "provisional measure" in that order was that Iran "should ensure the immediate release" of all the hostages. That order was not complied with, a fact that the Court, of course, noted in its judgment of May 24, 1980. However, the Court did not consider that Iranian noncompliance with its order relieved the United States from its duty to obey the provisional measures, which were addressed to both parties. One might read this as a ruling that there is no strict condition of reciprocity in regard to the interim measures. Noncompliance by one side

---

14. *Fisheries Jurisdiction (United Kingdom v. Iceland)*, Merits, Judgement, *I.C.J. Reports 1974*, p. 3.

does not mean the other party is free to ignore the order. However, non-compliance by Iran demonstrated that the Court's interim measures did not provide adequate remedies, and therefore (as noted above) the United States was free to take certain nonforcible countermeasures that otherwise would have been prohibited.

The second issue that merits consideration relates to the sanctions that the Court may impose on a state that acts in a way to undermine respect for the Court. There seems little doubt that the Court has the inherent authority to impose certain penalties on litigants that violate judicial requirements. For example, failure to produce documents may lead the Court to draw adverse inferences or to censure the party. The question of the Court's authority to impose penalties for noncompliance with an order of provisional measures is somewhat complicated by uncertainty as to the Court's jurisdiction over the noncomplying party. The reason for this is that the Court may order provisional measures on a showing of prima facie jurisdiction. Consequently, the Court may have reason to hesitate to impose severe sanctions on a party that has not definitively been shown to be subject to the Court's jurisdiction. However, the Court has been ready to censure or at least to note the failure of a party to comply with the provisional measures ordered.

A more important question is whether the Court may impose penalties when there is no reasonable doubt about its jurisdiction. In the hostages case, this question was pertinent in respect of both parties. With respect to Iran, the interesting question is whether the Court could have imposed penalties for the failure of Iran to appear before the Court. Iran's nonappearance was by no means unique. In the last decade, four other respondent (defendant) states have refused to appear before the Court even to challenge its jurisdiction. Iceland, Pakistan, Turkey, and France preceded Iran in this form of defiance of the Court. The four states, like Iran, did not entirely ignore the Court. They resorted to unofficial and unorthodox methods to bring to the Court's attention their objections to its jurisdiction. The Court considered these objections as if they had been officially presented on the ground that the Court, before finding on the merits, must satisfy itself that it has jurisdiction. In the hostages case it made that finding on the basis of three treaties by which Iran had accepted the obligatory jurisdiction of the Court. (It did so, incidentally, not in a separate decision on jurisdiction but by joining the jurisdiction to the case on the merits and disposing of the jurisdictional issue in the judgment of May 24.) There is no doubt that the Court reached the correct conclusion on jurisdiction, but the question may be asked whether it should not have shown its disapproval of Iran's defiance of the Court in another way. It could have declared Iran's objections irreceivable and thus made it clear that a state's failure to plead on the jurisdictional issue would have adverse consequences.[15]

Whether the Court should have imposed penalties against the United States for the rescue mission raises quite different questions from those relating to Iran. The United States as the applicant (plaintiff) was in a different position from the respondent. It sought the aid of the Court, and the Court was in a position to deny such aid for sufficiently serious reasons. The equitable doctrine of "clean hands" applied in domestic law provides an analogy. A plaintiff seeking relief from a Court may reasonably be denied such relief because of conduct that is contumacious or that interferes with the judicial process or anticipates its outcome. International tribunals have the same kind of authority and should exercise it whenever appropriate.

Would it have been appropriate to do so in the hostage case because of the U.S. rescue mission (as in fact two dissenting judges proposed)? The decision of the majority of the Court to do no more than rebuke the United States was a more reasonable way of dealing with the problem. To have withheld judgment would have been to ignore the comparative gravity of the misdeeds of the two parties. Iran had demonstrated its disrespect by not even appearing before the Court and by flouting the order of December 15, 1979. Even more important, as the Court noted, was "the extent and seriousness of the conflict between the conduct of the Iranian State and its obligations under the whole corpus of the international rules of which diplomatic and consular law is comprised, rules the fundamental character of which the Court must here again strongly affirm."[16] The Court also observed that neither the question of the legality of the rescue mission nor any "possible responsibility flowing from it" was before the Court.[17] It added that it could have no bearing on an evaluation of the conduct of the Iranian government more than six months earlier. These conclusions of the Court are logical and sensible. However, we should not forget that the rescue mission was the subject of censure by the Court. It cannot be said that such censure was entirely without effect. At the very least, it cast a cloud on the claim of the United States that it was seeking a solution through judicial, rather than military, measures.

It may be thought that this detailed discussion of the International

---

15. This position was advocated by Sir Gerald Fitzmaurice, a former judge of the Court, in an article entitled "The Problem of the Non-Appearing Defendant Government," 51 *British Yearbook of International Law* 98 (1980). Fitzmaurice suggested that the Court should inform the defendant government that unless it appears to challenge the jurisdiction the Court will assume jurisdiction and go on to hear the merits. It would not do so if a prima facie basis for jurisdiction is wholly nonexistent but only in those cases where there is a basis and the state concerned denies its validity or applicability in the particular circumstances.

16. *I.C.J. Reports 1980,* supra note 9, at 42, para. 91.

17. Ibid., at 43, para. 94.

Court's treatment of the rescue mission is excessive, since the point was only incidental to the main issues in the judgment. This may well be true, but it is also pertinent that the furtherance of international judicial settlement remains an important aim of the United States, as of many other states in the international community. Recourse to the Court by the United States in the hostage case contributed to that aim. The fact that the Court spoke with authority on the central issues underscored the importance and vitality of the international legal principles violated by Iran. From a broad perspective of future action, the decision in the hostage case will probably be a positive factor in encouraging greater use of the Court. But whether or not that is so, we would still wish to strengthen international judicial settlement. The questions raised by the Court in regard to the rescue mission are germane to that objective. They remind us that, if international adjudication is to be used more widely and effectively, the states of the world, and particularly the parties in the cases, should scrupulously respect the judicial process. This involves not only such obvious obligations as refraining from improper influence or doctoring evidence; it also includes the duty to refrain from action that would impede the judicial outcome or by unilateral action anticipate it. However, this duty cannot be categorical; it must allow, as the Charter does, for legitimate self-defense even during the period of judicial deliberation. By recognizing that qualification, we would remove a possible impediment to the use of judicial process by states reluctant to have their right to self-defense limited by their recourse to a tribunal. To deny this right in the hope that judicial protection would be adequate is less than realistic. It would make the best the enemy of the good.

PROTECTION OF DIPLOMATS AND REMEDIES FOR ABUSE

Iran's violation of international law pertaining to diplomats and diplomatic property was so clear that it has produced little analysis by international lawyers. The basic rules of diplomatic privileges and immunities that have evolved over centuries were recently codified in two major conventions: the 1961 Vienna Convention on Diplomatic Relations, and the 1963 Vienna Convention on Consular Relations. Most countries of the world are parties to these treaties; even the few that are not are regarded as subject to their rules, since the rules generally reflect customary law. Although this body of law is occasionally violated, it is on the whole well observed. The common interest of all states in diplomatic intercourse and the sanction of reciprocity have ensured a high degree of compliance. Even cynics about international law concede the effectiveness of diplomatic law in the daily business of foreign relations.

The Rule of Strict Diplomatic Inviolability

The hostage case gave new emphasis to the significance and vitality of these rules. The seizure brought virtually universal censure by the international community and by the Security Council acting unanimously. The magisterial pronouncements of the International Court underlined the importance of diplomatic inviolability to the conduct of international relations and bear quotation here:

> There is no more fundamental prerequisite for the conduct of relations between States than the inviolability of diplomatic envoys and embassies, so that throughout history nations of all creeds and cultures have observed reciprocal obligations for that purpose.
> . . . The institution of diplomacy, with its concomitant privileges and immunities, has withstood the test of centuries and proved to be an instrument essential for effective cooperation in the international community and for enabling States, irrespective of their differing constitutional and social systems, to achieve mutual understanding and to resolve their differences by peaceful means.[18]

In its judgment of May 24, 1980, the Court in an unusual exhortation declared:

> The Court considers it to be its duty to draw the attention of the entire international community, of which Iran has been a member since time immemorial, to the irreparable harm that may be caused by the events now before the Court. Such events cannot fail to undermine the edifice of law carefully constructed by mankind over a period of centuries, the maintenance of which is vital for the security and well-being of the complex international community of the present day.[19]

In addition to affirming the importance of diplomatic privileges and immunities and the obligations of inviolability and protection, the Court confirmed certain basic principles that underline the codified law of diplomatic relations. Consideration of these principles may be instructive in connection with future cases.

Were the Militants' Actions Imputable to the Iranian State?

The Court found it necessary to consider the question of "imputability," that is, whether the government of Iran could be held directly responsible for the

18. *United States Diplomatic and Consular Staff in Tehran,* Provisional Measures, Order of 15 December 1979, *I.C.J. Reports 1979* (The Hague: International Court of Justice), p. 19, paras. 38–39.

19. *I.C.J. Reports 1980,* supra note 9, at 43, para. 92.

acts of the militants in the first phases of the takeover of the premises and the seizure of the hostages. The Court noted that no suggestion was made that the militants, when they executed their attack on the embassy, had any form of official status as recognized agents or organs of the Iranian state. Consequently, this conduct could not be imputable to the state on that basis. The Court took account of Khomeini's declarations calling on students to "expand their attacks on the United States" in order "to force the return of the criminal Shah" and of his subsequent "congratulations" right after the seizure. But the Court thought it would be going too far to interpret these statements as an "authorization" from the state.[20]

The conclusion that Iran was responsible was based therefore not on direct responsibility but on violations of the "categorical obligations" of protection.[21] These duties applied to the premises, the archives and documents, and, of course, to the persons themselves. Their seizure violated a whole series of obligations laid down in the conventions and general international law, including freedom from attack and detention and rights of travel and communication. The "total inaction" of the Iranian authorities in the face of urgent and repeated requests for help showed that more than mere negligence or lack of means were the causes of the failure to protect.[22] The Court contrasted the behavior of the authorities in the November attack with other occasions in 1979 when the "Revolutionary Guards" and police intervened after the embassy was attacked. (The Guards freed the ambassador and his staff when they were taken prisoner in February 1979.) Thus there was no question that Iranian officials were aware of their obligations of protection and of the necessity to take urgent action. Moreover, they had the means to carry out their duty and completely failed to do so.

In the second phase of the seizure and occupation, the Iranian government incurred direct responsibility for multiple breaches of the conventions. Declarations of approval by Khomeini, his prohibition of any dealings with the U.S. emissary, and especially his decree of November 17 transformed the continuing occupation and detention into acts of state for which the state was directly and fully responsible. The Court made a special point of castigating the threats to put the hostages on trial or to compel them to bear witness, both of which are unequivocally forbidden by the conventions. None of these conclusions of the Court were surprising or broke new ground. Nonetheless, they are important for the amplitude of their interpretation of the obligations owed by host states to diplomatic and consular personnel.

20. Ibid., at 29, para. 59.
21. Ibid., at 30, para. 61.
22. Ibid., at 31, para. 64.

Diplomatic Immunity May Not Be Violated to Redress Grievances
The Court also dealt in unambiguous terms with the "justification" set forth
in Iranian statements that the hostage seizure was only a "marginal aspect"
of an overall problem created by "numerous crimes" perpetrated by the
United States against the Iranian people.[23] The alleged crimes included
complicity in the coup d'état of 1953 that restored the Shah to the throne. It
also included charges of espionage and subversive acts by U.S. diplomatic
agents attached to the embassy. With respect to those charges, the Court
noted that the conventions and customary law require diplomats to respect
the law of the receiving state and impose a duty not to interfere with its
internal affairs. However, they pointed out that violations of these obligations were subject to two remedies. One is to declare the individual diplomat
persona non grata and thus to compel his immediate withdrawal. The second and more radical remedy is to break off diplomatic relations with the
sending state and to close the offending mission. These remedies, the Courts
noted, are by their nature entirely efficacious yet do not violate the fundamental principle of inviolability. Iran did not have recourse to either of the
two remedies but resorted to coercive action that was unquestionably unlawful. The Court laid stress on the cumulative effect of Iran's multiple
violations, on the severe hardships inflicted on the individual hostages, and
on the "unique and particular gravity" of the state's direct responsibility as
a matter of policy for violations of basic and essential rules of international
conduct.[24]

While the decision and reasoning of the International Court are valuable contributions to international diplomatic law, they do not dispose of all
the questions that have been raised in regard to this aspect of the hostage
case. It may be useful, in view of their future relevance, to consider these
questions.

What Legal Measures Will Further Protect Diplomatic Personnel?
First, the question arises as to whether more effective legal measures may
be taken to strengthen protection of diplomats against attacks and infringements of inviolability. Is there a need to spell out more specifically the
receiving state's duty of protection? In large part, this had already been
done in the Convention on the Prevention and Punishment of Crimes
against Internationally Protected Persons, including Diplomatic Agents,
which was adopted by the United Nations in 1973 and now has fifty-nine
states as parties. The convention makes it clear that violent attacks or
threats of such attacks cannot be excused even if the worthiest motives are

23. Ibid., at 37, para. 81.
24. Ibid., at 42, para. 92.

involved. It is also obligatory on the states party to the convention either to extradite offenders or prosecute them. All states parties are obliged to cooperate in the prevention of the crimes covered. Similar provisions are included in the 1979 International Convention on the Taking of Hostages, which applies to the seizure or detention of any person in order to compel a third party to act or refrain from acting as a condition for the release of the hostage.

These conventions and those on diplomatic and consular immunities provide an adequate legal basis for measures of cooperation by all states to forestall attacks and seizures on any mission and to take protective steps when they are threatened or have occurred. It may prove advisable on that basis for governments whose embassies have been threatened to seek joint action by other states as soon as the threats have been made. Joint representations by a group of states may prove useful. In some situations joint protective measures may be taken, with contingency plans agreed upon in advance. A series of representations by ambassadors may convey to the host government that their states will withdraw their missions or leave token representation.

Manifestations of such common concerns by the diplomatic corps or by their governments in countries where one or two governments have been under virulent attack may induce the host governments to consider the political costs of their failure to extend the requisite protection.

It may also be salutary for such common concern to be expressed when hostile and inflammatory statements by officials or other leaders are made against foreign embassies. Such statements may well be regarded as incompatible with the duties of receiving states to provide adequate protection. It may be advisable to spell out more clearly the nature of such statements so as to avoid implications of infringement on free speech—not an easy task. However, some of the Iranian statements, such as those of the Ayatollah calling for "attacks" by students, would appear to constitute a direct incitement that should properly draw a critical response from the international community. Perhaps considered analysis and recommendation by international lawyers through their organizations (such as the Institut de Droit International) could produce a set of principles that would enable states to censure statements of an inflammatory character directed against foreign embassies.

Automatic Sanctions

A further remedy for future situations might be an international agreement that would provide for the imposition of sanctions against an offending state for denial of protection or incitement against diplomats. Arguments can be advanced that such sanctions should be automatic, that is, mandatory in all cases. This would on its face reduce selective application by states on the basis of their political relations. Even if one would expect some states to seek to escape their obligation to act against governments with which they have close friendly relations, a mandatory treaty obligation would carry with it a fairly high probability of action. It would be reasonable to expect it to have a deterrent effect.

One of the effective sanctions in such a treaty would be an undertaking to discontinue all air traffic with the offending country. By prohibiting their planes from flying to the offending country and by denying landing rights to the offending state's planes, the parties to the treaty would be able to inflict heavy costs on the wrongdoer without an excessive sacrifice on their part.

It is true that sanctions of this kind may be imposed by the Security Council under article 41, provided it finds a threat to the peace or breach of peace or act of aggression (as required by article 39). That finding does not necessarily follow from threats to or attacks upon diplomats, a point that was made in the Security Council by those opposing sanctions. In any case, the political factors in the Council and the veto render uncertain Council sanctions and their deterrent effect.

An automatic treaty obligation would be more certain, but that the threat of sanctions would have had any impact in Iran during the emotional outburst of anti-Americanism may be doubted. Future situations may not have that degree of emotionalism, though attacks on embassies are likely to occur in places where strong sentiments would prevail over rational calculation of political costs. Hence a treaty would not have deterrent effect in many cases, though it might be significant in some. It merits at least some consideration.

How Might Iran Have Better Addressed Its Grievances?

Another, rather different kind of problem is raised by the Iranian charges of subversion and espionage by U.S. diplomats and others whose center was the embassy. It is clear that the remedies in international law are expulsion of the offending diplomat and severance of diplomatic relations. The Court considered these remedies "entirely efficacious."[25] However, a state that used diplomats for subversion and was instrumental in the overthrow of a government is guilty of one of the gravest offenses in international law. Breaking diplomatic relations or expelling a diplomat surely falls short of the punitive and compensatory remedies called for by that offense.

Iran could have sought such remedies in the International Court, if the United States had made a special agreement on the Court's jurisdiction. Alternatively, Iran might have brought its case after accepting the com-

25. Ibid., at 40, para. 86.

pulsory jurisdiction of the Court under article 36(2) of the Court's Statute, already accepted by the United States. However, the United States might have interposed an objection based on its reservation by declaring it considered the matter exclusively within domestic jurisdiction. (The apparent absurdity of such an objection when Iran's complaint was U.S. subversion in Iran would probably not defeat the U.S. objection in view of the Connolly Reservation by which the United States reserved the right to determine for itself whether a matter fell within its domestic jurisdiction.)

Whether the United States would have attempted to resist a case against it by Iran is a matter for conjecture. But the question raised is not without relevance to future situations. If states desire to strengthen the role of the Court, as the United States purports to do, then one would suppose they should be prepared to accept the jurisdiction of the Court in cases brought against them on grounds of alleged subversion or other grave abuses of their diplomatic privileges. The United States might have announced, in the hostage crisis, that it was willing to have the charges against it heard in the Court or before a mutually agreed arbitral tribunal. It would have been appropriate to do so, particularly as the United States was also seeking the aid of the Court. Iran probably would not have gone to the Court because of its conviction that most of the judges would be dominated by European or U.S. influence. Its refusal to appear in the hostages case is evidence of that belief. More dispassionate observers are not likely to share that view. In fact, at least some Western governments are likely to believe the contrary, namely, that the composition of the Court and the political background of many of the judges would lead the Court to take very seriously charges of subversion and intervention by powerful Western states. That this may be the case should not be a sufficient reason for the United States to raise a jurisdictional barrier to a complaint by another state that feels itself wronged by illicit U.S. intervention. If the general policy of the United States is to seek to strengthen respect for law and to enhance the use of judicial settlement, it should be willing to meet charges against it in the International Court just as it has to in the political organs of the United Nations.

The political organs of the United Nations also provide a forum for hearing grievances of states arising from alleged subversion and espionage by foreign governments (whether through diplomats or other agents). In the hostage crisis, many of the governments concerned with resolving the crisis and bringing an end to the seizures thought it important to assure Iran that its grievances would be given full consideration. Statements in the Security Council during the early phases of the crisis, especially by Third World governments, emphasized this aspect. The United States did not oppose such proposals; indeed, it expressed its willingness to have the complaints of

Iran heard by an appropriate U.N. body and to cooperate with that body "once the hostages are released and have departed from Iran."[26] On its part, Iran called for an international commission of inquiry to investigate the "crimes against Iran" and to report to the relevant organs of the United Nations for appropriate action. However, the Iranian statements maintained that the release of the hostages could not be a prior condition for the inquiry but that it would be a "consequence" of the inquiry.[27]

As described in an earlier chapter, the Secretary-General, acting under a general mandate of the Security Council to continue his efforts to resolve the crisis, announced on February 20, 1980, the setting up of a five-member Commission "to undertake a fact-finding mission to Iran to hear Iran's grievances and to allow for an early solution of the crisis."[28] The United States and Iran had agreed to such a commission. The precise nature of the fact-finding to be done by the Commission was not made clear. What was meant by "finding" the facts was susceptible to different interpretations. For example, the May 1980 judgment of the International Court declared:

> [The Commission] was not set up by the Secretary-General as a tribunal to decide the matters of fact or of law in dispute between Iran and the United States; nor was its setting up decided by them on any such basis. On the contrary, he created the Commission rather as an organ or instrument for mediation, conciliation or negotiation to provide a means of easing the situation of crisis existing between the two countries; and this, clearly, was the basis on which Iran and the United States agreed to its being set up.[29]

This explanation by the Court was intended to distinguish the role of the Commission from the function of the Court in "deciding the matters of fact or of law in dispute." As we know, the Commission's mission to Iran and its related efforts to help in resolving the crisis were not successful. An insider's account of its deliberations and strategy might be of considerable interest as part of the history of the crisis, but none is now available.

For the present purpose, the experience of the Commission throws some light on the subtleties involved in providing an instrumentality to deal with the grievances of governments. It reminds us that it is not enough that the International Court and the Security Council are competent to deal with such grievances and that all that is needed for them to do so is the political will of the disputant states. It may be necessary in some cases, if the will of

26. U.N. Doc. 2/13705, December 22, 1979.
27. Report of Secretary-General, U.N. Doc. 2/13730, 1980, p. 3.
28. *I.C.J. Reports 1980,* supra note 9, at 21, para. 39.
29. Ibid., at 23, para. 43.

the two governments is to be obtained, to create an ad hoc mechanism that will meet the specific preoccupations of the governments. A critical factor may be the composition of the body, in particular the selection of members who, in the particular circumstances, will be regarded as likely to understand the positions of one or the other party and who in combination will be so balanced as to avoid the fatal defect of appearing to be one-sided. In addition, the ability of such a group to function quietly and flexibly is important. Its procedures might have to be tailored to fit the special exigencies. "Fact-finding," as the Court suggested, may really mean "mediation, conciliation or negotiation." In some cases, a calculated ambiguity as to aims and methods will be desirable for a body acting as an intermediary between two estranged contending states. Neither the Court nor the Council would normally meet these desiderata. Much as one might wish to fortify these principal organs of international authority, experience tends to show that "custom-made" mechanisms are often more likely to be effective in dealing with serious disputes.

Although the foregoing observations do not relate directly to international rules, they have a bearing on some conceptions (or misconceptions) of the role of law in the kind of case we are considering. They suggest the following advice for future guidance. One is recognition of the need to provide a satisfactory means of recourse for governments that consider themselves wronged by actions of other governments taken under cover of diplomatic or other official relations. Such grievances may appropriately be submitted to the International Court or to an alternative arbitral tribunal; the adjudications would almost surely strengthen international law. However, we should not consider adjudicatory procedures as the only means of vindicating international legal rights. Other instrumentalities such as the Security Council, a regional body, an ad hoc commission, or an individual intermediary (such as the Secretary-General) may serve that purpose. Any one of them or some in combination can help in resolving the dispute. International law does not impose any fixed or rigid requirement as to instrumentality; nor does it constitute a departure from international law for states to employ flexible settlement procedures designed for a particular set of circumstances. Despite the failure of the fact-finding Commission in the hostage case and the inability of the Secretary-General or Security Council to bring an end to the seizure, their efforts to facilitate a peaceful solution may enable governments and international bodies to cope more effectively with future clashes over the rights and wrongs of state conduct.

This somewhat optimistic observation may be regarded as unrealistic, particularly in view of the controversial aspects of information gathering by diplomats. Governments are likely to resist international inquiries into activities of their diplomats, and they almost certainly would oppose an international mechanism to uncover and condemn covert intelligence operations by official missions. Yet the fact that the United States was prepared to cooperate with the Commission in the hostage case with respect to Iranian charges of subversion suggests that at least in some circumstances there may be acceptance of third-party inquiries. While it is probably excessively idealistic to expect covert intelligence to disappear, it does not seem impractical to seek redress for some illegitimate activities, such as supplying funds and personnel to foment unrest or support a particular political faction. The persona non grata remedy, efficacious as it may be in many cases, does not always work to prevent abuse or provide adequate reparation. Nor does it meet the need for clarifying the proper limits of diplomatic conduct in doubtful areas. There is surely some room for further development of diplomatic law along these lines.

ECONOMIC AND OTHER NONMILITARY MEASURES

The economic and other nonmilitary measures taken by the United States in response to the seizures were generally regarded as permissible under international law, at least vis-à-vis Iran. Questions did arise as to the application of the measures insofar as they affected the sovereign rights of other states (mainly, the issue of extraterritorial application of the freeze). Doubts were also expressed regarding the selective investigations of Iranian students in the United States; to some extent these doubts were linked to international human rights. A further question of international law was raised by two of the judges in the International Court (as earlier mentioned) regarding the propriety of the measures adopted in April in view of the pendency of the case before the Court and the Court's "indications" in its order of December 1979 that no measures should be taken that would aggravate the tension between the parties.[30] I shall discuss these questions, but before doing so it may be of interest to consider in a more general way the international law principles applicable to the retaliatory measures taken by the United States and their implications for future cases.

The economic measures adopted in November 1979 included a ban on oil imports and a comprehensive freeze of assets belonging to Iran and entities controlled by it. The noneconomic measures included the investigations of Iranian students and (in December) restrictions on Iranian diplomatic personnel. It was only in April 1980 that the United States broke off diplomatic relations with Iran. In April also, it imposed an embargo on exports to Iran and banned travel there by U.S. citizens. All visas issued to Iranians for future entry to the United States were canceled. In addition,

30. I.C.J. Order, supra note 18, para. 47, 1B.

steps were taken to "facilitate" payment of claims of American nationals against Iran out of frozen assets in the United States.

Retorsion

The international law basis for these measures falls into two classes of permissible retaliatory action. The first, technically known as retorsion, applies to those measures a state is free to take under international law as its sovereign right and therefore may take against another state committing an unfriendly act. Thus states are generally free (apart from treaty obligations) to refrain from trade with other states or to control immigration from those states. Clearly, some of the anti-Iranian measures of the United States, such as the ban on imports and exports and the cancellation of visas, fell into this category, as did the severance of diplomatic relations. Whether the freeze did is more uncertain.

Reprisals

However, the legality of the freeze is not seriously in question, since it falls within the second category of permissible retaliatory acts, namely, reprisals. As previously indicated, reprisals are retaliatory acts that would be illegal if not for the prior illegal act of the state against which they are directed. As there was no doubt about the serious character of the Iranian act, otherwise illegal action by the United States was permissible as a reprisal. A reprisal need not be protective; it may be used as a way of vindicating a legal right. Its object might even be punitive. Hence, whether or not a freeze would have been permitted in the absence of a legal violation by Iran, its adoption by the United States in response to the seizure was within the area of legitimate action.

However, the right of an aggrieved state to take reprisals is not unlimited. It does not extend (as we already have seen) to the use of force contrary to the Charter. Nor, in my opinion, may reprisals be taken in violation of basic human rights or of the humanitarian laws of war. I believe this limitation would find wide approval as a legal principle. Whether or not there are other limitations on retaliatory measures is not quite as clear. The subject merits some comment here, since it may have a bearing on action in future cases.

Retaliation in General

Retaliatory action, whether retorsion or reprisal, has a coercive character in that it is intended to change the conduct of a foreign state or to punish it for its unfriendly or illegal action. The question of its legitimacy may arise if its aim has an illegal character—more particularly, if the coercion is intended to deprive the target state of its basic sovereignty and political independence. This principle has been expressed in various treaties (for example, the Pact of Bogotá) and in resolutions on nonintervention adopted in the United Nations by general consensus. It can be regarded as a general precept of international law linked to the basic concept of sovereignty. Stated in its abstract form, it is unexceptionable.

We may also infer from it some reasonable limits on retaliatory action. Thus the imposition of a trade boycott or freeze aimed at changing the government of a target state by requiring the ouster of the existing government or the participation of particular factions or individuals in the government would be prohibited. To make such action a condition of removing the economic embargo would be an illicit coercive act. This would also be true if the retaliatory action called for the surrender of a target state's territory. These are relatively easy cases that serve to give some content to the general principle.

More difficult judgments are required when the economic coercion is aimed at changing the behavior of the other state, even though that behavior is entirely legal, for example conditioning the removal of the sanction on the adoption by the target state of changes in its trade policy or foreign policy. Of course the U.S. action in the hostages case did not involve such conditions. Its demands that the hostages be released, that diplomats be accorded adequate protection, and that reparations be paid did not involve a curtailment of Iranian sovereignty or political independence. However, it is not far-fetched to envision other situations in which the retaliatory action may be directed to producing a change in the regime of the target state. Ample historical precedents exist in which a legitimate act of retaliation or defense was transformed into intervention to produce a new regime. It may therefore be important to reaffirm this basic limitation on the exercise of retorsion and reprisal.

Proportionality

The standard of proportionality (which we have already considered in relation to the use of force) is also pertinent to the application of economic and other nonforcible acts of retaliation. Trade embargos and blocking of assets may—and generally do—have considerable impact on the target state and the welfare of its population. When such measures are taken because of relatively isolated wrongs committed by the government of the target state, they may well be disproportionate to the wrongs that provoked them. On the whole, states do respect the limits imposed by proportionality. Violations of diplomatic privileges, infringements of economic treaties, frontier incursions occur with enough frequency to test the requirement of proportionality. In nearly all cases, the response of the injured state involves retaliation or protest in keeping with the nature and gravity of the offense and the necessity of countering its effect. The importance of this should not be minimized.

In the hostages case the idea of proportionality was also seen by some as calling for reciprocal retaliation, the tit-for-tat response. Why not take fifty-two Iranian diplomats into custody? (There were sixty Iranian diplomats and about one hundred and sixty consular officials in the United States in 1979.) This seemed obvious to some editorial writers. It would have been a "proportionate" reprisal, similar to the original act. It was rightly rejected by the United States. To have followed the Iranians in their departure from the rules would have compounded an odious violation. It would not have brought about the release of the American personnel, and it might well have been treated as a precedent for responding to legal violations involving diplomats.

A similar consideration applies to the treatment of Iranian nationals in the United States. Actions by the U.S. government that were aimed at making life more difficult for Iranian students may be questioned on the ground that such action involved a vindictive reaction against individuals who were not personally responsible for the outrages committed in Tehran. It is true that the special investigations of visa compliance by the students were permissible under U.S. law as well as under international law. However, the fact that the actions were taken because of the hostage seizure and were applied against Iranians to an extent and in a manner not followed in regard to other foreign students underscored the discriminatory character of the U.S. actions. It also carried with it an implication of collective guilt that was not in keeping with the principles of human rights generally advocated by the United States. That its actions vis-à-vis the students may plausibly be attributed to public indignation heightened by the frustration felt by the U.S. government does not imply justification; it rather indicates that governments that have been gravely wronged need to be especially on guard against vindictive acts that can serve only to lower the level of civilized behavior.

The Legality of the Freeze

The economic measures taken by the United States—the freeze, the ban on oil imports, and the general prohibition of exports—do not raise similar doubts as to their propriety. The freeze was justified in law on two grounds: first, as retaliation—a permissible reprisal—against the Iranian violation, and second, by the threat of Iran to withdraw all Iranian funds from U.S. banks. In his response to Judge Platon Morozov in the International Court hearings, Roberts Owen noted that the threat of withdrawal "constituted nothing less than an attack on the stability of the world economy and the international monetary system." He also referred to the threat of Iran to repudiate obligations owed to U.S. nationals.

> In response to Iran's effort to harm the U.S. economy and the dollar, and having in mind Iran's unlawful detention of American hostages, the President of the U.S. simply froze all Iranian assets in U.S. control for the time being, in part simply to make it possible for U.S. claimants to be made whole if the government of Iran carried through with its threats to repudiate all of its obligations to such claimants.[31]

It may be noted that the $12 billion in frozen assets was in excess of the totality of claims that could be asserted against Iran, but this could not be determined at the time. In any case, the gravity of Iran's violation was sufficient to justify the freeze as a reprisal.

The freeze applied only to assets of the Iranian state and entities under its control. It was not applied to deposits of private Iranian companies and individuals. Whether it could have been is uncertain. Arguments can be made that blocking individual assets of foreigners constitutes a deprivation of property that can be justified only for substantial reasons of national security or emergency. Such reasons may exist if the assets, though owned by private persons, are under the control of their government and could be used by that government for inimical purposes. In time of war the freezing of enemy assets has generally been accepted as legitimate even when extended to the assets of private persons. The situation in peace is not quite as clear. Governments that impose a freeze on privately owned assets in their jurisdiction would seek to justify it by referring to the threat to the economy or to the national security inherent in control of those assets by an unfriendly foreign government. If that position appears to have a reasonable basis, it too is likely to be acceptable to the international community and to be sustainable as a legal position.

As I previously indicated, the freeze of the Iranian assets was subjected to legal challenge on several grounds. One was the position of the two dissenting judges in the Court that the freeze was incompatible with the judicial process and also contrary to the order of interim measures. A second objection related to the application of the freeze to assets outside the United States. A third objection was that the economic sanctions against Iran were rejected by the Security Council, and therefore the United States could not adopt them unilaterally. I shall consider each of these objections.

As I noted earlier, the majority of the Court in its judgment made no reference to the question whether the economic measures were possibly

---

31. *Department of State Bulletin,* May 1980, p. 56.

incompatible with recourse to the judicial process or with the Court's order of interim measures. However the two dissenting judges (Morozov of the U.S.S.R. and Tarazi of Syria) suggested that the freeze and related measures involved an attempt to anticipate the outcome of the case by a coercive action based on the unilateral interpretation by the United States of its rights. In particular, they laid emphasis on indications that the United States intended to use the frozen assets for payments of claims of the hostages and their families. Judge Tarazi considered that this

> constituted an encroachment of the functions of the Court, for until the Court has ruled upon the principle of reparation the applicant State is not entitled to consider that its submissions have already been accepted and recognized as well founded.[32]

Judge Morozov referred to the U.S. proposals to pay claims out of Iranian assets as implying that "the United States is acting as a judge in its own cause."[33]

Although the majority opinion of the Court did not find it necessary to consider the propriety of the economic countermeasures *pendente lite,* the criticisms of the dissenting judges warrant a reply. Two reasons may be suggested as justification for the U.S. action. One is that the freeze and inventory of claims was a reasonable protective measure in light of the threats of Iran to withdraw the assets and of Iran's noncompliance with the Court's order of interim measures. If the Court had been able to protect the United States from Iranian withdrawal, there would have been no need for U.S. action. But clearly the Court could not have done so, as evidenced by Iran's defiance of the December 1979 order. In these circumstances, an irreparable injury to the United States would have occurred if it had not taken such action. A second point is that the freeze and inventory of claims was not a distribution of assets, nor did it involve action predicated on the determination of the validity of the claims. It was no more than a measure of conservation, a "freeze," not a taking of assets.

The argument is of interest, because it helps to clarify the still obscure notion of the right to self-help by a wronged state and the limits of that right. The broad conclusion is that, if a state seeks judicial aid to vindicate a legal wrong, it must not predetermine the outcome by its exercise of coercive authority except to prevent irreparable injury when the court is unable to provide adequate protection. In such case, a protective conservatory measure such as a freeze of assets should be available to the party affected.

Although the freeze of the Iranian assets may be seen as having a

32. *I.C.J. Reports 1980,* supra note 9, at 64.
33. Ibid., at 54.

punitive as well as a protective aim, the fact that the United States did not claim a right to expropriate the assets is significant. It underscores the limits of the U.S. retaliation. It also might counteract an implication that foreign-owned assets in the United States are potentially under risk of confiscation in retaliation for serious unfriendly international acts by foreign governments. However, that implication cannot be entirely discounted. Governments placing their funds in U.S. banks will almost surely have some concern that these funds may be frozen and their use blocked (hence, at least temporarily taken from them) as a consequence of a U.S. interpretation that the conduct of the foreign government involves a serious offense under international law. The problem raised by such apprehension may not seem pressing today, but from the standpoint of international financial stability it would be desirable to reduce the threat inherent in the power of a state to freeze or levy on foreign assets within its jurisdiction.

Two lines of approach suggest themselves. The first would seek agreement on the conditions under which a state may exercise control (including freezing) over foreign assets and to levy on such assets as reparation for legal violations by the foreign government. The second would seek agreement on mandatory third-party procedures (judicial, arbitral, or institutional) to pass on the rights of the host state to take action in respect to foreign assets within its jurisdiction. Neither agreement would be easy to obtain, but it would be in the interests of both the states that receive foreign assets and those that export capital to remove the uncertainty that exists at present regarding the freezing and taking of foreign assets.

The Relevance of Security Council Decisions and the Veto

The arguments about the legality of the economic countermeasures extended to the implications of decisions of the Security Council. In this respect, too, the Soviet judge on the Court expressed a critical view of the series of economic measures taken by the United States in April 1980, characterizing them as unilateral economic sanctions taken after the Security Council had rejected the proposal to adopt them. However, the significance of the Security Council actions for the legitimacy of U.S. sanctions was not discussed by the Court's majority in its judgment, since it was not considered germane to the issue before the Court.

Viewed in retrospect, two interesting legal questions were raised by the U.S. attempt to obtain a Security Council mandate under chapter VII of the Charter to impose economic sanctions—principally a trade boycott and blocking of assets by all states. It will be recalled that two resolutions were adopted by the Security Council in December 1979 that bear on sanctions. In the first, the Council called on Iran to release the U.S. personnel immediately.[34] It also characterized the situation as "one which could have grave consequences for international peace and security." The second referred to the Secretary-General's "opinion" that the crisis posed "a serious threat to international peace and security," a conclusion that has legal significance because it constitutes a basis for enforcement measures under chapter VII of the Charter.[35]

The resolution concluded with a decision of the Council to meet again "and in the event of non-compliance with this resolution to adopt effective measures under articles 39 and 41 of the Charter." The Council thus envisaged the possibility of nonmilitary sanctions. On January 10, 1980, the United States submitted a draft resolution that would have decided that, until such time as the hostages were released and had safely departed, all member states should prevent the sale, supply, or shipment by their nationals or from their territories of all items, commodities, or products except food, medicine, and medical supplies.[36] It also called on members to refuse to Iran or any person in Iran loans, deposit facilities, or increases in nondollar deposits and to prevent their nationals from engaging in new service contracts in support of Iranian industrial projects other than those concerned with medical care.

The preamble of the U.S. draft declared that the continued detention constituted a "continuing threat to international peace and security." It then referred expressly to the Council "acting in accordance with articles 39 and 41 of the Charter." The proposed resolution was thus clearly intended to impose mandatory sanctions of a broad economic character against Iran. The vote on the resolution was 10 in favor, 2 against (U.S.S.R. and the German Democratic Republic), with 2 abstentions (Bangladesh and Mexico), with China not participating in the vote. In view of the veto cast by the U.S.S.R., the draft resolution was not adopted.

The arguments made in the Council were almost entirely of a political character. The Afghanistan invasion by the U.S.S.R. was referred to by both sides, and charges of threats to the independence of Iran were leveled at both the United States and the Soviet Union. The legal arguments were less obvious but merit attention here.

One argument concerned the proposed determination of a threat to peace and security and its implications for other internal conflicts. The Mexican delegate referred to the "very nature of violent social changes that power temporarily disintegrated and that contending factions frequently caused unjust harm to foreigners." He then went on:

34. Security Council Resolution 457, December 4, 1979.
35. Security Council Resolution 461, December 31, 1979.
36. U.N. Doc. S/13735, 1980.

If the facts, however serious they might be, were to be characterized as a threat to peace and if sanctions were to be adopted against insurgent peoples simply because they had caused unfair harm to foreigners and had violated respected international rules, what might occur would be interference in the development of political change which must remain within the purview of the self-determination of peoples as stipulated in the Charter.[37]

Other views by nonsupporters (Bangladesh and China) stressed the importance of mediation and negotiation and suggested that sanctions would not lead to release of the hostages.

While these views were mainly political, they are pertinent to the legal basis of Security Council enforcement action. In particular, they point up the issue whether the Council has a right to enforce international law, that is, to take action against a lawbreaker, when there is no clear threat to the peace except by retaliatory military action of the aggrieved state.

The same issue has arisen in other situations before the Council. Dean Acheson maintained that the Council had no right to impose sanctions against a state even if it violated international law unless that state itself threatened the peace, but not if other states threatened to retaliate.[38] Others take a contrary view on the premise that a law-violating state creates a situation in which injured or outraged states are likely to use force in the absence of other available remedies. This is particularly likely where the aggrieved state is directly injured (as in the hostage case). It may also arise where the injury is not direct but a grave offense against rules considered fundamental by the international community. But both these examples link sanctions to responsibility.

It is not at all clear, however, that the Charter requires such linkage. Indeed, a better case can be made that the enforcement power of the Security Council is not limited to actions against wrongdoers and that it is free to take whatever action is necessary to maintain or restore peace and security when a threat to or breach of the peace has occurred.

In short, the Council was not set up as a court to pass on legal rights and wrongs but as a mechanism to bring about and even impose a peace. It would as a rule be expected to consider which states incited or provoked a threat or breach of peace, but it is not required to do so. Nor is it required to act against a lawbreaker unless it considers that such action would remove a threat to the peace or restore peace. It is by no means clear in retrospect that sanctions against Iran would have met that test.

37. *U.N. Chronicle,* March 1980, p. 24.
38. On this basis Acheson maintained that the Security Council sanctions against Southern Rhodesia were illegal. Senate Committee on Foreign Relations, *Hearings on U.N. Sanctions against Rhodesia,* 92nd Cong., 1st sess., July 7, 1971, pp. 37–38.

A second legal issue of consequence was raised by the position of the United States and Western European states that the draft resolution vetoed by the U.S.S.R. provided a legal ground for sanctions by member states. The arguments advanced were not given much attention at the time, but they have significant implications that extend beyond the hostage case.

One argument was a rather technical one. The U.S. representative on the Council, Donald McHenry, told the Council after the veto was cast that the Council's earlier Resolution 461 contained a binding obligation to take effective measures in the event of Iranian noncompliance. He referred to the last paragraph (quoted above) that the Council would meet "to adopt effective measures under articles 39 and 41 of the Charter." The idea that the Council had thereby bound itself to adopt sanctions at a future meeting is not quite persuasive. It implied that no veto could be exercised and that members were already obliged to vote for some measures, although they were not specified earlier.

A different argument was suggested by President Carter and by the foreign ministers of the Common Market countries. In April 1980, he announced the imposition of sanctions "in accordance with the sanctions approved by 10 members of the United Nations Security Council on January 13 in the resolution which was vetoed by the Soviet Union."[39] His official message to the Congress referred to the measures taken "in furtherance of the objectives of Resolution 461, adopted by the Security Council . . . and would have been specifically mandated by the Security Council on January 13, 1980, but for a veto by the Soviet Union."[40]

The Common Market foreign ministers requested their parliaments to impose sanctions against Iran "in accordance with the Security Council resolution on Iran of 10 January 1980, which was vetoed, and in accordance with the rules of international law."[41]

These references to the vetoed resolution as a legal basis for sanctions may be construed as no more than an effort to give a measure of international legitimacy to the sanctions and to underline the isolated opposition of the Soviet Union. It is also politically understandable that the United States would seek to use the Security Council majority vote to persuade its European allies to join in the sanctions. However, reliance on a vetoed resolution as if it conferred authority runs contrary to the basic principle of the Charter that nonprocedural decisions of the Council require the "concurring votes of the permanent members." The idea that a majority vote— even a nearly unanimous vote—may substitute for a legal decision of the

39. 16 *Weekly Compilation of Presidential Documents* 611, April 7, 1980.
40. Ibid., at 615, April 14, 1980.
41. See Reisman, "The Legal Effect of Vetoed Resolutions," 74 *American Journal of International Law* 904 (1980).

Council would go a long way toward eliminating the veto. At one time, this may have seemed a desirable advance to the United States, but it is quite clear that the elimination of the veto cannot be the present policy of the U.S. government. We must therefore assume that the statements of the President (and also the communiqué of the Common Market ministers) did not intend to erode the veto. But there is reason for concern in the attempt to find political advantage by relying on a majority vote that fell short of the legal requirement for a decision. This may, by force of precedent, introduce another class of authoritative decisions that would in time override the significance of the Council's unanimity rule. Apart from the law of the Charter, it is highly dubious that this would be a desirable development at present, but, whatever its possible long-run merits, the erosion of the veto should not be determined by statements made for short-run political benefits.

The Extraterritorial Reach of the Freeze

Controversial issues of international law were also raised by the application of the freeze to Iranian funds outside the United States. The U.S. Freeze orders extended to such funds on two bases. The first applied to the Iranian assets if they were "within the possession or control of persons subject to the jurisdiction of the United States."[42] On this basis, the freeze applied to Iranian deposits in foreign branches and subsidiaries of U.S. banks. The second ground for foreign application of the freeze was a provision in the order applicable to funds "subject to the jurisdiction of the United States." This presents the question whether Iranian funds on deposit in a local bank in Britain or France might be regarded as "subject to" U.S. jurisdiction. One answer was that dollar accounts held in European banks are "ultimately" or "really" located in the United States, because clearing takes place and debits and credits are recorded in New York.

To at least some Europeans the extension of U.S. law to accounts in their countries (whether or not the banks were U.S.-controlled) understandably appeared as an intrusion on their sovereignty. They maintained that local law applied to funds in their countries and that it was impermissible under international law for the United States to extend its legislation to transactions in their countries and to attempt to enforce that legislation against banks in those countries. Branches and subsidiaries of U.S. banks were equally subject to the law of the place in which they were operating, and that law could not be superseded by U.S. law based on the "nationality" of those branches and subsidiaries. A fortiori, the objection to U.S. law applied to European banks and their dollar accounts. The U.S. attempt to

42. Executive Order 12170, November 14, 1979, 44 *Federal Register* 65581 (1979).

apply and enforce the freeze orders (in the absence of U.N. compulsory sanctions or legislation of the foreign states) was therefore regarded in European circles as an excessive exercise of jurisdiction under international law that would undermine confidence in established banking practices.

It might be noted that the European reaction to the extraterritorial reach of the freeze was not as marked as resentment against other U.S. efforts to enforce U.S. law abroad, as in the "trading with the enemy" cases (such as the trade embargos on Cuba, and earlier China) and the antitrust and securities cases. U.S. attempts to compel foreign firms to provide documents or other information for American litigation were also a prominent ground for dissatisfaction. The adoption of legislation in several European countries designed to prevent the application of U.S. law in those countries reflects the continuing opposition of those states to U.S. extraterritorial measures. However, the European governments did not make any strong protests to the United States against the Iranian freeze.

The U.S. position was essentially that, in view of the gravity of the Iranian violations as well as the threat to U.S. creditors, it was appropriate to extend the freeze to all entities and transactions over which the United States could validly exercise jurisdiction under international law.

Nationality is a generally recognized basis of jurisdiction, hence branches and subsidiaries of U.S. banks could properly be subjected to U.S. requirements. Moreover, since dollar accounts were necessarily operated by transactions in the United States (for the reasons already noted), they were subject to U.S. jurisdiction. As both of these bases of jurisdiction have been accepted as valid in international law, the U.S. measures should not have been resisted by the states where the funds are located.

A subsidiary ground to support the validity of the U.S. measures was the implied "approval" of the freeze by the International Monetary Fund under a provision in the Fund's articles that allows "exchange control regulation" to be imposed for security reasons.[43] The United States had notified the IMF of the Iranian blocking orders and, although the IMF did not respond affirmatively, the absence of any challenge by the Fund within the time prescribed was deemed to constitute approval under the Fund's rules.

If we consider the issues from a more general legal aspect, the critical point seems to be whether there are international law criteria for deciding which of the two positions is correct. Clearly, each position rests on an accepted base of jurisdiction; the one, territoriality; the other, nationality. Yet a bank in London, Paris, or Frankfurt faced a penalty whatever it did, if each state enforced its law. Litigation had been started in Britain, France,

---

43. Articles of Agreement of the International Monetary Fund, article VIII, section 2(b), 29 *U.S. Treaties* 2203.

and Germany that would have decided the issue in respect of deposits in branches and subsidiaries of U.S. banks. The cases were not decided, however, because of the Iranian settlement agreement.

One way of deciding the issue is to conclude (with the Europeans) that jurisdiction based on territoriality requires priority under the basic international principles of territorial sovereignty. Thus banks would be required to comply with the law of the place where they do business and to disregard contrary U.S. measures. In view of the compulsion under which they acted, they should not be subject to penalties in the United States.

An alternative view would be to decide between the competing positions by considering the "reasonableness" of the claims of jurisdiction in light of the actual interests involved and the accepted policies of the international community. This approach, a type of "interest analysis," has found favor in some U.S. judicial decisions and in Article 40 of the Restatement (Second) of Foreign Relations Law, adopted by the American Law Institute in 1965. A new Draft Restatement of Foreign Relations Law (Revised), now under consideration and likely to be adopted, carries this approach somewhat further.[44] It holds that the presence of a jurisdictional base such as territoriality or nationality is legally required but does not in all cases give a state the right to prescribe or enforce its law. The connecting link is a necessary but not sufficient factor. Jurisdiction depends on an examination of "all relevant factors" and a judgment by a court (or other competent decision-maker) that its exercise in that case would be reasonable and fair. The Draft Restatement observes that courts (and other decision-makers) "are increasingly inclined to analyze various interests, examine contacts and links, give effect to justified expectations, search for the center of gravity of a given situation and develop priorities."[45]

A standard of reasonableness and a search for the "center of gravity" of a situation may seem to offer little guidance to courts or governmental officials faced with concrete decisions. To weigh the importance of relevant factors, to decide whether one interest should count for more than another, to determine which expectations are justified and which are not call for judgments that reflect underlying assumptions about political and social policy. This means that governments are likely to reach different conclusions about the reasonableness of many extraterritorial claims. However, such differences need not preclude—indeed, they should encourage—deliberate efforts on the part of the governments (and where appropriate, courts) to weigh the various elements in a case and to consider the sensitivities of other governments and the relative importance to each competing state of

---

44. American Law Institute, *Draft Restatement on the Foreign Relations Law of the United States (Revised)*, Tentative Draft No. 2, sections 401-403, pp. 87–114 (1981).

45. Ibid., at 95.

the action in question. To ignore these aspects and decide simply on the basis of the presence of a jurisdictional link such as territoriality or nationality would lead to decisions not likely to be tolerated by one or another of the states concerned. If conflicts over extraterritorial claims are to be resolved amicably, it seems essential that states moderate their jurisdictional rights by seeking solutions that take into account the diverse factors in each case and the reasonableness of the result.

The extraterritorial application of the Iranian assets freeze illuminates some aspects of the problem and suggests some practical conclusions. I have already referred to the different perceptions of the states regarding their interests. There is, in addition, another dimension of interests that requires consideration, namely, the wider interests of the international system. The Draft Restatement includes such interests in its list of relevant criteria for judging whether an extraterritorial claim is reasonable (Sec. 403); U.S. judicial decisions have also given weight to such community interests.

Governments sometimes justify their claims on grounds of international interests that appeal to other states and often to the private sector as well. Thus, in the Iranian freeze case, arguments against extraterritoriality urged that consideration be given to the international interest in stability in international financial relations, respect for the justified expectations of persons engaged in transnational activities, and recognition of territorial sovereignty as a basic tenet of the state system.

On the other side of the equation, as factors supporting the extraterritorial application of the freeze, it was possible to cite the recognized international interest in combating grave violations of international legal principles as well as the general interests of states in protecting important state interests and in exercising authority over their nationals, including their banks.

To be sure, listing of these diverse and competing interests does not provide an answer to the specific issues raised by the cases referred to earlier. However, the explicit recognition of these factors is a necessary and important step in arriving at a judgment of what is reasonable. I would go beyond this general observation and suggest two specific conclusions that are pertinent to action in future cases.

First, a state adopting reprisals or protective measures against a law-violator should not apply such sanctions to activities or persons outside of the country *solely* on the basis of a jurisdictional link such as nationality or objective effects. While one or another of such jurisdictional bases should be present, extraterritorial enforcement should not be pressed unless other compelling reasons exist to make that necessary.

In the case of the Iranian freeze, the extension to the dollar holdings in American banks abroad was adequately justified by the enormous dollar holdings of Iranian government entities in the American banks in Europe—a sum of about $6 billion out of the $12 billion affected by the freeze. On the other hand, the United States did not find it necessary to apply the freeze to the dollar accounts in foreign banks abroad (these were unblocked soon after the freeze was instituted) or to the nondollar accounts in branches and subsidiaries of the U.S. banks. Both of these examples of restraint exemplify our conclusion that it would not be reasonable to press a jurisdictional concept to its limits in cases where foreign sensitivities are strong and relatively little is to be gained by extraterritorial application.

The second conclusion involves international measures. It would be desirable to obtain explicit international affirmation of the following propositions: (1) that hostage taking is an offense against the international community and not merely against the target state and (2) that all states should cooperate with and assist the injured state in the legitimate retaliatory measures it has taken. A first step to this end has already been taken in the International Convention against the Taking of Hostages, adopted in 1979, to which a substantial number of states have adhered. The preamble of that treaty declares that "the taking of hostages is an offense of grave concern to the international community" and that

> it is urgently necessary to develop international cooperation between States in devising and adopting effective measures for the prevention, prosecution and punishment of all acts of taking of hostages as manifestations of international terrorism.[46]

These declaratory statements in a widely accepted treaty are supportive of the proposal made here for a declaration in which all states would recognize the *erga omnes* character of the offense of hostage taking and the corollary undertaking of cooperation and assistance.

It may be expected that on the basis of this declaration the executive and judicial authorities in the adhering states would refrain from ordering persons within their territories to disregard the relevant extraterritorial legislation and orders imposed on them by virtue of their nationality or other significant connection with the injured state. The fact that the territorial state had accepted an international agreement that it too has a legal interest in giving effect to retaliatory measures would almost surely deter its officials and courts from imposing conflicting requirements on persons subject to the injured state's orders. It would then be much easier for those governments and their courts to treat the matter as one in which they have a legitimate interest, so that they are not faced with a claim by the aggrieved state that is contrary to their national interest.

---

46. *International Legal Materials,* vol. XVIII (November 1979), p. 1457.

This position might be carried further to provide a basis for positive legislative and executive action by states in support of retaliatory measures by the injured state. One might expect states with close ties to the injured state to move in this direction when they felt, as in the Iranian case, a sense of outrage over the violation. The recognition of the *erga omnes* character of the offense[47] would not result in a legal obligation to take action (a result that might be resisted for various reasons), but it would provide a legal foundation for such action. It would in effect rebut a contention that the matter was none of the business of that state.

Action on these lines would not resolve all the complex problems raised by extraterritorial sanctions generally, but in the special circumstances of hostage taking and similar acts of terrorism they would be realistic measures to strengthen international collective action against the law-violating government.

THE VALIDITY OF THE SETTLEMENT AGREEMENTS

When the settlement agreements between the United States and Iran were concluded in January 1981, questions were raised by some international lawyers and in press comment as to the validity of the agreements under international law. The crux of the issue was the contention that the transfer of funds to Iran constituted a species of ransom payments and that the agreements were obtained by duress inherent in the threats to the hostages and their continued detention. These conclusions, it was argued, meant that the agreements violated article 52 of the Vienna Convention on the Law of Treaties, a provision said to constitute general international law and therefore to be binding on all states, whether or not parties to the convention. The issues raised by this argument are of sufficient interest to merit examination here.

It is noteworthy that the review carried out by the Reagan Administration before its decision to implement the agreements concluded that, while the agreements should be carried out in the overall interest of the United States, the administration "did not find it necessary to reach a conclusion as to the legally binding character of these agreements under international law."[48] It is not clear why the agreements might not have been "legally binding." If they were not, it could be either that they were not intended to

47. The *erga omnes* character of an offense refers to the principle that a violation of an international obligation is in some cases an offense against the international community as a whole, and therefore all states can be held to have a legal interest in protecting the right involved.

48. *Department of State Bulletin,* March 1981, p. 17.

be binding (a highly unlikely conclusion) or because they were invalid or void under article 52 of the Vienna Convention on the Law of Treaties.

If the agreements were void under international law, then they were without legal effect, and neither party has the right or option to declare them to be legally binding. The inference from the refusal of the Reagan Administration to pass on the legally binding character of the agreements is that this attribute is not essential to the U.S. decision to carry out the terms of the agreement. But one must ask whether an agreement that may be void (and not merely voidable) under international law could or should have been given effect by the President. Possibly the Reagan Administration wished only to satisfy those critics of the agreements who attacked them as payment of ransom under duress by leaving this as an unsettled question. Yet by refraining from taking a position in favor of the validity of the agreements, the U.S. government may have subjected itself to attack on the ground that its action in transferring assets and agreeing to the arbitral procedures lacked a proper legal foundation. Conceivably, Iran might on that basis refuse to perform its remaining obligations under the agreements (as, for example, by not replenishing the fund from which successful claimants against it would be paid).

Apart from this anomaly in the Reagan Administration's position, the question of the international validity of the agreement does not appear to be a serious question today. However, the question is of interest, because the debate about validity has shed light on some of the issues raised by article 52 of the Vienna Convention, an important provision that has given rise to considerable controversy.

Article 52 reads as follows:

Coercion of a state by the threat or use of force
> A treaty is void if its conclusion has been procured by the threat or use of force in violation of the principles of international law embodied in the Charter of the United Nations.

A preliminary question raised in the discussion relating to the Iranian settlement agreements was whether the United States was bound by article 52, considering that it is not a party to the Vienna Convention and that the rule in article 52 has never been applied and is arguably not customary law. The latter question is the critical one, since if article 52 expresses customary law (as do most other articles of the Vienna Convention) then the United States is subject to it even though not a party. (Incidentally, the United States relied on the Vienna Convention in its pleadings in the hostage case in the Court, thus recognizing the articles invoked as binding customary law.)

As to article 52, it is pertinent that the drafters of the convention and the states that adopted it in Vienna in 1969 considered it to declare existing law. The International Law Commission, the drafting body, had so concluded in its report to the conference.[49] The Commission observed that the development of international law exemplified in the Nuremberg Charter of 1945 and article 2(4) of the U.N. Charter consolidated an earlier trend and justified the conclusion that the invalidity of a treaty procured by the illegal threat or use of force is "a principle which is lex lata in the international law of today."[50] The Commission noted that the rule would not operate retroactively upon treaties concluded prior to the establishment of the rule against force in the Charter. The position taken by the Commission as to the customary law character of article 52 was affirmed without significant dissent by the conference of states that adopted the Vienna Convention. The United States supported that position in Vienna.

Some of the controversy relating to the settlement agreements focused on the claim that article 52 was undesirable and unlikely to be given effect without serious destabilizing consequences. It was argued that treaties concluding wars or other hostilities could be repudiated on the ground of article 52. It was further contended that the terms of article 52, particularly the threat of force, could be extended to coercion (such as economic pressure) and therefore give rise to attempts to evade treaty obligations. The arguments led some to conclude that article 52 should be repudiated as existing law by the United States.

In response, it was pointed out that it would be absurd to interpret article 52 as impugning the validity of peace treaties or armistice agreements. A peace treaty imposed against an aggressor state defeated in war was excluded by the language of article 52 (as well as by article 75 of the convention). But if an aggressor state that has used force contrary to article 29(4) sought to impose its terms by treaty, that treaty would be void. The other argument relating to the broad meaning of "force" and "threat of force" as including economic and political coercion was answered by reference to legislative history, which showed that the term "force" in article 52 meant armed force. A separate resolution condemning economic coercion in procuring treaties was adopted by the conference, thus making it clear (as was the express intention) that such coercion was not included in article 52.

Another issue arose from the fact that the Iranians clearly used force in seizing the hostages and the embassy and continued to threaten force against the hostages and indirectly against the United States. These facts were the basis for the argument that the settlement agreements were procured by the threat or use of force in violation of principles of international

49. *1966 Yearbook of the International Law Commission,* vol. II (United Nations Publication 1967, Sales No. 67.V.2), pp. 246–47.

50. Ibid., at 246, para. (1).

law embodied in the Charter. Some responded to this argument by maintaining that the Iranian seizures, though illegal, were not the use of force against the United States in the sense intended by article 2(4) of the Charter. This is perhaps debatable, since article 2(4) speaks of force used "in any other manner inconsistent with the purpose of the United Nations." One cannot say that the use of force by Iran was consistent with U.N. purposes.

A better response to the argument is that article 52 applies to a treaty embodying concessions procured by violence and threats of violence, and the settlement agreements do not fall into that category. The United States did not pay a "ransom" to Iran as a quid pro quo for the release of the hostages. The United States had $12 billion belonging to Iran (which it had frozen); it was prepared to return that property (and did so) on conditions that met U.S. interests in respect of the hostages and U.S. creditors. In fact, the agreements conferred on U.S. nationals some benefits that they would not have had if the hostages had not been taken.[51] The conclusion of the settlement agreements was "procured," because each party had what the other wanted. Iran presumably had other reasons as well for wanting the agreement. These facts, including the pressures and exigencies faced by Iran, show that this was not a ransom exacted by Iran. On the contrary, Iran received back only its own property and not even all of that.

In sum, we can conclude that article 52 did not apply to these agreements. We can reach that conclusion without impugning the validity of the agreements and without narrowing the ambit of article 2(4). This is a realistic and reasonable way of resolving the issues raised in this particular case. It does not, however, answer the hypothetical question whether an agreement involving a payment to release hostages or property would be void. There would be good reason to regard such agreements as void under article 52 and therefore as giving rise to a legitimate claim to reimbursement of the payment. The claimant government would then have the legal right to levy on the assets in its territory belonging to the law-violating state or, if sufficient assets were not available, to pursue the respondent state's assets elsewhere. Thus in these cases it would be reasonable to invoke article 52 against the lawbreaker.

Even if a state that was forced to enter into a treaty by threat of force should choose to allow that agreement to continue after it was freed from the threat of force, it would seem desirable to regard that treaty as void *ab initio*. This view was taken by the International Law Commission in its comments on article 52. It considered that this would enable the victim state to make

---

51. Roberts Owen, the State Department Legal Adviser at the time the settlement was made, has stressed this point. See chapter 8.

its decision on maintaining the treaty in a position of full equality with the other state. If the treaty were maintained, the Commission considered that in this case it would amount to a conclusion in effect of a new treaty and not recognition of the validity of a treaty "procured by means contrary to the most fundamental principles of the Charter of the United Nations."[52] It may be that these comments of the International Law Commission are excessively subtle and idealistic. However, they merit due consideration, for they emphasize the problems raised for states when they are coerced by illegal threat or use of force to enter into an agreement that they would otherwise reject. In the absence of effective international judicial machinery to deal with such coerced agreements, there is merit in affording the victim state a basis for treating the agreements as void ab initio.

The problems raised by the hostage crisis cast light on the complexities of legal responses to the use of force and the threat of force in violation of the Charter and other basic principles of international law. It is reasonable to conclude, however, that, while international law has not superseded factors of power and interest in combating illegal violence, it enables governments and their peoples to understand more clearly the normative choices they face and to perceive their common interests.

I have sought to show this in my analysis of the issues raised by the responses to the Iranian seizures. The legal analysis may seem to some to be arcane and remote from the imperatives of action. But action requires choices, and these choices cannot be divorced from conceptions of legitimacy shared by governments and their peoples. We look to the law for those conceptions, and we do so not merely on the abstract level of general principles but on the concrete level of specific rules and procedures. In this sense, the legal issues are of practical significance. They inform us about the kinds of action we should take in future cases, and they compel us to think hard about the international order we should strive for.

52. *1966 Yearbook of the International Law Commission*, p. 247.

10 LESSONS AND CONCLUSIONS

ABRAHAM A. RIBICOFF

This concluding chapter brings together some of the principal themes of the book and offers thoughts on the significance of the Iranian hostage crisis for the future. It is essential that decision-makers and opinion leaders, both in and out of government, study and reflect upon this experience for the broader lessons it teaches about the functioning of our institutions in time of great strain. If possible, we should identify ways to strengthen our preparation for the next crisis, for it is inevitable that there will be others. Whether the next crisis is another terrorist act, such as the taking of diplomatic hostages, or another instance of disintegration of the established order in a state of strategic importance to the United States, the probability of recurrence of more such challenges is unfortunately rather great. Ironically, what is *unlikely* to recur is the amount of pressure the United States could exert against Iran, because few other perpetrators of hostile acts will have such a large quantity of assets within ready reach. Thus we must face the prospect that the next crisis may be even more difficult to solve. This possibility only underscores the need to be thinking now of what we can learn from the Iranian hostage crisis.

Strategies for Resolving a Crisis
The Iranian hostage crisis provided dramatic proof of our nation's commitment to basic principles of international law and its affirmation of the use of existing international institutions for the peaceful settlement of disputes. For the first time in history, the United States brought a petition before the International Court of Justice on an issue of urgency and general importance to the world. The Court responded with unprecedented speed and unity with an order of interim relief and a final judgment in our favor. We similarly obtained unusual support and solidarity from the community of

nations in the form of overwhelming votes of support in the United Nations. We had some measure of cooperation from allied governments in connection with economic sanctions. Our government showed restraint in holding off from the use of military force for retribution or coercion and in avoiding the temptation to expropriate outright (or "vest") the frozen Iranian assets.

Several chapters in this volume have discussed the two-track strategy that motivated the administration's thinking throughout much of the crisis. On one track, the administration pursued every effort to negotiate with the Iranian side, while on the other it brought to bear increasing forms of economic and other pressure; in the background was the possibility of the use of force. In retrospect, the hardest question to answer is whether this was the best strategy or whether some other mix of negotiation, pressure, and force might have resolved the crisis sooner—or at lower costs to interests of the United States other than the lives of the individuals involved.

As Professor Louis Henkin has pointed out,[1] the United States had three different purposes: (1) to get the hostages out, (2) to defend its honor, and (3) to further its long-term interests, strategic and otherwise. The real problem was that those purposes could be contradictory. What might have achieved one purpose would have been counterproductive for another. The problem with analyzing the hostage situation was the difficulty in deciding which purpose was most important. In that strange and irrational context, some U.S. purposes counseled patience and avoiding radical measures, but the notion that there was not much that one could do was not a concept that the United States lived with easily.

The strongest retrospective argument for the administration's course of action is that it resulted in the release of all the hostages alive. The strategy also produced a package of agreements that put many (if not most) claimants against Iran in a better position than they were before the taking of the hostages. Our demonstrated commitment to peaceful settlement of disputes thus served its immediate purpose and affirmed our status as a nation that values human life and the rule of law.

There are widely differing views on whether the same result could have been achieved sooner and whether another approach to the use of force might have better served our long-term interests. Some people feel that more consistency with respect to the threat or use of force would have been desirable and that the administration suffered from the perception of a lack of will to invoke stronger measures than economic sanctions. It will always be a matter of argument whether the crisis could have been shortened by deliberate projection of a different image of the interplay between the economic and diplomatic offensive and the willingness to use force.

1. In the Council on Foreign Relations study group meeting. Cited with permission.

As Gary Sick notes in chapter 3, in the latter stages of the crisis an element of uncertainty was injected into the situation by the Reagan presidential campaign and subsequently by the anticipated change of power in the White House. The Iranians' awareness of candidate Reagan's heavy emphasis on military action during the campaign was probably a significant factor in Iran's almost frantic rush to complete formal action by the Majlis prior to November 4. After the election, Iranian apprehension about a new administration was quite valuable in establishing a credible deadline and enforcing it.

Warren Christopher's introduction and Harold Saunders's chapter 1 make a strong argument that the two-track strategy of negotiation, coupled with pressure, offered the best hope of producing the desired results and that the United States could do little to influence the internal political forces within Iran that prevented an earlier release of the hostages. I am in general agreement with Christopher's discussion of the role of military options. It is important to keep open the possibility of invoking military options, for an international lawbreaker like Iran may understand no other deterrent. The credible threat of a forcible response may have been the only factor that dissuaded the Iranians from trying or executing the hostages.

The relationship between peaceful settlement of disputes and the threat or use of force is not easy to harmonize. Is the threat or use of force compatible with a pending proceeding before the International Court of Justice, especially after the U.N. Security Council has failed to authorize collective enforcement measures? After studying Professor Schachter's analysis of this issue, I would advise against too much deference to international institutions, especially when their impotence to resolve a particular crisis has been amply demonstrated. The International Court of Justice performed to the best of its ability, but it had no power to induce Iranian compliance. Iran's flagrant disobedience of the Court's interim order and of the Security Council's call for release of the hostages should thus have released the United States from any legal obligation not to use self-help measures.

What are the prospects for a strengthened legal framework with more effective sanctions against governments that abet the taking of hostages? Many Americans deplored the fact that a Soviet veto prevented the United Nations from adopting binding sanctions and were greatly disappointed that a number of our allies had difficulty implementing sanctions in the absence of an international legal obligation to do so. The question has been raised whether swifter resort to the Security Council might have been more effective in obtaining favorable action on sanctions; as it happened, the Afghanistan invasion, which intervened during the delay, complicated the decision-making process and thwarted the imposition of sanctions. In any event, the inability of the United Nations or our allies to put timely and effective sanctions in place points to the need for a new international agreement with mandatory and possibly automatic sanctions, as suggested by Oscar Schachter in chapter 9.

Possible sanctions pursuant to such an agreement could be automatic withdrawal of ambassadors or severance of diplomatic relations, mandatory suspension of air or other transportation links between the offending state and the states participating in the agreement, or a mandatory embargo on trade relations or financial dealings with the offending state. Each of these possibilities has problems to be thought through before deciding on a mandatory program. For example, in the Iranian hostage crisis automatic severance of diplomatic relations might have been more harmful than helpful, since it would have eliminated valuable channels of communication through the Swiss, German, Algerian, and other embassies and would have restricted the sources of information about Iran available to the outside world. To the extent that Iran's domestic political turmoil fueled and perpetuated the crisis, even a concerted sanctions program might not have achieved the release of the hostages much sooner. And as with many forms of economic sanctions, it is true that the economic injury in a given case might be greater to the states implementing the sanctions than to the target.

It thus may be difficult to reach a common ground on a type of sanction that will be likely to be effective and that states will be willing to commit themselves to in advance. But the problems in working for an international agreement toward this end are not necessarily insurmountable. A possible model is the Bonn Declaration of 1978, entered into at a summit conference among the United States and its major allies,[2] which commits the participating governments (who carry two-thirds of free world air traffic) to suspend air transport services to states that offer sanctuary to air hijackers. If this type of sanction were expanded to include other forms of transportation as well, the offending state would quickly feel its isolation. Further study of the sanctions question may suggest other effective and appropriate measures. The United States government should therefore propose mandatory sanctions against governments that abet the taking of diplomatic hostages, in the form of either a United Nations convention or an agreement among the group of allies that have already adopted mandatory sanctions against governments that offer sanctuary to air hijackers.

Role of the United Nations

The basic premise of the United Nations is an inspiration. If adhered to, the principles of the United Nations could lead to world peace and international

2. *Department of State Bulletin*, September 1978, p. 5.

security, but member nations have too often been cynical in their use of the U.N. system. Consequently, its weaknesses in operation have many times failed to solve pressing global problems. And yet we must support and maintain the United Nations as a world instrumentality in the ultimate hope it will accept responsibility for the solution of world problems.

The United Nations and its constituent agencies are here to stay. So are our close political, financial, and commercial relationships with both our allies and the developing world. When the hostages were taken—and also before and on a number of occasions since—the United States has had discouraging experiences with the United Nations and its allies on sanctions and other actions involving global crises. While recognizing the inherent weaknesses of the United Nations system in solving many world problems, it is in our long-term interest to support and maintain it as an instrumentality for promoting order in the world.

I have long been concerned about the diminishing suasion exercised by the United States and its allies in U.N. institutions and activities. Drawing on my own personal experiences as a United States Representative to the 33rd Session of the United Nations General Assembly in 1978 and a 1977 study of United States participation in international organizations performed by the Senate Committee on Government Operations which I chaired,[3] I believe that the influence of the United States continues to be submerged in the United Nations, its constituent agencies, and their bureaucracies. I have noticed the elimination of Americans from top management positions in the U.N. agencies and their replacement with personnel put in key policy positions by Third World and socialist bloc countries. While many of these do their work with diligence and integrity, others are disposed, by ideology or from national motives, to condone U.N. activity hostile to U.S. interests. The result of U.S. neglect and others' persistence is that the influence of the United States is diminishing, and the United Nations is being progressively manipulated away from our own foreign policy objectives.

Assuming no change in this state of affairs, we must face the reality that we cannot count on support or even on friendly agreement within the established world institutions on moral or peace-threatening issues affecting our basic national interests no matter how rigorously we play by the rules for the submission of disputes for peaceful institutional resolution. We must always stand prepared to act alone.

If we were to tie our own hands, when we are able to apply meaningful sanctions, in favor of (probably fruitless) efforts to achieve a meaningless,

3. Report of the Senate Committee on Government Operations, *United States Participation in International Organizations*, 95th Cong., 1st sess., 1977, Doc. No. 95–50.

watered-down consensus in some unsympathetic international institutional setting, we would only encourage future outrageous behavior by our adversaries. There are limits to any nation's power, but it is essential that the world understand that we will not cave in to any other nation's stonewalling.

If we affirm our principles by invoking the established forums for promoting international order, we must not let that process deteriorate into a shallow, meaningless consensus. It is essential to stand firmly on our position of principle and be willing to affirm it alone. Thus we maintain our credibility as a world power.

As that wise and experienced man Governor William Scranton once observed, "our allies always complain about us when we take leadership. One of the things which I learned at the United Nations . . . was no matter what people say and this includes even the Third World, it is surprising how much respect they have for strength."[4] I agree.

Presidential Authority; Congressional-Executive Relations
The Iranian hostage crisis was the first significant test of several major pieces of legislation (passed in the aftermath of Vietnam and Watergate) that had redefined standards and procedures for the exercise of presidential authority in times of crisis. The National Emergencies Act of 1976 had replaced a hodgepodge of statutory provisions with a set of uniform procedures for the declaration and termination of states of emergency and had attempted to provide for a measure of congressional control over executive power. The International Emergency Economic Powers Act of 1977 (IEEPA) had established a new framework for the peacetime exercise of powers similar to those available under the Trading With the Enemy Act, while ending the president's power to vest foreign assets except in wartime. Both the National Emergencies Act and IEEPA were the product of several years of study and enjoyed broad bipartisan support at the time of enactment. In addition, the War Powers Resolution of 1973, a far more controversial enactment passed over President Nixon's veto, was also relevant to presidential options during the Iranian crisis.

President Carter's declaration of national emergency on November 14, 1979, was the first new emergency after the passage of the reform legislation. Pursuant to this declaration, the President exercised a wide range of extraordinary powers during the crisis, including the blocking of Iranian assets, the imposition of a trade embargo, and a ban on travel to Iran. The same emergency powers formed the basis for implementation of the settlement agreement concluded on January 20, 1981.

4. Study group meeting. Cited with permission.

The hostage crisis provided the U.S. government with its most extensive experience in the application of economic sanctions to achieve a foreign policy objective. Scores of unsung public servants proposed, promulgated, and administered an elaborate array of regulations and administrative procedures for the assets freeze, the oil embargo, export controls, and special immigration restrictions. The Treasury Department's Office of Foreign Assets Control and other involved agencies were able to draw upon earlier precedents for parts of the sanctions system, as pointed out by Robert Carswell and Richard Davis in chapter 4. But never before had such a large number of measures been used so systematically, with such potential for short- and long-term impact not only on the target of the sanctions but on American economic and commercial interests.

In light of our delicate system of checks and balances, the government officials involved in this program had to anticipate at each stage the requirements imposed by possible judicial review of official action. Judicial involvement began early in the crisis, and it required urgent and continuing efforts by government officials to impress upon judges across the country the importance of restraint, since premature ruling on the legal issues might have sent damaging signals to the Iranians and their friends regarding American resolve.

Policymakers confronted with a crisis situation in the future can hardly expect to have the kind of economic leverage that was available in the Iranian case. To the extent that there is a recurrence of comparable conditions, the legal framework for dealing with foreign assets is now more clearly established than it was during the Iranian crisis, because the precedents have been set and their validity confirmed through the judicial rulings concerning Iran. This body of experience can be drawn on in a future crisis.

One issue to be considered is whether the Iranian experience points up the need for any changes in the current emergency powers legislation. Those involved in making and implementing the Carter Administration's policies felt that in general the legal authorities in existence during the crisis were adequate and proper.[5] Where there were constraints on presidential authority, they were salutary ones, stemming from fundamental values in our Constitution and embodied in our laws. The constitutional and statutory limits on what the President could do without going to Congress for implementing legislation, as well as the ever-present possibility of court challenges to the exercise of presidential power, shaped the decision-making process from the outset of the crisis through its final resolution. Although there were doubtless many occasions when the President and his

5. This view was also shared by the diverse participants in the Council study group, who considered this issue at length.

key advisers might have wished for greater control or a wider range of options, in retrospect it is clear that conferring on the President more sweeping emergency powers than those available to him in the Iranian crisis would involve unacceptable changes in the allocation of responsibilities in our constitutional system.

Indeed, as several of the chapters in this volume point out, the existence of real and credible constraints on presidential power actually worked to U.S. advantage in the final negotiations. There were Iranian demands to which the U.S. negotiators could not and would not accede, because their authority was bounded by the rule of law. This is as it should be.

Thus, my comments about presidential authority in time of emergency relate not to changing the basic terms of the emergency powers legislation but rather to ensuring that the mechanisms for the exercise of authority function in the fullest manner. In this connection the Iranian hostage crisis offers a range of examples. One area of particular interest to me is the relationship between the President and Congress during an emergency.

From my perspective as a member of the Senate at the time, I believe that most of my colleagues from both houses and both parties were in general supportive of the President's efforts during the crisis and the attention given by the executive branch to keeping the Congress informed of developments. Cyrus Vance, in his book *Hard Choices*,[6] estimates that during the crisis he and Warren Christopher spent up to two hours each day in meetings or briefing sessions with members of Congress. This sustained effort to involve the Congress deserves commendation. Without it, especially in an election year, pressure might have built within the Congress for divisive debates on the President's policies or possibly even for mandating drastic action. As it was, the steady, behind-the-scenes briefings of members of Congress served the valuable purpose of keeping Congress behind the President's efforts to reach a negotiated and honorable resolution of the crisis.

On another level, the consultative process could have been enhanced through a more direct congressional involvement in *advance* of certain major decisions, particularly the decisions to block Iranian assets and to undertake a rescue mission involving members of the armed forces. After all, both the International Emergency Economic Powers Act and the War Powers Resolution call for consultation with the Congress "in every possible instance" *before* the critical steps are taken. The term "every *possible* instance" of course implicitly acknowledges that there may be circumstances under which the President could properly act first and consult later, but those circumstances should be the rare exception.

6. Cyrus Vance, *Hard Choices: Critical Years in America's Foreign Policy* (New York: Simon and Schuster, 1983), p. 14.

The most difficult questions of congressional-executive relations arise with respect to the decision to launch the rescue mission. President Carter, in his book *Keeping Faith,*[7] recounts that he met with Senator Robert Byrd the night of Wednesday, April 23, 1980—literally on the eve of the penetration of the force into Iran—primarily to develop a short list for congressional notification concerning "possible military action." The President did not then inform Senator Byrd that a rescue mission was to commence virtually immediately. The President's own account reflects considerable ambivalence about his discussion with Senator Byrd:

> After he [Byrd] left the White House I wondered if it would have been better to involve him more directly in our exact plans for the mission. His advice would have been valuable to me then—and also twenty-four hours later.

In the case of the assets freeze, Robert Carswell and Richard Davis have noted in chapter 4 that calls to congressional leaders were made in the brief interval between the report that Iran would pull its assets out of United States banks and the President's signing of the blocking order. I doubt that any member of Congress would have wanted that action to be delayed out of a formalistic insistence on giving more advance notice or involving more members of Congress. (On the other hand, the President might have initiated preliminary consultations on a possible freeze between November 4 and 13, although it is not clear whether Congress could have contributed meaningfully to assessing the highly fluid situation in those early days.)

These examples illustrate the difficult judgments that must be made in satisfying Congress's expectation of prior consultation "in every possible instance." The timing of consultation, the identification of members to consult, the detail of explanations to be given—all these depend so much upon circumstances that it would be questionable to impart too much specificity or rigidity to the concept of consultation.

Yet the Congress and the President, in a constructive manner, should establish some flexible guidelines for both sides of the consultation process, to be brought into play in crisis situations when grave risks and high stakes demand both congressional involvement and preservation of complete secrecy. There are various ways in which Congress could promote a more productive interchange between the branches in time of crisis while at the same time grappling with the factors that sometimes deter the executive from meaningful advance consultation. I would suggest consideration of the following points, for possible adoption by each house under its rule-making authority:

7. Jimmy Carter, *Keeping Faith: Memoirs of a President* (New York: Bantam Books, 1982), pp. 513–14.

DESIGNATION OF POINTS OF CONTACT. A simple and flexible structure could be established for designating the leadership of the two houses of Congress to act as liaison with the White House on the types of issues that might arise in an emergency. I would not favor a rigid listing of individuals or committees but rather a system under which the president could discuss the matter first with the majority and minority leaders of both houses and the Speaker of the House, who would then suggest to the President what additional members, if any, should be brought into the circle at what point in time. For certain types of emergency actions, this initial consultation would point toward involving one or more members of the appropriate com- mittee or committees—whether Foreign Relations, Armed Services, Intel- ligence, or another committee whose subject matter jurisdiction would be directly relevant. In other instances special expertise might indicate involv- ing a particular member at an early stage. For a highly secret, sensitive, and urgent matter such as the rescue mission, it might be appropriate for the congressional leadership to confirm the President's judgment that security concerns mandate the narrowest possible circle. Because of the wide range of possible circumstances, the consultation system should be deliberately flexible. Of course nothing would prevent the President from deciding on his own initiative to consult a broader group of members, and nothing would foreclose the vote or legislative prerogatives of any member of Congress.

SECURITY. The executive branch's fear of leaks is one of the most se- rious deterrents to consultation about sensitive operations. From my expe- rience as a member both of the Senate and the Cabinet, and on the basis of my long-time relationships with presidents and members of Congress, I believe that no serious risk of breach of security exists from consultation with the majority and minority leaders and the Speaker of the House. The President has been chosen by all the people of our nation, and the leadership is chosen by the elected representatives of the people. If the President and the congressional leadership cannot trust one another, then our democratic process can hardly function.

Concerning the broader issue of communications with larger numbers of members and congressional staff, there may be ways for Congress to improve its self-regulation with respect to classified executive branch com- munications. If Congress wishes to promote more effective consultation between the branches, it must do its part to create conditions under which the national security will not be jeopardized by inadvertence or poor judgment.

EFFICIENCY. Secretary Vance's estimate that he spent one-quarter of his time on congressional matters and (between himself and his deputy Warren Christopher) up to two hours a day with members of Congress concerning the hostage crisis alone is a troubling statistic. It raises the valid question whether Congress itself, by more efficient organization and procedures, could contribute to easing the burdens on officials who are already overworked with grave responsibilities. Consolidation of committees of overlapping jurisdiction, as recommended by the April 1983 Report of the Senate Study Group on Senate Practice and Procedure, on which I served, would be a step in the right direction. I also urge that we adopt Secretary Vance's suggestion that House and Senate committees of concurrent jurisdiction jointly hear the statements of executive branch officials. This would avoid unnecessary duplication.

Putting in place measures along these lines *before* the next all-consuming crisis could save valuable time and contribute to the quality of interaction between the branches. Careful efforts on the part of both branches to refine the consultation process can also help ensure that presidential actions in time of emergency will have the support of Congress and will not be made unnecessarily vulnerable to challenge on procedural grounds.

As a final comment on congressional-executive relations, both the International Emergency Economic Powers Act and the War Powers Resolution contain provisions for legislative veto by concurrent resolution, similar to the measure which the Supreme Court recently held unconstitutional in *Immigration and Naturalization Service v. Chadha*.[8] Under the constitutional and statutory framework as it existed during the Iranian crisis, the President was able to take swift and strong action, subject to the possibility that Congress might at some point attempt to exercise the legislative veto feature of the statutes under which he acted. Now that the Supreme Court has held the legislative veto unconstitutional, these statutes (as well as other statutes of considerable significance to the conduct of foreign affairs) are being studied by Congress to determine whether presidential authorities should be differently defined or subjected to some other form of congressional oversight.

As Congress reviews these statutes in light of the *Chadha* ruling, it will be important to preserve the President's flexibility to respond to future emergencies promptly and effectively, with a range of authorities that are adequate to the purpose. The Iranian crisis shows the value of having these authorities already in place for immediate use when emergency conditions arise. Congress should thus retain the existing scope of emergency powers and should not impair the President's flexibility to use the powers that were invoked in the Iran crisis.

Delegating the Crisis-Management Function

The President of the United States, according to his own account and the reports of all observers, made the resolution of the hostage crisis his central

8. 103 S. Ct. 2764, 51 U.S.L.W. 4907 (June 23, 1983).

concern for the 444 days from the seizure of the hostages until their release. The consequences of this intense concentration on a single issue were the subject of debate even while it was going on and are discussed in detail elsewhere in this volume. Warren Christopher properly asks, "Is there a better way?"

Christopher's proposal—that in a comparable crisis the president should consider delegating the crisis-management function out of the White House to an interagency task force of incumbent senior officials or to an individual of special stature and qualifications—offers the numerous advantages that its proponent has so ably described. Delegation of the day-to-day aspects of crisis response should contribute to freeing up the time of the President and his chief advisers, so that they can devote adequate attention to other important responsibilities, as well as enable them to approach crisis-related decisions from a more balanced perspective. It has been pointed out that various issues—Afghanistan is just one example—might have been handled more effectively if the Iranian crisis had not consumed such an overwhelming amount of the energies of the key participants. Also, it may frequently be advisable to draw on the knowledge of those outside the President's immediate circle, who have the historical memory of comparable experiences from the past.

In future crises, the President—early in the crisis—would thus be well-advised to consider whether the Christopher model could be used to enable him better to allocate his time and judgment to the range of international and domestic issues that will always require his personal involvement.

The advisability of adopting the Christopher proposal in any given crisis will depend on the nature of the crisis, the urgency of other matters competing for presidential attention, the President's style of interaction with his key advisers, and domestic political support for the President's policies, among other factors. If military involvement is likely or imminent, the President may need to continue to use a White House crisis-management system, because the consequences of decisions to initiate or respond to uses or threats of force admit of no substitute for the President's personal participation. For this among other reasons, it is not clear that the Christopher proposal could have been implemented during the first half of the Iranian crisis. But the successful functioning of the task force chaired by Deputy Secretary Christopher in the latter phase of the crisis may serve as a useful model in future crisis situations.

The Rescue Mission; Secrecy in a Crisis

Experienced military officers have pointed out that hostage recovery operations take on the nature of raids. Raids are among the most difficult of military operations. Indeed, it is rare that one succeeds completely. An operation to rescue hostages is made all the more difficult because its objective is nondestructive, the aim being to minimize loss of life while recovering hostages and delivering them to a place of safety. This is in sharp contrast to most raids, which involve violent action, including either the holding of an objective for a period of time or destroying something of importance, before withdrawing to friendly territory.

Furthermore, raids (including rescue attempts) depend heavily on adherence to three basic requirements: simplicity of plan, surprise in carrying out the operation, and speed of execution from start to finish. And finally, extraordinary care must be taken to examine all reasonable alternatives in developing a plan, and wherever and whenever possible the raiding party should include close to 100 percent redundancy in critical equipment.

A devastating fact, which was not sufficiently appreciated in advance of the rescue mission, is that raids have a high probability of failure. Failure can consist of nonachievement of the raid's objectives or of excessive casualties in light of the results achieved.[9] In the case of the Iranian hostage rescue mission, the President, the government, and the American public were not prepared for either the fact or the consequences of failure.

Whenever a mission in the nature of a raid is conducted, it is important for the President and the military command authorities to have a carefully thought-out plan on how to handle the communications media and the Congress in case of total or partial failure, especially if American casualties are involved. This aspect of planning was neglected in the Iranian crisis, in part because of the high emphasis on secrecy surrounding the plans for the rescue mission.

Secrecy of governmental processes in a crisis is inevitably both vital and troublesome, and the Iranian hostage crisis offers vivid illustrations of the tension between the need for secrecy and the problems it breeds. In the case of both the decision to impose the freeze on Iranian assets and the planning for the ill-fated rescue mission, secrecy was critical: advance knowledge of the proposed freeze could have enabled the Iranians to mitigate its impact, and even a hint of the imminence of a rescue mission could have ruined its chances for success.

With respect to the rescue mission, the President's advisers were understandably convinced that the prospects for the rescue mission depended

9. As an example, the Son Tay raid of a North Vietnamese prisoner of war camp was technically well executed but was a total failure in terms of its ultimate objective, because the prisoners had already been removed from the targeted camp. The Hammelburg raid of a prisoner of war camp behind German lines in World War II was only partly successful, because heavy combat with German forces ensued as the rescue force returned to friendly lines. The *Mayaguez* rescue achieved the objective of freeing the ship's crew, which had been held hostage, but losses in the rescuing force were heavy. Of recent incidents, the Israeli raid of the Entebbe airport is the rare exception in being highly successful in terms of rescuing virtually all the hostages with a minimum of casualties to friendly personnel.

upon complete surprise. No one would deny the legitimacy of this concern, for even a few hours' advance warning would have made it possible for the Iranian captors to move or harm the hostages. To preserve the possibility of total surprise, the planners for the mission insisted upon restricting the circle of persons involved to the barest minimum and taking the utmost precautions to safeguard operations security. But the sacrifices toward this end were substantial. On both the military and civilian sides, in retrospect it seems possible that the extreme preoccupation with operations security prevented the planners from taking measures to anticipate (and perhaps counter) some of the very obstacles that doomed the mission to failure.

On the military side, the issue of "a seemingly nondiscriminating over-emphasis on OPSEC [operations security]" was one of the principal concerns of the Rescue Mission Report commissioned by the Joint Chiefs of Staff to examine all military aspects of the rescue mission.[10] This report, prepared under the chairmanship of the former Chief of Naval Operations, Admiral James L. Holloway III, concluded that many things that "could have been done to enhance mission success were not done because of OPSEC considerations." Among the problems identified in the report were excessive compartmentalization of the planning function, lack of a comprehensive plans review and even of a detailed written plan for the mission, inadequate exchange of information (particularly as regards the dust cloud phenomenon and statistics on helicopter failure rate), and the failure to conduct a full-scale dress rehearsal of the activities to take place at Desert One. In the execution of the mission, the paramountcy of operations security concerns dictated the decisions to use only eight helicopters, not to send a weather reconnaissance flight or a C-130 Pathfinder, and to maintain total radio silence, among other critical constraints. In retrospect it seems possible that modest easing of the concern for operations security could have enhanced the probability that six working helicopters would arrive at Desert One and that the mission might have proceeded to a successful conclusion.

Without attempting to cover every aspect of the treatment of operations security in the Holloway Report (which merits reading in its entirety), several examples will illustrate the broader points. One serious disadvantage of the extreme concern for operations security was the failure to tap valuable experts and knowledge already existing in the military, because the persons who had access to that knowledge and expertise were not included in the sharply limited number of persons involved. Veterans of previous raids, who were available, were not consulted on how the mission

10. The "Rescue Mission Report" was distributed to the press and others in Washington, D.C., in a photocopied version in August 1980.

should be conducted. Although an effort was made to bring together the most highly qualified team for the job, there were a number of senior officers who could have contributed to the planning and training without any significant risk to the security of the mission, but they were not consulted because of the obsession with secrecy. Nor was there any independent evaluation of the adequacy of the plans for the mission other than by the Joint Chiefs of Staff themselves.

A poignant example of the detrimental effects of too much secrecy is the fact that the dust cloud phenomenon—one of the most significant factors contributing to the failure of the mission—was known within the military and even discussed in a Navy intelligence handbook, but the gap was never bridged between those who possessed this knowledge and those who might have been able to use it in planning and executing the mission. As Gary Sick noted in chapter 3 and as the Holloway Report confirms, the planners of the mission had not had this item drawn to their attention and thus could neither appreciate its significance, nor brief the crew, nor put into place the relatively simple remedies that might have allowed six helicopters to reach Desert One in operational condition.

The problem was that the ad hoc nature of the organization for the mission and the obsessive concern for operations security fed upon each other. One might have been manageable without the other; together the negative effects compounded each other with worse results than were anticipated. The military's study of this problem resulted in the Holloway Report's identification of a series of steps that might have enhanced the prospects for success of the mission without prejudicing operations security. The Report's first recommendation is the creation of a standing joint task force for counterterrorist operations, which would avoid the problems associated with an ad hoc organization and would facilitate planning, training, and maintenance of command relationships while at the same time making possible the more selective exercise of operations security measures. The Holloway Report also recommends creation of a special operations advisory panel, to be composed of carefully selected high-ranking officers (active or retired), to provide senior guidance to the planners of special operations. These measures, which have been adopted by the Joint Chiefs of Staff, should provide a cohesive structure for the best operational planning and training, as well as for drawing on the talents and knowledge of those with the most directly relevant backgrounds. Within such a structure, it should be possible to maximize the flow of pertinent information to those whose own lives—as well as the nation's security—depend on it.

It should be kept in mind that in Desert One human judgment was decisively influenced, even overridden, by technology. When machines failed to operate as anticipated, the mission was abandoned. The decision to abandon the mission was a purely human response to technological uncertainty. Such contingencies must be prepared for and the participants trained accordingly.

Knowledgeable and long-experienced military officers agree with the Holloway Report's conclusion that the ad hoc nature of planning, organizing, and executing the Iranian hostage rescue attempt severely hampered the conduct of the mission. I understand that the recommendation of the Holloway Report to establish a force capable of executing such missions in the future has been effectively carried out.

Nevertheless, military officers make the point that the President should not overlook the capability of the Joint Chiefs. It is generally preferable to use the established chain of command in planning, supporting, and executing as difficult an operation as a rescue attempt deep in hostile territory. The Joint Chiefs have operational resources at hand. They have means of handling the security problem; and the command organization provides for an orderly, thorough, and properly reviewed approach to planning and execution. With the revised organization resulting from the Holloway recommendations, a command structure and a force to carry out such missions will be available under any future conditions similar to the Iranian situation. Therefore, several good alternatives are now available. Forces within a unified command can be used for a rescue attempt under the control of a unified commander; or the special force resulting from the Holloway recommendations could be kept under the direct control of the Joint Chiefs or put under the control of a unified commander. In any event, the problem of "ad hocism" has been dealt with by the military's review, and responsible solutions are now in place.

These comments are not meant to imply criticism of President Carter's handling of the mission as Commander-in-Chief from the point of view of military command responsibilities. Military professionals, including the authors of the Holloway Report, agree that President Carter's handling of the military role in the hostage crisis should be considered the "textbook case" of the proper relationship between the Commander-in-Chief and his military subordinates. Whatever may be said about the rescue mission as a military failure, it did not fail because of second-guessing from the White House of decisions best left to the commander in the field or other military professionals. On this level the system worked as it is supposed to.

On the civilian side there has never been a review comparable to the military study of the rescue mission. It is important to ensure that the input of civilian agencies is brought to bear in timely fashion. From the accounts available in published sources, as well as what I understand from those who are in a position to know, it seems clear that key officials were either not consulted at all or were brought into the process so late that their advice could not be of maximum value. The Director of the National Security Agency, who surely cannot be suspected of any propensity to divulge official secrets and who surely had (or had access to) intelligence information of the highest utility, was not even told of the planning for the rescue mission until he requested an explanation for activities that came to his attention through his own agency sources. Secretary of State Vance's opportunity to participate in the process came only after the President's decision had already been taken, and Vance was not allowed to obtain the views of other State Department officials with expertise on such questions as the likely Soviet response. In all future crises, it will be important to maximize the quality of information available to the President even in circumstances when maximum secrecy is required.

The Role of the Press

John Chancellor of NBC once privately observed that the press is like fire or flood, in that it can sometimes be coaxed in certain directions but rarely forced against its natural inclinations. Was the press in the hostage crisis like a fire raging out of control or was it the administration that fanned the flames?[11]

Despite recurring criticisms that the crisis was excessively "hyped" by either the press or the White House or both, in my view it is not realistic to suggest that the press could or should have reduced the level of attention that it devoted to the crisis over the 444 days. The intense public interest in the crisis, the degree of concern devoted to it by the White House, and the level of media attention all were interdependent. But it is fair to ask whether there are lessons for the future to be drawn from assessing the nature and quality of press coverage.

Overall, I believe that the press performed commendably and responsibly during the crisis. Editors and journalists had to make difficult decisions about the printing of stories when lives were at stake. One example was that a number of journalists in Iran knew for weeks that six American diplomats were hidden in the Canadian Embassy. These journalists demonstrated admirable discretion in refraining from printing the story until after the diplomats could escape safely.

On the other hand, former administration officials have expressed some concern that certain disclosures might have jeopardized the welfare of the hostages, either by complicating the government's efforts to negotiate or by worsening the plight of individual hostages. This concern began early on. When Ramsey Clark and William Miller were sent as the President's personal emissaries, the news media's coverage even before the Ayatollah Kho-

11. The observation by Mr. Chancellor was made in a Council study group discussion.

meini had committed himself to receiving them was considered by many to have precipitated the rebuff they received. Determining cause and effect is probably impossible, however, in a situation involving so many unknowns and imponderables.

After the Clark-Miller experience, the administration tried—with mixed success—to preserve the secrecy of sensitive negotiating channels. Hamilton Jordan's book, *Crisis: The Last Year of the Carter Presidency,*[12] describes not only measures such as Jordan's clandestine travel in disguise but also a direct call from President Carter to publisher Katharine Graham aimed at preventing publication of the story of the "French connection" negotiations. These efforts may have postponed but did not prevent press coverage: Jordan's interlocutors themselves were apparently sources for some American journalists in Tehran.

With respect to individual hostages and their fate, the State Department was highly concerned about publication of any stories that might suggest intelligence backgrounds of any of the hostages. Such information (which was developed by some journalists but might not otherwise have been known to the Iranian captors) could have been fatal in the event espionage trials had ever commenced. Hostage families were concerned about release of this kind of information, as well as unconfirmed reports of hostage suicide attempts and other worrisome stories. In situations of this kind, the media had to balance the news value of the item against the concerns expressed by government representatives and family members.

The search for daily (and photogenic) developments had several negative by-products. There was a tendency, possibly inevitable but worth noting, to emphasize the short rather than the long term; beginning well before the hostage seizure, more could have been done to analyze long-term trends in Iranian society and Islam generally. Another unfortunate by-product of the intensity of media coverage was the spotlight for 444 days on the hostage families, who can hardly be said to have welcomed the attention.

Furthermore, the pressure to report something new each day produced incentives for making premature reports based on unconfirmed or unreliable sources. Former administration officials have criticized the media's treatment of several incidents where press sources were of dubious credibility. One such instance was press coverage of a fabricated letter of apology from Carter to Khomeini; it seemed to some officials that the Iranian version of the story was treated almost on a par with the administration's immediate denial. Other officials noted the absence of any factual basis for persistent speculation about a pre-election "October surprise" and pointed

12. Hamilton Jordan, *Crisis: The Last Year of the Carter Presidency* (New York: Putnam Publishing Group, 1982), pp. 149, 169.

to repeated errors in coverage of the content of the Algerian negotiations conducted by Warren Christopher.

In drawing lessons for the future from press coverage of the crisis, the relationship to other themes is apparent. As long as the President makes the crisis his top priority, the media will not be likely to do otherwise. Adoption of the Christopher proposal for crisis management would take the spotlight off the President and could result in better and more accurate news coverage. If there were a working group with a very good staff, its own experts, and a means for briefing the press, this would eliminate misconceptions and would be better for all concerned.[13] Under such conditions the crisis task force's liaison with the press could be either its head or a designated spokesman respected by the press. Referral of all press inquiries to the liaison could also assist in striking the proper balance between the interest in security of deliberations and diplomatic communications, on the one hand, and the public's right to know, on the other.

Promoting Understanding and Communication Between the United States and Developing Countries

Over and over again, the chapters in this volume illustrate the tremendous gulf in understanding between the United States and Iran. There is a deep ignorance in the United States concerning the thinking and culture of the developing countries of the world. We should establish stronger understanding on a global noncrisis basis. Cultural and educational exchanges should be promoted. We should make every effort to cultivate good relations through diplomatic representation of the highest quality, patiently learning long-term trends. By so doing, we will have greater resources to help solve problems between us in times of crisis.

We should use in a crisis the resources in our academic institutions. The Iranian hostage crisis underscores the need for the United States government to encourage language training and area studies both within and outside the government. In the crisis, it was indispensable to have Foreign Service officers and others who spoke Farsi to communicate with persons in Iran, and the government also drew heavily upon the understanding of the culture and religion of Iran among scholars in universities who could help interpret Iranian behavior. We should ensure that we are never short of such skills. This requires government officials to acquire unusual language skills. And it requires help for universities in establishing centers for scholars studying different cultures. Strengthening these institutions would serve the dual purpose of improving training over the long term and providing additional sources of knowledge to be consulted when needed.

13. Comment by John Chancellor, in the same discussion cited above in note 11.

In the wake of the Iranian hostage seizure, one of the questions that was frequently asked was why (after a considerable reduction from the 1,400 at the height of our relationship with Iran) we still had more than 65 members of our diplomatic and consular staff in that highly volatile country. Harold Saunders explained the government's reasoning in Chapter 1: our global interests require us to maintain a presence even in countries where the risk of personal danger is great. In the case of Iran, our long-term interests included oil supply, military coordination, intelligence exchange, and other relationships of both economic and geopolitical significance. Drawing down our diplomatic and consular staff and dependents was prudent at a time of extreme deterioration of relations, but even in retrospect it is hard to say that we should have withdrawn from Iran totally at any point between February and November 1979. Since we will never be able to eliminate all personal risks from our diplomacy, the sacrifices of the professional diplomats who run these risks should be appropriately recognized, with special compensation where circumstances warrant.

Two further observations should be made on the general subject of the Foreign Service. First, it is clear that the members of that organization who were held hostage by the Iranians acted throughout with great courage, dignity, and integrity. Isolated from almost all knowledge of what efforts were being made to secure their release, their spirits, while occasionally cast down, were never in despair. The nation was justly proud of their performance, and the risks and pressures under which the Foreign Service operates almost routinely in today's world deserve greater attention and regard than is usually given.

Second, the U.S. government—from the President down—kept the human dimension of the crisis constantly in mind. The attention and concern that were given to the families and relatives of those in Iran by the government was outstanding. There may have been occasional slips, and some family members inevitably felt these at times; but, overall, the continuous effort within the government to keep families informed, to seek information from all sources on the condition of the hostages, and to protect them from harm was precisely what Americans should expect from their government but do not always receive.

Severing relations is a step of last resort. Asymmetrical as it may have seemed at the time, the presence of some Iranian diplomats in the United States from November 1979 to April 1980 did keep open at least one formal channel of communication. Their expulsion was an appropriate symbolic gesture after it became clear that their continued presence would bring the crisis no closer to resolution. Our government quite properly complied with the requirements of the Vienna Convention on Diplomatic Relations at all times, resisting emotional cries for imprisoning the Iranian diplomats.

In the event of another embassy seizure or comparable crisis, we will need to rely, as we did in the Iranian crisis, on the assistance of third countries to substitute for our own disrupted channels of communication and sources of information and to help open up avenues to the authorities in the country involved. We owe an immense debt of gratitude to the Algerians, the Canadians, the Germans, the Panamanians, the Swiss, and people in numerous other countries whose support was invaluable during the crisis. The Iranian experience shows the value of maintaining constructive relationships with nonaligned countries throughout the world: when we are dealing with other nonaligned countries, their assistance may be more useful than that of our formal allies. It is also significant that well after the organs of the United Nations had ceased to be actively involved in attempting to resolve the crisis, the United Nations as an institution-in-being still had a role to play: Prime Minister Rajai in his visit to New York in the fall of 1980 experienced firsthand the disapproval of virtually the entire diplomatic community for Iran's continued holding of American diplomatic personnel.

Unconventional mediators and ad hoc methods of dispute resolution may become more common in future crises. In the Iranian crisis we coupled reliance on traditional international institutions—the U.N. Security Council and Secretary-General, the International Court of Justice—with innovative mechanisms brought into being for this special purpose. For a period of time in early 1980 it looked as though an ad hoc commission organized under U.N. auspices might be the vehicle for resolving the crisis rather than the permanent institutions whose weaknesses as well as strengths were evident during the crisis.

This nation has a wide range of transnational enterprises whose professional personnel have diplomatic as well as technical skills and a network of existing and potential contacts. The Iranian crisis provides a valuable case study of productive cooperation between the public and private sectors. Throughout, regular liaison was maintained between banks, businesses, their counsel, and government officials. The private communication lines supplemented government channels. Both the Christopher and Hoffman chapters attest to the fact that careful, selective, and controlled involvement of responsible individuals from the private sector can provide the government with a valuable resource in a crisis. Such individuals can serve a mediation role and facilitate solutions with a privacy not always maintained on a governmental level. We should be aware of this resource and use it.

In any future crisis it will be necessary to draw upon all the resources and insights at our disposal to understand the other side's objectives and motivations. This process is critical for crisis prevention as well as crisis resolution.

The Iranian hostage crisis was a crisis of the future. It was a time when our antagonists refused even to acknowledge the existence of basic norms that all nations had hitherto considered sacrosanct. The very premises of traditional international diplomacy were thrown to the winds. There were neither precedents nor solutions for the urgent challenges. In similar crises in the future, it will be wrong and indeed dangerous to assume that the other actors are motivated by the kinds of forces that shape American behavior. We cannot control or even predict the crises of the future, but we can continue in our search for ways to apply the lessons of the past.

DOCUMENTARY APPENDIX

APPENDIX A

Executive Order Blocking Iranian Property, November 14, 1979, and Report to the Congress by the President Concerning Blocking of Iranian Assets, November 14, 1979

EXECUTIVE ORDER

BLOCKING IRANIAN GOVERNMENT PROPERTY

Pursuant to the authority vested in me as President by the Constitution and laws of the United States including the International Emergency Economic Powers Act, 50 U.S.C.A. sec. 1701 et seq., the National Emergencies Act, 50 U.S.C. sec. 1601 et seq., and 3 U.S.C. sec. 301,

I, Jimmy Carter, President of the United States, find that the situation in Iran constitutes an unusual and extraordinary threat to the national security, foreign policy and economy of the United States and hereby declare a national emergency to deal with that threat.

I hereby order blocked all property and interests in property of the Government of Iran, its instrumentalities and controlled entities and the Central Bank of Iran which are or become subject to the jurisdiction of the United States or which are in or come within the possession or control of persons subject to the jurisdiction of the United States.

The Secretary of the Treasury is authorized to employ all powers granted to me by the International Emergency Economic Powers Act to carry out the provisions of this order.

This order is effective immediately and shall be transmitted to the Congress and published in the Federal Register.

Jimmy Carter

THE WHITE HOUSE

November 14, 1979

TO THE CONGRESS OF THE UNITED STATES:

Pursuant to Section 204(b) of the International Emergency
Economic Powers Act, 50 U.S.C.A. § 1703, I hereby report to
the Congress that I have today exercised the authority granted
by this Act to block certain property or interests in property
of the Government of Iran, its instrumentalities and controlled
entities and the Central Bank of Iran.

1. The circumstances necessitating the exercise of this
authority are the recent events in Iran and the recent actions
of the Government of Iran.

2. These events and actions put at grave risk the personal
safety of United States citizens and the lawful claims of
United States citizens and entities against the Government
of Iran and constitute an extraordinary threat to the national
security and foreign policy of the United States.

3. Consequently, I have ordered blocked all property
and interests in property of the Government of Iran, its
instrumentalities and controlled entities and the Central
Bank of Iran which are or become subject to the jurisdiction
of the United States or which are or come within the possession
of persons subject to the jurisdiction of the United States.
I have authorized the Secretary of the Treasury to employ all
powers granted to me by the International Emergency Economic
Powers Act to carry out the blocking.

4. Blocking property and property interests of the
Government of Iran, its instrumentalities and controlled
entities and the Central Bank of Iran will enable the
United States to assure that these resources will be
available to satisfy lawful claims of citizens and entities
of the United States against the Government of Iran.

5. This action is taken with respect to Iran for the
reasons described in this report.

[signature]

THE WHITE HOUSE,
NOV 1 4 1979

APPENDIX B
Order of the President and Secretary of State Delegating Authority to Warren M. Christopher, January 18, 1981

January 18, 1981

By the authority vested in the undersigned, as President and as Secretary of State, respectively, each of us hereby delegates to Warren M. Christopher, Deputy Secretary, Department of State, authority (1) to approve the texts of the Declaration of the Government of the Democratic and Popular Republic of Algeria relating to the release of the U.S. diplomats and nationals being held as hostages and to the resolution of claims of United States nationals against Iran, the Undertakings of the Governments of the United States and Iran with respect to such Declaration, and the Declaration of the Democratic and Popular Republic of Algeria concerning the settlement of claims by the Government of the United States of America and the Government of the Islamic Republic of Iran, to all of which the United States is today adhering, and to evidence such approvals by his initials or signature, and (2) to approve and to execute on behalf of the United States the Escrow Agreement and any other documents related to such Declarations and Undertakings.

THE WHITE HOUSE,

APPENDIX C

Telexes from the Government of Iran on the Basis of Which U.S. Banks Paid over $5.3 Billion, January 20, 1981

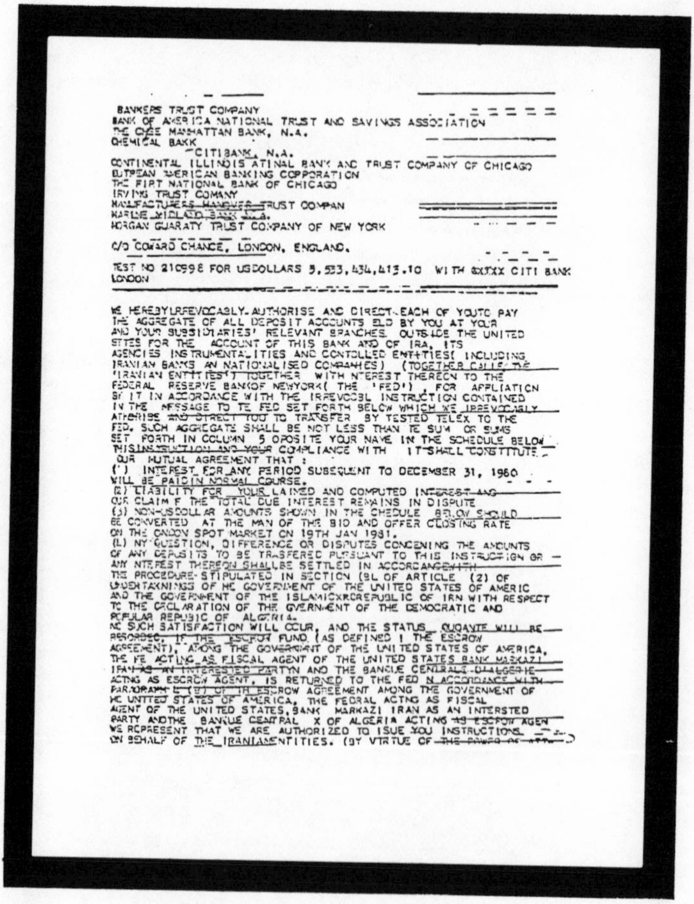

BANKERS TRUST COMPANY
BANK OF AMERICA NATIONAL TRUST AND SAVINGS ASSOCIATION
THE CHEE MANHATTAN BANK, N.A.
CHEMICAL BAKK
CITIBANK, N.A.
CONTINENTAL ILLINOIS ATINAL BANK AND TRUST COMPANY OF CHICAGO
EUTPEAN AMERICAN BANKING CORPORATION
THE FIRT NATIONAL BANK OF CHICAGO
IRVING TRUST COMANY
MANUFACTURERS HANOVER TRUST COMPAN
MARINE MIDLAND BANK N.A.
MORGAN GUARATY TRUST COMPANY OF NEW YORK

C/O COWARD CHANCE, LONDON, ENGLAND.

TEST NO 210998 FOR USDOLLARS 5,533,434,413.10 WITH XXXXX CITI BANK LONDON

WE HEREBYIRREVOCABLY-AUTHORISE AND DIRECT EACH OF YOUTO PAY THE AGGREGATE OF ALL DEPOSIT ACCOUNTS ELD BY YOU AT YOUR AND YOUR SUBSIDIARIES' RELEVANT BRANCHES OUTSIDE THE UNITED STTES FOR THE ACCOUNT OF THIS BANK AND OF IRA, ITS AGENCIES INSTRUMENTALITIES AND CONTOLLED ENTITIES(INCLUDING IRANIAN BANKS AN NATIONALISED COMPANIES) (TOGETHER CALLE THE 'IRANIAN ENTITIES') TOGETHER WITH NTEREST THEREON TO THE FEDERAL RESERVE BANKOF NEWYORK(THE 'FED') , FOR APPLIATION BY IT IN ACCORDANCE WITH THE IRREVOCBL INSTRUCTION CONTAINED IN THE MESSAGE TO TE FED SET FORTH BELOW WHICH WE IRREVOCABLY ATHORISE AND DIRECT YOU TO TRANSFER BY TESTED TELEX TO THE FED. SUCH AGGREGATE SHALL BE NOT LESS THAN TE SUM OR SUMS SET FORTH IN COLUMN 5 OPOSITE YOUR NAME IN THE SCHEDULE BELOW THISINSTRUCTION AND YOUR COMPLIANCE WITH IT SHALL CONSTITUTE OUR MUTUAL AGREEMENT THAT :
(') INTEREST FOR ANY PERIOD SUBSEQUENT TO DECEMBER 31, 1980 WILL BE PAIDIN NORMAL COURSE.
(2) LIABILITY FOR YOUR LAIMED AND COMPUTED INTEREST AND OUR CLAIM F THE TOTAL DUE INTEREST REMAINS IN DISPUTE
(3) NON-USDOLLAR AMOUNTS SHOWN IN THE CHEDULE BELOW SHOULD BE CONVERTED AT THE MAN OF THE BID AND OFFER CLOSING RATE ON THE ONDON SPOT MARKET ON 19TH JAN 1981.
(L) NY QUISTION, DIFFERENCE OR DISPUTES CONCENING THE AMOUNTS OF ANY DEPOSITS TO BE TRASFERED PURSUANT TO THIS INSTRUCTION OR ANY NTEREST THEREON SHALLBE SETTLED IN ACCORDANCE WITH THE PROCEDURE STIPULATED IN SECTION (9L OF ARTICLE (2) OF UNDERTAKNINGS OF HE GOVERNMENT OF THE UNITED STATES OF AMERIC AND THE GOVERNMENT OF THE ISLAMICXRCREPUBLIC OF IRN WITH RESPECT TO THE DECLARATION OF THE GVERNMENT OF THE DEMOCRATIC AND POPULAR REPUBIC OF ALGERIA.
NO SUCH SATISFACTION WILL CCUR, AND THE STATUS QUOANTE WILL BE RESORBED, IF THE ESCROW FUND (AS DEFINED I THE ESCROW AGREEMENT), AMONG THE GOVERNMENT OF THE UNITED STATES OF AMERICA, THE FE ACTING AS FISCAL AGENT OF THE UNITED STATES BANK MARKAZI IRAN AS AN INTERESTED PARTYN AND THE BANQUE CENTRALE D'ALGERIE ACTING AS ESCROW AGENT, IS RETURNED TO THE FED N ACCORDANCE WITH PARAGRAPH 5 (B) OF TH ESCROW AGREEMENT AMONG THE GOVERNMENT OF HE UNITED STATES OF AMERICA, THE FEDRAL ACTNG AS FISCAL AGENT OF THE UNITED STATES, BANK MARKAZI IRAN AS AN INTERSTED PARTY ANDTHE BANQUE CENTRAL X OF ALGERIA ACTING AS ESCROW AGEN
WE REPRESENT THAT WE ARE AUTHORIZED TO ISUE YOU INSTRUCTIONS ON BEHALF OF THE IRANIANENTITIES. (BY VIRTUE OF THE POWER OF ATT...)

Page 3:

```
MARINE
MIDLAND                        6,700,000.00            356,231.81
BANK, N.A.                                             ─ ─ ─ ─
EUROPEAN                                               ─ ─ ─ ─
AMERICAN                       6,800,000.00            991,422.22
BANKING                                                ─ ─ ─ ─ ─
CORP.

COL. 1                              COL. 4                         COL. 5
NAME OF BANK               XBOU.S.BANKS                            TOTAL
                           XXXXXXXXXX
                           CLAIMEDXXXXA

At
XBXXX
BANKERS TRUST COMPANY      DLRS.18,13,775.88    DCRST624,575,335.78
CITIBANK, N.A.            DLRS. 6,073,428.82    DLRS.521,386,973.37
THE CHASE MANHATTAN       DLRS.11,142,660.63    DLRS.460,63,63.68
BANK (N.A.)              (1530,000,000/DM90,000,000,000)
                                                DLRS 63,359,576.43

MORGAN GUARANTY TRUST  DLRSM WRGUUNDRWMT
OFANY OF N.Y.(DM50,000,00/YENLL,000,000,000)    DLRS. 98,163,445.23

IRVING TRUST COMPANY                            DLRS.216,443,822.00

CONTINENTAL ILLINOIS  CLUS.    682,831.17       DLS. 62,680,831.17
NATIONAL BANK AND TRUST
CPANY OF CHICAGO (DM30000,000/SF20,000,000)

                                                DLRS 27,95,854.40
FIRST-NAT-CTATE-BANK-    DLRS.   325,212.25     CLRS. 70,299,947.25
OF CHICAGO               (YEN 1,000,000000)

                                                DLRS.  5,756,019.00
XXXXXXXXBANKXXXXXXXXXXXXXXXXXXXXXXXXXXXXXXXX
CHEMICAL BANK                                   DLRS 23,675,163.63
BXXS

BANK OF AMERICA          DLRS.91,142,605.13     DLRS.2,608,331,740.51
N.T. NO S.A.

MANUFACTURERS                                   DLRS.460,532,155.87
HADER TRUST
COMPANY

MARINE MIDLAND           DLRS.    107,285.28    DLRS.  7,263,515.19
                                                            BANKS
EUROPEAN AMERICAN        DLRS.    173,162.93    DLRS.  7,961,583.1
BANKING CORP.

212399  MISK 1R
WE HAVE TRANSMITTED THE FOLLOWING INSTRCTION TO FEDRESERVE
NEWYORK
```

Page 2:

```
SCHEDULE

COL 1          COL 2
NAME OF        TOTAL PRINCIPAL O     ┌─────┐
BANK           DEPSIT                UCOOODITIONAL
               DOLLARS               INTEREST
                                     DOLARS
BANKERS
TRUST          533,234,15.91         70,788,721,778
COMPAN

CITIBANK,      445,024,827.77        70,788,721.778
N.A.

THE CHAS       393,213,876.13        55,46,147,10
MANHATTAN
BANK (N.A.)
              (SF20,000,000,000/DM50,000,000,000)
MORGAN GUARANTY  3,860,000.00        5,565,816.12
TRUST COMPANY
OF NEW YORK
              DM50,000,000/YEN44,000,000,000)
                                     12,185,532.00

                 45,000,000.00       411,000,000
IRVING TRUST
COMPANY          TE,750,00.00        31,639,822.00
CONTINENTAL
ILL INOIS                            8,454,500.00
NATIONAL BANK
AND TRUST
COMPANY OF
CHICAGO
              (DM90,000,000,000/SF20,000,000,000)
                 24,989,011.00       1,955,473.40
FIRST-
-NCL-)-7,(       7,000,700.00        9,774,705.00
S4,123-45)
              (YEN 1,000,000,000)
                 5,--716.00          57,703.00
CHEMICAL BANK    20,000,000.00       31,675,958.81
BANK OF        2,597,793,136.57      319,075,96.51
AMERICA
NAT. AND
S.A.
MLFACT-        410,053,855.87        70,499,100.00
URES HANOVER
TRST COMPANY
```

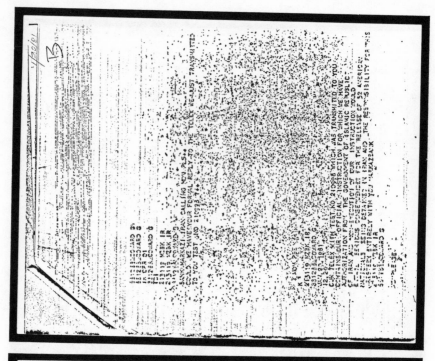

TO: FEDERAL RESERVE BANK, NEW YORK
FROM: BANK MARKAZI IRAN, TEHRAN

3,667,430,443.10 FROM THE BANKS NAMED   YOU WILL BE RECEIVING AN AGGREGATE
RELATING TO IRANIAN DEPOSITS OUTSIDE THE UNITED STATES,
THE FORM OF WHICH IS ATTACHED HERE TO DICK

YOU ARE AUTHORIZED TO TRANSFER SUCH AGGREGATE AMOUNT AND ANY
FUTURE AMOUNT RECEIVED UNDER SUCH INSTRUCTION TO THE BANK OF
ENGLAND ... IN THEIR BOOKS IN THE NAME OF
BANQUE CENTRALE D'ALGERIE, AS ESCROW AGENT UNDER THE ESCROW
AGREEMENT DATED JANUARY 19, 1981, AMONG THE GOVERNMENT OF THE
UNITED STATES OF AMERICA, THE FEDERAL RESERVE BANK OF NEW YORK,
ACTING AS FISCAL AGENT OF THE UNITED STATES, BANK MARKAZI
IRAN AS AN INTERESTED PARTY, AND BANQUE CENTRALE
D'ALGERIE AS ESCROW AGENT, YOU WILL APPLY THE FUNDS THUS
TRANSFERRED TO YOU, TOGETHER WITH THEIR FUNDS AS PROVIDED IN
SUCH ESCROW AGREEMENT UNDER THE UNDERTAKING OF THE GOVERNMENT OF
THE UNITED STATES OF AMERICA AND THE GOVERNMENT OF THE ISLAMIC
REPUBLIC OF IRAN WITH RESPECT TO THE DECLARATION OF THE GOVERNMENT OF

IN THE EVENT OF A RELEASE INSTRUCTION GIVEN PURSUANT TO SECTION
4.B OF THE ESCROW AGREEMENT, YOU WILL RECEIVE US DOLLARS
3,667,430,443.10 PURSUANT TO PAR 2.A OF THE UNDERTAKINGS. THE
US RELEASED AMOUNT TO PAR 2.A OF THE UNDERTAKINGS, THE
BY US UPON RECEIPT OF THE U.S. RELEASED AMOUNT, TO APPLY SUCH
U.S. RELEASED AMOUNT TO PAYMENT IN FULL OF ALL SYNDICATED
LOANS BY A BANK SYNDICATE OF WHICH A U.S. BANK OR ITS AGENCIES,
INSTRUMENTALITIES AND CONTROLLED ENTITIES, IS A MEMBER, IRANIAN
BANKS AND NATIONALIZED COMPANIES IN WHICH A U.S. BANK IS A
PARTICIPANT. IN ACCORDANCE WITH AN ORDER, DIRECTIVE OR LICENSE
HOLDING INTEREST IN SUCH ACCORD, FROM THE U.S. TREASURY DEPARTMENT
SINCE THE BANKS REFERRED TO ABOVE ARE PAYING INTEREST THROUGH
JANUARY 18, 1981 ON THE DEPOSITS TRANSFERRED BY ORDER OF BANK
MARKAZI, YOU SHALL NOT BE REQUIRED TO PAY FOR SUCH INTEREST ON SUCH
INDEBTEDNESS AT APPLICABLE NON-DEFAULT CONTRACT RATES THROUGH
JANUARY 18, 1981.

ANY PORTION OF THE U.S. RELEASED AMOUNT NOT APPLIED TO PAY
SUCH INDEBTEDNESS BECAUSE OF PREPAYMENT OF OTHERWISE SHALL
SEGREGATED IN A SEGREGATED ACCOUNT REFERRED TO IN PARAGRAPH
IN THE EVENT OF A TERMINATION INSTRUCTION GIVEN PURSUANT O
SECTION 4.B OF THE ESCROW AGREEMENT, YOU WILL REMIT ANY AMOUNT
BANKS IN THE RESPECTIVE AMOUNTS THAT THE TRANSFERRED DEPOSIT AS
RECEIPT (IN OUR INSTRUCTIONS TO THEM REFERRED TO ABOVE), ALL IN
ACCORDANCE WITH AN ORDER, DIRECTIVE OR LICENSE ISSUED BY THE
U.S. TREASURY, IN WHICH CASE THE STATUS QUO ANTE SHALL BE RESTORED.

YOURS FAITHFULLY
BANK MARKAZI IRAN, TEHRAN

WELL RECEIVED PLS?
THE CORRECTIONS WILL BE NECESSARY
WE WILL OBTAIN A CORRECTED TAPE AND RUN IT TO YOU AND ASK YOU
TO RELAY US SEIZE CONFIRMATION THAT IT IS CORRECT.
THIS WILL TAKE US A LITTLE TIME. WE WILL DO THIS AS QUICKLY AS
POSSIBLE
PLEASE CONFIRM UNLESS TODO??

APPENDIX D
Declarations, Undertakings, and Escrow Agreement of the Algerian Accords

DECLARATION OF THE GOVERNMENT OF
THE DEMOCRATIC AND POPULAR REPUBLIC OF ALGERIA

The Government of the Democratic and Popular Republic
of Algeria, having been requested by the Governments of
the Islamic Republic of Iran and the United States of
America to serve as an intermediary in seeking a mutually
acceptable resolution of the crisis in their relations
arising out of the detention of the 52 United States
nationals in Iran, has consulted extensively with the
two governments as to the commitments which each is
willing to make in order to resolve the crisis within the
framework of the four points stated in the Resolution
of November 2, 1980, of the Islamic Consultative Assembly
of Iran. On the basis of formal adherences received
from Iran and the United States, the Government of Algeria
now declares that the following interdependent commitments
have been made by the two governments:

GENERAL PRINCIPLES

The undertakings reflected in this Declaration are
based on the following general principles:

    A. Within the framework of and pursuant to the pro-
        visions of the two Declarations of the Government
        of the Democratic and Popular Republic of Algeria,
        the United States will restore the financial posi-
        tion of Iran, in so far as possible, to that which

- 2 -

existed prior to November 14, 1979. In this context, the United States commits itself to ensure the mobility and free transfer of all Iranian assets within its jurisdiction, as set forth in Paragraphs 4-9.

B. It is the purpose of both parties, within the framework of and pursuant to the provisions of the two Declarations of the Government of the Democratic and Popular Republic of Algeria, to terminate all litigation as between the government of each party and the nationals of the other, and to bring about the settlement and termination of all such claims through binding arbitration. Through the procedures provided in the Declaration relating to the Claims Settlement Agreement, the United States agrees to terminate all legal proceedings in United States courts involving claims of United States persons and institutions against Iran and its state enterprises, to nullify all attachments and judgments obtained therein, to prohibit all further litigation based on such claims, and to bring about the termination of such claims through binding arbitration.

POINT I: NON-INTERVENTION IN IRANIAN AFFAIRS

1. The United States pledges that it is and from now on will be the policy of the United States not to

intervene, directly or indirectly, politically or militarily, in Iran's internal affairs.

POINTS II AND III: RETURN OF IRANIAN ASSETS AND SETTLEMENT OF U.S. CLAIMS

2. Iran and the United States (hereinafter "the parties") will immediately select a mutually agreeable Central Bank (hereinafter "the Central Bank") to act, under the instructions of the Government of Algeria and the Central Bank of Algeria (hereinafter "the Algerian Central Bank") as depositary of the escrow and security funds hereinafter prescribed and will promptly enter into depositary arrangements with the Central Bank in accordance with the terms of this Declaration. All funds placed in escrow with the Central Bank pursuant to this Declaration shall be held in an account in the name of the Algerian Central Bank. Certain procedures for implementing the obligations set forth in this Declaration and in the Declaration of the Democratic and Popular Republic of Algeria Concerning the Settlement of Claims by the Government of the United States and the Government of the Islamic Republic of Iran (hereinafter "the Claims Settlement Agreement") are separately set forth in certain Undertakings of the Government of the United States of America and the Government of the Islamic Republic of Iran with Respect to the Declaration of the Democratic and Popular Republic of Algeria.

- 4 -

3. The depositary arrangements shall provide that, in the event that the Government of Algeria certifies to the Algerian Central Bank that the 52 U.S. nationals have safely departed from Iran, the Algerian Central Bank will thereupon instruct the Central Bank to transfer immediately all monies or other assets in escrow with the Central Bank pursuant to this Declaration, provided that at any time prior to the making of such certification by the Government of Algeria, each of the two parties, Iran and the United States, shall have the right on seventy-two hours notice to terminate its commitments under this Declaration. If such notice is given by the United States and the foregoing certification is made by the Government of Algeria within the seventy-two hour period of notice, the Algerian Central Bank will thereupon instruct the Central Bank to transfer such monies and assets. If the seventy-two hour period of notice by the United States expires without such a certification having been made, or if the notice of termination is delivered by Iran, the Algerian Central Bank will thereupon instruct the Central Bank to return all such monies and assets to the United States, and thereafter the commitments reflected in this Declaration shall be of no further force and effect.

- 5 -

Assets in the Federal Reserve Bank

4. Commencing upon completion of the requisite escrow arrangements with the Central Bank, the United States will bring about the transfer to the Central Bank of all gold bullion which is owned by Iran and which is in the custody of the Federal Reserve Bank of New York, together with all other Iranian assets (or the cash equivalent thereof) in the custody of the Federal Reserve Bank of New York, to be held by the Central Bank in escrow until such time as their transfer or return is required by Paragraph 3 above.

Assets in Foreign Branches of U.S. Banks

5. Commencing upon the completion of the requisite escrow arrangements with the Central Bank, the United States will bring about the transfer to the Central Bank, to the account of the Algerian Central Bank, of all Iranian deposits and securities which on or after November 14, 1979, stood upon the books of overseas banking offices of U.S. banks, together with interest thereon through December 31, 1980, to be held by the Central Bank, to the account of the Algerian Central Bank, in escrow until such time as their transfer or return is required in accordance with Paragraph 3 of this Declaration.

- 6 -

Assets in U.S. Branches of U.S. Banks

6. Commencing with the adherence by Iran and the United States to this Declaration and the Claims Settlement Agreement attached hereto, and following the conclusion of arrangements with the Central Bank for the establishment of the interest-bearing Security Account specified in that Agreement and Paragraph 7 below, which arrangements will be concluded within 30 days from the date of this Declaration, the United States will act to bring about the transfer to the Central Bank, within six months from such date, of all Iranian deposits and securities in U.S. banking institutions in the United States, together with interest thereon, to be held by the Central Bank in escrow until such time as their transfer or return is required by Paragraph 3.

7. As funds are received by the Central Bank pursuant to Paragraph 6 above, the Algerian Central Bank shall direct the Central Bank to (1) transfer one-half of each such receipt to Iran and (2) place the other half in a special interest-bearing Security Account in the Central Bank, until the balance in the Security Account has reached the level of U.S. $1 billion. After the U.S. $1 billion balance has

- 7 -

been achieved, the Algerian Central Bank shall direct all funds received pursuant to Paragraph 6 to be transferred to Iran. All funds in the Security Account are to be used for the sole purpose of securing the payment of, and paying, claims against Iran in accordance with the Claims Settlement Agreement. Whenever the Central Bank shall thereafter notify Iran that the balance in the Security Account has fallen below U.S. $500 million, Iran shall promptly make new deposits sufficient to maintain a minimum balance of U.S. $500 million in the Account. The Account shall be so maintained until the President of the arbitral tribunal established pursuant to the Claims Settlement Agreement has certified to the Central Bank of Algeria that all arbitral awards against Iran have been satisfied in accordance with the Claims Settlement Agreement, at which point any amount remaining in the Security Account shall be transferred to Iran.

Other Assets in the U.S. and Abroad

8. Commencing with the adherence of Iran and the United States to this Declaration and the attached Claims Settlement Agreement and the conclusion of arrangements for the establishment of the Security Account, which arrangements will be concluded within 30 days from the date of this Declaration, the United States will act to

- 9 -

Iran before the International Court of Justice and will thereafter bar and preclude the prosecution against Iran of any pending or future claim of the United States or a United States national arising out of events occurring before the date of this Declaration related to (A) the seizure of the 52 United States nationals on November 4, 1979, (B) their subsequent detention, (C) injury to the United States property or property of the United States nationals within the United States Embassy compound in Tehran after November 3, 1979, and (D) injury to the United States nationals or their property as a result of popular movements in the course of the Islamic Revolution in Iran which were not an act of the Government of Iran. The United States will also bar and preclude the prosecution against Iran in the courts of the United States of any pending or future claim asserted by persons other than the United States nationals arising out of the events specified in the preceding sentence.

- 8 -

bring about the transfer to the Central Bank of all Iranian financial assets (meaning funds or securities) which are located in the United States and abroad, apart from those assets referred to in Paragraphs 5 and 6 above, to be held by the Central Bank in escrow until their transfer or return is required by Paragraph 3 above.

9. Commencing with the adherence by Iran and the United States to this Declaration and the attached Claims Settlement Agreement and the making by the Government of Algeria of the certification described in Paragraph 3 above, the United States will arrange, subject to the provisions of U.S. law applicable prior to November 14, 1979, for the transfer to Iran of all Iranian properties which are located in the United States and abroad and which are not within the scope of the preceding paragraphs.

Nullification of Sanctions and Claims

10. Upon the making by the Government of Algeria of the certification described in Paragraph 3 above, the United States will revoke all trade sanctions which were directed against Iran in the period November 4, 1979, to date.

11. Upon the making by the Government of Algeria of the certification described in Paragraph 3 above, the United States will promptly withdraw all claims now pending against

-10-

POINT IV: RETURN OF THE ASSETS
OF THE FAMILY OF THE FORMER SHAH

12. Upon the making by the Government of Algeria of the certification described in Paragraph 3 above, the United States will freeze, and prohibit any transfer of, property and assets in the United States within the control of the estate of the former Shah or of any close relative of the former Shah served as a defendant in U.S. litigation brought by Iran to recover such property and assets as belonging to Iran. As to any such defendant, including the estate of the former Shah, the freeze order will remain in effect until such litigation is finally terminated. Violation of the freeze order shall be subject to the civil and criminal penalties prescribed by U.S. law.

13. Upon the making by the Government of Algeria of the certification described in Paragraph 3 above, the United States will order all persons within U.S. jurisdiction to report to the U.S. Treasury within 30 days, for transmission to Iran, all information known to them, as of November 3, 1979, and as of the date of the order, with respect to the property and assets referred to in Paragraph 12. Violation of the requirement will be subject to the civil and criminal penalties prescribed by U.S. law.

-11-

14. Upon the making by the Government of Algeria of the certification described in Paragraph 3 above, the United States will make known, to all appropriate U.S. courts, that in any litigation of the kind described in Paragraph 12 above the claims of Iran should not be considered legally barred either by sovereign immunity principles or by the act of state doctrine and that Iranian decrees and judgments relating to such assets should be enforced by such courts in accordance with United States law.

15. As to any judgment of a U.S. court which calls for the transfer of any property or assets to Iran, the United States hereby guarantees the enforcement of the final judgment to the extent that the property or assets exist within the United States.

16. If any dispute arises between the parties as to whether the United States has fulfilled any obligation imposed upon it by Paragraphs 12-15, inclusive, Iran may submit the dispute to binding arbitration by the tribunal established by, and in accordance with the provisions of, the Claims Settlement Agreement. If the tribunal determines that Iran has suffered a loss as a result of a failure by the United States to fulfill such obligation, it shall make an appropriate award in favor of Iran which may be enforced by Iran in the courts of any nation in accordance with its laws.

DECLARATION OF THE GOVERNMENT OF
THE DEMOCRATIC AND POPULAR REPUBLIC OF ALGERIA
CONCERNING THE SETTLEMENT OF CLAIMS BY
THE GOVERNMENT OF THE UNITED STATES OF AMERICA AND THE
GOVERNMENT OF THE ISLAMIC REPUBLIC OF IRAN

The Government of the Democratic and Popular Republic of Algeria, on the basis of formal notice of adherence received from the Government of the Islamic Republic of Iran and the Government of the United States of America, now declares that Iran and the United States have agreed as follows:

Article I

Iran and the United States will promote the settlement of the claims described in Article II by the parties directly concerned. Any such claims not settled within six months from the date of entry into force of this Agreement shall be submitted to binding third-party arbitration in accordance with the terms of this Agreement. The aforementioned six months' period may be extended once by three months at the request of either party.

Article II

1. An international arbitral tribunal (the Iran-United States Claims Tribunal) is hereby established for the purpose of deciding claims of nationals of the United States against Iran and claims of nationals of Iran against the United States, and any counterclaim which arises out of the same contract, transaction or occurrence that

---

-12-

SETTLEMENT OF DISPUTES

17. If any other dispute arises between the parties as to the interpretation or performance of any provision of this Declaration, either party may submit the dispute to binding arbitration by the tribunal established by, and in accordance with the provisions of, the Claims Settlement Agreement. Any decision of the tribunal with respect to such dispute, including any award of damages to compensate for a loss resulting from a breach of this Declaration or the Claims Settlement Agreement, may be enforced by the prevailing party in the courts of any nation in accordance with its laws.

Initialled on January 19, 1981

by _Warren M. Christopher_
Warren M. Christopher
Deputy Secretary of State
of the Government of the United States
By virtue of the powers vested in him by his Government
as deposited with the Government of Algeria

- 2 -

constitutes the subject matter of that national's claim, if such claims and counterclaims are outstanding on the date of this Agreement, whether or not filed with any court, and arise out of debts, contracts (including transactions which are the subject of letters of credit or bank guarantees), expropriations or other measures affecting property rights, excluding claims described in Paragraph 11 of the Declaration of the Government of Algeria of January 19 , 1981, and claims arising out of the actions of the United States in response to the conduct described in such paragraph, and excluding claims arising under a binding contract between the parties specifically providing that any disputes thereunder shall be within the sole jurisdiction of the competent Iranian courts, in response to the Majlis position.

2. The Tribunal shall also have jurisdiction over official claims of the United States and Iran against each other arising out of contractual arrangements between them for the purchase and sale of goods and services.

3. The Tribunal shall have jurisdiction, as specified in paragraphs 16-17 of the Declaration of the Government of Algeria of January 19 , 1981, over any dispute as to the interpretation or performance of any provision of that Declaration.

- 3 -

Article III

1. The Tribunal shall consist of nine members or such larger multiple of three as Iran and the United States may agree are necessary to conduct its business expeditiously. Within ninety days after the entry into force of this Agreement, each government shall appoint one-third of the members. Within thirty days after their appointment, the members so appointed shall by mutual agreement select the remaining third of the members and appoint one of the remaining third President of the Tribunal. Claims may be decided by the full Tribunal or by a panel of three members of the Tribunal as the President shall determine. Each such panel shall be composed by the President and shall consist of one member appointed by each of the three methods set forth above.

2. Members of the Tribunal shall be appointed and the Tribunal shall conduct its business in accordance with the arbitration rules of the United Nations Commission on International Trade Law (UNCITRAL) except to the extent modified by the Parties or by the Tribunal to ensure that this Agreement can be carried out. The UNCITRAL rules for appointing members of three-member tribunals shall apply mutatis mutandis to the appointment of the Tribunal.

3. Claims of nationals of the United States and Iran that are within the scope of this Agreement shall

- 4 -

be presented to the Tribunal either by claimants themselves or, in the case of claims of less than $250,000,
by the government of such national.

4. No claim may be filed with the Tribunal more than
one year after the entry into force of this Agreement
or six months after the date the President is appointed,
whichever is later. These deadlines do not apply to the
procedures contemplated by Paragraphs 16 and 17 of the
Declaration of the Government of Algeria of January 19,
1981.

Article IV

1. All decisions and awards of the Tribunal shall
be final and binding.

2. The President of the Tribunal shall certify,
as prescribed in paragraph 7 of the Declaration of the
Government of Algeria of January 19, 1981, when all
arbitral awards under this Agreement have been satisfied.

3. Any award which the Tribunal may render against
either government shall be enforceable against such
government in the courts of any nation in accordance with
its laws.

Article V

The Tribunal shall decide all cases on the basis of
respect for law, applying such choice of law rules and
principles of commercial and international law as the

- 5 -

Tribunal determines to be applicable, taking into account
relevant usages of the trade, contract provisions and
changed circumstances.

Article VI

1. The seat of the Tribunal shall be The Hague, The
Netherlands, or any other place agreed by Iran and the
United States.

2. Each government shall designate an Agent at the
seat of the Tribunal to represent it to the Tribunal
and to receive notices or other communications directed
to it or to its nationals, agencies, instrumentalities,
or entities in connection with proceedings before the
Tribunal.

3. The expenses of the Tribunal shall be borne
equally by the two governments.

4. Any question concerning the interpretation or
application of this Agreement shall be decided by the
Tribunal upon the request of either Iran or the
United States.

Article VII

For the purposes of this Agreement:

1. A "national" of Iran or of the United States, as
the case may be, means (a) a natural person who is a
citizen of Iran or the United States; and (b) a corporation or other legal entity which is organized under the
laws of Iran or the United States or any of its states or

- 6 -

territories, the District of Columbia or the Commonwealth of Puerto Rico, if, collectively, natural persons who are citizens of such country hold, directly or indirectly, an interest in such corporation or entity equivalent to fifty per cent or more of its capital stock.

2. "Claims of nationals" of Iran or the United States, as the case may be, means claims owned continuously, from the date on which the claim arose to the date on which this Agreement enters into force, by nationals of that state, including claims that are owned indirectly by such nationals through ownership of capital stock or other proprietary interests in juridical persons, provided that the ownership interests of such nationals, collectively, were sufficient at the time the claim arose to control the corporation or other entity, and provided, further, that the corporation or other entity is not itself entitled to bring a claim under the terms of this Agreement. Claims referred to the arbitration Tribunal shall, as of the date of filing of such claims with the Tribunal, be considered excluded from the jurisdiction of the courts of Iran, or of the United States, or of any other court.

3. "Iran" means the Government of Iran, any political subdivision of Iran, and any agency, instrumentality, or entity controlled by the Government of Iran or any political subdivision thereof.

- 7 -

4. The "United States" means the Government of the United States, any political subdivision of the United States, and any agency, instrumentality or entity controlled by the Government of the United States or any political subdivision thereof.

Article VIII

This Agreement shall enter into force when the Government of Algeria has received from both Iran and the United States a notification of adherence to the Agreement.

Initialed on January 19, 1981

by _Warren M. Christopher_
   Warren M. Christopher
   Deputy Secretary of State
   of the Government of the United States
By virtue of the powers vested in him by his Government
as deposited with the Government of Algeria

UNDERTAKINGS OF THE GOVERNMENT OF THE UNITED STATES OF AMERICA AND THE GOVERNMENT OF THE ISLAMIC REPUBLIC OF IRAN WITH RESPECT TO THE DECLARATION OF THE GOVERNMENT OF THE DEMOCRATIC AND POPULAR REPUBLIC OF ALGERIA

1. At such time as the Algerian Central Bank notifies the Governments of Algeria, Iran, and the United States that it has been notified by the Central Bank that the Central Bank has received for deposit in dollar, gold bullion, and securities accounts in the name of the Algerian Central Bank, as escrow agent, cash and other funds, 1,632,917.779 ounces of gold (valued by the parties for this purpose at U.S.$0.9397 billion), and securities (at face value) in the aggregate amount of U.S.$7.955 billion, Iran shall immediately bring about the safe departure of the 52 U.S. nationals detained in Iran. Upon the making by the Government of Algeria of the certification described in Paragraph 3 of the Declaration, the Algerian Central Bank will issue the instructions required by the following paragraph.

2. Iran having affirmed its intention to pay all its debts and those of its controlled institutions, the Algerian Central Bank acting pursuant to Paragraph 1 above will issue the following instructions to the Central Bank:

(A) To transfer U.S.$3.667 billion to the Federal Reserve Bank of New York to pay the unpaid principal of and interest through December 31, 1980 on (1) all loans and credits made by a syndicate of banking institutions, of which a U.S. banking institution is a member, to the

-2-

Government of Iran, its agencies, instrumentalities or controlled entities, and (2) all loans and credits made by such a syndicate which are guaranteed by the Government of Iran or any of its agencies, instrumentalities or controlled entities.

(B) To retain U.S. $1.418 billion in the Escrow Account for the purpose of paying the unpaid principal of and interest owing, if any, on the loans and credits referred to in Paragraph (A) after application of the U.S. $3.667 billion and on all other indebtedness held by United States banking institutions of, or guaranteed by, the Government of Iran, its agencies, instrumentalities or controlled entities not previously paid, and for the purpose of paying disputed amounts of deposits, assets, and interest, if any, owing on Iranian deposits in U.S. banking institutions. Bank Markazi and the appropriate United States banking institutions shall promptly meet in an effort to agree upon the amounts owing. In the event of such agreement, the Bank Markazi and the appropriate banking institution shall certify the amount owing to the Central Bank of Algeria which shall instruct the Bank of England to credit such amount to the account, as appropriate, of the Bank Markazi or of the Federal Reserve Bank of New York in order to permit payment to the appropriate banking institution. In the event that within 30 days any U.S. banking institution and the Bank Markazi are unable to agree upon the

ESCROW AGREEMENT

This Escrow Agreement is among the Government of the United States of America, the Federal Reserve Bank of New York (the "FED") acting as fiscal agent of the United States, Bank Markazi Iran, as an interested party, and the Banque Centrale d'Algerie acting as Escrow Agent.

This Agreement is made to implement the relevant provisions of the Declaration of the Government of Algeria of January 19, 1981 (the "Declaration"). These provisions concern the establishment of escrow arrangements for Iranian property tied to the release of United States nationals being held in Iran.

1. In accordance with the obligations set forth in paragraph 4 of the Declaration, and commencing upon the entry into force of this Agreement, the Government of the United States will cause the FED to:

(A) Sell, at a price which is the average for the middle of the market, bid and ask prices for the three business days prior to the sale, all U.S. Government securities in its custody or control as of the date of sale, which are owned by the Government of Iran, or its agencies, instrumentalities or controlled entities; and

-3-

amounts owed, either party may refer such dispute to binding arbitration by such international arbitration panel as the parties may agree, or failing such agreement within 30 additional days after such reference, by the Iran-United States Claims Tribunal. The presiding officer of such panel or tribunal shall certify to the Central Bank of Algeria the amount, if any, determined by it to be owed, whereupon the Central Bank of Algeria shall instruct the Bank of England to credit such amount to the account of the Bank Markazi or of the Federal Reserve Bank of New York in order to permit payment to the appropriate banking institution. After all disputes are resolved either by agreement or by arbitration award and appropriate payment has been made, the balance of the funds referred to in this Paragraph (B) shall be paid to Bank Markazi.

(C) To transfer immediately to, or upon the order of, the Bank Markazi all assets in the Escrow Account in excess of the amounts referred to in Paragraphs (A) and (B).

Initialed on January 19, 1981

by _Warren M. Christopher_
Warren M. Christopher
Deputy Secretary of State
of the Government of the United States
By virtue of the powers vested in him by his Government
as deposited with the Government of Algeria

- 2 -

(B) Transfer to the Bank of England as depositary for credit to accounts on its books in the name of the Banque Centrale d'Algerie, as Escrow Agent under this Agreement, all securities (other than the aforementioned U.S. Government securities), funds (including the proceeds from the sale of the aforementioned U.S. Government securities), and gold bullion of not less than the same fineness and quality as that originally deposited by the Government of Iran, or its agencies, instrumentalities or controlled entities, which are in the custody or control of the FED and owned by the Government of Iran, or its agencies, instrumentalities or controlled entities as of the date of such transfer.

When the FED transfers the above Iranian property to the Bank of England, the FED will promptly send to the Banque Centrale d'Algerie a document containing all information necessary to identify that Iranian property (type, source, character as principal or interest).

Specific details relating to securities, funds and gold bullion to be transferred by the FED under this paragraph 1 are attached as Appendix A.

- 3 -

2. Pursuant to the obligations set forth in paragraphs 5, 6 and 8 of the Declaration, the Government of the United States will cause Iranian deposits and securities in foreign branches and offices of United States banks, Iranian deposits and securities in domestic branches and offices of United States banks, and other Iranian assets (meaning funds or securities) held by persons or institutions subject to the jurisdiction of the United States, to be transferred to the FED, as fiscal agent of the United States, and then by the FED to the Bank of England for credit to the account on its books opened in the name of the Banque Centrale d'Algerie as Escrow Agent under this Agreement (the Iranian securities, funds and gold bullion mentioned in paragraph 1 above and deposits, securities and funds mentioned in this paragraph 2 are referred to collectively as "Iranian property").

3. Insofar as Iranian property is received by the Bank of England from the FED in accordance with this Agreement, the Iranian property will be held by the Bank of England in the name of the Banque Centrale d'Algerie as Escrow Agent as follows:

- 4 -

---- The securities will be held in one or more securities custody accounts at the Bank of England in the name of the Banque Centrale d'Algerie as Escrow Agent under this Agreement.

---- The deposits and funds will be held in one or more dollar accounts opened at the Bank of England in the name of Banque Centrale d'Algerie as Escrow Agent under this Agreement. These deposits and funds will bear interest at rates prevailing in money markets outside the United States.

---- The gold bullion will be held in a gold bullion custody account at the Bank of England, in the name of the Banque Centrale d'Algerie as Escrow Agent under this Agreement.

---- It will be understood that the Banque Centrale d'Algerie shall have no liability for any reduction in the value of the securities, bullion, and monies held in its name as Escrow Agent at the Bank of England under the provisions of this Agreement.

- 5 -

4. (a) As soon as the Algerian Government certifies in writing to the Banque Central d'Algerie that all 52 United States nationals identified in the list given by the United States Government to the Algerian Government in November, 1980, now being held in Iran, have safely departed from Iran, the Banque Centrale d'Algerie will immediately give the instructions to the Bank of England specifically contemplated by the provisions of the Declaration and the Undertakings of the Government of the United States of America and the Government of the Islamic Republic of Iran with respect to the Declaration of the Government of the Democratic and Popular Republic of Algeria, ~~and the Implementing Technical Classifications and Directions arising therefrom, all three of~~ which are made part of this Agreement.

The contractory parties should the notice is good faith to render any difficulty that could arise in the course of implementing this Agreement.

(b) In the event that

(i) either the Government of Iran or the Government of the United States notifies the Government of Algeria in writing that it has given notice to terminate its commitments under the Declaration referred to above; and

(ii) a period of 72 hours elapses after the receipt by the Government of Algeria of such notice, during which period the Banque Centrale d'Algerie has not given the Bank

- 6 -

of England the instruction described in subparagraph (a) above,

the Banque Centrale d'Algerie will immediately give the instructions to the Bank of England specifically contemplated by the provisions of the Declaration, and the Undertakings of the Government of the United States of America and the Government of the Islamic Republic of Iran with respect to the Declaration of the Government of the Democratic and Popular Republic of Algeria and the Implementing Technical Clarifications and Directions arising therefrom.

(c) If the certificate by the Government of Algeria referred to in subparagraph (a) has been given before the United States Government has effectively terminated its commitment under the Declaration, the Iranian property shall be transferred as provided in subparagraph (a) of this paragraph 4.

(d) The funds and deposits held by the Bank of England under this Agreement will earn interest at rates prevailing in money markets outside the United States after their transfer to the account of the Banque Centrale d'Algerie, as Escrow Agent, with the Bank of England, and such interest will be included as part of the Iranian property for the purposes of subparagraphs (a) and (b) of this paragraph 4.

- 7 -

5. On the date of the signing of this Agreement by the four parties hereto, the Banque Centrale d'Algerie and the FED will enter into a Technical Arrangement with the Bank of England to implement the provisions of this Agreement.

Pursuant to that Technical Arrangement between the FED, the Bank of England and the Banque Centrale d'Algerie, the FED shall reimburse the Bank of England for losses and expenses as provided in paragraph 10 thereof. The FED will not charge the Banque Centrale d'Algerie for any expenses or disbursements related to the implementation of this Agreement.

6. This Agreement will become effective as soon as it has been signed by the four parties to it and the Banque Centrale d'Algerie and the FED have entered into the Technical Arrangement with the Bank of England referred to in paragraph 5 of this Agreement.

7. Throughout its duration, this Agreement may be amended, canceled, or revoked only with the written concurrence of all four of the signatory parties.

8. Nothing in this Agreement shall be considered as constituting, in whole or in part, a waiver of any immunity to which the Banque Centrale d'Algerie is entitled.

ESCROW AGREEMENT

APPENDIX A

Securities, Gold Bullion, and Funds to be transferred by the Federal Reserve Bank of New York

International Bank for Reconstruction and Development Securities $35 million (face value)

Gold Bullion   1,632,917.746 fine ounces of gold, good delivery, London bars of a fineness of 995 parts per 1,000 or better

Funds   Approximately $1.38 billion

-8-

9. A French language version of this Agreement will be prepared as soon as practicable. The English and French versions will be equally authentic and of equal value.

10. This Agreement may be executed in counterparts, each of which constitutes an original.

In Witness whereof, the parties hereto have signed this Agreement on January 20, 1981.

For the Government of the United States of America

_____

For the Federal Reserve Bank of New York as fiscal agent of the United States

_____

For the Bank Markazi Iran

_____

For the Banque Centrale d'Algerie

_____

بسم الله

Téhéran, January 20th. 1981

I hereby, confirm that I agree with the following changes to the text of the ESCROW AGREEMENT among the Government of the United States of America, the Federal Reserve Bank of New York acting as fiscal agent of the United States, Bank Markazi Iran as interested party and the Banque Centrale d'Algérie acting as ESCROW agent.

1- At the end of paragraph 4 (A), after "attached to the declaration" the words "and the implementing technical clarifications and directions arising therefrom, all three of "are deleted, and the following sentence which is the last sentence of the said paragraph is added "The contracting parties resolve to work in good faith to resolve any difficulty that could arise in the course of implementing this agreement".

2- At the end of paragraph 4 (B) (II) the words "and the implementing technical clarifications and directions arising therefrom" are deleted.

Signed,

Esfandiar Rouchidpadeh

on behalf of Bank Markazi Iran

I HEREBY CERTIFY THAT THIS
ENGLISH-LANGUAGE DOCUMENT IS A TRUE
COPY OF A COPY OF THE ORIGINAL
DOCUMENT WHICH HAS BEEN OFFICIALLY
SUPPLIED TO US.

WAYNE G. MIELE

Study Group of the Council on Foreign Relations and the Association of the Bar of the City of New York

THE IRANIAN HOSTAGE CRISIS IN RETROSPECT: IMPLICATIONS FOR THE FUTURE

Chairman: Abraham A. Ribicoff, Special Counsel, Kaye Scholer Fierman Hays & Handler

Co-Directors: John Temple Swing, Vice President and Secretary, Council on Foreign Relations
                 Donald H. Rivkin, Senior Partner, Rivkin Sherman and Levy (now Schnader, Harrison, Segal & Lewis)

MEETINGS

March 30, 1982   The Diplomatic Negotiating Tracks
  Discussion Leader: Harold H. Saunders, Resident Fellow, American Enterprise Institute
  Commentator: I. William Zartman, Director of African Studies, School of Advanced International Studies, The Johns Hopkins University

May 4, 1982   The Role of Economic Sanctions—Part I
  Discussion Leaders: Robert Carswell, Partner, Shearman & Sterling
                          Richard J. Davis, Partner, Weil Gotshal & Manges

                        The Question of Military Intervention
  Discussion Leader: Gary G. Sick, Research Associate, Middle East Institute, Columbia University

May 27, 1982   The Role of Economic Sanctions—Part II
    Discussion Leaders: Robert Carswell
                                Richard J. Davis

                            The Problem of Settlement
    Discussion Leader: John E. Hoffman, Jr., Partner, Shearman &
                                    Sterling

September 29, 1982   The Role of the Media in Resolving the Crisis
    Discussion Leader: John Chancellor, Commentator, NBC
    Commentators: Jody Powell, Jody Powell and Associates, Inc.
                                Arnold Raphel, Deputy Director, Bureau of Politi-
                                    co-Military Affairs, Department of State

October 27, 1982   The Final Stage of the Hostage Crisis Negotiations
    Author: Roberts B. Owen, Partner, Covington & Burling

November 22, 1982   International Legal Issues Raised by the Crisis
    Author: Oscar Schachter, Professor of International Law
                                    and Diplomacy, Columbia Law School

December 13, 1982   Evolving Iranian Attitudes during and after the
                                    Crisis
    Discussion Leader: Shaul Bakhash, Visiting Associate Professor of
                                    Middle   Eastern   History,   Princeton
                                    University
    Commentator: Farhad Kazemi, Associate Professor of Politics
                                    and Director, Center for Near Eastern Stud-
                                    ies, New York University

January 10, 1983   Review of Saunders Chapter
    Author: Harold H. Saunders, Resident Fellow, American
                                    Enterprise Institute

January 27, 1983   Military Intervention in Crisis Situations
    Discussion Leaders: Major General Alfred Gray, USMC, Commanding
                                    General, Second Marine Division
                                Admiral James L. Holloway III, USN (Ret.), for-
                                    merly Chief of Naval Operations

April 12, 1983   Domestic Constitutional Aspects of the Crisis
    Discussion Leaders: Gerhard Casper, Dean, University of Chicago
                                    Law School

Lloyd N. Cutler, Partner, Wilmer Cutler & Pickering

October 3, 1983   Authors' Review Meeting
Presider: Abraham A. Ribicoff, Special Counsel, Kaye Scholer Fierman Hays & Handler

PARTICIPANTS

Abraham A. Ribicoff, Chairman—Kaye Scholer Fierman Hays & Handler
John Temple Swing, Group Co-Director—Council on Foreign Relations
Donald H. Rivkin, Group Co-Director—Rivkin Sherman and Levy (now Schnader, Harrison, Segal & Lewis)
Malcolm R. Schade, Rapporteur—Skadden Arps Slate Meagher & Flom
Kenneth Lee Adelman—U.S. Arms Control and Disarmament Agency
William P. Bundy—*Foreign Affairs*
Robert Carswell—Shearman & Sterling
Gerhard Casper—University of Chicago
John Chancellor—NBC News
Warren M. Christopher—O'Melveny & Myers
Lloyd N. Cutler—Wilmer Cutler & Pickering
Richard J. Davis—Weil Gotshal & Manges
Adrian W. deWind—Paul Weiss Rifkind Wharton & Garrison
William Diebold, Jr.—Council on Foreign Relations
Grace Darling Griffin—Council on Foreign Relations
Stephen R. Grummon—Department of State
Fred Haynes—Vought Corporation (now with LTV Aerospace and Defense Co.)
Louis Henkin—Columbia University
John E. Hoffman, Jr.—Shearman & Sterling
Moorhead C. Kennedy, Jr.—Cathedral Peace Institute (now with the Council for International Understanding)
Paul H. Kreisberg—Council on Foreign Relations
L. Bruce Laingen—National Defense University
Winston Lord—Council on Foreign Relations
Edward Marschner—Fox Glynn & Melamed
Michael J. O'Neill—formerly *The New York Daily News*
Roberts B. Owen—Covington & Burling
James B. Pearson—LeBoeuf Lamb Leiby and MacRae
Leland S. Prussia—Bank of America
Harold H. Saunders—American Enterprise Institute
Oscar Schachter—Columbia University
Elaine Sciolino—Council on Foreign Relations (now at *The New York Times*)

William W. Scranton—formerly Permanent Representative to the United
  Nations
Gary G. Sick—Ford Foundation
Gaddis Smith—Yale University
Admiral Stansfield Turner, USN (Ret.)—formerly Central Intelligence
  Agency
Cyrus R. Vance—Simpson Thacher & Bartlett
Robert B. von Mehren—Debevoise & Plimpton
I. William Zartman—Johns Hopkins University

NOTES ON SOURCES AND
ACKNOWLEDGMENTS

INTRODUCTION: WARREN CHRISTOPHER

In addition to my own memory and files and the thorough documentation provided by the chapters that follow, the recollections and views of President Carter and his senior advisers have all been set forth in their respective memoirs, and I have refreshed my memory with theirs: Jimmy Carter, *Keeping Faith: Memoirs of a President* (New York: Bantam Books, 1982); Cyrus R. Vance, *Hard Choices: Critical Years in America's Foreign Policy* (New York: Simon and Schuster, 1983); Harold Brown, *Thinking About National Security: Defense and Foreign Policy in a Dangerous World* (Boulder, Colo.: Westview Press, 1983); Zbigniew Brzezinski, *Power and Principle: Memoirs of the National Security Adviser, 1977–1981* (New York: Farrar, Straus, and Giroux, 1983); Jody Powell, *The Other Side of the Story* (New York: Morrow, 1984); Hamilton Jordan, *Crisis: The Last Year of the Carter Presidency* (New York: Putnam Publishing Group, 1982).

I also appreciate expert help in the preparation of this introduction from John Holum, Esq., a member of the State Department's Policy Planning Staff in 1979–81, now of the Washington, D.C. bar.

CHAPTERS 1, 2, AND 7: HAROLD H. SAUNDERS

In developing the outlines for chapters 1, 2, and 7, I drew initially on three documents, in addition to memory: One was a statement written by me in February 1981 and presented before several congressional committees as the starting point for my testimony in hearings on the settlement worked out with Iran that led to freeing the hostages. The second was an unclassified paper written by Foreign Service Officer Henry Precht entitled "The Hostage Crisis in Iran: 1979–81." It was released to the press as a public paper by the outgoing Carter Administration at the time of former President Carter's visit to Wiesbaden on January 22, 1981, to greet the returning hostages. These two documents, along with the other statements and testimony, are printed in *Iran's Seizure of the United States Embassy,* Hearings before the Committee on Foreign Affairs, House of Representatives, 97th Cong., 1st sess., February 17, 19, 25, and March 11, 1981, pp. 3–24 and 25–83. My statement along with others on the technical aspects of the Iranian-U.S. settlement also appear in *Iranian Asset Settlement,* Hearings before the Committee on Banking, Housing, and Urban Affairs, U.S. Senate, 97th Cong., 1st sess., To Explore the Intricacies of the Iranian Asset Agreement and the Role of U.S. Banks in the Fashioning of That Agreement, February 19, 1981. The third document was a personal communication to me by William Miller on the Ramsey Clark-William Miller mission in November 1979. The final text reflects detailed research in my own files and individual consultations and interviews with a number of my professional colleagues and with other sources, including American professors and foreigners who were in close communication with Iranians during the crisis but who have asked not to be cited by name.

No effort is made to duplicate the significant individual accounts of Washington policymaking already published: President Carter's own memoir, *Keeping Faith: Memoirs of a President* (New York: Bantam Books, 1982); Hamilton Jordan's account in *Crisis: The Last Year of the Carter Presidency* (New York: Putnam Publishing Group, 1982) of those negotiations in which he and I participated together; Zbigniew Brzezinski, *Power and Principle: Memoirs of the National Security Adviser, 1977–81* (New York: Farrar, Straus, and Giroux, 1983); and Cyrus R. Vance, *Hard Choices: Critical Years in America's Foreign Policy* (New York: Simon and Schuster, 1983). There is also the account of one negotiating track from a limited perspective in Pierre Salinger's *America Held Hostage: The Secret Negotiations* (Garden City: Doubleday, 1981).

Three other publications are useful for anyone approaching this subject:
- *The Iran Hostage Crisis: A Chronology of Daily Developments,* Report Prepared for the Committee on Foreign Affairs, U.S. House of Representatives, by Clyde R. Mark, the Foreign Affairs and National Defense Division, Congressional Research Service, Library of Congress (Washington, GPO, March 1981).
- *The Iran Hostage Crisis: A Chronology of Daily Developments, January 1–25, 1981* (as above, May 1981).
- "America in Captivity: Points of Decision in the Hostage Crisis," *The New York Times Magazine,* Special Issue, May 17, 1981.

I also appreciated reading the manuscript of Gary Sick's excellent forthcoming book, *All Fall Down: America's Encounter with the Iranian Revolution* (New York: Random House, Spring 1985), and am grateful for permission to cite sections covering both the Iranian revolution and the hostage crisis. It is invaluable for his personal account of most of the White House policy meetings and for the detailed attention he was able to focus on developments within Iran.

William Miller, now Associate Dean at the Fletcher School of Law and Diplomacy, provided a written personal account of the Clark-Miller mission.

Moorhead C. Kennedy, Jr., now Director of the Council for International Understanding in New York, shared with me the transcript of his interview with C. R. Devine, Chairman, International Federation of the Periodical Press and Vice President, *Reader's Digest.*

I owe particular thanks to more than two dozen former members of the Iran Working Group, to a number of the former hostages and their wives, and to other colleagues in the Department of State. Many of them read the next-to-last draft of these chapters, met with me for a long evening hosted by the Council on Foreign Relations, and provided detailed written comments. I also appreciate the perspectives of members of the study group formed by the Council on Foreign Relations and the Association of the Bar of the City of New York. The coauthors of this volume, most of them close colleagues and fast friends through the 444-day ordeal, were of course the ultimate critics.

I am grateful to the American Enterprise Institute for Public Policy Research in Washington for the opportunity since leaving government to study the larger question of U.S. relations with nations whose world view, political processes, and instruments of influence are different from ours. My experience with revolutionary Iran was a significant factor in moving me to that study.

Finally, very special thanks to Joan Rambo for making this project her own. She had an important hand in turning the final draft from a professional's dry account into a human story. She assembled the multitude of comments in an efficiently usable way and helped with the research. She made her own editorial suggestions, which I followed carefully. Her patience in transcribing, revising, and preparing the manuscript in presentable form was exceptional.

CHAPTER 3: GARY SICK

Except for specific citations, the information in chapter 3 is drawn from my unpublished personal notes. I am grateful to the members of the study group on the hostage crisis of the Council on Foreign Relations and the Association of the Bar of the City of New York for their helpful comments and suggestions. I particularly appreciate the efforts of Brenda S. Reger, Director of the Office of Information Policy and Security Review of the National Security Council, who coordinated the security review with such dispatch and sensitivity. However, the accuracy of all facts and judgments in this chapter is my sole responsibility.

CHAPTERS 4 AND 5: ROBERT CARSWELL and RICHARD J. DAVIS

Statements of fact and descriptions of events included in chapters 4 and 5 are based on specifically cited sources, published documents, our files located at the Treasury Department, or our recollections or those with whom we consulted. Various members of the Iran study group at the Council on Foreign Relations read portions or versions of the chapters and offered helpful suggestions and corrections. The chapters were also read and commented on by Robert H. Mundheim, former General Counsel of the Treasury Department, Dennis O'Connell, Director of the Office of Foreign Assets Control, and Robert R. Newcomb, Deputy (Trade, Tariff and Regulatory Affairs) to the Assistant Secretary of the Treasury (Enforcement and Operations). The portions of chapter 5 mentioning the Bank of England were discussed with Christopher W. McMahon, Deputy Governor, Bank of England. In addition, John E. Hoffman, Jr. (and Ruth Raymond, a talented paralegal who worked at Shearman & Sterling) read and commented on those aspects of the chapters relating to the bank negotiations. We are profoundly grateful to all these people, none of whom bears any responsibility for the result but all of whom enriched and refined our efforts to produce an accurate and comprehensive account of the crisis from our vantage point.

CHAPTER 6: JOHN E. HOFFMAN, JR.

Except where specifically noted, all the references and citations are from my personal notes and files. These include general notes on meetings and conversations and copies of all proposals and documents put forward by the parties to the discussions in which I participated. For any errors in recollections of conversations, I accept full responsibility; quotations from unpublished sources are—except when specifically noted—verbatim. I have had the benefit, which I appreciate, of comments on the chapter by a number of attorneys with whom I collaborated directly during the events described. They include Francis D. Logan and Peggy Grieve (Liddle) (both of Milbank, Tweed, Hadley & McCloy), Thomas W. Cashel (of Simpson, Thacher & Bartlett), C. Thorne Corse (Associate General Counsel, Bank of America, Retired), and Brigid Carroll (of Shearman and Sterling). Robert Carswell and Richard Davis also commented on those events in which they were direct participants.

CHAPTER 8: ROBERTS B. OWEN

The quotations and references to specific exchanges, conversations, and documents in this chapter are, except where otherwise noted, from my personal notes, files, and recollections. Where the text refers to provisions of the Algerian Accords (as they are frequently called) with quotation marks, the source is the material printed in the Documentary Appendix to this volume. Several people mentioned in the chapter have reviewed it and given me critically important corrections and suggestions; they include Warren Christopher, Harold Saunders, Robert Carswell, Arnold Raphel, and Mark Feldman.

CHAPTER 10: ABRAHAM J. RIBICOFF

My appreciation and gratitude go to the entire membership of the Council on Foreign Relations study group, which I chaired, and to the perceptive papers and ideas developed in our wide-ranging and intense discussions. Special thanks go to Lori Fisler Damrosch, whose patient research and other contributions were basic to this chapter. Thanks are also due Paul H. Kreisberg, John Temple Swing, Donald H. Rivkin, John E. Hoffman, Jr., Fred Haynes, and Edward C. Marschner for their helpful comments and suggestions, as well as to Malcolm Schade, whose digests of the group's discussions have been an indispensable resource.

INDEX

Abdullahi, Morteza, 250, 266
Abtahi, Saeed, 250
Acheson, Dean, 362
Act-of-state doctrine, 16
Afghanistan: communist coup, 37
Afghanistan, Soviet invasion of, 106; Car-
   ter's State of Union message on, 111–12;
   effect on Iran, 113, 114, 151
Agah, Ali, 141
Aguilar, Andres, 128
Ahmed, Rafeeuddin (Rafi), 108, 127, 131
Air Algérie, 320–21
Air traffic: discontinuance of as sanction,
   350
Algeria: as intermediary, 9, 209, 290, 293–
   96, 306–09, 313; Brzezinski–Bazargan–
   Yazdi meeting, 42–43, 59; France's finan-
   cial settlement with, 211n
Algerian Accords: drafting of, 21, 311–12;
   parallel declarations, 214–15; initialing
   of, 225, 273, 297, 321; "Undertakings,"
   225–27, 320; Implementing Technical
   Clarifications and Directions (ITCD), 225–
   28, 272–73, 321–22; Iran's blocked assets,
   230n; "cross-examination," 309, 313; process described, 314–15; categories of work
   on, 315; reproduced, 415–31. See also Algeria; Banks, U.S.; Escrow Agreement;
   Negotiations
Algerian Central Bank: Iran's investment
   in, 194n39; and Escrow Agreement, 225–
   27, 272, 317
Allies: economic sanctions, 8, 101–02, 110;
   cover account theory, 179n; multinational
   sanctions agreed upon, 195; and extraterritorial reach of freeze, 197; sanctions resisted, 198. See also Economic sanctions

Ambassadors: murder of, 57
America Held Hostage (Nightline), 25
American Law Institute, 366
Ammerman, Jim, 271
Anawaty, William, 179
Angermueller, Hans, 242
Anti-Americanism, 90–91, 285
Arbitration, international: procedures de-
   vised, 202; and Algerian Accords, 215;
   Iranian-courts clauses, 220, 312, 319;
   banks' objection to, 268; claims against
   Iran, 303–04; Iran agrees to, 309; site of,
   313; France–U.S., 341
Armed attack: seizure of hostages as, 328–
   29. See also Force—use of; Self-defense
Assets. See Freezing of Iran's assets
Association of Reserve City Banks, 204
Attachments, prejudgment; litigation over,
   185–88, 241–42; secured, 205–06; described, 299. See also Iranian-courts
   clauses; Litigation
Aubert, Pierre, 89
Automatic sanctions: for failure to protect
   diplomats, 349–50. See also Crisis management; Diplomatic privileges and immunities; Economic sanctions
AWACS, 97

Bani-Sadr, Abolhassan: and Iran's demands,
   81; removal of, 84; Carter's message to,
   89–90; as President, 120–21; and "secret
   plan," 130; order to remove dollar deposits
   in U.S., 176–77, 238; repudiation of debts,
   193, 240. See also Iranian revolution;
   Khomeni, Ayatollah
Bank of America, 206, 244, 245, 270